→ 1, (17-25), 4, (54-74), 5, (82-103), (

→ 2 (25.-43), 3, 4 (74-81), 5 (103-106), 6.

Second Edition

LEARNING
and
BEHAVIOR

James E. Mazur
Southern Connecticut State University

PRENTICE HALL

Englewood Cliffs, New Jersey 07632

Library of Congress Cataloging-in-Publication Data

MAZUR, JAMES E., [date]
  Learning and behavior / James E. Mazur. — 2nd ed.
    p.   cm.
  Includes bibliographical references.
  ISBN 0-13-528381-7
  1. Learning, Psychology of.   2. Conditioned response.   3. Behavior
modification.   4. Psychology, Comparative.   I. Title.
BF318.M38   1990
153.1'5--dc20   89-27214

Editorial/production supervision: *Edith Riker*
Cover design: *Ben Santora*
Manufacturing buyer: *Robert Anderson*

 © 1990 by Prentice-Hall, Inc.
A Division of Simon & Schuster
Englewood Cliffs, New Jersey 07632

Printed in the United States of America

10 9 8 7 6 5 4 3 2

ISBN   0-13-528381-7

Prentice-Hall International (UK) Limited, *London*
Prentice-Hall of Australia Pty. Limited, *Sydney*
Prentice-Hall Canada Inc., *Toronto*
Prentice-Hall Hispanoamericana, S.A., *Mexico*
Prentice-Hall of India Private Limited, *New Delhi*
Prentice-Hall of Japan, Inc., *Tokyo*
Simon & Schuster Asia Pte. Ltd., *Singapore*
Editora Prentice-Hall do Brasil, Ltda., *Rio de Janeiro*

To my parents,
Ann and Lou Mazur,
who responded to my early interests in science
with encouragement, understanding, and patience.

CONTENTS

PREFACE

The purpose of this book is to introduce the reader to the branch of psychology that deals with how people and animals learn, and how their behaviors are later changed as a result of this learning. This is a broad topic, for nearly all of our behaviors are influenced by prior learning experiences in some way. Because examples of learning and learned behaviors are so numerous, the goal of most psychologists in this field has been to discover general principles that are applicable to many different species and many different learning situations. What continues to impress and inspire me after many years in this field is that it is indeed possible to make such general statements about learning and behavior. This book describes some of the most important principles, theories, controversies, and of course experiments that have been produced by this branch of psychology in its first century.

This text is designed to be suitable for introductory or intermediate level courses in learning, conditioning, or the experimental analysis of behavior. No prior knowledge of psychology is assumed, but the reading may be a bit easier for those who have had a course in introductory psychology. Many of the concepts and theories in this field are fairly abstract, and to make them more concrete (and more relevant), I have included many real-world examples and analogies. In addition, most of the chapters include sections that describe how the theories and principles have been used in the applied field of behavior modification.

Roughly speaking, the book proceeds from the simple to the complex, both with respect to the difficulty of the material and the types of learning that are discussed. Chapter 1 discusses the nature of scientific theories and experiments, and it outlines the behavioral approach to learning and contrasts it with the cognitive approach. The first half of Chapter 2 has a historical tone, for it describes some of the earliest hypotheses about the learning process. To provide the reader with a different and important perspective, the second half of the chapter presents some theories about the physiological changes that may occur during learning. Chapter 3 discusses innate behaviors and the simplest type of learning, habituation. Many of the terms and ideas introduced here reappear in later chapters on classical conditioning, operant conditioning, and motor skills learning.

The next two chapters deal with classical conditioning. Chapter 4 begins with basic principles and ends with some therapeutic applications. Chapter 5 describes more recent theoretical developments and experimental findings in this area. Chapters 6 and 7 discuss the fundamental principles of operant conditioning, with Chapter 6 covering positive reinforcement and schedules of reinforcement and Chapter 7 covering negative reinforcement and punishment. Chapters 8, 9, and 10 have a more theoretical orientation (although many empirical findings are described here as well). Chapter 8 presents differing views on such fundamental questions as what constitutes a reinforcer and what conditions are necessary for learning to occur. Chapter 9 discusses the important topic of biological constraints on learning, and it explains why findings in this area have challenged the traditional views of classical and operant conditioning. Chapter 10 takes a more thorough look at generalization and discrimination than was possible in earlier chapters, and it also examines research on concept formation.

Chapter 11 surveys a wide range of findings in the rapidly growing area of animal cognition. Chapters 12 and 13 discuss two types of learning that are given little or no emphasis in many texts on learning: observational learning and motor-skills learning. These chapters were included because a substantial portion of human learning involves either observation or the development of new motor skills. Readers might well be puzzled or disappointed (with some justification) with a text on learning that included no mention of these topics. Finally, Chapter 14 presents an overview of the substantial body of behavioral research on choice behavior that has accumulated over the last few decades.

I owe thanks to many people for their help in different aspects of the preparation of this book. Many of my thoughts about learning and about psychology in general have been shaped by my discussions with Richard Herrnstein, my teacher, adviser, and friend. Dick also read several chapters of the book and provided useful comments. I am also grateful to several others who read portions of the book and gave me valuable feedback: Kenneth P. Hillner, South Dakota State University; Peter Holland, Duke University; Ann Kelley, Harvard University; Kathleen McCartney, University of New Hampshire; David Mostofsky, Boston University; Jack Nation, Texas A & M University; James R. Sutterer, Syracuse University; and E. A. Wasserman, University of Iowa. In addition, I thank Chris Berry, Paul Carroll, David Coe, Susan Herrnstein, Margaret Makepeace, Steven Pratt, and James Roach for their competent and cheerful help in numerous tasks which included typing, word processing, proofreading, searching for references, and collecting permissions. John Bailey and David Cook contributed some valuable library research for the second edition. I am grateful to Marge and Stan Averill for their careful proofreading of several chapters in this edition. I am also appreciative of the help and encouragement provided by John Isley, Susan Willig, and Susan Finnemore of Prentice-Hall. I thank my wife, Laurie Averill, for her extensive and tireless work on the preparation of this edition. Finally, Laurie and I thank our son Tom for his patience when both of us were working on this project.

ACKNOWLEDGMENTS

Figure 1-3: An adaptation of Figure 11 on page 276 from Miller, N. E., Liberalization of basic S-R concepts: Extensions to conflict behavior, motivation, and social learning. In S. Koch (Ed.), *Psychology: A study of a science* (Vol. 2). New York: McGraw-Hill, 1959. Copyright 1959 by McGraw-Hill Book Company Inc.

Figure 1-4: An adaptation of Figure 13 on page 278 from Miller, N. E., Liberalization of basic S-R concepts: Extensions to conflict behavior, motivation, and social learning. In S. Koch (Ed.), *Psychology: A study of a science* (Vol. 2). New York: McGraw-Hill, 1959. Copyright 1959 by McGraw-Hill Book Company Inc.

Figure 3-3: An adaptation of Figure 3 on page 150 from von Holst, E., Uber den Lichtruckenreflex bei Fischen. *Pubblicazioni della Stazione zoologica de Napoli, 15*, 143-158. Copyright 1935 by Francesco Giannini & Figli.

Figure 3-7: From Kandel, E. R., Small systems of neurons. *Scientific American*, September 1979, 68 and 75. Copyright 1979 by Scientific American, Inc. All rights reserved.

Figure 3-8: From Solomon, R. L. and Corbit, J. D., An opponent-process theory of motivation: I. Temporal dynamics of affect. *Psychological Review, 81*, 119-145. Figure 1, page 120. Copyright 1974 by the American Psychological Association. Reprinted by permission of the publisher and author.

Figure 3-9: From Solomon, R. L. and Corbit, J. D., An opponent-process theory of motivation: I. Temporal dynamics of affect. *Psychological Review, 81*, 119-145. Figure 4, page 128. Copyright 1974 by the American Psychological Association. Reprinted by permission of the publisher and author.

Figure 4-3: From Figure 4.2 on page 59 from Domjan, M. and Burkhard, B. *The principles of learning and behavior.* Copyright 1982 by Wadsworth, Inc. Reprinted by permission of Brooks/Cole Publishing Company, Monterey, California 93940.

Figure 4-5: An adaptation of Figure 1 on page 212 from Trapold, M. A. and Spence, K. W., Performance changes in eyelid conditioning as related to the motivational and reinforcing properties of the UCS. *Journal of Experimental Psychology, 59*, 209-213. Copyright 1960 by the American Psychological Association. Reprinted by permission of the publisher.

Figure 4-7: From Moore, J., Stimulus control: Studies of auditory generalization in rabbits. In Black and Prokasy (Eds.), *Classical conditioning II: Current theory and research.* 1972, page 214. Reprinted by permission of Prentice Hall, Inc., Englewood Cliffs, N. J. 07632.

Figure 6-3: Record of cat B on page 46 from Guthrie, E. R. and Horton, G. P., *Cats in a puzzle box.* New York: Rinehart & Company, 1946. Copyright 1946 by Edwin R. Guthrie and George P. Horton.

Figure 6-4: Record of cat G on page 52 from Guthrie, E. R. and Horton, G. P., *Cats in a puzzle box.* New York: Rinehart & Company, 1946. Copyright 1946 by Edwin R. Guthrie and George P. Horton.

Figure 6-10: From Mawhinney, V. T., Bostow, D. E., Laws, D. R., Blumenfeld, G. J., and Hopkins, B. L., A comparison of students' studying-behavior produced by daily, weekly, and three-week testing schedules. *Journal of Applied Behavior Analysis, 4*, 257-264. Figure 3, page 262. Copyright 1971 by the Society for the Experimental Analysis of Behavior. Reprinted by permission of the publisher.

Figure 6-11: From Weisberg, P., and Waldrop, P. B. Fixed-interval work habits of Congress. *Journal of Applied Behavior Analysis, 5*, 93-97. Figure 1, page 94. Copyright 1972 by the Society for the Experimental Analysis of Behavior. Reprinted by permission of the publisher.

Figure 7-4: From Skinner, B. F., *The behavior of organisms.* Figure 47, page 154. Copyright 1938 by D. Appleton—Century Co., Inc.

Figure 8-1: An adaptation of Figure 4 on page 267 from Tolman, E. C., and Honzik, C. H., Introduction and removal of reward, and maze performance in rats. *University of California Publications in Psychology, 4*, 257-275. Copyright 1930 by the University of California Press.

Figure 8-2: From Dicara, L. V., Learning in the autonomic nervous system. *Scientific American*, January 1970, page 33. Copyright 1970 by Scientific American, Inc. All rights reserved.

Figure 8-4: An adaptation of Figure 2 on page 381 from Mazur, J. E., The matching law and quantifications related to Premack's principle. *Journal of Experimental Psychology: Animal Behavior Processes, 1*, 374-386. Adapted by permission.

Figure 9-1: An adaptation of Figure 1 on page 124 from Garcia, J, Ervin, F. R., and Koelling, R. A., Learning with prolonged delay of reinforcement. *Psychonomic Science, 5*, 121-122. Copyright 1966 by the Psychonomic Society.

Figure 9-2: From Shettleworth, S. J., Reinforcement and the organization of behavior in golden hamsters: Hunger, environment, and food reinforcement. *Journal of Experimental Psychology: Animal Behavior Processes, 104*, 56-87. Figure 6, page 76. Copyright by the American Psychological Association, 1975. Reprinted by permission of the publisher.

Figure 9-3: From Jenkins, H. M. and Moore, B. R., The form of the auto-shaped response with food or water reinforcers. *Journal of the Experimental Analysis of Behavior, 20,* 163-181. Figure 2, page 175. Copyright 1973 by the Society for the Experimental Analysis of Behavior, Inc. Reprinted by permission of the publisher.

Figure 9-4a: An adaptation of Figure 3 on page 1034 from Baron, A., Kaufman, A., and Fazzini, D., Density and delay of punishment of free-operant avoidance. *Journal of the Experimental Analysis of Behavior, 12,* 1029-1037. Copyright 1969 by the Society for the Experimental Analysis of Behavior, Inc. Reprinted by permission of the publisher.

Figure 9-4b: An adaptation of Figure 1 on page 288 from Andrews, E. A. and Braveman, N. S., The combined effects of dosage level and interstimulus interval on the formation of one-trial poison-based aversions in rats. *Animal Learning & Behavior, 3,* 287-289. Copyright 1975 by the Psychonomic Society.

Figure 10-1: An adaptation of Figure 1 on page 81 from Guttman, N. and Kalish, H. I., Discriminability and stimulus generalization. *Journal of Experimental Psychology, 51,* 79-88. Copyright 1956 by the American Psychological Association. Reprinted by permission of the publisher.

Figure 10-2: From Jenkins, H. M. and Harrison, R. H., Effects of discrimination training on auditory generalization. *Journal of Experimental Psychology, 59,* 246-253. Figure 1, page 247, and Figure 2, page 248. Copyright 1960 by the American Psychological Association. Reprinted by permission of the publisher.

Figure 10-3: An adaptation of Figure 1 on page 324 from Hanson, H. M., Effects of discrimination training on stimulus generalization. *Journal of Experimental Psychology, 58,* 321-34. Copyright 1959 by the American Psychological Association. Reprinted by permission of the publisher.

Figure 10-6: An adaptation of Figure 1 on page 112 from Honig, W. K., Boneau, C. A., Burstein, K. R., and Pennypacker, H. S., Positive and negative generalization gradients obtained after equivalent training conditions. *Journal of Comparative and Physiological Psychology, 56,* 111-116. Copyright 1963 by the American Psychological Association. Reprinted by permission of the publisher.

Figure 10-7: An adaptation from Table 1 on page 222 from Gutman, A., Positive contrast, negative induction, and inhibitory stimulus control in the rat. *Journal of the Experimental Analysis of Behavior, 27,* 219-233. Copyright 1972 by the Society for the Experimental Analysis of Behavior, Inc. Reprinted by permission of the publisher.

Figure 10-9: From Warren, J. M. Primate learning in comparative perspective. In A. M. Schrier, H. F. Harlow, and F. Stollnitz (Eds.), *Behavior of nonhuman primates* (Vol. 1). New York: Academic Press, 1965. Figure 4, page 262. Copyright 1965 by the Academic Press.

Figure 11-2a: An adaptation of Figure 1 on page 210 from Grant, D. S., Proactive interference in pigeon short-term memory. *Journal of Experimental Psychology: Animal Behavior Processes, 1,* 207-220. Copyright 1975 by the American Psychological Association. Reprinted by permission of the publisher.

Figure 11-2b: An adaptation of Figure 1 on page 329 from D'Amato, M. R. and O'Neill, W., Effect of delay-interval illumination on matching behavior in the capuchin monkey. *Journal of the Experimental Analysis of Behavior, 15,* 327-333. Copyright 1971 by the Society for the Experimental Analysis of Behavior, Inc. Reprinted by permission of the publisher.

Figure 11-5: From Wagner, A. R., Rudy, J. W., and Whitlow, J. W., Rehearsal in animal conditioning. *Journal of Experimental Psychology, 97,* 407-426. Figure 11, page 421. Copyright 1973 by the American Psychological Association. Reprinted by permission of the publisher.

Figure 11-6: An adaptation of Figure 2 in Roberts, S., Isolation of an internal clock. *Journal of Experimental Psychology: Animal Behavior Processes, 7,* 242-268. Copyright 1981 by the American Psychological Association. Reprinted by permission of the publisher and author.

Figure 11-7: From Figure 2 in Mechner, F., Probability relations within response sequences under ratio reinforcement. *Journal of the Experimental Analysis of Behavior, 1,* 109-121. Copyright 1958 by the Society for the Experimental Analysis of Behavior, Inc. Reprinted by permission of the publisher.

Figure 11-8: From Figure 2 in Gillan, D. J., Premack, D., & Woodruff, G., Reasoning in the chimpanzee: I. Analogical reasoning. *Journal of Experimental Psychology: Animal Behavior Processes, 7,* 1-17. Copyright 1981 by the American Psychological Association. Reprinted by permission of the publisher.

Figure 12-1: From Bandura, A., Ross, D., and Ross, S. A., Imitation of film-mediated aggressive models. *Journal of Abnormal and Social Psychology, 66,* 3-11. Figure 1, page 8. Copyright 1963 by the American Psychological Association. Reprinted by permission.

Figure 12-3: An adaptation of Figure 1 on page 21 from Bandura, A., Grusec, J. E., and Menlove, F. L., Vicarious extinction of avoidance behavior. *Journal of Personality and Social Psychology, 5,* 16-23. Copyright 1967 by the American Psychological Association. Reprinted by permission of the publisher and author.

Figure 13-1: An adaptation from Table 2 on page 253 from Trowbridge, M. H., and Cason, H., An experimental study of Thorndike's theory of learning. *Journal of General Psychology, 7,* 245-260. Copyright 1932 by the Helen Dwight Reid Educational Foundation.

Figure 13-2: An adaptation of Figure 4 on page 11 from Hatze, H., Biomechanical aspects of a successful motion optimization. In P. V. Komi (Ed.), *Biomechanics V-B.* Copyright 1976 by University Park Press.

Figure 13-3: From Dore, L. R., and Hilgard, E. R., Spaced practice and the maturation hypothesis. *Journal of Psychology, 4,* 245-259. Figure 1, page 251. Copyright 1937 by the Helen Dwight Reid Educational Foundation.

Figure 13-4: An adaptation of Figure 1 on page 34 from Adams, J. A., and Reynolds, B., Effect of shift in distribution of practice conditions following interpolated rest. *Journal of Experimental Psychology, 47,* 32-36. Copyright 1954 by the American Psychological Association. Reprinted by permission of the publisher.

Figure 13-5: An adaptation of Figure 2 on page 240 from Newell, K. M., Knowledge of results and motor learning. *Journal of Motor Behavior, 6,* 234-244. Copyright by Hildref Publications.

Figure 13-7: An adaptation of Figure 1 on page 419 from Posner, M. I., and Keele, S. W., Attentional demands in movement. In *Proceedings of the 16th International Congress of Applied Psychology.* Copyright 1969 by Swets and Zeitlinger.

Table 14-1: Adapted from Figures 1 and 2 on page 268 from Herrnstein, R. J., Relative and absolute strength of response as a function of frequency reinforcement. *Journal of the Experimental Analysis of Behavior, 4,* 267-272. Copyright 1961 by the Society for the Experimental Analysis of Behavior, Inc. Reprinted by permission of the publisher and author.

Figure 14-1: An adaptation of Figure 1 on page 268 from Herrnstein, R. J., Relative and absolute strength of response as a function of frequency of reinforcement. *Journal of the Experimental Analysis of Behavior, 4,* 267-272.

Copyright 1961 by the Society for the Experimental Analysis of Behavior. Reprinted by permission of the publisher and author.

Figure 14-4: From Herrnstein, R. J., On the law of effect. *Journal of the Experimental Analysis of Behavior, 13,* 243-266. Figure 8, page 255. Copyright 1970 by the Society for the Experimental Analysis of Behavior. Reprinted by permission of the publisher and author.

Figure 14-5: An adaptation of Table 1 on page 147 from Rachlin, H., Green, L., Kagel, J. H., and Battalio, R. C., Economic demand theory and psychological studies of choice. In G. Bower (Ed.), *The Psychology of learning and motivation* (Vol. 10). Copyright 1976 by Academic Press Inc., 111 Fifth Avenue, New York, N. Y. 10003.

Figure 14-9: An adaptation of Figure 1 on page 486 from Ainslie, G. W., Impulse control in pigeons. *Journal of the Experimental Analysis of Behavior, 21,* 485-489. Copyright 1974 by the Society for the Experimental Analysis of Behavior, Inc. Reprinted by permission of the publisher and author.

CHAPTER

1

INTRODUCTION

THE PSYCHOLOGY
OF LEARNING AND BEHAVIOR

If you know nothing about the branch of psychology called *learning*, you may have some misconceptions about the scope of this field. I can recall browsing through the course catalog as a college freshman and coming across a course offered by the Department of Psychology with the succinct title, "Learning." Without bothering to read the course description, I wondered about the contents of this course. Learning, I reasoned, is primarily the occupation of students. Would this course teach students better study habits, better reading and note-taking skills? Or did the course examine learning in children, covering such topics as the best ways to teach a child to read, to write, to do arithmetic? Did it deal with children who have learning disabilities? It was difficult to imagine spending an entire semester on these topics, which sounded fairly narrow and specialized for an introductory-level course.

My conception of the psychology of learning was wrong in several respects. First of all, a psychology course emphasizing learning in the classroom would probably have a title such as "Educational Psychology" rather than "Learning." In fact, courses on classroom learning are more commonly offered by a college's Department of Education than by its Department of Psychology. My second error was the assumption that the psychology of learning is a narrow field. A moment's reflection reveals that students do not have a monopoly on learning. Children learn a great deal before ever entering a classroom, and adults must continue to adapt to an ever-changing environment. In recognition of the fact that learning occurs at all ages, the psychological discipline of learning places no special emphasis on the subset of learning that occurs in the classroom. Furthermore, since the human being is only one of thousands of species on this planet that have the capacity to learn, the psychological discipline of learning is by no means restricted to

1

the study of human beings. For reasons to be explained below, a large percentage of all psychological experiments on learning have used nonhuman subjects. Though they may have their faults, psychologists in the field of learning are not chauvinistic about the human species.

Although even specialists have difficulty defining the term *learning* precisely, most would agree that it is a process of change that occurs as a result of an individual's experience. Psychologists who study learning are interested in this process wherever it occurs—in adults, in school children, in other mammals, in reptiles, in insects. This may sound like a large subject matter, but the field of learning is even broader than this, because researchers in this area study not only the *process* of learning but also the *product* of learning—the long-term changes in an individual's behavior that result from a learning experience. An example may help to clarify the distinction between process and product. Suppose you glance out the window and see a raccoon near some garbage cans in the backyard. As you watch, the raccoon gradually manages to knock over a garbage can, remove the lid, and tear open the garbage bag inside. For the sake of this discussion, let us assume that the smell of food attracted the raccoon to the garbage cans, but that it has never encountered such objects before. If we were interested in studying this particular type of behavior, many different questions would probably come to mind. Some questions might deal with the learning process itself: Did the animal open the can purely by accident, or was it guided by some "plan of action"? What factors determine how long the raccoon will persist in manipulating the garbage can if it is not immediately successful in obtaining something to eat? If the first garbage can is opened simply by accident, will the raccoon still learn something that will make it more efficient in opening the next can? Such questions deal with what might be called the *acquisition* phase, or the period in which the animal is acquiring a new skill.

Once the raccoon has had considerable experience in dealing with garbage cans, it may encounter few surprises in its expeditions through the neighborhood. Although the acquisition process is essentially over as far as garbage cans are concerned, we can continue to examine the raccoon's behavior, asking somewhat different questions that deal with the *performance* of learned behaviors. The raccoon will have only intermittent success in obtaining food from garbage cans—sometimes a can will be empty and sometimes it will contain nothing edible. How frequently will the raccoon visit a given backyard, and how will the animal's success rate affect the frequency of its visits? The animal will probably be more successful at specific times of the day or week. Will its visits occur at the most advantageous times? Such questions concern the end product of the learning process, the raccoon's new behavior patterns. This text is entitled *Learning and Behavior* rather than simply *Learning* to reflect the fact that the psychology of learning encompasses both the acquisition process and the long-term behavior that results.

THE SEARCH FOR GENERAL PRINCIPLES OF LEARNING

Since the psychology of learning deals with all types of learning and learned behaviors in all types of creatures, its scope is broad indeed. Think, for a moment, of the different behaviors you performed in the first hour or two after rising this morning. Construct a mental list of these behaviors, and try to decide how many of them would not have been possible without prior learning. In most cases, the decision is easy to make. Getting dressed, washing your face, making your bed, and going to the dining room for breakfast are all examples of behaviors that depend mostly or entirely on previous learning experiences. (For instance, you had to learn how to get from your room to the dining room, and walking itself is of course dependent on previous learning.) The behavior of eating breakfast depends on several different types of learning, including the selection of appropriate types and quantities of food, the proper use of utensils, and the development of coordinated hand, eye, and mouth movements. Except for behaviors that must occur continuously for a person to survive, such as breathing and the beating of the heart, it is difficult to think of many human behaviors which are not obviously dependent on prior learning.

Considering all of the behaviors of humans and other creatures that involve learning, the scope of this branch of psychology may seem hopelessly broad. How can any single discipline hope to make any useful statements about all these different instances of learning? It should be clear that it would make no sense to study, one by one, every different example of learning that one might come across. This is not the approach of most researchers who study learning. Instead, their strategy has been to select, presumably on an arbitrary basis, a few learning situations that are studied in detail, and then to attempt to generalize from these situations to other instances of learning. Thus the goal of much of the research on learning has been to develop *general principles* that are applicable across a wide range of species and learning situations. B. F. Skinner, one of the most influential figures in the history of psychology, made his belief in this strategy explicit in his first major work, *The Behavior of Organisms* (1938). In his initial studies, Skinner chose white rats as subjects and lever pressing as a response. An individual rat would be placed in a small experimental chamber containing little more than a lever and a tray into which food was occasionally presented after the rat pressed the lever. A modern version of a chamber similar to the one Skinner used is shown in Figure 1-1. In studying the behavior of rats in such a sparse environment, Skinner felt that he could discover principles that govern the behavior of many animals, including human beings, in the more complex environments that are found outside the psychological laboratory. The work of Skinner and his students will be examined in depth beginning in Chapter 6, so you will have ample opportunity to decide for yourself whether Skinner's strategy has proven to be successful.

As the next few chapters will show, the search for general principles of learning did not begin with Skinner. Furthermore, this strategy is surely not unique to the psychology of learning. Attempts to discover principles or laws with wide applicability are a part of most scientific endeavors. If the notion of a *general principle* sounds vague, consider this simple example from phys-

FIGURE 1-1. An experimental chamber in which a rat can receive food pellets by pressing a lever. The pellets are delivered into the square opening below the lever. This chamber is also equipped with lights and a speaker, so that visual and auditory signals can be presented.

ics. A familiar principle of physics is the law of gravity, which predicts, among other things, the distance a freely falling object will drop in a given period of time. If an object starts from a stationary position and falls for t seconds, the equation $d=16t^2$ predicts the distance (in feet) that the object will fall. The law of gravity is certainly a general principle, because in theory it applies to any falling object, whether it is a rock, a baseball, or a skydiver. According to the law of gravity, neither the weight, chemical composition, shape, temperature, political persuasion, nor any other characteristic of the object is relevant: Notice that the above equation contains no terms for any of these properties. On the other hand, the law of gravity is not without its limitations. As with most scientific principles, it is applicable only when certain criteria are met. Two restrictions on the above equation are that it applies (1) only to objects close to the earth's surface and (2) only as long as no other force, such as air resistance, plays a role. If we chose to ignore these criteria it would be easy to "disprove" the law of gravity. We could simply drop a rock and a leaf and show that the leaf falls much more slowly. But once the restrictions on the law of gravity are acknowledged, our experiment proves nothing, since we did not eliminate the influence of air resistance. This example shows why it is frequently necessary to retreat to the laboratory in order to perform a meaningful test of a scientific principle. In the laboratory, the role of air resistance can be minimized through the use of a vacuum chamber. The leaf and the rock will fall at the same rate in this artificial environment, thereby verifying the law of gravity. For similar reasons, orderly principles of learning and behavior that might be obscured by a multitude of extraneous factors in the natural environment may be uncovered in a rarefied laboratory environment.

Once the restrictions on the law of gravity are specified, a naive reader might conclude that the law has no practical utility, because the natural environment provides no vacuums near the earth's surface. However, this conclusion is correct only if extremely precise measurements are demanded, because for many solid objects with a roughly spherical shape, the role of air resistance is so negligible that the law of gravity makes reasonably accurate predictions. Similarly, it would be naive to assume that a psychological principle has no relevance to the natural environment simply because that principle is most clearly demonstrated in the laboratory. Beginning with Chapter 2, every chapter in this text will introduce several new principles of learning and behavior, nearly all of which have been investigated in laboratory settings. To demonstrate that these principles have applicability to more natural settings, each chapter will also describe a number of real-world situations in which these principles play an important role. Many of the examples will come from the realm of *behavior modification*, a discipline that makes use of learning principles to help people cope with or cure a wide range of psychological problems.

THE NATURE OF SCIENTIFIC THEORIES

When a statement about the nature of the world is called a principle or a law, this suggests that there is general agreement among the experts that the statement is true, having been verified by numerous experiments. Because psychology is a relatively young science, few psychological statements have received such general accep-

tance, so the terms *theory* or *hypothesis* are more commonly used to label statements about behavior and its causes. It does not take a scientist to invent a theory of behavior, and nearly everyone has some theories about learning and learned behaviors. For instance, you may have a theory about how some people learn to enjoy smoking cigarettes, or about why your little brother throws a tantrum when he doesn't get his way. Since you probably already have plenty of such hypotheses about learning and behavior, a textbook must do more than simply give you additional theories and hypotheses to consider. This text will do more than this in two ways. One major purpose of this book is to describe the results of experiments that help us decide among competing hypotheses about behavior. A second purpose of the book is more general—to improve your ability to think clearly, logically, and scientifically about behavior and to develop your ability to distinguish between good hypotheses about the causes of behavior and weak ones.

Before beginning to examine any theories about learning, it is important to understand the major characteristics of scientific theories and the criteria frequently used to evaluate them. As with many abstract concepts, the characteristics of scientific theories may be best conveyed by considering a concrete example. Therefore, let us examine a specific theory of human behavior and evaluate its strengths and weaknesses as a scientific theory.

An Example of a Theory about Behavior: Biorhythm Theory

One Sunday in December, 1977, *The New York Times* contained an article entitled "The 12th man in huddle: A biorhythm expert." This article stated that at least five National Football League teams were using information about the biorhythms of their players and those of their opponents to help them plan game strategies. Proponents of biorhythm theory claim that simply by knowing a player's date of birth, they can consult a chart that will predict how well the player is likely to perform on a given day. If these claims are true, the implications for a game strategy are obvious. If your opponent's dangerous wide receiver is due for a poor performance, you can avoid using double coverage and make better use of your defensive players. If your halfback will have a favorable biorhythm pattern on Sunday, you should plan to rely more heavily on your running game. A head coach would be foolish not to take biorhythms into account if they can actually affect a player's performance. But what are biorhythms, and how are they supposed to affect behavior?

According to Bernard Gittelson (1977), one of the leading proponents of biorhythm theory, the basic idea is that every person's behavior is influenced by three bodily cycles—a physical cycle lasting 23 days, an emotional cycle lasting 28 days, and an intellectual cycle lasting 33 days. Figure 1-2 shows an example of a person's biorhythm cycles over a two-month period. Each of the three cycles is in the positive range for half of a cycle and in the negative range for the other half. The positive range of a cycle is supposedly associated with good performance (for instance, smart decisions, creative ideas, above-average physical skills). On the other hand, if a person's cycle is low, he or she will tend to make mistakes, have accidents, and simply perform worse than average on most everyday tasks. Besides these high points and low points of the three bodily cycles, the times when a cycle crosses the zero mark (as shown by the horizontal line in Figure 1-2) also play an important role in biorhythm theory. Days when a cycle crosses the zero point are called *critical days*, and these are also times when a person's behavior is likely to

be subpar. Gittelson explains the low performance predicted for critical days by likening them to the times when an electric light bulb is switched on or off—it is at these moments that the bulb is most likely to burn out.

The *Times* article described a number of cases that provide support for biorhythm theory. For instance, on November 19, 1977, when Ohio State football coach Woody Hayes punched a television cameraman on the sidelines as his team was losing, both his physical and intellectual cycles were low. On the following day, when Walter Payton of the Chicago Bears set a new NFL single-game rushing record, all three of his cycles were high. Biorhythm theorists suggest that examples such as these demonstrate how biorhythms can influence a person's performance, and the newspaper article cited several other examples from football and other sports.

How can the state of a person's biorhythms be determined simply by knowing the person's birthday? Biorhythm theory proposes that on the day a child is born, all three biorhythm cycles are at the zero position, and they begin by moving in the positive direction. Since the cycles are said to have periods of exactly 23, 28, and 33 days, the position of each cycle can be calculated for any future day. For instance, since the emotional cycle is said to have a period of 28 days, this cycle should reach a peak on the child's seventh day of life, return to zero on the fourteenth day, reach a low point on the twenty-first day, and so on.

If it is true that all people undergo such regular changes in their performance levels, and if a

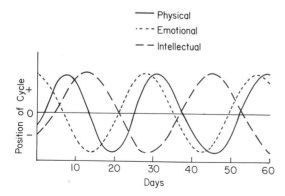

FIGURE 1-2. A typical pattern of a person's three bodily cycles over a two-month period, as hypothesized by biorhythm theory.

person's good and bad days can be predicted in advance, it should be obvious that biorhythms have implications that extend well beyond professional football. Persons who have occupations in which a faulty performance could cause injury to themselves or to others should be advised (or even required) to take a day off when their biorhythms will be low or critical. Gittelson (1977) described a number of examples of how biorhythm theory has been put into practice. At the time his book was written, over 5000 Japanese companies were using biorhythm charts for all their employees in an attempt to reduce occupational accidents. A large Japanese bus company was sending each of its drivers a warning card whenever the driver had a critical day, urging extra caution. Swissair adopted a rule that no plane could be flown by a pilot and copilot who were both experiencing critical days.

Biorhythm theory is an example of a theory about behavior—it attempts to predict when a person's behavior in a variety of everyday tasks will be above average, and when it will be below average. As a theory of behavior, biorhythm theory contains all the major components of the typical psychological theory. We can therefore use biorhythm theory as a means of examining the features that most psychological theories, and most scientific theories, have in common.

The Major Components of Scientific Theories

Science is an enterprise concerned with gaining information about *causality*, or the relationship between cause and effect. A simple example of a cause is the movement of a paddle as it strikes a Ping-Pong ball; the effect is the movement of the ball through the air. In psychology and other sciences, the word *cause* is often replaced by the term *independent variable*. This term implies that the experimenter is often "free" to vary the independent variable as he or she desires (for example, the experimenter can control the speed of the paddle as it strikes the ball). The term *dependent variable* replaces the word *effect*, and this term is used because the effect *depends* on some characteristic of the independent variable (the flight of the ball depends

on the speed of the paddle). The conventions of science demand that both the independent and dependent variables be observable events, as is the case in the Ping-Pong example. In the case of biorhythm theory, the independent variable is the number of days that have elapsed between a person's date of birth and some test day. The dependent variable is the person's level of performance on some specified task on the test day. Notice that although the experimenter is not free to choose a birthday for a given individual, persons with different dates of birth can be tested on the same day, or a single subject can be tested on several different days.

In order to predict the relationship between independent and dependent variables, many scientific theories make use of what are called *intervening variables*. Intervening variables are purely theoretical concepts that cannot be observed directly. To predict the flight of a Ping-Pong ball, Newtonian physics relies on a number of intervening variables, including *force, mass, air resistance*, and *gravity*. You can probably anticipate that the intervening variables of biorhythm theory are the three bodily cycles with their specified time periods. It should be emphasized that not all psychological theories include intervening variables, and some psychologists object to their use precisely because they are not directly observable. Later in this chapter the debate over the use of intervening variables will be examined.

The final major component of a scientific theory is its *syntax*, or the rules and definitions that state how the independent and dependent variables are to be measured, and that specify the relationships among independent variables, intervening variables, and dependent variables. It is the syntax of biorhythm theory that describes how to use a person's birthday to calculate the current status of the three cycles. The syntax also relates the cycles to the dependent variable, performance, by stating that positive cycles should cause high levels of performance whereas low or critical cycles should cause low performance levels. To summarize, the components of a scientific theory can be divided into four major categories: independent variables, dependent variables, intervening variables, and syntax.

Judging Scientific Theories

When reading about biorhythm theory for the first time, most people will form some opinion about its validity. Some may be convinced by the examples of Woody Hayes and Walter Payton and conclude that the theory is correct; others may decide the examples are merely coincidences and remain skeptical. In this text, however, we will be less concerned with how the average person thinks about behavior, and more concerned with how the scientist thinks about behavior. Let us therefore examine some of the major criteria used by scientists to evaluate a theory for its scientific merit, and we can try to determine how well biorhythm theory meets these criteria. Although there is no universally accepted list of standards for judging scientific theories, the following five criteria are generally thought to be among the most important. More extensive treatment of these issues is provided by Frank, 1949; Marx & Hillix, 1979; and Rosenthal & Rosnow, 1984.

1. *Testability (Falsifiability).* A theory should make unambiguous predictions that can be tested against the facts. This criterion is often called *falsifiability*, for it is generally agreed that a good theory is one that could, in principle, be proven wrong. One way a psychological theory might fail to meet this criterion is if it did not make any clear predictions about observable behavior. At first glance, it may seem that biorhythm theory makes very clear predictions: High biorhythm cycles predict good performance, and low or critical cycles predict poor performance. Unfortunately, the relationship between biorhythms and performance is not so straightforward, because on many days one or two cycles will be in a positive phase and the other one or two will be negative, and it is not clear what prediction to make from such a mixed pattern. Suppose we wish to predict the performance of a weight lifter for whom one cycle is low and the other two are high. Will the two positive cycles outweigh the negative to yield an above-average performance, or will the conflicting cycles more or less balance out, yielding an average performance? What would be predicted if the third cycle were critical rather than low?

Does it make any difference which of the three cycles is the critical one? Biorhythm theory, as it now stands, makes no clear predictions about these different combinations.

These uncertainties in prediction make biorhythm theory more difficult to test than it might be. The theory could be improved if its syntax were developed more completely, so that it specified a definite relationship between biorhythm pattern and level of performance. For instance, a better theory might state that the most favorable biorhythm pattern is three positive cycles, followed by two positive and one negative, then two positive and one critical, then one positive and two negative, and so on. Of course, the improvements need not take this specific form. The point is that a scientific theory must make definite predictions, because if there is room for reinterpretation and modification of the predictions after the data are collected, any result can be explained by the theory. If the weight lifter has a good performance, we could say that this was because of the two positive cycles (therefore, the theory is supported). If the weight lifter's performance is poor, we could attribute this to the one negative cycle (therefore, the theory is supported). This example shows how ambiguity about the relationship between hypothetical constructs and observable behavior can make a theory unfalsifiable, and a theory that cannot be proven wrong has no predictive value.

2. *Simplicity.* If two theories are equal in their ability to account for a body of data, the theory that does so with the smaller number of hypothetical constructs and assumptions is to be preferred (Popper, 1959). Without a competing theory with which to compare biorhythm theory, it is not possible to make any meaningful judgment about its simplicity. However, the dimension of simplicity can be illustrated by considering two theories about the solar system. Ptolemy proposed that the earth is at the center of the solar system. In order to account for the data (the motions of the sun, stars, and planets), he had to propose a cumbersome theoretical system involving numerous interconnected *cycles* and *epicycles*. By hypothesizing that the sun is at the center of the solar system, Copernicus was able to account for the same set of observations with

many fewer theoretical assumptions. Although both theories can predict the motions of objects in the night sky, Copernicus's theory is scientifically preferable because of its comparative simplicity (even if we ignore other, more modern observations that support Copernicus's theory but not Ptolemy's theory).

3. *Generality.* Theories that deal with more phenomena, with a greater range of observations, are usually judged to be better than theories of more restricted scope. If biorhythm theorists claimed that their theory only applied to football, it would be a less impressive theory. If it were then expanded to cover the performances of tennis players, pole vaulters, and all other athletes, it would become a more general theory of sports performance. Actually, biorhythm theory is even more general than this. We have seen that it has been applied to the performances of people in many different occupations, including airline pilots, bus drivers, and factory workers. This broad generality is a virtue of biorhythm theory.

4. *Fruitfulness.* An important property of a scientific theory is its ability to stimulate further research and further thinking about a particular topic. Part of the logic behind this criterion is that although a theory may eventually prove to be incorrect or of limited accuracy, it will have served a useful function if it provoked new studies that otherwise would not have been done. Often an experiment designed to test a particular theory will uncover a new phenomenon, one which the theory cannot explain. This can be a healthy state of affairs for a scientific discipline, because the new information can pave the way for the development of a more sophisticated theory. With respect to biorhythm theory, Gittelson (1977) described a very large number of studies that have been conducted to test the theory. It is possible that research on the patterns of good and bad job performances, though stimulated by biorhythm theory, might lead to a better understanding of occupational accidents, regardless of whether biorhythm theory is supported or refuted.

5. *Agreement with the Data.* This final criterion is the most obvious test of a theory—how well it coincides with the facts. If a theory makes predictions that clearly contradict some well-established facts, the theory must either be modified or discarded. On the other hand, if a theory accounts for some specified body of facts fairly well, it may be retained, at least temporarily. This criterion leads us to the complex topic of how research is conducted to test scientific hypotheses.

Issues and Techniques in Comparing Theory with Data

The evidence for biorhythm theory exemplifies three different methods that are frequently used to collect psychological data, each of which will be encountered in later chapters of this book. For the purposes of this introduction, only the most fundamental characteristics of these research methods will be discussed. (Many volumes have been written about the research strategies used in the behavioral sciences, providing interested readers with a wealth of information; for example, Barlow, 1984; Kirk, 1982; Schaughnessy & Zechmeister, 1985; Webb, Campbell, Schwartz, Sechrest, & Grove, 1981.)

Anecdotes or Case Histories. A major portion of the evidence in support of biorhythm theory takes the form of anecdotes about famous people such as Walter Payton and Woody Hayes. Gittelson (1977) cited numerous examples about celebrities who suffered from accidents or tragedies on days when their biorhythms were particularly unfavorable. For example, he reported that on the day when President Gerald Ford decided to grant Richard Nixon an unconditional pardon for any possible crimes committed during the Watergate affair (a decision that many political analysts felt was a mistake), Ford's intellectual and emotional cycles were low. As another example, actress Marilyn Monroe died of an overdose of sleeping pills on August 5, 1962, when, according to Gittelson, her physical cycle was critical and her emotional cycle was low. Gittelson's book is filled with dozens of examples of this nature. Although such anecdotes certainly make interesting reading, from a scientific point of view this type of evidence has serious shortcomings. Can you see any problems with these types of data?

Gittelson's use of anecdotes is in some ways similar to the *case history* approach used in some branches of psychology, including behavior modification (particularly in reports about patients with rare psychological disorders, where a clinician may encounter only one or two cases of the disorder). A concern that is frequently raised about the use of case histories is that the cases reported may represent a *biased sample*. That is, perhaps the psychologist has reported only those cases where treatment of the disorder was successful, and not those where the treatment was ineffective. To avoid this type of criticism, clinical psychologists usually report such information as the number of cases of the disorder they have encountered, the number of patients selected for treatment, the criteria used to select these patients, and the number of cases in which treatment was judged to be successful. However, with the anecdotal evidence for biorhythm theory, we are given no such information. Although the cases of Ford, Monroe, and others seem to support the theory, we do not know how many other cases Gittelson may have examined that did not support the theory. Perhaps Gittelson has reported 90 percent of the cases he has examined, or perhaps only 20 percent, with the remainder failing to support the theory. We have no way of knowing, and without this information the anecdotes are essentially worthless from a scientific standpoint.

Observational Techniques. This term will be used to denote a wide range of research techniques, including field observations (the simple observation of people or animals in natural environments), the use of surveys and questionnaires, and the use of archival data (the information contained in written documents and records). What these techniques have in common with the case-history method is that the experimenter is a more or less passive observer, making no effort to manipulate the variables that control a subject's behavior. Unlike the case-history approach, however, observational techniques always involve a systematic effort to obtain a representative sample from the population of interest. Gittelson (1977) reported a number of studies that exemplify the observational method. In one case, a researcher named Newcomb took a random sample of 100 accident reports from the files of a utility company. Because the sample was chosen at random, we can assume that it was an unbiased sample of the entire population (that is, of all the accident reports on file for this company). Newcomb found that 53 of these accidents occurred on a worker's critical day. Unfortunately, we are not told what criterion Newcomb used to define a critical day. If he counted only those days on which a cycle crossed the zero point, then his findings are impressive, for only about 20 accidents would be expected on critical days by chance. However, in his work, Gittelson also treats the days before and after a cycle crosses the zero point as critical days. If Newcomb also used this three-day criterion for critical days, the results are not remarkable, since it can be shown that by chance alone 50 of the accidents should occur on such loosely-defined critical days. The difference between the 50 accidents expected by chance and the 53 accidents actually counted could easily be the result of what statisticians call *sampling error*. That is, if several random samples of 100 accidents were drawn from the same files, there would almost certainly be differences in the number of critical-day accidents from sample to sample (perhaps 44 in the second sample, 58 in the third, 47 in the fourth, and so on).

The best solution to the problem of sampling error is to increase the amount of data in the sample, because with larger and larger samples we can have increasing confidence that the sample is representative of the entire population. A number of observational studies on traffic accidents with larger sample sizes have found no correspondence between biorhythm cycles and the frequency of accidents (Trinkhaus & Booke, 1982; Pitariu, Bostenaru, Lucaciu & Oachis, 1984). Because of their larger sample sizes, we can have more confidence in these studies than in Newcomb's.

Experimental Techniques. With observational methods, the researcher simply examines the independent and dependent variables as they already exist and tries to discern the relationship between them. In an experiment, the researcher actively manipulates the independent variable in some systematic way. The program of distributing warning cards to the drivers of a Japanese bus company on their critical days can therefore be called an experiment. The independent variable was whether or not the drivers were informed about their critical days. Accident rates from the year before the program began were compared with rates after the warning card program was adopted. The logic of this experiment was that if drivers were aware of their critical days, they might use extra caution and thereby reduce their chances of an accident. In the first year of the warning cards, the accident rate for this company decreased by nearly 50 percent.

Although on the surface this result seems to support biorhythm theory, most psychologists would be very cautious about drawing any conclusions from this study. The problem is that besides the warning cards, many other variables that could affect the accident rate might have changed from one year to the next. Perhaps the decrease in accidents occurred because in the second year many of the drivers were more experienced. Perhaps the bus company replaced some of its unreliable drivers with new ones. Perhaps, on the average, there were less-severe weather conditions during the second year. This sort of variable—one that is not of interest to the researcher but can nevertheless affect the results of an experiment—is called a *confounding variable*. In any experiment where a single group of subjects experiences two or more conditions in succession, there is always the possibility that a confounding variable can affect the results.

Although some of the possibilities just mentioned may sound farfetched, one alternative explanation of the drop in accident rate deserves serious consideration. In any study where the subjects realize they are participating in an experiment, there is the possibility that a *placebo effect* may be observed. In medical research, a *placebo* is a medically inactive pill which may be given to one group of patients while a second group receives an actual drug. If patients are told that the pills they are taking should cure some ailment, it is frequently found that patients from both groups will report that the pills were beneficial. Thus, although the placebo has no more curative powers than a spoonful of sugar, it seems that many patients report improvement simply because they expect the pill to help them. Whether this phenomenon is labeled a *placebo effect*, an *expectation effect*, or evidence for the power of suggestion, it can occur in behavioral research as well as in medicine. In the study of Japanese bus drivers, the drivers were certainly aware that the warning cards were designed to lower the accident rate, so it is possible that the decrease in accidents was merely a placebo effect. In this example, it is easy to speculate about the factors that could produce such an effect. When they received warning cards, the drivers probably devoted more thought to safety than they usually did. They may have considered how dangerous to their passengers and damaging to their careers an accident could be, and as a result they may have driven more slowly on those days.

The problems created by expectations do not necessarily disappear when subjects are not informed that they are participating in an experiment. Research by Rosenthal (1966) and others has shown that a sort of placebo effect can occur if only the person administering the experiment knows what sort of result is being sought. It is easy to imagine how the wishes of the experimenter can affect the outcome of an experiment. Suppose an experimenter is trying to prove that a particular type of training can help students solve simple geometry problems. One group, which is usually called the *experimental group*, receives the special training before taking the geometry test, whereas the second group, the *control group*, receives no initial training. If the experimenter who administers the test knows which subjects are experimental subjects and which are control subjects, the behavior of the experimenter (even one with the most honest intentions) may be slightly different for the two types of subjects. If an experimental subject rapidly solves a problem, the experimenter may say "correct" and have a hint of a smile. If a control subject gives a correct solution, the experimenter may again say "correct" but look worried or displeased. Such subtle differences in the experimenter's behavior can have large effects on a subject's performance.

To avoid placebo effects and experimenter effects, many studies employ a *double-blind* procedure, which means that neither the subject nor the person conducting the experiment knows whether that subject is in the control group or the experimental group. It often takes some ingenuity to devise a way to make the control subjects believe they are receiving some experimental treatment. Before reading further, can you think of a way to control for possible placebo effects in a study such as the one conducted with bus drivers in Japan?

If the accident rate of bus drivers decreases after they receive warning cards on critical days, this could be due to: (1) some confounding variable such as weather conditions, (2) a general increase in the drivers' concerns about safety, (3) a belief among drivers that they are receiving information that should help them avoid accidents, or (4) the opportunity to be more careful on critical days, when a driver might otherwise have an accident. Gittelson proposed that the fourth possibility is correct, but to be convinced we must control for the first three possibilities. One simple solution would be to place half of the drivers in an experimental group and half in a control group. Experimental subjects would receive warning cards on their critical days, as in the Japan study. Control subjects would receive just as many warning cards, but they would be distributed randomly, without consideration of the status of the driver's biorhythms. Neither the drivers nor their supervisors would know which drivers were receiving warning cards on critical days and which were receiving them randomly. You should return to the four possible explanations in the beginning of this paragraph to convince yourself that this procedure controls for the first three factors. That is, if the experimental group had substantially fewer accidents than the control group, we would have to conclude that this was because they were given warning cards specifically on their critical days.

Statistics and Significance Tests. In the hypothetical experiment just described, suppose the accident rate decreased 33 percent in the experimental group and 27 percent in the control group. This difference of 6 percent between groups might have resulted from the drivers' information about their biorhythms, or it could be simply the result of sampling error. How large a difference between two groups must we find before we can be confident that the result is due to our manipulation of the independent variable rather than to sampling error? In trying to answer this question, psychologists frequently rely on *inferential statistics* (so named because they assist the researcher in drawing inferences or theoretical conclusions from empirical results). The use of statistics in behavioral research is a vast topic, and there are many texts that describe the use of different statistical procedures and the logic behind them (for instance, Loftus & Loftus, 1988; Rosenthal & Rosnow, 1984; Sprinthall, 1987). The most common question addressed by a statistical test is: What are the chances that an observed difference between two groups is simply due to sampling error? If the likelihood that the results are due to chance is low, then it is said that the difference between groups was *significant*. In statistical jargon, the term *significant* implies nothing about the importance of a finding; it simply means that it is unlikely that the result occurred by chance. A result is usually called significant in psychological research if the probability that it occurred by chance is less than .05. We might read that a difference between an experimental group and a control group was "significant at the .05 level." This is another way of saying that so large a difference between groups would be expected only 5 times in 100 on the basis of chance alone. It is therefore highly probable that the difference was the result of the experimenter's manipulation of the independent variable.

BEHAVIORAL AND COGNITIVE APPROACHES TO LEARNING

The field of learning is frequently associated with a general approach to psychology called *behaviorism*, which was the dominant approach to the investigation of learning for the first half of the twentieth century. During the 1960s, however, the behavioral approach to learning found itself with a competitor. A new approach called *cogni-*

tive psychology began to develop, and one of the reasons for its appearance was that its proponents were dissatisfied with the behavioral approach. This book considers both perspectives, but it places more emphasis on the behavioral approach, so it is important for you to understand what the behavioral approach is and why cognitive psychologists objected to it. Two of the most salient characteristics of the behavioral approach are (1) the heavy reliance on animal subjects and (2) the emphasis on external events (environmental stimuli and overt behaviors) and a corresponding reluctance to speculate about processes inside the organism. Let us examine each of these characteristics in turn and see why cognitive psychologists objected to them.

The Use of Animal Subjects

A large proportion of the studies described in this text used animals as subjects, especially pigeons, rats, and rabbits. There are a number of reasons why researchers in this field frequently choose to conduct their experiments with nonhuman subjects. First of all, the possibility of a placebo effect or expectancy effect is minimized with animal subjects. Whereas a human subject's behavior may be drastically altered by the knowledge that he or she is being observed, this is unlikely with animal subjects. Most studies with animal subjects are conducted in such a way that the animal does not know its behavior is being monitored and recorded. Furthermore, it is unlikely that an animal subject will be motivated either to please or displease the experimenter, a motive that can ruin a study with human subjects. A second reason for using animal subjects is convenience. The species most commonly used as subjects are easy and inexpensive to care for, and animals of a specific age and sex can be obtained in any quantities the experimenter needs. Once animal subjects are obtained, their participation is as regular as the experimenter's—animal subjects never fail to show up for their appointments, which is unfortunately not the case with human subjects.

Probably the biggest advantage of domesticated animal subjects is that their environment can be controlled to a much greater extent than is possible with either wild animals or human subjects. This is especially important in experiments on learning, where previous experience can have a large effect on a subject's performance in a new learning situation. In the example of the wild raccoon opening a garbage can, our lack of information about the animal's previous experience with garbage cans would make it difficult to interpret its behavior. Likewise, if a human subject tries to solve some brain teaser as part of a learning experiment, the experimenter cannot be sure how many similar problems the subject has encountered in his lifetime. When animals are bred and raised in the laboratory, however, their environments can be constructed to make sure that they have no contact with objects or events similar to those they will encounter in the experiment.

A final reason for using animal subjects is that of comparative simplicity. Just as a child trying to learn about electricity is better off starting with a flashlight than a radio, researchers may have a better chance of discovering the basic principles of learning by examining creatures that are less intelligent and less complex than human beings. The assumption here is that although human beings differ from other animals in some respects, they are also similar in some respects, and it is these commonalities that can be investigated with animal subjects.

Criticisms of the use of animal subjects, by cognitive psychologists and others, seem to boil down to two major arguments. First, it is argued that many important skills, such as the use of language, reading, and solving complex problems, cannot be studied with animals. Although cognitive skills such as language and problem solving have been studied with animal subjects in recent years (see Chapter 11), most behavioral psychologists would agree that some complex abilities are unique to human beings. The difference between behavioral psychologists and cognitive psychologists seems to be only that cognitive psychologists are especially interested in precisely those complex abilities that only human beings possess, whereas behavioral psychologists are typically more interested in learning abilities that are shared by many species. This is nothing more than a difference in interests, and it is pointless to argue about it. The second argument against the use of animal subjects is that human beings are so different from any other animals that it is not possible to generalize from the behavior of animals to human behavior. This is not an issue that can be settled by debate; it is an empirical question that can only be addressed by conducting the appropriate experiments. As will be shown throughout this book, there is abundant evidence that research on learning with animal subjects produces findings that are also applicable to human behavior.

The Emphasis on External Events

This characteristic can be traced back to the very beginnings of behaviorism. The term *behaviorism* was coined by John B. Watson of Johns Hopkins University shortly after the turn of the century. Watson is usually called the first behaviorist, and his book *Psychology from the Standpoint of a Behaviorist* (1919) was very influential. In this book, Watson criticized the research techniques that prevailed in the field of psychology at that time. A popular research method was *introspection*, which involves reflecting upon, reporting, and analyzing one's own mental processes. Thus a psychologist might attempt to examine and describe his thoughts and emotions while looking at a picture or performing some other specific task. A problem with introspection was that it required considerable practice to master this skill, and even then two experienced psychologists might report different thoughts and emotions when performing the same task. Watson (1919) recognized this weakness, and he argued that verbal reports of private events (such as sensations, feelings, states of consciousness) should have no place in the field of psychology:

"States of consciousness," like the so-called phenomena of spiritualism, are not objectively verifiable and for that reason can never become data for science. In all other sciences the facts of observation are objective, verifiable and can be reproduced and controlled by all trained observers.... (p. 1)

...we may say that the goal of psychological study is the *ascertaining of such data and laws that, given the stimulus, psychology can predict what the response will be; or, on the other hand, given the response, it can specify the nature of the effective stimulus.* (p. 10, italics in original)

Watson's logic can be stated in the form of a syllogism:

Given that:	1.	We want psychology to be a science.
And that:	2.	Sciences deal only with events everyone can observe.
It follows that:	3.	Psychology must deal only with observable events.

According to Watson, the observable events in psychology are stimuli and responses; they are certainly not the subjective reports of trained introspectionists.

Whereas Watson argued against the use of unobservable events as psychological data, B. F. Skinner has repeatedly criticized the use of unobservable events in psychological theories. Skinner (1950, 1953, 1985) asserted that it is both dangerous and unnecessary to point to some unobservable event, or intervening variable, as the cause of behavior. Consider an experiment in which a rat is deprived of water for a certain number of hours and is then placed in a chamber where it can obtain water by pressing a lever. We would probably find an orderly relationship between the independent variable, the number of hours of water deprivation, and the dependent variable, the rate of lever pressing. The rule that described this relationship would be a part of the syntax of our theory, and this rule is represented by the arrow in Figure 1-3a. Skinner has pointed out that many psychologists would prefer to go further, however, and postulate an intervening variable such as *thirst*, which is presumably controlled by the hours of deprivation and which in turn controls the rate of lever pressing (see Figure 1-3b). According to Skinner, the inclusion of this intervening variable is unnecessary because it does not improve our ability to predict the rat's behavior—we can do just as well simply by knowing the hours of deprivation. The addition of the intervening variable needlessly compli-

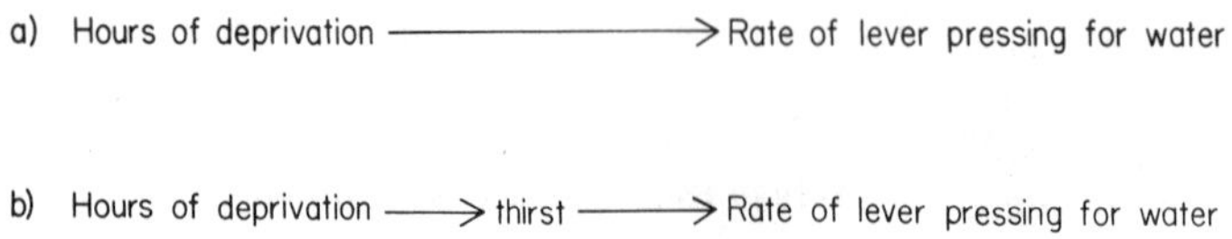

FIGURE 1-3.   (a) A schematic
diagram of a simple theory of
behavior with no intervening
variables. (b) The same theory
with an intervening variable
added. In this example, the
intervening variable, thirst, is
unnecessary, for it only
complicates the theory.

a) Hours of deprivation ――――――――――――> Rate of lever pressing for water

b) Hours of deprivation ――――> thirst ――――> Rate of lever pressing for water

cates our theory. Now our syntax must describe two relationships—the relationship between hours of deprivation and thirst, plus that between thirst and lever pressing. Since both theories are equally predictive, by the criterion of simplicity the theory without the intervening variable (Figure 1-3a) is preferable.

Skinner also argued that the use of an intervening variable such as thirst is dangerous because we can easily fool ourselves into thinking we have found the cause of a behavior when we are actually talking about a hypothetical and unobservable entity. Some other intervening variables that can find their way into a psychological theory are *anger, intelligence, stubbornness*, and *laziness*. To illustrate how an intervening variable can be treated as the cause of a behavior, suppose we ask a father why his 10-year-old son does not always do his homework. The father's answer might be, "Because he is lazy." In this case, laziness, an unobservable entity, is offered as an explanation, and accepting this explanation could prematurely curtail any efforts to improve the problem behavior. After all, if the cause of a behavior is inside the person, how can we control it? However, Skinner proposes that the causes of many behaviors can be traced back to the external environment, and by changing the environment we can change the behavior. Perhaps the young boy does not do his homework because he plays outside all afternoon, eats dinner with the family at a fairly late hour, and then is too tired to do his assignments. If so, a simple change in the boy's environment might improve his behavior. As just two possibilities, either the family dinner hour could be made earlier, or the boy could be required to come home an hour or two before dinner to do his homework. In short, the potential for controlling a behavior may be rec-

ognized if an intervening variable such as laziness is rejected and an external cause of the behavior is sought.

Neal Miller (1959), another psychologist with a behavioral orientation, took issue with Skinner's position that intervening variables are always undesirable. Miller suggested that intervening variables are often useful when several independent and dependent variables are involved. Starting with the example shown in Figure 1-3, he noted that the number of hours without water is only one factor that might influence a rat's rate of lever pressing for water. The rat's rate of pressing might also increase if it were fed dry food, or if it were given an injection of a saline solution. Furthermore, the rate of lever pressing is only one of many dependent variables that might be affected by hours of deprivation, dry food, or a saline injection. Two other dependent variables are the volume of water drunk, and the amount of quinine (which would give the water a bitter taste) that would have to be added to make the rat stop drinking. As shown in Figure 1-4a, Miller proposed that each of these three dependent variables would be influenced by each of the three independent variables. Once all of these variables are added, a theory without intervening variables would need to have a separate rule for describing each of the nine cause-and-effect relationships, as symbolized by the nine crossing arrows in Figure 1-4a. This fairly complicated theory could be simplified by including the intervening variable, thirst, as shown in Figure 1-4b. That is, we might assume that each of the three independent variables influences an animal's thirst, and the animal's level of thirst controls each of the three dependent variables (the three different measures of the animal's behavior). Figure 1-4b shows that

a.

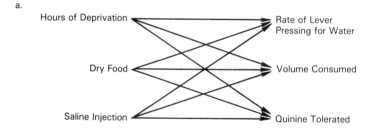

b.

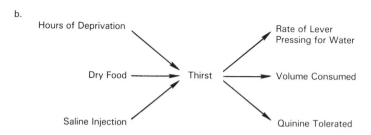

FIGURE 1-4. (a) The arrows represent the nine relationships between independent and dependent variables that must be defined by a theory without intervening variables. (b) The arrows represent the six relationships the theory must define if it includes the intervening variable of thirst. Neal Miller argued that the second theory is superior because it is more parsimonious. (After Miller, 1959)

once the intervening variable is included, only six cause-and-effect relationships have to be described—three to describe the relationship between each independent variable and thirst, and three more to describe the relationship between thirst and each dependent variable. In this case, the criterion of simplicity favors the theory with the intervening variable. Miller showed that the potential advantage of including intervening variables increases as a theory is expanded to deal with more and more independent variables.

As you might suspect, Miller's argument has not ended the debate over intervening variables. In reply to the sort of logic presented by Miller, Skinner's (1956a) position is that if so many variables affect thirst, and if thirst controls so many different behavior patterns, then whatever thirst is, it must be quite complicated, and the simpler theory depicted in Figure 1-4b does not do justice to this complexity. On the other side, those who favor the use of intervening variables also use another line of argument: They point out that intervening variables are commonplace in other, firmly established sciences. As already noted, many familiar concepts from physics (for instance, gravity) are intervening variables, since they are not directly observable. Some psycholo-

gists have therefore reasoned that progress in psychology would be needlessly restricted if the use of intervening variables were disallowed (Nicholas, 1984).

As the case of Neal Miller illustrates, it is not correct to say that all behaviorists avoid using intervening variables. As we will see, the theories of many psychologists of the behavioral tradition include them. The difference between theorists of the behavioral and cognitive approaches is only one of degree. As a general rule, cognitive psychologists tend to use intervening variables more freely and more prolifically than do behavioral psychologists. The theories of cognitive psychologists include a wide range of concepts that are not directly observable, such as short-term memory, long-term memory, sensory information storage, attention, rehearsal, and so on. Behavioral psychologists tend to use intervening variables more sparingly and more cautiously. (You should bear in mind that these stereotypes of behavioral and cognitive psychologists, as with all stereotypes, undoubtedly have many exceptions.)

The debate over the use of intervening variables has gone on for decades, and we will not settle it here. (For a variety of opinions on this matter, see Luce, 1984; Richelle, 1984; and other articles in the same issue of *The Behavioral and Brain Sciences.*) My own position (though hardly original) is that the ultimate test of a psychological theory is its ability to predict behavior. If a theory can make accurate predictions about behaviors that were previously unpredictable, then the theory is useful, regardless of whether or not it contains any intervening variables. In this text, we will encounter many useful theories of each type.

ON FREE WILL AND DETERMINISM

Determinism is a philosophical position that all the events of the world, including all human behaviors, are determined by physical causes which could, at least in principle, be discovered and analyzed with the techniques of science. A fair number of psychologists assume that this position is correct and use it as a starting point for their study of human behavior. On the other hand, many people find the determinist position unacceptable because it rules out the possibility of *free will*—the idea that some nonphysical entity such as the will or the soul can direct human behavior. For instance, many religions maintain that human beings are free to choose between good and evil. Those who believe in free will therefore claim that not all human behavior can be predicted or explained by a scientific analysis (which assumes there is a physical cause for every behavior).

Is it necessary to be a determinist to pursue the sort of scientific analysis of behavior that is described in this book? Certainly not. Regardless of your religious beliefs or your philosophical convictions, you can profit from reading this book as long as you are willing to observe that there is *some* regularity and predictability in the behaviors of both humans and nonhumans. It is probably not necessary to convince you that this is so, because this regularity is evident all around us. I am sure you can make some fairly accurate predictions about the behaviors of many individuals in your environment (such as what will happen if you request to borrow five dollars from your best friend, or what will happen if you walk toward a starling that is feeding in the grass, or what will happen to the flow of traffic as the light changes from green to yellow to red). Science is not needed to point out the regularities in behavior, but by using the scientific method as it has been described in this chapter we can gain a clearer understanding of these regularities and make more accurate predictions about future behavior. We can proceed in this fashion without taking any particular position on the free-will/determinism controversy.

2

SIMPLE IDEAS,
SIMPLE ASSOCIATIONS,
AND SIMPLE CELLS

The scientific investigation of learning did not begin until about the end of the nineteenth century. The first portion of this chapter presents some historical developments, both theoretical and experimental, that preceded the beginnings of this field and that had a strong influence on it. Most of these developments also preceded the emergence of the field of psychology itself. Although no single event marks the beginning of psychology as a separate discipline, an event frequently cited is the founding of the world's first psychological laboratory in Leipzig, Germany by Wilhelm Wundt in 1879. Prior to this time, the study of psychology was considered to be a part of the discipline of philosophy, and it was philosophers who most frequently lectured and wrote about psychological topics. The writings of a number of philosophers, who spanned several centuries but are now collectively called *Associationists*, constitute some of the earliest recorded thoughts about learning.

EARLY THEORIES ABOUT THE ASSOCIATION OF IDEAS

Aristotle

Aristotle (circa 350 B.C.) is generally acknowledged to be the first Associationist (although Aristotle did not use this term). He proposed three principles of association that can be viewed as an elementary theory of memory. Aristotle suggested that these principles describe how one thought leads to another. Before reading about Aristotle's principles, you have the opportunity to try something Aristotle never did—to conduct a simple experiment to test these principles. This experiment, which should take only a minute or two, might be called a study of *free association*. Get a piece of paper and a pencil, and write the numbers 1 through 12 in a column down the left side of the paper. Table 2-1 contains a list of words that are also numbered 1 through 12.

Read one word at a time, and write down the first two or three words that come to mind after reading each word. Do not spend much time on one word—your first few responses will be the most informative.

TABLE 2-1 Words for the Free Association Experiment

1. apple	7. girl
2. night	8. dentist
3. thunder	9. quiet
4. bread	10. sunset
5. chair	11. elephant
6. bat	12. blue

Once you have your list of responses to the twelve words, look over your answers and try to formulate some generalizations that describe the types of responses that are most likely to occur in such a task. Aristotle believed that the act of remembering is not a random process, but rather an orderly chain of thoughts that follow specific rules. By examining your responses you may be able to anticipate one or more of Aristotle's principles. Aristotle's first principle of association was contiguity. The more closely together (contiguous) in space or time two items occur, the more likely will the thought of one item lead to the thought of the other. For example, the response *chair* to the word *table* illustrates association by spatial contiguity, since the two items are often found close together. The response *lightning* to the word *thunder* is an example of association by temporal contiguity. Notice that an understanding of cause and effect is not necessary for such an association to develop. Although most adults understand that thunder and lightning are both products of the same electrical discharge, a young child or an uneducated adult might associate these two concepts without understanding the physical connection between them. Other examples of association by contiguity are *bread-butter* and *dentist-pain*.

Aristotle's other two principles of association were *similarity* and *contrast*. He stated that the thought of one concept often leads to the thought of similar concepts. Examples of association by similarity are the responses *orange* or *pear* to the prompt *apple*, or the responses *yellow* or *green* to the prompt *blue*. By *contrast*, Aristotle meant that an item often leads to the thought of its opposite (for instance, *night-day, girl-boy, sunset-sunrise*). Most people who try this simple free-association experiment conclude that Aristotle's principles of association have both strengths and weaknesses. On the negative side, the list of principles seems incomplete, and other factors that affect the train of thought may have already occurred to you. On the positive side, Aristotle's principles have some intuitive validity for most people, and they seem to be a reasonable first step in the development of a theory about the relationship between experience and memory.

The British Associationists: Simple and Complex Ideas

For Aristotle, the principles of association were simply hypotheses about how one thought leads to another. For many of the philosophers who wrote about Associationism several centuries later, this topic assumed a much greater significance: Associationism was seen as a theory of all knowledge. The *British Associationists* included Thomas Hobbes (1651), John Locke (1690), James Mill (1829), John Stuart Mill (1843), and others. These writers are also called the *British Empiricists* because of their belief that every person acquires all knowledge empirically—that is, through experience. This viewpoint is typified by John Locke's statement that the mind of a newborn child is a *tabula rasa* (a blank slate) onto which experience makes its mark. The Empiricists believed that every memory, every idea, and every concept a person has is based on one or more previous experiences. The opposite of Empiricism is *Nativism*, or the position that some ideas are innate, and do not depend on an individual's past experience. For instance, the Nativist Immanuel Kant (1781) believed that the concepts of space and time are inborn, and that through experience new concepts are built on the foundation of these original, innate concepts. The Empiricist position is the more extreme of the two because it allows for no counterexamples. That is, a demonstration that most concepts are learned through experience does no damage to the Nativist position, which acknowledges the role of experience. On the other hand, it takes only one example of an innate concept to refute the Empiricist position. As we shall see several times throughout the text (especially in Chapters 3 and 9, which emphasize biological contributions to behavior), modern research has uncovered many examples that are at odds with the extreme Empiricist position.

Fortunately, Associationism is not logically tied to extreme Empiricism. We can grant that some concepts are innate, but that many concepts are developed through experience. The British Empiricists offered some hypotheses both about how old concepts become associated in memory, and about how new concepts are formed. According to the Associationists, there is a direct correspondence between experience and memory. Experience consists of *sensations*, and memory consists of *ideas*. Furthermore, any sensory experience can be broken down into *simple sensations*. For instance, if a person observes a red box-shaped object, this sensation might be broken down into two simple sensations—*red* and *rectangular*. At some later time, the person's memory of this experience would consist of the two corresponding *simple ideas* of *red* and *rectangular*. Thus, as illustrated in Figure 2-1a, there is a one-to-one correspondence between simple sensations and simple ideas. A simple idea was said to be a sort of faint replica of the simple sensation from which it arose.

Now suppose that the person repeatedly encounters such a red box-shaped object. Through the principles of contiguity, an association should develop between the ideas of *red* and *rectangle*, as shown in Figure 2-1b. Once such an association is formed, if the person experiences the color red, this will not only invoke the idea of *red*, but by virtue of the association the idea *rectangular* will be invoked as well (Figure 2-1c).

It should be obvious how this sort of hypothesis can explain at least some of the results of a free-association experiment. For instance, the idea of *thunder* will "excite" the idea of *lightning* because of the association between them, an association developed according to the principle of contiguity. But many of our concepts are more complex than the simple ideas of *red, rectangu-*

lar, thunder, and *lightning*. In an attempt to come to grips with the full range of memories and knowledge of the world that all people have, several Associationists speculated about the formation of *complex ideas.* James Mill (1829) proposed that if two or more simple sensations are repeatedly presented together, a product of their union may be a complex idea. For instance, if the sensations *red* and *rectangular* occur together repeatedly, a new, complex idea of *brick* may form. Mill did not have much to say about how this event takes place, but Figure 2-1d shows one way to depict Mill's hypothesis graphically. Once such a complex idea is formed, it can also be evoked by the process of association when the sensation of either red or rectangle occurs. Mill went on to say that complex ideas could themselves combine to form *duplex ideas*. In short, Mill suggested that all complex ideas (1) can be decomposed into two or more simple ideas, and (2) are always formed through the repeated pairing of these simple ideas. In the following passage, Mill describes the formation of a hierarchy of ideas of increasing complexity:

Some of the most familiar objects with which we are acquainted furnish instances of these unions of complex and duplex ideas.

Brick is one complex idea, mortar is another complex idea; these ideas, with ideas of position and quantity, compose my idea of a wall....In the same manner my complex idea of glass, and wood, and others, compose my duplex idea of a window; and these duplex ideas, united together, compose my idea of a house, which is made up of various duplex ideas. (pp. 114-116)

This, then, was the view that all ideas, no matter how complex, are the product of simple ideas, which are in turn the product of simple sensations. As with Aristotle's principles of association, there are both strengths and weaknesses in this hypothesis. Some complex concepts are taught to children only after they have become familiar with the simpler ideas that compose them. For instance, it is only after a child understands the concepts of *addition* and *repetition* that the more complex concept of *multiplication* is presented, and it is often introduced as a procedure for performing repeated additions. For older students who know how to calculate the area of a rectangle, *integration* may be initially presented as a technique for calculating the total area of a series of very thin rectangles. In both of these examples, a complex idea is formed only after the mastery of simpler ideas, and it is difficult to imagine learning these concepts in the opposite order. However, other concepts do not seem to follow as nicely from Mill's theory, in-

cluding his own example of the concept of *house*. A two-year-old may know the word *house* and use it appropriately without knowing the "simpler" concepts of *mortar, ceiling,* or *rafter.* With *house* and many other complex concepts, people seem to develop at least a crude idea of the entire concept before learning all of the components of the concept, although according to Mill's theory this should not be possible. Thus although it appears to have validity in some cases, Mill's the-

FIGURE 2-1. Some principles of Associationism. (a) The one-to-one correspondence between simple sensations and simple ideas. (b) After repeated pairings of the two sensations, an association forms between their respective ideas. (c) Once an association is formed, presenting one stimulus will activate the ideas of both. (d) With enough pairings of two simple ideas, a complex idea encompassing both simple ideas is formed. The complex idea may now be evoked if either of the simple stimuli is presented.

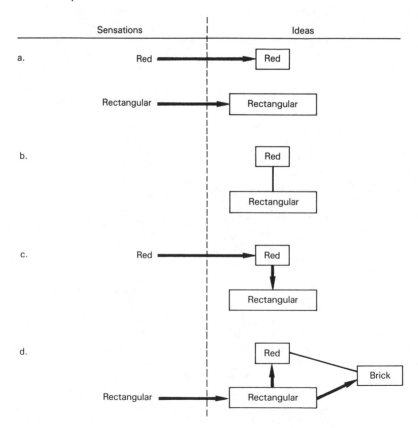

ory is at best incomplete. Some more recent theories about concepts and their formation will be presented in Chapter 10.

Thomas Brown's Secondary Principles of Association

As mentioned above, Aristotle's list of principles of association seemed incomplete. Another Associationist, Thomas Brown (1820) tried to remedy this situation by proposing nine secondary principles of association to supplement Aristotle's list. These principles are of more than historical interest, because in one way or another each of these principles has been investigated by modern researchers. Briefly, Brown's secondary principles were: (1) The *length of time* two sensations coexist determines the strength of association. (2) The *liveliness* or vividness of the sensations also affects the strength of the association. According to Brown, "brilliant objects" or "occasions of great joy or sorrow" will be more easily associated and better remembered. A stronger association will also occur (3) if the two sensations have been paired *frequently*, (4) if they have been paired *recently*, or (5) if both sensations are *free from strong associations* with other sensations. For instance, if you meet many new people at a party, you may find it easier to remember the name of someone who introduces himself as *Jeremiah* (a fairly unusual name) than someone called *John* (a name that you probably associate with quite a few people). Other factors that can affect the strength of an association are (6) *constitutional differences* among different individuals, (7) a person's current *emotional state*, (8) the momentary *state of the body* (healthy, ill, intoxicated), and (9) a person's *prior habits*.

The primary principles of Aristotle, the secondary principles of Thomas Brown, and James Mill's hypotheses about the development of complex ideas can be thought of as the earliest theories of learning, for they attempted to explain how people change as a result of their experiences. Yet although they had their theories, the Associationists conducted no experiments to test them. In retrospect, it is remarkable that despite an interest in principles of learning which spanned some 2000 years, no systematic experiments on learning were conducted until the end of the nineteenth century. This absence of research on learning was not a result of technological deficiencies—the first experiments on learning were so simple that they could have been performed centuries earlier.

EBBINGHAUS'S EXPERIMENTS ON MEMORY

Hermann Ebbinghaus (1885) was the first to put the Associationists' principles to an experimental test. In his memory experiments, Ebbinghaus might have used lists of words as study materials, but he felt that words were not ideal because any subject will have many preexisting associations between words (such as *coffee-hot*), and these previous associations will undoubtedly affect the subject's performance. To avoid this problem, Ebbinghaus invented the *nonsense syllable*—a meaningless syllable consisting of two consonants separated by a vowel (for instance, HAQ, PIF, ZOD). Ebbinghaus constructed a master list of some 2300 nonsense syllables, and by drawing from this list at random he could construct a list for study of any desired length.

Ebbinghaus himself served as his only subject in all of his studies, which continued for several years. This arrangement is not acceptable by modern standards, because the likelihood of experimenter bias is high in such an arrangement. Furthermore, any single subject might be somehow atypical and unrepresentative of people in general. Despite these potential pitfalls, Ebbinghaus's results have withstood the test of time: All of his major findings have been replicated by later researchers using the multiple-subject procedures that are standard in modern research. The basic plan of most of his experiments was to study a list of nonsense syllables until it was memorized perfectly, and then to determine how much of his memory remained at some later time. His method of study was always the same: Paced by the ticking of a watch, he would read through a list aloud at a steady rate. Upon finishing a list, he would return immediately to the start of the list and continue reading. Periodically he would attempt to recite the list by heart, at this same steady pace. These periods of reading and reciting would proceed without interruption until he had mastered the list. By counting the number of repetitions needed for one perfect recitation, Ebbinghaus had an objective measure of the difficulty of memorizing a list. But how could he measure what was left of this learning at a later time (say, 24 hours later)? Ebbinghaus's solution was to learn the list to perfection, then allow some time to pass, and finally relearn the list to perfection, again counting how many repetitions were necessary. His measure of the strength of memory was what he called *savings*, or the decrease in the number of required repetitions during the second learning period. For example, if a list required 20 repetitions during the initial learning, but only 15 repetitions during the relearning phase, this constituted a savings of 5 repetitions, or 25 percent. As shown below, the measurement of savings proved to be a sensitive way to gauge how the effects of an initial learning experience persisted over time.

Ebbinghaus's Major Findings

List Length. One of Ebbinghaus's simplest and least surprising results concerned the relationship between the length of a list and the number of repetitions needed to master it. Naturally, longer lists required more repetitions. Ebbinghaus found that he could learn a list of 12 nonsense syllables after about 17 repetitions. However, the number of necessary repetitions increased to 44 for a list of 24 items and to 55 for a list of 36 items. The general rule suggested by these results is that if the amount of material to be learned is doubled, the time needed to master the material is more than doubled. To put it another way, as list length increased, the study time required *per item* increased.

The Effects of Repetition. One of Thomas Brown's secondary principles of association states that the frequency of pairings directly affects the strength of an association. This principle is obviously supported by the simple fact that a list that is not memorized after a small number of repetitions will eventually be learned after more repetitions. However, one of Ebbinghaus's

findings offers some additional support for the frequency principle. Using a 16-item list, Ebbinghaus found that about 33 repetitions were necessary to achieve one perfect repetition, and after 24 hours he obtained a savings of about 33 percent. However, if he continued to study the list on the first day beyond the point of one perfect recitation (for instance, for an additional 10 or 20 repetitions), his savings after 24 hours increased substantially. In other words, even after he appeared to have perfectly mastered a list, additional study produced improved performance in a delayed test. Continuing to practice after performance is apparently perfect is called *overlearning*, and Ebbinghaus demonstrated that Thomas Brown's principle of frequency applies to periods of overlearning as well as to periods in which there is visible improvement during practice.

The Effects of Time. Thomas Brown's principle of recency states that the more recently two items have been paired, the stronger will be the association between them. Ebbinghaus tested this principle by varying the length of time that elapsed between his study and test periods. As shown in Figure 2-2, he examined intervals as short as 20 minutes and as long as one month. The graph in Figure 2-2 is an example of a *forgetting curve*, for it shows how the passage of time has a detrimental effect on performance in a memory task. The curve shows that forgetting is rapid immediately after a study period, but the rate of additional forgetting slows as more time passes. The shape of this curve is similar to the forgetting curves obtained by later researchers in numerous experiments with both human and animal subjects (Ammons, et al., 1958; Blough, 1959; Peterson & Peterson, 1959), although the time scale on the x-axis varies greatly depending on the nature of the task and the species of the subjects. Forgetting curves of this type provide strong confirmation of Thomas Brown's principle of recency.

The Role of Contiguity. The Associationists' principle of contiguity states that the more closely together two items are presented, the better will the thought of one item lead to the thought of the other. Ebbinghaus reasoned that if

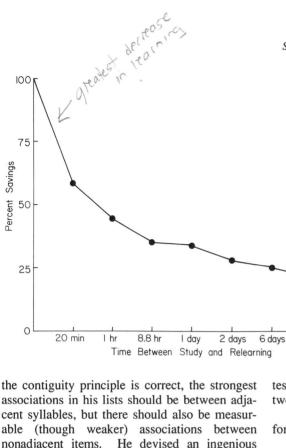

← greatest decrease in learning

FIGURE 2-2. Ebbinghaus's forgetting curve. The percentage savings is shown for various time intervals between his initial learning and relearning of lists of nonsense syllables. (After Ebbinghaus, 1885)

the contiguity principle is correct, the strongest associations in his lists should be between adjacent syllables, but there should also be measurable (though weaker) associations between nonadjacent items. He devised an ingenious method for testing this idea, which involved rearranging the items in a list after it was memorized, and then learning the rearranged list. His technique for rearranging lists is illustrated in Table 2-2. The designations I1 through I16 refer to the 16 items as they were ordered in the original list (List O). Once this list is memorized, there should be a strong association between I1 and I2, a somewhat weaker association between I1 and I3 (since these were separated by one item in the original list), a still weaker association between I1 and I4, and so on. There should be similar gradations in strength of association between every other item and its neighbors. The rearranged list called List 1 in Table 2-2 was used to test for associations between items one syllable apart. Observe that every adjacent item in List 1 was separated by one syllable in the original list. If there is any association between I1 and I3, between I3 and I5, and so on, then List 1 should be easier to learn than a totally new list (there should be some savings that are carried over from List O to List 1). In a similar fashion, List 2

tests for associations between items that were two syllables apart in the original list.

In this experiment, Ebbinghaus used a 24-hour forgetting period between his study of an original

TABLE 2-2 How Ebbinghaus rearranged an original list of 16 syllables (represented here by the symbols I1 through I16) to test for possible associations between items separated by one syllable, and by items separated by two syllables.

List 0 (Original list)	List 1 (One item skipped)	List 2 (2 items skipped)
I1	I1	I1
I2	I3	I4
I3	I5	I7
I4	I7	I10
I5	I9	I13
I6	I11	I16
I7	I13	I2
I8	I15	I5
I9	I2	I8
I10	I4	I11
I11	I6	I14
I12	I8	I3
I13	I10	I6
I14	I12	I9
I15	I14	I12
I16	I16	I15

list and his test with a rearranged list. If List 0 was simply relearned after 24 hours, there was about 33 percent savings. In comparison, Ebbinghaus found an average savings of 11 percent if List 1 was studied 24 hours after List 0, and a savings of 7 percent if List 2 was used. Although the amount of savings with these rearranged lists was not large, the pattern of results was orderly: As the number of skipped syllables increased in the rearranged lists, the amount of savings was diminished. These results are completely consistent with the principle of contiguity, because they imply that the strength of an association between two items depends on their proximity in the original list.

Backward Associations. In one experiment, Ebbinghaus learned a list one day and then attempted to learn the list in the opposite order the following day. As the British Associationists described it, the contiguity principle makes a straightforward prediction for this experiment. Since simply reversing the order of the items does not change the contiguity of any two items, and since the strength of an association is a function of contiguity, it should be just as easy to learn the reversed list as to relearn the original list. Ebbinghaus' experiment did not confirm this prediction, however. He obtained a savings of only 13 percent with reversed lists, much less than the 33 percent savings obtained when simply relearning original lists. There are many ways to interpret this result, but one explanation is that instead of a single, bidirectional association between two items (Figure 2-3a), there are actually two unidirectional associations between any two items (Figure 2-3b), and the strengths of these associations can vary independently. That is, a particular type of studying (such as studying item A followed by item B) may result in a strong association from item A to item B, but only a weak association from item B to item A.

Regardless of how we choose to interpret the results of the backward-list experiment, this study points out a limitation of the contiguity principle: If we wish to estimate the likelihood that presenting one item will lead to the recall of a second item, we must know not only how closely the items were paired in the period of

FIGURE 2-3. Two possible representations of the associations formed in memory when Item A is followed by Item B. (a) A strong bidirectional association. (b) A strong unidirectional association from A to B, and a weak association from B to A. The representation in (b) is more consistent with the results of Ebbinghaus's backward-list experiment.

study but also the *order* in which the items were presented. The backward-list experiment suggests that recall is better when items must be remembered in the same order in which they were originally studied.

Ebbinghaus and the Associationists Compared to Later Learning Theorists

Although both Ebbinghaus and the British Associationists preceded the beginnings of behaviorism and cognitive psychology, there are a number of parallels between the early writers and these two modern approaches to learning. The Associationists did not conduct experiments, but in their theoretical approach they were similar to modern cognitive psychologists. Like cognitive psychologists, the Associationists were interested in thought processes and in the nature of human knowledge. They speculated about the relationship between unobservable *simple ideas* and *complex ideas*. They showed little interest in observable behavior, or in how experience with various stimuli might alter a person's later behavior.

Ebbinghaus, on the other hand, was more representative of the behavioral approach. His experiments dealt with observable stimuli (the lists of nonsense syllables) and overt behavior (his recitation of the lists). Ebbinghaus's presentation of his results would satisfy the strictest behaviorist: His book is filled with tables that show how some objective measure of behavior (usually savings) depended on some clearly defined independent variable (such as the number of repetitions, the amount of time since original learning, list re-arrangement). For instance, the forgetting curve in Figure 2-2 plots the dependent variable, percent savings, as a function of the independent variable, time since original learning. As a strict behaviorist would surely argue, we need no intervening variables, no hypotheses about thought processes, to see the systematic manner in which the passage of time affects the ability to recall.

A behaviorist might also argue that this example shows that we do not need a theory about thought processes in order to put findings such as Ebbinghaus's to practical use. Thus the forgetting curve might suggest that if you must take an examination in which a good deal of rote memorization is involved (such as a history exam in which the names, places, and dates have little more inherent meaning to you than nonsense syllables), you should do your final studying as close to the time of the exam as possible. Ebbinghaus's forgetting curve suggests that a substantial fraction of this type of material may be lost after only a few hours. As another example, Ebbinghaus's experiment on overlearning suggests that you may be wise to continue to study even after you seem to have mastered the material to be remembered, because overlearning increased the amount of savings obtained at a later time. Finally, the experiment on backward lists indicates that the order in which you study the material can affect your ability to recall it. If you know that the exam will present you with a list of dates and require you to describe what events took place on those dates, you should study by using dates as stimuli and by responding with the appropriate event (rather than attempting to recall dates for various events). Notice that each of these conclusions can be reached simply by examining Ebbinghaus's results and generalizing to other situations where rote memorization is involved. They do not depend on a theory of knowledge, on an understanding of what *ideas* are or what *associations* are, or on a theory of what goes on in our brains when we learn. The point is that a strict behavioral approach, which emphasizes orderly relationships between stimuli and responses, can yield useful information about behavior without theorizing about internal events.

PHYSIOLOGICAL FACTS AND THEORIES RELATED TO ASSOCIATIONISM

Having examined some of the earliest theories and experiments on learning, we can now turn to a different set of questions. What goes on in a creature's nervous system when it is presented with some fairly simple stimulus, such as the color *red* or a *rectangular* shape? What happens in the nervous system when the stimuli *red* and *rectangular* are repeatedly paired and the animal begins to associate the two? How does a creature's sensory systems allow it to recognize more complex stimuli such as bricks, automobiles, or people's faces? Physiological psychologists have attempted to answer these questions, with varying degrees of progress so far. This section provides a brief overview of some of this research. This material should give you a different way to think about sensations, ideas, and associations, and it will provide a useful foundation for topics discussed in later chapters. In order to understand this material, it is necessary to have some understanding of how nerve cells or *neurons* function. The next section provides a short summary, but for more information you may want to read the section on neurons that can be found in nearly every textbook on introductory psychology.

The Basic Characteristics of Neurons

Despite large differences in their overall structures, the nervous systems of all creatures are composed of specialized cells called neurons, whose major function is to transmit information. The human brain contains about 10 billion neurons, and there are many additional neurons throughout the rest of the body. Whereas neurons vary greatly in size and shape, the basic components of all neurons, and the functions of those components, are quite similar. Figure 2-4 shows the structure of a typical neuron.

The three major components of a neuron are the *cell body*, the *dendrites*, and the *axons*. The cell body contains the *nucleus*, which regulates the basic metabolic functions of the cell, such as the intake of oxygen and the release of carbon di-

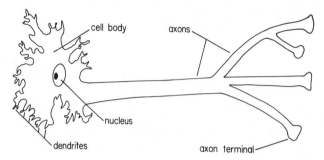

cell body

axons

nucleus

dendrites

axon terminal

FIGURE 2-4.   A schematic diagram of a neuron.

oxide.   In the transmission of information, the dendrites and the cell body are on the receptive side—they are sensitive to certain chemicals called *transmitters* that are released by other neurons.   When its dendrites and cell body receive sufficient stimulation, a neuron is said to "fire"— it exhibits a sudden change in electrical potential lasting only a few milliseconds (thousandths of a second).   The more stimulation a neuron receives, the more rapidly it fires: It may fire only a few dozen times a second with low stimulation but several hundred times a second with high stimulation. The axons are involved on the transmission side.   Each time a neuron fires, enlarged structures at the ends of the axons, the *axon terminals*, release a transmitter that may stimulate the dendrites of other neurons.   Thus, within a single neuron, the flow of activity typically begins with the dendrites, travels down the axons, and ends with release of transmitter by the axon terminals.

The term *synapse* refers to a small gap between the axon terminal of one neuron (called the *presynaptic neuron*) and the dendrite of another neuron (called the *postsynaptic neuron*). As Figure 2-5 shows, it is into the synapse that the presynaptic neuron releases its transmitter.   This transmitter can affect the postsynaptic neuron in one of two ways.   In an *excitatory synapse*, the release of transmitter makes the postsynaptic neuron more likely to fire.   In an *inhibitory synapse*, the release of transmitter makes the postsynaptic neuron less likely to fire.   A single neuron may receive inputs, some excitatory and some inhibitory, from thousands of other neurons.   At any moment, a neuron's firing rate re-

flects the combined influence of all its excitatory and inhibitory inputs.

Physiological Research on "Simple Sensations"

One theme of Associationism that has been uniformly supported by subsequent physiological findings is the hypothesis that our sensory systems analyze the complex stimulus environment that surrounds us by breaking it down into "simple sensations."   Quite a bit is now known about the traditional "five senses" (sight, hearing, touch, taste, and smell) and of several internal senses (which monitor the body's balance, muscle tensions, the position of the limbs, and so on). The evidence consistently shows that each of these sensory systems begins by detecting fairly basic characteristics of incoming stimuli.   A few examples will help to illustrate how this is accomplished.

The nervous system's only contact with the stimuli of the external environment comes through a variety of specialized neurons called *receptors*.   Instead of dendrites that are sensitive to the transmitters of other neurons, receptors have structures that are sensitive to specific types of external stimuli.   In the visual system, for example, the effective stimulus modality is, of course, light, and receptors sensitive to light are located on the *retina*.   As shown in Figure 2-6, light entering the eye is focused by the *cornea* and *lens*, passes through a gelatinous substance called the *vitreous humor*, and finally reaches the retina. If we make an analogy between the eye and a camera, then the retina is the counterpart of

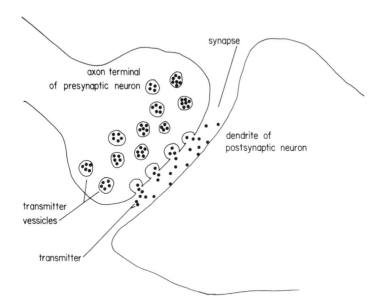

FIGURE 2-5. A schematic diagram of a synapse between two neurons. The chemical transmitter released by the axon terminal of the presynaptic neuron causes changes in the dendrite of the postsynaptic neuron that makes the neuron more likely to fire (in an excitatory synapse) or less likely to fire (in an inhibitory synapse).

photographic film. It is on the retina, which lines the inside surface of the eyeball, that a miniature inverted image of the visual world is focused. Some of the receptors on the retina are called *cones* (because of their shape), and different cones are especially sensitive to different colors in the spectrum of visible light. In the normal human eye, there are three classes of cones, which are most effectively stimulated by light in the red, green, and blue regions of the spectrum, respectively. A red-sensitive cone, for example, is most responsive to red light, but it will also exhibit a weaker response when stimulated by other colors in the red region of the spectrum, such as orange, violet, and yellow. Similarly, a green-sensitive cone is most effectively stimulated by green light, but it is also stimulated to some extent by blue and yellow light. Although we have

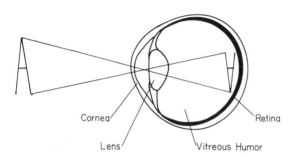

FIGURE 2-6. How light from an object in the environment enters the eye and is focused on the retina, in an inverted image.

only three types of cones, our ability to distinguish among a large number of subtle differences in color stems from the fact that different colors will produce different *patterns* of activity in the three types of cones. A particular shade of yellow, for example, will produce a unique pattern of activity—the red and green cones may be activated to approximately the same extent, and the blue cones will exhibit very little activity. Since no other color will produce exactly the same pattern of activity in the cones, this pattern is the visual system's method of encoding the presence of a particular shade of yellow.

We can think of cones as neurons that decompose the complex visual world into what the Associationists called "simple sensations." Notice that no matter how intricate a visual stimulus may be, a single red-sensitive cone can communicate only two primitive pieces of information to the rest of the nervous system. First, its activity signals the presence of light that is somewhere in the red region of the spectrum. Second, the cone's activity provides information about the location of the reddish light: The activation of a red-sensitive cone in, for example, the lower right portion of the retina indicates that the reddish light is coming from the upper left portion of the visual field (because the image projected onto the retina is inverted).

All the other sensory systems have specialized receptors that are activated by simple features of their respective sensory modalities. The skin contains a variety of tactile receptors, some sensitive to pressure, some to pain, some to warmth, and some to cold. In the auditory system, single neurons are tuned to particular sound frequencies, so that one neuron might be most sensitive to a tone with a frequency of 1000 cycles/second. Such a neuron would be less sensitive to equally intense tones of higher or lower pitches. Regarding the sense of taste, most experts believe that all gustatory sensations can be decomposed into four simple tastes—sour, salty, bitter, and sweet. Some very exacting experiments by Bekesy (1964, 1966) have shown that individual taste receptors on the tongue are responsive to one and only one of these four simple tastes. In short, the evidence from sensory physiology is unambiguous: All sensory systems begin by breaking down incoming stimuli into simple sensations.

Physiological Research on "Complex Ideas"

The essence of James Mill's theory of complex ideas is the notion of a hierarchy: At the bottom of the hierarchy are simple ideas, which can unite to produce complex ideas. Complex ideas can unite to form duplex ideas, and so on. Although Mill was concerned with the memories (ideas) of *past* sensations, his concept of a hierarchy of increasing complexity must certainly have some relevance to the processing of *current* sensations. After all, whereas our visual systems start by detecting the basic features of a stimulus—color, brightness, position, and so on—each of us can recognize complex visual patterns, such as the face of a friend or a written word. Somehow, the simple sensory attributes detected by the receptors on the retina must be combined to yield more "complex ideas," such as *my friend Paul* or the written word *music*. Although the mechanisms of visual pattern recognition are still largely a mystery, some impressive research by Hubel and Wiesel (1965, 1979) offers a few clues about how neurons higher in the visual pathways respond to more complex stimulus features than do the cones on the retina. The general procedure used by Hubel and Wiesel can be summarized briefly. They would isolate a single neuron somewhere in the visual system of an anesthetized monkey (or cat) and record the electrical activity of that neuron while presenting a wide range of visual stimuli (varying in color, size, shape, and location in the visual field) to the animal. The electrical activity of the neuron was recorded by piercing it with a *microelectrode* (a very thin wire), which was connected to suitable amplifying and recording equipment. The question Hubel and Wiesel wished to answer was simple: What type of "detector" is this neuron? That is, what type of visual stimuli would make the neuron fire most rapidly?

For our purposes, the neurons of greatest interest are those in the *visual cortex*, an area in the back of the head, just beneath the skull. Recall that on the retina, a receptor can be stimulated by a simple point of light: If the point of light is sufficiently bright and if it strikes the receptor, the receptor will respond. In the visual cortex, however, Hubel and Wiesel found individual neurons that responded to more complex shapes. One class of cells, which Hubel and Wiesel call *simple cells*, fired most rapidly when the visual stimulus was a line of a specific orientation, presented in a specific part of the visual field. For example, one simple cell might fire most rapidly to a line at a 45-degree angle from the horizontal, projected on a specific part of the retina. If the orientation of the line were changed to 30 degrees or 60 degrees, the cell would fire less rapidly, and with further deviations from 45 degrees the cell would respond less and less. It is tempting to speculate about what sort of neural connections from the retina to the visual cortex might explain why a simple cell is most responsive to a line of a specific orientation. In the mammalian visual system, cells in the visual cortex are separated from the receptors on the retina by a chain of several intervening neurons (and, of course, several intervening synapses). Nevertheless, it is an appealing hypothesis to suppose that

a simple cell in the cortex receives (indirect) excitatory inputs from individual receptors that are positioned in a row on the surface of the retina, as diagramed schematically in Figure 2-7. Furthermore, let us assume that receptors on either side of this row have inhibitory connections to the simple cell (as represented by the minus signs in Figure 2-7). Since each of the rods becomes active when light falls on it, and since the simple cell's activity level is increased by excitatory inputs and decreased by inhibitory inputs, you should be able to see that this simple cell will be maximally excited by a line of 45 degrees. You should also see why lines of somewhat different orientations will produce some lesser degrees of activity in the simple cell.

It should be emphasized that this discussion of the neural connections between the retina and the visual cortex is mere speculation—no one has yet managed to trace the "wiring diagram" for a simple cell. Nevertheless, since all receptors on the retina are responsive to single points of light, it seems logically inescapable that some such integration of information must occur between the retina and the line-detecting cells in the visual cortex. Therefore, it is probably not too great a

FIGURE 2-7. (a) A schematic diagram of a portion of the retina illustrating the possible connections between receptors on the retina and a simple cell in the visual cortex. The plus signs mark receptors with excitatory inputs to the cortical cell, and the minus signs mark receptors with inhibitory inputs to the cortical cell. (b) If a line of 45 degrees is projected onto this portion of the retina, the cortical cell becomes highly active because of the many excitatory inputs. (c) A line of less than 45 degrees stimulates some receptors that inhibit the cortical cell and fewer receptors that excite the cortical cell, so as a result the cortical cell fires less rapidly.

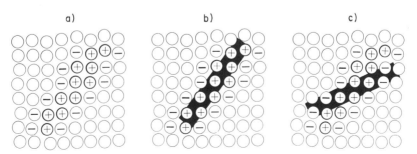

distortion of James Mill's views to say that a visual receptor on the retina is the physical counterpart to a simple idea (a point of light), that a simple cell in the visual cortex is the physical counterpart to a more complex idea (a line of a specific orientation) and that it is some sort of union of the information from several simple ideas that makes the more complex idea possible.

A line of a specific orientation is admittedly still quite simple compared to some of the complex ideas about which Mill wrote—bricks, mortar, walls, windows. Unfortunately, relatively little is known about how the visual system reacts to such complex stimuli. However, Hubel and Wiesel did find some cells a bit more sophisticated than their simple cells. Other cells in the visual cortex, which they called *hypercomplex* cells, were maximally excited by stimuli with two edges intersecting at a specific angle. For instance, one hypercomplex cell might respond to the corner of a rectangle—two edges forming a 90-degree angle. Another hypercomplex cell might be most responsive to part of a triangle—two edges that formed an angle of say, 45 degrees. Among the most complex visual detectors ever reported are cortical neurons in macaque monkeys that could be called "hand detectors" and "face detectors" (Desimone, Albright, Gross, & Bruce, 1984; Gross, Rocha-Miranda, & Bender, 1972). For instance, the face detectors responded vigorously to human or monkey faces, whereas a variety of other stimuli (shapes, textures, pictures of other objects) evoked little or no response.

This type of evidence for visual feature detectors has led some sensory psychologists to espouse the *single neuron doctrine* of perception (Barlow, 1972). According to this view, the visual system (and probably other sensory systems) is arranged in a hierarchy of increasing complexity, and at the highest levels are neurons that respond to very specific features. Are there single neurons that are activated by such complex stimuli as the face of a friend or a 1976 Pinto? Those who favor the single neuron doctrine believe that the brain may indeed contain such specialized neurons. But this is only one possibility. Another is that an entire cluster of neurons may be activated by a complex visual stimulus, and it is the activity of this entire group of cells that corresponds to a complex idea. Still another view is that a large portion of the neurons in the visual cortex are activated by a complex visual stimulus, and it is not *which neurons* are active so much as the specific *pattern* of activity that encodes the nature of the stimulus (Lashley, 1929, 1950; Pribram, 1966). At the present time, no one knows which of these possibilities is most accurate. As an empiricist, James Mill believed that experience is at the root of all simple and complex ideas. However, when Hubel and Wiesel (1963) examined cells in the visual cortex of newborn kittens with no previous visual experience, they found feature detectors similar to those found in adult cats (though the neurons of kittens were more sluggish in their responsiveness to visual stimuli). If we wish to call feature detectors the physiological counterparts to Mill's ideas (either simple or complex), then we must grant that, at least in cats, these ideas are innate: Individual cells in a kitten's visual cortex are pre-wired to respond to specific visual features (lines, angles) before the kitten has seen any visual patterns whatsoever. Yet despite the fact that feature detectors are present at birth, experience plays an important role in two ways. First, visual experience keeps the feature detectors functioning well. Hubel and Wiesel (1970) found that if kittens were deprived of visual stimulation during certain *critical periods* of their young lives, the feature detectors of these kittens would deteriorate and become nonfunctional. Second, the response characteristics of such feature detectors can be modified depending upon the type of visual stimulation a kitten receives. Blakemore and Cooper (1970) raised some kittens in an environment with large vertical stripes on the walls and other kittens in an environment with horizontal stripes. The feature detectors of kittens raised with vertical stimuli responded primarily to edges of approximately vertical orientation, and few cells responded to horizontal lines. The opposite was found for kittens raised with horizontal stimulation. These studies with young kittens show that heredity and environment both contribute to the types of visual feature detectors that will be found in the adult animal.

Physiological Research on Associative Learning

Over the years, psychologists have proposed two general classes of theories about what takes place at the cellular level during learning. One possibility is that neurons may grow new axons and/or new dendrites as a result of a learning experience, so that totally new synapses are formed. A second possibility is that learning involves only changes in already existing synapses. Let us briefly examine each of these possibilities.

Some of the best evidence for the hypothesis that new synapses are developed as a result of experience comes from studies in which animals were exposed to enriched living environments. Rosenzweig and his colleagues (Rosenzweig, 1966; Rosenzweig, Mollgaard, Diamond, & Bennet, 1972) placed young rats in two different environments to determine how early experience influences the development of the brain. At about 25 days of age, some rats were placed in an environment rich in stimuli and in possible learning experiences. These animals lived in groups of 10 to 12, and their cage contained many objects to play with and explore—ladders, wheels, platforms, mazes, and the like. In a second group, the rats were raised in a much more impoverished environment. Each animal lived in a separate, empty cage, and it could not see or touch other rats. Subjects in this condition certainly had far fewer sensory and learning experiences. Rosenzweig and his colleagues wanted to see how 80 days of experience in an enriched or an impoverished environment affected the brains of these rats. They expected to find only subtle differences in chemical composition, but to their surprise, they found that the brains of the enriched subjects were significantly heavier than those of impoverished subjects. Differences in weight were especially pronounced in the cerebral cortex, which is thought to play an important role in the learning process. These findings, which have been replicated many times, suggest that the complexity of an animal's environmental experiences during adolescence affects the growth of brain tissue. Other studies have shown that exposure to enriched environments can produce similar changes in adult animals, and that in

some cases very brief exposure can have significant effects. For instance, Ferchmin and Eterovic (1983) found increased brain weights in young rats after only four 10-minute periods in an enriched environment.

What types of changes at the cellular level accompany these differences in overall brain size? Microscopic examinations have revealed a variety of changes in the brain tissue of rats exposed to enriched environments, including more branching of dendrites (indicative of more synaptic connections between axons and dendrites) and synapses with larger surface areas (Rosenzweig, 1984). Other studies have found that more structured types of learning experiences can produce cellular changes in more localized areas of the brain. Spinelli, Jensen, and DiPrisco (1980) trained young kittens on a task in which they had to flex one foreleg to avoid a shock to that leg. After a few brief sessions with this procedure, each kitten's somatosensory cortex (an area of the cortex that is responsive to tactile stimuli) was examined. The experimenters found that (1) a larger region of the cortex was responsive to stimulation of the foreleg involved in the avoidance training (compared to the cortical region responsive to the other, untrained foreleg) and (2) there was a marked increase in the number of dendritic branches in this specific area of the cortex. These studies provide compelling evidence that relatively brief learning experiences can produce significant increases in the number, size, and complexity of synaptic connections.

Changes that can be detected by observing brain tissue with a microscope (changes in the size or number of synapses) do not exhaust the possible ways that learning might affect individual neurons. Indeed, the time needed for the growth of axons or dendrites may be too slow to account for the rapidity of learning found in many experiments with both animal and human subjects. For this reason (and as a result of several types of experimental evidence), physiological psychologists have speculated that learning may also be represented by a number of different chemical changes at the synaptic level. One possibility is that as a result of a learning experience the axon terminal of the presynaptic neuron acquires the capacity to release more (or for that matter, less) chemical transmitter in a single action potential. Another general possibility is that the cell membrane of the postsynaptic neuron becomes more (or less) sensitive to the transmitter, so that although the amount of the transmitter released by the presynaptic neuron may be the same, the response of the postsynaptic neuron will be altered. A large body of research has investigated such possible chemical changes, and some of this research will be presented in later chapters. For the moment, it will be sufficient to realize that from the perspective of physiological psychologists, a learning experience might produce (1) a change in the number or physical size of some synapses somewhere in the nervous system, or (2) more subtle chemical changes in some synapses. There is evidence to provide some encouragement for each of these possibilities.

Before concluding this brief survey of the physiological approach to learning, we should take one final look at James Mill's concept of complex ideas. The work of Hubel and Wiesel showed that the visual system has individual neurons that respond to features such as lines, edges, angles, and corners. Calling these stimuli "complex" may be exaggeration, but at least cortical neurons respond to more complex features than the receptors on the retina. Further research suggested that kittens are born with these feature detectors. However, many of our complex ideas, and presumably those of animals as well, are developed through experience. What happens at the physiological level when a child learns the concept *house* or when a kitten learns to recognize and respond appropriately to a *snake*? Unfortunately virtually nothing is known about the physiological changes that accompany the learning of a new complex idea. Nevertheless, this scarcity of information has not stopped psychologists from speculating about possible underlying physiological processes. A number of writers (such as Konorski, 1967; Wickelgren, 1979) have proposed that in addition to innate feature detectors like those found by Hubel and Wiesel, the cerebral cortex may contain many unused or dormant neurons, perhaps with weak inputs from various feature detectors. As a result of an animal's learning experiences, one (or possibly several) of these dormant neurons might come to respond selectively to a particular complex object. To take a simple example, after an animal has had sufficient exposure to the complex object we call an *apple*, some cortical neuron might develop excitatory inputs from detectors responsive to the apple's red color, roughly spherical shape, specific odor, and other characteristics. Once the appropriate set of excitatory inputs was established, this neuron would respond specifically to the presence of an apple. In this way, an animal that at birth had no complex idea of an apple might develop the ability to recognize apples as a result of its experience.

This sort of theory uses physiological terminology and concepts to speculate about the same issues James Mill discussed several centuries ago—the nature of our knowledge of the world and the simple and complex ideas that are part of that knowledge. It must be stressed that, because of our present ignorance in these matters, physiological theories about the formation of complex ideas can tell us only what is possible, not what actually happens.

CHAPTER

3

INNATE BEHAVIOR PATTERNS AND HABITUATION

When any animal is born, it is already endowed with a variety of complex abilities. Its immediate survival depends on the ability to breathe and to pump blood through its veins. If it is a mammal, it has the ability to regulate its temperature within narrow limits. If its survival depends on the ability to flee from predators, it may start to walk and run within minutes after birth. Newborn animals are also equipped with a range of sensory capacities. As Hubel and Wiesel (1963) have shown, kittens have inborn visual cells responsive to colors, edges, and probably other aspects of the visual world. Such innate sensory structures are by no means limited to kittens, nor to the visual system.

One major purpose of this chapter is to provide a selective (but, it is hoped, representative) survey of the types of behavioral abilities that an animal may already possess as it enters the world. There are good reasons for examining innate behavior patterns in a book about learning. First of all, many learned behaviors are deriva-

tives, extensions, or variations of innate behaviors. Second, many of the features of learned behaviors (for example, their control by environmental stimuli, their mechanisms of temporal sequencing) have parallels in inborn behavior patterns. The second purpose of this chapter is to examine the phenomenon of *habituation*, which is often said to be the simplest type of learning.

Most of the examples of innate behavior patterns described in this chapter are based on the work of *ethologists*—scientists who study how animals behave in their natural environments. Although both ethologists and psychologists in the field of learning study animal behavior, their purposes and strategies are different. The testing environments of learning psychologists tend to be barren and artificial, for their goal is to discover general principles of learning that do not depend on specific types of stimuli. Ethologists usually conduct their experiments in the animal's natural habitat or in a seminaturalistic setting, because their purpose is to determine how an animal's behavior helps it to survive in its environment. Ethologists are interested in both learned and innate behaviors, and many of the behavior patterns they have studied in detail are *species-specific* (unique to a single species). In recent years, psychologists who study learning have shown increasing interest in innate behaviors and species-specific behaviors. As a result, the work of ethologists is having greater impact on both research and theory in the field of learning.

One characteristic that is common to many behaviors, both learned and unlearned, is that they appear to be purposive, or goal-directed. As we will see, this is true of some of our most primitive reflexes as well as our most complex skills. For this reason, it will be useful to begin this chapter with some concepts from *control systems theory*, a branch of science that deals with goal-directed behaviors in both living creatures and inanimate objects.

Characteristics of Goal-Directed Systems

Control systems theory provides a general framework for analyzing a wide range of goal-directed systems. The terminology used here is based on the work of McFarland (1971). A relatively simple example of an inanimate goal-directed system is a house's heating system. The goal of the heating system is to keep the house temperature above some minimum level, say

65° F. If the house temperature drops below 65°, the heating system "spontaneously" springs into action, starting the furnace. Once the temperature goal is reached, the activity of the heating system ceases. Of course, we know there is nothing magical about this process. The activity of the heating system is controlled by the thermostat, which relies on the fact that metals expand when heated and contract when cooled. The cooling of the metals in the thermostat causes them to bend and close an electrical switch, thus starting the furnace. Heating of the metals opens the switch and stops the furnace. The thermostat is an example of a fundamental concept in control systems theory, the *comparator*. As shown in Figure 3-1, a comparator receives two types of input, called the *reference input* and the *actual input*. The reference input is often not a physical entity but a conceptual one (the temperature that, when reached, will be just enough to open the switch and stop the furnace). On the other hand, the actual input measures some actual physical characteristic of the present environment—the air temperature in the vicinity of the thermostat in this case.

Any comparator has rules that it follows to determine, based on the current actual input and reference input, what its output will be. In the case of a thermostat, the output is an on/off command to the furnace, which is an example of an *action system*. The rules that the thermostat follows might be: (1) If the furnace is off and the air temperature becomes one degree lower than the reference input, turn on the furnace, and (2) If the

FIGURE 3-I. The concepts of control systems theory as applied to a house's heating system.

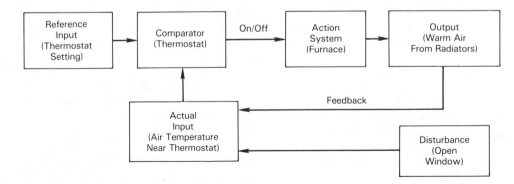

furnace is on and the air temperature becomes one degree higher than the reference input, turn off the furnace. With a setting of 65°, these rules would keep the air temperature between 64° and 66°. As this illustration suggests, a comparator usually tolerates a certain range of discrepancy between reference input and actual input. If it did not, the furnace would constantly flicker on and off with every slight change in air temperature.

The product of the action system is simply called the *output*—the entry of warm air from the radiators in this example. As Figure 3-1 shows, the output of the action system feeds back and affects the actual input to the comparator. For this reason, such a goal-directed system is frequently called a *feedback system* or a *closed-loop system*. The output of the action system (warm air) and the actual input to the comparator (air temperature) seem closely related, and you may wonder why two separate terms are needed to describe them. The reason is that there is not always a close relationship between the output of the action system and the actual input, for other factors can affect the actual input. One example is the *disturbance* depicted in Figure 3-1. If a window is open on a cold day, this will also affect the air temperature near the thermostat, which may then be very different from the temperature of the air coming out of the radiators.

In summary, this example illustrates six of the most important concepts of control systems theory: comparator, reference input, actual input, action system, output, and disturbance. We will encounter many examples of goal-directed behaviors in this book, and it will often be useful to try to identify the different components of the feedback loop in these examples. The next section is the first of many in this book that will make use of the concepts of control systems theory.

REFLEXES

A *reflex* is a stereotyped pattern of movement of a part of the body that can be reliably elicited by presenting the appropriate stimulus. You are probably familiar with the *patellar* (knee-jerk)

reflex: If a person's leg is supported so that the foot is off the ground and the lower leg can swing freely, the light tap of a hammer just below the kneecap will evoke a small kicking motion from the leg. As with all reflexes, the patellar reflex involves an innate connection between a stimulus and a response. The stimulus in this example is the tapping of the tendon below the kneecap, and the response is of course the kicking motion.

A normal newborn child displays a variety of reflexes. A nipple placed in the child's mouth will elicit a sucking response. If the sole of the foot is pricked with a pin, the child's knees will flex, pulling the feet away from the painful stimulus. If an adult places a finger in the child's palm, the child's fingers will close around it in a grasping reflex. Some of the newborn's reflexes disappear with age. Others, such as the dilation of the pupils and the closing of the eyes in response to a bright light, or coughing in response to a throat irritation, persist throughout life.

The newborn's reflexes have been exhaustively catalogued, and the absence of some of these reflexes may be a sign of neurological or physiological impairments. Yet besides simply enumerating the reflexes of newborns, of adults, and of other animals, scientists have attempted to discover properties that many or all reflexes have in common. An early researcher who worked toward this goal was Sir Charles Sherrington (1906).

Sherrington's Principles of Reflex Action

Sherrington conducted most of his research on *spinal animals*, which are animals whose spinal cords have been severed to remove all neural connections to and from the brain. In the spinal animal the brain can neither receive sensory inputs from the body nor exert any control over the muscles, so any reflexes observed are controlled by neurons in the spinal cord and in the body itself. Spinal animals were used to gain information about the neural control of reflexes, but the principles Sherrington discovered apply to reflexes in normal animals as well. He demonstrated several ways in which a reflexive response changes with the intensity of the eliciting stimulus. These changes can be illustrated with the *flexion* or *withdrawal reflex* of a dog's hind leg in response to a pin prick applied to the bottom of the hind paw. First of all, in order to elicit a response, the intensity of the stimulus must exceed some minimum value, called the *threshold.* A subthreshold stimulus will produce no response at all. As soon as the threshold is exceeded, however, a leg-flexion response is observed—the dog's leg bends at the knee and pulls the paw away from the painful stimulus. If the intensity of the pin prick is further increased, the *latency* of the flexion response decreases. That is, a response that begins only after one second with a weak stimulus may begin in one-half of a second with a stronger stimulus. If the intensity of the stimulus is increased still further, a phenomenon Sherrington called *irradiation* may be observed: Muscles that were previously inactive now become part of the response. With a suitably intense stimulus, the reflexive response "spreads" to the upper leg, and the leg now flexes at both the knee and the hip. With a very intense stimulus, the opposite hind leg and then the foreleg are extended as the stimulated leg is withdrawn. This more vigorous response is clearly adaptive, for its effect is to maximize the distance between the paw and a potentially harmful stimulus.

As this description implies, the more vigorous withdrawal reflex involves the coordinated action of many different muscles. Sherrington emphasized, however, that the coordination of different muscles also occurs in more localized reflexes. Muscles are usually arranged in antagonistic pairs consisting of *flexors* (which cause the withdrawal of a limb) and *extensors* (which produce limb extension). If a stimulus evokes the reflexive contraction of a flexor muscle, it invariably produces a relaxation of the opposing extensor muscles, thereby ensuring that the antagonistic muscles will not fight each other. Conversely, if a stimulus excites the extensor muscle it will simultaneously inhibit the flexor muscle. Sherrington called this property *reciprocal inhibition.*

Most of the more familiar reflexes, such as the eyeblink, the knee jerk, and withdrawal reflexes, are called *phasic reflexes,* which means that the

duration of the response is brief. In contrast, *tonic reflexes,* such as those involved in balance and posture, consist of a continuous series of adjustments in muscle tension. While always brief, some phasic reflexes such as the dog's *scratch reflex* involve more than a single discrete movement. If a spot on the back of a dog is touched or brushed lightly, the hind leg will come up and scratch the back. Sherrington used a mild electrical current to simulate an itch, and as long as the stimulus persisted, a rhythmic scratching motion continued at a rate of four repetitions per second. Although this rhythmic scratch reflex appears stereotyped and mechanical, Sherrington suggested that it also has a purposive or adaptive character, because the direction of the scratching corresponds to the location of the irritating stimulus. This may not sound surprising, since scratching would be pointless if it were not directed toward the itch. However, this directionality of the scratch reflex was found in spinal dogs as well as in normal dogs. Thus the ability to aim the scratch response toward the itch does not depend on the influence of the brain.

One general conclusion that can be drawn from Sherrington's work is that even the simplest reflexes are more complex than they may first appear. The sophistication of simple reflexes becomes especially clear when their goal-directed properties are examined.

Goal-Directedness in the Flexion Reflex

If you ever accidentally placed your hand on a hot stove, you probably exhibited a flexion reflex—a rapid withdrawal of the hand caused by a bending of the arm at the elbow. The response has such a short latency because the association between sensory and motor neurons occurs directly in the spinal cord. Figure 3-2 depicts a cross-section of the spinal cord and some of the neural machinery involved in this reflex. The hand contains sensory neurons sensitive to pain, and their lengthy axons travel all the way into the spinal cord before synapsing with other neurons. In the flexion reflex, one or more small neurons called *interneurons* separate the sensory neurons from motor neurons. The motor neurons have

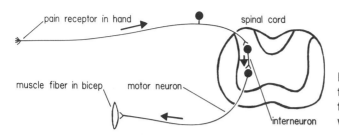

FIGURE 3-2. A cross-section of the spinal cord is shown, along with the components of the spinal withdrawal reflex.

cell bodies within the spinal cord, and their axons exit through the front of the spinal cord, travel back down the arm, and synapse with individual muscle fibers in the arm. When excited, the muscle fibers contract, thereby producing the response. The physiology of this reflex is sometimes called the *spinal reflex arc*, after the shape of the path of neural excitation shown in Figure 3-2. Of course, not one but many of such sensory neurons, interneurons and motor neurons are involved in producing the reflexive response.

So far this description of the chain of connections in the spinal reflex arc is consistent with the standard definition of a reflex—a stimulus elicits a response. There is more to the story of the spinal reflex arc, however, so now let us see how this reflex can be viewed as a feedback system. Within the muscles of the arm are structures called *stretch receptors*, which serve as the comparators of the feedback system. We will not go into detail about how this happens, but the stretch receptors compare (1) the goal or reference input—the commands sent from the motor neurons to the muscle fibers telling them to contract, and (2) the actual amount that the muscles have contracted. Notice that the mere fact that some motor neurons have sent their commands to the muscle does not guarantee that the arm is safely withdrawn from the dangerous object. There might be a disturbance—an obstruction that impedes the movement of the arm. Or the muscles may be in a state of fatigue and therefore fail to respond sufficiently to the commands of the motor neurons. If the muscles have not contracted sufficiently for any such reason, the stretch receptors begin to stimulate the motor neurons (which in turn stimulate the muscle fibers more vigorously), and this stimulation continues until the contraction is completed. In

short, the comparators (the stretch receptors) continue to stimulate the action system (the motor neurons and muscle fibers) until the goal (a successful muscle contraction) is achieved.

This analysis of the spinal reflex arc shows that feedback can play a crucial role in even the simplest reflexive behaviors. Stretch receptors or neurons with similar functions have been found in many parts of the human body and in other animals. In all cases, the function of these cells is to determine whether or not the commands of the motor neurons have been carried out. As we turn to other classes of innate behaviors, we will find further examples of closed-loop movement systems.

TROPISMS AND ORIENTATION

Whereas a reflex is the stereotyped movement of a part of the body, a *tropism* is a movement or change in orientation of the entire organism. The first to study tropisms was Jacques Loeb (1900), who called tropisms "forced movements," to suggest that no intelligence, will, or choice was involved. For example, a *geotropism* is an orienting movement that relies on a sensitivity to gravity. Loeb conducted a simple experiment in which an actinian (a sea anemone) was placed with its head down in a test tube. Within minutes the actinian had regained its normal head-up orientation. Loeb cautioned against inferring from this sort of purposeful movement that a creature has "a mind" or intelligence, because plants also exhibit geotropisms. Regardless of how a seed is oriented when planted in the ground, it will grow its roots downward and its stalk upward, which shows that plants can also exhibit goal-directed "behavior." Loeb was interested in uncovering the physical and chemical bases of such forced movements in both plants and animals. Later researchers (such as Fraenkel & Gunn, 1940) grouped tropisms into two major categories, *kineses* (plural of *kinesis*) and *taxes* (plural of *taxis)*.

Kineses

A frequently cited example of a kinesis is the humidity-seeking behavior of the wood louse. This creature, though actually a small crustacean, resembles an insect, and it spends most of its time under a rock or a log in the forest. Gunn (1937) showed that the wood louse must remain in humid areas in order to survive—if the air is too dry it will die of dehydration in a matter of hours. Fortunately for the wood louse, nature has provided it with a simple yet effective technique for finding and remaining in moist areas. A series of studies by Gunn and his colleagues uncovered the wood louse's strategy. In one experiment, a number of wood lice were placed in the center of a chamber in which the air was moist at one end and dry at the other. Fraenkel and Gunn (1940) described the results as follows:

After a further quarter of an hour or so, most of the animals are seen to have collected in the moist side of the chamber, where they mostly stay still. From time to time one starts walking and goes into the dry side, but seldom or never does it stop there. The woodlice walk in both moist air and dry; they often stop and remain stationary for long periods in moist air, but they usually keep on walking in the dry. That is to say, their average linear velocity, counting intervals of rest as well, is higher in dry air than in moist....We might say that woodlice like moist air and dislike dry, or that they seek the one and fear the other. But it is quite unnecessary to make any such assumptions about what goes on in the animals' minds. We can describe the behaviour in mechanical terms.... (p. 13)

What is noteworthy about this behavior (and what distinguishes a kinesis from a taxis) is that the *direction* of the movement is random with respect to the direction of the humid areas. The wood louse does not head directly toward a moist area or away from a dry one because it has no means of sensing the humidity of a distant location—it can only sense the humidity of its present location. Nevertheless, its tendency to keep moving when in a dry area and stop when in a moist area is generally successful in keeping the creature alive.

Without belaboring the obvious, it is worth noting that the wood louse's humidity-seeking behavior is another example of a feedback system. Although we do not know exactly how the wood louse measures humidity, its behavior tells us that it must have a comparator that can detect the actual input (current humidity) and compare it to the reference input (the goal of high humidity). The action system in this case is the creature's locomotion system—the motor neurons, muscles, and legs that allow it to move about. Locomotion is, of course, the output of this action system, and in this example there is no necessary connection between this output and the actual input to the comparator. That is, the wood louse may move about incessantly if it finds itself in a dry location, but if there are no humid areas nearby, the goal of high humidity will not be achieved as a result of this locomotion.

Taxes

Unlike kineses, in a taxis the direction of movement bears some relationship to the location of the stimulus. One example of a taxis is a maggot's movement away from any bright light source. If a bright light is turned on to the maggot's right, it will promptly turn to the left and move in a fairly straight line away from the light. The maggot accomplishes this directional movement by using a light-sensitive receptor at its head end. As the maggot moves, its head repeatedly swings left and right, and this oscillating movement allows it to compare the brightness of light in various directions and to move toward the direction where the light is less intense.

The maggot's taxis is primitive, for it can only point the organism in a single direction—away from the light. A more sophisticated taxis is exhibited by the ant, which can use the sun as a navigational aid when traveling to or from its home. On a journey away from home, the ant travels in a straight path by keeping the sun at a constant angle to its direction of motion. To return home, the ant changes the angle by 180 degrees. The ant's reliance on the sun can be demonstrated by providing it with an artificial sun that the experimenter can control. If this light source is gradually moved, the ant's direction of travel will change to keep its orientation with respect to the light constant (Schneirla, 1933).

In some cases it can be shown that an organism's bodily orientation is controlled by more than one stimulus. For example, many fish remain in an upright position by using both gravity and a sensitivity to light (which is normally most intense directly overhead). Figure 3-3 illustrates the findings of von Holst (1935), who varied the direction from which light was projected into an aquarium in order to study the orienting mechanisms of the fish *Crenilabrus*. On the left is a *Crenilabrus* whose gravity-sensing apparatus has been removed. This subject's orientation is totally controlled by the direction of the light. If the light is projected from the side, the fish continues to aim its back directly toward the light; if the light is projected from below, the fish swims upside down. On the right is a *Crenilabrus* whose gravity-sensing apparatus is intact. With

light coming from the side, the visual and gravitational stimuli are placed in conflict, and the fish strikes a compromise between the two. However, when the light comes from below and is thus maximally discrepant from the gravitational stimulus, the fish apparently ignores the light and relies on the gravitational cues. This last result makes more sense once we understand that the fish's usual method of adjusting to the direction of the light is to equalize the intensity of the light striking its two eyes. With the light coming from below, the intact fish can both respond to the gravitational cues and equalize the light intensity (or lack of intensity) in its two eyes by remaining upright.

SEQUENCES OF BEHAVIOR

So far we have considered innate behaviors consisting of either a brief movement (phasic reflexes) or a continuous series of adjustments (tonic reflexes and tropisms). The innate behavior patterns we will now examine are more com-

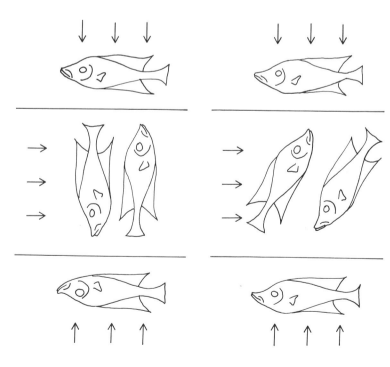

FIGURE 3-3. On the left is a fish with its gravity-sensing mechanism removed. Regardless of the direction of incoming light (as shown by the arrows), this fish orients itself so that the light is directly overhead. On the right is a normal fish. When light comes from the side, the fish's orientation represents a compromise between the visual and gravitational cues. (After von Holst, 1935)

plex, for they consist of a series of different movements that are performed in an orderly sequence.

Fixed Action Patterns

The ethological term *fixed action pattern* has been used to describe some of these behavioral sequences. Although some ethologists (Eibl-Eibesfeldt, 1975) include simple reflexes in the broader category of fixed action patterns, this category also encompasses more elaborate sequences of behavior. A fixed action pattern has the following characteristics: (1) it is a part of the repertoire of all members of a species, and it may be unique to that species, (2) suitable experiments have confirmed that the animal's ability to perform the behavior is not a result of prior learning experiences, and (3) if it consists of a sequence of behaviors, these behaviors occur in a rigid order regardless of whether they are appropriate in a particular context. That is, once a fixed action pattern is initiated, it will continue to completion without further support from environmental stimuli.

As an example of a fixed action pattern, Eibl-Eibesfeldt (1975) described the nut-burying behavior of a particular species of squirrel:

The squirrel *Sciurus vulgaris L.* buries nuts in the ground each fall, employing a quite stereotyped sequence of movement. It picks a nut, climbs down to the ground, and searches for a place at the bottom of a tree trunk or a large boulder. At the base of such a conspicuous landmark it will scratch a hole by means of alternating movements of the forelimbs and place the nut in it. Then the nut is rammed into place with rapid thrusts of its snout, covered with dirt by sweeping motions and tamped down with the forepaws. (p. 23)

Although all members of the species exhibit this behavior pattern, this does not prove that the behavior is innate. Each squirrel may learn how to bury nuts by watching its parents early in life. In order to determine whether the behavior pattern is innate, Eibl-Eibesfeldt conducted a *deprivation experiment*, in which all possible means of learning the behavior were removed. A squirrel was separated from its parents at birth and raised in isolation so that it had no opportunity to observe other squirrels burying nuts (or doing anything else, for that matter). In addition, the squirrel received only liquid food and it lived on a solid floor, so it had no experience in handling food nor in digging or burying objects in the ground. The animal was kept well fed, so that it had little chance of discovering that storing away food for a time of need is a good strategy. When the squirrel was full grown, Eibl-Eibesfeldt finally gave it some nuts, one at a time. At first the squirrel ate the nuts until apparently satiated. When given additional nuts, it did not drop them but carried them around in its mouth as it searched around the cage. It seemed to be attracted by vertical objects, such as a corner of the cage, where it might drop the nut. Obviously it could not dig a hole in the floor, but it would scratch at the floor with its forepaws, push the nut into the corner with its snout, and make the same covering and tamping-down motions seen in the burying sequence of a wild squirrel. This careful experiment demonstrates conclusively that the squirrel's nut-burying repertoire is innate. The caged squirrel's scratching, covering, and tamping-down motions in the absence of dirt show how the components of a fixed action pattern will occur in their usual place in the sequence even when they serve no function.

As with simple reflexes, it usually takes a fairly specific stimulus, which ethologists call a *sign stimulus*, to initiate a fixed action pattern. In the case of the squirrel, the sign stimulus is clearly the nut, but without further experiments we cannot tell which features—its size, shape, color, and so on—are essential ingredients for eliciting the response. For other fixed action patterns, systematic investigation has revealed which features of a stimulus are important and which are irrelevant. The results are often surprising. Consider, for example, the innate begging response of newborn Herring Gulls. When a parent enters the nest, the young gulls beg for food by pecking at the parent's beak. This pecking acts as a sign stimulus for the parent, who responds by regurgitating food to feed the chicks. But what aspects of the parent's appearance elicit the chicks' begging responses in the first place? By presenting the chicks with a series of models that mimicked an adult gull to various degrees, Tinbergen and Perdeck (1950) determined that a red spot on the otherwise yellow beak of the parent is an important sign stimulus. A yellow beak with a blue spot elicited fewer pecks, and a solid yellow beak fewer still. But while the presence and color of this small red spot were quite important, other aspects of the model's appearance mattered very little. For instance, the young gulls would peck energetically at a hand-held yellow pencil-shaped rod, especially one with a red spot near the tip.

The tendency for fixed action patterns to be elicited by a seemingly poor imitation of the natural sign stimulus is prevalent in adult animals as well as in newborns. A classic example is the territorial defense response of the male three-spined stickleback (Tinbergen, 1951). During the mating season, this fish will fiercely defend its territory against intrusion by other male sticklebacks. (Female sticklebacks are allowed to enter.) The male's stereotyped threat behaviors are elicited by the sight of a red patch on the underside of the intruding male. If the intruding male stickleback does not have a red patch (which can only happen if the spot has been painted over by a devious experimenter), it will not be attacked. On the other hand, the defending male will attack pie-shaped or cigar-shaped pieces of wood that are placed in its territory if they have a red patch on the bottom.

A more surprising finding is that sometimes an unrealistic model can elicit a stronger response than the actual sign stimulus itself. One example is provided by the oyster catcher, a bird that lays white eggs with brown spots. If one of its eggs rolls out of its nest, the bird will retrieve it with stereotyped head and neck movements. However, if given a choice between one of its own eggs and a replica that is four times as large, it prefers this *supernormal stimulus* to the normal one, and strains to bring this "egg" to its nest (Figure 3-4).

One conclusion to be drawn from this discussion of sign stimuli is that whereas it is fairly easy to determine what stimulus elicits a fixed action pattern, it requires systematic research to discover exactly which features of the stimulus actually control the animal's behavior. We might have expected the shape of an intruding fish to be a crucial variable in eliciting the defensive response of the male stickleback, but it turns out that shape is relatively unimportant. As we will see in later chapters, this same question can be asked about any learned behavior that occurs in the presence of a specific stimulus: Which characteristics of the stimulus are controlling the behavior, and which are irrelevant? In attempting to answer this question, researchers in the field of learning use techniques that are fundamentally the same as those used by ethologists.

FIGURE 3-4. An oyster catcher attempts to roll a supernormal egg back to its nest. (After Tinbergen, 1951)

Reaction Chains

Ethologists distinguish between fixed action patterns and what are sometimes called *reaction chains*. The difference is that whereas fixed action patterns continue until completion once started, in a reaction chain the progression from one behavior to the next depends on the presence of the appropriate external stimulus. If the stimulus is not present, the chain of behaviors will be interrupted. On the other hand, if a stimulus for a behavior in the middle of a chain is presented at the outset, the earlier behaviors will be omitted.

An interesting example of such a sequence of behaviors, all innate, is provided by the hermit crab. The hermit crab has no shell of its own; instead it lives in the empty shells of gastropods (mollusks). Frequently during its life the hermit crab grows too large for its present shell and must find a larger one. The crab's current shell may also be less than ideal in other ways—it may be too heavy or too brightly colored—so it spends a good deal of time examining empty shells. Reese (l963) identified at least eight separate fixed action patterns that usually occur in a sequence as this creature searches for and selects a new shell. A crab with no shell or with an inadequate shell exhibits a high level of locomotion. Eventually during its travels the crab spots a shell visually, at which point it approaches the shell and touches it. The crab grasps the shell with its two front legs, and then climbs on top of it. Its cheliped (claw) is used to feel the texture of the surface—a rough texture is preferred. The crab then climbs down and rotates the shell in its legs, exploring the external surface. When the aperture of the shell is located, this too is explored by inserting the cheliped as far as possible. If there is sand or other debris in the aperture, it is removed. Once the aperture is clear, the crab turns around and inserts its abdomen deeply into the shell, and then withdraws it. This entering and exiting often occurs several times in rapid succession, and it may serve to help determine whether the size of the interior is acceptable. If the shell is suitable, the crab turns the shell upright, enters it once again, and then goes on its way.

The behaviors in this sequence and the stimuli that prompt them are diagramed in Figure 3-5.

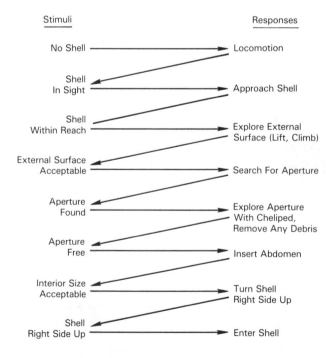

FIGURE 3-5. The hermit crab's reaction chain of shell searching and selecting behaviors. The behaviors form a chain because each successive behavior usually (but not always) eventually leads to the stimulus for the next behavior in the chain.

This figure helps to emphasize what is the distinguishing characteristic of reaction chains—that the performance of one behavior usually produces the stimulus that elicits the next behavior in the chain. For instance, the first behavior of the chain, locomotion, eventually results in visual contact with a shell, which is the stimulus for the second response, approach. The response of approach brings the crab into close proximity with the shell, which is the stimulus for the third response, lifting, and so on. Unlike the behaviors of a fixed action pattern, those of a reaction chain do not always occur in this complete sequence. The sequence can stop at any point if the stimulus required for the next step is not forthcoming. For example, Reese (1963) found that shells filled with plastic were similar enough to usable shells to elicit the first six behaviors of Figure 3-5. However, since the aperture was not open, the seventh behavior did not occur, and the crab would eventually walk away. On the other hand, the initial steps of the sequence may be omitted if the stimulus for a behavior in the middle of the sequence occurs. When crabs were presented with a suitable shell with the aperture directly in front of them, they would often omit the first five behaviors and proceed with the last four behaviors of the sequence. This dependence on external stimulus support makes the behaviors of a reaction chain more variable, but at the same time more adaptable, than those of a fixed action pattern.

Before leaving the topic of reaction chains it is worth noting that the concepts of control systems theory are just as applicable here as they are for reflexes and tropisms. Indeed, we can usually find feedback loops at several different levels in a complex behavioral sequence. At the broadest level, the entire shell selection repertoire of the hermit crab can be viewed as a large feedback loop. The crab's goal is a suitable shell; if it does not have one, a complex pattern of behaviors is activated, and these searching and selecting behaviors continue until a suitable shell is found. This large feedback loop is depicted in Figure 3-6a. For simplicity, the reference input, actual input, and comparator have been collapsed into one box representing the comparison process. The comparison can be expressed as a question:

Does the crab have a suitable shell? If the answer is yes, the crab will move on to other behaviors. If the answer is no, the search and selection process will proceed. The action system and its output have been collapsed into a box representing the behaviors that occur when the crab's goal of a suitable shell is not yet realized. This diagram shows that the searching and selecting behaviors will continue until the crab obtains a suitable shell.

As Figure 3-6b shows, the reaction chain of searching and selection behaviors (which we have treated as the action system and output of a large feedback loop) actually consists of a series of smaller feedback loops. The reference input for the first feedback loop is the visual detection of a shell. Until this goal is reached, the crab will engage in locomotion. When a shell is sighted, the next feedback loop is initiated, in which the response of approaching the shell continues until the goal for this loop (having the shell within reach) is achieved. In a similar fashion, the other behaviors of the response sequence can also be viewed as smaller feedback systems. It should be clear that despite its greater complexity, Figure 3-6b is still an oversimplification. For instance, it does not show that the sequence may stop if one goal (such as finding the aperture, in step 4) is not reached after some unspecified amount of time. The point of Figure 3-6 is merely to show how feedback loops can be found at various levels of detail in a complex behavioral sequence. These behaviors of the hermit crab are all innate, but Miller, Galanter, and Pribram (1960) have eloquently argued that the nesting of smaller feedback loops within larger feedback loops occurs in most learned behaviors as well.

HABITUATION

For his vacation, Dick has rented a cottage on a picturesque lake deep in the woods. The owner of the cottage has advised Dick that although the area is usually very quiet, members of the fish and game club just down the shore often engage in target practice for a few hours during the evening. Despite this forewarning, the first loud rifle shot elicits a *startle reaction* from Dick—he

a.

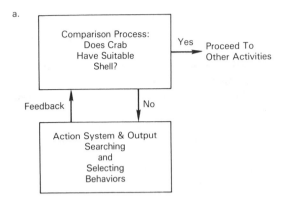

b.

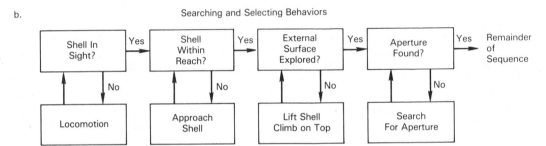

FIGURE 3-6. (a) The entire sequence of shell searching and selecting behaviors can be viewed as a large feedback loop. If the hermit crab has no shell, the searching and selecting behaviors continue until this situation is rectified. (b) The individual behaviors of the reaction chain can each be viewed as separate feedback loops.

practically jumps out of his chair, and then his heart beats rapidly and he breathes heavily for several seconds. After about half a minute Dick has fully recovered and is just returning to his novel when he is again startled by a second gunshot. This time the startle reaction is not as great—his body does not jerk quite as dramatically, and there is not so large an increase in heart rate. With additional gunshots, Dick's startle response decreases until it has disappeared completely—the noise no longer disrupts his concentration on his novel.

This example illustrates the phenomenon of *habituation*, which is a decrease in the strength of a response after repeated presentation of a stimu-

lus that elicits the response. In principle, any elicited response can exhibit habituation, but in practice habituation is most evident in the body's automatic responses to new and sudden stimuli. The startle reaction is one example of such a response. Another is the *orienting response*: If a new sight or sound is presented to a dog or other animal, the animal may stop its current activity, lift its ears and its head, and turn in the direction of the stimulus. If the stimulus is presented repeatedly but is of no consequence, the orienting response will disappear. An important characteristic of habituation (which distinguishes it from both sensory adaptation and muscular fatigue) is that it is *stimulus specific*. Thus after Dick's startle reaction to the sound of gunfire has habituated, he should still exhibit such a reaction if the back door slams.

The function habituation serves for the organism should be clear. In its everyday activities an organism encounters many stimuli, some potentially beneficial, some potentially dangerous, and many neither helpful nor harmful. It is to the organism's advantage to be able to ignore the many insignificant stimuli it repeatedly encounters. To be continually startled or distracted by such stimuli would be a waste of the organism's time and energy. Consider, for example, the aggressive behavior of a male three-spined stickleback to another male entering its territory. This aggression against an intruder is important because it allows the stickleback to keep its territory, without which it cannot mate. However, since other males have staked out their own territories in adjacent areas, one male will repeatedly see these neighboring males as they patrol the borders of their territories. It would be harmful to all parties if neighboring males continually fought at their borders. But such fights between neighbors are rare, and a study by Peeke and Veno (1973) suggests that habituation is involved. Once a male stickleback had established its territory in an aquarium, a second male (protected inside a glass tube) was presented at the edge of the territory. The owner of the territory initially made many biting responses toward the intruder in the glass tube, but over the course of 30 minutes the frequency of biting responses decreased by more than 50 percent. Peeke and Veno showed that this habituation of an aggressive response was stimulus-specific by again presenting an intruder after an interlude of 15 minutes. If the intruder was the same fish as before, the owner's biting responses were infrequent (that is, the effects of the preceding habituation were still evident). If the intruder was a different fish, however, then all evidence of habituation disappeared, and the owner's biting responses were as frequent as when the first intruder appeared. This sort of habituation of aggressive responses to familiar males evidently helps to maintain relative peace among neighboring sticklebacks.

The usefulness of habituation is witnessed by its universality throughout the animal kingdom. The most primitive nervous systems found on our planet are those of coelenterates (jellyfish, sea anemones, hydra), consisting of diffuse networks of neurons. Yet research on hydra shows that they are capable of habituation. If a bright light is presented or if the surface to which the hydra is attached is vibrated, the hydra contracts. Rushford and his colleagues found that after several hundred presentations of a vibratory stimulus, the probability of a contraction response decreased from nearly 1.0 to about 0.2. This decline in responsiveness was not due to simple muscular fatigue, because when the vibratory stimulus was replaced with a light, the probability of a contraction increased immediately (Rushford, Burnett, & Maynard, 1963; Rushford, 1965). This study therefore demonstrated the stimulus specificity that is part of the accepted definition of habituation. There have also been reports of habituation in protozoa (one-celled organisms). Evidence for even the most primitive type of learning in protozoa is surprising because they have no nervous systems (by definition, since a nervous system is composed of many cells). In one study, Wood (1973) found a decline in the contraction response of the protozoan *Stentor coeruleus* with repeated presentations of a tactile stimulus. At the same time, the *Stentor's* responsiveness to another stimulus, a light, was undiminished.

General Principles of Habituation

Anyone who questions the feasibility of discovering general principles of learning applicable to a wide range of species should read the extensive literature on habituation. We have seen that habituation occurs in species as different as *Stentor coeruleus* and *Homo sapiens*. Furthermore, the mere existence of habituation is not all that is shared by such diverse species. In a frequently cited article, Thompson and Spencer (1966) listed some of the most salient properties of habituation, properties that have been observed in human beings, other mammals, and invertebrates. Several of Thompson and Spencer's principles are described below.

1. *The Course of Habituation.* Habituation of a response occurs whenever a stimulus is repeatedly presented. The decrements in responding from trial to trial are large at first but get progressively smaller as habituation proceeds.

2. *The Effects of Time.* If after habituation the stimulus is withheld for some period of time, the response will recover. The amount of recovery depends on the amount of time that elapses. To draw a parallel to Ebbinghaus's findings, we might say that habituation is "forgotten" as time passes. Suppose that after Dick's startle response to the gunshots has habituated, there are no more gunshots for 30 minutes but then they begin again. Dick is likely to exhibit a weak startle reaction to the first sound of gunshot after the break. (Thus there is some savings over time but also some forgetting.) In comparison, if there were no further shooting until the following evening, Dick's startle reaction after this longer time interval would be larger.

3. *Relearning Effects.* Whereas habituation may disappear over a long time interval, it should proceed more rapidly in a second series of stimulus presentations. In further series of stimulus presentations, habituation should occur progressively more quickly. To use Ebbinghaus's term, there are savings from the previous periods of habituation. For example, although Dick's initial startle response to the sound of gunfire on the second evening of his vacation might be almost as large as on the first evening, the response should disappear more quickly the second time.

4. *The Effects of Stimulus Intensity.* We have already seen that a reflexive response is frequently stronger with a more intense stimulus. Such a response is also more resistant to habituation. Habituation proceeds more rapidly with weak stimuli, and if a stimulus is very intense there may be no habituation at all.

5. *The Effects of Overlearning.* As in Ebbinghaus's experiments, further learning can occur at a time when there is no longer any change in observable behavior. Thompson and Spencer called this *below-zero* habituation because it occurs at a time when there is no observable response to the stimulus. Suppose that after 20 gunshots Dick's startle response has com-

pletely disappeared. After a 24-hour interval, however, he might exhibit little savings from the previous day's experience. If there were 100 gunshots on the first evening, he would probably show less of a startle response on the second evening. In other words, although the additional 80 gunshots produced no additional changes in Dick's behavior at the time, they did increase his long-term retention of the habituation.

6. *Stimulus Generalization.* The transfer of habituation from one stimulus to new but similar stimuli is called *generalization.* For example, if on the third evening the sounds of the gunshots are somewhat different (perhaps because different types of guns are being used), Dick may have little difficulty ignoring these sounds. The amount of generalization depends on the degree of similarity between the stimuli, and it is always the subject, not the experimenter, who is the ultimate judge of similarity. For example, in the experiment of Peeke and Veno (1973), a human observer might have expected considerable generalization of habituation from the first intruding male stickleback to the second, because to the human the two fish appeared very similar. However, to the stickleback whose territory was invaded, the two intruders were evidently quite discriminable, since the fish exhibited little transfer of habituation of its aggressive responses to the new intruder.

Physiological Mechanisms of Habituation

Because the principles of habituation are common to a wide range of creatures, simple and complex, some psychologists have speculated that the physiological mechanisms of habituation may also be similar in different species. Of course, this speculation could be wrong—it is certainly conceivable that two species that exhibit similar patterns of habituation from a behavioral perspective might have very different physiological mechanisms producing this habituation. Nevertheless, this possibility has not deterred some researchers from investigating the physiological changes accompanying habituation in fairly primitive creatures.

Eric Kandel and his colleagues (Castellucci, Pinsker, Kupferman & Kandel, 1970; Kandel & Schwartz, 1982) have devoted extensive study to both the behavior and the nervous system of *Aplysia*, a large marine snail (see Figure 3-7a). They chose to study this animal because its nervous system is relatively simple—it contains only a few thousand neurons, compared to the billions in a mammal's nervous system. Furthermore, the precise number, shape, position, and synaptic connections of *Aplysia's* neurons are remarkably uniform from one individual to the next, so that researchers can give labels to individual neurons and trace their inputs and outputs. Kandel and colleagues investigated the process of habituation in one of *Aplysia's* reflexes, the *gill-withdrawal reflex*. If the creature's siphon (described as a "fleshy spout") is touched lightly, its gill contracts and is drawn inside the mantle for a few seconds. The neural mechanisms that control this reflex are well understood. The siphon contains 24 sensory neurons that respond to

tactile stimulation. Six motor neurons control the gill-withdrawal response. The cell bodies of both the sensory and motor neurons are located in the abdominal ganglion, a collection of a few hundred cell bodies. It is here that the axons of the siphon's sensory neurons make contact with the motor neurons. Each of the 24 sensory neurons has a *monosynaptic* connection (that is, a direct connection that involves just one synapse) with each of the six motor neurons. In addition, other axons from the sensory neurons are involved in *polysynaptic* connections (indirect connections mediated by one or more interneurons) with these same motor neurons. Figure 3-7b depicts a small portion of this neural circuitry.

If the siphon is stimulated about once every minute for 10 or 15 trials, the gill-withdrawal reflex habituates. Complete habituation lasts for about an hour, and partial habituation may be observed for as long as 24 hours. If such trials are given on three or four successive days, long-term habituation (lasting several weeks) can be ob-

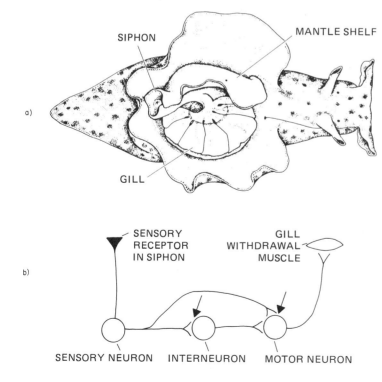

FIGURE 3-7. (a) The marine snail, *Aplysia.* (b) A small portion of the neural circuitry involved in the gill-withdrawal reflex. The sensory receptors in the siphon synapse either directly with a gill motor neuron or with an interneuron. In either case, Kandel and his associates found that habituation occurs in the first synapse of the chain, as indicated by the arrows. (From Kandel, 1979)

served. What changes at the physiological level are responsible for this habituation? Through a series of elaborate tests, Kandel's group was able to determine that during habituation, a decrease in excitatory conduction always occurred at the synapses involving the axons of the sensory neurons (at the points marked by arrows in Figure 3-7b). They also found that there was no change in the postsynaptic neuron's sensitivity to the transmitter. What had changed was the amount of transmitter released by the presynaptic (sensory) neurons—with repeated stimulus presentations less transmitter was released into the synapse. In the case of long-term habituation, Bailey and Chen (1983) found that the *active zones* of the sensory neurons (locations on the axon terminals from which transmitter is released) had decreased in both size and number. Kandel (1979) noted that this mechanism of habituation is not unique to *Aplysia*. Physiological investigations of habituation in two other species (the crayfish and the cat) also found decreases in the amount of transmitter released by the sensory neurons.

Having determined exactly which neurons underwent changes during the habituation of the gill-withdrawal reflex, Kandel proceeded to ask questions at a deeper level: What chemical mechanisms are responsible for the depressed transmitter release of the sensory neurons? Each time a neuron fires there is an influx of calcium ions into the axon terminals, and this calcium current is thought to cause the release of transmitter into the synapse. Perhaps this calcium current into the axon terminals becomes progressively weaker with repeated stimulation of the sensory neuron. The appropriate studies (Klein & Kandel, 1978; Klein, Shapiro & Kandel, 1980) supported this hunch: The calcium current grew weaker during habituation, and in the recovery period after habituation both the calcium current and the response of the postsynaptic (motor) neuron increased at the same rate. The experimenters concluded that a decrease in the calcium current causes a decrease in the amount of transmitter released into the synapse, which in turn decreases the excitation of the motor neuron, producing a weakened gill-withdrawal response.

The work of Kandel and his associates nicely illustrates the potential advantages of the "simple systems" strategy in physiological research on learning. Because of the comparative simplicity of *Aplysia's* neural networks, they have been able to pinpoint the neural changes responsible for habituation, and to make some preliminary hypotheses about the chemical processes involved as well. In Kandel's (1985) view, this research shows that, at least in some cases, learning depends on changes at very specific neural locations, not on widespread changes in many parts of the nervous system. Furthermore, this learning involved no anatomical changes, such as the growth of new axons, but merely changes in the effectiveness of existing synapses. It remains to be seen whether similar neural and chemical mechanisms are involved in habituation in higher animals.

Habituation in Emotional Responses: The Opponent-Process Theory

Richard Solomon and John Corbit (1974) proposed a theory of emotion that has attracted a good deal of attention. The theory is meant to apply to a wide range of emotional reactions. The type of learning they propose is quite similar to the examples of habituation we have already examined—in both, a subject's response to a stimulus changes simply as a result of repeated presentations of that stimulus. Opinions about the Opponent-Process Theory differ greatly, and as you read this section, you might want to form your own opinion about the theory's scientific merit, using the criteria for scientific theories discussed in Chapter 1.

The Temporal Pattern of an Emotional Response. Imagine that you are a pre-medical student taking a course in organic chemistry. You received a C+ on the midterm, and your performance in laboratory exercises was fair. You studied hard for the final exam, but there were some parts of the exam that you could not answer. While leaving the examination room, you overheard a number of students say that it was a difficult test. A few weeks later you receive your grades for the semester, and you learn to your surprise that your grade in organic chemistry was an A-! You are instantly ecstatic, and you tell the good news to everyone you see. You are too excited to do any serious work, but as you run some errands none of the minor irritations of a typical day (long lines, impolite salespersons) bother you in the least. By evening, however, your excitement has settled down, and you experience a state of contentment. The next morning, you receive a call from the registrar's office. There has been a clerical error in reporting the grades, and it turns out that your actual grade in organic chemistry was B-. This news provokes immediate feelings of dejection and despair. You reevaluate your plans about where you will apply to medical school, and wonder whether you will go at all. Over the course of a few hours, however, your emotional state gradually recovers and returns to normal.

This example illustrates all of the major features of a typical emotional episode as proposed by Opponent-Process Theory. Figure 3-8 presents a graph of your emotional states during this imaginary episode. The solid bar at the bottom marks the time during which some emotion-eliciting stimulus is present. In our example, it refers to the time when you believed your grade was A-. The y-axis depicts the strength of an individual's emotional reactions both while the stimulus is present and afterward. (Solomon and Corbit always plot the response to the stimulus itself in the positive direction, regardless of whether we would call the emotion "pleasant" or "unpleasant.") According to the theory, the onset of such a stimulus produces the sudden appearance of an emotional reaction, which quickly reaches a peak of intensity (the initial ecstasy in our example). This response then gradually declines to a somewhat lower level or plateau (your contentment during the evening). With the offset of the stimulus (the telephone call), there is a sudden switch to an emotional after-reaction that is in some sense the opposite of the initial emotion (the dejection and despair). This after-reaction gradually declines and the individual's emotional state returns to a neutral state.

To strengthen their arguments, Solomon and Corbit reviewed some experimental data from a

FIGURE 3-8. The typical pattern of an emotional response, according to Opponent-Process Theory. The solid bar shows the time in which an emotion-eliciting stimulus is present. (From Solomon & Corbit, 1974)

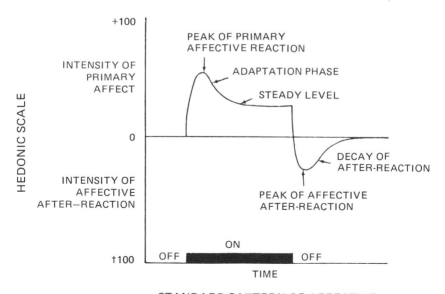

STANDARD PATTERN OF AFFECTIVE
DYNAMICS

situation where the initial emotional response was decidedly negative, but where heart rate was used as an objective measure of a subject's emotional reaction. In this experiment (Church, Lo-Lordo, Overmier, Solomon, & Turner, 1966) dogs were restrained in harnesses and received a number of 10-second shocks. During the first few shocks a dog's overt responses were typically those of terror—it might shriek, pull on the harness, urinate or defecate, and its hair might stand on end. At the termination of the shock, a typical dog's behavior was characterized as "stealthy, hesitant, and unfriendly." Intuitively, we might not feel that these after-reactions are the "opposite" of terror, but they are certainly different from the initial reaction. After a short time the stealthiness would disappear and the dog's disposition would return to normal—"active, alert, and socially responsive." Heart-rate measures provided more compelling support for the pattern in Figure 3-8: During the shock, heart rate rose rap-

idly from a resting state of about 120 beats/minute to a maximum of about 200 beats/minute and then began to decline. At shock termination there was a rebound effect in which heart rate dropped to about 90 beats/minute, then returned to normal after 30 or 60 seconds.

The a-process and b-process. Solomon and Corbit describe several other examples of emotional episodes, but let us now turn to the intervening variables of their theory—the internal processes that, they propose, underlie an individual's observable emotional responses. They hypothesize that the pattern shown in Figure 3-8 is the result of two antagonistic internal processes that they call the *a-process* and the *b-process*. The a-process is largely responsible for the initial emotional response, and the b-process is totally responsible for the after-reaction. The left half of Figure 3-9 shows how these two processes supposedly combine to produce the pat-

FIGURE 3-9. According to Opponent-Process Theory, a person's emotional reaction (or "manifest affective response") is jointly determined by the underlying a- and b-processes. The proposed time course of these processes during the first few presentations of an emotion-eliciting stimulus is shown on the left. The right side shows the predicted patterns after many repetitions of the same stimulus. (From Solomon & Corbit, 1974)

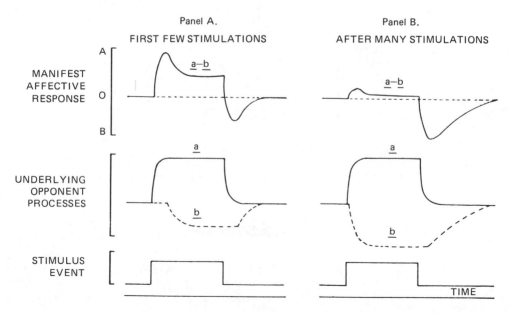

tern of Figure 3-8. Solomon and Corbit describe the a-process as a fast-acting response to a stimulus that rises to a maximum and remains there as long as the stimulus is present. When the stimulus ends, the a-process decays very quickly (see the middle left graph in Figure 3-9). In the heart-rate study, the a-process would be some hypothetical internal mechanism (perhaps the flow of adrenalin?) that produces, among other responses, an increase in heart rate. The antagonistic b-process is supposedly activated only in response to the activity of the a-process, and it is supposedly more sluggish both to rise and to decay. The middle left graph in Figure 3-9 also shows the more gradual increase and decrease in the b-process. In the heart rate example, the b-process would be some internal mechanism causing a decrease in heart rate.

Note that in Figure 3-9, the b-process begins to rise while the stimulus (the shock) is still present. Solomon and Corbit propose that when both the a-process and the b-process are active to some degree, the resulting emotional response can be predicted by simple algebraic summation. That is, the action of the a-process will be countered to some extent by the action of the b-process, and the emotional response will be weaker. According to the theory, it is the rise in the b-process that causes the drop in the initial emotional reaction from the peak to the plateau. When the stimulus ends and the a-process quickly decays, all that remains is the b-process, which produces the emotional after-reaction. Before reading further, you should make sure you see how the two processes in the middle left graph of Figure 3-9 combine to produce the pattern in the upper left graph.

The Effects of Repeated Stimulation. To this point, the discussion has been restricted to an individual's first encounter with a new stimulus. However, a crucial feature of the Opponent-Process Theory is its predictions about how the pattern of an emotional response changes with repeated presentations of the same stimulus. To put it simply, the theory states that with repeated exposures to a stimulus the primary emotional response exhibits a sort of habituation—it becomes progressively smaller—while at the same time

there is a marked increase in the size and duration of the after-reaction. The top right graph in Figure 3-9 shows the predicted pattern of an emotional response after many stimulations. The middle right graph shows that, according to the theory, this change is the result of an increase in the size of the b-process. Solomon and Corbit propose that whereas the a-process does not change, the b-process is strengthened with use and weakened with disuse. With repeated stimulations, the b-process rises more quickly, reaches a higher maximum, and is slower to decay after the stimulus is terminated.

Solomon and Corbit supported these predictions by describing the pattern of responding after dogs received a number of shocks in the Church et al. (1966) study. After several sessions, there was little if any heart-rate increase during the shock. However, after shock termination, heart rate decreased by as much as 60 beats/minute, and it took from two to five minutes (instead of a minute or less) for heart rate to return to normal. The dogs' overt behaviors also exhibited changes with experience:

During shocks, the signs of terror disappeared. Instead, the dog appeared pained, annoyed, anxious, but not terrified. For example, it whined rather than shrieked, and showed no further urination, defecation, or struggling. Then, when released suddenly at the end of the session, the dog rushed about, jumped up on people, wagged its tail, in what we called at the time "a fit of joy." Finally, several minutes later, the dog was its normal self: friendly, but not racing about. (Solomon & Corbit, 1974, p. 122)

In short, with extended experience the dog's overt behaviors paralleled its heart-rate response: The reaction to the shock was smaller than before, but the after-reaction was larger and of longer duration.

Other Examples. Solomon and Corbit claim that Opponent-Process Theory describes the temporal dynamics of many different types of emotional experiences, and a few more of their examples will give some indication of the generality of the theory. They discuss the emotional responses of parachutists on their initial jumps and on later jumps, as reported by Epstein (1967).

Overall, the emotional experiences of parachutists resemble those of the dogs in the heart rate study. Novice parachutists appear terrified during a jump; after the jump they look stunned for a few minutes, then return to normal. Experienced parachutists appear only moderately anxious during a jump, but afterward they report feelings of exhilaration and euphoria that can last for hours. They claim that this feeling of euphoria is one of the main reasons they continue to jump.

A graphic example involving a pleasurable initial reaction followed by an aversive after-reaction deals with the use of opiates. After a person's first opiate injection, an intense feeling of pleasure (a "rush") is experienced. This peak of emotion declines to a less intense state of pleasure. As the effect of the drug wears off, however, the aversive after-reactions set in—nausea, insomnia, irritability, anxiety, an inability to eat, and other physical problems, along with feelings of craving for the drug. The withdrawal symptoms can last for hours or a few days.

For an experienced opiate user the pattern changes. The injection no longer brings an initial rush, but only mild feelings of pleasure, if any. This decrease in the effects of a drug with repeated use is called *tolerance*, and it is observed with many drugs besides opiates. Some theorists have suggested that drug tolerance is a good example of habituation (for example, Baker & Tiffany, 1985). According to the Opponent-Process Theory, however, tolerance is the product of a strengthened b-process. The stronger b-process also explains why, with repeated opiate use, the withdrawal symptoms become more severe, and they may last for weeks or longer. At this stage the individual does not take the opiate for pleasure but for temporary relief from the withdrawal symptoms. In terms of the Opponent-Process Theory, each injection reinstates the a-process, which counteracts the withdrawal symptoms produced by the b-process. Unfortunately, each injection also further strengthens the b-process, so the individual is caught in a vicious cycle. Solomon and Corbit propose that their theory provides a framework for understanding not only opiate use but all addictive behaviors (such as smoking, alcoholism, and the use of barbiturates and amphetamines). We will see in Chapter 5,

however, that other researchers who study drug use disagree with the details of Opponent-Process Theory.

Why is it that many emotional reactions include both an a-process and an antagonistic b-process? Solomon and Corbit suggest that the b-process is the body's mechanism, albeit imperfect, of avoiding prolonged, intense emotions. Extremes of emotion, whether positive or negative, are taxing on the body's resources, so when any a-process persists for some time the corresponding b-process is evoked to counteract it, at least in part. If this is indeed the function of the b-process, then the examples of addictive behaviors clearly demonstrate that this mechanism is imperfect.

A Brief Evaluation. A fair number of experiments have supported the predictions of Opponent-Process Theory (Solomon, 1980). Nevertheless, a common criticism of the theory is that there is little concrete evidence about the actual physiological mechanisms that might correspond to the hypothetical a- and b-processes. Of course, this situation could be remedied if researchers find physiological processes that behave as the theory predicts. Critics also point out that the different examples used by Solomon and Corbit exhibit vastly different time courses. In the heart-rate studies with dogs, the b-process lasts only seconds or a few minutes. In an addiction, the b-process may continue for months. Is it likely that the same physiological mechanisms are involved in emotional events whose durations differ by a factor of ten thousand or more? Critics have argued that there may be nothing more than a superficial resemblance among the different examples Solomon and Corbit present.

In defense of Opponent-Process Theory, we might assert that as long as emotional responses conform to the predictions of the theory, it does not matter whether these patterns are based on a single physiological mechanism or on a dozen different ones. On a strictly descriptive level, the major characteristics of emotional episodes emphasized by Opponent-Process Theory (the peak, the plateau, the after-effect, the changes with repeated stimulation) appear to be fairly well documented by case histories, systematic observations, and experiments. Whether or not these patterns share a common physiological mechanism, the data suggest that the theory captures some characteristics of emotional responses that are quite general. Though it has been called a weakness, the theory's ambitious attempt to unite diverse emotional situations in a single framework may actually be its greatest virtue. The broad viewpoint provided by Opponent-Process Theory allows us to see commonalities among our emotions that would probably go unnoticed in a more myopic analysis of individual emotional responses.

4

BASIC PRINCIPLES
OF CLASSICAL CONDITIONING

PAVLOV'S DISCOVERY AND ITS IMPACT

Part of the excitement of conducting scientific research arises from the ever-present possibility that a routine experiment, conducted with a fairly mundane objective in mind, can produce an unexpected finding of great importance. The history of science records many stories of such serendipitous discoveries, and in one such story the main character was the Russian scientist Ivan Pavlov.

Although he eventually became one of the most famous figures in the history of psychology, Pavlov was trained as a physiologist, not as a psychologist. He conducted a substantial amount of research on the physiology of the digestive system, and in 1904 he was awarded the Nobel Prize in Medicine and Physiology for this work. Pavlov was interested in the various substances that are secreted by an animal's digestive system

to break down the food eaten. He analyzed the chemical composition of the digestive juices, measured the times they were secreted during the course of a meal, and attempted to discover the neural mechanisms controlling these physiological responses. One of the digestive juices Pavlov studied was saliva, which is the first secretion to make contact with any ingested food. The subjects in Pavlov's studies were dogs, and he developed a surgical technique that enabled him to redirect the saliva from one of the dog's salivary ducts through a tube and out of the mouth, so that it could be measured. Figure 4-1 pictures Pavlov's experimental apparatus, which included a harness to restrain the subject and the devices for recording each drop of saliva.

In Pavlov's research, a single dog might be subjected to several test sessions on successive days. In each session the dog would be given food, and its salivation would be recorded as it ate. Pavlov's important observation came when

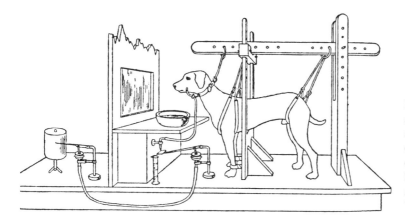

FIGURE 4-1. Pavlov's salivary conditioning situation. A tube redirects drops of saliva out of the dog's mouth so they can be recorded automatically. (From Yerkes & Morgulis, 1909)

studying dogs that had been through the testing procedure several times. Unlike a new subject, an experienced dog would begin to salivate even before the food was presented. Pavlov reasoned that some stimuli that had regularly preceded the presentation of food in previous sessions, such as the sight of the experimenter, had now acquired the capacity to elicit the response of salivation. Since it was not the original purpose of this experiment to study salivation as a response to some nonfood stimulus, Pavlov might have treated this phenomenon as an annoyance, a confounding variable to be eliminated. Instead, however, he recognized the significance of this unexpected result, and he spent the rest of his life studying this phenomenon, which is now known as classical conditioning. Pavlov realized his subjects were exhibiting a simple type of learning: Salivation, which began as a reflexive response to the stimulus of food in the dog's mouth, was now elicited by a new (and initially ineffective) stimulus. Pavlov speculated that many of an animal's learned behaviors might be traced back to its innate reflexes, just as a dog's learned behavior of salivating when the experimenter appeared developed from the initial food-salivation reflex. If so, then we might be able to discover a good deal about an animal's learning mechanisms by studying the development of learned or conditioned reflexes in the laboratory. With this goal in mind, Pavlov developed a set of procedures for studying classical conditioning that are still in use today.

The Standard Paradigm of Classical Conditioning

To conduct an experiment in classical conditioning, an experimenter must first select some stimulus that reliably elicits a characteristic response. The stimulus of this pair is called the *unconditioned stimulus*, and the response is called the *unconditioned response*. The term *unconditioned* is used to signify the fact that the connection between the stimulus and response is unlearned (innate). In Pavlov's experiments on the salivary response, the unconditioned stimulus (abbreviated US) was the presence of food in the dog's mouth, and the unconditioned response (UR) was the secretion of saliva. The third element of the classical-conditioning paradigm is the *conditioned stimulus* (CS), which can be any stimulus that does not initially evoke the UR (for instance, a bell). The term *conditioned stimulus* indicates that it is only after conditioning has taken place that the bell will elicit the response of salivation.

Figure 4-2 diagrams the sequence of events on a single trial of classical conditioning. In its simplest form, a classical-conditioning trial involves the presentation of the CS (say, a bell) followed by the US (for instance, the food). On the initial trials only the US will elicit the response of salivation. However, as the conditioning trials continue, the dog will begin to salivate as soon as the CS is presented. Any salivation that occurs dur-

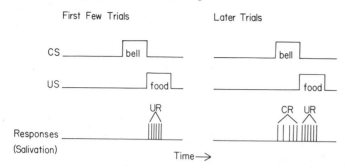

FIGURE 4-2. The events of a classical-conditioning trial both before a conditioned response is established (left) and after (right).

ing the CS but before the US is referred to as a *conditioned response* (CR), since it is only because of the conditioning procedure that the bell now elicits salivation.

The abbreviations for the four basic elements of the classical-conditioning paradigm will appear repeatedly in this and later chapters, so be sure that you have no confusion about what each term represents. The two components of the initial stimulus-response pair are the US and the UR. Through the procedures of classical conditioning, a new stimulus, the CS, begins to elicit responses of its own, and these responses to the CS are called CRs (since they are learned, or conditioned responses). In salivary conditioning, the CR and the UR are both salivation, and in many other conditioning situations the CR closely resembles the UR. However, we will soon see that in some types of classical conditioning the form of the CR is very different from that of the UR.

The Variety of Conditioned Responses

As Chapter 3 showed, the bodies of both humans and animals exhibit a large number of reflexive responses. Some of these reflexes involve overt muscular movements, and others involve the internal responses of various glands and organs. Classical conditioning has been observed in many of these reflexes. Schlosberg (1928) conducted one of several studies on the knee-jerk reflex. The US was the tap of a hammer on the tendon below the kneecap, and the UR was the rapid jerking of the lower leg, a movement due mainly to the flexion of the quadriceps muscle. With different subjects, Schlosberg tested several different stimuli

as CSs—a tone, a click, a buzz, and tactile pressure on a finger. On conditioning trials the CS preceded the US by a fraction of a second. On occasional test trials the CS was presented without the US, and on a substantial fraction of these test trials a conditioned response was observed: The CS elicited a knee-jerk response similar to that produced by the hammer. In similar studies, successful classical conditioning has been obtained with a number of other muscular reflexes in different parts of the body, including the ankles and toes, the abdomen, and the Achilles tendon (Hull, 1934). One study examined the pupillary reflex—the contraction of the pupil of the eye when a bright light is presented. By repeatedly pairing a bell (the CS) with a bright light (the US), Watson (1916) was able to produce a weak pupillary contraction to the bell presented by itself.

The term *interoceptive conditioning* refers to situations in which either the CS or the US is the stimulation of some internal gland or organ. A number of studies have shown that it is possible to classically condition various organs such as the heart, the stomach, the liver, and the kidneys. For example, in one study on classical conditioning of the kidneys (Bykov, 1957), dogs were given injections of 100 cc of water as a US, and the UR was the secretion of urine by the kidneys. After many trials in which some CS (such as a whistle) was paired with the injection of water, these animals exhibited CRs—large increases in the secretion of urine to the CS alone. Numerous studies of this type have shown that the reflexive responses of glands and organs, like muscular reflexes, can be controlled by the procedures of classical conditioning. In fact, it is probably only a slight exaggeration to state that any reflexive response (that is, any response that is reliably elicited by some US) can be classically conditioned, given a sufficient number of pairings between the US and some CS. Of course, the speed and reliability of conditioning can vary greatly depending on the stimuli and responses that are involved.

Although classical conditioning has been observed with dozens of different reflexes, today only a handful of conditioned responses are studied to any great extent. The reasons for this are strictly pragmatic. Insofar as the goal of a researcher is to discover general principles of conditioning, the exact response system under investigation is basically irrelevant. Over the years, researchers in classical conditioning have converged on a small number of conditioning *preparations* (that is, conditioning situations utilizing a particular US, UR, and species of subject) that can be studied easily and efficiently. As the number of studies involving a specific preparation grows, it gains the additional advantage of the accumulated technical knowledge surrounding that preparation. For these reasons, on subsequent pages we will repeatedly encounter studies employing the same conditioning preparations. The following conditioning situations, among others, have been used in a large number of experiments on classical conditioning.

Eyeblink Conditioning. Conditioning of the eyeblink reflex has been studied with both humans and rabbits as subjects. Figure 4-3 shows a typical procedure for eyeblink conditioning with rabbits. The subject is placed in a tight compartment to restrict its movement. The US in this case is a puff of air directed at the eye, and the UR is of course an eyeblink. Both the timing and magnitude of an eyeblink are recorded by a potentiometer, which measures the movement of a thread attached to the rabbit's eyelid. In other eyelid conditioning studies the US is a mild electric shock delivered to the skin in the vicinity of the eye, a stimulus that also reliably elicits an eyeblink as a UR. In such studies the CS may be a light, a tone, or some tactile stimulus such as a vibration of the experimental chamber, and the duration of the CS is typically about one second. Like the UR, the CR is an eyeblink, but its form is different. Whereas the unconditioned eyeblink is a large and rapid eyelid closure, the conditioned response is a smaller and more gradual eyelid movement. The most common measure of the strength of conditioning is the percentage of trials on which a CR is observed. Eyeblink conditioning requires a large number of CS-US pairings. For example, it may take well over 100 pairings before a CR is observed on 50 percent of the trials.

Conditioned Suppression. In this procedure, which is also called the *conditioned emotional response* (CER) procedure, the subjects are usually rats, and the US is an aversive event such as a brief electric shock delivered through the metal bars that form the floor of the experimental chamber. The unconditioned response to shock may include several different behaviors—the ani-

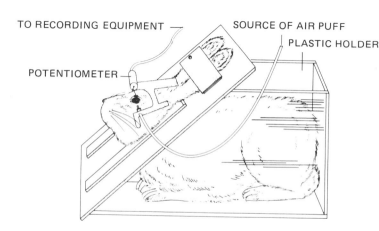

TO RECORDING EQUIPMENT — SOURCE OF AIR PUFF

PLASTIC HOLDER

POTENTIOMETER

FIGURE 4-3. An eyeblink conditioning arrangement. The potentiometer measures the movement of the rabbit's eyelid in response to either an air puff or some conditioned stimulus.

mal may jump, squeal, and temporarily stop what it was doing before the shock occurred. The measure of conditioning in this situation is the suppression of ongoing behavior when the CS (which signals that a shock is forthcoming) is presented. So that "ongoing behavior" can be measured automatically and reliably, a separate task on which the subject will respond at a fairly steady rate is included in this procedure. Most frequently, hungry rats are given the opportunity to press a lever, and occasionally a lever press will result in the delivery of a food pellet. It is fairly easy to schedule the delivery of food pellets in such a way that the animal will press the lever slowly but steadily for an hour or more, now and then earning a bit of food.

As in eyeblink conditioning, the CS may be visual, auditory, or tactile, but the duration of the CS is generally much longer in the conditioned suppression procedure—CSs of one minute or more are commonplace. When the CS is first presented, it may have little effect on the subject's lever-pressing behavior. The rat may pause for a few seconds to notice this novel stimulus (an orienting response), but it will soon resume its lever pressing. However, after a few pairings of the CS and shock (in which the shock arrives at the end of the one-minute CS and lasts for perhaps one second), the subject's behavior is markedly different—its rate of lever pressing suddenly decreases as soon as the CS is presented, and the animal may make only a few lever presses during the minute that the CS is present. If you observed a rat in this situation, you might say that the rat looked "afraid" during the CS, which is why this is sometimes called a conditioned emotional response procedure or a conditioned fear procedure. We do not need to speculate about the rat's emotions, however, to make use of the objectively measurable change in the animal's behavior. The extent to which lever pressing is suppressed provides us with a measure of the strength of conditioning. To calculate the level of suppression, the rate of lever pressing during the CS is usually compared to the rate just prior to the onset of the CS. For example, if the rat was pressing the lever at a rate of 40 responses per minute before the CS and this rate dropped to 10 responses per minute in the

presence of the CS, this would constitute a suppression of 75 percent.

Conditioning takes place in far fewer trials in the conditioned suppression procedure than in the eyeblink procedure, perhaps partly because the shock is more intense than the air puffs or mild shocks used in eyeblink conditioning. Whatever the reasons, strong conditioned suppression can often be observed in fewer than 10 trials, and in some cases significant suppression to the CS is found after just one CS-US pairing.

The Galvanic Skin Response (GSR). This conditioning preparation has been used fairly little in recent years, but it was quite popular during the first half of the twentieth century. The subjects in these studies were always humans, and the GSR is a change in the electrical conductivity of the skin. To measure a person's GSR, two coin-shaped electrodes are attached to the palm, and the electrodes are connected to a device that measures momentary fluctuations in the conductivity of the skin (caused by small changes in perspiration). The conductivity of the skin is altered by emotions such as fear or surprise, which is why the GSR is often one measure used in lie detector tests. One stimulus that reliably produces a large increase in skin conductivity is electric shock, and a similar increase in conductivity can be conditioned to any CS that is paired with shock. For instance, the CS might be a tone, the US a shock to the left wrist, and the response an increase in conductivity of the right palm. One reason for the interest in the GSR is that since it provides a response that can be quickly and reliably conditioned with human subjects, many complex stimuli (such as spoken or written words) can be examined as CSs.

Taste-Aversion Learning. This conditioning procedure has been extensively investigated since about the late 1960s. Rats are frequently the subjects in this research, but other species (pigeons, quail, guinea pigs) have also been used. By definition the CS in this procedure is the taste of something the subject eats or drinks. In many cases, the food is one that the subject has never tasted before. After eating or drinking, the subject is given an injection of a poison (the US) that makes the animal ill. Several days later, after the subject has fully recovered from its illness, it is again given the opportunity to consume the substance that served as the CS. The usual result is that the animal consumes little or none of this food. Thus the measure of conditioning is the degree to which the subject avoids the food.

In such an experiment, further information must be supplied before we can be certain that a specific association between food and illness is responsible for the animal's avoidance of that food. It is conceivable that the animal would eat little of *any* food as a result of its recent illness. One way to dismiss this possibility is to include two groups of subjects. Subjects in the experimental group receive a pairing of the food and poison; control subjects receive only the poison. If in the subsequent test, control subjects consume large amounts of this food but experimental subjects do not, this difference between groups must be due to the pairing of food and poison in the experimental group. In studies of this type, experimental subjects do in fact consume considerably less of the test food than control subjects (Garcia, McGowan, & Green, 1972).

There are a number of reasons why taste-aversion learning has received so much attention in recent years. For one thing, as will be discussed in detail in Chapter 9, some psychologists have suggested that taste-aversion learning is not an ordinary example of classical conditioning, but that it violates some of the general principles that apply to most examples of classical conditioning. Second, a taste aversion often develops after just one conditioning trial, and this rapidity of conditioning is advantageous for certain theoretical questions. Third, a taste aversion is something that many people experience at least once in their lives. Perhaps there is some type of food that you refuse to eat because you once became ill after eating it. You may find the very thought of eating this food a bit nauseating, although most people may enjoy the food. If you have such a taste aversion you are not unusual—one study found that over half of the college students surveyed had at least one taste aversion (Logue, Ophir, & Strauss, 1981). A taste aversion may develop even if the individual is certain that the food was not the cause of the subsequent illness. I once attended a large dinner party where the main

course was chicken tarragon. Besides passing food around the table, we evidently passed around an intestinal virus, because many of the guests became quite ill that evening. For some, the illness lasted for over a week. The result of this accidental pairing of food and illness was that several years later, some of these guests still refused to eat chicken tarragon or any food with tarragon spicing. Taste aversion can be strong and long lasting!

Pavlov's Stimulus Substitution Theory

Pavlov was the first to propose a theory of classical conditioning that is now called the *stimulus substitution theory*. On a behavioral level, the theory simply predicts the changes that supposedly take place among the observable events of conditioning—the stimuli and responses. The theory states that by virtue of the repeated pairings between CS and US, the CS becomes a substitute for the US, so that the response initially elicited by only the US is now also elicited by the CS. At first glance, this theory seems to provide a perfectly satisfactory description of what takes place in many common examples of classical conditioning. In salivary conditioning, initially only food elicits salivation, but later the CS also elicits salivation. In eyeblink conditioning, both the UR and the CR are eyelid closures. In GSR conditioning, an increase in skin conductance is first elicited by a shock, and after conditioning a similar increase in skin conductance occurs in response to some initially neutral stimulus.

Despite these apparent confirmations of the stimulus substitution theory, this theory has been criticized on a number of counts. First of all, the CR is almost never an exact replica of the UR. For instance, it was already noted that whereas an eyeblink UR to an air puff is a large, rapid eyelid closure, the CR that develops is a smaller and more gradual eyelid closure. That is, both the size and the temporal pattern of the CR differ from those of the UR. This fact, however, only allows us to reject the strictest interpretation of stimulus substitution theory, one that states that the CR will be identical to the UR in all details. In defense of stimulus substitution theory, Hilgard (1936) argued that since the intensity and stimulus modality of the CS and US may be different, such differences in response magnitude and timing are to be expected. After all, URs of different sizes can be obtained simply by changing the intensity of the US—a strong shock will produce a large eyeblink UR, and a weak shock will produce a smaller UR. Given such variability among URs themselves, it seems unrealistic to expect that the CR will be identical to the UR in all respects.

A somewhat larger problem for stimulus substitution theory is that whereas many USs elicit several different responses, as a general rule not all of these responses are later elicited by the CS. For example, Zener (1937) noted that when a dog is presented with food as a US, a number of responses such as chewing and swallowing of the food occur in addition to salivation. Yet although a well-trained CS such as a bell will elicit salivation, it will generally not elicit the chewing and swallowing responses. Thus not all of the components of the UR are present in the CR. Conversely, a CR may include some responses that are *not* part of the UR. For instance, using a bell as a CS, Zener found that many dogs would turn their heads and look at the bell when it was rung. Sometimes a dog would move its entire body closer to the ringing bell. Obviously these behaviors were not a normal part of the dog's UR to food. Because of such results, it was clear that stimulus substitution theory had to be modified if it were to remain a viable theory of classical conditioning. Hilgard (1936) suggested two ways in which the theory might be amended. First, it should be acknowledged that only some components of the UR are transferred to the CR. Hilgard noted that some components of the UR may depend on the physical characteristics of the US, and they will not be transferred to a CS with very different physical characteristics. Thus although a dog will chew and swallow food when it is presented, it cannot chew and swallow food that is not there (when the bell is rung). Second, it should be recognized that a CS such as a bell frequently elicits unconditioned responses of its own, and these may become part of the CR. For instance, when it first hears a bell, a dog may exhibit an orienting response—it may raise its ears, look in the direction of the bell, and possibly approach the bell. Although such orienting responses usually habituate if the bell is inconsequential, they persist or increase if the bell is paired with food. A more recent theory of classical conditioning called the *sign-tracking* theory (Hearst & Jenkins, 1974) emphasizes precisely this aspect of an animal's response to a CS. It states that animals tend to orient themselves toward, approach, and explore any stimuli that are good predictors of important events such as the delivery of food. It is not very surprising that some components of the orienting response to the CS are retained as part of the CR. In short, the form of the CR may reflect both the unconditioned response to the US and the unconditioned response to the CS itself.

Possibly the strongest argument against stimulus substitution theory arises from the finding that in some cases the direction of the CR is opposite to that of the UR. For instance, one response to an electric shock is an increase in heart rate, but in studies with guinea pigs Black (1965) observed conditioned heart rate *decreases* to a CS paired with shock. Another example involves studies in which animals (usually rats) are given a morphine injection as the US. One of the URs to morphine is hyperthermia, or an increase in body temperature. In experiments where some CS is repeatedly paired with morphine, two types of CRs have been observed. Sometimes the CR is an increase in body temperature, as predicted by stimulus substitution theory, but in other cases the CR is a decrease in body temperature. Conditioned responses that are the opposite of the UR have been called *conditioned compensatory responses* (Siegel, 1982) or examples of *paradoxical conditioning* (Finch, 1938).

Regardless of their label, such examples of paradoxical conditioning may seem to imply that stimulus substitution theory is inadequate as a general theory of classical conditioning. Nevertheless, a number of theorists have suggested that these examples are not as damaging to stimulus substitution theory as they appear on the surface (Eikelboom and Stewart, 1982; Wagner, 1981). Eikelboom and Stewart asserted that classical conditioning always involves stimulus substitution, and that all apparent counterexamples involve cases where either the CR or the UR was not measured correctly. Their arguments are discussed in more detail in Chapter 5, but we can get a feeling for their approach by considering their analysis of the conditioned temperature responses that occur when morphine is used as a US. They point out that the UR to morphine actually consists of two components—the initial response of hyperthermia eventually gives way to hypothermia (lower-than-normal body temperature) as the morphine leaves the animal's system. (This pattern is consistent with the Opponent-Process Theory of Solomon and Corbit.) Which of these two temperature responses is transferred to the CS may depend on a number of factors, such as the exact temporal relationship between the CS and US. In any case, once it is realized that the UR to morphine involves both hyperthermia and hypothermia, it becomes difficult to argue that either type of CR constitutes a clear counterexample to stimulus substitution theory.

As can be seen, although potential difficulties with stimulus substitution theory have been known for decades, there are still those who assert that the theory is fundamentally correct. Yet even if the proponents of stimulus substitution theory are right, the version of the theory that emerges is one with fairly little predictive power. We began with the simple view that the CR mimics the UR. But several qualifications had to be added to keep the theory consistent with the facts: (1) The sizes and temporal patterns of the CR and UR may differ, (2) Not all components of the UR become part of the CR, (3) The CR may include response components that are not part of the UR, and (4) The CR is sometimes opposite in direction to the UR (or at least to the most obvious part of the UR). With all of these qualifications, it becomes difficult to predict in advance what the CR will look like in a specific instance.

Having surveyed the arguments for and against stimulus substitution theory as a descriptive theory, let us now turn to Pavlov's speculations about possible physiological mechanisms involved in classical conditioning. Pavlov had limited information about the physiology of the brain, and some of the specific details of his theory have since been proven wrong. On a more general level, however, his speculations still constitute a viable physiological theory of conditioning.

Pavlov proposed that there is a specific part of the brain that becomes active whenever a US (such as food) is presented, and he called this part of the brain the *US center*. Similarly, for every different CS (a tone, a light), there is a separate *CS center*, which becomes active whenever that particular CS is presented. From what we know about the physiology of the sensory systems (Chapter 2), these assumptions seem quite reasonable, especially since the exact nature of CS centers and US centers is not important to Pavlov's theory. It does not matter, as far as this theory is concerned, whether a CS center or US center is a single neuron, a group of neurons with similar functions, or even a particular pattern of activity in a set of neurons. Pavlov also assumed that for every UR (say, salivation) there is part of the brain that can be called a *response center*, and it is the activation of this response center that initiates the neural commands that ultimately produce the observed response. Furthermore, since the US elicits the UR without any prior training, Pavlov assumed that there is an innate connection between the US center and the response center (see Figure 4-4). Finally, Pavlov proposed that somehow an association develops during the course of classical conditioning, so that now the CS produces activity in the response center (and a CR is observed).

As Figure 4-4 suggests, there are at least two types of new associations that would give the CS the capacity to elicit a CR. On one hand, a direct association between the CS center and the response center might develop during conditioning. Since this association is between a stimulus and a response, it is sometimes called an *S-R association*. On the other hand, the connection between the CS and response centers might be less direct. Perhaps an association between the CS center and the US center is formed during conditioning. Later, when the CS is presented, this activates the CS center, which activates the US center (through the newly formed association), which in turn activates the response center (through the innate association). This hypothesis constitutes the position that an *S-S association* is formed during classical conditioning. Pavlov tended to favor

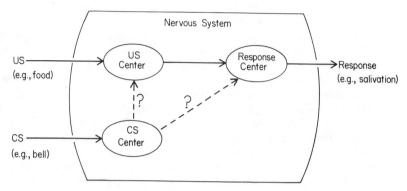

FIGURE 4-4. Two possible versions of Pavlov's stimulus substitution theory. During classical conditioning, an association might develop from the CS center to the US center, or from the CS center directly to the response center.

the S-S position, but he had little empirical support for this view. More recently, however, experimenters have devised a number of clever techniques to try to distinguish between these two alternatives. The next section describes one such procedure.

S-S or S-R Connections?

In the absence of physiological information about what neural changes take place during classical conditioning, how can we distinguish between the S-S and S-R positions? Rescorla (1973) used the following reasoning. If the S-S position is correct, then after conditioning the occurrence of a CR depends on the continued strength of two associations—the learned association between the CS center and the US center, and the innate association between the US center and the response center (see Figure 4-4). If the US-response connection is somehow weakened, this should cause a reduction in the strength of the CR, since the occurrence of the CR depends on this connection. On the other hand, if the S-R position is correct, the strength of the CR does not depend on the continued integrity of the US- response association, but only on the direct association between the CS center and the response center. But how can a reflexive US-response association be weakened? Rescorla's solution was to rely on habituation.

Rescorla used a conditioned suppression pro-

TABLE 4-1   Design of Rescorla's (1973) Experiment

Group	Phase 1	Phase 2	Test
Habituation	Light→Noise	Noise (habituation)	Light
Control	Light→Noise	No stimuli	Light

cedure with rats, but instead of the usual electric shock, a loud noise was used as the US. Rescorla's previous work had indicated that a conditioned suppression of lever pressing would develop to any CS paired with the noise, but also that the noise was susceptible to habituation if it was repeatedly presented. The design of the experiment is shown in Table 4-1. In Phase 1, two groups of rats received identical classical conditioning with a light as the CS and the noise as the US. In Phase 2, the habituation group received many presentations of the noise by itself, so as to habituate the subjects' fear of the noise. The control subjects spent equal amounts of time in the experimental chamber in Phase 2, but no stimuli were presented, so there was no opportunity for the noise to habituate in this group. In the test phase of the experiment, both groups were presented with the light by itself for a number of trials, and the subjects' levels of suppression of lever pressing were recorded. Rescorla found high levels of suppression to the light in

Rescorla
S-S theorist

the control group, but significantly lower levels of suppression in the habituation group. He therefore concluded that the strength of the CR is dependent on the continued strength of the US-response association, as predicted by the S-S position but not the S-R position.

The technique of decreasing the effectiveness of the US after an excitatory CS has been created is called *US devaluation*. In Rescorla's study, devaluation was accomplished by habituating fear of the noise, but other techniques have also been used. For instance, if the US is food, it can be devalued by satiating the subject (Holland & Recorla, 1975). Other research on the associations formed during classical conditioning will be described in Chapter 5. For now, it will be sufficient to understand how questions about the workings of the nervous system can be addressed in a meaningful way without actually tracing any specific neural connections.

Pavlov's Influence on Psychology

It is difficult to overstate Pavlov's importance in the history of psychology. Pavlov continued to study classical conditioning for the first few decades of the twentieth century, and during that time he trained scores of students in his research techniques. Classical conditioning was vigorously studied in Russia, and Pavlov's ideas also influenced many learning theorists in America, including John B. Watson, Clark Hull, and Kenneth Spence. At present, investigation of the principles of classical conditioning continues at many universities in the United States, the Soviet Union, Europe, and elsewhere. One measure of Pavlov's importance to the field of learning is the fact that nearly all of the terms and concepts discussed in this chapter (including all of the phenomena described in the next section) were first identified by Pavlov.

BASIC CONDITIONING PHENOMENA

Acquisition

In most classical conditioning experiments, several pairings of the CS and the US are necessary before the CR becomes fully developed. On the first few trials, there may be little or no conditioned responding to the CS. With additional pairings, conditioned responding gradually increases in strength. The part of a conditioning experiment in which the subject first experiences a series of CS-US pairings, and during which the CR gradually appears and increases in strength, is called the *acquisition phase*. Figure 4-5 shows the results of an acquisition phase in an experiment on eyeblink conditioning with human subjects (Trapold & Spence, 1960). The measure of conditioning is the percentage of trials on which a conditioned eyeblink response was recorded. Subjects in Group A received 130 trials with a strong air puff as a US, and this group exhibited a typical acquisition curve. The likelihood of a CR gradually increased over the first 50 trials or so, and subsequently there was little or no additional increase in the percentage of CRs with additional conditioning. The pattern of results suggests that even if Group A received many more conditioning trials, the percentage of CRs would probably never rise above about 55 percent. This value— the stable maximum level of conditioned responding that is gradually approached as conditioning proceeds—is called the *asymptote*. That is, for Group A it might be reported that "the percentage of CRs approached an asymptote of approximately 55 percent."

One factor that has a major influence on the asymptote of conditioning is the size or intensity of the US. In general, if a stronger stimulus is used as a US (a stronger puff of air, a larger amount of food), the asymptote of conditioning will be higher (a higher percentage of conditioned eyeblinks, more salivation). This point is demonstrated by the results from Group B in Figure 4-5. For the first 90 trials, these subjects experienced the same conditioning procedures as did Group A. However, beginning on trial 91, a weaker air puff was used as a US for Group B. You can see that shortly after this, the percentage of CRs in Group B decreased and approached a stable level of about 30 percent. Evidently, this was the asymptote of conditioning for the less intense US, or the highest level of conditioned responding that could be maintained with the weak air puff.

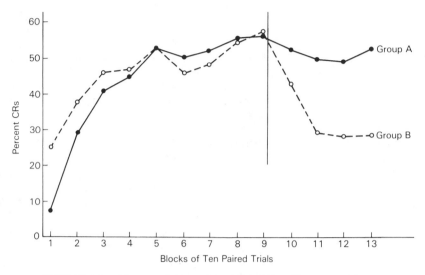

FIGURE 4-5. The acquisition of eyeblink CRs of human subjects. Subjects in Group A received 130 trials with a strong air puff as the US. Subjects in Group B received 90 trials with a strong air puff followed by 40 trials with a weaker air puff. (After Trapold & Spence, 1960)

The intensity of the US can affect not only the asymptote of conditioning but also the rate of learning. For instance, Annau and Kamin (1961) found that the intensity of shock in a conditioned suppression procedure was directly related to the rate at which subjects reached their asymptotic levels of suppression. With intense shocks, rats exhibited complete suppression of lever pressing during the CS as early as the second day of conditioning. With a weaker shock, another group of rats showed a more gradual development of conditioned suppression that continued over about four days of conditioning. To summarize, as the intensity of the US increases, acquisition proceeds more quickly, and the final (asymptotic) size of the CR is larger.

The intensity of the CS can also affect the rate of acquisition. Imagine one conditioning experiment in which a faint tone was used as a CS, and another with a very loud tone as a CS. It should come as no surprise that conditioning will occur more rapidly with the loud tone. On the other hand, the intensity of the CS generally does not affect the asymptote of conditioning. For in-

stance, suppose that for the Group A in Figure 4-5, a much more intense CS were used. The asymptote of conditioning might have been reached in considerably fewer than 50 trials, but it would still be about 55 percent. Thus whereas both CS and US intensity determine how quickly conditioning will proceed, only the US determines the asymptotic size of the CR.

Extinction

The mere passage of time has relatively little effect on the strength of a conditioned response. Suppose we conducted an experiment in salivary conditioning, repeatedly pairing a bell and food until our subject reliably salivated as soon as the bell was rung. We could then remove the dog from the experimental chamber and allow a week, a month, or even a year to pass before returning the subject to the chamber. At this later time, upon ringing the bell, we would most likely still observe a CR of salivation (though perhaps not quite as much salivation as on the last trial of the initial training session). The point is that the simple passage of time will not cause an animal to "forget" to produce the CR once the CS is again presented.

This does not mean, however, that a conditioned response, once acquired, is permanent. A simple technique for producing a reduction and eventual disappearance of the CR is the procedure of *extinction*, which involves repeatedly presenting the CS *without* the US. For example, suppose we followed the acquisition phase of our experiment on salivary conditioning with an extinction phase, in which the bell was presented for many trials but no food was delivered. The first two panels in Figure 4-6 show, in an idealized form, the likely results of our hypothetical experiment. Like the acquisition phase, the course of extinction is usually gradual. In the beginning of an extinction phase, there are large reductions in the amount of salivation from trial to trial. Toward the end of the extinction phase, the decreases in conditioned responding occur more slowly, but eventually the CR will disappear altogether.

When the extinction phase is completed, we have a dog that behaves like a dog that is just beginning the experiment—the bell is presented and no salivation occurs. On the basis of this observation alone, we might conclude that the procedure of extinction simply reverses the effects of the previous acquisition phase. That is, if the animal has formed an association between the CS and the US during the acquisition phase, perhaps this association is gradually destroyed during the extinction phase. The simplicity of this hypothesis is appealing, but Pavlov had a different theory of what takes place during extinction. We can call the initial association (formed during the acquisition phase) an *excitatory* association, be-

cause by virtue of this association the CS now excites, or activates, the US center. Pavlov proposed that during the course of extinction, a parallel, but *inhibitory*, association is developed. When extinction is complete, the effects of the excitatory and inhibitory associations cancel out, so that the US center is no longer activated by the presentation of the CS.

The concept of a conditioned inhibitory association should not sound strange, because we have seen that there are both excitatory and inhibitory synapses in the nervous system. However, you may wonder why Pavlov suggested that the animal is left with two associations (one excitatory and one inhibitory) at the end of an extinction phase. Would it not be simpler to assume that a single, excitatory association is formed during acquisition and destroyed during extinction? The answer is that Pavlov had discovered two additional phenomena, *spontaneous recovery* and *disinhibition*, which convinced him that the excitatory association developed during conditioning is not destroyed during extinction.

Spontaneous Recovery

The third panel of Figure 4-6 illustrates the phenomenon of spontaneous recovery. Suppose that after an acquisition phase on Day 1 and an extinction phase on Day 2, we return our subject to the experimental chamber on Day 3 and conduct another series of extinction trials with the bell. Figure 4-6 shows that on the first several trials of Day 3, we are likely to see some conditioned responding to the bell, even though no CRs were observed at the end of Day 2. Pavlov called this reappearance of conditioned responding *spontaneous recovery*, and treated it as proof

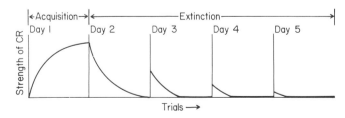

FIGURE 4-6. Idealized changes in the strength of a CR across one acquisition day followed by four days of extinction.

that the excitatory CS-US association is not permanently destroyed in an extinction procedure. Pavlov's conclusion was obviously correct: If extinction serves to undo or erase the learning that occurred in acquisition, why would CRs spontaneously reappear without further conditioning trials? Whatever happens during extinction, it is not a simple erasure of the previous learning.

Pavlov explained the phenomenon of spontaneous recovery in the following way. He proposed that an inhibitory CS-US association is formed during extinction, but that inhibitory associations (or at least newly formed ones) are more fragile than excitatory associations, and they are therefore more severely weakened by the passage of time. With respect to Figure 4-6, Pavlov would say that at the end of Day 2, the inhibitory CS-US association is strong enough to completely counteract the excitatory association, so no CRs are observed. However, in the time between Day 2 and Day 3, the inhibitory association is weakened, so at the beginning of Day 3 it can no longer fully counteract the excitatory association, and some CRs are therefore observed. Further extinction trials on Day 3 strengthen the inhibitory association (just as they did on Day 2), and so conditioned responding once again disappears.

If we were to conduct further extinction sessions on Days 4, 5, 6, and so on, we might again observe some spontaneous recovery, but typically the amount of spontaneous recovery would become smaller and smaller until it no longer occurred (see Figure 4-6). Pavlov would claim that with repeated extinction sessions the inhibitory association becomes progressively less fragile, until it can withstand the passage of time as well as the excitatory association.

The existence of spontaneous recovery is firmly established, but many psychologists are skeptical about Pavlov's explanation of this phenomenon. The assumptions about conditioned inhibition and its temporary fragility seem a bit contrived. Other theories of spontaneous recovery (Boakes & Halliday, 1975; Estes, 1955; Skinner, 1950) are too complex to be presented here, but consider this simplified explanation: After Day 2, our dog has experienced one session in

which the bell was followed by food and one session in which it was not. At the start of Day 3, the animal cannot know whether this session will be like that of Day 1 or like that of Day 2, and its behavior (some weak CRs at the start of the session) may be a reflection of this uncertainty.

Disinhibition

During the acquisition phase of classical conditioning, any sort of distraction may prevent the occurrence of a CR on any given trial. If, for example, a novel stimulus such as a buzzer is presented a few seconds before a CS-US pairing, the CS may fail to elicit a CR on that trial. Pavlov called this effect *external inhibition*, because some external stimulus seemed to inhibit or block a response that otherwise would have occurred.

During an extinction session, Pavlov discovered an effect that is in some ways the opposite of external inhibition. Suppose that an extinction phase has progressed to the point where the CS (a bell) no longer evokes any salivation. Now, if a novel stimulus such as a buzzer is presented a few seconds before the bell, the bell may once again elicit a CR of salivation. Pavlov called this effect *disinhibition* because he believed that the presentation of a distracting stimulus (the buzzer in this example) disrupts the fragile inhibitory link that supposedly develops during extinction. According to Pavlov, the more stable excitatory association is less affected by the distracting stimulus than the inhibitory association. The net result is a slight excitatory tendency that is manifested in the reappearance of the conditioned salivary response.

As in the discussion of spontaneous recovery, let us be sure to separate data from theory. Because it has been observed a number of times in different experiments (Bottjer, 1982; Brimer, 1970; Winnick & Hunt, 1951), we can be confident that disinhibition is a real phenomenon. On the other hand, Pavlov's theory about why disinhibition occurs may or may not be accurate. In any case, Pavlov's discovery of disinhibition and spontaneous recovery were enough to convince him that a conditioned inhibitory association is developed during the course of extinction.

Conditioned Inhibition

Although not everyone accepts Pavlov's theory of extinction, there is general agreement that a CS can develop inhibitory properties as a result of certain conditioning procedures (see Miller & Spear, 1985). If it can be shown that a CS prevents the occurrence of a CR, or that it reduces the size of the CR from what it would otherwise be, then this CS is called an *inhibitory CS* or a *conditioned inhibitor* (sometimes designated as a CS⁻). Pavlov discovered what is probably the simplest and most effective procedure for changing a neutral stimulus into a conditioned inhibitor. This procedure involves the use of two different CSs, such as a metronome and a flashing light. Suppose that in the first phase of an experiment we repeatedly pair the sound of the metronome with the presentation of food, until the subject shows a stable salivary response to the metronome. The metronome can now be called an *excitatory CS* (or CS⁺), because it regularly elicits a CR. In the second phase of the experiment, the dog receives two types of trials. Some trials are exactly like those of phase one (metronome plus food). However, on occasional trials (selected at random), both the metronome and the flashing light are presented simultaneously, but no food is delivered. For obvious reasons, the term *compound CS* is sometimes used to describe the simultaneous presentation of two or more CSs, such as the metronome and the light. At first, the dog may salivate both on trials with the metronome and on trials with the compound CS. As phase two continues, however, the dog eventually learns that no food ever occurs on trials with the compound CS. The result is that the dog continues to salivate on trials with the metronome alone, but little or no salivation occurs on trials with both the metronome and the flashing light.

There are two ways to interpret the results of such an experiment. One possibility is that the light has become a conditioned inhibitor. On the surface it seems to satisfy the definition of a conditioned inhibitor—its presence causes a reduction in the size of the CR from what it would otherwise be. But notice that we have only tested

the light in a single context (in compound with the metronome). Another possibility is that the dog has learned nothing about the light by itself, but only about the metronome-plus-light compound. In other words, perhaps the dog has learned something about the compound CS as a unit (that it is not followed by food), but if presented with the flashing light without the metronome the dog may treat this as a totally new (and neutral) stimulus. To determine whether the light by itself has developed general inhibitory properties, some test of the light in a new context is needed.

Pavlov recognized this problem, and he developed a test that offers a much more convincing demonstration of the inhibitory properties of a stimulus such as the flashing light. Suppose that a third stimulus, a tactile stimulus applied to the dog's leg, is developed into an excitatory CS (that is, it reliably elicits salivation). Now suppose that, for the first time, the dog receives a trial with a compound CS consisting of the tactile stimulus and the flashing light. This procedure of testing the combined effects of a known excitatory CS and an expected inhibitory CS is called a *summation test*. If the flashing light is truly a conditioned inhibitor, it should have the capacity to reduce the CR produced by any CS, not simply that of the metronome with which it was originally presented. Based on the results of Pavlov and others, we would probably find that the flashing light reduced or eliminated the CR to the tactile stimulus, even though these two stimuli were never presented together before. This type of result indicates that the flashing light is a general conditioned inhibitor, because it evidently has the ability to block or diminish the conditioned salivary response elicited by any excitatory CS.

A second method for determining whether a stimulus is inhibitory is to measure how long it takes to turn the stimulus into an excitatory CS. Suppose that one group of dogs, the experimental group, has received the training with the metronome and flashing light described earlier, so we believe the flashing light is a conditioned inhibitor. A second group of dogs, the control group, has not been exposed to the flashing light before, so it is presumably a neutral stimulus for this group. (Ideally, except for exposure to the flashing light, the experience of the two groups should be as similar as possible. For this reason, the control subjects might receive the same number of conditioning trials as the experimental group, but the CSs would be the metronome and some stimulus other than the flashing light.) Now suppose that both groups receive a series of trials with the flashing light paired with food. Since the flashing light is supposedly a conditioned inhibitor in the experimental group, the acquisition of conditioned responding should be slower in this group. This is because any excitatory conditioning that occurs must first offset the inhibitory properties of the CS before a CR is observed. This technique of testing for the inhibitory properties of a CS is called a *retardation test* (Rescorla, 1969), because the development of conditioned responding should be retarded with a CS that is initially inhibitory. The retardation test and the summation test are the two most common techniques for showing that a CS is a conditioned inhibitor.

Why does the procedure described before (metronome→food, metronome plus flashing light→no food) turn the flashing light into a conditioned inhibitor? The following rule of thumb may make this phenomenon easier to understand: A stimulus will become a conditioned inhibitor if it reliably signals the absence of the US in a context where the US would otherwise be expected to occur. In our example, the metronome provided the "context" in which food was normally presented. Because the flashing light signaled the absence of an otherwise imminent US, it became an inhibitory CS.

Generalization and Discrimination

After classical conditioning with one CS, other, similar stimuli will also elicit CRs, although these other stimuli have never been paired with the US. This transfer of the effects of conditioning to similar stimuli is called *generalization*, and it is illustrated in Figure 4-7. In this experiment on eyeblink conditioning, rabbits received a few hundred trials with a 1200 Hz tone as the CS and a shock near the eye as a US.

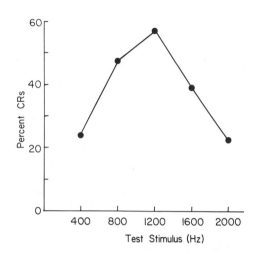

FIGURE 4-7. A typical generalization gradient. Rabbits in an eyeblink conditioning experiment received several hundred pairings of a 1200 Hz tone and a shock. The graph shows the results from a subsequent generalization test in which the 1200 Hz tone and four others were presented but never followed by the US. (From Moore, 1972)

The data shown in Figure 4-7 were collected on a test day, when tones of five different frequencies were repeatedly presented in a random sequence, but no US occurred on any trial. In other words, these tests were conducted under extinction conditions. As can be seen, the 1200 Hz tone elicited the highest percentage of CRs. The two tones closest in frequency to the 1200 Hz tone elicited an intermediate level of responding, and the more distant tones elicited the fewest responses. The function in Figure 4-7 is a typical *generalization gradient*, in which the x-axis plots some dimension along which the test stimuli are varied, and the y-axis shows the strength of conditioned responding to the different stimuli. In general, the more similar a stimulus is to the training stimulus, the greater will be its capacity to elicit CRs.

If all the stimuli tested vary along a single physical dimension (tone, frequency, wavelength of light, size, brightness), predicting which new stimuli will elicit the most generalized responding is simple. However, in some cases it is much more difficult to anticipate which stimuli a subject will find most similar to the CS used in conditioning. Consider a classical conditioning experiment by Razran (1949) that involved human subjects and printed words as CSs. After conditioning with a small set of words, Razran looked for generalization to other words that were either phonetically or semantically similar to the conditioned words. Generalization to a newly introduced word was measured as a percentage of the size of response to the conditioned word. One clear conclusion from this research was that generalization among words cannot be predicted merely on the basis of their physical similarity. For example, after conditioning to the word *day*, subjects showed generalization of 19.6 percent to the word *may* (which is similar in appearance and sound but not in meaning), and generalization of 39.8 percent to *week* (which is similar in meaning but not in appearance or sound). In this case and others, similarity of meaning was more important than physical similarity. The rules for generalization among linguistic stimuli may be similar to those that predict performance on a free-association task (see Chapter 2), for Razran also found evidence for the Associationists' principle of contrast (considerable generalization from *day* to *night*, and from *dark* to *light*). Such patterns of generalization among semantically related words are obviously dependent upon a person's experience—a person who did not understand English would exhibit little generalization from *day* to *week* or *night*.

The opposite of generalization is *discrimination*, in which a subject learns to respond to one stimulus but not to a similar stimulus. We have seen that if a rabbit's eyeblink is conditioned to a 1200 Hz tone, there will be substantial generalization to an 800 Hz tone. However, if the 800 Hz tone is never followed by food but the 1200 Hz tone is always followed by food, the animal will eventually learn a discrimination in which the 1200 Hz tone elicits an eyeblink and the 800 Hz tone does not. This type of discrimination learning is important in many real world situations. For instance, impala and other species of prey on the African plains can learn to discriminate between wild dogs that have just eaten (and

will not attack again) and wild dogs on the hunt (which are very dangerous). The latter will elicit an obvious fear reaction in the prey, whereas the former will not.

Because of the limitations in a subject's sensory capabilities, some discriminations may be difficult to learn. Pavlov described a study by one of his colleagues, Shenger-Krestovnikova, in which a discrimination was made progressively more difficult. At first, a dog learned to discriminate between the images of a circle and an ellipse projected on a screen, as shown in Figure 4-8a. The circle was followed by food, while the ellipse was not, and the dog readily mastered this discrimination. Then the ellipse was gradually changed to look more and more like the circle (b, c, and d in Figure 4-8). In the final condition, with a nearly circular ellipse, the dog managed to develop a weak discrimination at first (with somewhat less responding to the ellipse than to the circle). After several weeks of conditioning with the difficult discrimination, however, the discrimination was lost and the dog's behavior

FIGURE 4-8. Stimuli presented to a dog in the experiment of Pavlov and Shenger-Krestovnikova. An initial discrimination between a circle and an ellipse (a) was made progressively more difficult (b, c, and d).

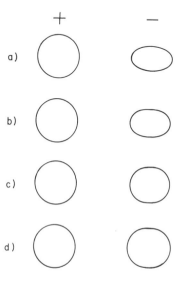

changed in other ways as well. When taken into the experimental chamber, the dog would bark, squeal, and bite whatever parts of the apparatus it could reach. These were dramatic and disturbing behaviors from an animal that had previously been quiet and well behaved. Now when the dog was returned to the easiest discrimination, it still showed no difference in responding to the ellipse versus the circle. With additional training, the initial discrimination was eventually recovered, but only after twice as many trials as it took to learn this easy discrimination in the first place. Pavlov called the deterioration in the subject's behavior an *experimental neurosis* (that is, an experimentally induced behavior disturbance). He believed that the dog's emotional behaviors were analogous to the psychological problems that can arise when a person is required to perform demanding tasks for long periods of time—the individual may exhibit a variety of negative emotions, and easy tasks may now seem impossible.

Whereas the concepts of generalization and discrimination are easy to describe, a number of theoretical problems have puzzled psychologists since the time of Pavlov. Why does conditioning with one stimulus cause a "spread of excitation" to similar stimuli? Can we predict, in advance, what stimuli a subject will treat as similar? How does experience affect the shape of a generalization gradient? What types of training will produce the most accurate levels of performance in a task where a difficult discrimination is required? These and other questions about generalization and discrimination will be examined in Chapter 10.

TEMPORAL RELATIONSHIPS BETWEEN CS AND US

In any experiment on classical conditioning, the precise timing of the CS and the US can have a major effect on the results. All of the experiments discussed so far involved what is called *short-delay conditioning* (see Figure 4-9), in which the CS begins a second or so before the US. It is well established that this temporal ar-

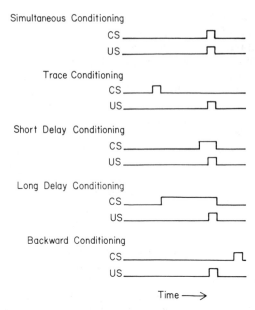

FIGURE 4-9. The temporal relationships between CS and US in five types of classical conditioning.

rangement produces the strongest and most rapid conditioning.

Several studies have shown that the early onset of the CS is important: In *simultaneous conditioning*, where the CS and US begin at the same moment (Figure 4-9), conditioned responding is much weaker than in short-delay conditioning (Smith & Gormezano, 1965; White and Schlosberg, 1952). This may be so for a number of reasons. For one thing, if the US begins at the same moment as the CS, the subject may be so busy responding to the US that it fails to notice the CS. Furthermore, if the CS does not precede the US, it cannot serve to signal or predict the arrival of the US. As we will see again and again, the predictiveness of a CS is an important determinant of the degree of conditioning the CS undergoes, and of whether this conditioning is excitatory or inhibitory. The following rules of thumb, though not perfect, are usually helpful in predicting the outcome of a conditioning arrangement: To the extent that a CS is a good predictor of the presence of the US, it will tend to become excitatory. To the extent that a CS is a good predictor of the absence of the US, it will tend to become inhibitory. It should help to keep these rules in mind when examining the other conditioning arrangements discussed in this section.

As shown in Figure 4-9, *trace conditioning* refers to the case in which the CS and US are separated by some time interval in which neither stimulus is present. The term *trace conditioning* is derived from the notion that since the CS is no longer physically present when the US occurs, the subject must rely on a "memory trace" of the CS if conditioning is to occur. In a number of studies, the amount of time elapsing between CS and US presentations, or the *CS-US interval*, was systematically varied. That is, one group of subjects might receive a series of conditioning trials with a two second CS-US interval, another group with a five second CS-US interval, and so on. The results of such studies showed that as the CS-US interval is increased, the level of conditioning declines systematically (Ellison, 1964; Lucas, Deich & Wasserman, 1981). In some cases, the decreases in conditioning are quite dramatic. For instance, in eyeblink conditioning there is virtually no evidence of conditioned responding if the CS and US are separated by as little as two seconds (Schneiderman, 1966).

A similar pattern emerges in *long-delay conditioning*, where the onset of the CS precedes that of the US by at least several seconds, but the CS continues until the US is presented (see Figure 4-9). In long-delay conditioning, CS-US interval refers to the delay between the onsets of the CS and US. Here, too, the strength of the conditioned responding decreases as the CS-US interval increases, but the effects of delay are usually not as pronounced as in trace conditioning (which is understandable, since in long-delay conditioning the subject does not have to rely on its memory of the CS). In both trace and delay conditioning, studies of the CS-US interval provide impressive support for the Associationists' principle of contiguity. However, the results are also consistent with the predictiveness rule, because as the CS-US interval increases, it becomes increasingly difficult for the subject to predict the exact moment when the US will occur.

In long-delay conditioning, Pavlov noted that the temporal location of the CRs changed over trials. Early in training, a dog would salivate as soon as the CS was presented, although the CS-US interval might be ten seconds. As conditioning trials continued, however, these early CRs would gradually disappear, and the dog would salivate shortly before the food was presented (eight or nine seconds after CS onset). This pattern indicates, first of all, that the dog had learned to estimate the duration of the CS quite accurately. In addition, it is consistent with the rule that the stimulus that is the best predictor of the US will be the most strongly conditioned. In this example, what stimulus is a better predictor of the US than CS onset? Obviously, it is the compound stimulus, CS onset plus the passage of about ten seconds. Consequently, it is this latter stimulus that ultimately elicits the most vigorous CRs.

The bottom of Figure 4-9 diagrams an example of *backward conditioning*, in which the CS is presented after the US. Even if the CS is presented immediately after the US, the level of conditioning is markedly lower than in simultaneous or short-delay conditioning. From the perspective of the contiguity principle, this does not make sense: If the CS and US are equally contiguous in short-delay conditioning and in backward conditioning, the contiguity principle predicts that equally strong CRs should develop. As with Ebbinghaus's backward-list experiment (Chapter 2), the weakness of backward conditioning points to a limitation of the contiguity principle—besides their temporal proximity, the order of the stimuli is important. Although backward conditioning may result in a weak excitatory association (Ayres, Haddad, & Albert, 1987; Champion & Jones, 1961), other studies have found that after a sufficient number of trials a backward CS becomes inhibitory (Larew, 1986; Siegel & Domjan, 1971). The reasons for this inhibitory conditioning are quite complex (see Tait & Saladin, 1986; Wagner & Larew, 1985), but once again the predictiveness rule can serve as a useful guide: In backward conditioning, the onset of the CS signals a period of time in which the US will be absent. That is, as long

Differential Contingency?

as the backward CS is present, the subject can be certain that no US will occur.

CS-US Correlations

In each of the conditioning arrangements discussed so far, the temporal pattern of stimulus presentations is exactly the same on every trial. For example, in long-delay conditioning the onset of the US always follows the onset of the CS by the same amount of time, and the US never occurs at any other time. We can describe this perfect correlation between CS and US with two probabilities: The probability that the US will occur in the presence of the CS, denoted p(US/CS), is 1.0; the probability that the US will occur in the absence of the CS, p(US/no CS), is 0.0. In the real world, however, the relationships between stimuli are seldom so regular. A rabbit in the forest must learn to recognize stimuli that could indicate that a predator is nearby. The rustling of leaves could be a predator, or it could be simply a breeze. On some occasions the sound of a snapped twig may mean a hunter is nearby; on other occasions it may not. There are also times when a predator's attack is not preceded by any perceptible stimulus. These less-than-perfect correlations between signals and consequences can also be stated in probabilistic terms. Given a particular stimulus, the probability of an attack by a predator may be high (but not 1.0). In the absence of the stimulus, the probability of an attack may be lower (but not 0.0). Although the relationships among stimuli are variable and uncertain in the real world, the ability to detect those imperfect correlations that do exist between signals and consequences has obvious advantages. It is important for an animal to know which stimuli are the most dependable signals of possible danger. In the laboratory, classical conditioning procedures can be used to evaluate an animal's ability to detect imperfect correlations between stimuli.

A series of experiments by Rescorla (1966, 1968) showed how the two probabilities p(US/CS) and p(US/no CS) interact to determine the size of the CR. In a conditioned suppression procedure with rats, the CS was a two minute tone that was presented at random intervals aver-

aging eight minutes. For one group of subjects, Group .4-.2, there was a .4 probability that a shock would occur during a two-minute CS presentation, and there was a .2 probability that a shock would occur in any two-minute period when the CS was not present. The US might occur at any moment during the presence or absence of the CS. Notice that neither the presence nor absence of a CS was a definite signal that a US would occur, and neither provided any information about the timing of a US (since a shock could occur at any time). The only information the CS provided was whether the probability of shock was high or low.

The full experiment included ten groups of subjects with different values of p(US/CS) and p(US/no CS). The results can be summarized as follows. Whenever p(US/CS) was greater than p(US/no CS), the tone became an excitatory CS (that is, response suppression occurred when the tone was presented). The amount of suppression depended on the size of the difference between p(US/CS) and p(US/no CS). For instance, there was a high level of suppression to the tone in Group .4-0, a moderate level of suppression in Group .4-.1, and only weak suppression in Group .4-.2. When the probability of shock was the same in the presence and absence of the CS (Group .4-.4, Group .2-.2), there was no suppression at all to the tone. In another experiment, Rescorla included a group in which p(US/CS) was actually lower than p(US/no CS)—that is, the CS signaled a relative level of safety from shock—and he demonstrated that the CS became inhibitory in this group.

Based on these results, Rescorla concluded that the traditional view of classical conditioning, which states that the *contiguity* of CS and US is what causes an association to develop, is incorrect. Notice that in the groups with equal probabilities of shock in the presence and absence of the CS, there were many pairings of the CS and US, yet there was no conditioning to the CS. Rescorla therefore proposed that the important variable in classical conditioning is not the contiguity of CS and US but rather the *correlation* between CS and US. If the correlation is positive (that is, if the CS predicts a higher-than-normal probability of the US), the CS will become excitatory. If there is no correlation between CS and US (if the probability of the US is the same whether or not the CS is present), the CS will remain neutral. If the correlation between CS and US is negative (if the CS signals a lower-than-normal probability of the US), the CS will become inhibitory.

The correlational approach to classical conditioning is substantially different from an analysis based on contiguity, for it implies that an animal can learn about the long-term relation between CS and US. (A short time sample from a conditioning session could give very inaccurate estimates of the probabilities of shock in the presence and absence of the US. Only with long time samples can accurate estimates of these probabilities be made.) Although exactly how animals can accomplish this fact is still a matter for debate, Rescorla's studies show that animals can learn about the correlation between CS and US even in the absence of a recurring and predictable temporal pattern.

OTHER CONDITIONING ARRANGEMENTS

So far we have examined only procedures in which a CS is paired with (or correlated with) a US. However, other classical conditioning procedures involve the pairing of two CSs instead of a CS and a US. Two such conditioning arrangements are described next.

Higher-Order Conditioning

In *second-order conditioning*, a CR is transferred from one CS to another. Pavlov described the following experiment to illustrate this process. First, the ticking of a metronome was firmly established as a CS in salivary conditioning, by pairing the metronome with food. Because it was paired with the US, the metronome is called a *first-order CS*. Then another stimulus, a black square, was presented and immediately followed by the metronome on a number of occasions, but no food was presented on these trials. After a few trials of this type, the black square began to elicit salivation on its own, despite the fact that this stimulus *was never paired directly with the food* (but only with the metronome, a CS that was frequently paired with the food). In this example, the black square is called a *second-order CS* because it acquired its ability to elicit a CR by being paired with a first-order CS, the metronome.

Pavlov also reported that, although it was quite difficult to obtain, he sometimes found evidence of *third-order conditioning* (the transfer of a CR from a second-order CS to yet another stimulus). He believed that these examples of second- and higher-order conditioning were important because they broadened the scope of classical conditioning. If there were no such thing as higher-order conditioning, then the only time an animal could learn through the process of classical conditioning would be when it encountered some US (food, water, a predator). But since higher-order conditioning is possible, new CRs may be acquired any time the animal encounters an already conditioned CS along with some new, neutral stimulus. As more and more stimuli become CSs as a result of an animal's everyday experiences, the opportunities for further learning through higher-order conditioning will expand at an increasing rate.

The following example illustrates how higher-order conditioning can play an important role in an animal's ability to avoid dangerous situations in its environment. Although wolves are among the major predators of deer, the sight of a wolf does not elicit an unconditioned fear reaction in a young whitetail deer. Instead, the sight of a wolf must become a CS for fear as a result of a young deer's experience. This conditioning might occur in at least two ways. The sight of a wolf might be followed by an attack and injury to the young deer. More likely, however, the sight of wolves is simply paired with visible signs of fear in other deer. (For simplicity, let us assume that the sight of fear reactions in other deer elicits an innate fear reaction in the young deer.) In either case, the sight of wolves eventually becomes a first-order CS for a fear response in the young deer. Once this happens, higher order conditioning can occur whenever some initially neutral stimulus is paired with the sight of wolves. Perhaps certain sounds or odors frequently precede the appearance of wolves, and through second-order conditioning, these may come to elicit fear. Or perhaps wolves are usually encountered in certain parts of the forest, and so the deer becomes fearful and cautious when traveling through these places. Although these examples are only speculative, they show how an initially neutral stimulus (the sight of wolves) can first develop the capacity to elicit a fear response, and can then transfer this response to other stimuli.

Sensory Preconditioning

Sensory preconditioning is similar to second-order conditioning, except that the two CSs are repeatedly paired *before* the US is introduced. For example, let us return to Pavlov's experiment on second-order conditioning with the black square, metronome, and food. To conduct a parallel experiment on sensory preconditioning with these same stimuli, we would first expose a dog to many trials on which the black square was paired with the metronome. In the second phase of the experiment, the metronome would be paired with food, and of course the metronome would eventually elicit salivation. In the final phase of the experiment (the test phase), we would present the black square by itself to determine whether it would now also elicit a CR of salivation. If it did, this would be a successful demonstration of sensory preconditioning. A number of studies with this type of design have demonstrated the existence of sensory preconditioning (Brogden, 1939; Pfautz, Donegan, & Wagner, 1978; Prewitt, 1967). Such results provide further evidence for the existence of S-S associations, and they show that these associations can form between two "neutral" stimuli as well as between a CS and a US.

CLASSICAL CONDITIONING OUTSIDE THE LABORATORY

Few psychologists now believe that the bulk of our learned behaviors arise directly from the principles of classical conditioning. Whereas classical conditioning can explain how reflexive behaviors are transferred from a US to some new

stimulus, it cannot account for behaviors that have no obvious eliciting stimulus (such as walking, playing, cooking a meal) nor for totally novel behaviors (uttering a sentence never heard before, solving a problem in calculus). In later chapters we will examine other principles of learning that are more applicable to such "spontaneous" and "creative" behaviors. Yet although Pavlov probably overestimated the importance of classical conditioning for everyday human behaviors, we should be careful not to make the opposite mistake of underestimating its importance. Classical conditioning is relevant to behaviors outside the laboratory in at least two ways. First, it offers a means of understanding behaviors we usually call "involuntary"—behaviors that are automatically elicited by certain stimuli whether we want them to occur or not. As will be discussed, many emotional reactions seem to fall into this category. Second, research on classical conditioning has led to several major treatment procedures for behavior disorders. These procedures can be used to strengthen desired "involuntary" responses or to weaken undesired responses. The remainder of this chapter examines the role of classical conditioning in these non-laboratory settings.

Classical Conditioning and Emotional Responses

For the most part, emotional responses such as feelings of pleasure, happiness, anxiety, or excitement are difficult to measure in another person, and this makes them difficult to analyze scientifically. However, if we temporarily dispense with scientific rigor and examine our introspections, it should become clear that these sorts of emotional reactions are frequently triggered by specific stimuli. Furthermore, it is often obvious that the response-eliciting properties of the stimulus were acquired through experience. Suppose you open your mailbox and find a letter with the return address of a close friend. This stimulus may immediately evoke a pleasant and complex emotional reaction that you might loosely call affection, warmth, or fondness. Whatever you call the emotional reaction, there is no doubt that this particular stimulus—a person's handwritten address on an envelope—would not elicit the response from you shortly after your birth, nor would it elicit the response now if you did not know the person who sent you the letter. The envelope is a CS that elicits a pleasant emotional response only because the address has been associated with your friend. Other stimuli can elicit less pleasant emotional reactions. For many college students, examination period can be a time of high anxiety. This anxiety can be conditioned to stimuli associated with the examination process—the textbooks on one's desk, a calendar with the date of the exam circled, or the sight of the building where the exam will be held.

It is instructive to look for examples of classical conditioning in your daily life. In the following example, many readers will probably understand the emotional reaction of my friend Phil. Like the video games that have largely replaced them, pinball games can evoke a high level of enjoyment and excitement in some people. I once watched as Phil took his turn on a pinball machine which awarded a free game for a high score. During the course of play, the winning of a free game was signaled by a loud clunk. As Phil reached the critical score and heard the loud clunk, he smiled with satisfaction and exclaimed, "That's the most beautiful sound in the world!" Of course, objectively speaking the clunk was not a beautiful sound at all. What Phil probably meant was that for him, the sound evoked a pleasant emotional response. By being repeatedly paired with the winning of a free game, this ordinary sound gained the capacity to elicit the emotional response of excitement.

A final, personal example shows that conditioned emotional responses are not under voluntary control, and that they are not necessarily guided by logic or by a knowledge of one's environment. Before my wife, Laurie, and I were married, our jobs required us to live over two hundred miles apart. We visited each other on weekends, about twice a month. Laurie owns a very distinctive winter coat—a white coat with broad horizontal stripes of red, yellow, and green. It is easy to find her in a crowd when she is wearing that coat. One day when Laurie was at her job and I was at mine, I was walking across the campus, when I saw, ahead of me, someone wearing a coat just like Laurie's. My immediate reaction was a good example of a conditioned response—my heart started pounding rapidly, as when a person is startled by a loud noise. This response persisted for 10 or 20 seconds. What is noteworthy about the response is that it did not make sense—I knew Laurie was several hundred miles away, and the person wearing the coat could not possibly be her. In addition, whereas Laurie has a full- length coat, the coat I saw was short, and the person wearing it was a man with a beard. Yet none of these discrepancies was enough to prevent my conditioned heart-rate response, and my galvanic skin response undoubtedly exhibited a large increase as well.

The Acquisition of Sexual Deviations

Whereas the private nature of emotional responses can make them difficult to examine, emotional reactions sometime lead to overt behaviors, and these behaviors are not always tolerated by society. One class of such behaviors is that of *sexual deviations*, which includes a variety of abnormal sexual preferences and practices. After investigating the case histories of 45 sexual deviants, McGuire, Carlisle, and Young (1965) came to the conclusion that sexual deviations frequently develop through simple classical conditioning. McGuire et al. began with the observation that one US for sexual arousal is the manual stimulation of the genitals (masturbation). They proposed that any stimulus that is repeatedly paired with masturbation will eventually evoke sexual arousal by itself. Furthermore, the stimulus need not be physically present during masturbation; if the individual repeatedly imagines or fantasizes about a specific stimulus during masturbation, the result can be the same—the stimulus will become a CS for sexual arousal.

By examining a few of the case descriptions provided by McGuire et al., we can begin to understand the circumstances that can prompt an individual to engage in an unusual fantasy during masturbation. The following excerpt describes the cases of two *exhibitionists*—individuals who gain sexual pleasure by exposing their genitals to members of the opposite sex:

We found that the initial incident need not even have been of sexual interest to the individual at the time it occurred. For example, two patients separately reported that they had on one occasion been urinating in a semipublic place when they were surprised by a passing woman. At the time each had felt embarrassed and left hurriedly. It was only later that the sexual significance of the encounter was appreciated and each of them had then masturbated frequently to the memory of the incident till the thought of self-exposure had acquired, by conditioning, such strong sexual stimulus value that each had in the end taken to public exposure. Neither patient had had the slightest interest in such behavior prior to the incident. (McGuire, et al., 1965, pp. 188-189)

The last sentence is particularly important, because it implies that a chance occurrence (in this case, being seen urinating by a woman) was the event that inspired the masturbation fantasies. These men would probably not have become exhibitionists if they had not been seen by a woman at the critical moment. On the other hand, it would be a gross mistake to assume that the onset of exhibitionism was an inevitable result of that incident. McGuire et al. claim that the repeated masturbation to the memory of the incident was an essential ingredient in the development of this sexual deviation. What needs to be explained is why these men chose repeatedly to recall this incident while masturbating. Other persons might experience a similar embarrassing incident and soon forget it. McGuire et al. reported that in a majority of cases, one or both of these additional factors was present and may have contributed to the outcome: (1) The precipitating incident was often the person's first actual sexual experience (that is, excluding secondhand experiences from books or movies). (2) Many individuals believed, for a variety of reasons, "that a normal sex life was not possible for them" (p. 186). Therefore, when by happenstance they experienced an unusual event with sexual implications, they were ready to seize it and fantasize about it. The following case provides a good example of such a situation:

This 28-year-old patient, married at the age of 24, had had normal sexual interests. However, his wife proved

to be totally frigid so that the marriage was never consummated. In the early months of his marriage, while sexually frustrated, he observed that a young lady in the opposite flat was in the habit of stripping in a lighted room with the curtains open. (The patient's wife confirmed this story.) The patient found this very stimulating sexually. The marriage had not been consummated when the couple moved house. In his new environment the patient sought opportunities of seeing women undressing and developed the habit of masturbating on these occasions. It is interesting to note that the patient retained all the circumstances of the early stimulus and had no interest in nudist films or striptease shows. He came to our notice after his fourth conviction for a "Peeping-Tom" offense. (p. 189)

If the hypothesis of McGuire et al. is correct, it follows that sexual preferences are surprisingly malleable: Given repeated pairings with a state of sexual arousal, a wide range of objects and situations can become sexually stimulating. These reports of the development of sexual deviations, as well as corresponding reports of the procedures used to eliminate sexual deviations, are among the most striking examples of the potency of classical conditioning.

Applications in Behavior Therapy

Systematic Desensitization for Phobias. One of the most widely used procedures of behavior therapy is systematic desensitization, a treatment for phobias that arose directly out of laboratory research on classical conditioning. A *phobia* is an excessive and irrational fear of an object, a place, or a situation. Phobias come in numerous forms—fear of closed spaces, of open spaces, of heights, of water, of crowds, of speaking before a group, of taking an examination, of insects, of snakes, of dogs, of birds. Some of these phobias may sound almost amusing, but they are no joke to those who suffer from them, and they are frequently quite debilitating. A fear of insects or snakes may preclude going to a picnic or taking a walk in the woods. A fear of crowds may make it impossible for a person to go to the supermarket, to a movie, or to ride on a bus or train. A fear of birds or of open spaces may literally make an individual a prisoner in his or her home.

How do phobias arise? Although there are

probably several ways that a phobia can develop (see Minecka, 1985), it is not surprising that after Pavlov's discovery, classical conditioning was seen as one possible source of irrational fears. This hypothesis was bolstered by a famous (or, more accurately, infamous) experiment by John B. Watson and Rosalie Rayner (1921). Watson and Rayner used classical conditioning to develop a phobia in a normal 11-month-old infant named Albert. Before the experiment, there were few things that frightened Albert, but one stimulus that did was the loud noise of a hammer hitting a steel bar. Upon hearing the noise, Albert would start to cry. Since this stimulus elicited a reliable response from Albert, it was used as the US in a series of conditioning trials. The CS was a live white rat, which initially produced no signs of fear in Albert. On the first conditioning trial, the noise was presented just as Albert was reaching out to touch the rat, and as a result Albert began to cry. Albert subsequently received seven more conditioning trials of this type. After this experience, Albert's behavior indicated that he had been classically conditioned—he cried when he was presented with the white rat by itself. This experimentally induced fear also generalized to a white rabbit and to other white furry objects, including a ball of cotton and a Santa Claus mask. After a month had passed, these stimuli still elicited some fear in Albert, although his reactions to them were somewhat diminished.

If this experiment sounds cruel and unethical, rest assured that modern legal safeguards for the protection of human subjects would make it difficult or impossible for a psychologist to conduct such a study today. In any case, Watson and Rayner concluded that a long-lasting fear of an initially neutral stimulus may result from the pairing of that stimulus with some fearful event. In short, the principles of classical conditioning may explain how some phobias are acquired.

If this analysis is correct, then the principles of classical conditioning should also describe how a phobia can be cured. To be specific, if the CS (the phobic object or event) is repeatedly presented without the US, the phobia should extinguish. Yet numerous case histories indicate that phobias can be extremely persistent. Why is it that phobias do not gradually disappear on their own? For example, if a teen-ager's fear of crowds stems from a childhood experience in which he was lost in a crowd, why doesn't the phobia extinguish as a result of repeated exposures to crowds with no aversive consequences? One obvious explanation is simply that the individual carefully avoids the phobic object or event, and without exposure to the CS, extinction cannot occur. Another possible explanation is the self-sustaining nature of some phobias. Thus if a person is fearful of crowds, any attempt to attend a movie, a football game, or the like will result in fear, discomfort, and possibly embarrassment if the person becomes so anxious that he must leave abruptly. If this happens, the phobic stimulus has once again been paired with aversive consequences, and the phobia may be strengthened.

Systematic desensitization can be viewed as a procedure in which the patient is exposed to the phobic object in a gradual way, so that fear and discomfort are kept to a minimum and extinction is allowed to occur. The treatment has three parts—the construction of a *fear hierarchy*, training in relaxation, and the gradual presentation of items in the fear hierarchy to the patient. The fear hierarchy is a list of fearful situations of progressively increasing intensity. At the bottom of the list is an item that evokes only a very mild fear response in the patient, and at the top is the most highly feared situation.

After the fear hierarchy is constructed, the patient is given training in *progressive relaxation*, or *deep muscle relaxation*. This technique, developed by Wolpe (1958), is a means of inducing a state of bodily calm and relaxation by having the person alternately tense and relax specific groups of muscles. For instance, the patient is first instructed to make a fist and to tense all the muscles of the hand as tightly as possible. After holding this tension for 5 to 10 seconds, the patient is instructed to release the tension, and to concentrate on making the muscles of the hand as relaxed and as limp as possible for 15 to 20 seconds. This same procedure is used for muscles in the arms, neck, head, trunk, and legs. The idea behind this procedure is that many people have a high level of muscle tension without being aware of it, and if simply told to "completely relax" a set of muscles they will be unable to do so.

However, by contrasting a high degree of muscle tension with subsequent relaxation, a person can learn to relax the muscles on cue. The progressive relaxation procedure takes about 20 minutes, and when it is completed patients usually report that they feel very relaxed. At this point the extinction of the phobia can begin.

The therapist begins with the weakest item in the hierarchy, describes the scene to the patient, and asks the patient to imagine this scene as vividly as possible. For example, in the treatment of a teenager who developed a fear of driving after an automobile accident, the first instruction was to imagine "looking at his car as it was before the accident" (Kushner, 1965). Because the patient is in a relaxed state, and because the lowest item did not evoke much fear to begin with, it usually can be imagined with little or no fear. The patient is instructed to continue to imagine the scene for about 20 seconds. After a short pause in which the patient is told to relax, the first item is again presented. If the patient reports that the item produces no fear, the therapist moves on to the second item on the list, and the procedure is repeated. The therapist slowly progresses up the list, being certain that the fear of one item is completely gone before going on to the next item. A typical fear hierarchy contains 10 or 15 items, but there have been cases in which lists of over 100 items were constructed. The hierarchy for the patient with a fear of driving included the following nine items:

1. Imagine looking at your car as it was prior to the accident.
2. Imagine leaning against your car.
3. Imagine sitting in your car with the ignition turned off.
4. Imagine sitting in your car and turning on the ignition, with the car stationary but the motor idling.
5. Imagine backing out of your driveway and turning the car so you are in a position to drive off.
6. Imagine driving the car around the block on which you live.
7. Imagine driving along a straight road with no intersections.
8. Imagine you are approaching an intersection with no traffic appearing.

9. Imagine approaching the same intersection with another car nearing the intersection to your right, where there is a stop sign. (This was the situation leading to the patient's accident).

(paraphrased from Kushner, 1965, pp. 194-195)

In this case, the patient made rapid progress, and after only six sessions the young man could again drive his car without fear. A three-month follow-up found no return of the phobic symptoms.

This case history is a bit unusual in the brevity of therapy (10 to 20 sessions are more typical) but not in its final outcome. Paul (1969) reviewed about 75 published reports on the use of systematic desensitization that together involved thousands of patients. In most of these reports about 80 to 90 percent of the patients were cured of their phobias—a very high success rate for any type of therapy in the realm of mental health. There were only a few reports of relapses, and no evidence of *symptom substitution* (the appearance of a new psychological disorder after the original problem disappears). This mass of evidence suggests that systematic desensitization is an effective and efficient treatment for phobias.

Aversive Counterconditioning. Although it may sound paradoxical, people are frequently very poor at controlling their own behaviors. Consider several classes of behavior that are all too common in our society—overeating, excessive drinking, smoking, drug abuse. Whereas many people who engage in these behaviors know they are potentially harmful and claim they would like to stop, they also claim that they are unable to do so. The problem is that although the behaviors are detrimental to one's health, there are strong sources of motivation for continuing the behaviors. The motives may be of different types: Performing the behavior may be highly enjoyable, or refraining from the behavior may be unpleasant, or both. To put it simply, these behaviors have short-term advantages and long-term disadvantages. We will examine such conflicting motives in more detail in Chapter 14, but for now let us consider one behavioral technique designed to combat these unwanted behaviors.

The goal of aversive counterconditioning is to develop an aversive CR to stimuli associated with the undesirable behavior. For instance, if the patient is an alcoholic, the procedure may involve conditioning the responses of nausea and queasiness of the stomach to the sight, smell, and taste of alcohol. The term *counterconditioning* is used because the technique is designed to replace a positive emotional response to certain stimuli (such as alcohol) with a negative one. In the 1940s, Voegtlin and his associates conducted extensive research on the use of aversive counterconditioning as a treatment for alcoholism (Voegtlin, 1940; Lemere, Voegtlin, Broz, O'Hallaren, & Tupper, 1942). Over the years, more than 4000 alcoholics volunteered to participate in Voegtlin's distinctly unpleasant therapy. Over a 10-day period, a patient received about a half dozen treatment sessions in which alcoholic beverages were paired with an *emetic*—a drug that produces nausea. Conditioning sessions took place in a quiet, darkened room in which a collection of liquor bottles were illuminated to enhance their salience. First, the patient received an emetic, and soon the first signs of nausea would begin. The patient was then given a large glass of whiskey, and was instructed to look at, smell, taste, and swallow the whiskey until vomiting occurred (which was usually no more than a few minutes). In later conditioning sessions, the whiskey was replaced with a variety of other liquors to ensure that the aversion was not limited to one type of liquor. It is hard to imagine a more unpleasant therapy, and the patients' willingness to participate gives an indication both of their commitment to overcome their alcoholism and of their inability to do so on their own.

Since a number of different treatments for alcoholism are known to promote short-term abstinence, the real test of a treatment's effectiveness is its long-term success rate. Figure 4-10 shows the percentages of former patients who were totally abstinent for various lengths of time after the therapy. As can be seen, the percentage of individuals who were totally abstinent declined over time. The diminishing percentages may reflect the process of extinction: If over the years a person repeatedly encounters the sight and smell of alcohol (at weddings, at parties, on television) in the absence of the US (the emetic), the CR of nausea should eventually wear off. At least two types of evidence support the role of extinction. First, patients who received "booster sessions" (further conditioning sessions a few months after the original treatment) were, on the average, abstinent for longer periods of time. Such reconditioning sessions probably counteracted the effects of extinction. Second, those who continued to associate with old drinking friends (and were thereby exposed to alcohol) were the most likely to fail.

If the declining percentages in Figure 4-10 seem discouraging, several points should be

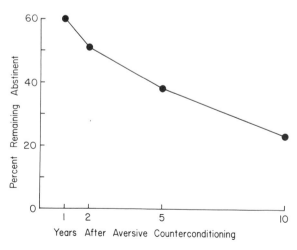

FIGURE 4-10. The percentages of Voegtlin's clients who remained completely abstinent for various amounts of time following aversive counterconditioning for alcoholism. (After Lemere & Voegtlin, 1950)

made. First of all, a similar pattern of increasing relapses over time occurs with every known treatment for alcoholism, and in fact Voegtlin's success rates are quite high compared to those of other treatments. Furthermore, these percentages are extremely conservative estimates of the success of Voegtlin's procedures because he employed a very strict criterion for success—total abstinence. Persons who drank with moderation after the treatment were counted as failures, as were those who suffered a relapse, received reconditioning sessions, and were once again abstinent. Figure 4-10 therefore presents the most pessimistic view possible regarding the effectiveness of this treatment. In the United States, the use of aversive counterconditioning as a treatment for alcoholism has increased substantially since the mid-1970s, with success rates remaining about the same as in Figure 4-10 (Wiens & Menustik, 1983).

Aversive counterconditioning has been used for a number of problems besides alcoholism, including drug abuse, cigarette smoking, and sexual deviations. For example, Marks and Gelder (1967) used electric shock as a US to eliminate a male client's fetish for female clothing. Before therapy, the client was aroused (as measured by penile erection) by a photograph of a nude female (which is considered normal), but also by the sight of female panties, a slip, a skirt, and pajamas. The client then received 20 trials in which the panties were paired with shock, after which they no longer elicited arousal. The other items continued to produce arousal, however. Next, the other pieces of clothing were paired with shock, one at a time, until only the nude photograph (never paired with shock) elicited arousal. In this way, the man's abnormal sexual attraction to clothing was eliminated while leaving his sexual attraction to females intact.

In some procedures designed to help smokers break the habit, cigarette smoke itself is used as an aversive US. This strategy relies on the fact that, whereas smokers enjoy inhaling cigarette smoke in moderate amounts, excessive inhalation becomes aversive to them. (This finding will not surprise nonsmokers, many of whom find any amount of cigarette smoke unpleasant.) In one version of this procedure, a fan blows warm, smoky air into the face of the client while she smokes. In another variation called the *rapid smoking* technique, the client is required to take a puff every six seconds until she claims she cannot tolerate another puff. A typical treatment program involves five or ten one-hour sessions. The initial results of this type of procedure are frequently quite impressive: Over 90 percent of those who complete the program are abstinent at first. However, the long-term follow-ups are less encouraging, and a typical finding is that after six months perhaps only 30 percent of these individuals are still not smoking. As with all types of aversive counterconditioning, the problem may be that the aversion extinguishes over time.

In summary, aversive counterconditioning is a procedure that attempts to decrease unwanted behaviors by conditioning aversive reactions to stimuli associated with the behaviors. Its effectiveness is variable. It appears to be a useful procedure for eliminating certain sexual deviations. When used as a treatment for smoking or alcoholism, generally less than half of all clients remain abstinent for as long as six or twelve months. Nevertheless, these percentages are significantly higher than those found when individuals try to stop drinking or smoking without professional help. The effectiveness of aversive counterconditioning can be enhanced by offering periodic reconditioning sessions and by instructing clients to avoid stimuli associated with the problem behavior (bars, drinking companions, smoke-filled rooms, and the like).

Treatment of Nocturnal Enuresis. Children usually learn to use the toilet instead of wetting their pants by about age three or four. For most children, the control of nighttime elimination occurs shortly afterward. However, a substantial portion of children continue to wet their beds at ages five or older, and this behavior becomes an increasing problem for both child and parents. The problem is aggravating for the parents, who must do all the extra laundry. Among the disadvantages for the child are the discomfort, the anger of one's parents, and often the reluctant declining of invitations to be an overnight guest with friends or relatives. Fortunately, most cases of nocturnal enuresis can be cured by a straight-forward procedure developed by Mowrer and Mowrer (1938). A water-detecting device is placed beneath the child's sheets, and a single drop of urine will activate the device and sound an alarm (a buzzer or a bell) to wake up the child. The child is instructed in advance to turn off the alarm, go to the toilet and urinate, and then go back to sleep. The sensor and alarm are used every night until the problem disappears.

In developing this procedure, the Mowrers were guided by an understanding of the principles of classical conditioning. The alarm is a US that elicits two responses in the child: (1) awakening, and (2) the tightening of those muscles necessary to prevent further urination (responses that occur because the child has no difficulty retaining urine when awake). The goal of the procedure is to transfer either or both of these responses to an internal CS—the pattern of bodily sensations that accompany a full bladder. For simplicity, let us call the CS a full bladder. By repeatedly pairing a full bladder with the alarm, the response of awakening and/or tightening the muscles so as to retain one's urine would eventually be elicited by the full bladder alone, before the alarm sounds. Notice that either awakening and going to the bathroom or retaining one's urine is an appropriate response in this situation.

The classical conditioning explanation of the alarm system has not gone unchallenged, and other analyses of this procedure have been suggested (including the view that avoidance learning, as described in Chapter 7, is involved). Regardless of which is the most appropriate explanation, the procedure is largely successful. A number of studies have found success rates of about 80 percent, and in some of the "unsuccessful" cases the children, though not completely symptom-free, were improved. Relapses are a frequent problem, however, with perhaps 25 percent of the children eventually experiencing a return of bedwetting (Johnson, 1981). These relapses can be readily treated with a period of reconditioning, but Young and Morgan (1972) tried a modified procedure in an effort to minimize relapses. With the alarm system active, children were given a type of overlearning in which they drank two pints of liquid just before going to bed (thus making the task of remaining dry more difficult). Only 10 percent of the children trained with this procedure had relapses, compared to 20 percent without the overlearning procedure.

Summary of the Classical Conditioning Therapies. Behavior therapies based on principles of classical conditioning have been used to strengthen, eliminate, or replace behaviors. The Mowrer's treatment for nocturnal enuresis is an example of a procedure designed to strengthen a behavior—nighttime retention. Systematic desensitization is used to eliminate the emotional responses of fear and anxiety. Aversive counter-conditioning is designed to replace pleasant emotional responses to such stimuli as alcohol and cigarette smoke with aversion. Each of these procedures has its share of failures and relapses, but each can also boast of long-term successes for a significant percentage of those who receive treatment.

CHAPTER

5

MODERN THEORIES AND RESEARCH ON CLASSICAL CONDITIONING

Chapter 4 described some of the most basic terms and concepts of classical conditioning and some of the ways it can affect our daily lives. Most of the concepts presented in that chapter either were developed by Pavlov or can be traced back to some of his ideas. Pavlov saw classical conditioning as a simple, mechanical, rule-governed type of learning, yet one that might account for a good deal of our learned behaviors. The present chapter examines some of the ways in which psychologists' conceptions of classical conditioning have changed over the years. Perhaps the clearest theme emerging from modern research on classical conditioning is that although it is one of the simplest types of learning, it is more complicated than was once believed. This is not to say that modern conditioning experiments have obtained chaotic results that follow no rules; rather, it is simply that the modern rules (theories) of conditioning have become more complex and more sophisticated.

This chapter will survey some current themes and issues in the field of classical conditioning. The chapter is divided into four sections, each of which addresses different questions. The first section, "Theories of Associative Learning," is concerned with the conditioning *process,* and the question of *when* conditioning takes place: Under what conditions will a stimulus become an excitatory CS, or become an inhibitory CS, or remain neutral? What factors determine whether the stimulus will become a strong CS or a weak CS? These are certainly very basic questions, and this section will describe a few well-known theories that attempt to answer them. The second section deals with the *products* of conditioning: *What types of associations* are developed in different conditioning situations? In Chapter 4 (under "S-S or S-R Associations?"), we examined some evidence that an S-S association between the CS center and the US center is developed during simple conditioning. We will see, however, that a CS-US association is only one of many possible associative products of the classical conditioning process.

Associations are not directly observable, but another product of the conditioning process, the conditioned response, certainly is. The third section of this chapter presents modern theories that try to predict *what form* the conditioned response will take. Will the CR be similar to the UR, the opposite of the UR, or something entirely different? We will see that besides its theoretical importance, this issue has significant practical consequences, as when a stimulus that has been associated with a drug might later elicit a response that either mimics or opposes the reaction to the drug itself. The final section of this chapter examines both the process and products of classical conditioning from a neurophysiological perspective. This section will describe some research that examines how classical conditioning alters the functioning of individual neurons, and some that investigates what areas of the brain are involved.

THEORIES OF ASSOCIATIVE LEARNING

One of the oldest principles of associative learning is the principle of frequency—the more frequently two stimuli are paired, the more strongly will an individual associate the two. Thomas Brown (1820) first proposed this principle, and we have seen data from Ebbinghaus and from classical conditioning experiments that support this principle. The principle was also the cornerstone of several influential mathematical theories of learning (Bush & Mosteller, 1955; Estes, 1950; Hull, 1943). The details of these theories need not be presented here. It is sufficient to say that each predicted a learning curve of the general shape shown in Figure 4-6: The strength of conditioning increases rapidly at first, but with additional trials it slows down and approaches an asymptote.

Because of this widespread acceptance of the frequency principle, it is not surprising that an experiment by Kamin (1968) that contradicted this principle attracted considerable attention. After Kamin's experiment was published, violations of the frequency principle were found in many other conditioning situations. We will examine Kamin's experiment on the *blocking effect* in the next section. We will then go on to consider several different theories of classical conditioning that have been developed in an effort to avoid the limitations of the frequency principle and provide a more adequate analysis of the processes of associative learning.

The Blocking Effect

In order to make the description of Kamin's experiment and others in this chapter easier, some notational conventions will be adopted. Because these experiments included not one but several CSs, let us use capital letters to represent different CSs (for instance, T will represent a tone, and L will represent a light). Usually only one US is involved, but it may be present on some trials and absent on others, so the superscripts + and o will represent, respectively, the presence and absence of the US. For example, T^+ will denote a trial on which one CS, a tone, was presented by itself and was followed by the US. The notation TL^o will refer to a trial on which two CSs, the tone and the light, were presented simultaneously, but were not followed by the US. It should be noted that nearly all of the experiments described below employed counterbalancing procedures in which the roles of L and T were reversed for half of the subjects in each group. For instance, if half of the subjects in one group received some T^+ trials and some TL^o trials, the other half of the subjects would receive L^+ trials and LT^o trials. The purpose of this counterbalancing is to ensure that the results of an experiment are not affected by some uninteresting differences between CSs of different modalities. To avoid unnecessary confusion, however, there will be no mention of this counterbalancing in the descriptions of the experiments.

Kamin's original experiment used rats in a

TABLE 5-1 Design of Kamin's (1968) Blocking Experiment

Group	Phase 1	Phase 2	Test Phase	Result
Blocking	L+	LT+	T	T elicits no CR
Control	—	LT+	T	T elicits a CR

conditioned suppression procedure, but the results have been replicated many times using other conditioning situations. Table 5-1 outlines the design of the experiment. There were two groups of rats, a blocking group and a control group. In the first phase of the experiment, subjects in the blocking group received a series of L^+ trials, and by the end of this phase L elicited a strong CR. In Phase 2, the blocking group received a series of LT^+ trials. These trials were exactly the same as Phase 1 trials except that a second CS, T, occurred along with L. In the test phase, T was presented by itself in extinction for several trials so as to measure the strength of conditioning to this CS.

The conditions for the control group were identical except for one important difference—in Phase 1 no stimuli were presented at all. Thus the first time these subjects were exposed to L, T, and the US was in Phase 2. It is important to realize that both groups in this experiment received exactly the same number of pairings of stimulus T and shock. Because of the equal number of pairings, the frequency principle predicts that conditioning to T should be equally strong in the two groups. However, Kamin obtained a strikingly different result: Whereas he observed a strong CR to T in the control group, he recorded essentially no conditioned responding at all to T in the blocking group. Since the only difference between the two groups was that the blocking group received conditioning trials with L in Phase 1 but the control group did not, Kamin concluded that this prior conditioning with stimulus L somehow "blocked" the later conditioning of stimulus T.

An intuitive explanation of Kamin's blocking experiment is not difficult to construct: To put it simply, stimulus T is redundant in the blocking group; it supplies no new information. By the end of Phase 1, subjects in the blocking group have learned that stimulus L is a reliable predictor of the US—the US always oc-

curs after L has occurred, and never at any other time. The addition of T to the situation in Phase 2 adds nothing to the subject's ability to predict the US. This experiment suggests that conditioning will not occur if a CS adds no new information about the US. In the control group, on the other hand, the subjects have learned nothing about any of the stimuli at the start of Phase 2. For these animals, both stimuli L and T provide valuable information about an otherwise unpredictable US, so perhaps these animals learn to associate both stimuli with the US. (Kamin showed that L also produces a conditioned response in the control group.)

This experiment forces us to conclude that the simple frequency hypothesis is not completely correct. We cannot predict the strength of conditioning to T simply by counting the number of times T is paired with the US. We must also take into account what other CSs are present, and what their prior conditioning histories have been. In short, Kamin's experiment showed that conditioning is not the automatic result of the pairing of CS and US. Conditioning will occur only if the CS is informative, only if it is predictive of something important, such as an upcoming shock. This view seems to imply that the subject has a more active role in the conditioning process than was previously thought—the subject is a selective learner, learning about informative stimuli and ignoring uninformative ones. For two psychologists, Robert Rescorla and Allan Wagner, the blocking effect and related findings underscored the need for a new theory of classical conditioning, one that could deal with these loose notions of informativeness and predictiveness in a more rigorous, objective way. The results of their collaborative efforts was the Rescorla-Wagner model, now one of the most famous theories of classical conditioning.

The Rescorla-Wagner Model

An Intuitive Introduction. It will require some effort to master the principles of the Rescorla-Wagner model—it is one of the more difficult theories presented in this book. However, the basic ideas behind the theory are quite simple and reasonable, so let us begin by examining these ideas in an informal way. We can start with the assumption that it is useful for an animal to be able to predict or anticipate important events in its environment, both favorable and unfavorable. It is useful for the animal to know both *what type* of event is coming and the *size* of that event. Classical conditioning can be viewed as a means of learning about signals (CSs) for important events (USs). The Rescorla-Wagner model assumes that each time a particular CS is presented, one of three things can happen: (1) the CS might become more excitatory, (2) the CS might become more inhibitory, or (3) there might be no change in the CS. The predictions of the Rescorla-Wagner model regarding which of these will happen may be easier to understand if we compare what an animal "expects" on a given trial with what actually happens. If the actual US is larger than expected, (for example, the animal expects no shock but then receives one), there will be some excitatory conditioning of the CS. If the actual US is smaller than expected (for instance, if the animal expects a shock but does not receive one), there will be some inhibitory conditioning. Finally, if what the animal expects is what actually happens, there will be no additional learning.

With these three general rules in mind, let us now examine the model in more detail. How can an animal anticipate what type of US is forthcoming? The S-S theory of classical conditioning provides a simple explanation: A direct link from a specific CS center (such as a tone center) to a specific US center (such as a food center) is formed during conditioning. This link may explain how the subject can predict the arrival of food, since the occurrence of the tone will now produce activity in the food center through this link.

This reasoning may explain how the animal can predict *what type* of event is coming (food as opposed to water, sexual stimulation, or pain), but how can the animal predict the *size* of that event? A straightforward idea is that the *strength of the association* reflects the size of the event: If the tone signals a large amount of food, a strong association will eventually form between the tone center and the food center. If the amount of food is small, only a weak association will develop. Rescorla and Wagner adopted this assumption that when learning is complete (that is, when conditioning has reached its asymptote), the strength of association will be directly related to the size or intensity of the US. Stating this relationship in a slightly different way, they propose that the amount of associative strength a US center will support at asymptote depends on the size of the US.

A specific example will illustrate this property. Suppose that a rat is placed in a conditioned suppression procedure in which a light is repeatedly paired with a 1 mA shock. Let us use the notation A_1 to denote the amount of associative strength a 1 mA shock can support at asymptote. (The letter A stands for asymptote; the subscript 1 indicates that we are now concerned with 1 mA shock.) As conditioning proceeds, the strength of the association between light and shock will approach A_1. The *associative strength* of the light will be labelled V_L (where V will always refer to the strength of some CS-US association, and L signifies the light). Speaking casually, we might say that A_1 reflects the size of the observed event (the actual shock), and that V_L is a measure of the subject's current "expectation" about the size of the shock. Over the course of conditioning, the Rescorla-Wagner model predicts that V_L will approach A_1 (that the subject's expectations will come closer and closer to the actual event). Both V_L and A_1 are intervening variables, for they cannot be observed directly. What we can observe, however, is that the size of the CR (which the model states is directly related to V_L) increases and approaches some asymptote that depends on the size of the US (as illustrated by the results shown in Figure 4-5, for example).

A second example will illustrate the model's predictions for a situation in which there are two CSs. Suppose a new subject is given conditioning trials in which a light and a tone are presented simultaneously and followed by a 1 mA shock. Both V_L and V_T (the associative strength of the tone) will increase over trials, but neither will approach A_1 in this case. Instead, the model states that it is the sum of their associative strengths, V_{sum}, that will approach A_1 in such a situation (where $V_{sum} = V_L + V_T$). This assumption can be explained as follows: Presumably, an animal will use all available stimuli to predict the occurrence and the size of a US. Since the light and tone are always presented together, the animal will use both of these signals, and it will be able to predict the size of the shock accurately when the sum of their associative strengths equals A_1. If the light and the tone are equally salient, their associative strengths will increase at the same rate, so at asymptote V_L and V_T will both equal $A_1/2$. On the other hand, if the light is more salient than the tone, at asymptote its associative strength will be greater than the tone's, but their total strength will still equal A_1.

We are now in a position to state more formally the three rules mentioned at the beginning of this section. Let us define A_j as the asymptote of associative strength a given US, j, will support. The model states that on each conditioning trial, the type of learning that occurs depends on a comparison of the two quantities, A_j and V_{sum}. There are, again, just three possibilities:

1. If $A_j > V_{sum}$, there will be excitatory learning — each CS present on that trial will receive an increase in associative strength. This possibility corresponds to the situation in which the US is "underpredicted." That is, the total associative strength of all the CSs present was not large enough to signal the full size of the US, as reflected in A_j.

2. If $A_j < V_{sum}$, there will be inhibitory learning — each CS present on that trial will receive a decrease in associative strength. An example of such a situation is an extinction trial. Because no US is presented on an extinction trial, $A_j = 0$. If the CSs presented on that trial have any positive associative strength at all because of prior conditioning, V_{sum} will be greater than A_j (greater than 0), and the as-

sociative strength of each will be weakened. In this case, the US is "overpredicted"—the CSs signal that a US will be forthcoming, but no US is presented.

3. If $A_j = V_{sum}$, there will be no learning. This corresponds to the situation where the size of the US is well predicted by the CSs which preceded it.

These rules state whether learning will occur on a given trial and whether it will be excitatory or inhibitory. All that remains is to predict *how much* learning will occur on each trial. For any given CS, the model states that the amount of increase or decrease in associative strength will always be proportional to the discrepancy between V_{sum} and A_j. If this discrepancy is large, the change in associative strength will be large. If the discrepancy is small, there will be proportionately less change in associative strength. Finally, the model states that the change in associative strength also depends on the salience of the CS. Therefore, if two CSs are present on a conditioning trial, but one is intense and the other is weak, there will be a larger change in the associative strength of the more intense stimulus.

Although it is fairly easy to memorize and recite these rules, for most people it will take more work to acquire a solid understanding of this model. The best way to gain such an understanding is actually to use the model to make predictions for a variety of conditioning situations. We will now work through several such examples using numerical and graphic aids to make the predictions concrete. Since neither the associative strength of any CS nor A_j can be measured directly, any numbers assigned to these quantities are completely arbitrary. In each of the following examples, let us consider a conditioned suppression procedure with a 1 mA shock as the US, and let us set A_1 equal to 100. That is, we will assume that this shock will support 100 units of associative strength.

Acquisition. Consider the first conditioning trial on which a light is paired with the 1 mA shock. If the light is the only CS present, then $V_{sum} = V_L$, and $V_L = 0$ because there has been no prior conditioning with the light. Therefore, the discrepancy $(A_1 - V_{sum}) = (100 - 0) = 100$, and there will be some excitatory conditioning on this

V = assoc. strength of CS-US

trial. The model states that the amount of learning will be proportional to this discrepancy, with the proportion depending on the salience of the light. We need to introduce another variable, S_L, which is a measure of the salience of the light. According to the Rescorla-Wagner model, S_L must have a value between 0 and 1. Let us assume that with the particular light used as the CS, $S_L = .2$. This value of .2 means that on any trial on which the light is present, the change in V_L will equal 20 percent of the discrepancy between A_1 and V_{sum}. Therefore, on the first trial V_L will be incremented by $.2 \times 100 = 20$ units. This process of incrementation is depicted graphically in Figure 5-1.

On trial 2, V_L (and therefore V_{sum}) begins at 20, so the discrepancy between A_1 and V_{sum} is 80. The increment in V_L on trial 2 is $.2 \times 80 = 16$, and so after 2 trials $V_L = 20 + 16 = 36$ (see Figure 5-1). Notice because of the smaller discrepancy between A_1 and V_{sum} on trial 2, the amount of learning is smaller than on trial 1 (16 units instead of 20). Figure 5-1 shows that the increment in associative strength should drop to 12.8 on trial 3 and to 2.7 by trial 10. By the end of trial 10, V_L has risen to 89.3, and with additional trials it would get closer and closer to the asymptote of 100. As already mentioned, the values chosen for A_1 and S_L are arbitrary, but the

model's predictions about the overall shape of the acquisition curve are the same no matter what values are used. That is, the model predicts that the initial increases in V_L will be the largest, and the increments will become smaller and smaller as the asymptote is approached.

In this simple example, V_L and V_{sum} were always equal, so the plotting of both quantities in Figure 5-1 may seem redundant. However, the next example shows that if more than one CS is involved, it is necessary to know both V_{sum} and the associative strengths of all the individual CSs.

Overshadowing. In a conditioning experiment with a compound CS consisting of one intense stimulus and one weak one, Pavlov discovered a phenomenon he called *overshadowing*. After a number of conditioning trials, the intense CS would produce a strong CR if presented by itself, but the weak CS by itself would elicit little if any conditioned responding. It was not the case that the weak CS was simply too small to become an effective CS, because if it were paired with the US by itself it would soon elicit CRs on its own. However, when presented in conjunction with a more intense CS, the latter seemed to mask or overshadow the former.

It is easy to show how the Rescorla-Wagner

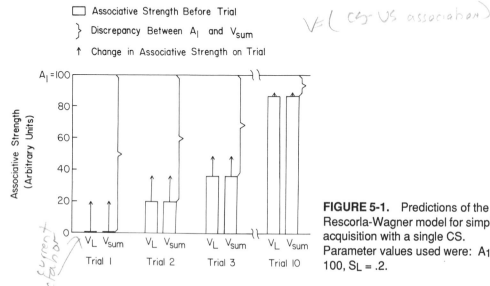

□ Associative Strength Before Trial

} Discrepancy Between A_1 and V_{sum}

↑ Change in Associative Strength on Trial

FIGURE 5-1. Predictions of the Rescorla-Wagner model for simple acquisition with a single CS. Parameter values used were: $A_1 = 100$, $S_L = .2$.

model accounts for the phenomenon of overshadowing. Let us assume that we begin a new conditioning experiment with two CSs, the same light used in the previous example ($S_L = .2$) and a very loud noise (salience of the noise = $S_N = .5$). Figure 5-2 shows the results of several conditioning trials with this compound CS. On trial 1, $V_{sum} = V_L + V_N = 0$, so the discrepancy between A_1 and V_{sum} is 100 as in the previous example. Unlike the previous example, however, there are two CSs whose associative strengths must be incremented. For V_L, the increment is the same as in trial 1 of the first example: $.2 \times 100 = 20$. For the more salient noise, however, the increment is $.5 \times 100 = 50$. Thus, after trial 1, $V_{sum} = 20 + 50 = 70$. At the start of trial 2, therefore, the discrepancy between A_1 and V_{sum} has already been reduced to 30. The increment in V_L on trial 2 is $.2 \times 30 = 6$, and the increment in $V_N = .5 \times 30 = 15$. The total increment in V_{sum} is 21, so that after two trials $V_{sum} = 70 + 21 = 91$. Figure 5-2 also shows the predictions for trials 3 and 10. Notice that with the two CSs, V_{sum} approaches A_1 much more rapidly than in Figure 5-1, and by trial 10 the increments in associative strength are too small to show in the graph. At this point, $V_L = 28.6$, $V_N = 71.4$, and $V_{sum} \approx 100$ (although to be precise V_{sum} will never reach a value of exactly 100).

The model's prediction of overshadowing can be seen clearly by comparing the course of V_L in Figures 5-1 and 5-2. The only difference between these two conditioning situations is the addition of the noise in the second example. In Figure 5-1, V_L has reached a value of 89.3 after 10 trials, and with further trials it will approach 100. In Figure 5-2, V_{sum} has nearly reached 100 by trial 10, but because the more salient noise has usurped over 70 units of associative strength, V_L will never rise above 30. In short, it is because the total strength of both CSs in the compound can never rise above 100 that the model predicts the light will be overshadowed—the level of conditioning will never be what it would be in the absence of the noise.

Blocking. The model's explanation of the blocking effect is similar to that of overshadowing. Recall that in the blocking group, stimulus L receives many pairings with the shock in Phase 1 (see Table 5-1), so that by the end of this phase $V_L \approx 100$ (assuming once again that the asymptote is 100). In the blocking experiment, it does not matter whether stimulus L is more or less salient than stimulus T; what matters is that by the end of Phase 1, L has usurped essentially all of the associative strength the US can support. At the start of Phase 2, with $V_L \approx 100$, $V_T = 0$, and

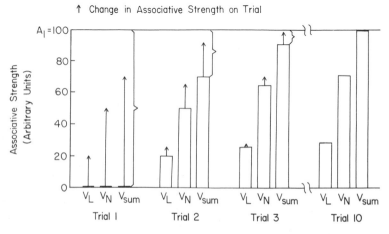

☐ Associative Strength Before Trial

⟩ Discrepancy Between A_1 and V_{sum}

↑ Change in Associative Strength on Trial

FIGURE 5-2. Predictions of the Rescorla-Wagner model for a case where an intense noise overshadows a light. Parameter values used were: $A_1 = 100$, $S_L = .2$, $S_N = .5$.

$V_{sum} \approx 100$, there is virtually no discrepancy between V_{sum} and A_1, and therefore no further changes in associative strength for either stimulus. This explanation of the blocking effect is really quite simple: The light is a perfect prediction of the shock, so there is nothing left to learn when the tone is added.

Extinction. Let us return for a moment to the simple example depicted in Figure 5-1, in which a single CS, L, is paired with a 1 mA shock ($A_1 = 100$). Suppose there have been enough acquisition trials to bring V_L to a value of 90, and then extinction trials begin. In Chapter 4 we saw that if a CS is repeatedly presented without the US, the conditioned response gradually weakens and disappears. The Rescorla-Wagner model provides a simple explanation of this, as depicted in Figure 5-3. The only trick to understanding its predictions for an extinction situation is to realize that $A_0 = 0$ (that is, the intensity of the US on an extinction trial is zero, since there is no US). Therefore, as long as V_{sum} has any positive value at all, V_{sum} will be greater than A_0, and inhibitory learning will occur. On the first extinction trial of this example, with $V_{sum} = V_L = 90$ and $S_L = .2$, the change in associative strength will be $.2 \times (0 - 90) = -18$. This means that on the first extinction trial V_L will decrease from 90 to 72. This weaker associative strength is still greater than the asymptote of 0, so on the second extinction trial V_L will decrease by 14.4 units to 57.6. With additional extinction trials V_L will drop closer and closer to 0.

An extinction trial is a simple example of a situation in which the US is "overpredicted"—a CS predicts that a US will occur but it does not. The next example shows that a conditioned inhibitor can be developed in a slightly different case of overprediction.

Conditioned Inhibition. Suppose that, as in the previous example, stimulus L has acquired an associative strength of 90 and then extinction trials begin. The only difference is that on all extinction trials a second CS, T, with a salience the same as L ($S_T = .2$) is presented in addition to L. Figure 5-4 shows that according to the model, stimulus T should become a conditioned inhibitor during these extinction trials. The reason is, of course, that regardless of the presence of T on these extinction trials, the US will be overpredicted because of the associative strength of L. The model states that if the US is overpredicted (that is, if $A_j < V_{sum}$), then the associative strength of all the CSs present on the trial will be decremented. Since V_T is initially zero, any decrements in associative strength will push

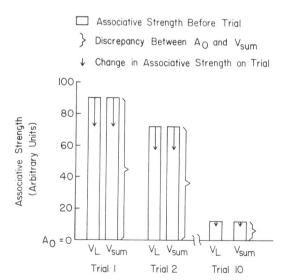

☐ Associative Strength Before Trial

} Discrepancy Between A_0 and V_{sum}

↓ Change in Associative Strength on Trial

FIGURE 5-3. Predictions of the Rescorla-Wagner model for a case of simple extinction. Parameter values used were: $A_0 = 0$, $S_L = .2$, starting value of $V_L = 90$.

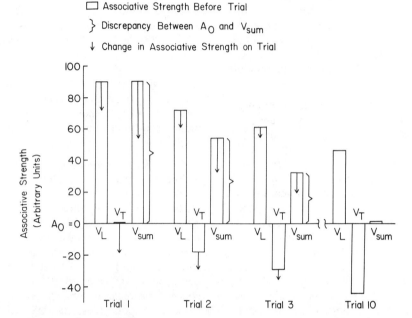

FIGURE 5-4. Predictions of the Rescorla-Wagner model for a case where T should become a conditioned inhibitor. Parameter values used were: $A_0 = 0$, $S_L = .2$, $S_T = .2$, starting value for $V_L = 90$.

V_T into the negative range, making it a conditioned inhibitor. To be more precise, on trial 1, the change in V_T will be $.2 \times (0 - 90) = -18$. Similarly, V_L will drop 18 units of associative strength to 72.

The second trial shown in Figure 5-4 is noteworthy because it is the first example we have encountered in which both an excitatory CS and an inhibitory CS are present. With $V_L = 72$ and $V_T = -18$, Figure 5-4 shows that $V_{sum} = 54$ (it is less than V_L). With additional extinction trials, V_L will become less positive, V_T will become more negative, and V_{sum} will approach an asymptote of zero. But notice that at this asymptote (which Figure 5-4 shows is nearly reached by trial 10), V_L retains a positive associative strength of approximately 50. The associative strength of V_T is approximately -50, and because there is almost no discrepancy between A_0 and V_{sum}, there will be almost no further changes in the associative strength of either stimulus with additional extinction trials.

The Overexpectation Effect. Besides being able to account for existing data, another characteristic of a good theory (called *fruitfulness* in Chapter 1) is the ability to stimulate new research by making novel predictions that have not been previously tested. The Rescorla-Wagner model deserves good grades on this count, because since 1972, scores of experiments have been conducted to test some of the model's many unique predictions. The model's prediction of a phenomenon known as the over-expectation effect is a good case in point.

Table 5-2 presents the design of an experiment which tests the overexpectation effect. Two CSs, L and T, are involved. For Phase 1, the notation "L+, T+" is used to indicate that on some trials L is presented by itself and followed by shock, whereas on other trials T is presented by itself and followed by shock. The two types of trials, L+ and T+, are randomly intermixed in Phase 1. Consider what should happen on each type of trial, assuming once again that a 1 mA shock is the US ($A_1 = 100$). On L+ trials, V_L will continue to increase and eventually

TABLE 5-2　Design of an Experiment on the Overexpectation Effect

Group	Phase 1	Phase 2	Test Phase	Result
Overexpectation	L^+, T^+	LT^+	L, T	moderate CRs
Control	L^+, T^+	no stimuli	L, T	strong CRs

approach 100. Similarly, on T^+ trials, V_T will grow and also approach the asymptote of 100. Note that because L and T are never presented together, the strengths of both stimuli can approach the asymptote. Let us assume that by the end of Phase 1, $V_L = V_T \approx 100$.

In Phase 2, subjects in the control group receive no stimuli, so in the test phase V_L and V_T will continue to equal about 100, and a strong CR to each stimulus should be observed on the first several test trials (which are extinction trials). However, subjects in the overexpectation group receive a series of trials with the compound stimulus, LT, followed by shock. On the first trial of Phase 2, V_{sum} will equal almost 200, much more than the asymptote of 100. Loosely speaking, we might say that the subject expects a larger US on the compound trial because two strong CSs are presented, but all it receives is the same 1 mA shock. Thus compared to what it actually receives, the animal has an overexpectation about the size of the US, and the model states that under these conditions all CSs will lose some of their associative strength. With enough trials in Phase 2 for the overexpectation group, V_{sum} should drop from 200 toward the asymptote of 100. When tested in the next phase, the individual stimuli L and T should exhibit weaker CRs in the overexpectation group because of the decreased values of V_L and V_T. Experiments have confirmed this prediction that CRs will be weaker in the overexpectation group than in the control group (Kremer, 1978).

The model's accurate prediction of the overexpectation effect is especially impressive because the prediction is counter-intuitive. If you knew nothing about the Rescorla-Wagner model when you examined Table 5-2, what result would you predict for this experiment? Notice that subjects in the overexpectation group actually receive more pairings of each CS and the US, so the frequency principle would predict stronger CRs in the overexpectation group. Based on the frequency principle, a weakening of CS-US associations as a result of additional CS-US pairings is the last result we would expect. Yet this result is predicted by the Rescorla-Wagner model, and the prediction turns out to be correct. The overexpectation effect is only one of several counter-intuitive predictions of the Rescorla-Wagner model which have been supported by subsequent research.

The Equations. The discussion of the past several pages was meant to show that it is not necessary to feel comfortable with abstract algebraic equations to comprehend the fundamental notion underlying the Rescorla-Wagner model—that learning occurs whenever there is a discrepancy between a subject's expectations about some important event (a US) and the event itself. However, for the sake of completeness and for the mathematically inclined, the assumptions of the theory will now be stated in the form of two mathematical equations. As we have seen, the model makes predictions on a trial-by-trial basis: For each trial it predicts the increment or decrement in associative strength for every CS that is present. Let ΔV_i signify the change in associative strength that occurs for any CS, i, on a single trial. The model states that

$$\Delta V_i = S_i(A_j - V_{sum}).$$

All of the other terms of the equation have already been defined, but the definition of V_{sum} merits repeating:

$$V_{sum} = \sum_{i=1}^{n} V_i$$

where stimuli i through n are present on a given trial. That is, V_{sum} is the total associative strength of all CSs present (and only those present) on that trial. It should be clear that ΔV_i will be positive whenever $A_j > V_{sum}$ and negative whenever $A_j < V_{sum}$.

Theories of CS Effectiveness

The Rescorla-Wagner model might be called a theory about US effectiveness: It states that an unpredicted US is effective in promoting learning, whereas a well-predicted US is ineffective. This model has been successfully applied to many conditioning phenomena, but it is not perfect. Some well-established phenomena are difficult for the model to explain. For this reason, other psychologists have proposed alternative theories of classical conditioning that are based on fairly different assumptions about the learning process. One such class of theories can be called theories of CS effectiveness, because they assume that the conditionability of a CS, not the effectiveness of the US, is what changes from one situation to another. A phenomenon called the CS preexposure effect provides one compelling piece of evidence for this assumption.

The CS Preexposure Effect. Consider a simple conditioning experiment with two groups of subjects. The control group receives simple pairings of one CS with a US. The only difference in the CS preexposure group is that before the conditioning trials the CS is presented by itself a number of times. The comparison of interest concerns how quickly conditioned responding develops in these two groups. The common finding is that conditioning proceeds more rapidly in the control group than in the CS preexposure group (Lubow & Moore, 1959; Lubow, Markman, & Allen, 1968). A common-sense explanation of this result is that a sort of habituation occurs in the CS preexposure group—because the CS is presented repeatedly but initially predicts nothing, the subject gradually pays less and less attention to this stimulus. We might say that the subject learns to ignore the CS because it is not informative, and for this reason the subject takes longer to associate the CS with the US when conditioning trials begin and the CS suddenly becomes informative.

Although it is a well-established phenomenon, the Rescorla-Wagner model does not predict the CS preexposure effect. Let us examine what the model has to say about the first preexposure trial, on which the CS is presented by itself. Since there have been no prior conditioning trials, $V_{sum} = 0$, and since no US is presented, $A_j = 0$. Because $A_j = V_{sum}$, there should be no learning of any kind on the first preexposure trial, and exactly the same logic applies to all subsequent preexposure trials. In short, the model predicts that no learning will occur when a novel CS is presented by itself. But evidently subjects do learn something on CS preexposure trials, and what they learn hinders their ability to develop a CS-US association during the later conditioning phase.

One way to discuss the CS preexposure effect in the framework of the Rescorla-Wagner model would be to suppose that the salience of a CS can change as a result of a subject's experience with that CS. Recall that the parameter S_i represents the salience of the CS. In their initial description of the model, Rescorla and Wagner (1972) implied that the value of S_i is a fixed property of a CS, with the value depending on the intensity of the CS as well as on the subject's sensory capabilities. However, the CS preexposure effect suggests that some alteration of these assumptions is in order: Assuming that the general framework of the Rescorla-Wagner model is correct, the data suggest that S_i decreases when a CS is repeatedly presented without consequence. We can easily change the value of S_i in a mathematical equation, but what does such a change mean from a psychological perspective? Some learning theorists have proposed that this change consists of a decrease in the organism's *attention* to stimulus i. They claim that during the CS preexposure trials the subject learns that it is pointless to pay attention to that stimulus, so when the stimulus is later paired with a US it takes longer for an association to develop.

If the CS preexposure effect and other similar phenomena are to be explained by the Rescorla-Wagner model, it seems that the only recourse is to concede that the parameter S_i is not a fixed property of the CS. Rather, this parameter probably reflects both the physical properties of the CS and the subject's previous experience with the

CS. Once it is granted that S_i can change, the Rescorla-Wagner model itself becomes, in part, a theory of CS effectiveness (as well as of US effectiveness). However, we will now turn to two other theories that assume that *only* the effectiveness of the CS, and not that of the US, can change with experience.

Mackintosh's Theory of Attention. In cognitive psychology, attention has been a popular concept for many years. The basic notion is that an individual is continually bombarded by numerous stimuli in many sensory modalities, but a person's ability to process this information is fairly limited. As a result, an individual must selectively process some of this information at the expense of ignoring the remainder. A common example that illustrates the phenomenon of selective attention is the so-called *cocktail party phenomenon*. If you are at a party where there are many conversations going on at once, you have the ability to choose which conversation you attend to. Without moving, you could decide to listen to the person in front of you for a while, then listen for a while to a conversation taking place in back of you, and so on. Laboratory experiments have shown that if a subject listens to one of two voices speaking simultaneously, the subject can later recall virtually nothing about what the other voice had said. At least within the domain of speech, it seems that a person's attentional capacity is very limited, for with only two sources of speech it is difficult or impossible to learn from both simultaneously.

It seems reasonable to suppose that nonhumans must also have such limits of attentional capacity, and that these should affect their ability to learn from their experiences. Theories of attention in animals propose that on a conditioning trial where several stimuli are presented simultaneously, the subject will attend to only one or a few of these stimuli, and learning (that is, changes in associations) will only occur for those stimuli to which the animal attends. Without attention, there will be no learning. Starting with such ideas, Mackintosh (1975) proposed a theory of attention and classical conditioning that is considered to be a major competitor of the Rescorla-Wagner model. Without going into

great detail, the major tenets of Mackintosh's theory can be illustrated by showing how it explains Kamin's blocking effect. Mackintosh rejects the most important principle of the Rescorla-Wagner model, that the amount of learning depends on the discrepancy between V_{sum} and A_j. Mackintosh instead assumes that S_i changes with experience in the following way. If we have two stimuli, L and T, and L is a better predictor of the US than T, then S_L will increase and S_T will decrease and eventually reach zero. In other words, the subject will attend to the more informative stimulus L and not attend to stimulus T. Now consider what this theory predicts for the second phase of Kamin's blocking experiment, as diagrammed in Table 5-1. In the blocking group, stimulus L will be more informative than T by virtue of the conditioning that took place in Phase 1. Therefore S_L will increase and S_T will drop toward zero. If the decline in S_T is rapid, then there will be little learning about T in Phase 2.

It is important to note the Mackintosh's theory predicts that blocking will not occur on the first trial of Phase 2. This is because the subject cannot know in advance that T will be uninformative, and at least for the first trial S_T will be greater than zero, so some association between T and the US should form. In support of this prediction, Mackintosh cites some further research by Kamin that showed that there was some weak conditioning to stimulus T in the blocking group, and that most of this conditioning occurred on the first trial of Phase 2. On the surface, this finding seems to favor Mackintosh's theory over the Rescorla-Wagner model. However, we should realize that the Rescorla-Wagner model predicts that there will be complete blocking only if V_L (and therefore V_{sum}) has reached A_j in Phase 1. If V_L does not reach A_j in Phase 1, then both V_L and V_T will increase in Phase 2. The results of Kamin's experiments can therefore be explained both by the Rescorla-Wagner model and by Mackintosh's attentional theory.

A somewhat different theory of CS effectiveness was developed by Pearce and Hall (1980). The details of this theory will not be presented here, but in essence the theory states that CSs become ineffective whenever the US is already well predicted. If the situation is then changed so that the US is again surprising (by making the US more intense, for example), the theory asserts that the CSs will quickly regain their effectiveness, and additional conditioning can then occur. Like Mackintosh's theory, the Pearce-Hall theory predicts that blocking should not occur on the first trial of Phase 2, because a CS cannot lose its effectiveness until it is presented at least once with no surprising consequences.

Experiments designed to distinguish between the Rescorla-Wagner model and the theories of CS effectiveness have produced mixed results, with some of the evidence supporting each theory (Balaz, Kasparow, & Miller, 1982; Hall & Pearce, 1983; Hall, Kaye, & Pearce, 1985). Perhaps these findings indicate that both classes of theory are partly correct. That is, perhaps the effectiveness of both CSs and USs can change as a result of a subject's experience. If a US is well predicted, it may promote no conditioning, as the Rescorla-Wagner model states. Likewise, if nothing surprising follows a CS, the CS may become ineffective, at least until the situation changes.

Comparitor Theories of Conditioning

Despite their differences, the Rescorla-Wagner model and theories of CS effectiveness have two features in common: (1) their predictions are based on trial-by-trial calculations, and (2) they assume that the presence of one CS can interfere with the subject's *learning* about other CSs, as in the blocking procedure. In contrast, some recent theories of classical conditioning take a different position on both points (Gibbon & Balsam, 1981; Miller & Schachtman, 1985). These theories might be called *comparitor theories* because they assume that the animal compares the likelihood that the US will occur in the presence of the CS with the likelihood that the US will occur in the absence of the CS. This idea may sound familiar, because it is fairly similar to Rescorla's (1968, 1969) analysis of CS-US correlations, which was discussed in Chapter 4.

Let us see how comparitor theories differ from those already discussed. First, comparitor theories do not make predictions on a trial-by-trial

basis, because they assume that what is important is not the events of individual trials but rather the overall, long-term correlation between a CS and the US. Second, these theories propose that the comparison of CS and context does not affect the *learning* of a conditioned response but rather its *performance*. As a simple example, suppose that the probability of a US is .5 in the presence of some CS, but its probability is also .5 in the absence of this CS. The comparator theories predict that this CS will elicit no CR, which is what Rescorla (1968) found, but not because the CS has acquired no excitatory strength. Instead, the theories assume that both the CS and *contextual stimuli*—the sights, sounds, and smells of the experimental chamber—have acquired equal excitatory strengths, because both have been paired with the US 50 percent of the time. The theories also assume that a CS will not elicit conditioned responding unless it has greater excitatory strength than the contextual stimuli. Unlike the Rescorla-Wagner model, however, they assume that an animal in this situation has indeed learned something about the CS—that the US sometimes occurs in its presence—but it will not respond to the CS unless it is a better predictor of the US than the context.

Supporters of comparitor theories have obtained several types of experimental results that are consistent with these theories but pose problems for the Rescorla-Wagner model. For example, suppose that after conditioning, an animal exhibits only a weak response to the CS because both the CS and the contextual stimuli have some excitatory strength. According to the comparitor theories, one way to increase the response to the CS would be to extinguish the excitatory strength of the context by keeping the subject in the context and never presenting the US. Since the response to the CS depends on a comparison of the CS and the context, extinction of the context should increase the response to the CS. Experiments of this type have shown that extinction of the context does increase responding to the CS (Matzel, Brown, & Miller, 1987). The Rescorla-Wagner model does not predict this effect, because it states that the associative strength of a CS cannot change if the CS itself is not presented. This theoretical debate is not settled, however, because other results favor the Rescorla-Wagner model over the comparitor theories (Ayres, Bombace, Shurtleff, & Vigorito, 1985; Randich & Ross, 1984).

Summary

In this section, we have carefully examined an influential theory of classical conditioning, the Rescorla-Wagner model, and we have taken a briefer look at two alternative types of theories—theories of CS effectiveness and comparitor theories. Since these theories are at the forefront of research on classical conditioning, it is not yet possible to say which is best. In dealing with experimental results, each of these theories has its strengths and weaknesses. The weaknesses suggest that a perfect theory of classical conditioning has not yet been formulated.

Nevertheless, substantial progress has been made toward the goal of understanding the process of classical conditioning. Although these three types of theories differ in many ways, they share one common theme: The predictiveness or informativeness of a CS is a critical determinant of whether or not a conditioned response will occur. And the predictiveness or informativeness of a CS cannot be judged in isolation: It must be compared to the predictiveness of other stimuli that are also present in the animal's environment.

TYPES OF ASSOCIATIONS

Associations in First-Order Conditioning

Chapter 4 considered the question of whether an S-S or an S-R association is formed during simple first-order conditioning. Remember that an S-S association would be a link between the CS center and the US center, which are hypothetical areas of the subject's brain that are activated by these two stimuli. According to the S-S position, a conditioned response occurs because presentation of the CS activates the CS center, which activates the US center, which in turn activates the response center (see Figure 4-4). According to the S-R position, a direct link between the CS center and the response

center is formed during conditioning. Later, activation of the CS center will directly activate the response center through the S-R link, and the US center is not involved. Chapter 4 showed that experiments employing US devaluation (in which the ability of the US to evoke a UR is diminished in one way or another after the CS has been conditioned) tended to support the S-S position. That is, any change that decreases the ability of the US to evoke a response also decreases the ability of the CS to evoke this response. These results favor the S-S position, and the more indirect route from CS center to response center in Figure 4-4, because the response-eliciting capacity of the CS seems to be tied to the response-eliciting capacity of the US.

Associations in Second-Order Conditioning

Compared to the findings on first-order conditioning, studies on the associations formed during second-order conditioning have painted a more complex and confusing picture. Imagine an experiment with rats in which a light is paired with food, and the conditioned response to the light is an increase in activity (as if the animals are restlessly waiting for the food). Food is the US, and light is CS1 (the first-order conditioned stimulus). Next, a tone (the second-order conditioned stimulus, CS2), is repeatedly paired with the light, and second-order conditioning is eventually demonstrated—the tone now also elicits an increase in activity. What sorts of associations make the conditioned response to the tone possible? Based on the discussion in the preceding paragraph, you might guess that the activation of brain centers follows the path: tone→tone center→light center→food center→response center→response. This is a sensible guess, but it is wrong. When Holland and Rescorla (1975) conducted this experiment, they found evidence for a direct S-R association between the tone center and the response center. Their method involved devaluing the US by satiating the rats and then retesting their responses to the tone. Activity responses in the presence of the tone were not diminished, even though the animals showed little interest in eating the food.

First-order conditioning → S-S assoc.
Second " " → S-R assoc.

What is surprising about this result is that the conditioned response to the CS2 (the tone) persisted even after devaluation of the US that was responsible for the acquisition of this response in the first place. Yet with another group of rats that received direct pairings of the tone and food (first-order conditioning), Holland and Rescorla found evidence for an S-S (tone-food) association. They therefore concluded that S-S associations are formed in first-order conditioning, but that S-R associations are formed in second-order conditioning.

Other studies have also found evidence for S-R associations in second-order conditioning. In some of this research, a different procedure was used: After a conditioned response to CS2 was developed, CS1 was extinguished. (This could have been done in the Holland and Rescorla experiment by first extinguishing conditioned responses to the light and then testing the tone.) Several studies have found that conditioned responses to CS2 persisted after extinction of CS1, once again supporting the S-R position (Amiro & Bitterman, 1980; Nairne & Rescorla, 1981; Zamble, Hadad, Mitchell, & Cutmore, 1985). However, as if this difference between first-order and second-order associations were not puzzling enough, other experiments have found evidence for second-order S-S associations (Rashotte, Griffin, & Sisk, 1977; Rescorla, 1982). Why S-S associations are found in some cases of second-order conditioning and S-R associations are found in others is still not fully understood, but certain procedural differences (such as whether CS2 and CS1 are paired by presenting them simultaneously or in succession) can make a big difference (Holland, 1985; Rescorla, 1982). In any case, one general conclusion we can draw about associations in second-order conditioning is that they do not fall into any single category: Both S-S and S-R associations can and do occur.

Associations Involving Contextual Stimuli

No experiment on classical conditioning takes place in a vacuum. Besides the stimuli the experimenter uses as CS and US, the experimental chamber inevitably contains a variety of distinctive sights, sounds, and smells that are collectively called contextual stimuli, as mentioned above. These contextual stimuli are more or less continuously present in the chamber (the experimenter cannot turn them on or off), and it might seem convenient to try to ignore them, but it is becoming increasingly clear that they play an important role in many conditioning situations (see Balsam & Tomie, 1985). Let us briefly consider a few examples of their effects.

When a stimulus is repeatedly presented in one experimental chamber, an association can develop between the contextual stimuli and that stimulus. For instance, if a light is occasionally presented in the chamber, the subject may form a context-light association, and we might say the subject learns to "expect" the light when it is placed in the chamber. If the light is now an expected event, this might help to explain the CS preexposure effect—the finding that if a CS has been repeatedly presented in the experimental context, it becomes harder to condition when it is later paired with a US. The possibility of a context-CS association suggests an explanation of the CS preexposure effect that is somewhat different from Mackintosh's (1975). Mackintosh proposed that the CS preexposure effect occurs because animals stop paying attention to uninformative CSs. According to the present explanation, the problem is not that the CS is uninformative but that it is expected. And just as there is little learning when the US is expected (an idea that is at the heart of the Rescorla-Wagner model), there may be little learning when the CS is expected.

One way to test this theory is to try to extinguish the context-CS association by giving the subject several sessions in the experimental chamber with no CS presentations (a boring phase of the research for both experimenter and subject, no doubt, since nothing happens in the experimental chamber). If the context-US association is weakened, this should reverse the effects of CS preexposure, and the CS should now be easier to condition when paired with a US. Wagner (1978) obtained just such a result in an eyeblink conditioning study with rabbits. Evidence for context-CS associations has been obtained in other ways as well (Rescorla, 1984), leaving little doubt that such associations can be formed.

Other studies have provided parallel evidence for the existence of context-US associations. A phenomenon analogous to the CS preexposure effect is the *US preexposure effect*, in which initial presentations of the US by itself result in slower conditioning in later CS-US pairings. For instance, Domjan and Best (1980) gave rats in an experimental group several injections of an illness-inducing drug, and this drug was subsequently paired with a novel taste (saccharin). These rats developed less of an aversion to the saccharin than control animals that did not receive the drug preexposure. If we think of the context in which the drug injections took place as a stimulus in its own right, this experiment is very similar to Kamin's (1968) blocking experiment. That is, since the drug was repeatedly paired with the context, the rats might have learned to expect the drug in that context. When the drug was then paired with both context and saccharin, the saccharin was a redundant CS, and so there was little learning about the saccharin. This explanation of the US preexposure effect is therefore known as *context blocking*. Domjan and Best provided evidence for context blocking by giving another group of rats the drug-preexposure trials in one chamber and the saccharin-drug pairing in a distinctly different chamber. For these animals, the US preexposure effect was reduced, but not completely eliminated. Based on these and similar findings, it appears that the development of a context-US association is one cause of the US preexposure effect, but not the only one (Abramson & Bitterman, 1986; Klein, Becker, Boyle, Krug, Underhill, & Mowrer, 1987; Randich & Ross, 1985).

Other research has suggested that, in several respects, associations involving contextual stimuli behave similarly to associations involving CSs and USs. For instance, Rescorla, Durlach, and Grau (1985) demonstrated several standard conditioning phenomena with context-US associations—acquisition, extinction, discrimination, and discrimination reversal (in which the roles of CS+ and CS- are reversed). In a survey of the effects of contextual stimuli, Balsam (1985) concluded that they can play several different roles

in conditioning situations. For example, contextual stimuli can *compete* with a CS for associative strength, as in the phenomenon of context blocking. They can also *summate* with a normal CS, so that the CS elicits stronger conditioned responses when presented in the same context where conditioning originally took place than in a different context (Bouton & Bolles, 1985). They can serve as a point of comparison with a normal CS, as the preceding section on comparitor theories showed. In many respects, contextual stimuli are similar to ordinary CSs.

CS-CS Associations

We have already seen that in a typical conditioning situation, associations may develop between CS and US, between context and CS, and between context and US. If a compound CS (such as a light and tone presented simultaneously) is paired with a US, an association can also form between the two CSs. The existence of sensory preconditioning (Chapter 4) provides one type of evidence for CS-CS associations. An experiment on taste-aversion learning by Rescorla and Cunningham (1978) offered another type of evidence, because it showed that extinction of one element of a compound CS causes a reduction in responding to the other, non-extinguished element. Rats initially drank a solution that was composed of two different tastes, such as salt and quinine, after which they were given an injection of poison to make them ill. This procedure was designed to develop aversions to the salt and quinine tastes. Next, the aversion to one of the two tastes (say, quinine) was extinguished for one group of rats by having them drink a quinine solution in the absence of the poison. A control group received no such extinction sessions with quinine. Finally, when given the opportunity to drink a salt solution, the quinine-extinction group showed less aversion to the salt solution than the control group.

This result shows that in the initial pairing of the salt-quinine solution with illness, the rats not only developed associations between each taste and illness, but also between salt and quinine. Because of this salt-quinine association, a decrease in the aversion to quinine produced a decrease in the aversion to salt. This sort of association between the elements of a compound CS has been called a *within-compound association.* Other studies have provided additional evidence for such within-compound associations (Heth, 1985; Rescorla & Durlach, 1981). Rescorla (1986) has found that stronger within-compound associations develop when the two elements of the compound are perceptually similar (such as two solid colors) than when they are dissimilar (such as a solid color and a striped pattern).

Occasion Setting

A CS⁺ tends to elicit a conditioned response, and a CS⁻ tends to prevent the occurrence of a conditioned response. Until recently, it was generally believed that these are the only two ways a CS can affect an animal's behavior. However, experiments by Holland (1983; 1985; Ross & Holland, 1981) suggest a third possibility. Holland has found that under certain circumstances, a stimulus can control a conditioned response in an indirect way: It can determine whether or not the subject will respond *to another CS.* For instance, in one experiment with rats, Ross and Holland (1981) arranged two types of trials. On half of the trials, a light was presented for a few seconds, followed by a tone for a few seconds, followed by food. On the other trials, the tone was presented by itself, and there was no food. Thus the presence of the light meant that the tone would be followed by food. From previous research, the experimenters knew that when a tone is paired with food, it elicits a distinctive "head-jerk" CR in rats—the animal repeatedly moves its head from side to side (as if it is looking for the source of the sound). In this experiment, Ross and Holland found that the tone elicited this head-jerk response when it was preceded by the light, but not otherwise. In other words, the light seemed to regulate the conditioned response to the tone. Ross and Holland called the light an *occasion setter*, because it signaled those occasions on which the tone would be paired with food (and those occasions on which the tone would elicit a CR).

Exactly how an occasion setter does its job is not yet certain. Holland has favored the idea that an occasion setter regulates a specific CS-US association. This possibility is illustrated in Figure 5-5, using the stimuli of the Ross and Holland experiment. We can think of the occasion setter (the light) as a sort of switch that must be turned on to complete the connection between tone and food. If this idea is correct, the occasion setter should only influence responding to the tone; it should not affect responding to other CSs (such as a bell that has been paired with food). Holland (1983) reported some evidence for such specificity of function. On the other hand, Davidson and Rescorla (1986) have found that an occasion setter can affect the responses to more than one stimulus. They first trained rats in two occasion-setting procedures: A tone served as an occasion setter for a flashing light, and a steady light served as an occasion setter for a clicker. In the test phase, the roles of the two occasion setters were switched, and it was found that the tone now controlled responses to the clicker, and the steady light controlled responses to the flashing light. These results seem to contradict the simple switching idea illustrated in Figure 5-5, because according to this theory an occasion setter for one stimulus should not affect responses to a different stimulus in any way (just as a switch on one's radio does not control the operation of the television, or vice versa). Because of results like these, Rescorla (1985) has proposed that an occasion setter's role is actually one of *facilitation*—it regulates the degree to which the US center can be activated by any CS, not just the CS that has

FIGURE 5-5. One theory of how a light can act as an occasion setter for a tone. The light might act like a switch that completes the tone-food connection.

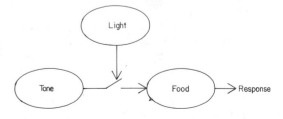

been paired with the occasion setter in training. On the other hand, Holland (1986) questioned the facilitation hypothesis, because he has found that the ability of an occasion setter to control responding to different CSs is quite limited. Yet although their nature is still a matter of controversy, occasion setters have attracted considerable attention because they appear to be distinctly different from ordinary excitatory or inhibitory CSs (LoLordo & Ross, 1987; Rescorla, 1987).

Summary

Some of the types of associations we have examined are summarized in Figure 5-6, which depicts the possible consequences of repeatedly pairing a compound CS (a light and a tone) with a food US. In addition to the light-food and tone-food associations, within-compound associations can form between the light and the tone, and each of these three stimuli can become associated with the context. Still other associations can develop in second-order conditioning and occasion-setting situations. In addition, each type of association can be either excitatory or inhibitory. Thus although classical conditioning might be loosely described as a procedure in which the subject learns to associate a CS and a US, in reality a rich array of associations can develop in any classical conditioning situation.

FIGURE 5-6. The associations that may form when a compound stimulus composed of a light and a tone are paired with food.

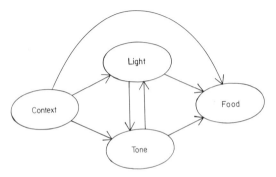

OPPONENT PROCESSES IN CLASSICAL CONDITIONING

As we have already seen, predicting the form of a conditioned response has proven to be a difficult task. In some cases, the CR is quite similar to the UR, and in others it is the opposite of the UR. When a CR is the opposite of the UR, it is sometimes called a *compensatory CR*, because it tends to compensate for, or counteract, the UR (just as the b-process in opponent-process theory is thought to counteract the a-process). In this section, we will first investigate how classical conditioning can affect an individual's reaction to a drug. In this area of research, both mimicking and compensatory CRs have been observed. We will then examine some theories that try to explain why CRs assume the variety of forms that they do.

Drug Tolerance as a Conditioned Response

A heroin user's first injection produces a highly pleasurable response of euphoria, but with later injections of the same dosage, the intensity of this positive emotional response becomes smaller and smaller. The decrease in effectiveness of a drug with repeated use is called *tolerance*, and it is found with many drugs. Several hypotheses about why tolerance occurs have been proposed. Typical pharmacological explanations attribute tolerance to possible physiological changes, such as a change in metabolism that allows the drug to pass through the body more quickly. According to the Solomon and Corbit theory, drug tolerance is the result of an increase in the b-process, which tends to counteract the a-process (the initial drug effect). The increase in tolerance with successive drug administrations is supposedly due to an automatic strengthening of the b-process over trials. Both the pharmacological explanations and the Solomon and Corbit theory therefore attribute drug tolerance to a change in the individual's body that alters the way the body reacts to the drug. However, based on his research on morphine and other drugs, Shepard Siegel (1975) has proposed a very different explanation of tolerance, one based on classical conditioning. In short, Siegel claims that drug tolerance is, at least in part, due to a compensatory CR that is elicited by contextual stimuli that regularly precede a drug administration. A description of a few of his experiments will illustrate how Siegel came to these conclusions.

One of the URs produced by morphine is *analgesia*, or a decreased sensitivity to pain. In one experiment, Siegel (1975) found that a decrease in analgesia over successive morphine injections (that is, tolerance of the analgesic response) was controlled by contextual stimuli. Siegel's subjects were rats, and he tested their sensitivity to pain by placing them on a metal plate that was heated to an uncomfortably warm temperature of about 54° C. When a rat's paws become painfully hot, the rat makes an easily measurable response—it lifts its forepaws and licks them. By measuring the latency of this paw-lick response, Siegel had a measure of the animal's sensitivity to pain.

Rats in a control group received four test trials (separated by 48 hours) on which they were brought into a special experimental room, given an injection of a saline solution (as a placebo), and later placed on the metal surface. The paw-lick latencies for these control subjects were roughly the same on all four trials, averaging 13 seconds. The procedure for one experimental group was exactly the same, except that these rats received a four morphine injections, not saline injections. On the first trial, the average paw-lick latency for this group was 24 seconds— nearly double that of the control group. This result shows that the morphine had its expected analgesic effect. However, the latencies for this group decreased over the next three trials, and on the fourth trial their latencies were about the same as those of the control group. Thus in four trials these rats had developed a tolerance to the morphine—it no longer had an analgesic effect.

According to Siegel's hypothesis, this tolerance occurred because the contextual stimuli that accompanied each morphine injection (the sights, sounds, and smells of the experimental room) acquired the capacity to elicit a compensatory CR of *hyperalgesia*, or an increased sensitivity to pain. By trial 4, this compensatory CR of hyper-

algesia completely counteracted the UR of analgesia, so the net effect was no change in pain sensitivity. If this hypothesis is correct, it should be possible to eliminate the tolerance simply by changing the contextual stimuli on the final trial. Siegel attempted to do this in a third group by giving these rats their first three morphine injections in their home cages. On trial 4, these rats received their morphine injections in the experimental room for the first time. Since this context was completely novel, it should elicit no compensatory CRs. Indeed, these animals showed a strong analgesic response, and their mean paw-lick latency was 28 seconds! Thus although this was the fourth morphine injection for these rats, their analgesic response was like that of animals that had never received a morphine injection before. This big difference between the two morphine groups was obtained simply by *changing the room* in which the morphine was injected.

If a rat's tolerance to morphine is indeed a conditioned response, it should be possible to extinguish this response by presenting the CS (the context) without the US (morphine). In another study, Siegel, Sherman, and Mitchell (1980) demonstrated such an extinction effect. Rats first received three daily injections of morphine, during which they developed tolerance to its analgesic effects. They then received nine extinction trials, in which they were transported to the experimental room and were given an injection as usual, except that they received saline instead of morphine. These can be called extinction trials because the CS (the experimental room and injection routine) was presented without the morphine. The extinction trials were followed by one final test with morphine, and the experimenters found that the morphine again produced a modest analgesic response—the rats' tolerance to morphine had been partially extinguished as a result of the saline trials.

Whereas Siegel's findings provide a strong case that morphine tolerance can come under the control of environmental stimuli, his theory that this tolerance is due to the presence of a compensatory CR has been challenged. Baker and Tiffany (1985) proposed that Siegel's results are due to a type of context-specific habituation: Because the context allows the animal to anticipate the upcoming morphine injection, the effects of this injection are diminished. Others have suggested that both the compensatory-CR theory and the context-specific habituation theory may be part of the story of drug tolerance (Paletta & Wagner, 1986).

Some of the most convincing evidence for the compensatory-CR theory has come from studies in which the CS is presented without the drug US, and a compensatory CR has been observed directly. For instance, Rozin, Reff, Mack, and Schull (1984) showed that for regular coffee drinkers, the smell and taste of coffee can serve as a CS that elicits a compensatory CR counteracting the effects of caffeine. In addition to its effects on arousal and alertness, caffeine normally causes an increase in salivation. However, for regular coffee drinkers, this increase in salivation is minimal (a tolerance effect). Rozin et al. had their subjects drink a cup of coffee that either did or did not contain caffeine (and the subjects were not told which). After they drank coffee with caffeine, subjects showed only a small increase in salivation, as would be expected of habitual coffee drinkers. However, after they drank coffee without caffeine, these subjects showed a substantial *decrease* in salivation. The experimenters concluded that this decrease was a compensatory CR elicited by the stimuli that were usually paired with caffeine (the smell and taste of coffee). In addition, when these subjects drank a cup of hot apple juice containing caffeine, they showed substantial increases in salivation, which shows that they had not developed a general tolerance to the salivation-increasing effects of caffeine—their tolerance was found only when the caffeine was paired with the usual CS, coffee. In summary, Rozin et al. demonstrated that coffee can come to elicit a compensatory CR, a decrease in salivation, after it has been repeatedly paired with caffeine. Similar evidence for compensatory CRs has been obtained with morphine (Mucha, Volkovskis, & Kalant, 1981; Paletta & Wagner, 1986), and with many other pharmacological agents, including adrenalin (Russek & Pina, 1962) and alcohol (Crowell, Hinson, & Siegel, 1981).

If it is generally true that classical conditioning contributes to the phenomenon of drug tolerance, it should be possible to find evidence for this effect in nonlaboratory settings. Siegel and his colleagues (Siegel, Hinson, Krank, & McCully, 1982) present some evidence from regular heroin users who died, or nearly died, after a heroin injection. Of course, an overdose of heroin can be fatal, but in some cases the dosage that caused a death was one the user had tolerated on the previous day. Siegel proposes that in some cases of this type, the user may have taken the heroin in an unusual stimulus environment, where the user's previously acquired compensatory CRs to the heroin injection would be decreased. He states that survivors of nearly fatal injections frequently report that the circumstances of the drug administration were different from those under which they normally injected the drug.

In summary, Siegel proposes that drug tolerance is due, at least in part, to the acquisition of a compensatory CR that tends to counteract the effects of the drug itself. He has demonstrated that morphine tolerance is stimulus-specific, and that it can be acquired and extinguished like any other CR. It is hard to imagine how a theory of drug tolerance focusing on general physiological changes (and not allowing for the contribution of classical conditioning) could account for the phenomena Siegel and others have observed.

Stimulus Substitution Revisited

Despite the compelling evidence that a CR's form is frequently the opposite of the UR's form, some theorists still contend that Pavlov's stimulus substitution theory is basically correct. To maintain this position, these theorists must assert that in cases where compensatory CRs have been observed, either the CR or the UR has not been correctly measured. In several articles, Eikelboom and Stewart (1982; Stewart, de Wit, & Eikelboom, 1984) make this claim about the compensatory CRs that are found in many conditioning situations involving pharmacological agents.

To begin, Eikelboom and Stewart note that even within a single response system there can be both mimicking and opposing CRs. For instance, one UR to ethanol is a decrease in body temperature, and a CS paired with ethanol elicits an opposing response, an increase in body temperature. In contrast, whereas morphine produces an increase in body temperature, a CS paired with morphine later produces a mimicking response, an increase in body temperature. The picture is confusing indeed, but Eikelboom and Stewart suggest that it can be clarified by being careful about defining the term *UR*. They claim that all true URs are initiated by the organism's central nervous system (CNS), which consists of the brain and the spinal cord. If the CNS is not involved in a response, the response should not be called a UR, and we should not expect any CR to mimic this response.

The logic behind this definition of a UR can be illustrated by using insulin as an example. (Insulin's effects on the body are numerous and complex, but the following discussion has been simplified to make it easier to explain the Eikelboom and Stewart theory.) When an animal is given a low dose of insulin, one initial reaction is a decrease in blood glucose levels. If we were careless, we might call this decrease a UR. However, Eikelboom and Stewart maintain that this decrease in blood glucose is not a UR because the CNS is not involved in this reaction: Insulin acts directly on cells in the body, increasing their uptake of glucose and therefore leaving less glucose in the blood. However, blood glucose levels do affect an animal's CNS in the following way. Blood glucose levels are monitored in a part of the brain called the *hypothalamus*. When blood glucose levels are low, the hypothalamus initiates a chain of commands to certain organs that ultimately leads to an increase in blood glucose. According to Eikelboom and Stewart, then, the real UR to an insulin injection—the response initiated by the CNS—is an increase in blood glucose, even though the initial bodily response to insulin is a decrease in blood glucose.

Once the actual UR is identified, Eikelboom and Stewart claim that predicting the form of the CR is straightforward: The CR will always mimic the UR, as Pavlov's stimulus substitution theory proposed. Thus a CS that is repeatedly paired with an insulin injection should produce a CR of increased blood glucose, and this prediction has been confirmed by experimental results. Eikelboom and Stewart reviewed the evidence for several different pharmacological agents, and as a general rule they proposed that cases where the CR appears to be the opposite of the UR are all cases where the UR has not been properly identified. Although the simplicity of this theory is appealing, it is by no means clear that the theory can be applied to all cases of compensatory CRs. Even for the few substances Eikelboom and Stewart consider (glucose, insulin, morphine, ethanol, atropine, and a few others) the data are incomplete and sometimes contradictory. The theory may have an even more difficult time accounting for compensatory CRs that are found in conditioning situations that do not involve drugs.

Conditioned Opponent Theories

Schull (1979) has developed a very different theory about compensatory CRs. He calls his theory a *conditioned opponent theory* to reflect the fact that he accepts most of the assumptions of the Solomon and Corbit theory but makes one important change. Schull accepts the assumption that a typical emotional experience involves the elicitation of an a-process followed by an opposing b-process. However, he does not accept the idea that the b-process is automatically strengthened with use and weakened with disuse. Instead, he assumes that the b-process may appear to grow because any stimulus that is paired with the emotional experience will become a CS that can later elicit the b-process (but not the a-process, which Schull assumes is not transferable to a CS). To put it another way, whereas Solomon and Corbit proposed that the b-process is increased by a nonassociative strengthening mechanism, Schull proposes that any increase in the size of b-process is a CR elicited by one or more CSs.

Schull's theory may be easier to understand if we consider a specific example. As discussed in Chapter 3 in the section on the Solomon and Corbit theory, a person's response to an initial heroin injection is a very pleasurable sensation followed by unpleasant withdrawal symptoms.

The initial pleasure is the a-process, and the unpleasant after-effect is the b-process. Now, according to Schull, only the b-process is conditionable. Let us assume that stimuli that accompany the heroin injection—the needle, the room, and so on—serve as CSs that, after a few pairings with heroin, begin to elicit the withdrawal symptoms by themselves. These CSs have several effects. First, they tend to counteract the a-process, so a heroin injection no longer produces much of a pleasurable sensation. Second, they combine with the b-process to produce more severe and longer-lasting withdrawal symptoms. Third, when no morphine is available, the presence of these stimuli can still produce withdrawal symptoms and cravings for the drug. Thus Schull proposes that classically conditioned stimuli may contribute to many of the debilitating characteristics of drug addiction.

Whereas Schull's conditioned opponent theory deals exclusively with the conditioning of b-processes, Wagner and his associates (Donegan & Wagner, 1987; Mazur & Wagner, 1982; Wagner, 1981) have developed a general theory of classical conditioning that is meant to apply to all CRs, whether or not we would want to call them "b-processes." Wagner calls this theory a *sometimes opponent process* (SOP) theory because it predicts that in some cases a CR will be the opposite of the UR, whereas in other cases a CR will mimic the UR. How can we predict what type of CR we will see in a particular conditioning situation? According to SOP, the CR will mimic the UR if the UR is *monophasic*, but it will be the opposite of the UR if the UR is *biphasic*. In essence, the terms *monophasic* and *biphasic* concern whether or not a b-process can be observed in the UR. For example, the heart-rate UR to shock is biphasic because it consists of an increase in heart rate when the shock is on, followed by a decrease in heart rate *below baseline* when the shock is terminated. Because the UR exhibits such a "rebound effect," SOP predicts that the CR will be the opposite of the UR, and Black's (1965) research has demonstrated that this is the case. On the other hand, the UR of an eyeblink to a puff of air is monophasic: The eye closes, then opens, but there is no rebound—the eye does not open wider than it was initially. For this reason, SOP predicts that the CR will mimic the UR in eyeblink conditioning, which is of course the case.

If SOP is correct, we should be able to make predictions in two directions. First, by observing the entire UR, we should be able to predict the form of the CR. For instance, a rat's typical response to foot shock is a brief period of hyperactivity followed by a longer period of decreased activity ("freezing"). SOP predicts that the CR will resemble the latter response, freezing, which is the case (Fanselow, 1980). Second, SOP predicts that if a CR appears to be the opposite of the UR, careful observation will reveal that the UR is actually biphasic. For example, whereas decreased activity is typically observed in rats after a morphine injection, stimuli paired with morphine elicit a CR of hyperactivity. By observing rats' activity levels for many hours after a morphine injection, Paletta and Wagner (1986) found that the initial period of decreased activity is indeed followed by a period of hyperactivity, as SOP predicts. Results from a number of other conditioning situations are also consistent with SOP's predictions (Wagner & Brandon, in press), as are some of the neurophysiological findings discussed in the next section.

PHYSIOLOGICAL RESEARCH ON CLASSICAL CONDITIONING

The final topic of this chapter complements each of the previous ones. Regardless of their theoretical perspectives, just about everyone who studies classical conditioning agrees that our understanding of this type of learning would be greatly enhanced if we knew what changes take place in the nervous system during the acquisition and subsequent performance of a new conditioned response. This topic has been the focus of intense research efforts in recent years. Much has been learned about the physiological mechanisms of classical conditioning, and the following discussion can provide only a brief survey of some of the major developments in this area.

Research with Primitive Creatures

Kandel's research on the neural mechanisms of habituation in the mollusk *Aplysia* was discussed in Chapter 3. Kandel and his associates have also studied classical conditioning in *Aplysia* in several different ways. In some early studies, Kandel and Tauc (1964, 1965) produced a conditioning-like effect in a three-neuron configuration of *Aplysia*. Figure 5-7 illustrates their methods. Electrodes were inserted into the cell bodies of neurons 1 and 2, and delivering a weak electrical current through either electrode would cause the corresponding neuron to fire. Before conditioning, it was found that the firing of neuron 1 did not cause neuron 3 to fire, whereas the firing of neuron 2 did cause neuron 3 to fire. However, the firing of neuron 1 did produce a small depolarization in the membrane of neuron 3, which indicated that there was an ineffective synaptic connection between neurons 1 and 3. Given this initial state of affairs, Kandel and Tauc treated the stimulation of neuron 1 as the CS, and the stimulation of neuron 2 as the US, which produced the UR of the firing of neuron 3. After several CS-US pairings (the stimulation of neuron 1, then neuron 2), Kandel and Tauc found that the CS now elicited a response of its own— the stimulation of neuron 1 now caused neuron 3 to fire. This new synaptic association was not permanent: It lasted for about 20 minutes and then disappeared. However, the researchers were able to demonstrate this conditioning-like effect in several sets of neurons. They also showed that the effect depended on the temporal contiguity of

CS and US—unpaired stimulations of neuron 1 and neuron 2 did not produce the effect.

The results of Kandel and Tauc illustrate how simple the neural mechanisms of classical conditioning might be, at least in some creatures. Since there are three distinct elements in any classical conditioning situation—the CS, the US, and the response—a minimum of three neurons must be involved. What is significant about the results of Kandel and Tauc is that working with this absolute minimum of three neurons they were able to demonstrate something resembling classical conditioning.

In their more recent work, Kandel and his associates have begun to examine classical conditioning in the gill-withdrawal reflex of *Aplysia*. In their conditioning arrangement, the US was a shock to the tail, and the UR was the gill-withdrawal response (refer to Figure 3-7). The CS was weak stimulation of the siphon, which initially produced only a minor gill-withdrawal response. After several pairings of the CS and US, however, the CS began to elicit a full gill-withdrawal response (Carew, Hawkins, & Kandel, 1983). Hawkins, Carew, and Kandel (1983) found that the precise temporal arrangement of CS and US was crucial. Optimal learning occurred with short-delay conditioning (with the CS preceding the US by 0.5 seconds), and there was no evidence of conditioning with a delay of 2 seconds. Further investigation revealed that this enhanced response to siphon stimulation was due to an increase in the amount of transmitter released by the sensory neurons of the siphon. It is interesting to note that precisely the opposite

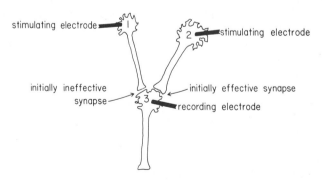

stimulating electrode

initially ineffective synapse

stimulating electrode

initially effective synapse

recording electrode

FIGURE 5-7. A schematic diagram of the procedure used by Kandel and Tauc (1964) to obtain an effect resembling classical conditioning in only three neurons of *Aplysia*. Before conditioning, stimulation of neuron 2 produced a strong response in neuron 3, but stimulation of neuron 1 did not. After several "conditioning" trials on which neuron 1 and neuron 2 were stimulated in rapid succession, neuron 1 now developed the capacity to produce a response in neuron 3.

neural change (decreased transmitter release by the sensory neurons) was found to be responsible for habituation of the gill-withdrawal response. Because of results like these, Hawkins and Kandel (1984) express the hope that other conditioning phenomena, such as generalization, second-order conditioning, and blocking, may also be traced to equally simple changes at the cellular level. Along these lines, Kandel's group has recently discovered a chemical process that may underlie the phenomenon of conditioned inhibition (Mackey, Glanzman, Small, Dyke, Kandel, & Hawkins, 1987).

Research with Mammals and Other Vertebrates

Because of the staggering complexity of the nervous systems of higher animals such as mammals, the task of uncovering the physiological mechanisms of classical conditioning is extremely difficult. Nevertheless, substantial progress has now been made on several different fronts.

One line of research has investigated which major sections of the brain are involved in the conditioning process. For example, in baboons, a certain part of the hypothalamus appears to be intimately involved in the conditioned heart-rate changes that are elicited by CSs paired with shock. If this part of the hypothalamus is destroyed, heart-rate CRs disappear, whereas unconditioned heart-rate responses are unaffected (Smith, Astley, DeVit, Stein & Walsh, 1980). In other species, a number of different brain sites have been implicated in heart-rate conditioning, including parts of the amygdala, hypothalamus, and cingulate cortex (Schneiderman, McCabe, Haselton, Ellenberger, Jarrell & Gentile, 1987). From our perspective, the important point is not the names of these specific areas but the finding that certain brain sites are essential for learned responses (CRs) but not for unlearned responses (URs).

For another common classical conditioning preparation, rabbit eyeblink conditioning, the neural circuitry has been studied in great detail. Many studies have shown that the cerebellum, a part of the brain that is important for many skilled movements, plays a critical role in eyeblink conditioning. It is interesting to observe that, as in heart-rate conditioning, different neural pathways are involved in unconditioned eyeblink responses and conditioned eyeblink responses. The eyeblink UR to a US such as an air puff directed at the eye seems to be controlled by two distinct pathways—a fairly direct pathway in the brainstem and a more indirect pathway passing through the cerebellum (Thompson, 1986). There is considerable evidence that the eyeblink CR is controlled by this second, indirect pathway. If sections of this pathway in the cerebellum are destroyed, eyeblink CRs disappear and cannot be relearned (Lavond, Hembree, & Thompson, 1985; Yeo, Hardiman, & Glickstein, 1985). If neurons in this same part of the cerebellum are electrically stimulated, eyeblink responses similar to the CR are produced (Thompson, McCormick, & Lavond, 1986).

Wagner and Donegan (in press) point out that there is an intriguing correspondence between these physiological findings and the predictions of Wagner's SOP model. As discussed in the preceding section, SOP suggests that a CR mimics the later portions of the UR but not its initial portions. The findings just described may explain why this is so, at least in the case of eyeblink conditioning: The CR is activated by the same neural pathways as is the later part of the UR. This relation between SOP and neurophysiological evidence provides a nice example of how theories of learning and neurophysiological research can be mutually supportive. The assumptions of SOP are bolstered by the evidence of dual neural pathways, and as Wagner and Donegan explain, SOP makes a number of specific predictions that can give direction to further physiological investigations.

A somewhat different line of research has examined individual cells whose activity appears to be related to the acquisition of conditioned responses. For example, McCormick and Thompson (1984) found that the firing rates of certain cells in the cerebellum are correlated with behavioral measures of the eyeblink CR. That is, when a rabbit is presented with a series of conditioning trials with a CS such as a tone, the activity of these cells increases at about the same rate as eyeblink response. When the eyeblink CR decreases during extinction, so does the activity of these cells. Moreover, the cellular activity within a single presentation of the CS parallels the pattern of the eyeblink, with the neuron's activity preceding the eyeblink response by about 30 milliseconds. Along with other evidence, this finding suggests that these cells play an important role in the development of the CR. Such neurons are not unique to the cerebellum, however, because neurons with similar properties have been found in the hippocampus, a brain structure suspected of playing a role in learning and memory (Berger & Weisz, 1987). The discovery of neurons whose activity is so closely related to overt behavior is an important development. Exactly how these neurons in different parts of the brain actually contribute to the conditioning process is not yet known, however.

As we have seen, physiological research on classical conditioning is proceeding at a number of different levels, including research on entire brain structures, on individual neurons, and on chemical mechanisms. Both primitive and more advanced species are being studied. Our understanding of the physiological underpinnings of classical conditioning should increase greatly in the years to come. It will be interesting to see whether the cross-species generality of conditioning principles that is so evident at the behavioral level is accompanied by equally general neural mechanisms.

6
BASIC PRINCIPLES
OF OPERANT CONDITIONING

Although it undeniably affects the behavior of both people and animals in many important ways, classical conditioning is not the universal mechanism of learning Pavlov thought it might be. Its major limitation is that it applies only to reflexive behaviors—behaviors that are reliably elicited by some specific stimulus. Contrary to the speculations of Sechenov (1863) and Pavlov (1927), most of the behaviors of human beings and of higher animals are not reflexive in this sense. Behaviors such as walking, talking, eating, drinking, working, and playing do not occur automatically and with machinelike regularity in response to any particular stimulus. In the presence of a stimulus such as food, a creature might eat or it might not, depending on a multitude of factors such as the time of day, the time since its last meal, the presence of other members of its species, the other activities available at the moment, and so on. Because it appears that a creature can choose whether or not to engage in behaviors of this type, people sometimes call them "voluntary" behaviors and contrast them with the "involuntary" behaviors that are part of unconditioned and conditioned reflexes. Some learning theorists state that whereas classical conditioning is limited to involuntary behaviors, operant conditioning influences our voluntary behaviors. The term *voluntary* is difficult to define in a precise, scientific way, and therefore it may be a mistake to use this term to refer to all of our nonreflexive behaviors. However, regardless of what we call nonreflexive behaviors, this chapter should make one thing clear: Just because there is no obvious stimulus preceding a behavior, this does not imply that the behavior is unpredictable. Indeed, the extensive research on operant conditioning might be characterized as an effort to discover general principles that can predict what nonreflexive behaviors a creature will produce, and under what conditions.

THE LAW OF EFFECT

Thorndike's Experiments

E. L. Thorndike (1898; 1911) was the first researcher to systematically investigate how an animal's nonreflexive behaviors can be modified as a result of its experience. In Thorndike's experiments, a hungry animal (a cat, a dog, or a chicken) was placed in a small chamber that he called a *puzzle box*. If the animal performed the appropriate response, the door to the puzzle box would be opened, and the animal could exit and eat some food placed just outside the door. For some subjects, the required response was simple—pulling on a rope, pressing a lever, or stepping on a platform. Figure 6-1 shows one of Thorndike's more difficult puzzle boxes, which required a cat to make three separate responses—pulling a string (which lifted one bolt), stepping on the platform (which lifted the other bolt), and reaching through the bars and turning one of the two latches in front of the door. The first time a subject was placed in a puzzle box (whether simple or complex), it usually took a long time to escape. A typical subject would move about inside the puzzle box, explore the various parts of the chamber in a seemingly haphazard way, and during the course of this activity it would eventually perform the response that opened the door. Based on his careful observations of this behavior, Thorndike concluded that an animal's first production of the appropriate response occurred purely by accident.

To determine how a subject's behavior would change as a result of its experience, Thorndike would return an individual animal to the same puzzle box many times. His measure of performance was *escape latency*—the amount of time it took the subject to escape on each trial. Figure 6-2 presents a typical result from one of Thorndike's cats, which shows that as trials progressed the cat's latency to escape gradually declined (from 160 seconds on the first trial to just 7 seconds on the twenty- fourth trial). Thorndike attributed this gradual improvement over trials to the progressive strengthening of a S-R connection: the stimulus was the inside of the puzzle box, and the response was whatever behavior opened the door. To account for the gradual strengthening of this connection, Thorndike formulated a principle of learning that he called the *Law of Effect*:

Of several responses made to the same situation, those which are accompanied or closely followed by satisfaction to the animal will, other things being equal, be more firmly connected with the situation, so that, when it recurs, they will be more likely to recur; those which are accompanied or closely followed by discomfort to the animal will, other things being equal, have their connections with that situation weakened, so that, when it recurs, they will be less likely to occur. The greater the satisfaction or discomfort, the greater the strengthening or weakening of the bond (p. 244).

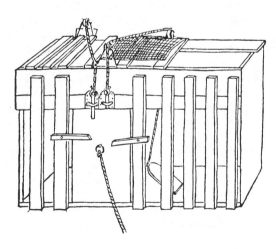

FIGURE 6-1. One of Thorndike's puzzle boxes. A cat could escape from this box by pulling a string, stepping on the platform, and turning one of the two latches on the front of the door. (From Thorndike, 1898)

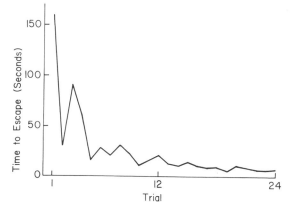

FIGURE 6-2. The number of seconds required by one cat to escape from a simple puzzle box on 24 consecutive trials. (From Thorndike, 1898)

How are we to know what is satisfying or discomforting for an animal subject? Thorndike was careful to define these terms in a way that did not rely on the observer's intuition:

By a satisfying state of affairs is meant one which the animal does nothing to avoid, often doing such things as attain and preserve it. By a discomforting or annoying state of affairs is meant one which the animal commonly avoids and abandons (p. 245).

The application of the Law of Effect to the puzzle-box experiments is straightforward: Certain behaviors, those that opened the door, were closely followed by a satisfying state of affairs, escape and food, so when the animal was returned to the same situation it was more likely to produce those behaviors than it had been at first. In modern psychology, the phrase "satisfying state of affairs" has been replaced by the term *positive reinforcer*, but the Law of Effect (or the principle of *reinforcement*) remains as one of the most important concepts of learning theory.

Guthrie and Horton: Evidence for a Mechanical Strengthening Process

Two researchers who followed Thorndike, E. R. Guthrie and G. P. Horton (1946), provided more convincing evidence that the learning that took place in the puzzle box involved the strengthening of whatever behavior happened to be followed by escape and food. They placed

cats in a puzzle box with a simple solution: A pole in the center of the chamber had only to be tipped in any direction to open the door. A camera outside the chamber photographed the cat at the same instant that the door swung open, thereby providing a permanent record of exactly how the subject had performed the effective response on each trial. The photographs revealed that after a few trials each cat settled upon a particular method of manipulating the pole that was quite consistent from trial to trial. However, different subjects developed quite a variety of methods for moving the pole—one cat would always push the pole with its left forepaw, another would always rub the pole with its nose, and another would lie down next to the pole and roll over into it. Figure 6-3 shows the results from the first 24 trials for one cat. At first the cat's behavior at the moment of reinforcement varied greatly from trial to trial. By the ninth or tenth trial, however, the cat began to develop a stereotyped method of operating the pole—it would walk to the left of the pole and brush against it with its backside. This method of moving the pole was produced in a very regular fashion on trials 15 through 24. Figure 6-4 shows the behavior of another cat, beginning on trial 52. This cat had developed the behavior of moving the pole by biting it while standing in a particular position.

The findings of Guthrie and Horton can be summarized by stating that after their subjects mastered the task, there was relatively little variability from trial to trial for a given subject, but

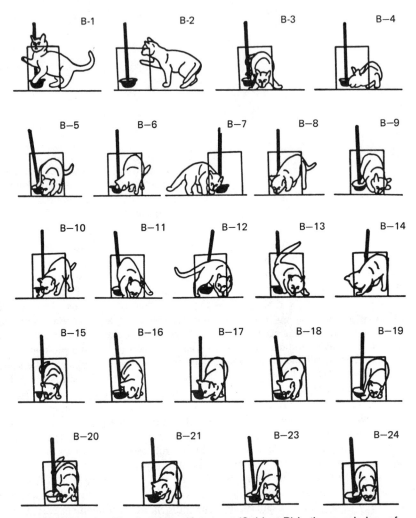

FIGURE 6-3. The behavior of one cat (Subject B) in the puzzle box of Guthrie and Horton. The 24 pictures show the cat's position at the moment of reinforcement on the cat's first 24 trials in the puzzle box, where any movement of the vertical pole caused the door to open. (From Guthrie & Horton, 1946)

considerable variability between subjects. These results provide evidence for a particular version of the Law of Effect that Brown and Herrnstein (1975) aptly called the *stop-action principle*. According to this principle, there is a parallel between the action of the camera and the reinforcer in the experiments of Guthrie and Horton. Like the camera, the occurrence of the reinforcer serves to stop the animal's ongoing behavior and strengthen the association between the situation (the puzzle box) and those precise behaviors that were occurring at the moment of reinforcement. (The term *stop-action* is particularly appropriate because Guthrie [1935] believed that a behavior was strengthened not because it was followed by a reinforcer but because it was the last behavior

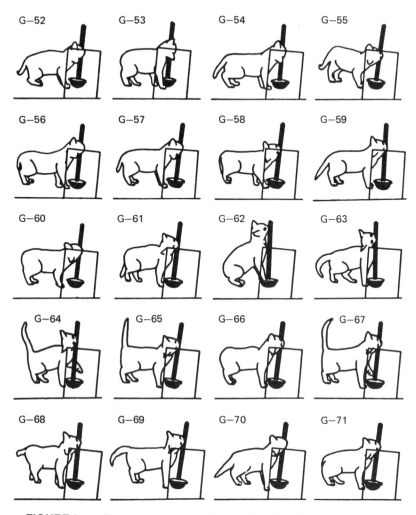

FIGURE 6-4. The behavior of another cat (Subject G) at the moment of reinforcement on trials 52 through 71 in the puzzle box. (From Guthrie & Horton, 1946)

to occur in the chamber. However, today the prevailing view is that Thorndike's position, which emphasized the importance of the reinforcer, is the correct one.)

The stop-action principle states that because of this strengthening process, the specific bodily position and the muscle movements occurring at the moment of reinforcement will have a higher probability of occurring on the next trial. Of course, a single reinforcer may not be enough to

guarantee the prompt recurrence of a behavior on the next trial, and by chance some other pattern of movement might displace the pole. This is shown by the fact that a cat's behavior varied considerably from trial to trial at first. However, one of these initial behaviors will eventually produce a second reinforcer, thereby further strengthening that S-R association, and making it more likely that that behavior will occur again (and be strengthened still further). This sort of positive feedback process should eventually produce one S-R connection that is so much stronger than any other that its particular pattern of response will occur with high probability, trial after trial. This reasoning provides a simple explanation of why different cats developed different stereotyped techniques for moving the pole. For each cat, whatever random behavior happened to get reinforced a few times would become dominant over other behaviors.

More recently, Moore and Stuttard (1979) challenged this interpretation of the Guthrie and Horton experiments. Moore and Stuttard showed that many of the stereotyped behaviors Guthrie and Horton observed in their cats (for instance, rubbing against the pole with their sides or with their heads) can be elicited by the mere presence of human beings. Presenting the reinforcers of food and escape were unnecessary. Moore and Stuttard speculated that since the cats could see through the glass walls and door of Guthrie and Horton's puzzle box, the sight of the experimenters may have elicited these feline behaviors. They proposed that the cats in the puzzle box were not learning any new behaviors; they were simply performing instinctive behaviors. In short, Moore and Stuttard asserted that it is not necessary to use reinforcement to get catlike behaviors from a cat.

This criticism by Moore and Stuttard seems to miss the point of Guthrie and Horton's experiments. In their book, Guthrie and Horton readily admitted that they had nothing to say about where a cat's initial behaviors in the puzzle box came from. They could not explain why on the first trial one cat may hit the pole with its paw, or why another may bite the pole, except to note that these behaviors must be products of the animal's heredity and its previous learning experiences. What they could explain, however, is why different cats develop different yet consistent patterns of moving the pole, and why a single behavior pattern emerges from the multiplicity of behaviors seen on the first few trials. Presumably, we should be able to predict on the basis of a cat's first few trials what stereotyped behavior will eventually emerge for that subject. Consider the first six trials of the cat shown in Figure 6-3. The behavior of brushing

against the pole with its right side is reinforced three times (trials 3, 5, and 6), whereas other behaviors (moving the pole with the head, with the paw, or by rolling into it) are only reinforced once apiece. The stop-action principle would predict that the behavior of brushing the pole with the right side has the greatest chance of recurring on future trials, and this prediction is confirmed.

In summary, Guthrie and Horton realized that a cat's initial behaviors in the puzzle box were samples from its natural repertoire. The work of Moore and Stuttard showed that the presence of the experimenters may have influenced which of the cat's many behaviors might be especially likely to occur at first. Furthermore, Moore and Stuttard are correct in claiming that the stop-action principle does not explain how new behaviors are learned. What the principle does explain, however, is how old behaviors can be strengthened through reinforcement and thereby become more likely to occur in the future.

Superstitious Behaviors

The mechanical nature of the stop-action principle suggests that behaviors may sometimes be strengthened "by accident." We have already seen this sort of fortuitous strengthening at work in the experiments of Guthrie and Horton. Different cats developed different styles of moving the pole, apparently as a consequence of what behaviors happened to precede reinforcement on each cat's first few trials in the puzzle box. The stereotyped way a particular cat responded in the puzzle box is an example of a *superstitious behavior*, because although some behavior that moved the pole was necessary for reinforcement, there was no requirement that the subject use approximately the same motion each time.

Skinner (1948) conducted a famous experiment, now often called the *superstition experiment*, which made a strong case for the power of accidental reinforcement. The subjects were pigeons, and each was placed in a separate experimental chamber in which grain was presented every 15 seconds regardless of what the pigeon was doing. After a subject had spent some time in the chamber, Skinner observed the animal's behavior. He found that six of his eight subjects had developed clearly defined behaviors that they performed repeatedly between food presentations. One bird made a few counterclockwise turns between reinforcers, another made pecking motions at the floor, and a third repeatedly poked its head into one of the upper corners of the chamber. A fourth bird was observed to toss its head in an upward motion, and two others swayed from side to side. These behaviors occurred repeatedly despite the fact that no behavior was required for reinforcement.

According to Skinner, these distinctive behaviors developed for the same reasons that the cats of Guthrie and Horton developed distinctive styles of moving the pole: Whatever behavior happened to be occurring when the reinforcer was delivered was strengthened. If the first reinforcer occurred immediately after a pigeon had tossed its head upward, this behavior of head tossing would be more likely to occur in the future. Therefore, there was a good chance that the next reinforcer would also follow a head tossing motion. The accidental strengthening process is self-perpetuating, because once any one behavior develops a somewhat higher frequency of occurrence than all other behaviors, it has a greater chance of being reinforced, which increases its frequency still further, and so on.

Skinner (1948) proposed that many of the superstitious behaviors people perform are produced by the same mechanism that caused his pigeons to exhibit such peculiar behaviors:

Rituals for changing one's luck at cards are good examples. A few accidental connections between a ritual and favorable consequences suffice to set up and maintain the behavior in spite of many unreinforced instances. The bowler who has released a ball down the alley but continues to behave as if he were controlling it by twisting and turning his arm and shoulder is another case in point. These behaviors have, of course, no real effect on one's luck or upon a ball half way down an alley, just as in the present case the food would appear as often if the pigeon did nothing—or, more strictly speaking, did something else (p. 171).

Richard Herrnstein (1966) refined Skinner's analysis of human superstitions. Herrnstein notes that Skinner's analysis is most applicable to idio-

syncratic superstitions, like those of the gambler or the bowler. It seems likely that such personalized superstitions arise out of an individual's own experience with reinforcement. On the other hand, superstitions that are widely held across a society (for example, the belief that it is bad luck to walk under a ladder, or that the number 13 is unlucky) are probably acquired through communication with others, not through individual experience. How these more common superstitions first arose is not known, but Herrnstein suggests that some may be the residue of previous contingencies of reinforcement that are no longer in effect. As an example, he cites the belief that it is bad luck to light three cigarettes on a single match. This superstition arose in the trenches during World War I. At that time, there was some justification for this belief, because every second that a match remained lit increased the chances of being spotted by the enemy. This danger is not present in everyday life, but the superstition is still passed on from generation to generation. Herrnstein speculates that it may be perpetuated by stories of occasional individuals who violate the rule and meet with an unfortunate fate. Thus Herrnstein claims that some superstitions were originally valid beliefs, and are now perpetuated by rumor and/or occasional coincidental events. However, while it is easy to imagine how some superstitions (such as the one about walking under a ladder) may have begun, the origins of others are less clear.

Skinner's analysis of his superstition experiment has not gone unchallenged. Staddon and Simmelhag (1971) conducted a careful replication of the superstition experiment, recorded the pigeons' behaviors more thoroughly than Skinner did, and came to different conclusions. In their superstition experiment, Staddon and Simmelhag found that certain behavior patterns tended to occur frequently in many or all of their subjects during the intervals between food deliveries. They found that these behaviors could be grouped in two major categories, which they called *interim behaviors* and *terminal behaviors*. Interim behaviors were defined as those that were frequent in the early part of the interval, when the next reinforcer was still some time away. Interim behaviors included pecking toward the floor, turning, and moving along the front wall of the chamber. Terminal behaviors were defined as behaviors that seldom occurred early in the interval but increased in frequency as the time of food delivery approached. Two of the most frequent terminal behaviors were orienting toward the food magazine and pecking in the vicinity of the magazine. To recapitulate, interim behaviors are those that occur frequently early in the interval between reinforcers, and terminal behaviors are those that occur frequently toward the end of the interval.

Staddon and Simmelhag used their data to challenge Skinner's conclusions in several respects. First of all, they proposed that some of the behaviors that Skinner called "superstitious behaviors," such as turning in circles, may actually have been interim behaviors. But interim behaviors are seldom followed by the delivery of food, because they do not often occur at the end of the interval. In other words, Staddon and Simmelhag argued that it is not accidental reinforcement that causes interim behaviors to increase in frequency. Instead, they proposed that interim behaviors are simply behaviors that a subject has an innate predisposition to perform when the likelihood of reinforcement is low. In short, interim behaviors are a reflection of an organism's hereditary endowment, not of the reinforcement process.

Secondly, Staddon and Simmelhag claimed that they were proposing a view of the reinforcement process that was substantially different from Skinner's. They agreed that some of the superstitious behaviors Skinner observed may have occurred so frequently because they were followed by food. (These were most likely to be terminal behaviors.) However, instead of saying that reinforcement "stamps in" or "strengthens" those behaviors that it follows, Staddon and Simmelhag proposed that reinforcement is a more passive process of "selection." They proposed that the reinforcement process depends on the operation of two classes of principles: *principles of variation* and *principles of reinforcement*. The principles of variation determine what behaviors occur when a creature is first exposed to a new situation, before reinforcement has a chance to operate. The principles of variation include such factors as the subject's inherited behavior tendencies, level of motivation, and previous experiences in similar situations. The principles of reinforcement operate, not by strengthening the behavior that is followed by reinforcement, but rather by the gradual elimination of behaviors that do not produce reinforcement. Staddon and Simmelhag draw a parallel between their two types of principles and Darwin's (1859) theory of evolution, which states that the pressures of survival select among members of a species who have differing traits by eliminating all but the "fittest" individuals.

Although the Staddon and Simmelhag article presented some important data and several fresh ideas about the nature of reinforcement, it could be argued that the distinction between reinforcement as strengthening and reinforcement as selection is little more than a difference in semantics. If the difference were important, it should be possible to design an experiment for which the two conceptions of reinforcement make clearly different predictions. However, Staddon and Simmelhag proposed no such experiment. Nevertheless, their analysis is important because it shows that not all the behaviors that arise when periodic free reinforcers are delivered are the result of an accidental pairing with reinforcement. Some of the behaviors may simply be interim behaviors, which become highly probable when the next reinforcer is some time away, and the subject must do something to "pass the time." Despite the arguments of Staddon and Simmelhag, however, it seems clear that Skinner was correct in his assertion that some behaviors both inside and outside the laboratory increase in frequency as a result of an accidental pairing with reinforcement. For instance, many of the idiosyncratic superstitions of athletes (wearing a certain pair of socks, or eating a certain food before a big game) are the product of the success that followed these behaviors in the past, as the athletes themselves will admit.

Problems with the "Stop-Action Principle"

Despite the evidence in its favor, it has long been recognized that the stop-action principle has its problems. A number of classic experiments demonstrated that animals learn much more than a single pattern of movements during the course of operant conditioning. In a study by Muenzinger (1928), guinea pigs had to run down an alley and then press a lever in order to obtain a piece of lettuce. Over hundreds of trials, Muenzinger observed the movements a guinea pig used to press the lever, classifying them into three categories—pressing with the left paw, pressing with the right paw, and gnawing on the lever with the teeth. He reasoned that one of these three categories should eventually dominate the others. To see why, suppose that in the first 50 trials there were 25 left-paw responses, 20 right-paw responses, and 5 teeth responses. These early responses might reflect nothing more than a slight initial preference for the left paw. But since each response is supposedly strengthened by reinforcement, and since the left-paw response received more strenthenings than right-paw responses, the animal's initial preference for the left paw would be amplified. On the second 50 trials we might expect to see perhaps 30 left-paw responses, 18 right-paw responses, and 2 teeth responses. On later trials, the additional strengthening of left-paw responses should make this behavior more and more frequent.

Muenzinger's results did not follow this pattern, however. Most of his subjects displayed response styles that varied unaccountably over trials, with left-paw responses in the majority at some times, right-paw responses at other times, and teeth responses at still other times. The stop-action principle offers no way to explain this variability in response styles.

One interpretation of Muenzinger's results might run as follows: Reinforcement strengthens, not one particular movement pattern, but an entire class of interchangeable movements. The three response types Muenzinger observed are all members of the same class because they all have the same effect on the environment—the lever is depressed. Therefore, when one member of the class (for example, a right-paw response) is reinforced, the future probability of all members of the class are strengthened. This analysis provides no explanation of the fluctuations in response types observed by Muenzinger; instead, it treats them as uninteresting, random variations within a class of interchangeable behaviors.

Lashley (1924) conducted a series of studies that provided stronger evidence for this view that reinforcing one specific behavior strengthens an entire class of behaviors with equivalent functions. In one study, rats had to wade through a maze filled with a few inches of water to reach a food reward. After the rats had learned to travel through the maze without errors, the water level was raised so that the rats had to swim instead of wade. If all the rats had learned was a specific set of muscle movements, it would be necessary for them to learn the maze anew, since the muscle movements of swimming are quite different from those used in wading. However, no such relearning was necessary, and the subjects swam through the maze correctly on their first trial with the deeper water. Lashley concluded that what rats learn in a maze is a sequence of turns, each of which brings them closer to the goal. This sequence of turns is not linked to any single pattern of muscle movements.

Studies such as those of Muenzinger and Lashley showed that even the simplest operant responses exhibit a remarkable degree of adaptability and flexibility. If you are not impressed with this flexibility, consider how difficult it would be to build a robot with similar adaptability of movement. If you happen to be skilled in mechanics and electronics, given sufficient time and money you might be able to build a robot that could walk through a maze and learn from its incorrect turns. Yet imagine how much more difficult it would be to build a robot with the adaptability of movement possessed by an average mammal. Such a robot would be able to swim through the maze if it were flooded, to hop on one foot if the other foot were injured, to crawl using its arms and elbows if both legs were paralyzed, and so on. The task of building such a skillful robot would be immense. Similarly, the task of discovering how animals can exhibit such flexibility of movement has proven to be a difficult one for psychologists and physiologists. Chapter 13 will survey some of what is known about how animals and people learn to perform new skilled movements.

THE PROCEDURE OF SHAPING, OR SUCCESSIVE APPROXIMATIONS

Whereas the experiments of Guthrie and Horton favored the view that a specific set of muscle movements and bodily positions was strengthened at the moment of reinforcement, Figures 6-3 and 6-4 show that in its strictest sense this viewpoint is incorrect. Although the stereotyped nature of these cats' behaviors is unmistakable, a certain amount of variability in bodily position from trial to trial is evident as well. This variability in behavior might annoy a meticulous theorist interested in predicting behaviors precisely, but it is actually an indispensable commodity for psychological researchers, animal trainers, and behavior therapists. Variability in behavior provides the means by which a totally new behavior, never performed by an individual before, can gradually be developed. The procedure that makes use of behavioral variability is known as *shaping* or the *technique of successive approximations.*

Shaping Lever Pressing in a Rat

Suppose that as part of your laboratory work in a psychology course, you are given a rat in an experimental chamber equipped with a lever the rat can press and a pellet dispenser. You have a remote-control button that, when pressed, delivers one food pellet to the food tray in the chamber. Your task is to train the rat to press the lever at a modest rate. Since you have learned about Thorndike's experiments, you may believe that this task will be very simple: Your strategy is simply to wait until the rat presses the lever by accident and then deliver a food pellet. This reinforcer should strengthen the response of pressing the lever, and your plan is to deliver a food pellet for every lever press, thereby gradually increasing the probability of this response.

Although this plan sounds reasonable, there are at least two ways it might fail. Suppose that after a few minutes in the chamber your rat presses the lever, and you immediately press the button to deliver a food pellet. However, the operation of the pellet dispenser makes a loud click

that startles the rat and causes it to freeze for 10 or 15 seconds. It is only about a minute later that the animal finally discovers the food pellet in the tray and eats it. We have seen that the contiguity between response and reinforcer is an important requirement of the Law of Effect—whatever behavior immediately precedes reinforcement will be strengthened. In this case the behavior that immediately preceded the rat's discovery of the food pellet was not pressing the lever (as you had intended) but rather approaching the food tray. If it did anything, the reinforcer may have strengthened the rat's tendency to approach or explore the food tray.

The problem is that you need a reinforcer that you can be sure the animal will receive immediately after the correct response is made. A common solution to this problem is to develop the sound of the pellet dispenser into a *conditioned reinforcer.* A conditioned reinforcer is a previously neutral stimulus that has acquired the capacity to strengthen responses because that stimulus has been repeatedly paired with food or some other *primary reinforcer.* (A primary reinforcer is a stimulus that naturally strengthens any response it follows. Primary reinforcers include food, water, sexual pleasure, and comfort.) If you repeatedly expose your subject to the sound of the pellet dispenser followed by the delivery of a food pellet, the sound of the dispenser should become a conditioned reinforcer. You can be sure that this has been accomplished when the rat will quickly return to the food tray from any part of the chamber as soon as you operate the dispenser.

At this point, your initial plan might work. If you present the sound of the dispenser immediately after the rat presses the lever, the response of lever pressing should be strengthened. However, there is yet another difficulty you might encounter. Suppose the lever is five inches above the floor of the chamber, and it takes an effortful push from your subject to fully depress the lever. Under these circumstances, you might wait for hours and the rat might never depress the lever. And of course, you cannot reinforce a response that never occurs.

It is in this situation that the variability inherent in behavior becomes helpful. A good way to start would be to wait until the rat is below the lever and then to reinforce any detectable upward head movement. After five or ten reinforcers for such a movement, the rat will probably exhibit an upward head movement soon after consuming the previous food pellet. Once this behavior is well established, the procedure of shaping consists of gradually making your criterion for reinforcement more demanding. For example, the next step might be to wait for an upward head movement of at least one-half inch. At first your subject may make a few head movements of less than one-half inch (which you do not reinforce), but because of the variability in such behaviors a movement of the required size will most likely occur. Each reinforcement of such a larger movement will increase the probability of another similar response, and soon the rat will be making these responses regularly. You can then go on to demand upward movements of one inch, one and one-half inches, and so on, until the animal is bringing its head close to the lever. The next step might be to require some actual contact with the lever, then contact with one forepaw, then some downward movement of the lever, and so on, until the rat has learned to make a full lever press.

Figure 6-5 provides a graphic illustration of how the procedure of shaping makes use of the variability in the subject's behavior. Suppose that before beginning the shaping process, you simply observed the rat's behavior for five minutes, making an estimate every five seconds about the height of the rat's head above the floor of the chamber. Figure 6-5 provides an example of what you might find: The y-axis shows the height of the rat's head to the nearest half inch, and the x-axis shows the number of times this height occurred in the five-minute sample. The resulting frequency distribution indicates that the rat usually kept its head about 1.5 inches from the floor, but sometimes its head was lower and sometimes much higher. Given such a distribution, it might make sense to start the shaping process with a requirement that the rat raise its head to a height of at least 2.5 inches before it is reinforced. Figure 6-5 also illustrates how the frequency distribution would probably shift after the shaping process began.

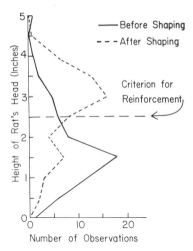

FIGURE 6-5. Hypothetical distributions showing the height of a rat's head as observed at regular intervals before shaping (solid line) and after selective reinforcement of head heights greater than 2.5 inches (dotted line). Rachlin (1970) presents a similar analysis of the shaping process.

Shaping Behaviors in the Classroom

The procedure of successive approximations can be used to produce totally new behaviors in people as well as in laboratory rats. At many colleges and universities, there are stories about how the students in a large lecture course collaborated to shape the behavior of their professor. In one such story, a professor who usually stood rigidly behind the lectern was reinforced by his students for any movement, and by the end of the hour he was pacing back and forth and gesturing wildly with his arms. I happen to know more details about a similar story at Harvard, where at one time the professor in an introductory psychology course lectured from an elevated stage. The students secretly agreed to reinforce the professor for any movement to the left. The reinforcers they used were listening attentively, nodding their heads in apparent understanding of what he was saying, and taking notes. Whenever the professor moved to the right, however, they stopped delivering these reinforcers—they would stop taking notes, yawn, look bored, and look around the room. This systematic delivery of reinforcers for movement to the left was apparently quite successful, for legend has it that about halfway through the lecture the professor fell off the left side of the stage (which was only about 18 inches high).

Stories of this type suggest that shaping can work even when the subject is unaware of what is going on. If the professors in these stories realized what their students were doing, they probably would have resisted this behavioral control (perhaps on the stubborn belief that it is the behavior of students that should be shaped in the classroom, not the professor's).

Shaping Speech in an Institutionalized Adult

Not all examples of shaping are as frivolous as those described in the last section. Shaping is frequently used in behavior therapy for individuals with severe behavior problems. As one example, Isaacs, Thomas, and Goldiamond (1960) used this procedure to reinstate speech in a 40-year-old patient in a mental institution. This patient, who was classified as a catatonic schizophrenic, had not spoken at all since he entered the institution 19 years earlier. At this point, a behavior therapist began to work with the patient, meeting with him about three times a week. More or less by accident, the therapist found that gum could be used as a reinforcer for this patient.

During the first two weeks, the therapist would hold up a stick of gum and wait for the patient's eyes to look toward the gum. As soon as they did, he would give the patient the gum. By the end of the second week, the patient's eyes looked toward the gum as soon as it was presented. In the third and fourth weeks, the therapist's criterion was any detectable lip movement, and soon lip movements occurred as soon as the gum was presented. The therapist then required any audible vocalization before giving the gum, and then attempted to get the patient to say the word *gum* by holding up the gum and saying, "Say gum, gum." At the end of the sixth week, the patient suddenly said, "Gum, please." He

subsequently answered questions about his name and age.

This patient's case was by no means a total success, because after additional reinforcement procedures he began to talk to other members of the hospital staff but not to other patients or visitors. The difference between these two classes of individuals was that the hospital staff was instructed to respond only to verbal communications of the patient, whereas patients and visitors would reinforce the patient's silent gestures by attempting to understand them and give the patient what he wanted. Of course, these two patterns of behavior provide further support for the effects of reinforcement on the patient's verbal behavior: He would speak in those situations where only speech was reinforced, but he would communicate with gestures in those situations where gestures were reinforced with attention and compliance with his requests.

Some might find it interesting to speculate why this patient had been mute for so many years. In light of his rapid recovery of speech after the first word was spoken, it seems unlikely that the patient was unable to speak. Was it the case, however, that he believed he was unable to speak? Was he mute because he was reinforced for his silence, or because he was punished in some way when he did speak? Unfortunately, we will never know the answers to these questions. What we do know, however, is that 19 years of the standard hospital treatment (along with whatever "common sense" strategies the hospital staff may have used to try to encourage speech) were totally unsuccessful for this patient. In contrast, after only 18 one-hour sessions of behavior therapy, a modest level of speech was restored. Although the technique of successive approximations may sound simple, it is by no means a procedure that is so obvious that it occurs to every professional in the field of mental health. The literature on behavior modification records many such cases where the use of shaping or some other straightforward behavioral technique was never considered by those in charge of a patient, but where the patient made rapid progress once the recommendations of a specialist in behavior modification were followed.

Versatility of the Shaping Process

We have already seen that the applicability of classical conditioning is relatively limited as a theory of learned behaviors: Classical conditioning applies only to those behaviors that are reliably elicited by some stimulus (the US). In comparison, the Law of Effect is much more widely applicable, even if we consider only the strict stop-action approach favored by Guthrie and Horton. The stop-action principle applies not only to behaviors that are preceded by a specific stimulus but to any behavior the subject produces. As long as a behavior such as pressing a lever, stepping on a platform, or pulling a chain occurs once in a while, we can patiently wait for the desired behavior to occur, follow it with a reinforcer, and the frequency of that behavior should increase. To put it simply, the stop-action principle can be used to increase the frequency of any behavior that is part of the subject's repertoire. However, once the procedure of shaping is added to the Law of Effect, its applicability is extended still further. The procedure of shaping utilizes the variability inherent in a creature's behavior to develop totally new behaviors, which the subject has never performed before and probably would never perform in the absence of a shaping program. For instance, a rat can be taught to press a lever that is high above its head, or one that requires so much effort to operate that the animal must get a running start and throw all of its weight onto the lever. In principle, at least, the applicability of the shaping process is limited only by the capabilities of the subject—if the subject is capable of making the desired behavior, the careful employment of the technique of successive approximations should eventually be successful in producing the appearance of the behavior.

THE RESEARCH OF B. F. SKINNER

Whereas Thorndike deserves credit for the first systematic investigations of the principle of reinforcement, it was B. F. Skinner who was primarily responsible for the increasing interest in this topic during the middle of the twentieth century. Skinner himself discovered many of the most basic and most important properties of reinforcement. In addition, he trained several generations of students whose ongoing research continues to enrich our knowledge about the ways that reinforcement affects the behavior of people and animals.

Skinner used the terms *operant conditioning* or *instrumental conditioning* to describe the procedure in which a behavior is strengthened through reinforcement. Both of these terms reflect the large degree of control the subject has over the most important stimulus in the environment—the reinforcer. The delivery of the reinforcer is contingent on the subject's behavior—no reinforcer will occur until the subject makes the required response. For example, in Thorndike's puzzle box the reinforcer (escape and food) might occur after 5 seconds or after 500 seconds, depending entirely on when the animal made the appropriate response. The term *operant conditioning* reflects the fact that the subject obtains reinforcement by operating on the environment in this paradigm. The term *instrumental conditioning* is suggestive of the fact that the subject is instrumental in obtaining the reinforcer.

The Free Operant

In his research on operant conditioning, Skinner modified Thorndike's procedure in a simple but very important way. Research with the puzzle box involved a *discrete trial procedure*: A trial began each time a subject was placed in the puzzle box, and the subject could make one and only one response on each trial. The primary dependent variable was response latency. After each trial the experimenter had to intervene, physically returning the subject to the puzzle box for the next trial. This procedure was time-consuming and cumbersome, and only a small number of trials could be conducted each day (due to the fatigue of both subject and experimenter). Other operant conditioning procedures that were popular in the early part of the century, such as those involving runways or mazes with a reinforcer at the end, shared these same disadvantages.

Skinner's innovation was to make use of a response that the subject could perform repeatedly without the intervention of the experimenter. When experimenting with rats, researchers of the Skinnerian tradition typically use lever pressing as the operant response. When the subjects are pigeons, the most frequently measured response is the *key peck*: One or more circular plastic disks, called response keys, are recessed in one wall of the experimental chamber (see Figure 6-6), and the bird's pecks at these keys are recorded. Procedures that make use of lever pressing, key pecking, or similar responses are called *free operant procedures*, so as to distinguish them from the discrete trial procedures of the puzzle box or maze. The distinguishing characteristics of a free operant procedure are that (1) the operant response can occur at any time, and (2) the operant response can occur repeatedly for as long as the subject remains in the experimental chamber. Indeed, responses such as lever pressing and key pecking require so little effort that a subject can make thousands of responses in a single session. Along with this change in procedures came a change in independent variables: Instead of using latency as a measure of response strength, Skinner used *response rate* (most commonly measured as responses per minute). One major advantage of the free operant procedure,

FIGURE 6-6. A pigeon pecking at a lighted key in a typical operant conditioning chamber. Grain is provided as a reinforcer through the square opening beneath the key.

with its large number of responses, is that the experimenter can observe and record the moment-to-moment variations in response rate that occur as a subject learns about the experimental situation or as some external stimulus is changed.

Critics of the Skinnerian paradigm often point to the artificiality of the typical operant conditioning chamber. It is certainly true that the natural environments of pigeons, rats, and people bear little resemblance to the barren experimental chambers used in most operant research. Rats in the wild do not obtain their food by pressing levers, and pigeons do not do so by pecking at illuminated plastic disks. Since Skinner was certainly aware of these facts, why did he choose to study behavior in this way? To make sure that you are not puzzled by the rationale behind the Skinnerian approach to research, let us recapitulate some of the points discussed in Chapter 1. First of all, the use of an artificial, simplified environment is one of the most universal characteristics of scientific research. The reason for creating an artificial environment is to give the experimenter as much control as possible over the independent variables, and to eliminate as many of the confounding variables as possible. Furthermore, Skinner's selection of the "unnatural" responses of lever pressing and key pecking was deliberate. His purpose was to investigate general principles of operant conditioning, principles that applied to many different species, many different behaviors, and many different reinforcers. He assumed that such general principles could be discovered by selecting on a more or less arbitrary basis any species of subject, any response, and any reinforcer.

Of course, the burden of proving that it is possible to discover general principles of learning in the operant conditioning chamber rests with those who conduct such experiments. Operant conditioners have provided such evidence in at least three ways. First, if a particular characteristic of operant behavior can be demonstrated with several fairly different species, albeit in a laboratory setting, this in itself constitutes evidence that a principle with some cross-species generality has been discovered. The early volumes of the *Journal of the Experimental Analysis of Behavior*, a journal devoted to operant research, contain considerable evidence of this type. One study might employ a particular reinforcement procedure with pigeons as subjects, and other studies might employ the same type of procedure with rats, children, or retarded adults. In most cases the similarity of results across different species was unmistakable. A second line of evidence involves drawing parallels between laboratory experiments and real-world situations that have similar rules for the delivery of reinforcement. What must be shown is that there are similarities in the behaviors produced in these two situations. A later section of this chapter, which discusses reinforcement schedules, draws a number of parallels of this type. A third type of evidence consists of showing that principles of operant conditioning that were discovered in the laboratory can be used in behavior therapy to modify problem behaviors. Several applications of this type are discussed at the end of this chapter.

The Three-Term Contingency

In its simplest form, a contingency is a rule that states that some event, B, will occur if and only if another event, A, occurs. Simple classical conditioning provides one example of such a contingency: The US will occur if and only if the CS first occurs. It is sometimes said that in operant conditioning, there is a contingency between response and reinforcer—the reinforcer occurs if and only if the response occurs. Skinner pointed out, however, that there are actually three components in the operant conditioning contingency: (1) the context or situation in which a response occurs (that is, those stimuli that precede the response), (2) the response itself, and (3) the stimuli that follow the response (that is, the reinforcer). To be more specific, Skinner noted that the contingency in operant conditioning usually takes the following form: In the presence of a specific stimulus, often called a *discriminative stimulus*, the reinforcer will occur if and only if the operant response occurs. Because of the three components—discriminative stimulus, response, and reinforcer—Skinner called this relationship a *three-term contingency*.

Suppose a pigeon learns to peck a key for food pellets in a chamber that has a bright yellow light just above the key. When the light is on, each response produces a food pellet, but when the light is off, no food pellets are delivered. If the light is periodically turned on and off during the course of the experiment, the pigeon will learn to discriminate between these two conditions and respond only when the light is on. This type of discrimination learning is important in many real-world situations, because a response that is reinforced in one context may not be reinforced in another. For example, a child must learn that the behavior of telling jokes may be reinforced if it occurs during recess but punished if it occurs during math class. The term *stimulus control* refers to the broad topic of how stimuli that precede a behavior can control the occurrence of that behavior. Chapter 10 will examine this topic in detail.

Other Basic Principles: Acquisition, Extinction, Spontaneous Recovery, Generalization, and Conditioned Reinforcement

All of these principles have counterparts in classical conditioning that we have already examined, so a brief discussion of them will suffice here. Thorndike's results (as in Figure 6-2) demonstrate that the acquisition of an operant response, like that of a CR, is usually a gradual process. In operant conditioning, the procedure of extinction involves no longer following the operant response with a reinforcer, and as in classical conditioning the response will weaken and eventually disappear. If the subject is returned to the experimental chamber at some later time, spontaneous recovery of the operant response will typically be observed. Thus the idealized response patterns shown in Figure 4-6 could represent the acquisition, extinction, and spontaneous recovery of an operant response just as well as a classically conditioned response.

In the preceding section, we saw that discrimination learning can occur in operant conditioning as well as in classical conditioning. The opposite of discrimination, generalization, is also a common phenomenon in operant conditioning. Let us return to the example of the pigeon that learned to discriminate between the presence and absence of a bright yellow light. Suppose the color of the light were now changed to green or orange, and no more reinforcers were delivered. Despite this change in color, the subject would probably continue to peck at the key for a while, until it learned that no more reinforcers were forthcoming. In other words, the pigeon generalized from the yellow light to a light of another color, even though it had never been reinforced for pecking in the presence of this other color. If we tested a number of different colors, we would probably obtain a typical generalization gradient in which responding was most rapid in the presence of yellow and less and less rapid with colors less and less similar to yellow.

In operant conditioning, the phenomenon of conditioned reinforcement (also called *secondary reinforcement*) is in many ways analogous to second-order classical conditioning. As discussed in Chapter 4, if some CS, (such as a light), is repeatedly paired with a US, that CS can then take the place of the US in classical conditioning with a second CS, (say, a tone). If the tone is now repeatedly paired with a light, the tone will start to elicit CRs, which is the same thing that would happen if the tone were paired with the US itself. We might say that the first-order CS, the light, acts as a surrogate for the US in second-order conditioning. In operant conditioning, the counterpart to the US is the primary reinforcer. The counterpart to the first-order CS is the initially neutral stimulus that becomes a conditioned reinforcer through repeated pairings with the primary reinforcer. The conditioned reinforcer can then act as a surrogate for the primary reinforcer, increasing the strength of any response that it follows. In an early study on conditioned reinforcement, Skinner (1938) presented rats with repeated pairings of a clicking sound and food. No responses were required of the subjects during this phase of the experiment. In the second phase of the experiment, food was no longer presented; nevertheless, the rats learned to press a lever when this response produced only the clicking sound. Of course, since the clicking sound was no longer paired with food, it is not surprising that the lever pressing did not persist for long. This is another way in which first-order CSs and conditioned reinforcers are similar: If a conditioned reinforcer is no longer paired with a primary reinforcer it eventually loses its capacity to act as a reinforcer, just as a first-order CS loses its ability to condition a second-order CS if it is repeatedly presented without the US.

Skinner used the term *generalized reinforcers* to refer to a special class of conditioned reinforcers—those that are associated with a large number of different primary reinforcers. Perhaps the best example of a generalized reinforcer is money. The potency of this reinforcer in maintaining the behaviors of workers in our society is clear— few employees would remain on the job if informed that their employer could no longer pay them any salary. Money is a generalized reinforcer (and a very powerful one) precisely because it can be exchanged for so many different stimuli that are inherently reinforcing for most people—food, clothing, material possessions, entertainment, exciting vacations. Although money is a powerful reinforcer, it should be clear that its power, like that of all conditioned reinforcers, is dependent on its continued association with primary reinforcers. If money could no longer be exchanged for any primary reinforcers, it would be difficult to find individuals who were willing to work simply to obtain green pieces of paper.

Some everyday human behaviors are maintained by conditioned reinforcers that are several times removed from any primary reinforcer. Consider a college student who is diligently studying for an upcoming midterm exam in elementary calculus. If there is nothing inherently reinforcing about studying calculus for this student, why is the behavior occurring? Skinner would attribute this behavior to the student's past experience with the conditioned reinforcer of a good grade—the student has presumably had numerous experiences throughout her life in which studying for an exam was followed by a good grade on the exam. A good grade on an exam is not a primary reinforcer, however; it simply brings the student one step closer to another conditioned reinforcer—a good final grade in the course. A good course grade makes it more likely that the woman will obtain a good job after graduation (another conditioned reinforcer), which will provide a decent salary (another conditioned reinforcer), which can finally be exchanged for a wide range of primary reinforcers. Considering all the steps that separate the behavior of studying from primary reinforcement, it is not surprising that this behavior has a low frequency of occurrence among some students, especially when they have no inherent interest in the subject matter of a course.

Response Chains

In Chapter 3, we examined the concept of a reaction chain, which is a sequence of innate behaviors that occur in a fixed order. A similar concept involving learned behaviors is the *response chain*, which is defined as a sequence of behaviors that must occur in a specific order, with the primary reinforcer being delivered only after the final response of the sequence. Some of the clearest examples of response chains are displayed by animals trained to perform complex sequences of behavior for circus acts or other public performances. Imagine a hypothetical performance in which a rat climbs a ladder to a platform, pulls a rope that opens a door to a tunnel, runs through the tunnel to another small platform, slides down a chute, runs to a lever, presses the lever, and finally receives a pellet of food.

Ignoring for the moment how the rat could be trained to do this, we can ask what maintains the behavior once it has been learned. The first response, climbing the ladder, brings the rat to nothing more than a platform and a rope. These are certainly not primary reinforcers for a rat. Skinner would claim, however, that these stimuli act as conditioned reinforcers for the response of climbing the ladder because they bring the animal closer to primary reinforcement than it was before. Besides serving as conditioned reinforcers, the platform and rope also act as discriminative stimuli for the next response of the chain, pulling the rope. The conditioned reinforcer for this response is the sight of the door opening, for this event brings the subject still closer to primary reinforcement. Like the platform and rope, the open door also serves a second function—it is a discriminative stimulus for the next response, running through the tunnel. We could go on to analyze the rest of the response chain in a similar fashion, but the general pattern should be clear by now. Each stimulus in the middle of a response chain is assumed to serve two functions: It is a conditioned reinforcer for the previous response and a discriminative stimulus for the next response of the chain. This analysis is depicted graphically in Figure 6-7, where S^D stands for

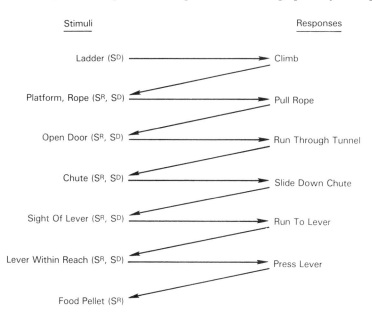

Stimuli   Responses

Ladder (S^D) ————————————→ Climb

Platform, Rope (S^R, S^D) ←———————→ Pull Rope

Open Door (S^R, S^D) ←———————————→ Run Through Tunnel

Chute (S^R, S^D) ←————————————→ Slide Down Chute

Sight Of Lever (S^R, S^D) ←——————→ Run To Lever

Lever Within Reach (S^R, S^D) ←——→ Press Lever

Food Pellet (S^R) ←

FIGURE 6-7. The alternating sequence of stimuli and responses in the hypothetical response chain described in the text. Each stimulus within the chain serves as a conditioned reinforcer for the previous response and as a discriminative stimulus for the next response.

"discriminative stimulus" and S^R stands for "reinforcing stimulus."

How would an animal trainer go about teaching a rat to perform this sequence? One very effective strategy, sometimes called *backward chaining*, is to start with the last response of the chain and work backward. After teaching the rat where to obtain its food reinforcement and establishing the sound of the food dispenser as a conditioned reinforcer, the trainer could start to shape the last response of the chain, pressing the lever. Once this response was well established, the trainer might place the rat on the bottom of the chute. It is very likely that the rat would move from this position to the lever, since the lever will now act as a conditioned reinforcer (having been previously paired with food). By additional shaping, the rat could be trained to slide down the chute to reach the lever, then to travel through the tunnel to reach the chute, and so on. Some shaping with food as a primary reinforcer might be required for some links of the chain (for instance, pulling the rope). Once the response was established, however, the primary reinforcement could be removed and the behavior would be maintained by the conditioned reinforcement provided by the next stimulus of the chain, a stimulus that signalled that the animal was one step closer to the primary reinforcer.

A comparison of this sort of learned response chain and innate reaction chains (for example, the shell-selection behaviors of the hermit crab described in Chapter 3) reveals both similarities and differences. Both innate and learned behavior sequences consist of an alternating pattern of stimuli and responses (compare Figure 3-5 with Figure 6-7). In both cases, each successive stimulus acts to terminate the preceding behavior and to "set the occasion" for the next behavior of the chain. Because of this property, each stimulus in a response chain might be called a sub-goal, and it should be clear that we could characterize a learned response chain as a series of feedback loops, just as the hermit crab's reaction chain was so characterized in Chapter 3 (see Figure 3-6). A major difference between innate and learned response chains, however, is that only the latter depends on reinforcement for its continued integrity. If a reaction chain is completely in-

nate, its component behaviors are not dependent on any external reinforcer, nor can they be modified by experience—each behavior will continue to be highly probable whenever its eliciting stimuli are present. In contrast, the behaviors of a learned response chain will eventually disappear if the primary reinforcement is eliminated. It is also interesting to observe what happens if one of the conditioned reinforcers in the middle of the chain is eliminated. The general rule is that all behaviors that occur before the "broken link" of the chain will be extinguished, whereas those that occur after the broken link will continue to occur. For example, suppose that pulling the rope no longer opens the door to the tunnel. The response of rope pulling will eventually stop occurring, as will the behavior of climbing the ladder that leads to the platform and rope. On the other hand, if the rat is placed beyond the broken link (inside the tunnel or at the top of the chute), the remainder of the chain should continue to occur as long as the final response is followed by the primary reinforcer. Because they are the furthest from the primary reinforcer, responses near the beginning of a response chain should be the weakest, or the most easily disrupted. Behavior therapists frequently make use of this principle when attempting to break up a response chain that includes some unwanted behaviors (such as walking to the drugstore, buying a pack of cigarettes, opening the pack, lighting a cigarette, and smoking it). Efforts to interrupt this chain should be most effective if applied to the earliest links of the chain.

REINFORCEMENT SCHEDULES

Among Skinner's many achievements, one of his most noteworthy was his categorization and experimental analysis of *reinforcement schedules*. A reinforcement schedule is simply a rule that states under what conditions a reinforcer will be delivered. To this point, we have considered only one such rule, where *every* occurrence of the operant response is followed by a reinforcer. This schedule is called *continuous reinforcement* (abbreviated CRF), but it is only one of an infinite number of possible rules for delivering a reinforcer. The real world provides numerous examples of situations in which a particular response is sometimes but not always followed by a reinforcer. A predator may make several unsuccessful attempts to catch a prey before it finally obtains a meal. A salesman may knock on several doors in vain for every time he succeeds in selling a magazine subscription. A typist may type dozens of pages, comprised of thousands of individual keystrokes, before finally receiving payment for a completed job. Recognizing that most behaviors outside the laboratory receive only intermittent reinforcement, Skinner devoted considerable effort to the investigation of how different schedules of reinforcement produce different patterns of behavior (Ferster & Skinner, 1957).

Plotting Moment-to-Moment Behavior: The Cumulative Recorder

Besides developing the free operant procedure, which makes it possible to collect a large amount of data from a single subject each session, Skinner constructed a simple mechanical device, the *cumulative recorder*, which records these responses in a way that allows any observer to see at a glance the moment-to-moment pat-

terns of a subject's behavior. Figure 6-8 shows how the cumulative recorder works. A slowly rotating cylinder pulls a roll of paper beneath a pen at a steady rate, so the x-axis of the resultant graph, the *cumulative record*, represents time. If the subject makes no response, a horizontal line is the result. However, each response causes the pen to move up the page by a small increment (in a direction perpendicular to the movement of the paper), so the y-axis represents the cumulative number of responses the subject has made since the start of the session. For instance, if every response moves the pen 0.01 inches up the page, and if the height of the graph is 5.6 inches above its starting position, we know that the subject has made 560 responses so far.

As Figure 6-8 shows, a cumulative record tells much more than the overall number of responses. Segments of the record that have a fairly even linear appearance correspond to periods in which the subject was responding at a steady rate—the greater the slope, the faster the response rate. Figure 6-8 also shows how an acceleration or deceleration in response rate would appear in the cumulative record. Finally, small downward deflections in a cumulative record generally indicate those times at which a reinforcer was delivered. With these points in mind, we can

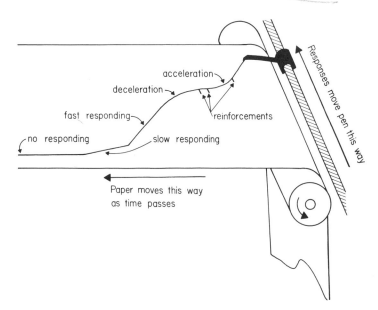

FIGURE 6-8. A simplified drawing of a cumulative recorder and the type of graph it produces.

now examine how the schedule of reinforcement determines a subject's pattern of responding.

The Four Simple Reinforcement Schedules

Fixed Ratio. The rule for reinforcement in a fixed ratio (FR) schedule is that a reinforcer is delivered after every *n* responses, where *n* is the size of the ratio. For example, in a FR 20 schedule, every 20 responses will be followed by a reinforcer. If an animal begins with a FR 1 schedule (which is the same as continuous reinforcement) and then the ratio is gradually increased, the subject can be trained to make many responses for each reinforcer. For example, many animals will respond for food reinforcement on FR schedules where 100 or more responses are required for each reinforcer. The behavior of many species (including pigeons, rats, monkeys, and human beings) on FR schedules have been studied, and in most cases the general characteristics of the behavior are similar. After a subject has performed on a FR schedule for some time and has become ac-

quainted with the requirements of the schedule, a distinctive pattern of responding develops. As Figure 6-9 shows, responding on a FR schedule exhibits a "stop-and-go" pattern: After each reinforcer, there is a pause in responding that is sometimes called a *postreinforcement pause.* Eventually this pause gives way to an abrupt continuation of responding. Once responding begins, the subject typically responds at a constant, rapid rate (note the steep slopes in the cumulative record) until the next reinforcer is delivered.

Outside the laboratory, perhaps the best example of fixed-ratio schedules is the "piecework" method used to pay factory workers in some companies. For instance, a worker operating a semiautomatic machine that makes door hinges might be paid 10 dollars for every 100 hinges made. As I worked in a factory for several summers while I was an undergraduate, I had the opportunity to observe workers who were paid by the piecework system. Their behavior was quite similar to the FR pattern shown in Figure 6-9. Once a worker started up the machine, he almost always worked steadily and rapidly until the counter on the machine indicated that 100 pieces

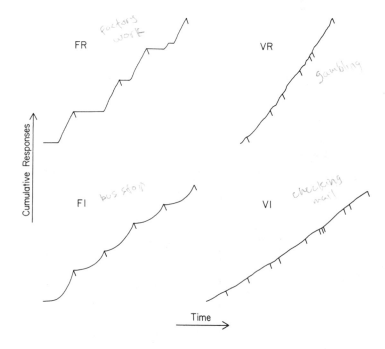

FIGURE 6-9. Idealized cumulative records showing the typical patterns of behavior generated by the four simple reinforcement schedules.

had been made. At this point, the worker would record the number completed on a work card and then take a break—he might chat with friends, have a soda or a cup of coffee, or glance at a newspaper for a few minutes. After this pause, the worker would turn on the machine and produce another 100 hinges. It is worth noting that these workers needed very little supervision from their boss. The boss did not have to prod them to work faster or chastise them for taking excessively long breaks. The schedule of reinforcement, which delivered reinforcers in direct proportion to the amount of work done, was sufficient to maintain the performance of these workers.

Several other features of performance on FR schedules deserve mention. First, the average size of the postreinforcement pause increases as the size of the ratio increases. For example, with a pigeon pecking a key, the average pause may be only a second or so with a FR 20 schedule, but it may be several minutes long with a FR 200 schedule. In contrast, the subject's rate of responding after the postreinforcement pause decreases fairly gradually as the size of the ratio increases (Crossman, Bonem, & Phelps, 1987; Powell, 1969). With very large ratios, however, the animal may start to exhibit long pauses at times other than right after reinforcement. The term *ratio strain* is sometimes used to describe the general weakening of responding that is found when large response:reinforcer ratios are used.

Other factors besides the size of the ratio also have a comparatively large effect on the size of the postreinforcement pause and little or no effect on response rate after the pause. For instance, the average pause will be shorter if a subject receives more food after completing each ratio (Powell, 1969), and longer if the subject's motivational level is lowered by giving it food before the experimental session (Sidman & Stebbins, 1954). In general, then, a subject's behavior on a FR schedule can be divided into two fairly distinct categories—either the subject is responding at a rapid, steady rate, or it is not responding at all. Variables such as ratio size and amount of reinforcement seem to change a subject's behavior mainly by determining the lengths of the pauses, and they

have less effect on the rate of steady responding once it begins.

Variable Ratio. The only difference between a FR schedule and a variable ratio (VR) schedule is that on the latter the number of required responses is not constant from reinforcer to reinforcer. To be specific, the rule for reinforcement on a VR *n* schedule is that *on the average*, a subject will receive one reinforcer for every *n* responses, but the exact number of responses required at any moment may vary widely. When an experiment is controlled by a computer, a VR schedule is sometimes implemented by giving the computer a list of possible ratio sizes from which it selects at random after each reinforcer to determine the number of responses required for the next reinforcer. For example, a list for VR 10 might contain the ratios 1, 2, 3, 4, 5, 6, 10, 19, and 40. In the long run an average of 10 responses will be required for each reinforcer, but on a given trial the required number may be as little as 1 or as large as 40. In a special type of VR schedule called a *random ratio* (RR) schedule, each response has an equal probability of reinforcement. For instance, in a RR 20 schedule every response has one chance in 20 of being reinforced regardless of how many responses have occurred since the last reinforcer.

Figure 6-9 shows a typical cumulative record from a VR schedule. The pattern of responding might be described as rapid and fairly steady. The major difference between FR performance and VR performance is the absence of long postreinforcement pauses on VR schedules. Although it is sometimes stated that there are no postreinforcement pauses on VR schedules, this is not strictly correct. With VR schedules of modest length, regular postreinforcement pauses are found (Kintsch, 1965; Webbe, DeWeese, & Malagodi, 1978); however, they are several times smaller than those found on FR schedules with equal response:reinforcer ratios (Mazur, 1983). Intuitively, the reason for the shorter postreinforcement pauses on VR schedules seems clear: After each reinforcer, there is at least a small possibility that another reinforcer will be delivered after only a few additional responses.

Many forms of gambling are examples of VR schedules. Games of chance such as slot machines, roulette wheels, and lotteries all exhibit the two important characteristics of VR schedules: (1) A person's chances of winning are directly proportional to the number of times the person plays, and (2) the number of responses required for the next reinforcer is uncertain. It is the combination of these two features that makes gambling an "addiction" for some people—gambling behavior is strong and persistent because the very next lottery ticket or the very next coin in a slot machine could turn a loser to a big winner. Ironically, the characteristics of a VR schedule are strong enough to offset the fact that in most forms of gambling the odds are against the player, so that the more one plays, the more one can be expected to lose.

Although games of chance are among the purest examples of VR schedules outside the laboratory, many other real-world activities, including most sports activities, have the properties of a VR schedule. Consider the behavior of playing golf. As one who is very fond of this activity, I know that this behavior is maintained by quite a few different reinforcers, such as companionship, exercise, sunshine, fresh air, and picturesque scenery. Most of these reinforcers are delivered on a schedule that is approximately continuous reinforcement—that is, they occur almost every time one goes golfing. Yet these are certainly not the only reinforcers at work, because each of these reinforcers could be obtained just as easily (and without paying greens fees) by taking a hike in the woods with friends. And although I also enjoy a walk in the woods, I can attest (as can, I am sure, millions of other golfers) that the game of golf offers additional reinforcers that a walk in the woods does not. These are the thrill and satisfaction that come from playing well, either through an entire round or on a single shot. Nearly every golfer can boast of a few outstanding shots, and of occasional days when every iron shot happened to land on the green and every putt seemed to drop. Regardless of what factors cause such occasional excellent performances, what is important from a behavioral perspective is that they are unpredictable. Each time a golfer walks to the first tee, there is a chance that this round will be his or her best. On each shot when the flagstick is within the golfer's range, there is a chance that the ball will end up in the hole or very close to it. This continual possibility of an outstanding round or at least a spectacular shot is probably an important reason why the average golfer keeps returning to the course again and again.

The long list of other behaviors that are reinforced on VR schedules includes: playing practically any competitive sport, fishing, hunting, playing card games or video games, watching the home team play, going to mixers. You should be able to see that the delivery of reinforcers for each of these activities fits the definition of a VR schedule: The occasion of the next reinforcer is unpredictable, but in the long run the more often the behavior occurs, the more rapidly will reinforcers be received.

Fixed Interval. In all interval schedules, the presentation of a reinforcer depends both on the subject's behavior and on the passage of time. The rule for reinforcement on a fixed interval (FI) schedule is that the first response after a fixed amount of time has elapsed is reinforced. For example, in a FI 60-second schedule, immediately after one reinforcer has been delivered a clock starts to time the next 60-second interval. It does not matter whether the subject makes no responses during this interval or 100 responses—none of them will do any good whatsoever. However, at the 60-second mark a reinforcer is "stored" (that is, the apparatus is now set to deliver a reinforcer), and the next response will produce the reinforcer. If the subject had either a perfect sense of time or access to a clock, the optimal behavior on a FI schedule would be to wait exactly 60 seconds and then make one response to collect the reinforcer. However, because no subject has a perfect sense of time and because a clock is usually not provided for the subject to watch, subjects on FI schedules typically make many more responses per reinforcer than the one that is required. Figure 6-9 shows the typical pattern of responding found on FI schedules. As on FR schedules, there is a postreinforcement pause, but after this pause the subject starts by responding quite slowly (unlike the abrupt switch to rapid responding on a FR schedule). As the interval progresses, the animal responds more and more rapidly, and just before reinforcement the response rate is quite rapid. For obvious reasons, the cumulative record pattern from this class of schedule is sometimes called a *fixed-interval scallop.*

The FI schedule has few close parallels outside the laboratory, because few real-world reinforcers occur on such a regular temporal cycle. However, one everyday behavior that approximates the typical FI pattern of accelerating responses is waiting for a bus. Imagine that you are walking to a bus stop, and that just as you arrive you see a bus leave. Suppose that you are not wearing a watch, but you know that a bus arrives at this stop every 20 minutes, so in the meantime you sit down on a bench and start to read a book. In this situation, the operant response is looking down the street for the next bus. The reinforcer for this response is simply the sight of the next bus. (This may seem like a fairly weak reinforcer, but once you see the bus coming you can walk up to the curb and make sure the driver sees you and stops.) At first, the response of looking for the bus may not occur at all, and you may read steadily for 5 or 10 minutes before your first glance down the street. Your next glance may occur one or two minutes later, and now you may look down the street every minute or so. After 15 minutes you may put away the book and stare down the street almost continuously until the bus arrives.

Other situations in which important events occur at regular intervals can produce similar patterns of accelerating behavior. In a clever experiment, Mawhinney, Bostow, Laws, Blumenfeld, and Hopkins (1971) examined one such situation. These researchers measured the study behavior of college students in a psychology course, and they found that the pattern of this behavior varied quite predictably depending on the schedule of examinations. As mentioned earlier, the conditioned reinforcer of a good grade on an exam is an important reinforcer for studying. So that the students' study behavior could be measured, all the readings for the course were available only in a special room in the library, and the materials could not be taken out of this

room. The amount of time each student spent studying in this room was recorded by observers who watched through a one-way mirror.

During the first two weeks of the course, a short quiz (worth 5 points) was scheduled for each class meeting. In the next three weeks there were no quizzes, but a longer exam (worth 60 points) was given at the end of the third week. The second half of the term mimicked the first half, with two weeks of daily quizzes followed by three weeks with a large exam at the end. The weeks with daily quizzes approximated a CRF schedule of reinforcement, for every day of studying might be reinforced with a good grade on the next day's quiz. The exams after three weeks were more like a FI schedule, for there was no immediate reinforcer for studying during the early parts of the three-week period. This arrangement is not exactly like a FI schedule, because on a FI schedule no response except the last has any effect, whereas studying early in the three-week period presumably had some beneficial effect in terms of the grade on the exam. Despite this difference, Figure 6-10 shows that the patterns of the students' study behavior during the two three-week periods were similar to typical FI performance—there was little studying during the early parts of the three-week period, but the amount of studying steadily increased as the exam approached. In contrast, study behavior was more stable from day to day when the students had daily quizzes. This experiment demonstrates that an instructor's selection of a schedule of quizzes or exams can have a large effect on the study behavior of the students in the course. If an instructor wants students to study at a steady pace throughout the term, the common method of scheduling a few widely spaced exams is not optimal.

Variable Interval. Variable interval (VI) schedules are like FI schedules except that the amount of time that must pass before a reinforcer is stored varies unpredictably from reinforcer to reinforcer. For example, in a VI 60-second schedule, the time between the delivery of one reinforcer and the storage of another might be 6 seconds for one reinforcer, then 300 seconds for the next, 40 seconds for the next, and so on. As

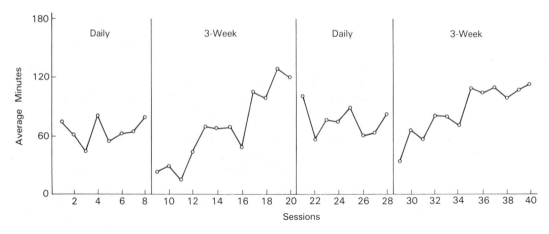

FIGURE 6-10. The results obtained by Mawhinney et al. (1971) in their experiment on the study habits of college students. The y-axis shows the average number of minutes of study per day when the instructor gave daily quizzes, and when a larger exam was given at the end of a three-week period.

on FI schedules, the first response to occur after a reinforcer is stored collects that reinforcer, and the clock does not start again until the reinforcer is collected.

As Figure 6-9 shows, VI schedules typically produce a steady, moderate response rate. At an intuitive level, this manner of responding seems sensible in light of the characteristics of the schedule. Since a reinforcer might be stored at any moment, a long pause after reinforcement would not be advantageous. By maintaining a steady response rate, the subject will collect each reinforcer soon after it is stored, thus keeping the VI clock moving most of the time. On the other hand, a very high response rate, such as that observed on a VR schedule, would produce only a minor increase in the rate of reinforcement.

An example of an everyday behavior that is maintained by a VI schedule of reinforcement is checking for mail. The reinforcer in this situation is simply the receipt of mail. Most people receive mail on some days but not on others, and the days when one will find something reinforcing (such as letters, as opposed to junk mail or bills) in the mailbox are usually impossible to predict. The delivery of mail approximates a VI schedule because (1) it is unpredictable, (2) if a reinforcer is stored (the mail has been delivered)

only one response is required to collect it, and (3) if the reinforcer has not yet been stored, no amount of responding will bring it forth. The resultant behavior is moderate and steady: Most people check the mail every day, but only once a day (or at most only a few times a day if there is some uncertainty about whether the mail carrier has come yet.)

One way in which the delivery of mail differs from the laboratory VI schedule is that the mail will continue to be delivered even if a person has not collected the previously delivered mail. As already mentioned, in the traditional VI schedule the clock stops once a reinforcer has been stored, and it will not begin to run again until a subject collects the stored reinforcer. Therefore, no more than a single reinforcer can be stored at once. However, Vaughan (1976, 1982) has studied the behavior generated under what he calls *stored VI* schedules, in which the VI clock runs at all times, and any uncollected reinforcers are saved until the animal collects them. For example, if there has been a long pause in responding and three reinforcers have been stored, the subject's next three responses will each produce one of the stored reinforcers. One might think that this variation from the standard VI schedule would produce very different behavior. For example, in a one-hour session with a stored VI 1-minute schedule (which would store an average of 60 reinforcers per session), a subject could obtain all of these reinforcers simply by waiting until the end of the session and then making 60 responses. However, Vaughan found that the behavior of pigeons on stored VI schedules was not discriminably different from their behavior on traditional VI schedules—response rates were moderate and steady. An intuitive explanation of this result is that a sprinkling of reinforcers throughout the hour, even at the cost of making many ineffective responses, is preferable to waiting until the end of the session, when each reinforcer could be collected with a single response. We could say the same thing about the person who checks for mail every day—this mode of responding is evidently preferable to waiting until the end of the week before checking the mail, when the probability of receiving a reinforcing piece of mail would be much higher.

Extinction and the Four Simple Schedules

Suppose that an experimenter takes five pigeons and trains them on five different schedules—one on a schedule of continuous reinforcement (CRF), and one each on a FR, VR, FI, and VI schedule. Each subject receives ten sessions, and each session, regardless of the reinforcement schedule, lasts until 50 reinforcers have been delivered. For each subject, the eleventh session starts with the same schedule as before, but after five reinforcers have been delivered each animal is switched to an extinction schedule. Which subject (ignoring the possibility of individual differences among the pigeons) will make the most responses during extinction before quitting? How many responses will the different subjects make?

Of course, the answers to these questions would depend in part on the numerical value of each schedule (for instance, whether the FR schedule was FR 5 or FR 100), but some general rules about the *resistance to extinction* of the different simple schedules can be stated. One general finding is that extinction is more rapid after CRF than after a schedule of intermittent

reinforcement. This finding is called the *partial reinforcement extinction effect*, an effect that seemed paradoxical to early researchers because it violates Thomas Brown's principle of frequency. Why should a response that is only intermittently followed by a reinforcer be stronger (more resistant to extinction) than a response that has been followed by a reinforcer every time it has occurred? This question has been named *Humphrey's paradox*, after the psychologist who first demonstrated the partial reinforcement extinction effect. At least a half dozen explanations of this paradox have been proposed, some of which were subsequently shown to be inadequate. We will examine two of the more widely accepted explanations of this phenomenon.

One explanation, first proposed by Mowrer and Jones (1945), is called the *discrimination hypothesis*. It states that in order for a subject's behavior to change once extinction begins, the subject must be able to discriminate the change in reinforcement contingencies. With CRF, where every response has been reinforced, the change to extinction (where no response is reinforced) is a highly discriminable event, and so it does not take long for responding to disappear. In a FR or FI schedule, the switch to extinction is less distinct, because subjects are accustomed to making many responses that are not reinforced. Therefore, subjects should make more responses during extinction after FR or FI reinforcement before they stop. The discrimination problem becomes still more difficult in the two variable schedules, VR and VI. Because of the nature of these schedules, a subject will have experienced occasional long stretches in which many unreinforced responses were eventually followed by a reinforcer. It should therefore take still longer for responding to cease in extinction following VR or VI reinforcement. Consistent with these predictions, research has shown that extinction takes place fairly quickly after CRF, more slowly after FR or FI reinforcement, and still more slowly after VR or VI reinforcement.

The discrimination hypothesis will probably also coincide with your predictions about some real-world reinforcement schedules. A vending machine usually dispenses reinforcers (candy, soda) on a schedule of continuous reinforcement: Each time the correct change is inserted, a reinforcer is delivered. If the schedule is switched to extinction (the machine breaks down), a person will not continue to put coins in the machine for long. At the other extreme is another machine into which people insert coins, the slot machine, which dispenses reinforcers on a VR schedule. If a slot machine broke down in such a way that it appeared to be functioning normally but could never produce a jackpot, a gambler might continue to pour many coins into the machine before giving up (especially if the gambler had been reinforced on that machine in the past).

Despite the intuitive appeal of the discrimination hypothesis, experimental evidence suggests that it is not completely correct, and that a slightly different hypothesis, the *generalization decrement hypothesis* (Capaldi, 1966, 1967) is better. Generalization decrement is simply a term for the decreased responding one observes in a generalization test when the test stimuli become less and less similar to the training stimulus. For instance, if a pigeon is reinforced for pecking at a yellow key, we should observe a generalization decrement (less rapid responding) if the key is blue in a generalization test. According to the generalization decrement hypothesis, responding during extinction will be weak if the stimuli present during extinction are different from those that prevailed during reinforcement, but strong if these stimuli are similar to those encountered during reinforcement. According to Capaldi, one class of important stimuli are the numbers of consecutive unreinforced responses that have been followed by a reinforced response. Imagine a subject that has always been reinforced on a CRF schedule, and has now made five or ten responses without reinforcement. This stimulus situation (having made a string of unreinforced responses) is quite unlike anything the subject has encountered before, so there should be considerable generalization decrement, and responding should soon stop. Now suppose another subject faces extinction after FR 50. Even after 100 responses, the stimulus situation (having made many consecutive unreinforced responses) is not that different from the stimuli experienced under FR 50, so responding may continue for a while longer.

Do not be discouraged if the generalization decrement hypothesis sounds exactly like the discrimination hypothesis, for the difference between them is subtle. Simply stated, the difference is this: The discrimination hypothesis assumes that responding continues during extinction because the subject *cannot discriminate* the extinction condition from the preceding reinforcement schedule. According to the generalization decrement hypothesis, the subject may well be able to discriminate the change, but there is nevertheless enough similarity between the extinction condition and conditions in which reinforcers were presented in the past to maintain responding for a while. In one type of experiment that supports the generalization decrement hypothesis, one group of subjects is first exposed to some schedule of intermittent reinforcement, then to a long period of CRF, and then switched to extinction. A second group receives only the period of CRF, then extinction. For both groups, the transition from CRF to extinction should be easy to detect, so according to the discrimination hypothesis extinction should be rapid. However, the generalization decrement hypothesis predicts that extinction should be slower for the first group because of these subjects' earlier experiences with intermittent reinforcement. That is, these subjects will continue to respond when their responses are not reinforced because this situation is similar to ones in which they were eventually reinforced in the past. The results of several studies (Jenkins, 1962; Rashotte & Surridge, 1969) supported the generalization decrement hypothesis—extinction was retarded for those animals that had previous experience with intermittent reinforcement.

Other Reinforcement Schedules

Although the four simple reinforcement schedules have been the most thoroughly investigated, they are only four of an infinite number of possible rules for delivering reinforcement. Many other rules for reinforcement have been named and studied, and we can examine a few of the more common ones.

Under a schedule of *differential reinforcement of low rates* (DRL), a response is reinforced if and only if a certain amount of time has elapsed since the previous response. For example, under DRL 10 seconds, every response that occurs after a pause of at least 10 seconds is reinforced. If a response occurs after 9.5 seconds, this not only fails to produce reinforcement but it resets the 10-second clock to zero, so that now 10 more seconds must elapse before a response can be reinforced. As you might imagine, DRL schedules produce very low rates of responding, but they are not as low as would be optimal. Since subjects cannot estimate the passage of time perfectly, the optimal strategy would be to pause for an average of 12 or 15 seconds and then respond. In this way, if the subject erred from this average on the short side, the pause might still be longer than 10 seconds and produce a reinforcer. The usual finding, however, is that the average pause is somewhat less than 10 seconds, and as a result considerably more than half of the subject's responses go unreinforced. Some subjects seem to use a regular sequence of behaviors to help pace their operant responses. For example, a pigeon on a DRL 5-second schedule might peck at the key, then peck at each of the four corners of the chamber, then peck at the key again.

The opposite of the DRL contingency is the *differential reinforcement of high rates* (DRH), whereby a certain number of responses must occur within a fixed amount of time. For example, a reinforcer might occur each time the subject makes 10 responses in 3 seconds or less. Since rapid responding is selectively reinforced by this schedule, DRH can be used to produce higher rates of responding than those obtained with any other reinforcement schedule.

Other common reinforcement schedules are those that combine two or more simple schedules in some way. In a *concurrent schedule*, the subject is presented with two or more response alternatives (for instance, several different levers), each associated with its own reinforcement schedule. With more than one reinforcement schedule available simultaneously, psychologists can determine which schedule the subject prefers and how much time is devoted to each alterna-

tive. In *chained schedules*, the subject must complete the requirement for two or more simple schedules in a fixed sequence, and each schedule is signalled by a different stimulus. For instance, in a chain FI 1-minute FR 10, a pigeon might be presented with a yellow key until the FI requirement is met, then a blue key until 10 more responses are made, and then the reinforcer would be presented. The subject's behavior during each link of the chain is usually characteristic of the schedule currently in effect (an accelerating response pattern during the FI component, and a stop-and-go pattern during the FR component). As in the response chains discussed earlier, the strength of responding weakens as a schedule is further and further removed from the primary reinforcer. Thus a FI schedule will produce less responding if instead of leading to reinforcement it simply leads to a FR schedule.

Another schedule that consists of two simple schedules is the *conjunctive schedule*, in which the requirement of each schedule must be satisfied before the reinforcer is delivered. For instance, in a conjunctive FI FR schedule a reinforcer will be delivered only if (1) the required amount of time has passed and (2) the required number of responses have been made. Contingencies that approximate a conjunctive FI FR schedule seem to control the behavior of the U. S. Congress. In an analysis of the behavior of Congress, Weisberg and Waldrop (1972), suggested that adjournment is a major reinforcer for this legislative body, and that its major behavior is the passage of legislation. The FR requirement facing Congress is that all the pending legislation be disposed of in some way. The FI requirement is that Congress take most of the year to finish its work—imagine the public outcry that would result if our representatives finished their work in only five months and took the rest of the year off. To demonstrate how these contingencies affect the behavior of Congress, Weisberg and Waldrop plotted the cumulative number of bills passed during the years 1947-1954. As Figure 6-11 shows, the FI component seems to play a dominant role in this situation, for the cumulative record of Congressional behavior provides a fine illustration of the FI scallop.

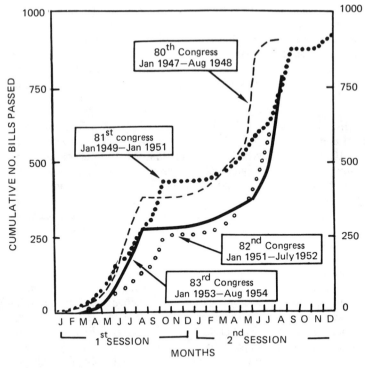

FIGURE 6-11. The work habits of the U. S. Congress between the years 1947 and 1954. The scalloped patterns show that each Congress passed bills at an accelerating rate as the scheduled date of adjournment approached. (From Weisberg & Waldrop, 1972)

THE EXPERIMENTAL ANALYSIS OF REINFORCEMENT SCHEDULES

Throughout the preceding discussions of reinforcement schedules, the explanations of why particular schedules produce specific response patterns have been casual and intuitive. For example, we noted that it would not "make sense" to have a long postreinforcement pause on a VR schedule, or to respond on a very rapid rate on a VI schedule. This level of discussion can make the basic facts about reinforcement schedules easier to learn and remember. However, such imprecise statements are no substitute for a scientific analysis of exactly which independent variables (which characteristics of the reinforcement schedule) control which dependent variables (which aspects of the subject's behavior). This section presents a few examples that show how a scientific analysis can either improve upon intuitive explanations of behavior or distinguish among different explanations, all of which seem intuitively reasonable.

The Cause of the FR Postreinforcement Pause

Why do animal subjects pause after reinforcement on FR schedules? Several possible explanations seem intuitively reasonable. Perhaps the postreinforcement pause is the result of fatigue: The subject has made many responses, has collected a reinforcer, and now it rests to alleviate its fatigue. A second possibility is satiation: The consumption of the food reinforcer causes a slight decrease in the animal's level of hunger. To be sure, the small amount of food that is typically presented as a reinforcer cannot do much to satisfy the animal's hunger, but perhaps it is enough to produce a small and short-lived decrease in hunger, which results in a brief interruption in responding. A third explanation of the postreinforcement pause emphasizes the fact that on a FR schedule the subject is furthest from the delivery of the next reinforcer immediately after the occurrence of the previous reinforcer. According to this position, a subject's behavior on a

FR schedule is similar to a response chain. We have already seen that the initial responses in the chain, those farthest removed from the primary reinforcer, are the weakest. Ferster and Skinner (1957) stated this last possibility in a slightly different way by noting that the occurrence of one reinforcer serves as a distinctive discriminative stimulus that signals the absence of further reinforcement in the near future. For convenience, let us call these three explanations of the FR postreinforcement pause the *fatigue hypothesis*, the *satiation hypothesis*, and the *remaining-responses hypothesis*.

Each of these hypotheses sounds plausible, but how can we determine which is correct? Several types of evidence help to distinguish among them. First, there is the finding that postreinforcement pauses become larger as the size of the FR increases. This finding is consistent with both the fatigue and remaining-responses hypotheses, but there is no reason why a subject should become more satiated on a long FR schedule than on a short one. Indeed, since the subject can collect reinforcers at a faster rate on a short FR schedule, if anything its level of hunger should be lower (and pauses therefore longer) on shorter FR schedules.

Data that help to distinguish between the fatigue and remaining-responses hypothesis are provided by studies that combine two or more different FR schedules into what is called a *multiple schedule*. In a multiple schedule, the subject is presented with two or more different schedules, one at a time, and each schedule is signalled by a different discriminative stimulus. For example, Figure 6-12 illustrates a portion of a session involving a multiple FR 10 FR 100 schedule. When the response key is blue, the schedule is FR 100; when it is red, the schedule is FR 10. The key color remains the same until a reinforcer is earned, at which point there is a .50 probability that the key color (and schedule) will switch. The behavior shown in Figure 6-12, though hypothetical, is representative of the results from several studies that used multiple FR FR schedules (Crossman, 1968; Mintz, Mourer, & Gofseyeff, 1967). Examine the postreinforcement pauses that occurred at points a, b, c, d, e, and f. Half of these pauses occurred after a ratio of 100 (a, d, f) and half after a ratio of 10 (b, c, e). Notice that there is a long pause at f, as might be expected from the fatigue hypothesis, but contrary to this hypothesis there are only short pauses after FR 100 at points a and d. The pause after FR 10 is short at point b, but long at points c and e. It turns out that we are unable to predict the size of the postreinforcement pause by knowing how many responses the subject has produced in the *preceding* ratio. This fact forces us to reject the fatigue hypothesis. On the other hand, it is possible to predict the size of the pause by knowing the size of the *upcoming* ratio. Notice that the pause is short whenever the key color is red (points a, b, and d), which is the discriminative stimulus for FR 10. The pause is long when the key color is blue (points c, e, and

FIGURE 6-12. A hypothetical but typical pattern of response from a multiple schedule where the blue key color signaled that the schedule was FR 100 and the red key color signaled that the schedule was FR 10. The text explains how results like these can be used to distinguish between different theories of the postreinforcement pause.

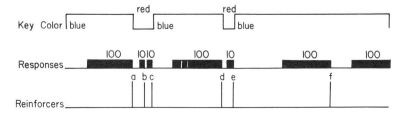

f), the discriminative stimulus for FR 100. This pattern is exactly what would be predicted by the remaining-responses hypothesis: The size of the postreinforcement pause is determined by the upcoming FR requirement.

This type of analysis has demonstrated quite clearly that the size of the postreinforcement pause depends heavily on the upcoming ratio requirement, and that the factors of satiation and fatigue play at most a minor role.

Comparisons of VR and VI Response Rates

We will now turn from a question with a fairly clear answer to one whose answer is still being debated: Why is the rate of response faster on VR schedules than on VI schedules? One thing that is certain is that the faster response rates on VR schedules are not simply due to higher rates of reinforcement. A clever procedure known as *yoking* proves this point conclusively. Two subjects are simultaneously placed in two separate chambers. The behavior of the subject in the first chamber (let us call it the *controlling chamber*) determines what happens to the subject in the second chamber (the *yoked chamber*). In a study conducted by Catania, Matthews, Silverman, and Yohalem (1977), the subject in the controlling chamber responded on an ordinary VR schedule. Each time this subject completed the VR requirement, two things would happen: (1) this subject would receive a reinforcer, and (2) a reinforcer would also be stored in the yoked chamber, and the next response of the yoked subject would collect it. Because the times of storage were irregular, the schedule in the yoked chamber was a VI. Since every reinforcer in the controlling chamber was paired with a reinforcer in the yoked chamber, this procedure equated both the number of reinforcers in the two chambers and their distribution over time. Catania et al. tested several pairs of birds in these chambers, and in every case the results were the same: Despite the equal reinforcement rates, the subjects on the VR schedules always developed faster response rates than their counterparts on the VI schedules.

Having ruled out the possibility that differences in reinforcement rate cause the higher response rates on VR schedules, let us turn to two other explanations that cannot be so easily dismissed. One theory can be classified as a *molecular* theory, which means that it focuses on small-scale events—the moment-by-moment relationships between responses and reinforcers. The other theory is a *molar* theory, or one that deals with large-scale measures of behavior and reinforcement. Of course, the terms *small-scale* and *large-scale* are relative, but to be more specific, molecular theories usually discuss events that have time spans of less than one minute, whereas molar theories discuss relationships measured over at least several minutes and often over the entire length of an experimental session. The issue of VI and VR response-rate differences is one of several areas where there are opposing molar and molecular explanations, and we will encounter others in later chapters.

For the present issue, the most popular molecular theory is the *IRT reinforcement theory*, where IRT stands for *interresponse time*—the time between two consecutive responses. In essence, this theory states that response rates are slower on VI schedules than on VR schedules because long IRTs (long pauses between responses) are more frequently reinforced on VI schedules. This theory was first proposed by Skinner (1938), and among its more recent proponents are Anger (1956), Shimp (1969), and Platt (1979). Imagine that a subject has just been switched from CRF to a VI schedule. Some of this subject's IRTs will be short (for instance, less than one second will elapse between two responses) and others will be larger (for example, a pause of five or ten seconds will separate two responses). On the VI schedule, which of these two responses is more likely to be reinforced—a response after a pause of 0.5 seconds, or a response after a pause of 5 seconds? The answer is the latter, because the more time that elapses between two responses, the greater is the probability that the VI clock will time out and store a reinforcer. For example, if the schedule is VI 60 seconds, the probability of reinforcement is roughly ten times higher for an IRT of 5 seconds than for an IRT of 0.5 seconds. The direct relationship between IRT size and the probability of reinforcement on VI schedules is not theory but fact. IRT reinforcement theory states that as a consequence of this relationship, longer IRTs will be selectively strengthened on VI schedules.

Next, let us examine the relationship between IRT size and the probability of reinforcement on a VR schedule. Stated simply, there is no such relationship, because time is irrelevant on a VR schedule—the delivery of reinforcement depends entirely on the number of responses emitted, not on the passage of time. Therefore, unlike VI schedules, there is no selective strengthening of long pauses on VR schedules, and this in itself could explain the VI-VR difference. However, Skinner (1938) went a bit further by noting that when a subject is first switched from CRF to a VR schedule, its responses are not distributed uniformly over time. Instead, responses tend to occur in clusters or "bursts," perhaps simply because the subject makes several responses while in the vicinity of the key or lever, then explores some other part of the chamber, then returns and makes a few more responses, and so on. Skinner suggested that this tendency to respond in bursts could lead to a selective strengthening of short IRTs on a VR schedule. For simplicity, let us suppose that each burst consists of exactly five responses, each separated by 0.5 seconds, and each pause between bursts is at least five seconds long. In each burst of responses, there is only one chance for a long IRT to be reinforced (the first response after the pause), but there are four chances for a 0.5 second IRT to be reinforced (the next four responses). Skinner therefore concluded that short IRTs were selectively strengthened on a VR schedule simply because they were reinforced more frequently.

To provide empirical support for their viewpoint, proponents of IRT reinforcement theory have arranged schedules that reinforce different IRTs with different probabilities. For example, Shimp (1968) set up a schedule in which only IRTs between 1.5 and 2.5 seconds or between 3.5 and 4.5 seconds were reinforced. As the theory of selective IRT reinforcement would predict, IRTs of these two sizes increased in frequency. In another experiment, Shimp (1973) mimicked the pattern of IRT reinforcement that occurs in a typical VI schedule: He did not use a VI clock, but simply reinforced long IRTs with a high probability and short IRTs with a low probability. The result of this "synthetic VI" schedule was a pattern of responding that was indistinguishable from that of a normal VI schedule—moderate steady responding with a mixture of long and short IRTs.

Critics have raised a number of objections against IRT reinforcement theory, some of which are too lengthy and technical to repeat here. However, a frequent criticism is that simply showing that the selective reinforcement of certain classes of IRTs can change an organism's behavior in *some* situations (such as in Shimp's experiments) does not prove that this same mechanism controls behavior in other situations (that is, in standard VI and VR schedules). An empirically based objection is that even in situations where only long IRTs are reinforced, such as in DRL schedules, subjects typically continue to produce a large number of short IRTs. That is, the tendency to respond in bursts is not completely eliminated even when this manner of responding is never reinforced. At the very least, this finding implies that other factors besides the probability of reinforcement influence the sizes of IRTs a subject produces.

A molar theory of the VI-VR difference might be called the *response-reinforcer correlation theory*. Instead of focusing on the last IRT to occur before reinforcement, this theory emphasizes a relationship between responses and reinforcement of a much more global nature (Baum, 1973; Green, Kagel, & Battalio, 1987). Figure 6-13 depicts the properties of VI and VR schedules that underlie the response-reinforcer correlation theory. This figure shows the relationship between a subject's average response rate and overall reinforcement rate for a typical VR schedule and a typical VI schedule. On VR 60, as on all ratio schedules, there is a linear relationship between response rate and reinforcement rate. For instance, a response rate of 60 responses per minute will produce 60 reinforcers per hour, and a response rate of 90 responses per minute produces 90 reinforcers per hour. The relationship on the VI 60-second schedule (as on all VI schedules) is very different. No matter how rapidly the subject responds, it cannot obtain more than the scheduled 60 reinforcers per hour. The

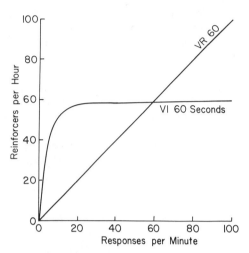

FIGURE 6-13. The relationship between a subject's rate of response and the rate of reinforcement on a VR 60 schedule and a VI 60-second schedule.

reason that reinforcement rate drops with very low response rates is that the VI clock will sometimes be stopped (having stored a reinforcer), and it will not start again until the subject makes a response and collects a reinforcer. But as long as the subject responds at a modest rate it will obtain close to 60 reinforcers per hour.

It should be emphasized that the relationships depicted in Figure 6-13 apply only in the long run. Because of the variable nature of VI and VR schedules, in the short run the actual rate of reinforcement will often be much higher or much lower. According to the response-reinforcer correlation theory, however, the organism is able to ignore these short-term fluctuations and learn about the long-term relationships between response rate and reinforcement rate. To see how this could cause the response rate difference between VI and VR, suppose that after extensive experience on VR 60 a pigeon's response rate stabilizes at about 60 responses per minute (where the two functions cross in Figure 6-13), producing about 60 reinforcers per hour. Now suppose the schedule is switched to VI 60 seconds, under which this same response rate would also produce 60 reinforcers per hour. However,

the subject's response rate is not completely steady, and by occasionally responding at rates above and below 60 responses per hour, the subject learns that variations in response rate have little effect on reinforcement rate on the VI schedule. The subject's behavior may gradually drop to, say, 20 responses per hour without a substantial decrease in the rate of reinforcement. Speaking loosely, we could say that on VI 60 seconds the subject has learned that the extra 40 responses per hour are "not worth it," for they would produce only a negligible increase in reinforcement rate.

To date, neither proponents of the molecular approach nor those of the molar approach have succeeded in making a thoroughly convincing case for their position. Critics of the response-reinforcer correlation theory have argued that it makes excessive intellectual demands on the subject, and that animal subjects may not be capable of making accurate long-term estimates of response rate and reinforcement rate. As a further criticism, Catania et al. (1977) noted that in their yoking procedure, the response rate difference between VR subjects and VI subjects emerged after only one or two sessions. It seems unlikely that a subject could gain an understanding of the relationship between response rate and reinforcement rate (as shown in Figure 6-13) with such a small sampling of reinforcers.

Perhaps the best way to decide between the molar and molecular theories is to use a schedule in which the molar contingencies favor rapid responding and the molecular contingencies favor slow responding (or vice versa). This is not possible with normal VR or VI schedules, but Vaughan (1987) designed some complex schedules that had these properties. For instance, one schedule had the molar features of a VR schedule (with more reinforcers for faster response rates) but the molecular features of a VI schedule (with reinforcement more likely after a long IRT). As predicted by IRT reinforcement theory, pigeons responded slowly on this schedule (and thereby lost reinforcers in the long run). Conversely, pigeons responded rapidly on a schedule in which the molecular contingencies favored rapid responding (short IRTs) but the molar contingencies favored slow responding (so once again the pigeons lost reinforcers in the long run). These results clearly favor the molecular approach, for they indicate that the animals were sensitive to the short-term consequences of their behavior, but not the long-term consequences.

APPLICATIONS OF OPERANT CONDITIONING

Within the field of behavior modification, operant conditioning principles have been applied to so many different behaviors that they are too numerous to list, let alone describe in any detail, in a few pages. Operant conditioning principles have been used to help people who wish to improve themselves by losing weight, smoking or drinking less, or exercising more. They have been applied to a wide range of children's problems, including classroom disruption, poor academic performance, fighting, tantrums, extreme passivity, and hyperactivity. They have been used in attempts to improve the daily functioning of adults and children who have more serious behavioral problems and must be institutionalized. These principles have also been applied to problems that affect society as a whole, such as litter and pollution, the waste of energy and resources, workplace accidents, delinquency, shoplifting, and other crimes. In light of the number and diversity of these applications, it should be clear that this section can do no more than describe a few representative examples. For those who wish to know more, there are many books devoted primarily or exclusively to the systematic use of operant conditioning principles in real-world settings (O'Leary & Wilson, 1987; Peterson & Tannenbaum, 1986; Hersen & Van Hasselt, 1987; Kanfer & Goldstein, 1985; Martin & Pear, 1983).

Teaching Language to Autistic Children

Autism is a severe disorder which affects about 2 to 4 of every 10,000 children (Wing, 1972), usually appearing when a child is a few years old. One major symptom of autism is extreme social withdrawal. The child shows little of the normal interest in watching and interacting with other people. Autistic children do not acquire normal language use: They either remain silent or exhibit *echolalia*, which is the immediate repetition of any words they hear. Autistic children frequently spend hours engaging in simple repetitive behaviors such as rocking back and forth or spinning a metal pan on the floor. Despite considerable research, the causes of autism remain a mystery, but one certainty is that typical psychiatric and institutional care produce little if any improvement in these children (Kanner, Rodriguez, & Ashenden, 1972). Individuals diagnosed as autistic frequently spend all of their childhood and adult lives in a state institution.

During the 1960s, Ivar Lovaas developed an extensive program based on operant conditioning principles designed to train autistic children to speak, to interact with other people, and in general to behave more normally (Lovaas 1967, 1977). Lovaas's program makes use of many of the operant conditioning principles we have already discussed, plus some new ones. At first, a therapist uses a spoonful of ice cream or some other tasty food as a primary reinforcer, and starts by reinforcing the child simply for sitting quietly and looking at the experimenter. Next, using the procedure of shaping, the child is rewarded for making any audible sounds, and then for making sounds that more and more closely mimic the word spoken by the therapist. For instance, if the child's name is Billy, the therapist may say the word "Billy" as a discriminative stimulus, after which any verbal response that approximates this word will be reinforced. To avoid the necessity of relying entirely on the primary reinforcer of food (which would lose its effectiveness rapidly because of satiation), the therapist begins to develop other stimuli into conditioned reinforcers. Before presenting the food, the therapist may say "Good!" or give the child a hug—two stimuli that can eventually be used as reinforcers by themselves.

Early in this type of training, the therapist may use her hand to aid the child in his mouth and lip movements. This type of physical guidance is one example of a *prompt*. A prompt is any stimulus that makes a desired response more likely. In this example, the therapist's prompt of moving the child's lips and cheeks into the proper shape makes the production of the appropriate response more likely. Whenever a prompt is used, it is usually withdrawn gradually, in a procedure known as *fading*. Thus the therapist may do less and less of the work of moving the child's lips and cheeks into the proper position, then perhaps just touch the child's cheek lightly, then not at all. This type of training demands large amounts of time and patience on the part of the therapist, especially in the beginning, when progress is slowest. It may take several days of training, conducted for several hours each day, before the child masters his first word. It may be a few more days before a second word is mastered, and a few more before the therapist can say either of the two words and reliably receive the appropriate imitative response (assuming that the child is not echolalic to begin with). However, the pace of a child's progress quickens as additional words are introduced, and after a few weeks the child may master several new words each day. At this stage of training, however, the child is only imitating words he hears, and the next step is to teach him the meanings of these words. The training begins with concrete nouns such as *nose*, *shoe*, and *leg*. The child is taught to identify the correct object in response to the word as a stimulus (for example, by rewarding an appropriate response to the instruction, "Point to your nose"), and to produce the appropriate word when presented with the object (Therapist: "What is this?" Billy: "Shoe."). As in the imitative phase, the child's progress accelerates as the labeling phase proceeds, and soon the child is learning the meanings of several new words each day. Later in training, similar painstaking techniques are used to teach the child the meanings of verbs and adjectives, of prepositions such as *in* and *on*, and of abstract concepts such as *first, last, more, less, same*, and *different*.

Lovaas's language training program requires many months of daily sessions between therapist and autistic child. To make it more likely that the child's newly learned behavior of speaking to the therapist will generalize to other adults, several different therapists, male and female, will usually work with the child at different times. Although this program demands large amounts of

time and effort from skilled instructors, it can produce dramatic improvements in the behavior of children who typically show negligible improvement from any other type of therapy. Over the course of several months, Lovaas's typical result is that a child who was initially aloof and completely silent becomes friendly and affectionate, and learns to use language to answer questions, to make requests, or to tell stories.

How successful is this behavioral treatment in the long run? Lovaas (1987) compared children who had received extensive behavioral treatment for autism (40 hours a week for two or more years) with children who had received minimal treatment (10 hours a week or less). The children were assigned to these "treatment" and "control" groups at random. (As many children as possible were assigned to the treatment group, but because of the limited staff size, many more children had to be assigned to the control group.) At age six or seven, all children were given some standard IQ tests, and their performance in school was evaluated. The differences between groups were dramatic: Nearly half of the children from the treatment group had normal IQs and academic performance, as compared to only 2 percent of the children from the control group. These results are very encouraging, for they suggest that if extensive behavioral treatment is given to young autistic children, it can essentially eliminate the autistic symptoms in some of them (though not all). Lovaas proposed that the chances for success are best if the behavioral treatment begins at the earliest possible age.

The Token Economy

In a token economy, the principle of conditioned reinforcement is used in an attempt to improve the behaviors of entire groups of individuals. Token economies have been employed in classrooms, mental institutions, prisons, and homes for juvenile delinquents (see Kazdin, 1977, for a comprehensive review). What all token economies have in common is that each individual can earn tokens by performing any of a number of different desired behaviors, and can later exchange these tokens for a variety of "backup" or primary reinforcers. The tokens may be physical objects such as poker chips or gold stars on a bulletin board, or they may simply be points added in a record book.

An early report by Schaefer and Martin (1966) provides a good example of a token system. In a large state hospital, Schaefer and Martin studied the behavior of 40 adult female patients diagnosed as chronic schizophrenics. They noted that one of the major characteristics of hospitalized schizophrenics is that they appear "apathetic" and seem to lack "interest and motivation": For instance, a patient may stare at a wall all day, or may continually pace around the ward. Schaefer and Martin sought to determine whether the contingent delivery of tokens for more varied and normal behaviors would improve the behavior of these patients. The patients were randomly divided into two groups. Patients in the control group received a supply of tokens regardless of their behavior. Patients in the experimental group were reinforced with tokens for specific behaviors from three broad categories: personal hygiene, social interaction, and adequate work performance. Some examples of reinforced behaviors in the first category were thoroughness of showering, toothbrushing, hair combing, use of cosmetics, and maintenance of an attractive appearance. Among the reinforced social behaviors were everyday greetings (such as "Good morning"), speaking in group-therapy sessions, and playing cards with other patients. The work assignments that were reinforced with tokens varied from individual to individual, but some examples were emptying wastepaper baskets, wiping tables, and vacuuming. Notice that all of the reinforced behaviors would generally be considered normal and desirable not only within the hospital but also in the outside world. The tokens were used to purchase both necessities and luxuries, including food, cigarettes, access to TV, recreational activities, and so on. The token program remained in effect for three months, and nurses on the ward periodically made observations of the patients in both the experimental and control groups.

The single most important finding of this study was that over the three-month period the variety and frequency of "adaptive" behaviors increased in the experimental group, whereas there was no visible change in the control group. The results of this and many other studies on token economies in mental institutions leave no doubt that such procedures can produce impressive improvements in the personal, social, and work-related behaviors of patients. An important question, however, is whether patients who are exposed to a token economy ultimately fare better when they are released from the hospital—that is, whether their more adaptive behaviors will generalize to the outside world, where there are no tokens for good hygiene or for performing household chores. Although the evidence is not as overwhelming as we might hope, a number of findings suggest that there may be long-term benefits from carefully designed token economies. For example, Schaefer and Martin found that only 14 percent of the patients in the experimental group who were eventually discharged later returned to the hospital, as compared to the hospital's average return rate of 28 percent. Not all accounts of token economies have reported such long-term benefits. However, it seems that those token economies from which the patient is removed gradually rather than abruptly, and those that stress independence and self-reliance are the most likely to produce lasting improvements (Kazdin, 1983).

Since about the mid-1970s, the use of token economies in mental hospitals and other institutions has been severely restricted by a series of legal rulings. In the most famous of these judicial decisions (*Wyatt v. Stickney*), the court ruled that many of the backup reinforcers most commonly used in token economies were constitutionally guaranteed rights of all patients, and therefore they could not be made contingent on a patient's behavior. The list of such rights included nutritionally adequate meals, having visitors, a comfortable bed, the opportunity to exercise several times a week, to be outdoors regularly and frequently, to interact with the opposite sex, and to watch television in a common room. The intent of this ruling was, of course, to protect the rights and well-being of institutionalized persons. Unfortunately, however, this list of rights includes nearly all of the most potent reinforcers available to therapists. In an article critical of the *Wyatt v. Stickney* decision, Wexler

(1973) pointed out that with chronic schizophrenics, these reinforcers may be the only ones that work. It would be ironic if in the name of freedom and personal rights, the courts removed the only promising method of restoring adaptive behaviors and providing the patient with the skills necessary in the outside world. It is also worth noting that, unlike individuals in mental institutions, all other members of our society are afforded no assurances that they will receive such "constitutionally guaranteed rights" as nutritionally balanced meals and a comfortable bed. In any case, to cope with the *Wyatt v. Stickney* decision, some behavior therapists have resorted to using personalized and idiosyncratic reinforcers such as a personal television in one's room, the opportunity to feed kittens, and the purchase of items from a mail-order catalog (Wexler, 1973). To date, no court has ruled that such reinforcers are constitutionally guaranteed.

Reinforcing Employee Performance

In recent years, many businesses, both large and small, have begun to use the principles of operant conditioning to increase productivity and to decrease employee absenteeism and workplace accidents. A study by Wallin and Johnson (1976) illustrates the potential benefits of this approach. In a small electronics company where worker tardiness and absenteeism had become a problem, workers were allowed to participate in a monthly lottery if their attendance record had been perfect for the past month. The names of all workers who had perfect attendance records were placed in a basket, and a random drawing determined the winner of a 10-dollar prize. Since the lottery was an example of a RR schedule, we might predict that it should produce steady behavior, assuming that the size of the reinforcer was sufficient. Apparently it was, for in the first 11 months of the lottery system, employee absenteeism was 30 percent lower than in the previous 11 months. This simple program, which cost only $110, saved the company over $3100 in sick-leave expenditures during the initial 11-month period. Since this study included no control group, it is of course possible that the results were produced by chance or by a placebo effect.

However, another study (Pedalino & Gamboa, 1974) compared an experimental group with a lottery to three control groups without a lottery, and only the lottery group showed a reduction in absenteeism.

Reinforcement procedures have also been used to decrease workplace accidents. For instance, Fox, Hopkins, and Azrin (1987) described how workers in two open-pit mines were given trading stamps (exchangeable for various types of merchandise) for accident-free performance. The workers could earn stamps in a variety of ways: by completing a year without a lost-time accident, by following safety standards, and so on. They lost stamps if someone in their group had an accident or damaged equipment. Following the adoption of the trading-stamp program, lost-time accidents decreased by more than two-thirds in both mines and continued at this lower level over a period of several years. The program was also very cost effective for the mining companies: The monetary savings from reduced accident rates were at least 15 times greater than the cost of the trading-stamp program.

Contingency Contracts

In each of the previous examples, the behavioral control was one-sided: The therapist or employer set the rules, and the patient or employee was required to follow them. In contrast, a *contingency contract* encourages a reciprocal exchange of reinforcers between two or more parties. Behavioral contracts have been formed between therapist and patient, between parents and child, and between spouses. In most cases, each party plays an active role in creating the contract and indicates his or her agreement with the terms of the contract by signing it. A contingency contract lists in detail the duties (behaviors) required of each party and the privileges (reinforcers) that will result if the duties are performed (Stuart, 1971).

In a description of behavioral marriage therapy, Jacobson and Dallas (1981) reported that contingency contracts are often used in the initial phases of therapy to promote more positive interactions between partners. They note that in unhappy married couples, each spouse tends to resort to threats, punishment, and retaliation in an attempt to get what he or she wants from the other. A contingency contract can help to encourage the exchange of reinforcers and to let each partner know what behaviors the other desires. For instance, in part of such a contract the husband may agree to do the dishes in the evening if and only if the wife took the children to school that morning. Conversely, the wife agrees to take the children to school the next morning if and only if the husband did the dishes the night before. Jacobson and Dallas claim that the use of a written contract has several advantages: "it constitutes a public commitment to change; it decreases the likelihood of forgetting; and it prevents each spouse from retrospectively distorting the terms of the agreement" (1981, p. 390). For couples with severe problems, the use of a contingency contract may be only the first step in treatment, and later they are given training in communication and problem-solving skills. One review concluded that roughly half of the couples who received behavioral marriage therapy showed at least some improvement in their relationship, and in some cases the improvement was quite substantial (Jacobsen, Follette, Revenstorf, Baucom, Hahlweg & Margolin, 1984).

Summary

The successful application of the principles of reinforcement to a wide array of behavioral problems provides one of the strongest pieces of evidence that the research of the operant conditioning laboratory is relevant to real-world behavior. However, one common criticism of behavior modification is that these principles are nothing new, and that people have always used reward and punishment to try to control the behavior of others. Kazdin (1980) argues that this criticism is wrong for several reasons. First of all, many people are apparently quite unaware of how their own actions affect the behavior of others, and as a result they inadvertently reinforce the very behaviors they would like to eliminate. The parent who eventually gives in to a child's demands after the child whines or has a tantrum is reinforcing whining and tantrums on a VI schedule. The psychiatric nurse who listens sympathetically when a patient complains of imaginary illnesses or tells unbelievable stories is reinforcing this unusual verbal behavior with attention. These and countless other examples show that many people have little understanding of the basic principles of reinforcement.

Kazdin also notes that whereas the rules for reinforcement are applied systematically and consistently in a behavior-modification program, they seldom are when the average person uses reinforcers. A parent may begin with a rule that a child can earn an allowance by drying the dishes each night. However, the parent may sometimes excuse the child and give the allowance anyway if the child complains she or he is tired (and complaining is thereby reinforced). On another day, when the parent is in a bad mood, the same complaint of being tired might result in a spanking.

One final argument against the statement that the principles of operant conditioning are "common sense" is that knowing something about the principles of reinforcement is not the same as knowing everything. Behavior modifiers certainly do not know everything about how reinforcement works, but they do know much more than the average person. Consider how many of the principles of operant conditioning you understood (at least at a common sense level) before you read this chapter compared to those you know now. You may have had some idea of how primary and conditioned reinforcers can alter behavior, but unless you have had experience training animals you were probably unfamiliar with the principles of shaping, backward chaining, prompting, fading, and discrimination learning. You would probably find it difficult to predict the different behavior patterns that are produced by the four simple reinforcement schedules, either during acquisition or subsequent extinction. (If you do not believe this, try describing the four simple schedules to a friend with no training in psychology and see whether he or she can predict the different behaviors these schedules generate.) The subtleties and complexities of operant behavior are not obvious, and it has taken careful experiments to uncover them. With further research in this area, psychologists should continue to develop a more complete understanding of how "voluntary" behaviors are affected by their consequences.

7

AVOIDANCE AND PUNISHMENT

Everyone knows that some stimuli are "pleasant" or "satisfying" (to use Thorndike's term), whereas others are "unpleasant" or "aversive." Furthermore, since everyone is familiar with the terms "reward" and "punishment," people seem to know these two types of stimuli can have different effects on our behavior. However, because the terms "pleasant" and "unpleasant" are based on our introspections, psychologists have struggled to find more objective ways to define these concepts. Chapter 8 will describe the story of some of these efforts. For our present purposes, however, we can get by with the everyday meanings of these terms, along with Thorndike's observation that a pleasant stimulus is one that the organism seeks to attain and preserve, and an unpleasant stimulus is one that the organism seeks to avoid or terminate.

Chapter 6 was entirely devoted to the topic of *positive reinforcement*, which might be described as a procedure in which the occurrence of a behavior is followed by a pleasant stimulus. Skin-

ner has noted, however, that positive reinforcement is only one of four possible contingencies between a behavior and its consequences. Figure 7-1 presents these four possibilities in the form of a two-by-two matrix. First of all, there are two classes of stimuli (excluding hedonically neutral stimuli), pleasant and unpleasant. Secondly, each type of stimulus can either be presented or removed if a behavior occurs. Since we have already examined the procedure in cell 1 of the matrix, this chapter will focus on the other three cells. We can begin with some definitions. With *negative reinforcement* (cell 4), the occurrence of a certain behavior is followed by the removal of an unpleasant stimulus. One example of negative reinforcement is when an individual takes an aspirin and this is followed by the termination of a headache. In this case, the individual *escapes* from or removes an unpleasant stimulus by performing some behavior. The term *negative reinforcement* also encompasses instances of *avoidance,* in which a response prevents an un-

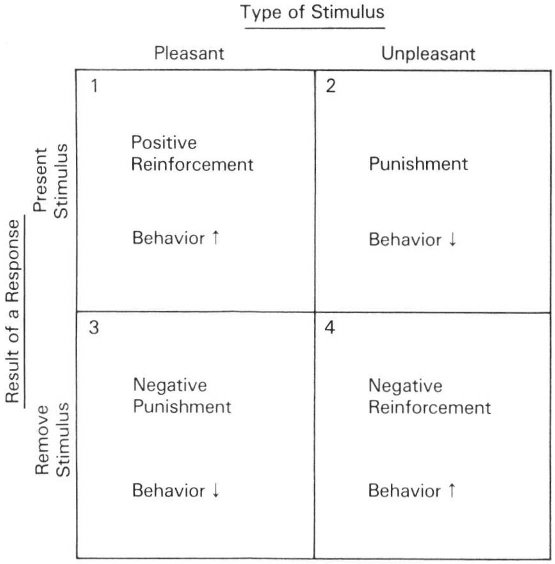

Type of Stimulus

	Pleasant	Unpleasant
Present Stimulus	1 Positive Reinforcement Behavior ↑	2 Punishment Behavior ↓
Remove Stimulus	3 Negative Punishment Behavior ↓	4 Negative Reinforcement Behavior ↑

(Result of a Response)

FIGURE 7-1. A two-by-two matrix depicting two types of reinforcement and two types of punishment.

pleasant stimulus from occurring in the first place. For example, the behavior of paying one's income tax avoids the unpleasant consequences of failing to do so. It has been conclusively shown that both positive and negative reinforcement act to strengthen or increase the likelihood of the behavior involved. The term *positive* indicates that a stimulus is presented if a behavior occurs; the term *negative* indicates that a stimulus is subtracted (removed or avoided entirely) if a behavior occurs.

Procedurally, cells 2 and 3 are similar to cells 1 and 4, respectively, except that the opposite type of stimulus is used. Cell 2 represents the procedure of *punishment,* in which a behavior is followed by an unpleasant stimulus. To emphasize the fact that a stimulus is presented, we might call this procedure *positive punishment,* but this term is seldom used. Cell 3 represents *negative punishment,* in which a pleasant stimulus is removed or omitted if a behavior occurs. The term *omission* is often used instead of *negative punishment.* An example of negative punishment is when a parent refuses to give a child his or her usual weekly allowance after the child has performed some undesirable behavior (such as staying out too late).

The first portion of this chapter surveys a number of experiments on negative reinforcement, and it discusses some of the theoretical issues about avoidance that psychologists have debated over the years. Next, we will look at the two types of punishment procedures. Although punishment is the opposite of positive reinforcement from a procedural standpoint, this does not necessarily mean that it also has the opposite effect on behavior. Some psychologists have concluded that, behaviorally as well as procedurally, punishment is the opposite of positive reinforcement, but others have concluded that punishment is not an effective form of behavioral control. We will consider the evidence and attempt to draw our own conclusions. Finally, we will examine some of the many ways that punishment has been used in behavior modification.

AVOIDANCE

A Representative Experiment

Solomon and Wynne (1953) conducted an experiment that illustrates many of the properties of negative reinforcement. Their subjects were dogs, and their apparatus a *shuttle box*—a chamber with two rectangular compartments separated by a barrier several inches high. A subject could move from one compartment to the other simply by jumping over the barrier. Each compartment had a metal floor that could be electrified to deliver an unpleasant stimulus, shock. The only other noteworthy features of the chamber were two overhead lights that separately illuminated the two compartments. In each experimental session, a dog received ten trials on which it could either escape or avoid a shock by jumping over the barrier to the other compartment. Every few minutes, the light above the dog was turned off (but the light in the other compartment remained on). If the dog remained in the dark compartment, after ten seconds the floor was electrified and the dog received a shock until it hopped over the barrier to the other compartment. Thus the dog could *escape* from the shock by jumping over the barrier. However, the dog could also *avoid* the shock completely by jumping over the barrier before the ten seconds of darkness had elapsed. On the next trial the contingencies were the same, except that the response required to escape or avoid the shock was jumping back into the first compartment.

On each trial, Solomon and Wynne measured the latency of the hurdling response from the moment the light above the dog went out. The latencies for a subject's first few trials were usually longer than ten seconds, so they could be classified as *escape* responses—the hurdling response occurred only after the shock had begun. However, by perhaps the fifth trial, a dog's response latency decreased to less than ten seconds, so now it was making an *avoidance* response—by hurdling soon after the light went out, the dog did not receive the shock.

After a few dozen trials, a typical dog's response latencies declined to an average of about two or three seconds, and they might be consistently less than ten seconds for the last several sessions of the experiment. In fact, Solomon and Wynne found that many dogs never again experienced a shock after their first avoidance response—all subsequent latencies were less than 10 seconds. Results such as these had led earlier theorists (Mowrer, 1947; Schoenfeld, 1950) to ponder a question that is sometimes called the *avoidance paradox*: How can the *nonoccurrence*

of an event (shock) serve as a reinforcer for the avoidance response? Notice that escape responses pose no problem for a reinforcement analysis, because here the response produces a change in a hedonically important stimulus—the presence of shock changes to the absence of shock when the escape response is made. On the other hand, consider a trial on which one of Solomon and Wynne's dogs made a response five seconds after the light was turned off. Such an avoidance trial involved no change in the shock conditions—there was no shock before the response, and no shock after the response. The early avoidance theorists felt it did not make sense to say that a shock that is not experienced can act as a reinforcer for some behavior. It was this puzzle about what motivated avoidance responses that led to the development of an influential theory of avoidance known as *two-factor theory* or *two-process theory*.

Two-Factor Theory

Mowrer (1947) was one of the most important figures in the development of two-factor theory. The two factors or processes of this theory are classical conditioning and operant conditioning, and according to the theory both of these processes are necessary for avoidance responses to occur. The proposed role of each of these factors can be illustrated by referring to the experiment of Solomon and Wynne. One unconditioned response to shock is fear, and this response plays a critical role in the theory. Through classical conditioning, this fear response is transferred from the US, shock, to some CS, a stimulus that precedes the shock. In the Solomon and Wynne experiment, the CS was clearly the 10 seconds of darkness that preceded each shock. After a few trials, a subject would presumably respond to the darkness with fear. This conditioning of a fear response to an initially neutral stimulus is the first process of the theory.

Mowrer (1947) reasoned that besides being a response, fear has various stimulus properties—a subject can sense changes in heart rate, breathing, and other visceral responses. I think everyone would agree that the sensations that accompany a fear reaction are unpleasant. It therefore follows from the definition of negative reinforcement (cell 4, Figure 7-1) that a reduction in fear can serve as a reinforcer for any response that it follows. According to Mowrer, a so-called "avoidance response" is reinforced by the reduction in fear that accompanies the removal of the fear-eliciting CS. In the Solomon and Wynne experiment, a subject could escape from a dark compartment to an illuminated compartment by jumping over the barrier. Thus the operant conditioning component of two-factor theory is the reinforcement of an avoidance response by the reduction in fear that occurs when the CS (darkness in this example) is terminated.

It should be emphasized that in two-factor theory, what we have been calling "avoidance responses" are redefined as escape responses. The reinforcer for an avoidance response is supposedly not the avoidance of the shock but rather the escape from a fear-eliciting CS. This theoretical maneuver is two-factor theory's solution to the avoidance paradox. If the theory is correct, we no longer have to wonder how the nonoccurrence of an event such as shock can reinforce a behavior. The removal of a fear-evoking CS is an observable change in the stimulus environment that certainly might act as a negative reinforcer. In short, according to two-factor theory the termination of the signal for shock in avoidance behavior has the same status as the termination of the shock in escape behavior—both are actual changes in stimulation that can serve as reinforcers.

Evidence Supporting Two-Factor Theory

Since the role of the fear-eliciting CS is so crucial to two-factor theory, it is not surprising that many experiments have investigated how CSs can influence avoidance behavior. This research has provided support for two-factor theory in several ways. One class of experiments (Rescorla, 1967; Rescorla & LoLordo, 1965; Weisman & Litner, 1969) has involved creating a fear-eliciting CS in one context and observing its effects when it is presented during a different situation, where an animal is already making avoidance responses. For example, Rescorla and LoLordo (1965) first trained dogs in a shuttle box, where jumping into the other compartment postponed a shock. Then the dogs received conditioning trials in which a tone was paired with shock. Finally, the dogs were returned to the avoidance task, and occasionally the tone was presented (but no longer followed by shock). Rescorla and LoLordo found that whenever the tone came on, the dogs dramatically increased their rates of jumping over the barrier. This result shows that a stimulus that is specifically trained as a CS for fear can amplify ongoing avoidance behavior.

Conversely, several studies have demonstrated that a stimulus that is trained as a conditioned inhibitor for shock depresses avoidance responding (Morris, 1974; Rescorla & LoLordo, 1965). For instance, in another part of their research, Rescorla and LoLordo found that the presentation of such a CS⁻ decreased the rate at which the dogs jumped over the barrier. A CS⁻ for fear is sometimes called a "safety signal," because its presence is correlated with the absence of shock. Weisman and Litner (1969) have shown that animals in an avoidance situation will work to obtain such a safety signal, even though this stimulus had no effect in the avoidance task. Based on findings like these, some theorists have proposed a variation of two-factor theory called the *safety-signal hypothesis* (Weisman & Litner, 1972). According to this hypothesis, any stimulus that follows a response in a typical avoidance task (for instance, the illuminated compartment a dog reached by hurdling over the barrier in the Solomon and Wynne experiment) acts as conditioned positive reinforcer because it is a signal for a shock-free period. Notice that whereas the operant conditioning component of traditional two-factor theory is negative reinforcement (removal of a fear-eliciting CS), in the safety-signal hypothesis it is positive reinforcement (presentation of a safety signal). This hypothesis is supported by evidence that presenting an explicit stimulus each time a shock is terminated (which we can think of as a safety signal) can reduce an animal's fear of the situation (Minecka, Cook, & Miller, 1984). The reduction in fear only occurs, however, when the intertrial interval is long, and therefore signals a long shock-free period (Rosellini, DeCola, & Warren, 1986). A similar theory is Denny's (1971) relaxation theory, which states that a period of relaxation that follows an avoidance response is a positive reinforcer for that response. Although distinctions can be made among traditional two-factor theory, the safety-signal hypothesis, and relaxation theory (see Mineka, 1979), for our purposes their similarities will be emphasized: (1) All three theories stress the importance of conditioned fear (or its absence), and (2) all three assume that the two factors, classical conditioning and operant conditioning, each play indispensable roles in avoidance behavior.

Other experiments supporting two-factor theory have shown that the signal for shock in a typical avoidance situation does indeed develop aversive properties, and that animals can learn a new response when the only consequence of that response is the removal of that signal. In an early experiment, Miller (1948) attempted to develop a white compartment into an aversive stimulus by shocking rats while they were in that chamber. From this point on, no further shocks were presented, but Miller found that a rat would learn a new response, turning a wheel, when this response opened a door and allowed the rat to escape from the white chamber. In the next phase, wheel turning was no longer an effective response; instead a subject could escape from the white chamber by pressing a lever. Eventually Miller's subjects learned this second novel response. Miller reported that the rats learned these new responses by "trial and error": Whatever response produced the opportunity to escape from the white chamber eventually increased in frequency. You should see the parallel between Miller's results and the experiments of Thorndike, where food was used as the reinforcer. Here, the only consequence of a response was the chance to escape from the white chamber, and since the appropriate response increased, this was by definition an example of negative reinforcement. Miller concluded that fear is an "acquirable drive," and that fear reduction can serve as a reinforcer.

The studies just described provide support for two-factor theory by showing that a CS for shock can accelerate ongoing avoidance behavior, and its removal can reinforce totally new responses.

However, not all the evidence on two-factor theory has been favorable, and the next section discusses some of the major problems with the theory.

Problems with Two-Factor Theory

Avoidance without Observable Signs of Fear. One problem with two-factor theory concerns the relationship between fear and avoidance responses. It has long been recognized that this relationship is not as neat as the theory predicts. If the theory is correct, we should be able to observe an increase in fear when the signal for shock is presented, and then a decrease in fear once the avoidance response is made. To conduct such a study, an experimenter must select some objective measure that is thought to be a measure of fear. An animal's heart rate is a commonly used measure. In a study which supported two-factor theory, Soltysik (1960) found heart-rate increases in dogs before the avoidance response and decreases after the response. Unfortunately, the results of other studies are not as encouraging for two-factor theory. Black (1959) observed that dogs' heart rates continued to increase after the avoidance responses were made. In a study with human subjects, Bersch, Notterman, and Schoenfeld (1956) found no heart-rate increases when the signal for shock was presented to well-practiced subjects.

Beginning with some of the earliest studies on avoidance learning, evidence began to accumulate that observable signs of fear disappear as subjects become more experienced. For example, Solomon and Wynne (1953) noted that early in their experiment, a dog would exhibit various signs of fear (whining, urination, shaking) when the light was turned off. However, once the subject became proficient in making the avoidance response, such overt signs of emotion disappeared. But according to two-factor theory, fear should be greatest when avoidance responses are the strongest, since fear is supposedly what motivates the avoidance response. Other studies have corroborated the observations of Solomon and Wynne, using the conditioned suppression procedure (see Chapter 4) to measure a subject's fear. Kamin, Brimer, and Black (1963) and Starr and

Mineka (1977) first trained different groups of rats with different numbers of trials on a signaled avoidance task. Next, while subjects pressed a lever for food reinforcement, the signal for shock from the avoidance task was presented, and the suppression of lever pressing was used as a measure of fear. In both studies, there was less suppression (and presumably less fear of the stimulus) after 27 avoidance trials than after 9 avoidance trials. Of course, two-factor theory predicts that fear should be greater after more trials on the avoidance task.

Why does fear decrease as an animal gains experience on an avoidance task? One possibility is that fear decreases as the animal learns that it has control over the shocks. Studies have shown that animals who can control the shocks are less fearful of the conditioning situation than animals who receive exactly the same pattern of CS and shock presentations but have no control over these stimuli (Neuenschwander, Fabrigoule, & Mackintosh, 1987). There is also evidence that the sensory feedback that occurs when an animal makes an avoidance response causes an overall reduction in fear, presumably because this feedback has been paired with the termination of shock (Cook, Mineka, & Trumble, 1987). Yet, regardless of the reasons for this reduction in fear with experience, it still poses a problem for two-factor theory, which states that fear is the cause of all avoidance responses.

Extinction of Avoidance Behavior. As described earlier, many of the dogs in the Solomon and Wynne experiment quickly became proficient at the avoidance task, so that after a few trials they never again received a shock. From the perspective of two-factor theory, each trial on which the shock is avoided is a classical-conditioning extinction trial: The CS (darkness) is presented, but the US (shock) is not. According to the principles of classical conditioning, the CR (fear) should gradually weaken on such extinction trials until it is no longer elicited by the CS. But if the darkness no longer elicits fear, the avoidance response should not occur either. Thus two-factor theory predicts that avoidance responding should gradually deteriorate after a series of trials without shock. However, once

avoidance responses fail to occur, the subject will again receive darkness-shock pairings, and the CR of fear should be reconditioned. Then, as soon as avoidance responses again start to occur, the fear of the darkness should once again start to extinguish. In short, two-factor theory seems to predict that avoidance responses should repeatedly appear and then disappear in a cyclical pattern.

Unfortunately for two-factor theory, such cycles in avoidance responding have almost never been observed. Indeed, one of the most noteworthy features of avoidance behavior is its extreme resistance to extinction. The classic work of Solomon and Wynne provided a good example of this resistance to extinction. They report that after producing an initial avoidance response, many of their dogs responded for several hundred trials without receiving a shock (Solomon, Kamin, & Wynne, 1953; Solomon & Wynne, 1954). In addition, they found that response latencies continued to decrease during these trials even though no shock was received. This suggests that the strength of the avoidance response was increasing, not decreasing, during these shock-free trials. Such findings were perplexing for two-factor theorists, but Solomon and Wynne (1954) attempted to deal with these results by proposing the notions of *conservation of anxiety* and *partial irreversibility*. By conservation of anxiety, Solomon and Wynne postulated that if response latencies become very short (as they often do) in an avoidance task, the avoidance response may actually occur before the fear response. If the fear response never occurs, they suggested, then there is no opportunity for it to extinguish. In their principle of partial irreversibility, Solomon and Wynne proposed that if classical conditioning involves an extremely intense and traumatic US, then complete extinction of the fear of the CS may become impossible. With these two principles, they felt they could account for the persistence of avoidance responding. However, from a scientific point of view *post-hoc* explanations of unexpected results are never very convincing, and many psychologists view the slow extinction of avoidance behavior as evidence, not for the principles of conservation of anxiety and partial irreversibility, but of the weaknesses of two-factor theory. Given these weaknesses, it is not surprising that other theories of avoidance behavior have been proposed. Two major alternatives to two-factor theory are discussed next.

One-Factor Theory

To put it simply, one-factor theory states that the classical conditioning component of two-factor theory is not necessary. There is no need to assume that fear reduction is the reinforcer for an avoidance response, because, contrary to the assumptions of two-factor theory, avoidance of a shock can in itself serve as a reinforcer. Herrnstein (1969) described some of the major pieces of evidence for one-factor theory, which consist largely of experiments in which there is no signal for shock, no potential CS to become fear-provoking. The experiments of Sidman (1953) and Herrnstein and Hineline (1966) are among the best-known studies relevant to one-factor theory.

The Sidman Avoidance Task. Murray Sidman (1953) developed an avoidance procedure that is now called either by his name or by the term *free-operant avoidance*. In this procedure, there is no signal preceding shock, but if the subject makes no responses, the shocks occur at perfectly regular intervals. For instance, in one condition of Sidman's experiment, a rat would receive a shock every 5 seconds throughout the

session if it made no avoidance response (see Figure 7-2a). However, if the rat made an avoidance response (pressing a lever), the next shock did not occur until 30 seconds after the response. Each response postponed the next shock for 30 seconds (Figure 7-2b). In this procedure, a rat could not accumulate a large interval of shock-free time—a burst of 10 consecutive responses would still delay the next shock 30 seconds after the last response. Nevertheless, by responding regularly (say, once every 20 to 25 seconds), a rat could avoid all the shocks. In practice, Sidman's rats did not avoid all the shocks, but they did respond frequently enough to avoid many of them.

On the surface, these results seem consistent with one-factor theory and problematic for two-factor theory because there is no signal before a shock. If there is no stimulus to elicit fear, why should an avoidance response occur? Actually, it is not difficult to construct an answer that is consistent with two-factor theory, as Sidman himself realized. The logic proceeds as follows: Although Sidman provided no external stimulus, the passage of time could serve as a stimulus because the shocks occurred at regular intervals. That is, once a subject was familiar with the procedure, fear might increase as more and more time elapsed without a response. The animal could associate fear with the stimulus "a long time since the last response," and it could remove this stimulus (and the associated fear) by making a response.

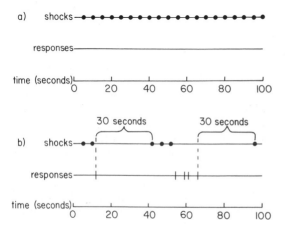

FIGURE 7-2. The procedure in one condition of Sidman's (1953) avoidance task. (a) If the subject makes no responses, a shock is delivered every five seconds. (b) Each response postpones the next shock for 30 seconds.

Since it is known that the passage of time can control behavior in other contexts (see Chapter 11), it is difficult to argue with the logic of the two-factor explanation. To make a stronger case for one-factor theory, we need an experiment in which neither an external stimulus nor an unobservable stimulus such as the passage of time might function as a CS for fear. The next experiment meets these requirements.

The Herrnstein and Hineline (1966) Experiment. The procedure of this experiment was complex, but in essence a rat's lever-press responses switched the animal from a schedule that delivered shocks at a rapid rate to one that delivered shocks at a slower rate. Technically, these schedules of shock delivery might be called *random time* (RT) schedules, because the shocks occurred at unpredictable times, but probability that a shock might occur in a given two-second interval was constant on each schedule. For example, in one condition the probability of a shock after each two-second interval was .3 if the rat had not recently pressed the lever, but only .1 if the rat had recently made a lever press. Clearly, to reduce the number of shocks the animal should remain on the .1 schedule as much as possible. A single response switched the animal to the .1 schedule, which remained in effect until, by

chance, a shock finally occurred. Then the animal was switched back to the .3 schedule, where it remained until another lever press occurred.

A hypothetical 100-second segment of a session is shown in Figure 7-3. The imaginary subject began the session on the .3 schedule, and received four shocks in the first 20 seconds before a response switched the animal to the .1 schedule. The animal's second response had no effect, since it was still on the .1 schedule. The .1 schedule remained in effect for 22 seconds, after which a shock occurred and the .3 schedule was reinstated. Notice that during these 22 seconds on the .1 schedule, the animal avoided four shocks that would have occurred on the .3 schedule. A third response at about 55 seconds switched the animal to the .1 schedule for another 14 seconds, during which three more shocks were avoided. But responding is not always reinforced by a shock-free period. The animal's fourth response was, by chance, followed almost immediately by a shock delivered by the .1 schedule. This example shows that responses in this procedure only produced a lower rate of shocks on the average; they did not guarantee any fixed shock-free time.

Herrnstein and Hineline (1966) found that 17 of their 18 rats eventually acquired the avoidance response, although for some subjects several sessions (and thousands of shocks) were required

FIGURE 7-3. A hypothetical 100-second segment of a session in the Herrnstein and Hineline (1966) experiment. Each response temporarily switched a rat from a schedule where the probability of shock was .3 every two seconds to a schedule where the probability was .1, A subject could avoid many shocks (open circles) by responding, but a response did not guarantee any specific amount of shock-free time.

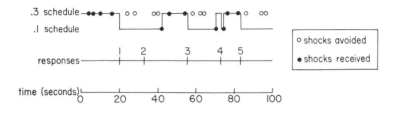

before any stable level of responding was reached. They concluded (1) that animals can learn an avoidance response when neither an external CS nor the passage of time is a reliable signal for shock, and (2) in order to master this task, animals must be sensitive to the average shock rates in the presence and absence of responding. In arguing for one-factor theory, Herrnstein (1969) reasoned that if animals are sensitive to these two rates of shock, then postulating that an unobservable fear controls the behavior is a needless complication: Why not simply assume that a reduction in shock rate is the reinforcer for the avoidance response? The one-factor theorist's solution to the avoidance paradox is thus to deny that it is a paradox. In the more traditional signaled avoidance procedure (which prompted the earliest discussions of the avoidance paradox), the difference in shock rates is extreme—certain shock if no response occurs, and no shock if a response occurs. Given this large difference in shock rates, the rapid acquisition of responding in the signaled avoidance task is not surprising. In addition, Herrnstein suggested that the signal that precedes shock becomes a discriminative stimulus which speeds the acquisition of the avoidance response. These two features may explain why acquisition was much slower in the Herrnstein and Hineline experiment than in a typical signaled avoidance procedure.

Slow Extinction as a Failure of Discrimination. One-factor theory, which relies solely on the principles of operant conditioning, has a simple explanation for the persistence of avoidance responses during extinction. Recall that one popular explanation of why extinction is slower after variable schedules of reinforcement than after fixed schedules is that it is more difficult for the subject to discriminate a change in the contingencies. This same explanation can be extended to the extinction of avoidance responses. We have seen that once an avoidance response is acquired, the subject may avoid every scheduled shock by making the appropriate response. Now suppose that at some point the experimenter turns off the shock generator. From the subject's perspective, the subsequent trials will appear no different than the previous trials: The stimulus comes on, the

subject responds, the stimulus goes off, no shock occurs. Since the subject can discriminate no change in the conditions, there is no change in behavior either, according to this reasoning.

Cognitive Theory

Seligman and Johnston (1973) proposed a cognitive theory of avoidance which they suggested was superior to both the two-factor and one-factor theories. On a very general level, the Seligman and Johnston theory bears some resemblance to the Rescorla-Wagner model of classical conditioning. Recall that two important concepts in the Rescorla-Wagner model are the observed size of the US and the subject's expectancy about the size of the US. Learning occurs only when there is a discrepancy between observation and expectation; with no discrepancy, there is no learning. Similarly, Seligman and Johnston propose that a subject's behavior will change in an avoidance task whenever there is a discrepancy between expectancy and observation. To be more specific, Seligman and Johnston propose that there are two important expectations in an avoidance situation: (1) an expectation about the consequences of a response, and (2) an expectation about the consequences of not responding. On the first trial of a signaled avoidance experiment, a subject can have no expectation that a particular response will avoid a shock, nor that shock will occur if it does not respond. Consequently, the subject makes no avoidance response on the first trial. However, over the course of the acquisition phase, the subject gradually develops the expectations that (1) no shock will occur if a response is made, and (2) shock will occur if a response is not made. Assuming that the animal prefers situation 1 over situation 2 (a very reasonable assumption), the animal will make a response.

Once these two expectations have been formed, Seligman and Johnston assume that the animal's behavior will not change until one or both of the expectations are violated. This assumption can account for the slow extinction of avoidance behavior. As long as the animal responds on each extinction trial, it can observe only that a response is followed by no shock.

This observation is consistent with the animal's expectation, so there is no change in its behavior. Presumably, extinction will only begin to occur if the subject eventually fails to make a response on some trial (perhaps by mistake, or because the subject is distracted by a random noise, by an itch, and so on). It is only on such trials that the subject can observe an outcome (no response followed by no shock) that is inconsistent with the animal's expectations.

The Procedure of Response Blocking (Flooding). The slow extinction of avoidance responses is not inevitable: An experimenter can hasten the course of extinction by using a procedure called *response blocking* or *flooding.* As its name suggests, response blocking involves presenting the signal that precedes shock but preventing the subject from making the avoidance response. For example, Page and Hall (1953) conducted an avoidance experiment in which rats learned to avoid a shock by running from one compartment to another. After the response was learned, one group of rats received normal extinction trials. A second group had the extinction trials preceded by five trials in which a subject was retained in the first compartment for 15 seconds, with the door to the second compartment closed. Thus these subjects were prevented from making the avoidance response, but unlike in the acquisition phase they received no shocks in the first compartment. Page and Hall found that extinction proceeded much more rapidly in the response-blocking group. The other term for this procedure, *flooding,* connotes the fact that subjects are "flooded" with exposure to the stimulus that used to precede shock. (In the Page and Hall experiment, this stimulus was simply the inside of the first compartment.) There is now considerable evidence that response blocking is an effective way to speed the extinction of avoidance responses (Baum, 1966, 1976).

Cognitive theory provides a convenient explanation of why response blocking works. The subject is forced to observe a set of events—no response followed by no shock—that is discrepant from the animal's expectation that no response will be followed by shock. A new expectation, that no shock will follow no response, is gradually formed, and as a result, avoidance responses gradually disappear.

Can the other theories of avoidance behavior account for the effects of response blocking? An obvious explanation based on two-factor theory is that the forced exposure to the CS produces extinction of the conditioned response of fear. Findings that the effectiveness of response blocking is dependent on the number of trials and their duration are consistent with this theory. An explanation based on one-factor theory might proceed as follows: Normal avoidance extinction is slow because there is no discriminative stimulus that signals the change from acquisition to extinction conditions. The procedure used to prevent the avoidance response represents a drastic stimulus change: It gives the subject a cue that things are now different from the preceding acquisition phase. It is therefore not surprising that subsequent extinction proceeds more quickly.

Seligman and Johnston claim that one-factor theory actually makes no clear prediction about the effects of response blocking. That is, if it had turned out that response blocking was ineffective, a one-factor theorist could always argue that the response-blocking part of the experiment is so different from the acquisition and extinction phases that there is no generalization to the extinction phase. However, Seligman and Johnston fail to note that both cognitive theory and two-factor theory could find similar "excuses" if response blocking were ineffective. Like the one-factor theorist, the cognitive theorist and the two-factor theorist could also claim that the subject simply treats the response-blocking phase and the extinction phases as two separate situations, and so the subject does not generalize from one phase to the other. It seems, therefore, that all three theories are equally vague in their predictions about the effects of response blocking: Each can account for the more rapid extinction, but none would be hopelessly embarrassed if it had turned out that response blocking did not alter the course of extinction.

When Avoidance Responses Become Ineffective. According to cognitive theory, a second way to hasten the extinction of avoidance responses would be to present the shock whether or not a response occurs. This contingency would violate a subject's expectation that a response leads to no shock, and therefore avoidance responding should decline. Several studies have shown that following avoidance responses with shock does lead to rapid extinction of those responses (Davenport & Olson, 1968; Seligman & Campbell, 1965). Of course, this result is not surprising, and you should be able to see that both two-factor theory and one-factor theory can easily account for this finding. The presentation of a shock following an avoidance response is a dramatic change in conditions that should quickly produce changes in the subject's behavior.

Conclusions About the Theories of Avoidance

Although two-factor theory has been a popular theory of avoidance behavior, it suffers from several weaknesses. Avoidance learning can occur when there is no external signal for shock (Herrnstein and Hineline, 1966). Although fear plays a crucial role in this theory, the bulk of the evidence suggests that fear disappears yet avoidance responses continue as subjects become experienced at the avoidance task. Finally, two-factor theory offers no convincing explanation for the slowness of extinction in avoidance tasks.

Both one-factor theory and cognitive theory avoid the major problems of two-factor theory by assuming that fear is not an indispensable part of avoidance behavior. But we have reviewed a number of studies showing that fear does play a role in some avoidance situations (Miller, 1948; Rescorla and LoLordo, 1965). Because of such findings, it seems that one-factor theory and cognitive theory would be most accurate if they acknowledged that fear *can* play a role in avoidance situations, although it is not a *necessary* role. Indeed, Seligman and Johnston included an "emotional component" in their theory of avoidance that is basically a statement that classical conditioning of fear responses can influence avoidance behavior.

Seligman and Johnston claim that one-factor theory makes no specific predictions about such matters as extinction and response blocking. However, we have seen that the predictions of

one-factor theory are no more ambiguous than those of cognitive theory. In the final analysis, the differences between these two theories are to a large extent semantic: Wherever cognitive theory speaks of a violation of expectations or a change in expectations, one-factor theory can point to changes in discriminative stimuli. Those who like to speculate about an animal's expectations will probably favor cognitive theory; strict behaviorists, who avoid such speculation about internal events, will prefer the terminology of one-factor theory.

Flooding as Behavior Therapy

Regardless of which theory best accounts for the effects of response blocking or flooding, this procedure has been adopted by some behavior therapists as a treatment for phobias. The major difference between flooding and systematic desensitization (Chapter 4) is that the hierarchy of fearful events or stimuli is eliminated. Instead of beginning with a stimulus that elicits only a small amount of fear, a therapist using a flooding procedure starts immediately with a highly feared stimulus, and forces the patient to remain in the presence of this stimulus until the patient's external signs of fear subside. For example, an individual with a snake phobia might be required to remain in a small room where the therapist is handling a live snake. Of course, it is the therapist's duty to describe the details of the flooding procedure to the patient in advance, to point out that the fear the patient will experience may be quite unpleasant, and to obtain the patient's consent before proceeding. In spite of these safeguards for protecting the rights of the patient, the use of flooding in behavior therapy has been challenged on both practical and moral grounds. Morganstern (1973) reviewed a number of studies that compared the effectiveness of flooding and systematic desensitization, and he concluded that these procedures are about equally effective. Since systematic desensitization (which never allows the patient to experience a high level of fear) is clearly a more pleasant form of therapy, Morganstern argued that there is little justification for using flooding in therapy.

Whereas Morganstern's position seems reasonable, flooding can sometimes succeed in eliminating a phobia when systematic desensitization has failed. Yule, Sacks, and Hersov (1974) report the case history of an 11-year-old boy who had a fear of loud noises—balloons bursting, cap guns, motorcycles, pneumatic drills, and so on. Several weeks of systematic desensitization had produced little improvement. As a last resort, the therapists described a flooding procedure, and the boy agreed to try it. In the first session, the boy entered a small room filled with some 50 balloons. The mere sight of the balloons made the boy very nervous, and he began to cry when the therapist started to break them, one at a time. The therapist continued, however, and eventually he persuaded the boy to break the balloons, first with his feet (while covering his ears with his hands) and later with his hands. The first session ended after several dozen balloons had been broken. At the beginning of the second session, the boy still appeared anxious, but the therapist reported that after breaking several hundred more balloons he almost seemed to enjoy it. After the second session, the boy no longer seemed to fear loud noises, so the therapy was discontinued. A follow-up inquiry 25 months later found that the boy had experienced no recurrences of the phobia.

Although flooding was successful in this case, Yule et al. suggest that it should be used with caution. They suggest that long-duration sessions are essential—the therapist should first observe the onset of fear, and then continue with the procedure until a definite reduction in fear is seen. If the session is terminated too soon, the patient's phobia might actually increase. Indeed, there are a few reports of cases where patients' fears worsened after short-duration therapy sessions of this type (Staub, 1968). Despite these drawbacks, flooding can be an effective form of treatment for phobias when used carefully (James, 1986; Morris & Kratochwill, 1983). There is also evidence that its effectiveness can be enhanced by having patients perform some task, such as playing a video game, to distract their attention during the exposure to the fear-eliciting stimulus. The reasons for this effect are not known, but a similar phenomenon has been observed in rats, whereby a distracting stimulus such as a loud noise can increase the effectiveness of a flooding procedure (Baum, 1987; Baum, Pereira, & Leclerc, 1985).

UNCONTROLLABLE AND UNPREDICTABLE AVERSIVE EVENTS

As has been described, Seligman and Johnston's (1973) cognitive theory proposes that animals develop certain expectations during the course of avoidance learning. These expectations dealt with a specific set of circumstances (for instance, in the presence of the noise, a lever press will be followed by no shock). However, Seligman and his colleagues (Maier & Seligman, 1976; Overmier & Seligman, 1967; Seligman, 1975) have proposed that in certain circumstances, animals can develop expectancies of a much more general character: They may develop the expectation that their behavior has little effect on their environment, and this expectation may generalize to a wide range of situations. Seligman calls this general expectation *learned helplessness*. This section will examine some of the data and theories about learned helplessness, plus other research on what happens when aversive stimuli are uncontrollable and/or unpredictable.

Learned Helplessness

Consider the following experiment. A dog is first placed in a harness where it receives several dozen inescapable shocks. On the next day, the dog is placed in a shuttle box, where it receives escape/avoidance trials very similar to those administered by Solomon and Wynne (1953): Ten seconds of darkness is followed by shock unless the dog jumps into the other compartment. But whereas the dogs in Solomon and Wynne's study learned the task within a few trials, about two thirds of the dogs in Seligman's procedure never learned either to escape or avoid the shock. (In Seligman's procedure the shock ended after 60 seconds if a dog did not respond.) For a few trials, a dog might run around a bit, but eventually the dog would simply lie down and whine when the shock came on, making no attempt to escape.

Seligman's conclusion was that in the initial training with inescapable shock the dog developed an expectation that its behavior has no effect on the aversive consequences it experiences, and this expectation of helplessness carried over to the shuttle box.

Parallel experiments have been conducted with human subjects. For instance, in one study (Hiroto & Seligman, 1975), college students were first presented with a series of loud noises that they could not avoid. They were then asked to solve a series of anagrams. These students had much greater difficulty solving the problems than students who were not exposed to the unavoidable noises. A typical control subject solved all the anagrams, and got faster and faster as the trials proceeded. A typical subject in the noise group would fail on most of the problems, apparently giving up on a problem before the allotted time had expired. Eventually, after many trials, a subject in the noise condition might begin to make some slow progress on the anagrams.

Seligman's explanation is the same for both of these examples: Early experience with uncontrollable aversive events produces a sense of helplessness that carries over into other situations, leading to learning and performance deficits. To be more specific, Maier and Seligman (1976) claimed that there are three components of learned helplessness: motivational, cognitive, and emotional. By a motivational impairment, they meant that subjects lose the motivation to try to control events in their environment, or if they do try at first, they give up easily. The cognitive impairment is a lowered ability to learn from one's experience. Some studies have shown that even when "helpless" subjects are given the same number of successes as control subjects, they learn more slowly. For example, one study found that exposure to inescapable shocks later impaired rats' abilities to learn which of two arms in a maze would allow them to escape from a shock (Jackson, Alexander, & Maier, 1980). After a few successful anagram solutions, students in the helpless group did not improve as rapidly on subsequent problems as did control subjects. (Not all studies have found such cognitive deficits, however; see Anisman, Hamilton, & Zacharko, 1984.) Finally, Maier and Seligman

(1976) summarized a number of emotional problems that have been shown to follow exposure to inescapable aversive events: rats developed ulcers, cats ate less, humans experienced temporary increase in blood pressure, and monkeys became ill. Seligman proposed that this complex pattern of motivational, cognitive, and emotional problems is the result of exposure to inescapable aversive events.

The phenomenon of learned helplessness has been the topic of considerable attention and controversy for at least two reasons. First, many psychologists do not believe that animals are capable of making such an abstract and sweeping generalization as "My behavior has no control over the aversive events I experience," especially after only one session of exposure to inescapable aversive stimuli. Other explanations of the phenomenon have been proposed. Second, as both an experimental psychologist and a clinician, Seligman (1975) has suggested that this laboratory phenomenon is similar in several ways to the severe and prolonged periods of depression some unfortunate people experience. As one example, Seligman described the case of a middle-aged woman whose children had gone off to college, and whose husband was often away on business trips. These unpleasant events were out of the woman's control—nothing she did could bring her family back. Apparently as a result of these experiences, the woman developed a case of profound depression. She often stayed in bed most of the day, for just getting dressed seemed like a great chore. As with Seligman's dogs, the simplest of tasks became difficult for this woman. One implication of the parallel Seligman draws between helplessness and depression is that research on ways to prevent or cure the former might be successfully applied to the latter.

In later writings, Seligman and his colleagues have reformulated their theory of helplessness in humans and have suggested that there may be differences between helplessness in humans and in animals (Abramson, Seligman, & Teasdale, 1978; Peterson & Seligman, 1984). Briefly, they suggest that helplessness in humans can vary along three dimensions: (1) The sense of helplessness may be specific to one situation or fairly global, (2) The person may attribute his or her helplessness to internal or external factors, and (3) The person may view this helplessness as stable (long-term) or unstable (short-term). The severity of the problem and strategy for treatment will depend heavily on which of these characteristics applies in a given case. For instance, if a student attributes his failure in math to specific, external factors ("That was a very difficult course"), this will be less debilitating than if the failure is attributed to internal, global factors ("I'm just incapable of college-level work"). Seligman and his colleagues admit that they do not know whether these three dimensions are applicable to helplessness in animals.

Despite these possible differences between animal and human helplessness, Seligman's work has suggested possible treatment procedures that might be helpful in both cases. One form of treatment has already been alluded to: If helpless dogs are guided across the barrier for enough trials, they will eventually start making the response on their own. In more general terms, Seligman suggests that the best treatment is to place the subject in a situation where it cannot fail, so that gradually an expectation that one's behavior has some control over the consequences that follow will develop. More interesting are studies showing that learned helplessness can be prevented in the first place by what Seligman calls "immunization." That is, the subject is first exposed to a situation where some response (such as turning a wheel) provides escape from shock. Thus the animal's first exposure to shock occurs in a context where the animal can control the shock. Then, in a second situation, inescapable shocks are presented. Finally, the animals are tested in a third situation where a new response (say, switching compartments in a shuttle box) provides escape from shock. It has repeatedly been shown that this initial experience with escapable shock blocks the onset of learned helplessness (Maier & Seligman, 1976; Williams & Lierle, 1986). As one possible implication of this finding, Seligman (1975) suggests that feelings of helplessness in a classroom environment may be prevented by making sure that a child's earliest classroom experiences are ones where the child succeeds (ones where the child demonstrates a mastery over the task at hand).

Other Effects of Uncontrollable Shocks

The type of exposure to uncontrollable shocks that gives rise to learned helplessness can also produce many other changes in an animal, not all of which are encompassed by Seligman's theory. Alternative theories have been developed to deal with these effects. For example, it is known that many species react to aversive stimuli by freezing. One theory of learned helplessness states that because animals become inactive when receiving inescapable shocks, and because this inactivity carries over to the avoidance task, they have difficulty learning to make the avoidance response (Bracewell & Black, 1974). Another theory states that the stress of experiencing inescapable shock depletes some neurochemicals involved in movement, so subsequently the subject learns the avoidance task more slowly (Weiss, 1971). There is indeed evidence that uncontrollable shock depletes noradrenaline levels, thereby causing decreased activity (Weiss, Goodman, Losito, Corrigan, Charry, & Bailey, 1981). In contrast, animals exposed to controllable shocks experience much smaller decreases in noradrenaline levels (Tsuda & Tanaka, 1985).

Uncontrollable shock affects other brain chemicals as well, and some of these effects are related to pain sensitivity. Many studies have shown that exposure to inescapable shock or other aversive stimuli causes a temporary analgesic effect, wherein animals become less sensitive to pain (for example, Jackson, Maier, & Coon, 1979). This analgesia is due partly, but not entirely, to the endogenous opiod system, which is the body's natural mechanism for decreasing sensitivity to pain (see Maier & Keith, 1987). Here, too, the distinction between controllable and uncontrollable shocks is important. The opiod portion of the analgesic response does not occur if escapable shocks are used (Drugan, Ader, & Maier, 1985). In addition, if animals are initially exposed to escapable shocks, they develop an "immunity" similar to that found in learned helplessness. In this case, they become immune to the analgesic effects of the inescapable shocks that are subsequently presented—these inescapable shocks produce no analgesia (Moye, Hyson,

Grau, & Maier, 1983). Such similarities suggest that a common set of learning principles may be responsible for both learned helplessness and this type of stress-induced analgesia.

Predictable and Unpredictable Shocks

In a typical experiment on learned helplessness, subjects are initially exposed to shocks that are both uncontrollable and unpredictable. Some theorists have therefore suggested that many of the debilitating effects of this procedure do not occur because the shocks are uncontrollable, but rather because the animals cannot predict when they will occur and when they will end (Averill, 1973; Overmier & Wielkiewicz, 1983). There is some evidence to support this hypothesis. For example, Volpicelli, Ulm, and Altenor (1984) found learned helplessness in a group of rats that were exposed to uncontrollable and unpredictable shocks, but not in a group that received the same uncontrollable shocks when each was followed by a 3-second stimulus (darkness). Notice that these stimuli did not afford much predictability—they signaled that the shock was over and would not return for at least 3 seconds, but they provided no information about when the next shock would begin. Still, this limited predictiveness was enough to preclude the learned helplessness effect.

It appears unlikely that all of the reported effects of uncontrollable shock were actually due to their unpredictability, because a number of studies have shown that unpredictability and uncontrollability have separate and distinct effects on behavior (Maier & Warren, 1988; Rosellini, Warren, & DeCola, 1987). Nevertheless, whether aversive events are predictable or unpredictable can make a big difference to the animal. We have already seen that animals are less fearful in situations where shocks are predictable than when they are unpredictable. Other studies have shown that animals will choose signaled versus unsignaled shocks in a choice situation. This preference has been found regardless of whether the shocks can be avoided or not. For example, Badia, Culbertson, and Harsh (1973) found that rats would press a lever that switched them from unsignaled shocks to shocks that were two or three times more intense but were signaled by a 5-second tone. This preference for signaled shocks does not necessarily imply, however, that situations involving signaled shock are less stressful for the animals. Some studies have found that situations with signaled shock are less stressful, but others have found that they are more stressful, and there is still intense disagreement about how these conflicting results should be interpreted (Abbott & Badia, 1986; Abbott, Schoen, & Badia, 1984; Arthur, 1986).

PUNISHMENT

Figure 7-1 suggests that punishment has the opposite effect on behavior as positive reinforcement: Reinforcement produces an increase in behavior, and punishment produces a decrease in behavior. Whether this statement is correct is an empirical question, and such illustrious psychologists as Thorndike and Skinner have concluded that it is not. Based on their own research, each concluded that the effects of punishment are not exactly opposite to those of reinforcement. However, their experiments are not very convincing. For example, Skinner (1938) placed two groups of rats on VI schedules of lever pressing for three sessions, and then each animal had two sessions of extinction. For one group, nothing unusual happened during extinction, and this group produced the upper cumulative record in Figure 7-4: Responding gradually decreased over the two sessions. For the second group, however, each lever press during the first 10 minutes of extinction was punished—whenever a rat pressed the lever, the lever "slapped" upward against the rat's paws. This mild punishment was enough to reduce the number of responses during these 10 minutes to a level well below that of the first group. However, when the punishment was removed, response rates increased, and by the end of the second session the punished animals had made just about as many responses as the unpunished animals. From these results, Skinner concluded that the effects of punishment are not permanent, and that punishment produces only a "temporary suppression" of responding.

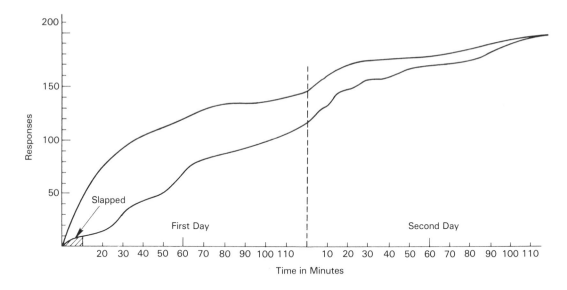

FIGURE 7-4. Cumulative records during two days of extinction from the two groups of rats in Skinner's (1938) experiment on punishment. The upper record is from the group that received normal extinction. The lower record is from the group whose responses were punished during the first 10 minutes of extinction.

The problem with Skinner's conclusion is that although the effects of punishment were certainly temporary, so was the punishment itself. It is not clear what an analogous experiment with positive reinforcement would look like, but we know that the effects of positive reinforcement are also "temporary" in the sense that operant responses will extinguish after the reinforcer is removed. Since Skinner's early experiment, many studies have addressed the question of whether punishment is the opposite of reinforcement in its effects on behavior. The following section describes a few of these studies.

Is Punishment the Opposite of Reinforcement?

We can attempt to answer this question by examining the two words used by Skinner—"temporary" and "suppression." If, unlike in Skinner's experiment, the punishment contingency is permanent, is the decrease in behavior still temporary? Sometimes it is, for a number of studies

have shown that subjects may habituate to a relatively mild punisher (Azrin, 1960; Rachlin, 1966). In Azrin's (1960) experiment, once pigeons were responding steadily on a VI schedule, punishment was introduced—each response produced a mild shock. Response rates decreased immediately, but over the course of several sessions they returned to their preshock levels. Despite such results, there is no doubt that suitably intense punishment can produce a long-term decrease or disappearance of the punished behavior. When Azrin used more intense shocks, there was little or no recovery in responding over the course of the experiment.

Although Skinner did not define the term "suppression," later writers (Estes, 1944) have taken it to mean a decrease in behavior that does not depend on a contingency between the behavior and the aversive event. It does not take a punishment contingency to cause a decrease in behavior. For example, in the frequently-used conditioned-suppression procedure, a CS for shock is presented as an animal is responding for food reinforcement. After a few pairings of the CS and shock, responding for food slows or stops completely during the CS, even though these responses are not punished, and no behavior on the part of the subject can prevent the shock. In short, an aversive event can cause a general decrease in a subject's ongoing behavior. Does a contingency between a specific behavior and an aversive event do more than this? Does it cause a greater decrease in this behavior than the same event delivered on a noncontingent basis? An experiment by Schuster and Rachlin (1968) investigated this question. Pigeons could sometimes peck at the left key in a Skinner box, and at other times they could peck at the right key. Both keys offered identical VI schedules of food reinforcement, but then different schedules of shock were introduced on the two keys. When the left key was lit (signaling that the VI schedule was available on this key), some of the pigeon's keypecks were followed by shock. On the other hand, when the right key was lit, shocks were presented regardless of whether the pigeon pecked at the key. Under these conditions, responding on the left key decreased markedly, but there was little change in response rate on the right key. In another study, Goodall (1984) found that the strength of the response-shock contingency determined the degree of response reduction. A strong response-shock contingency (in which responses were frequently followed by shock) caused much greater reductions in responding than a weak contingency (in which responses were only occasionally followed by shock). In a control group where shocks were delivered on a noncontingent basis, there was little reduction in responding regardless of the frequency of the shocks.

Studies like these have firmly established the fact that a punishment contingency does more than simply cause a general decrease in activity. When a particular behavior is punished, that behavior will exhibit a large decrease in frequency while other, unpunished behaviors show no substantial change in frequency. To summarize, contrary to the predictions of Thorndike and Skinner, empirical results suggest that the effects of punishment are directly opposite to those of rein-

forcement: Reinforcement produces an increase in whatever specific behavior is followed by the hedonically positive stimulus, and punishment produces a decrease in the specific behavior that is followed by the aversive stimulus. In both cases, we can expect these changes in behavior to persist as long as the reinforcement or punishment contingency remains in effect.

Factors Influencing the Effectiveness of Punishment

We now know a good deal more about punishment besides the fact that its effects can be permanent and that the response-punisher contingency is important. Operant conditioners have examined a number of variables that determine what effects a punishment contingency will have. Azrin and Holz (1966) reviewed some of these variables, and to their credit all of their major points appear as true now as when their chapter was published. Several of these points are described next.

Manner of Introduction. If one's goal is to obtain a large, permanent decrease in some behavior, then Azrin and Holz recommend that the punisher be immediately introduced at its full intensity. We have already seen that subjects can habituate to a mild punisher, and several studies have shown that this habituation seems to generalize to higher intensities of punishment. The end result is that a given intensity of punishment may produce a complete cessation of behavior if introduced suddenly, but it may have little or no effect on behavior if it is gradually approached through a series of successive approximations. Azrin, Holz, and Hake (1963) reported that a shock of 80 volts following each response was sufficient to produce a complete suppression of pigeons' key-peck responses if the 80-volt intensity was used from the outset. However, if the punishment began at lower intensities and then slowly increased, the pigeons would continue to respond even when the intensity was raised to as much as 130 volts. Since a behavior modifier's goal when using punishment is to eliminate an undesirable behavior, not to shape a tolerance of the aversive stimulus, the punisher should be at its maximum intensity the first time it is presented.

Immediacy of Punishment. Just as the most effective reinforcer is one that is delivered immediately after the operant response, a punisher that immediately follows a response is most effective in decreasing the frequency of the response (Baron, Kaufman & Fazzini, 1969; Goodall, 1984). Baron et al. (1969) studied the behavior of rats who were responding on a Sidman avoidance task. Some of the rats' avoidance responses were punished with shock, but in different conditions the delay between a response and the punishment was varied between 0 and 60 seconds. Baron et al. obtained an orderly relationship between punishment delay and response rate: the more immediate the punishment, the greater the decrease in responding. Along these same lines, Hineline (1970) found that rats would press a lever to postpone shocks, even though the total number of shocks they received was the same regardless of whether they responded or not. The importance of contiguity in a punishment contingency may explain why many commonly used forms of punishment are ineffective. For example, the mother who tries to decrease a child's misbehavior with the warning, "Just wait until your father gets home" is describing a very long delay between a behavior and its aversive consequences. It would not be surprising if this contingency had little effect on the child's behavior.

Schedule of Punishment. Like positive reinforcers, punishers need not be delivered after every occurrence of a behavior. Azrin and Holz conclude, however, that the most effective way to eliminate a behavior is to punish every response rather than to use some intermittent schedule of punishment. A common way to assess the effects of different punishment schedules is first to establish responding for some positive reinforcer on a schedule that is the same throughout the experiment (for instance, a VI 60-second schedule). Then a variety of different punishment schedules are superimposed on the reinforcement schedule to examine their effects. In one such experiment, Azrin, Holz, and Hake (1963) delivered punishment on FR schedules ranging from FR 1 (every response followed by shock) to FR 1000 (every 1000th response followed by shock). As you might expect, the smaller FR punishment schedules produced the greater decreases in responding.

The schedule of punishment can affect the patterning of responses over time as well as the overall response rate. When Azrin (1956) superimposed a FI 60-second schedule of punishment on a VI 3-minute schedule of food reinforcement, he found that pigeons' response rates declined toward zero as the end of each 60-second interval approached. In other words, the effect of the FI schedule of punishment (a decelerating pattern of responding) was the opposite of that typically found with FI schedules of reinforcement (an accelerating pattern of responding). In a similar fashion, Hendry and Van-Toller (1964) punished rats' lever presses on a FR 20 schedule and found that response rates decreased as the twentieth response was approached. Response rates increased suddenly after each shock was delivered. This pattern is also the opposite of that produced by FR reinforcement schedules, in which there is a pause after each reinforcer is delivered. In other research, Galbicka and his colleagues showed that certain lengths of interresponse times (IRTs) could be decreased through punishment: When long IRTs were punished, monkeys produced fewer long IRTs and more short IRTs (Galbicka & Branch, 1981; Galbicka & Platt, 1984). This result parallels the studies showing that certain durations of IRTs can be increased through selective reinforcement (Chapter 6).

These and other studies on schedules of punishment bolster the argument that punishment is the opposite of reinforcement in its effects on behavior: Where a particular reinforcement schedule produces an accelerating response pattern, the same schedule of punishment produces a decelerating pattern; where reinforcement produces a pause-then-respond pattern, punishment produces a respond-then-pause pattern; where reinforcement increases IRTs of certain sizes, punishment decreases them.

Motivation to Respond. Azrin and Holz note that the effectiveness of a punishment procedure is inversely related to the intensity of the subject's motivation to respond. Azrin, Holz, and Hake (1963) demonstrated this point quite clearly by observing the effects of punishment on pigeons' food-reinforced responses when the birds were maintained at different levels of food deprivation. Punishment had little effect on response rates when the pigeons were very hungry, but when these animals were only slightly food-deprived the same intensity of punishment produced a complete cessation of responding. This finding is not surprising, but it does emphasize a strategy for increasing the effectiveness of a punishment procedure without increasing the amount of punishment: Attempt to discover what reinforcer is maintaining the behavior, and decrease the value of that reinforcer. Thus if a mother believes that her young child engages in destructive behaviors as a way of getting the mother's attention, she can (1) punish the undesired behaviors and simultaneously (2) give the child more attention before the child resorts to the undesirable behaviors. A related strategy, as discussed next, is to deliver the same reinforcer for a different, more desirable response.

Availability of Alternative Behaviors. Azrin and Holz reported a result that we might easily predict, using common sense. A pigeon could peck at a single response key for food reinforcement on a FR 25 schedule. When each response was punished by a mild shock, the subject's response rate decreased, but only by about 10 percent. However, in another condition, a second key also provided food on a FR 25 schedule, but only responses on the first key were punished. It should come as no surprise that the pigeon ceased responding on the first key and responded exclusively on the second. The more general point, however, is that punishment is much more effective when the subject is provided with an alternative way to obtain the reinforcer that has been maintaining some unwanted response. For this reason, when behavior modifiers decide it is necessary to use punishment to eliminate some unwanted behavior (such as fighting among children), they almost always pair this punishment with reinforcement for an alternative behavior that is incompatible with the unwanted behavior (for instance, cooperative play).

Punishment as a Discriminative Stimulus. This observation is less obvious than those of the last few paragraphs. Besides having aversive properties, a punisher can also sometimes function as a discriminative stimulus—a signal predicting the availability of other stimuli, either pleasant or unpleasant. Imagine an experiment in which a pigeon's responses go unpunished during some portions of the session but are followed by shock during other parts of the session. Each time the shock begins, the pigeon's response rate *increases*! This behavior seems paradoxical until we learn that the pigeon can obtain food only during those periods when its responses are punished; an extinction schedule is in effect during the periods when responses are not shocked (Holz and Azrin, 1961). In other words, the shocks following responses served as discriminative stimuli for the availability of food reinforcement, for they were the only stimuli that differentiated between the periods of reinforcement and extinction. Azrin and Holz suggest that similar explanations may account for some instances of *masochism*—self-injurious behaviors that appear equally paradoxical at first glance. Because self-injurious behaviors often bring the reinforcers of sympathy and attention to the individual, the aversive aspects of this type of behavior (pain) may serve as discriminative stimuli that reinforcement is imminent.

Disadvantages of Using Punishment

Although Azrin and Holz conclude that punishment can be a method of behavior change that is at least as effective as reinforcement, they warn that it can produce a number of undesirable side effects. First, they note that punishment can sometimes lead to a general suppression of all behaviors, not only the behavior being punished. Second, the use of punishment can elicit a number of emotional effects, such as fear and anger, that are generally disruptive of behavior and therefore undesirable. These first two side effects are usually temporary, but other disadvantages of punishment are not. A third problem is that in real-world situations, the use of punishment demands the continual monitoring of the individual's behavior, whereas the use of reinforcement does not necessarily demand such monitoring. This is because it is in the individual's interest to point out instances of a behavior that is followed by a reinforcer. If a child receives a reinforcer for cleaning up her room, she will probably make sure her parents see the room after it is cleaned. On the other hand, if the child is punished for a messy room, she is unlikely to call her parents to see the messy room so that the punishment contingency can be enforced.

Along the same lines, a practical problem with the use of punishment is that individuals may try to circumvent the rules or escape from the situation entirely. Azrin and Holz described the behavior of a clever rat that was scheduled to receive shocks for some of its lever presses while working for food reinforcement. The rat learned to avoid the shocks by lying on its back while pressing the lever, thereby using its fur as insulation from the shocks delivered via the metal floor of the chamber. We might expect people to be even more ingenious in their tricks to circumvent a punishment contingency. If punishment is a teacher's primary method of behavioral control, a child may try to hide evidence of misbehavior. In addition, the child may attempt to escape from the situation by feigning sickness or by playing hooky.

Another disadvantage of using punishment is that it can lead to aggression, against either the punisher or whomever happens to be around. The constant risk of bodily harm faced by prison guards (and by prisoners) attests to this fact. Aggression as a response to aversive stimulation is not unique to humans. Ulrich and Azrin (1962) reported a study in which two rats were placed in an experimental chamber. The animals behaved peaceably until they began to receive shocks, at which point they began to fight. Similar results have been obtained with pigeons, mice, hamsters, cats, and monkeys.

Given the numerous disadvantages of punishment, Azrin and Holz suggest that it should be used reluctantly, and with great care. A final argument against using punishment is an ethical one. If an individual's behavior can be changed in the desired way with either reinforcement or punishment, why should the more unpleasant procedure of punishment be used? Of course, there are some circumstances where reinforcement is ineffective and punishment must be used. Furthermore, Azrin and Holz point out that punishment will always be a part of our environment. They admit that it might be possible to legislate punishment out of existence in institutions such as prisons and schools. It would be much more difficult, however, to eliminate punishment in everyday interpersonal interactions (between parent and child, between spouses, and so forth). Finally, the physical environment is full of potential punishers that are impossible to eliminate. Just think of the possible punishing consequences that might follow the wrong behavior while one is driving a car, walking through a forest, swimming, skiing, cooking, or performing almost any behavior. Since punishment cannot be eliminated from our environment, it is important for behavioral psychologists to continue to study this phenomenon so as to increase our understanding of how it influences behavior.

Negative Punishment

Cell 3 in Figure 7-1 represents negative punishment, in which a pleasant stimulus is removed if a response occurs. Several studies have shown that this procedure produces a decrease in responding. In a study where pigeons pecked a key for food on a VI schedule, Ferster (1958) demonstrated the effect of a time-out from positive reinforcement. While the VI schedule was in effect, the color of the response key would occasionally turn blue, which signaled that further pecking at the key would result in a 10-minute time-out (during which reinforcement was not available). However, the subject could avoid the time-out by not pecking when the key was blue. As the pigeons became familiar with this contingency, response rates dropped to zero when the key was blue, even though the VI schedule was still in effect during this stimulus.

We have already seen that the positive punishment procedure reduces behavior because of the contingency between response and punisher, not simply because the presence of aversive stimuli causes a general suppression of behavior. Similarly, it has been shown that an omission procedure causes a decrease in responding because of the specific contingency between a response and the omission of a pleasant stimulus, not simply because the decrease in these stimuli causes a general reduction in behavior (Wilson, Boakes, & Swan, 1987). Thus in both positive and negative punishment, the contingency between a response and its consequences is much more important than any change in the number of pleasant or aversive stimuli *per se*. Because it is a means of reducing behavior without using an aversive stimulus, negative punishment has become a popular tool in behavior modification, as discussed at the end of this chapter.

Some Theories of Punishment

Although it is now generally agreed that punishment causes reductions in behavior, there are several conflicting theories about why it does so. A theory called the *avoidance theory of punishment* attempts to explain the effects of punishment within the framework of two-factor theory. One proponent of this theory, James Dinsmoor (1954, 1955, 1977), begins with the assumption that any response (such as a lever press) can be viewed as a chain of behaviors (walking to the lever, raising one's paw, pressing the lever). When the final response of this chain produces an aversive stimulus such as shock, earlier behaviors in the chain begin to elicit fear (through the rules of classical conditioning). This fear is, of course, aversive, but the subject can escape from the fear by interrupting the chain and performing some other behavior (for instance, walking away from the lever). This other behavior is reinforced by the escape from fear, and it therefore increases in frequency. To recapitulate, according to Dinsmoor, a typical sequence of events in a punishment situation might be: (1) A rat walks toward the lever; some fear is elicited, (2) The rat raises its paw; more fear is elicited, (3) The rat moves away from the lever; fear is terminated, and (4) The frequency of moving away from the lever increases because it has been reinforced by the termination of fear. According to this theory, then, the function of punishment is to *increase other behavior,* which *indirectly* causes a decrease in the punished response simply because the animal spends more time doing something else. The avoidance theory of punishment postulates no mechanism for directly weakening or decreasing the punished behavior.

The major alternative to the avoidance theory of punishment is sometimes called the *negative law of effect* (Rachlin and Herrnstein, 1969). This phrase was coined by Thorndike (1911), who initially proposed that punishment is the opposite of reinforcement before changing his opinion about its effectiveness. Stated simply, this theory proposes that punishment acts directly to weaken the punished behavior, not indirectly as proposed by the avoidance theory. The theory might also be called the *one-factor theory of punishment* because, like the one-factor theory of avoidance, it postulates that the classical conditioning factor (fear elicitation and termination) is not an important or necessary part of the punishment process.

Distinguishing between these two theories of punishment has proven to be more difficult than it might seem at first. By recording a number of different behaviors both before and during punishment, Dunham (1972; Dunham & Grantmyre, 1982) has found that when one behavior is punished, the frequency of some other behavior increases. For instance, when rats received shocks as they drank, drinking decreased and wheel running increased. Does this finding mean that the avoidance theory of punishment is correct? That is, did the rats learn to avoid the shocks by running, and was the decrease in drinking only a byproduct of the increased running? Not necessarily. The opposite chain of events may be applicable: Drinking may have decreased as a direct result of the punishment (as one-factor theory asserts), thereby giving the animal more time for wheel running. Based on their work with similar procedures, Baker, Woods, Tait, and Gardiner (1986) concluded that the avoidance theory is incorrect. Their reasoning is subtle, but in essence they found similar increases in an alternative behavior regardless of whether one behavior, eating, was punished or was simply precluded by removal of the food. They argued that the avoidance theory cannot explain the similar effects of these two procedures except by attributing them to coincidence.

Perhaps the most revealing comparison of these two theories is based on recent mathematical analyses of choice behavior. Because an understanding of this research depends on a familiarity with other work on choice behavior, a discussion of this topic will be postponed until Chapter 14.

THE USE OF PUNISHMENT IN THERAPY

Wherever possible, behavior therapists avoid using punishment, because the comfort and happiness of the patient is one of their major concerns. However, if a behavior is dangerous or otherwise undesirable, and if other techniques are impractical or unsuccessful, the use of punishment may be deemed preferable to doing nothing at all. This section describes some representative situations in which behaviors have been reduced or eliminated with punishment. As will be seen, the aversive stimuli employed are frequently quite mild. The examples that follow provide further support for some of Azrin and Holz's rules about punishment.

Punishment of "Voluntary" Behaviors

One nonphysical form of punishment that is frequently used by parents and teachers is scolding and reprimanding a child for bad behavior. This tactic can certainly influence a child's behavior, but not always in the way the adult wants. The problem is that a reprimand is a form of attention, and we have already seen that attention can be a powerful reinforcer. Furthermore, a child who is scolded or reprimanded frequently also receives attention from siblings or classmates, and this attention from peers may serve as further reinforcement for the undesired behavior. This does not mean, however, that scolding or reprimanding can never achieve their intended results (see Abramowitz, O'Leary, & Rosen, 1987.) O'Leary, Kaufman, Kass, and Drabman (1970) found that the manner in which a repri-

mand is given is a major factor determining its effectiveness. They observed that most teachers use loud or public reprimands that are heard not only by the child involved but by all others in the classroom. In a second-grade classroom, O'Leary et al. began by simply measuring the frequency of disruptive behaviors when the teacher used this form of discipline. In the second phase of the study, they instructed the teacher to use "soft" or private reprimands wherever possible (that is, to walk up to the child and speak quietly, so that no other children could hear). O'Leary et al. found a decrease in disruptive behavior of roughly 50 percent when such soft reprimands were used.

Studies in classroom situations have shown that praise from the teacher can be an effective positive reinforcer for good behavior ("I like the way you are working." "You did a good job on that problem."). However, the exclusive use of positive reinforcement may not be sufficient to maintain order in a classroom, simply because disruptive behaviors such as talking out of turn or fighting have strong reinforcers of their own (other children laugh, the child gets possession of a desired object, and the like). Nearly all grade-school teachers therefore rely on some form of punishment to reduce disruptive behaviors. The work of O'Leary et al., along with other similar research, suggests that an effective strategy for teachers is the combination of praise for desirable behaviors and private reprimands for undesirable behaviors.

Stronger forms of punishment are sometimes necessary when a child's behavior is a more serious problem than a mere classroom disturbance. For example, some retarded, autistic, or schizophrenic children engage in self-injurious behaviors such as repeatedly slapping themselves in the face, biting deep into their skin, or banging their heads against any solid object. The causes of these behaviors are not clear, but because of the risk of severe injury these children are sometimes kept in physical restraints around the clock except when a therapist is in the immediate vicinity. Under such conditions, there is little opportunity for the child to learn more appropriate behaviors. For such extreme behavioral disorders, electric shock has been successfully used as a punisher. A report by Prochaska, Smith, Marzilli, Colby, and Donovan (1974) describes the treatment of one nine-year-old profoundly retarded girl named Sharon.

When she was unrestrained and not under the influence of a tranquilizer, Sharon would hit her nose and chin with her fist at a rate of about 200 blows per hour. The behavior therapists first tried to decrease her head banging with negative punishment and with positive reinforcement for other behaviors, but in this case these procedures were ineffective. They then began to use a shock to Sharon's leg as a punisher for head banging, and her rate of head banging decreased dramatically. Unfortunately, Azrin and Holz's observation about the need for continual monitoring was supported in this case, because there was little generalization of this learning to Sharon's home or school environments. Evidently Sharon had learned that head banging was punished only in the clinic, with the electrodes on her leg and with the therapist watching her. Obviously, other tactics were necessary if her head banging were to be totally eliminated.

To reduce Sharon's head banging in her normal environments, the therapists made use of a remote-control unit to deliver the shocks, and her behavior was continuously monitored at school and at home. Under these new conditions, Sharon's head banging dropped to zero within a week. The disappearance of head banging generalized to times when the shock generator was removed, and eventually the punishment procedures were terminated with no return of the behavior. The elimination of head banging was accompanied by improvements in other behaviors—Sharon's crying spells (previously frequent) ceased, so she could now go with her parents to public places such as shopping centers and restaurants.

Prochaska et al. suggested that their final punishment program was successful because they followed several of the suggestions of Azrin and Holz: Punishment was delivered immediately after the unwanted behavior, it was delivered after each occurrence of the behavior, there was no way to escape from the contingency, and other, desirable behaviors such as playing with classmates were reinforced. The use of shock as a punisher with children is a controversial matter, and there will probably always be individuals who are unconditionally opposed to it for moral reasons. To be fair, however, the aversive features of this procedure must be weighed against the negative consequences of failing to implement the punishment procedure. In Sharon's case, the pain of several dozen half-second shocks seems small when compared to the alternative—a life of self-injury, physical restraint, and the inability to play with peers or go out in public.

Punishment of "Involuntary" Behaviors

You may be surprised to learn that so-called "involuntary" or reflexive behaviors, which seem to occur automatically in response to some stimulus, can be reduced through punishment. Heller and Strang (1973) described the use of a mild punisher to reduce the frequency of bruxism in a 24-year-old male. *Bruxism* is the gnashing and grinding of one's teeth while asleep, a problem found in about 5 percent of all college students. This behavior sometimes results in serious tooth damage. To measure the rate of bruxism automatically, Heller and Strang used a voice-operated relay that was activated by the sound of the teeth grinding. The client wore an earplug while he slept, and each instance of bruxism recorded by the voice-operated relay was followed immediately by a three-second burst of noise in the client's ear. As soon as this punishment contingency was introduced, the rate of bruxism decreased from a baseline rate of about 100 occurrences per hour to about 30 occurrences per hour. The therapists reported that the remaining instances of bruxism were often too soft to trigger the equipment and therefore went unpunished. It is interesting to note that although the client was asleep when the bruxism occurred, the character of this behavior changed in a way that partially circumvented the punishment contingency (it became quieter). Presumably, the rate of bruxism would have decreased further if more sensitive recording equipment were employed.

Creer, Chai, and Hoffman (1977) reported a

case in which another involuntary behavior, coughing, was controlled with punishment. A 14-year-old boy first developed a loud, grating cough as the result of a cold, but the cough persisted long after the cold had ended. Visits to a number of doctors and several types of medication did not help. In school, the boy's cough first elicited laughter in his classmates, but after a while the laughter turned to ridicule. The boy's teachers were annoyed with the disruption the coughing caused, and finally he was expelled and told he could not return to school until his coughing had stopped.

When he was referred to the therapists (at an asthma center), the boy received a thorough medical examination, but no abnormalities were found. The therapists then tried both systematic desensitization and hypnosis, but these did not solve the problem. At this point, the therapists discussed the possibility of using shock as a punisher for coughing, and both the boy and his parents agreed that it was worth a try. The procedure involved administering a mild one-second shock to the boy's forearm each time he coughed. The results were dramatic. During a one-hour baseline, 22 instances of coughing were recorded. Under the punishment contingency, the boy coughed once, received a shock, and then did not cough again for the rest of the hour. The shock electrodes were then removed, and no coughing reappeared. At home that evening he continued to be symptom-free, and he returned to school the next day. Follow-ups over a two-and-a- half-year period revealed that the chronic cough had never reappeared.

The suddenness with which the cough disappeared in this case is unusual, but other attempts to eliminate uncontrolled coughing or sneezing with punishment have also been successful (Alexander, Chai, Creer, Miklich, Renne, & Cardoso, 1973; Kushner, 1968). In addition, aversive stimuli have been used to eliminate several other types of involuntary behaviors, including muscle spasms (Sachs & Mayhall, 1971), frequent vomiting (Cunningham & Linscheid, 1976), gagging (Glasscock, Friman, O'Brien, & Christopherson, 1986), and hallucinations (Bucher & Fabricatore, 1970). Of course, we should not expect a punishment contingency to eliminate a symptom caused by some physical disorder (for example, coughing due to a respiratory illness). However, if physicians have determined that no medical problem is responsible for a persistent behavioral symptom, punishment may be an effective (albeit unpleasant) treatment.

Negative Punishment: Response Cost and Time-out

It is easy to incorporate a negative punishment contingency in any token system: Whereas tokens can be earned by performing desirable behaviors, some tokens are lost if the individual performs an undesirable behavior. The loss of tokens, money, or other conditioned reinforcers following the occurrence of undesirable behaviors is called *response cost*. Token economies that include a response cost arrangement have been used with children, prison inmates, and patients in mental institutions. Phillips (1968) described how response cost was used as part of a token system for "predelinquent" boys. These boys, in their early teens or younger, had each been guilty of minor violations of the law, and authorities believed that their behaviors would get worse unless some action were taken. They were therefore sent to Achievement Place, a home in the community supervised by two "house parents." While at Achievement Place, each boy was on a token system under which he could earn points through such behaviors as doing homework, getting good grades, keeping his room clean, and doing household chores. The points could be used to purchase snacks or an allowance, or for privileges such as watching TV, staying up late, or going into town. Behaviors that lost points were arguing or fighting, disobeying the house parents, displaying poor manners, or being late. For example, a boy lost a certain number of points for every minute he was late in returning from school or late in going to bed. By recording the boys' behaviors before and after the response-cost contingency went into effect, Phillips showed conclusively that this contingency improved their behaviors. As might be expected, the loss of points affected only those behaviors that were included under the rule. For instance, when fines were established for being late from school, the boys became prompt in returning home from school, but not in returning from errands.

We have seen that the most common form of negative punishment is *time-out,* in which one or more desirable stimuli are temporarily removed if the individual performs some unwanted behavior. Time-out is often used with children, as when a parent tells a child to go to his or her room for misbehaving. Of course, it is an empirical question whether a particular form of time-out is punishing. If the child's room is filled with toys and games, it may actually serve as a reinforcer. Research has shown that time-outs in which a child is sent to an isolated room can reduce aggressive or disruptive behaviors in classroom situations. For example, Drabman and Spitalnik (1973) used 10-minute time-outs as punishment for aggressive and out-of-seat behavior in a class of emotionally disturbed children. If an observer determined that a child's behavior was sufficiently disruptive (according to certain objective criteria), the teacher was given a signal. The teacher then told the child, "You have misbehaved. You must leave the class." The child was then sent to the barren isolation room for 10 minutes. Both aggression and time out of seat were substantially reduced as soon as the time-out contingency was put into effect. It seems likely that this procedure was effective at least in part because a child could not engage in any social interactions while in the isolation room. Both time-out and response-cost procedures have become increasingly popular with teachers and behavior therapists because they are effective ways to reduce unwanted behaviors without presenting any aversive stimulus.

CHAPTER

8

THEORETICAL ISSUES ABOUT BEHAVIOR AND REINFORCEMENT

The theoretical issues examined in this chapter are very broad, and they deal with matters of importance to the entire field of learning. The topics concern such basic issues as what ingredients, if any, are essential for learning to take place, and under what conditions will a supposed reinforcer strengthen the behavior it follows. Most of the issues we will examine have been pondered by learning theorists for many years. Some have now been fairly well resolved, but others are the subject of continuing research.

The issues of this chapter can be divided into three general categories. First, we will consider whether both the performance of a response and the reinforcement of that response are necessary for learning to take place. Hypotheses about the importance of the reinforcer have varied enormously. Some writers have suggested that reinforcement is essential for any learning to occur, others that reinforcement is involved in operant conditioning but not in classical conditioning, and still others that reinforcement is not essential

for either type of learning. We will weigh the relative merits of each of these positions. Second, we will trace the history of attempts to develop a method for predicting which stimuli will be effective reinforcers for a given subject and which will not. A successful method for predicting the effectiveness of a reinforcer would have obvious practical utility, and we will see that it would be equally important from a scientific standpoint. Finally, we will survey recent efforts to analyze the effects of reinforcers using concepts from economics.

THE ROLE OF THE RESPONSE

Operant conditioning might be described as "learning by doing": An animal performs some response and experiences the consequences, and the future likelihood of that response is changed. For Thorndike, the performance of the response was a necessary part of the learning process.

After all, if a response does not occur, how can it be strengthened by reinforcement? Convinced that a pairing of response and reinforcer is essential for learning, Thorndike proposed the following experiment:

Put the rat, in a little wire car, in the entrance chamber of a maze, run it through the correct path of a simple maze and into the food compartment. Release it there and let it eat the morsel provided. Repeat 10 to 100 times according to the difficulty of the maze under ordinary conditions....Then put it in the entrance chamber free to go wherever it is inclined and observe what it does. Compare the behavior of such rats with that of rats run in the customary manner. (1946, p. 278)

Thorndike predicted that a rat that was pulled passively through a maze would perform like a naive subject in the later test, since the animal had no opportunity to perform a response. On this and several other issues, Thorndike's position was challenged by Edward C. Tolman (Tolman, 1932, 1951, 1959) who might be characterized as an early cognitive psychologist (although he worked decades before the emergence of the field of cognitive psychology). According to Tolman, operant conditioning involves not the simple strengthening of a response but the formation of an *expectation*. In a maze, for example, a rat develops an expectation that a reinforcer will be available in the goal box. In addition, he proposed that the rat acquires a "cognitive map" of the maze—a general understanding of the spatial layout of the maze. Tolman proposed that both of these types of learning could be acquired by passive observation as well as by active responding, so that animals should be able to learn something in the type of experiment Thorndike described.

One study fashioned according to Thorndike's specifications was conducted by McNamara, Long, and Wike (1956), who used two groups of rats in an elevated T-maze. Subjects in the control group ran through the maze in the usual fashion, and a correct turn at the choice point brought the animal to some food. If the subject went to the wrong arm of the maze, it was confined there for one minute. Control subjects received 16 trials in the maze, and by the end of training they made the correct turn on 95 percent of the trials.

Subjects in the experimental group received 16 trials in which they were transported through the maze in a wire basket. Each experimental subject was paired with a control subject; that is, it was transported to the correct or incorrect arm of the maze in exactly the same sequence of turns that its counterpart in the control group happened to choose (therefore receiving the same number of reinforcers as its counterpart). This training was followed by a series of extinction trials in which all subjects ran through the maze, but no food was available. During extinction, control subjects chose the previously correct turn on 64 percent of the trials, and experimental subjects on 66 percent of the trials. Thus the experimental animals performed equally well despite the fact that they had never been reinforced for running through the maze.

Similar findings of learning without the opportunity to practice the operant response have been obtained in other studies (Dodwell & Bessant, 1960; Patten & Rudy, 1966). Dodwell and Bessant found that rats benefited substantially from riding in a cart through a water maze with eight choice points. This shows that animals can learn not only a single response but also a complex chain of responses without practice. These studies make it clear that, contrary to Thorndike's prediction, active responding is not essential for the acquisition of an operant response. However, the results do not imply that it is necessary to adopt Tolman's concepts of expectations and cognitive maps. A behaviorist could argue that passive subjects acquire stimulus-stimulus associations during their rides through the maze via classical conditioning. That is, because the last choice point of the maze is repeatedly paired with food, an S-S association develops. Similarly, an association is formed between the second-to-last turn and the last turn, and so on. Psychologists can debate whether the behavioral or cognitive explanation is preferable, but either way it is clear that Thorndike's prediction was incorrect: Performance of a response is not essential for operant conditioning to occur. Given this fact, we can now turn to the question of whether the other component of the operant conditioning contingency, the reinforcer, is a necessary ingredient in the learning process.

THE ROLE OF THE REINFORCER

Is Reinforcement Necessary for Operant Conditioning?

From a literal point of view, the answer to this question is obviously yes, since by definition operant conditioning consists of presenting a reinforcer after the occurrence of a specific response. But we have seen that, loosely speaking, operant conditioning can be called a procedure for the learning of new "voluntary" or nonreflexive behaviors. A better way to phrase this question might be: "Is reinforcement necessary for the learning of all new voluntary behaviors?" Prominent early behaviorists such as Thorndike, Clark Hull (1943), and Mowrer (1947) believed that it was, but on this issue as well Tolman took the opposite position. A famous experiment by Tolman and Honzik (1930) called the *latent learning experiment* provided evidence on this issue.

In the Tolman and Honzik experiment, rats received 17 trials in a maze with 14 choice points, one trial per day. The rats were divided into three groups. Group 1 was never fed in the maze; when they reached the goal box they were simply removed from the maze. Rats in Group 2 received a food reinforcer in the goal box on every trial. In Group 3, the conditions were switched on day 11: For the first 10 trials there was no food in the goal box, but on trials 11-17 food was available.

On each trial, Tolman and Honzik recorded the number of errors (wrong turns) a rat made, and Figure 8-1 shows the averages from each group. Rats in Group 2 (consistently reinforced) displayed a typical learning curve, with the number of errors decreasing to about three per trial by the end of the experiment. Rats in Group 1 (never reinforced) showed much poorer performance. Their error rate dropped slightly but leveled off at about seven errors per trial. The results from Group 3 are the most interesting. On the first 11

FIGURE 8-1. Mean number of errors on each trial for the three groups in the Tolman and Honzik (1930) experiment on latent learning.

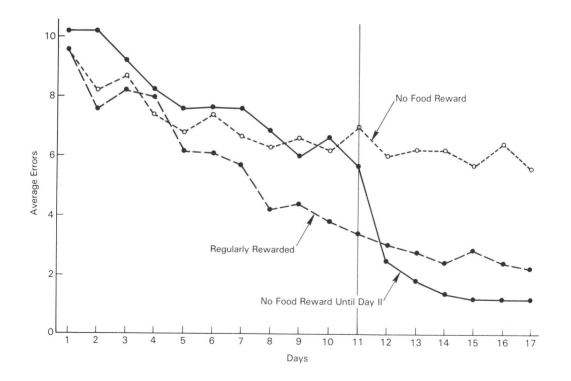

trials their results resembled those of Group 1. This makes sense since both groups received no food on trials 1-10, and on trial 11 subjects in Group 3 had no way of knowing that food was available until they reached the goal box. On trial 12, however, (that is, after only one reinforced trial) the performance of Group 3 improved dramatically, and their average number of errors was actually slightly lower than that of Group 2 for the remainder of the experiment. In other words, as soon as rats in Group 3 learned that food was available in the goal box, their performance became equal to that of rats that had been consistently reinforced since the beginning of the experiment.

Since Group 2 required some 12 trials to drop to an error rate of three per trial, it would be implausible to propose that Group 3 learned an equivalent amount on a single trial (trial 11). Instead, Tolman and Honzik asserted that although they received no food on trials 1-10, subjects in Group 3 nevertheless learned just as much about the maze as subjects in Group 2. However, because they initially received no food in the maze, Group 3 subjects were not motivated to display what they had learned. Only after food was available did subjects in Group 3 translate their learning into performance. Tolman and Honzik concluded that reinforcement is not necessary for the *learning* of a new response, but it is necessary for the *performance* of that response. All learning theorists are now acutely aware of the distinction between learning and performance, largely because of Tolman's influential work.

Several dozen experiments on latent learning were conducted between the 1920s and 1950s, and a majority of them found evidence that learning can occur when the experimenter provides no obvious reinforcer such as food (MacCorquodale & Meehl, 1954). Yet although the existence of the latent learning phenomenon cannot be disputed, Tolman's opponents did not concede that this proved that learning could occur without reinforcement. A frequent counterargument was that although there was no food on the early trials for Group 3, other, more subtle reinforcers may have been present, such as being removed from the maze after reaching the goal box. Notice that on the first 10 trials, there was some small de-

crease in errors in both Groups 1 and 3 despite the absence of food reinforcement. According to Tolman's own reasoning, this improvement in performance suggests that some sort of weak reinforcer was at work.

The issue of whether or not reinforcement is necessary for learning has never been fully resolved, because it is always possible to postulate the existence of some undetected reinforcer. Nevertheless, the theorist who steadfastly maintains that no operant responses can be learned without reinforcement is placed in an uncomfortable theoretical position for two reasons. First, the proposed reinforcer for learning is of uncertain nature and is out of the experimenter's control (unlike the traditional reinforcers of food, water, and the like, which the experimenter can control). Second, the theorist must admit that the rate of learning is not greatly affected by the amount of reinforcement: Groups 2 and 3 in the Tolman and Honzik experiment evidently learned about the same amount on trials 1-10 despite the absence of food in Group 3. On the other hand, the amount of reinforcement had a large effect on performance. Therefore, the latent learning experiments show that operant learning can occur with at best a minimum of reinforcement, but operant performance is greatly influenced by the amount of reinforcement.

Expectations about the Reinforcer

Although latent learning can occur without a reinforcer, the strengthening power of a reinforcer is shown most clearly when a reinforcer *is* presented after the required response is made. In such situations, exactly what is the function of the reinforcer? Some theorists, such as Thorndike (1946) and Hull (1943), suggested that the reinforcer is merely a sort of catalyst—it strengthens an S-R association between the discriminative stimulus and the operant response, but the reinforcer itself is not included in that association. Opposing this view is the idea that a reinforcer not only stimulates associative learning but also becomes a part of the associative network (Mackintosh & Dickinson, 1979; Tolman, 1932). If so, the associative learning in operant conditioning would involve three distinct elements—

the discriminative stimulus, the operant response, and the reinforcer. According to this view, we might say that the animal "develops an expectation" that a particular reinforcer will follow a particular response.

An early experiment by Tinklepaugh (1928) tested these competing ideas. A monkey was first trained on a discrimination task in which a slice of banana was placed beneath one of two containers. After a wait of a few seconds, the monkey could choose one of the containers, earning the slice of banana if it chose correctly. The monkey almost always succeeded on this easy task. Then, on a test trial, the experimenter secretly replaced the slice of banana with a piece of lettuce (a less potent reinforcer for the monkey). If the monkey had learned nothing more than an S-R association (between the correct container and the reaching response), then the switch to lettuce should go unnoticed. If, however, the monkey had developed an expectation about the usual reinforcer, the lettuce should come as a surprise. Tinklepaugh found that the switch in reinforcers did indeed affect the animal's behavior: The monkey appeared surprised and frustrated, and it refused to accept the lettuce. The monkey had evidently developed a strong expectation about what type of reinforcer was forthcoming.

In more recent work, Colwill and Rescorla (1985a) obtained similar findings with rats under more controlled conditions. Two different responses produced two different reinforcers: pressing a lever earned food pellets, and pulling a chain earned a few drops of sugar water. The rats learned to make both responses. Later, each rat was given either free food pellets or free sugar water (with the lever and chain unavailable), and then each animal was made ill with a poison. This procedure was designed to devalue one of the two reinforcers by associating that food with illness. In the test phase, each rat was again presented with the lever and the chain, but this time no food was available. The question of interest was whether a subject would respond more on one manipulandum than on the other in the extinction test. Colwill and Rescorla found that rats poisoned after eating food pellets made few lever presses but many chain pulls, and the opposite was true for those rats poisoned after drinking

sugar water. They concluded that the rats associated lever pressing with food pellets and chain pulling with sugar water, and the animals avoided whichever response was associated with the food paired with illness.

In another experiment, Colwill and Rescorla found evidence that a rat's expectation about the type of reinforcer it will receive can be quite specific. The design was similar to the previous experiment, except that the reinforcers were two different types of food pellets. The rats first learned to press a lever for one type of pellet and to pull the chain for the other type. Instead of using poison, this time one of the two types of pellets was devalued through satiation: Each animal was repeatedly presented with one type of pellet until it refused to eat any more of them. (Previous studies had shown that rats can become satiated to one food yet still accept another, just as you might not want to eat another mouthful of lasagna after a big dinner yet still be willing to have dessert.) In the subsequent extinction test, the rats made most of their responses on the manipulandum that had previously earned the pellets that had not been presented to the point of satiation. Colwill and Rescorla concluded that a rat's knowledge about what type of reinforcer follows a specific response is quite detailed, because the animal can distinguish not only between solid and liquid reinforcers but also between two flavors of food pellets.

This research shows quite clearly that reinforcers are more than catalysts that strengthen S-R associations. During operant conditioning, animals develop associations between specific responses and specific reinforcers. The response-reinforcer association is an important part of the learning, because if the reinforcer is devalued, the response will be weakened. In other words, animals will not produce responses that were reinforced in the past if they no longer value the reinforcer that was used to strengthen those responses. To be more accurate, we should say that the previously-reinforced responses will be weaker, not that they will disappear entirely, because no experiment on reinforcer devaluation has succeeded in completely eliminating the operant response (Adams, 1982; Colwill & Rescorla, 1985b). For reasons that are not yet understood, it seems that the response-strengthening effect of a reinforcer cannot be completely reversed by devaluing the reinforcer—the response continues to persist at a greater level than before the operant conditioning took place.

Colwill and Rescorla (1986, 1988) presented evidence that animals also develop associations between the discriminative stimulus and both the operant response and the reinforcer during typical operant conditioning. For instance, they found that rats learned to associate two different discriminative stimuli with two different reinforcers (a light with food pellets and a noise with sugar water, or vice versa). They concluded that associations are formed among all of the three main components of Skinner's three-term contingency (the discriminative stimulus, the operant response, and the reinforcer). These findings parallel those that demonstrate the existence of associations among the three main components of classical conditioning situations (the CS, the US, and the response; see Chapter 5). Thus in both classical and operant conditioning, subjects appear to develop a richer and more diverse array of associations than was once supposed.

Is Reinforcement at Work in Classical Conditioning?

The diversity of associations is only one feature shared by classical and operant conditioning. A number of phenomena, including extinction, spontaneous recovery, generalization, discrimination, and others, are found with both conditioning procedures. Because of these similarities, a persistent issue debated by learning theorists is whether these two procedures correspond to two different learning processes, or whether a single learning process is at work in both procedures. In theoretical debates that began before theories of avoidance learning were developed (Chapter 7), two-factor theorists were those who believed that the two conditioning procedures depend on two different learning processes. On the other hand, one-factor theorists believed that a common learning mechanism is at work in both classical and operant conditioning.

Among those who favored the two-factor position were Miller and Konorski (1928), Skinner

(1935), Mowrer (1947), and Kimble (1961). These writers did not agree on exactly how classical and operant conditioning were different. For our present purposes, however, we will focus on the hypothesis that reinforcement is involved in operant conditioning but not in classical conditioning. For example, Konorski and Miller (1937) proposed that although operant responses are clearly controlled by their consequences, classically conditioned responses are not. They asserted that the appearance of a CR depends only on temporal contiguity between CS and US, whereas the appearance of an operant response depends on the reinforcement of that response.

One prominent one-factor theorist was Clark Hull (1943), who maintained that reinforcement is a necessary part of both operant and classical conditioning. Hull proposed that although the experimenter does not explicitly program a reinforcer in classical conditioning, there are nevertheless hidden reinforcers that strengthen and maintain the CR, and without such reinforcers no CR would appear. In effect, Hull was claiming that classical conditioning is actually a disguised form of operant conditioning, and that the one factor common to both procedures is reinforcement. Similar positions have been taken by others (Kendler & Underwood, 1948; Miller, 1951a; Smith, 1954).

It does not take much imagination to speculate about the "built-in" reinforcers that might operate in some common classical conditioning paradigms. In Pavlov's experiments on salivary conditioning, the US was dry food, so it seems plausible that by salivating a dog could increase the palatability of the food (Hebb, 1956). Such increased palatability would be a reinforcer that was contingent on the response: The food would be more palatable on trials with a salivary response and less palatable on trials without salivation. Could it be that this CR of salivation is actually an operant response? In eyeblink conditioning, it seems very likely that a CR might alter the aversiveness of the US, particularly when the US is an air puff to the eye that can be avoided by closing the eyelid (Schlosberg, 1937). Is eyeblink conditioning actually an example of avoidance learning? Other CRs might be the byproducts of operant responses. For instance, when a CS is repeatedly paired with shock, human subjects exhibit a change in the electrical conductance of the skin called the galvanic skin response. Smith (1954) suggested that the galvanic skin response is actually a by-product of muscular tensing that occurs in anticipation of the shock. The reinforcer for these muscular responses might be a decrease in the painfulness of the shock.

If CRs are controlled by their consequences, as one-factor theorists maintain, then it should be possible to increase or reduce the frequency of CRs by adding an explicit reinforcer to a classical conditioning situation. Gormezano and Coleman (1973) describe several experiments of this type. In one, they used rabbits in an eyeblink conditioning procedure, with a shock near the eye as the US. Rabbits in what we will call the *classical group* received a 5 mA shock as the US on every trial whether they made a response or not. (In other words, this group received normal classical conditioning, in which the US was not dependent on the subject's behavior.) However, in what we will call the *omission group* a subject could eliminate the US entirely by making a conditioned eyeblink response to the CS, a tone. That is, in this group the US intensity was 5 mA if there was no CR, but 0 mA if a CR did occur.

A one-factor analysis of this experiment might proceed as follows. In the classical group, eyeblink CRs will appear because these responses somehow produce a reduction in the aversiveness of the shock. In the omission group, acquisition should be more rapid and the asymptote of learning should be higher, because for these subjects the reinforcer for a CR is the complete avoidance of a shock. The results of Gormezano and Coleman did not support these predictions, however. Acquisition was slower in the omission group, and at asymptote CRs occurred on about 80 percent of the trials, compared to nearly 100 percent in the classical group. The poorer performance of the omission group is understandable in terms of the principles of classical conditioning (since some trials had no US and were therefore "extinction trials"), but it is exactly the opposite of what a reinforcement analysis would predict.

Results like this weaken the one-factor position, for they indicate that CRs are not easily influenced by experimenter-controlled reinforcers or punishers. Such results do not completely settle the issue, however, since as Kimble (1961) has noted, one can always propose that some reinforcer is at work in classical conditioning. Along these lines, Herrnstein (1977) suggested that the internal, sensory feedback from a CR may be a strong reinforcer for that CR, and that any reinforcer or punisher the experimenter might apply would be weak in comparison. For instance, a rabbit may receive strong reinforcement from the sensory feedback from an eyeblink when it occurs in the presence of a CS frequently associated with an air puff. The major disadvantage of this line of reasoning is that it is unfalsifiable—there is no way to control this sensory feedback or determine whether it is indeed a strong reinforcer. In summary, although there may be no way to eliminate completely the possibility that reinforcement is responsible for the occurrence of CRs in classical conditioning, research such as that of Gormezano and Coleman provides little encouragement for this position.

Can Reinforcement Control Visceral Responses?

This question, like that of the previous section, initially arose out of attempts to find a clear behavioral distinction between classical conditioning and operant conditioning. Two-factor theorists such as Konorski and Miller (1937) and Mowrer (1947) suggested that reinforcement can control the behavior of the skeletal muscles (those involved in movement of the limbs) but not visceral responses (the behavior of the glands, organs, and the smooth muscles of the stomach and intestines). On the other hand, one-factor theorists claimed that reinforcement controls all learned behaviors, including visceral responses.

For many years it was impossible to perform a meaningful experiment on this question, because scientists had no way to separate skeletal and visceral responses. Suppose a misguided one-factor theorist offered to deliver a reinforcer, a 20-dollar bill, if you increased your heart rate by at least 10 beats per minute. You could easily accomplish this by running up a flight of stairs or by doing a few push-ups. This demonstration of the control of heart rate through reinforcement would not convince any two-factor theorist, who would simply point out that what the reinforcer increased was the activity of the skeletal muscles, and the increase in heart rate was an automatic, unlearned response to the body's increase in activity. That is, the increase in heart rate was not a direct result of the reinforcement; rather, it was a byproduct of skeletal activity. To perform a convincing study, it would be necessary to eliminate any possible influence of the body's skeletal muscles.

During the 1960s, Neal Miller and his colleagues devised a procedure that met this requirement. Their subjects were rats that were temporarily paralyzed by an injection of a drug called *curare*. Curare blocks movement of the skeletal muscles, including those necessary for breathing, so an artificial respirator was needed to keep the subjects alive. The normal activity of the glands and organs is not affected by curare, so it might be possible to observe the direct control of visceral responses by reinforcement. But what could serve as an effective reinforcer for a paralyzed rat? To solve this problem, Miller made use of a finding by Olds and Milner (1954) that a mild, pulsating electrical current delivered via an electrode to certain structures in the brain acts as a powerful reinforcer. Although it is not known why *electrical stimulation of the brain* (ESB) is a reinforcer, it can be used to strengthen

responses in many species of subjects. Rats will press a lever at high rates for many hours, ceasing only at the point of exhaustion, if ESB is made contingent on this response.

Figure 8-2 shows the experimental procedure used by Miller and his colleagues in many of their experiments. A curarized rat is artificially respirated, has an electrode implanted in its brain for the delivery of ESB, and is connected to recording equipment to monitor heart rate (or other visceral responses). In an early set of experiments, Miller and DiCara (1967) attempted to increase or decrease the heart rates of different rats using ESB as reinforcement. After measuring a rat's baseline heart rate (which averaged about 400 beats per minute), the experimenters began a shaping procedure. If the goal was an increase in heart rate, reinforcement would be provided for some small (for instance, 2 percent) increase. The criterion for reinforcement was then gradually raised. With other rats, Miller and DiCara used a similar procedure to try to shape heart-rate decreases. They obtained substantial heart-rate changes in both directions: By the end of a session, the average heart rate was over 500 beats per minute for subjects reinforced for a rapid heart rate, and about 330 beats per minute for subjects reinforced for a slow heart rate.

Miller's research group also found that reinforcement could control many visceral responses besides heart rate (see DiCara, 1970, for a review). They found that curarized rats could either

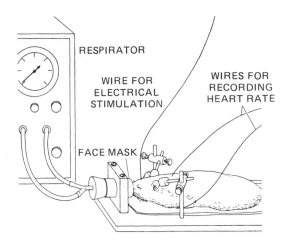

FIGURE 8-2. The experimental arrangement used by Miller and DiCara in their experiments on the operant control of heart rate. (From DiCara, 1970)

dilate or constrict the blood vessels of the skin, increase or decrease the activity of the intestines, and increase or decrease the rate of urine production by the kidneys. The specificity of these responses made it difficult to argue that they were caused by some general property of the drug, of the artificial respiration procedure, and so forth. It would be very difficult to explain how some property of curare could cause an increase in heart rate in one subject (with no change in intestinal activity), a decrease in heart rate in another subject (with no change in intestinal activity), an increase in intestinal activity in yet another subject (with no change in heart rate), and so on. It seems much more reasonable to accept the position that these visceral responses were being influenced by the ESB reinforcement. Furthermore, Miller's group used shock avoidance as a reinforcer in some of their studies to show that the results were not limited to ESB as a reinforcer.

The position that reinforcement can control many visceral responses would have been incontestable if it were not for some developments that took place in the early 1970s. Both Miller and other researchers found it difficult to replicate the early results that showed control of heart rate by ESB reinforcement. Sometimes such control was demonstrated, but often it was not, and there was no obvious pattern in the successes and failures (Miller & Dworkin, 1974). Thus the operant control of heart rate, which appeared to be robust and easily obtainable in the early studies, later proved to be a perplexingly evanescent phenomenon.

Perhaps because of these difficulties, there appears to have been little further research on this issue since the mid-1970s. If we must try to draw some conclusions from the data that are available, it seems that reinforcement can exert direct control over some visceral responses when the activity of the skeletal muscles has been eliminated, but this control is not as easy to obtain as the early studies seemed to suggest. Yet despite these unresolved theoretical issues, interest in the practical and therapeutic applications of visceral learning has grown at an enormous rate. If individuals can learn to control such visceral responses as heart rate, blood pressure, and intestinal activity (through operant conditioning or any other means), the potential health benefits are numerous. Interest in these matters has given rise to a new term, *biofeedback,* and a new area of intense research activity.

Biofeedback

Chapter 3 discussed the importance of feedback in behaviors ranging from simple reflexes to reaction chains. Sensory feedback is essential for the smooth execution of most movements. Imagine how difficult it would be to write a letter or walk around a house in complete darkness, or to eat a meal without biting your tongue or gums after a dentist has anesthetized a large portion of your mouth. Recognizing the importance of feedback in the control of movement, many psychologists have speculated that one reason we have so little control over many of our bodily functions is that feedback from our organs and glands is weak or nonexistent. The term *biofeedback* encompasses any procedure designed to supply the individual with amplified feedback about some bodily process. The reasoning is that with this improved feedback may come the possibility of better control.

The general design of many biofeedback experiments can be illustrated by examining one study on the control of muscle tension in the forehead. Excessive tension in the forehead muscles is the cause of muscle contraction headaches, which some people experience at a high frequency. Budzynski, Stoyva, Adler, and Mullaney (1973) attempted to train a group of individuals who suffered from chronic muscle-contraction headaches to relax these muscles. These people experienced some headache pain almost every day before the start of treatment. During therapy sessions, each patient received *EMG (electromyogram) biofeedback*—electrodes attached to the patient's forehead monitored muscle tension, and the level of tension was translated into a continuous train of clicks the patient could hear. The patient was instructed to slow down the rate of clicking, thereby decreasing the tension in these muscles. Patients learned to accomplish this task almost immediately, and their average muscle tension levels were about 50 percent lower in the first biofeedback session than in the preceding baseline sessions.

Although this finding is interesting in its own right, the important therapeutic questions are the following: (1) Could patients continue to relax forehead muscles in the absence of the biofeedback? (2) Did their headaches become less frequent? (3) Did the treatment produce long-term benefits? (4) How does EMG biofeedback compare to other treatment procedures for tension headaches? Regarding the first question, Budzynski et al. showed that after biofeedback training, patients could produce low forehead tension without the biofeedback equipment, and this ability was retained in a three-month follow-up. Patients were instructed to practice this muscle relaxation at home, twice a day for about 20 minutes. In answer to questions 2 and 3, this combination of biofeedback training and home practice led to a marked reduction in headache activity in about 75 percent of the patients, and these improvements were maintained in a three-month follow-up. On the average, patients reported a decrease of about 80 percent in the frequency and severity of their headaches, and many were able to decrease or eliminate medication they had been taking.

The answer to the fourth question is not as clear. Some later studies found that other procedures such as deep-muscle relaxation were just as effective as EMG biofeedback. It therefore seems fair to ask whether the biofeedback training (which involves expensive equipment and therapist time) is necessary at all. There is still no definite answer to this question, but after reviewing all the relevant studies Qualls and Sheehan (1981) concluded that, at least for some individuals, EMG biofeedback may be more effective than simple relaxation techniques in the treatment of tension headaches.

For a different class of medical problems, the superiority of EMG biofeedback over other therapeutic techniques has been more firmly established. Beginning with the work of Marinacci and Horande (1960), a number of physicians have used EMG biofeedback to restore voluntary movement in limbs paralyzed by disease or accident. A study by Johnson and Garton (1973) illustrates the potential usefulness of biofeedback. The patients in this study were ten individuals suffering from hemiplegia (paralysis on one side

of the body) who could walk only with the aid of a leg brace. All patients had suffered from this problem for at least a year, and they had failed to improve with traditional muscular-rehabilitation training. With electrodes connected to the paralyzed muscles of the leg, a patient received auditory feedback on the level of muscle tension (which was initially very low, of course). Any increase in muscle tension would produce a louder sound, and a patient's task was to increase the loudness of the signal. All patients rapidly learned how to do this. They received daily biofeedback sessions, first in the hospital and later at home with a portable EMG feedback device. All patients showed some improvement in muscle functioning, and five improved to the point where they could walk without the leg brace. This study and others have demonstrated quite convincingly that EMG biofeedback can be a useful supplement to traditional rehabilitation therapy for certain muscular disorders, producing improvements that would not be obtained without the biofeedback.

Feedback from an EMG device is only one of many types of biofeedback; some other examples include feedback on heart rate, cardiac irregularities, blood pressure, skin temperature, electrical activity of the brain, stomach acidity, and intestinal activity. The degree of voluntary control that is possible and the therapeutic benefits of the different types of biofeedback vary considerably (see reviews by Blanchard and Young, 1974; Burish, 1981; and Ford, 1982). For instance, we have seen that EMG biofeedback is beneficial for many hemiplegic patients. In contrast, attempts to lower the blood pressure of hypertensive patients using biofeedback have seldom produced medically significant changes. Opinions on the future of biofeedback vary from the optimistic appraisals of some biofeedback researchers to the conclusions of some critics that biofeedback offers nothing of use to the medical profession. Considering the variety of procedures encompassed by the term biofeedback, both of these positions appear to be overly general and extreme. Evaluations of the effectiveness of biofeedback should be made on a problem-by-problem basis. For some medical problems, biofeedback may be totally ineffective. For other problems it may be only as effective as other, less expensive treatments. For still others it may produce health improvements that are superior to those of any other known treatment.

HOW CAN WE PREDICT WHAT WILL BE A REINFORCER?

The past several chapters should leave no doubt that the principle of reinforcement is one of the most central concepts in the behavioral approach to learning. This concept has also been the subject of considerable debate and controversy between behavioral psychologists on one hand and critics of the behavioral approach on the other. Critics have frequently argued that the definition of reinforcement is circular, and therefore that the concept is not scientifically valid (Chomsky, 1959, 1972; Postman, 1947). This is a serious criticism, so let us examine what they mean by the term *circular*.

A brief definition of a reinforcer is "a stimulus that increases the future probability of a behavior which it follows." Suppose a behavioral psychologist presents a stimulus, a small quantity of beer, to a rat each time the rat presses a lever, and the probability of lever pressing increases. By the foregoing definition, the psychologist would conclude that beer is a reinforcer for the rat. This conclusion, however, provides no explanation; it is nothing more than a restatement of the facts. If asked, "Why did the rat's lever pressing increase?" our behaviorist would answer, "Because it was reinforced by the presentation of beer." If asked, "How do you know beer is a reinforcer?" the reply would be, "Because it caused an increase in lever pressing." The circularity in this sort of reasoning should be clear: A stimulus is called a reinforcer because it increases some behavior, and it is said to increase the behavior because it is a reinforcer. As stated, this simple definition of a reinforcer makes no specific predictions whatsoever. If there were no increase in lever pressing in the beer experiment, this would pose no problem for the behavioral psychologist, who would simply conclude, "Beer is not a reinforcer for the rat."

If there were nothing more to the concept of a reinforcer than this, then critics would be correct in saying that the term is circular and unpredictive. Because of the seriousness of this criticism, behavioral psychologists have made several attempts to escape from this circularity by developing independent criteria for determining which stimuli will be reinforcers and which will not. The problem boils down to finding some rule that will tell us *in advance* whether or not a stimulus will act as a reinforcer. If we can find such a rule, one which makes new, testable predictions, then the circularity of the term reinforcer will be broken. Several attempts to develop this sort of rule are described next.

Need Reduction

In his earlier writings, Clark Hull (1943) proposed that all primary reinforcers are stimuli that reduce some biological need, and that all stimuli that reduce a biological need will act as reinforcers. The simplicity of this rule is appealing, and it is certainly true that many primary reinforcers serve important biological functions. We know that food, water, warmth, and avoidance of pain are all primary reinforcers, and each also plays an important role in the continued survival of an organism. Unfortunately, it does not take much thought to come up with exceptions to this rule. For example, sexual stimulation is a powerful reinforcer, but despite what you may hear some people claim, no one will die if deprived of sex indefinitely. (To be sure, sexual behavior is essential to the survival of a species, so any species for which sex was not a reinforcer would probably become extinct very quickly. However, the principle of need reduction is meant to apply to the survival needs of an individual creature, not of an entire species.) Another example of a reinforcer that serves no biological function is saccharine (or any other artificial sweetener). Saccharine has no nutritional value, but because of its sweet taste it is a reinforcer for both humans and nonhumans. People purchase saccharine and add it to their coffee or tea, and rats choose to drink water that is flavored with saccharine over plain water.

Besides reinforcers that satisfy no biological needs, there are also examples of biological necessities for which there is no corresponding reinforcer. One such example is vitamin B1 (thiamine). Although intake of thiamine is essential for maintaining good health, animals such as rats apparently cannot detect the presence or absence of thiamine in their food by smell or taste. As a result, rats suffering from a thiamine deficiency will not immediately select a food that contains thiamine. If they have the opportunity to sample various diets over a period of days, however, they will eventually settle on the diet that improves their health (Rodgers & Rozin, 1966). This result shows that it is better health, not the presence of thiamine in the rat's food, that is actually the reinforcer for selecting certain foods.

It makes sense that most biological necessities will function as reinforcers, because a creature could not survive if it were not strongly motivated to obtain these reinforcers. As a predictor of reinforcing capacity, however, the need reduction hypothesis is inadequate because there are numerous exceptions to this principle—reinforcers that satisfy no biological needs, and biological needs that are not translated into reinforcers.

Drive Reduction

Recognizing the problem with the need reduction hypothesis, Hull and his student Neal Miller (1948, 1951b) became two of the most vigorous advocates of the *drive reduction* theory of reinforcement. This theory states that strong stimulation of any sort is aversive to an organism, and any reduction in this stimulation acts as a reinforcer for the immediately preceding behavior. The term *drive reduction* was chosen because many of the strong stimuli an animal experiences are frequently called drives (the hunger drive, the sex drive, and so on). Of course, the theory asserts that other strong stimuli, which are not normally called drives (such as loud noise, intense heat, and fear), will also provide reinforcement when their intensity is reduced. A reduction in stimulation of any sort should serve as a reinforcer.

There are at least two major problems with the drive reduction theory. First, it is not always easy to measure the intensity of stimulation (or a reduction in stimulation) objectively. Suppose we

place an animal in a chamber where the temperature is 100°F, and an operant response lowers the temperature to 75°F for a few minutes. The animal would probably produce the operant response at a steady rate, thereby keeping the temperature at 75° most of the time. This behavior is consistent with the drive reduction hypothesis, because the reinforcer consists of a reduction in a certain stimulus, heat. Now suppose the temperature of the chamber is 25°F, and the operant response again produces a 25° reduction in temperature, to 0°. Most animals would not make the operant response in this case, evidently preferring an air temperature of 25° to one of 0°. In this case, the reduction in stimulation does not act as a reinforcer. An advocate of drive reduction theory would undoubtedly argue that this example portrays a naive interpretation of what is meant by a reduction of stimulation, since living organisms are not thermometers. As discussed in Chapter 2, there is fairly good evidence that animals have some sensory receptors that are stimulated by heat, and other receptors that are stimulated by cold. A drive reduction theorist might propose that a reduction in either type of stimulation (extreme heat or extreme cold) acts as a reinforcer, and experimental results verify this idea. The problem is that if we abandon the physicist's measure of heat as a stimulus (temperatures as measured by a thermometer), we are once again in the position where we cannot predict in advance whether a given reduction in temperature will serve as a reinforcer—we must know something about the subject's sensory receptors and how they operate. Still, this is not a fatal flaw for drive reduction theory, because we might be able to begin with physiological research on a creature's sensory system and then use this information to predict whether a particular increase or decrease in temperature should serve as a reinforcer.

The second problem with drive reduction theory is more serious. There are numerous examples of reinforcers that either produce no decrease in stimulation or actually produce an increase in stimulation. Sheffield, Wulff, and Backer (1951) found that male rats would repeatedly run down an alley when the reinforcer was a female rat in heat. This reinforcer produced no decrease in the male's sex drive because the rats were always separated before ejaculation occurred, yet the male rat's high speed of running continued trial after trial. Similarly, we know that sexual foreplay is reinforcing for human beings even when it does not culminate in intercourse. People will engage in a variety of behaviors for the opportunity to engage in sexual activities that do not include orgasm and the resultant reduction in sex drive. The popularity of pornographic magazines and movies provides further evidence on this point.

Reinforcers that consist of an actual increase in stimulation are common for creatures of a wide range of species and ages. Human infants, kittens, and other young animals spend long periods of time playing with toys and other objects that produce ever-changing visual, auditory, and tactile stimulation. Butler (1953) found that monkeys would learn a complex response when the reinforcer was simply the opening of a window that let them see outside the experimental chamber. Myers and Miller (1954) observed that rats would press a lever when the reinforcer was the chance to explore a novel environment. Adult humans are reinforced by a great variety of stimuli and activities that increase their sensory stimulation—music, engaging in sports and exercise, mountain climbing, skydiving, horror films, and the like. There seems to be no way to reconcile these facts with the drive reduction hypothesis.

Trans-Situationality

The failures of the need reduction and drive reduction theories suggest that there is no simple way to classify reinforcers and nonreinforcers on the basis of their biological or stimulus properties. The problem is compounded by the existence of individual differences within a given species—horror films may be reinforcers for some people but not for others. Because of these difficulties, theorists such as Paul Meehl (1950) turned to a more modest theoretical position, but one that still offered the possibility of making new predictions and thereby avoiding the circularity of the term *reinforcer*. Meehl invoked the concept of *trans-situationality,* which simply means that a stimulus that is determined to be a

reinforcer in one situation will also be a reinforcer in other situations. Suppose that at the outset we do not know whether water sweetened with saccharine will be a reinforcer for a mouse. By performing a simple experiment, we might find that the mouse will learn to run in an activity wheel if every several revolutions of the wheel are reinforced with a few seconds of access to the saccharine solution. After we have determined that saccharine is a reinforcer in this one experiment, the principle of trans-situationality implies that we should be able to make new predictions. For instance, we should be able to use saccharine as a reinforcer for lever pressing, climbing a ladder, learning the correct sequence of turns in a maze, and so on.

In reality, the principle of trans-situationality works quite well in many cases. Reinforcers such as food, water, and escape from pain can be used to strengthen a multitude of different behaviors. The crucial question, however, is whether the principle of trans-situationality offers a foolproof method of predicting which stimuli will act as reinforcers. Is it universally true that a stimulus that acts as a reinforcer in one situation will act as a reinforcer in all other contexts? The first person to document clear exceptions to the principle of trans-situationality was David Premack, whose influential experiments and writings changed the way many psychologists think about reinforcement.

Premack's Principle

The procedure of reinforcement is frequently said to include a contingency between a behavior (the operant response) and a stimulus (the reinforcer). An implication of this description is that the two elements of a reinforcement contingency are members of two distinct classes of events—reinforceable behaviors on one hand and reinforcing stimuli on the other. One of Premack's major contributions was to demonstrate that there is no clear boundary between these two classes of events, and in fact it may be counterproductive to talk about two separate classes at all. Premack followed the lead of earlier writers such as Sheffield (Sheffield, 1948; Sheffield, Wulff, & Backer, 1951) in pointing out that nearly all reinforcers involve both a stimulus (such as food) and a behavior (such as eating), and it may be the latter that actually strengthens the operant response. Is it water or the act of drinking that is a reinforcer for a thirsty animal? Is a toy a reinforcer for a child or is it the behavior of playing with the toy? Is a window with a view a reinforcer for a monkey or is it the behavior of looking? Premack proposed that it is more accurate to characterize the reinforcement procedure as a contingency between one behavior and another than as a contingency between a behavior and a stimulus. For example, he would state that in many operant conditioning experiments with rats, the contingency is between the behavior of lever pressing and the behavior of eating—eating can occur if and only if a lever press occurs.

At least for the moment, let us accept Premack's view and see how it relates to the principle of trans-situationality. If the principle is correct, then there must be some subset of all behaviors that we might call *reinforcing behaviors* (for instance, eating, drinking, playing) and another subset of behaviors that are *reinforceable behaviors* (for example, lever pressing, running in a wheel, pecking a key). According to the principle of trans-situationality, any behavior selected from the first subset should serve as a reinforcer for any behavior in the second subset. However, Premack's experiments have shown a number of ways in which trans-situationality can be violated.

In one experiment (Premack, 1962), rats were deprived of water for 23 hours before each session, and they were then placed in a chamber where they could run in an activity wheel or drink water from a drinking tube. In *baseline* sessions, both of these behaviors could occur at any time, and not surprisingly the rats spent much more time drinking than running in the wheel. In the next condition, drinking was made contingent on running: A rat received a few seconds of access to water each time it ran in the wheel for a certain number of revolutions. As expected, the amount of running increased greatly above its baseline level, so by definition drinking was a reinforcer for running under these conditions.

The next phase of the experiment was the crucial one, for it showed that the roles of reinforcer and reinforced behavior could be reversed by changing the subjects' motivational states. Now the rats had free access to water in their home cages, and in baseline sessions they did little drinking and much more running. Next, running was made contingent on drinking: The running wheel was normally locked in a stationary position, but a rat could unlock the wheel for a 10-second period by drinking water for a few seconds. In this condition, running served as a reinforcer for drinking (the amount of drinking increased above its baseline level by about a factor of four). This experiment provides a clear case in which the principle of trans-situationality was violated: Drinking was a reinforcer for running in one context, but running was a reinforcer for drinking in another context.

Premack did more than criticize the principle of trans-situationality; he proposed an alternative theory (1959, 1965), now called *Premack's principle,* which provides a straightforward method for determining whether one behavior will act as a reinforcer for another. The key is to measure the durations of the behaviors in a baseline situation, where all behaviors can occur at any time without restriction. Premack's principle states that *more probable behaviors will reinforce less probable behaviors.* The phrase "more probable behavior" means the behavior that the subject performed for a larger fraction of the time in the baseline session. Let us see how Premack's principle accounts for the results of his 1962 experiment. When the rats were water-deprived, drinking was the more probable behavior in the baseline sessions, so Premack's principle correctly predicts that drinking should reinforce running. When the rats had free access to water in their home cages, running was more probable than drinking in the baseline sessions. In this case, when running was made contingent on drinking, the amount of drinking increased above baseline levels (that is, running reinforced drinking).

Premack suggested that instead of postulating two categories of behaviors—reinforceable behaviors and reinforcing behaviors—we should rank behaviors on a scale of probability that ranges from behaviors of high probability to those of zero probability. Behaviors higher on the probability scale will reinforce behaviors lower on the probability scale. A study Premack (1963) conducted with Cebus monkeys highlights the advantages of Premack's principle and the weaknesses of the trans-situationality principle. These monkeys are inquisitive animals that will explore and manipulate any objects placed in their environment. Premack therefore used the manipulation of different mechanical objects as the tested behaviors.

Premack's findings can be illustrated by examining the results from one monkey, Chicko. Figure 8-3 shows that in baseline conditions, operating a lever had the highest probability, operating a plunger had the lowest, and opening a small door had an intermediate probability. In subsequent contingency sessions, different pairs of items were presented. One item served as the "operant response" and the other as the potential "reinforcer"—the reinforcer was locked and could not be operated until an operant response occurred. In six different phases, every possible combination of operant response and reinforcer was tested, and Figure 8-3 shows the results. The lever served as a reinforcer for both door opening and plunger pulling. Door opening reinforced plunger pulling but it did not reinforce lever pressing. Plunger pulling did not reinforce either of the other behaviors. You should see that each of these six results is in agreement with the principle that more probable behaviors will reinforce less probable behaviors. In addition, notice that door opening, the behavior of intermediate probability, violated the principle of trans-situationality. When it was contingent on plunger pulling, door opening was a reinforcer. When it led to the availability of lever pressing, it played the role of a reinforceable response. Which was door opening, then—a reinforcer or a reinforceable response? Premack's answer is that it can be either, depending on the behavior's relative position on the scale of probabilities. A behavior will act as a reinforcer for behaviors that are lower on the probability scale, and it will be a reinforceable response for behaviors higher on the probability scale. For this reason, Premack's principle is sometimes called a principle of *reinforcement relativity:* There are no absolute categories of re-

L = Lever Pressing
D = Door Opening
P = Plunger Pulling

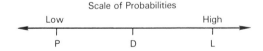

Scale of Probabilities

| | Low | | High | |

| | P | D | L | |

Contingency Conditions	Result	Conclusion
1. D → L	D Increases	L Reinforces D
2. P → L	P Increases	L Reinforces P
3. L → D	L Does Not Increase	D Does Not Reinforce L
4. P → D	P Increases	D Reinforces P
5. L → P	L Does Not Increase	P Does Not Reinforce L
6. D → P	D Does Not Increase	P Does Not Reinforce D

FIGURE 8-3. The procedure used in Premack's (1963) experiment, and the results from one monkey, Chicko. The notation D→L means that Chicko was required to open the door before being allowed to operate the lever.

inforcers and reinforceable responses, and which role a behavior plays depends on its *relative* location on the probability scale.

Premack's Principle and Punishment. Premack (1971) proposed a principle of punishment that is complementary to his reinforcement principle: *Less probable behaviors will punish more probable behaviors.* Since a subject may not perform a low-probability behavior if given a choice, it is necessary to require that the low-probability behavior be performed in order to demonstrate that this principle is correct. One way to accomplish this is to use a *reciprocal contingency,* which ensures that two behaviors occur in a fixed proportion. An experiment I conducted (Mazur, 1975) illustrates the characteristics of a reciprocal contingency. In one condition, a rat was required to engage in 15 seconds of wheel running for every 5 seconds of drinking. At the start of a session, the running wheel was free to rotate but the drinking tube (which contained sugar water) was retracted out of the animal's reach. After the rat ran for a total of 15 seconds, the wheel was locked in position, and the drinking tube became available. This situation remained in effect until the rat drank for a total of 5 seconds, at which point the original condition (wheel free, drinking tube retracted) was restored. These cycles of 15 seconds of running and 5 seconds of drinking continued throughout

the session, as long as the subject continued to meet the schedule requirements. This reciprocal contingency therefore required approximately three times as much running as drinking. Notice, however, that the total durations of these activities were completely controlled by the subject—the rat could spend most of its time either running or drinking, or it could choose not to perform these behaviors at all.

The results from one typical rat (Subject 1) will show how this experiment simultaneously verified Premack's reinforcement and punishment rules. In baseline sessions, this rat spent about 17 percent of the session drinking and about 10 percent of the session running, as shown in Figure 8-4. In the reciprocal contingency described in the preceding paragraph, the percentage of time spent running increased to 16 percent, while drinking time decreased to just over 5 percent of the session time. In other words, the higher probability behavior, drinking, reinforced running, and at the same time the running requirement punished drinking. Naturally, the exact percentages varied from subject to subject, but for all five rats, drinking was the behavior with the higher probability in baseline. In the reciprocal contingency, drinking time decreased and running time increased for all subjects, as Premack's principles of reinforcement and punishment predict. Quite a few other studies have provided similar support for Premack's rules

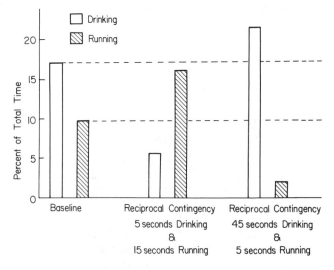

FIGURE 8-4. The performance of one rat in Mazur's (1975) experiment. In the first reciprocal contingency, running time increased and drinking time decreased compared to their baseline levels. In the second reciprocal contingency, running time decreased and drinking time increased compared to their baseline levels.

(Hundt & Premack, 1963; Terhune and Premack, 1970).

The Use of Premack's Principle in Behavior Modification.

Although we have focused on the theoretical implications of Premack's principle, this theory has had a large impact on the applied field of behavior modification. It has contributed to the practice of behavior modification in at least two ways. First, it has stressed that behaviors themselves can serve as reinforcers, thereby encouraging behavior therapists to use such reinforcers in their work. Therapists now frequently instruct clients to use "Premackian reinforcers" such as reading, playing cards, phoning a friend, or watching television as reinforcers for desired behaviors such as exercising, studying, or avoiding smoking. Premackian reinforcers have also been widely adopted in institutional settings. Imagine the difficulties the staff of a mental institution would face in setting up a token economy if they relied only on tangible reinforcers such as food, beverages, cigarettes, money, and the like. The costs of reinforcing patients with such items would be prohibitive, and problems of satiation would be commonplace. However, by making certain activities contingent upon good behavior, therapists gain access to a wide variety of inexpensive reinforcers.

The second advantage of Premack's principle is that it gives therapists clues about what events will be reinforcers for individuals who may not be affected by typical reinforcers. For example, Mitchell and Stofelmayr (1973) used Premack's principle to improve the behavior of a group of extremely inactive schizophrenics. These patients spent most of their time sitting motionless, and occasionally they would pace up and down the ward, but they did little else. The therapists tried to get the patients to engage in some productive work (not to obtain a source of free labor, of course, but for therapeutic reasons). These patients refused items such as candies, cigarettes, fruit, and biscuits, so they could not be used as reinforcers. However, since sitting was a highly probable behavior for these patients, the therapists decided to make sitting contingent on a small amount of labor. A patient was required to work for a few minutes on a simple task and was then allowed to sit down for a while. Using this passive behavior as a reinforcer, Mitchell and Stofelmayr succeeded in getting these patients to engage in some useful activity for the first time. This contingency would presumably be the first step in a therapy program that rewarded the patients for performing adaptive behaviors such as washing themselves, cleaning their rooms, and so on. In any case, this example illustrates how a therapist can discover effective reinforcers simply by observing what a patient normally does.

In a very different setting, Homme, deBaca, Devine, Steinhorst, and Rickert (1963) used Premack's principle to control the behavior of a class of nursery-school children. Among the most probable behaviors of these children were running around the room, screaming, pushing chairs around, and so on. The teacher's instructions and commands initially had little impact on the children's behaviors. A program was then established in which these high-probability behaviors were made contingent on low-probability behaviors such as sitting quietly and listening to the teacher. After a few minutes of such a low-probability behavior, the teacher would ring a bell and give the instructions "Run and scream," at which point the children could perform these high-probability behaviors for a few minutes. Then the bell would ring again, and the teacher would give instructions for another behavior, which might be either one of high or low probability. (One of their favorite high- probability behaviors was pushing the teacher around in a desk chair with coasters.) After a few days, the children's obedience of the teacher's instructions was nearly perfect.

These examples illustrate just two of the many ways Premack's principle has been used in applied settings. Although we shall soon see that this principle has its limitations, it has proven to be a successful rule of thumb for deciding which events will be reinforcers and which will not.

Response Deprivation Theory

Research has shown that Premack's principle will reliably predict reinforcement and punishment effects (1) if a schedule requires more of the low-probability behavior than of the high-probability behavior, or (2) if a schedule requires equal amounts of the two behaviors. However, if a schedule requires much more of the high-probability behavior than the low-probability behavior, Premack's principle may be violated. My experiment with rats in a reciprocal contingency between running and drinking (Mazur, 1975) illustrates how this can happen.

Recall that Subject 1 spent about 17 percent of the time drinking and 10 percent running in baseline sessions (Figure 8-4). This animal's ratio of drinking time to running time was therefore about 1.7 to 1. In one of the reciprocal contingencies, 45 seconds of drinking were required for every 5 seconds of running. Notice that this reciprocal contingency demanded a 9-to-1 ratio of drinking to running, which is higher than the ratio exhibited in the unrestricted, baseline conditions. Figure 8-4 shows that in this reciprocal contingency, running time decreased to about 2 percent of the session time, while drinking time actually increased to 21 percent. Thus, contrary to Premack's principle, in this case a low-probability behavior actually reinforced a high-probability behavior. Eisenberger, Karpman, and Trattner (1967) were the first to show that this can happen if a schedule requires large amounts of the high-probability behavior and small amounts of the low-probability behavior.

To accommodate results of this type, Timberlake and Allison (1974) proposed the *response deprivation theory* of reinforcement, a theory that is actually a refinement of Premack's principle. To see how the theory works, let us consider once again the results from Subject 1 shown in Figure 8-4. According to response deprivation theory, the baseline ratio of the two behaviors is a crucial number. For Subject 1, the baseline ratio of drinking time to running time was 1.7:1. Timberlake and Allison would assume that Subject 1 preferred this ratio of drinking to running above all others, since in baseline the animal was free to choose any ratio. Response deprivation theory therefore predicts that any schedule that lowers this ratio is depriving the animal of its preferred level of drinking. It is this restriction on the opportunities for drinking that makes drinking a reinforcer. For example, in the

condition where 5 seconds of drinking alternated with 15 seconds of running, the drinking:running ratio was 1:3, a large decrease from the baseline ratio. Notice that if the animal simply maintained its baseline amount of running (10 percent), its drinking time would be only 3.3 percent, compared to a baseline level of 17 percent. Timberlake and Allison propose, in effect, that the animal strikes a compromise between drinking and running—it increases its running time (to 16 percent in this case) so as to bring its drinking time somewhat closer to its baseline level (to just over 5 percent in this case). Upon observing this increase in running time compared to baseline, we say that drinking has reinforced running.

Response deprivation theory accounts for the reinforcement of drinking by running using similar logic: Whenever the required drinking:running ratio is *larger* than in baseline, this amounts to a deprivation of running, so running can serve as a reinforcer. In the condition requiring a 9:1 ratio of drinking to running, Subject 1 had relatively little opportunity for running, so by increasing its drinking time above baseline levels the animal earned a bit more running time.

In summary, response deprivation theory states that unless a schedule happens to require exactly the same ratio of two behaviors that a subject chooses in baseline conditions, one of the behaviors becomes a relatively precious commodity because of its restricted availability. Regardless of whether it is the high- or low-probability behavior, the more-restricted behavior will act as a reinforcer for the less-restricted behavior.

Although it is more complicated than Premack's principle (and more difficult to understand), response deprivation theory is the most reliable predictor of reinforcer effectiveness of all the theories we have examined. The theory allows us to predict whether an activity will serve as a reinforcer by observing the probability of that behavior (and of the behavior to be reinforced) in a baseline situation. Because it allows us to make predictions in advance that are usually correct, the circularity of the term *reinforcer* is avoided. It is not particularly important whether the theory is always correct; it is sufficient to ask whether we can make better predictions about behavior with the theory than without it, and the answer is certainly affirmative.

Behavior Regulation Theories

The success of response deprivation theory has stimulated the development of a new class of theories about reinforcement that can be called *behavior regulation theories* (for example, Allison, 1976; Hanson & Timberlake, 1983; Lea, 1983; Rachlin, 1978). These theories assume that the way an animal distributes its behavior in an unrestricted (baseline) situation is, from the animal's perspective, the most preferred way to spend its time. An animal's baseline distribution of behavior is sometimes called its *bliss point* because it is assumed that this pattern of behavior maximizes the animal's satisfaction. When the animal cannot reach its bliss point because it is constrained by some contingency, it will behave in a way that brings it as close to the bliss point as possible.

The concepts of control systems theory (Chapter 3) can help us to understand the main premises of behavior regulation theories. The bliss point is the animal's "goal" or reference input, since it represents the ideal way to spend its time in a particular situation. For instance, in an hour-long baseline session where a rat can run in a wheel and drink sugar water, its bliss point may consist of spending 20 minutes drinking, 10 minutes running, and 30 minutes doing something else. If a reinforcement schedule places a constraint on how the animal can spend its time, the actual input (the way the animal actually distributes its time) may have to differ from the reference input. Thus if a reciprocal contingency requires equal amounts of running and drinking, there is no way the animal can achieve its bliss point of 20 minutes of drinking and 10 minutes of running. How will the rat respond to this situation? Like response deprivation theory, behavior regulation theories predict that, when constrained by a schedule in this way, an animal strikes some compromise between the different behaviors.

If the rat spent 10 minutes running, it would be very far from its bliss point for drinking (10

minutes as compared to the bliss point of 20 minutes). Behavior regulation theories therefore predict that the amount of running will increase above baseline levels, which will reduce the discrepancy between the actual and ideal amounts of drinking. The theories do not predict precisely where the animal will stop, but as an example, suppose the rat spent 15 minutes running, 15 minutes drinking, and 30 minutes doing something else. With this compromise, the discrepancies between the actual and ideal durations would be only 5 minutes for both running and drinking. Because the amount of running increased under this schedule, we could say that drinking reinforced running. But from the perspective of behavior regulation theories, the important point is that whenever a creature's behavior is constrained by the requirements of some schedule, the animal will allocate its behavior in a way that brings it as close as possible to its bliss point. According to this view, the process we call "reinforcement" is really not so much the strengthening of one particular response as it is the redistribution of time to adapt to the constraints imposed by the environment.

BEHAVIORAL ECONOMICS

This chapter has described quite a few different theories about reinforcement. In an effort to achieve a better understanding of this concept, some psychologists have turned to theories from the field of economics. Microeconomics, which is concerned with the behavior of individual consumers, and the study of operant conditioning, which is concerned with the behavior of individual organisms, have several common features (Lea, 1978). Both disciplines examine how the individual works to obtain relatively scarce and precious commodities (consumer goods in economics, reinforcers in operant conditioning). In both cases, the resources of the individual (money in economics, time or behavior in operant conditioning) are limited. Both disciplines attempt to predict how individuals will allocate their limited resources so as to obtain scarce commodities.

Because of these common interests, some psychologists and economists have begun to share theoretical ideas and research techniques. The new field of *behavioral economics* is a product of these cooperative efforts (Allison, 1983; Green & Kagel, 1987). This section describes a few of the ways in which economic concepts have been applied to human and animal behavior, both inside and outside the laboratory.

Optimization: Theory and Research

Optimization as a Basic Assumption in Microeconomics. A basic question for microeconomists is how individual consumers will distribute their incomes among all the possible ways it can be spent, saved, or invested. Suppose a woman brings home $400 a week after taxes. How much of this will she spend on food, on rent, on household items, on clothing, on entertainment, on charitable contributions, and so on? Optimization theory provides a succinct and reasonable answer: The consumer will distribute her income in whatever way maximizes her "subjective value," (or loosely speaking, in whatever way gives her the most satisfaction). Although this principle is easy to state, putting it into practice can be extremely difficult. How can we know whether buying a new pair of shoes or giving that same amount of money to a worthy charity will give the woman greater satisfaction? For that matter, how does the woman know? Despite these difficulties, optimization theory maintains that people can and do make such judgments and then distribute their income accordingly.

A simple example may help to illustrate the assumptions of optimization theory. Suppose that you are an avid reader of both autobiographies and science fiction, and that as a birthday present you receive a gift certificate good for any ten paperbacks at a local bookstore. How many autobiographies will you buy, and how many books of science fiction? Naturally, optimization theory cannot give us a definite answer, but it does provide some guidelines. A common assumption is that as a consumer obtains more and more items of a given type, the value of each additional item of that same type decreases. For example, the

value of one new science fiction novel may be relatively high, but a second science fiction novel will be a bit less valued, and the tenth new science fiction novel may have fairly little value. This assumption is based on the concept of satiation—you may grow weary of vicariously traveling to yet another unexplored planet in the twenty-third century. Similarly, your first new autobiography should be the most valued, the second a bit less valued, and so on. These assumptions are illustrated graphically in the two left panels of Figure 8-5. The y-axis shows the (hypothetical) cumulative value of different numbers of science fiction novels (left panel) and autobiographies (center panel). The steps depict the additional value provided by one more paperback of each type. The consistently higher curve for science fiction novels means that for this illustration we will assume that you enjoy science fiction novels somewhat more than autobiographies. From these two graphs, the total value of any possible combination of science fiction novels and autobiographies can be calculated. The results are plotted in the right panel of Figure 8-5. Even before looking at this graph, you should realize that the optimal package will consist of some mixture of the two types of books, since the first autobiography has more value than the tenth science fiction novel, and the first science fiction novel has more value than the tenth autobiography. For the specific functions drawn in the two left panels, it turns out that the combination of 6 science fiction novels and 4 autobiographies leads to the highest total value. Optimization theory therefore predicts that this combination would be chosen by a person who had this particular set of preferences for the two types of books.

The decisions of anyone who earns an income are obviously much more complex than in this simple example, but optimization theory suggests that the decision-making process is essentially the same—the consumer searches for the maximum subjective value. Although a good deal of economic theory is based on this principle, uncertainty about the exact shape of any individual's value functions makes the principle of optimization difficult to test. The next section shows that the principle has also been applied to

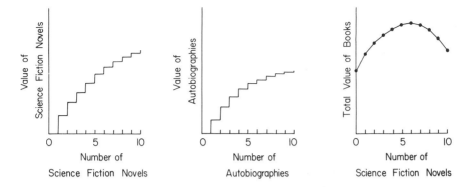

FIGURE 8-5. An illustration of the predictions of optimization theory for a case where a person must choose any combination of science fiction novels and autobiographies, for a total of ten books. The left panel shows that the subjective value of a set of science fiction novels increases with each additional novel, but the increment in value is progressively smaller. The center panel shows a similar pattern for autobiographies. The right panel shows that a person with precisely these preferences for the two types of books would maximize subjective value by choosing six science fiction novels and four autobiographies.

animal behavior, where researchers have been more successful in gathering concrete evidence to support it.

Optimization and Behavioral Ecology. Behavioral ecologists study the behaviors of animals in their natural habitats or in semi-naturalistic settings, and they attempt to determine how the behavior patterns of different species are shaped by environmental factors and the pressures of survival. It is easy to see why the concept of optimization is appealing to behavioral ecologists, with their interest in the relationship between evolution and behavior: Animals whose behaviors are more nearly optimal should increase their chances of surviving and of breeding offspring that will have similar behavior tendencies. Behavior ecologists have documented many cases where animals' behaviors are close to optimal, involving such varied pursuits as foraging for food, searching for a mate, and choosing group size (Krebs & Davies, 1978). Two quite different examples are described below.

When searching for its prey, any predator must make decisions. If a large prey is encountered, it should of course be captured. On the other hand, if a small prey is encountered, the predator's decision is trickier. If a long time is required to chase, capture, and eat the small prey, it may not be worthwhile to go after it, because during this time the predator will miss the opportunity to capture any larger prey that might come along. Theorists have developed complex equations which specify the optimal choice for a predator in any particular situation (Charnov, 1976; Schoener, 1971), but perhaps you can get a feel for their predictions without resorting to any mathematics. A general rule is that if the density of large prey is low (so that encounters with large prey are rare), the predator should go after any prey, large or small. If the density of large prey is high, however, the predator should ignore all small prey, because in chasing them it would lose valuable time during which a large prey might come along.

Werner and Hall (1978) tested these predictions by placing ten bluegill sunfish in a large aquarium with three sizes of prey (smaller fish). When prey density was low (20 of each type), the sunfish ate all three types of prey as often as they were encountered. When prey density was high (350 of each type), the sunfish ate only the largest prey. When prey density was intermediate (200 of each type), the sunfish ate only the two largest prey types. By measuring the time required to capture and eat prey of each type, Werner and Hall were able to show that the behaviors of the sunfish were exactly what optimization theory predicted for all three situations.

In an ingenious (if not enviable) piece of field research, Parker (1978) applied optimization theory to the mating behavior of the dung fly. This insect is so named because the female deposits its fertilized eggs in cow dung, where the larvae then develop. Dung flies generally mate in the vicinity of a fresh pat of cow dung, because females prefer fresh deposits over older ones. The males tend to locate themselves near a fresh pat and wait for a female to arrive. Parker calculated the optimal time a male should wait near one pat before moving to a fresher pat, based on the behavior he observed in the females and on the level of competition among males for the prime locations. The amounts of time the males actually stood pat before moving on were close to the optimal durations. Other aspects of the dung flies' behaviors, such as the amount of time spent copulating as opposed to searching for another mate, were also approximately optimal.

These examples show how scientists have applied optimization theory to the behaviors of animals in naturalistic settings. In the psychological laboratory, optimization theory can be put to a more rigorous test, and its predictions can be compared to those of alternative theories. Some of this research will be described in Chapter 14.

Elasticity and Inelasticity of Demand

In operant research, there have been many studies on how behavior changes as the requirements of a reinforcement schedule become more severe, as when a ratio requirement is increased from FR 10 to FR 100. This question is very similar to the economic question of how the *demand* for a commodity changes as its prices increases. Economists say the demand for a commodity is *elastic* if the amount purchased decreases mark-edly when its price increases. Demand is typically elastic when close substitutes for the product are readily available. For example, the demand for a specific brand of cola would probably drop dramatically if its price increased by 50 percent, because people would switch to other brands, which taste about the same. Conversely, demand for a product is called *inelastic* if changes in price have relatively little effect on the amount purchased. This is generally the case for products with no close substitutes. In modern society, the demand for gasoline is fairly inelastic because many people have no alternative to driving their cars to work, school, shopping centers, and so on.

Lea and Roper (1977) conducted an experiment with rats that demonstrated a similar relation between the availability of substitutes and elasticity of demand. By pressing one lever, rats could earn food pellets on FR schedules, which ranged from FR 1 to FR 16 in different conditions. The availability of a substitute food was also varied across conditions. When no substitute was available, demand for the food pellets was fairly inelastic: On FR 16, the rats earned almost as many pellets as on FR 1, even though the price was 16 times higher. When a fairly close substitute (sucrose pellets) could be obtained by pressing a second lever, demand for the food pellets was more elastic, with a greater decrease in the number of food pellets earned with the higher ratios. Finally, demand was very elastic when a perfect substitute (identical food pellets) could be earned by pressing the second lever. Lea and Roper therefore obtained, in this simple experiment with rats, the same relation between substitution and elasticity that economists find when people purchase goods in the marketplace. Other laboratory experiments with animals have found a similar connection between substitute availability and elasticity (Hursh & Bauman, 1987).

Income Level and Demand

Another factor that affects the demand for different products is a person's income level. When a consumer's income is low, he might spend more on product A than on product B. If his income increases, however, he might then spend more on product B than on product A, even if the prices of A and B have not changed. Does this mean that the person's preferences have changed? Not necessarily. This change in relative expenditures may occur because A is a necessity (such as bread, milk, or vegetables) and B is a luxury item (such as lobster, champagne, or chocolates). As the individual's income rises, he may have no need to purchase more of product A, but he can indulge himself by buying more of product B. In describing this phenomenon, economists state that different products have different *income elasticities.* That is, different products vary in the extent to which changes in income lead to changes in demand for these products.

A number of laboratory experiments have demonstrated such reversals in relative expenditures with changes in income (Elsmore, Fletcher, Conrad, & Sodetz, 1980; Kagel, Dwyer, & Battalio, 1985). In these experiments, "expenditure" is measured by counting responses, not money, and "income" is varied by changing the reinforcement schedule, which determines how many reinforcers the subject can "purchase" before the session ends. Shurtleff, Warren-Boulton, and Silberberg (1987) recorded rats' responses on two separate but equally long VI schedules, one of which delivered food and the other water flavored with saccharin. The saccharin water can be considered a luxury item because the rats had free access to ordinary water. When the VI schedules delivered few reinforcers, the rats spent most of their time on the VI schedule for food. When the schedules delivered many reinforcers, the rats spent more time on the VI schedule for saccharin water, thereby demonstrating a shift toward the luxury item when their responses bought more reinforcers.

Economic theory predicts that under certain circumstances, an increase in income can produce an actual decrease in the demand for a certain product. According to the theory, a consumer's demand for *inferior goods,* such as inferior but inexpensive cuts of meat, may decrease with increasing income, because the consumer can then afford goods of higher quality, such as better cuts of meat. Silberberg, Warren-Boulton, and Asano (1987) demonstrated such an effect with monkeys. On each trial of their exper-

iment, a monkey chose between a small food pellet and a larger but bitter food pellet. The bitter pellet was the inferior good, of course. Under low-income conditions (when there were fairly few trials each day), the monkeys frequently choose the bitter pellets, presumably because they could not get enough food if they only chose the smaller pellets. When income level was increased (by providing more trials per day), the monkeys chose more small pellets, but they actually chose fewer bitter pellets than before, even though there were more opportunities to earn the pellets. In other words, they abandoned the inferior good in favor of the superior good as their income level increased.

Consumption-Leisure Tradeoffs

In some cases, animal experiments have been used to test economic ideas that would be impractical or expensive to test with people. One such idea is the *negative income tax,* which has sometimes been proposed as an alternative to the current welfare system of the United States. With a negative income tax, the government would give money to people with very low incomes, thereby guaranteeing a minimum income for every citizen. For example, suppose the minimum was $4000 a year for every adult. A person who had no income at all would receive a subsidy of $4000. For every dollar a person earned, this subsidy would be reduced by some fraction of a dollar, such as one half. For instance, someone who earned $4000 a year would still get a subsidy of $2000, thereby increasing his total income to $6000.

An advantage of the negative income tax is that it guarantees each person some minimal income without encouraging unemployment: No one can earn more money by remaining unemployed than by working, whereas this can happen under the current welfare system. Critics of the negative income tax argued, however, that it would encourage those who are currently working but earning low wages to work less. Consider someone who works 20 hours a week and earns $8000 a year. Without the negative income tax, if this person dropped back to 15 hours a week, his yearly income would drop to $6000. With the negative income tax (that is, with the specific formula described above), this person could work 15 hours a week, earn $6000, and get a subsidy of $1000, so his total yearly income would be $7000. Critics have therefore predicted that because of the subsidies it provides to low-income workers, a negative income tax would encourage these workers to work less.

Several experiments with animals have supported this prediction (Allison & Boulter, 1982; Battalio & Kagel, 1985). In an experiment by Green, Kagel, and Battalio (1987), pigeons first earned food on an ordinary variable-ratio schedule. The experimenters recorded the number of responses made and amount of food earned in each 40-minute session. In the next condition, there were two changes: (1) Each pigeon was given a "subsidy"—free food was delivered at random times throughout the session, and (2) the VR schedule delivered less food than before. These two changes were designed so that if the bird made as many responses as in the first condition, it would receive the same total amount of food as before. What actually happened, however, was that the birds drastically reduced their response rates, and even with the subsidy included, they obtained less food than before. The researchers interpreted this result as a trade-off between work and leisure. Because the birds received free food, and because it was now harder to earn food on the VR schedule, they chose to respond less, thereby settling for a bit less food and more leisure time. This experiment, which mimicked the characteristics of a negative income tax program, therefore suggested that a decrease in work can indeed occur in this type of situation. This problem with the negative income tax is not necessarily insurmountable, however, and ways to minimize the reduction in responding have been suggested (Timberlake, 1984).

Summary

Research on behavioral economics with animal subjects can serve a number of useful functions. First, it can demonstrate the generality of an economic principle by showing that it applies to animals as well as people. Second, it can provide inexpensive and well-controlled tests that would be nearly impossible to conduct in the real world. Third, it can help to identify the weaknesses and limitations of an economic theory, and it may suggest principles from learning theory as alternative explanations of consumer behavior. The collaboration between economists and psychologists may therefore help to advance both disciplines.

CHAPTER
9
BIOLOGICAL CONSTRAINTS ON LEARNING

Largely because of the work of ethologists, most psychologists now take it for granted that all animals possess a variety of innate behavior patterns, and that some of these patterns may be unique to one or just a few species. For example, the hermit crab's complex sequence of shell-selection behaviors (Chapter 3) is largely innate, and psychologists are not disturbed by the fact that no other aquatic creatures exhibit such behaviors. Similarly, psychologists do not find it theoretically puzzling that squirrels are born with nut-burying repertoires, whereas most other mammals are not. With innate behavior patterns, variety is accepted as the rule rather than the exception.

On the other hand, when it comes to learned behaviors, many psychologists have suggested that it is possible to discover principles of learning that are applicable across a wide range of species. The section "General Principles of Learning" in Chapter 1 showed that this was the assumption upon which B. F. Skinner based his

entire program of research. With few exceptions, Skinner's many students and followers took a similar position on this issue. Pavlov (1928), Spence (1947), and others have stated quite clearly their belief that with learned behaviors, generality should be the rule (see Garcia, McGowan, & Green, 1972). According to this line of reasoning, the same general principles of learning will be discovered regardless of what species of subject, what response, what reinforcer, and what discriminative stimulus one chooses to study. If this assumption turned out to be incorrect, the extensive research on the arbitrary responses (for instance, lever pressing, key pecking) of a small number of species (rats, pigeons) in artificial environments would make little sense. Why would psychologists care, for example, about a rat's pattern of lever pressing with a FI schedule of food reinforcement if unpredictably different patterns were likely with different mammals, or with different reinforcers?

To recapitulate, probably the most fundamental assumption underlying research on animal learning is that it is possible to discover general principles of learning that are not dependent in any important way on an animal's biological makeup. During the 1960s, researchers began to report findings that questioned the validity of this assumption. For the most part, these findings took the form of alleged exceptions to one or another well-established general principle of learning. As this type of evidence began to accumulate, some psychologists started to question whether the goal of discovering general principles of learning was realistic (Lockard, 1971; Rozin & Kalat, 1971; Seligman, 1970). Their reasoning was that if we find too many exceptions to a rule, what good is the rule?

This chapter examines the evidence against the general-principle approach and attempts to come to some conclusions about its significance for the psychology of learning. For convenience, this evidence is grouped into three broad categories: (1) attacks on the contiguity principle, (2) attacks on an assumption called the equipotentiality premise, and (3) evidence for the intrusion of innate behaviors in operant conditioning procedures. These three categories pose problems of what I consider to be increasing seriousness for the general-principle approach to learning.

ATTACKS ON THE CONTIGUITY PRINCIPLE

As discussed in Chapter 2, the principle of contiguity is the oldest and most persistent principle of association, having been first proposed by Aristotle. We have seen that CS-US contiguity is an important independent variable in classical conditioning: In trace conditioning, the separation of CS and US by only a few seconds can produce large decreases in both the rate and asymptote of conditioning. Similarly, studies showed that delays of only a few seconds between response and reinforcer severely impaired the acquisition of an operant response. The opinion on the effects of delay that prevailed through the early 1960s was summarized in a popular textbook on learning: "At the present time it seems unlikely that learn-

ing can take place at all with delays of more than a few seconds. This statement applies to negative as well as to positive reinforcers" (Kimble, 1961, p. 165).

Given this opinion about the importance of contiguity in both classical and operant conditioning, it is easy to see why the work of John Garcia and his colleagues on long-delay learning attracted considerable attention. Garcia's research involved a classical conditioning procedure in which poison was the US and some novel taste was the CS. In one study (Garcia, Ervin, & Koelling, 1966), rats were given the opportunity to drink saccharine-flavored water (which they had never tasted before) and they later received an injection of an emetic that produces nausea in a matter of minutes. For different subjects the interval between the termination of drinking and the injection varied from 5 to 22 minutes. Although these durations were perhaps one hundred times longer than those over which classical conditioning was generally thought to be effective, all subjects subsequently exhibited an aversion to water flavored with saccharine. Furthermore, there was no orderly relationship between CS-US interval and degree of aversion: Subjects with delays of 20 minutes or more showed, on the average, just as much suppression of drinking as those with delays of 5 or 10 minutes. (These tests were conducted three days later to make sure that the subjects had completely recovered from their illnesses.)

A second experiment by the same researchers found that aversions to the taste of saccharine could be established with CS-US intervals of over an hour. Later investigators showed that taste-aversion learning was possible with still longer CS-US intervals. For instance, Etscorn and Stephens (1973) found aversions to saccharine when a full 24 hours separated the CS from the poison US.

Of course, to make a convincing case that such long-delay learning is possible, it was necessary to rule out some alternative explanations of the results. One possibility was that the avoidance of the CS was an instance of *sensitization*. That is, perhaps the (widely separated) pairing of CS and US was unnecessary, and that after an illness an animal is hesitant about ingesting *any* substance. This possibility has been disproven in at least two ways. First, aversion to the CS is much greater in experimental groups (which receive one or more trials with both the CS and the US) than in control groups (which are exposed only to the poison). Second, it has been repeatedly shown that the aversion is specific to the CS; it is not a general avoidance of all foods or all liquids. For example, in their study with a 24-hour CS-US interval, Etscorn and Stephens found that before the conditioning trial, rats preferred saccharine-flavored water to plain water, but after the conditioning trial this preference was reversed. The aversion was specific to the saccharine taste.

Another possible explanation of the long-delay learning of taste aversions is that the actual delays are not really as long as they appear. The reasoning is that some trace of the food may persist long after an animal is finished eating or drinking, and this stimulus (for instance, an aftertaste, the sensation of food in the stomach) may bridge the delay between ingestion and illness. A number of clever experiments have ruled out this possibility. Garcia, Hankins, Robinson, and Vogt (1972) gave rats dry food on some days and the same food moistened with water on other days, and only the dry food (or for other subjects, only the wet food) was followed by poison a few hours later. By that time, a subject's stomach contents would be the same regardless of whether it had eaten wet or dry food. Nevertheless, rats poisoned after eating the dry food learned to avoid the dry food but not the wet food, and rats poisoned after wet food selectively avoided wet food. Garcia, McGowan, and Green (1972) described another study that was also designed to eliminate the possibility of a lingering taste or stomach sensation. Each rat drank a very small amount of sour-tasting water. This slightly acidic water would presumably mix with and be masked by acids of much higher concentrations in the rat's stomach. In addition, the rat was then allowed to eat dry food for an hour, and finally the subject was exposed to cobalt 60 radiation, which causes a temporary illness known as "radiation sickness." Although there was certainly no lingering sensation of the sour water by the time the subjects became ill, they still developed an aversion to the sour water.

Besides providing convincing evidence against the "aftertaste" hypothesis, the last experiment is interesting because it suggests that taste aversions do not develop only for the last substance eaten. In fact, the rats probably did not develop an aversion to the dry laboratory food they consumed after the sour water. Revusky and Bedarf (1967) showed that the novelty of a food is a much more important determinant of taste-aversion learning than whether or not it was the last food eaten before the onset of illness. Several other studies have also showed that the novelty of a taste is important: If a new food is first presented without illness, it later becomes more difficult to develop a taste aversion to that food (Best, 1982).

It is now generally accepted that taste aversions can be acquired by animals of many different species when the CS-US interval is several hours long, and that this learning is not dependent on any aftertaste or other stimulus that might fill the delay between ingestion and illness. Many writers have argued that such a learning ability is adaptive: If an animal in the wild eats a poisonous food, it may not become ill until many hours later. Creatures that have the ability to associate their illness with what they have previously eaten will be able to avoid that food in the future and thereby have a better chance of survival. Nonetheless, because the effective CS-US intervals are many times longer than in traditional experiments on classical and operant conditioning, some psychologists proposed that taste-aversion learning is a special type of learning, one that does not obey the principle of contiguity. Thus taste-aversion learning was seen by some as an exception to one of the most basic principles of association. As the next section shows, taste-aversion learning was also involved in a second line of attack on the general-principle approach.

ATTACKS ON THE "EQUIPOTENTIALITY PREMISE"

As already mentioned, a crucial assumption underlying most research on classical and operant conditioning is that the experimenter's choice of stimulus, response, reinforcer, and species of subject is relatively unimportant. Suppose, for example, an experimenter wishes to test some hypothesis about learning using the salivary conditioning preparation. The subjects will be dogs, and the US will be food powder, but what stimulus should be used as the CS? According to what Seligman and Hager (1972) call the *equipotentiality premise*, it does not matter what stimulus is used; the decision is entirely arbitrary. The following quotation from Pavlov (1928, p. 86) documents his belief in the equipotentiality premise: "Any natural phenomenon chosen at will may be converted into a conditional stimulus...any visual stimulus, any desired sound, any odor, and the stimulation of any part of the skin." Similarly, for operant conditioning, the equipotentiality premise states that any stimulus can serve as a discriminative stimulus, and any response can be chosen as an operant response, to be strengthened through the use of reinforcement.

From the outset, we should dismiss a very strict interpretation of the equipotentiality premise. If it were taken to mean that all stimuli and all responses will result in *equally rapid* learning, this idea could be disproven very easily. Pavlov himself recognized that different CSs will condition at different rates: A bright light will acquire a CR more rapidly than a dim light. Likewise, two operant responses may differ in how easily they can be strengthened by reinforcement: With a pigeon, for example, it may be easier to shape a key-peck response than a chain-pulling response. A more lenient version of the equipotentiality premise is one that states that although stimuli (or responses) certainly differ in their conditionability, a stimulus (or response) that is difficult to condition in one context should also be difficult to condition in other contexts. For example, if a dim light is a poor CS in a salivary conditioning experiment, it should also be a poor CS in an eyeblink conditioning experiment. In short, this more moderate version of the equipotentiality premise states that a given stimulus will be an equally good (or equally bad) CS in all contexts. Similarly, it should be possible to classify an operant response as "easy to shape" or "difficult to shape," and a response's categorization should

not depend on what reinforcer is used or what discriminative stimulus might be involved.

A considerable amount of evidence has shown that even this moderate version of the equipotentiality premise is incorrect. The following sections describe some of the major pieces of evidence and present some theoretical alternatives to the equipotentiality premise.

Preparedness in Taste-Aversion Learning

Garcia and Koelling (1966) conducted an important experiment that showed that the same two stimuli can be differentially effective in different contexts. Two groups of rats were each presented with a compound stimulus consisting of both taste and audiovisual components. Each rat received water that had a distinctive flavor, and whenever the rat drank the water it was presented with flashing lights and a clicking noise. For one group, the procedure consisted of typical taste-aversion learning: After drinking the water, a rat was injected with a poison, and it soon became ill. For the second group there was no poison; instead, a rat's paws were shocked whenever it drank. Thus both groups of rats received pairings of both taste and audiovisual stimuli with an aversive event, but the aversive event was illness for one group and shock for the other.

Garcia and Koelling wanted to determine how strongly the two types of stimuli (taste and audiovisual) were associated with the two different aversive consequences. To do so, they conducted extinction tests (no shock or poison present) in which the taste and audiovisual stimuli were presented separately. Half of the subjects in each group first received the flavored water without the audiovisual stimulus, and their consumption was measured. Later, they were presented with plain water, but their drinking was now accompanied by the audiovisual stimulus. To control for possible order effects, the other half of the subjects received these stimuli in the opposite order.

Figure 9-1 shows the results of this experiment. For each group, the bar graphs show the amount of water consumed in each of the two tests, measured as a percentage of that group's consumption in baseline tests conducted before

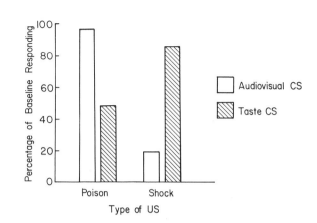

FIGURE 9-1. Results from the experiment of Garcia and Koelling (1966). The first two bars show the amount of water consumed in the presence of two different CSs by the group for which poison was the US. The second two bars show the consumption by the group with shock as the US.

any poison or shock was presented. The group that received poison showed a greater aversion to the taste stimulus than to the audiovisual stimulus. However, exactly the opposite pattern was observed for the group that received the shock. For these animals, consumption of the flavored water was almost the same as in baseline, but consumption of water accompanied by the audiovisual stimulus decreased to less than 20 percent of its baseline level.

What can we conclude about the stimuli used in this experiment? Which was the better stimulus, taste or the audiovisual stimulus? What was the more effective aversive event, shock or illness? The results shown in Figure 9-1 imply that there is no simple answer to these questions. Taste was a more effective stimulus when the aversive event was poison, but the audiovisual stimulus was more effective when the aversive event was shock. Garcia and his colleagues therefore concluded that before we can predict the strength of a conditioned response, we must know something about the *relationship* between the CS and the US. They suggest that because of a rat's biological makeup, it has an innate tendency to associate illness with the taste of the food it had previously eaten. The rat is much less likely to associate illness with visual or auditory stimuli that are present when a food is eaten. On the other hand, the rat is more likely to associate a painful event like shock with external auditory and visual stimuli than with a taste stimulus.

Seligman (1970) suggested that some CS-US

associations might be called *prepared* associations because the animal has an innate propensity to form such associations quickly and easily (for example, a taste-illness association). Other potential associations might be called *contraprepared* associations, because even after many pairings a subject may have difficulty forming an association between the two stimuli (such as taste and shock). In between are *unprepared* associations—those for which the creature has no special predisposition, but which can nevertheless be formed after a moderate number of pairings. In the Garcia and Koelling experiment, the association between the audiovisual stimulus and shock may be an example of an unprepared association. It is hard to imagine why rats would have an innate predisposition to associate a strange flashing light and clicking sound with shock to the forepaws, but they were able to associate these two stimuli after a number of pairings.

It should be clear that Seligman's concept of preparedness is at odds with the equipotentiality premise. It implies that in order to predict how effective a particular CS will be, it is not enough to know how effective this CS has been in other contexts. We must also know what US will be used, and whether this CS-US pair is an example of a prepared, unprepared, or contraprepared association. To further complicate matters, other experiments have shown that the predisposition to associate two stimuli can vary across different species. Although rats may be predisposed to associate taste stimuli with illness, other animals may not be. Wilcoxon, Dragoin, and Kral (1971) compared the behaviors of rats and bobwhite quail when illness followed ingestion of water that had a distinctive (sour) taste, or water with a distinctive (dark blue) color, or water that was both sour-tasting and dark blue. As we would expect, rats displayed aversions to the sour taste but not the blue color. In contrast, quail developed aversions both to the sour water and the blue water, and the blue color was actually the more effective stimulus for these animals.

Wilcoxon and colleagues hypothesized that the differences between rats and quail are related to their respective methods of obtaining food in the natural environment. Rats have excellent senses of taste and smell but relatively poor vision, and they normally forage for food at night. Quail are daytime feeders, and they have excellent vision, which they use in searching for food. It makes sense that those stimuli that are most important for a given species at the time of ingestion are also those that are most readily associated with illness. An implication of this conclusion is that an analysis of a creature's lifestyle in its natural environment may provide clues about which associations are prepared, unprepared, and contraprepared for that creature. Another implication is that attempting to generalize about preparedness or ease of learning from one species to another can be a dangerous strategy.

It is interesting to speculate about which food-related stimuli are most readily associated with illness by people. Based on what you know about the past and present eating habits of the human species, which stimulus modality do you suspect is the most likely to be the focus of an illness-induced aversion to certain foods? Logue, Ophir, and Strauss (1981) used questionnaires to query several hundred college students about any food aversions they might have that developed as a result of an illness that occurred after they ate the food. Of the 65 percent who reported at least one aversion, 83 percent claimed that the taste of the food was now aversive to them. Smaller percentages claimed they found other sensory characteristics of the food aversive: The smell of the food was aversive for 51 percent, the texture of the food for 32 percent, and the sight of the food for only 26 percent. These percentages suggest that

people are more similar to rats than to quail when it comes to the acquisition of food aversions following illness. In many cases, people develop an aversion to some food even though they know that their illness was caused by something completely unrelated to the food, such as the flu or chemotherapy treatment (Bernstein, Webster, & Bernstein, 1982; Logue, Logue, & Strauss, 1983).

The results of these surveys also show that people can develop aversions to more than one sensory characteristic of a food or liquid. The same is true with other species. Recall that quail could develop aversions to either the color or taste of water, but that aversions to color developed more easily. Braveman (1977) describes a number of studies showing that various mammals, including rats and other rodents, can develop an aversion to the visual appearance of a food or liquid, although several pairings of food and illness may be required. In short, although animals may be predisposed to develop aversions to stimuli of one sensory modality, aversions can be learned to stimuli of other modalities, only with greater difficulty.

One way to enhance the development of an aversion to a nontaste stimulus is to present it along with a taste stimulus as a compound CS (see, for example, Holder & Garcia, 1987; Kucharski & Spear, 1985). This enhancement is called *potentiation*. For instance, Rusniak, Hankins, Garcia, and Brett (1979) found that rats developed only a weak aversion to an almond scent that was paired with poison. However, if the almond scent was paired with a saccharin taste and poison, rats developed a strong aversion to the almond scent. Taste stimuli can also potentiate conditioned aversions to visual stimuli (Best & Meachum, 1986; Lett, 1984). The phenomenon of potentiation has attracted a good deal of attention because it is the opposite of the familiar phenomenon of overshadowing, wherein the presence of a strong CS decreases rather than facilitates conditioning to a weaker CS.

Preparedness in Avoidance Learning

In his article on preparedness in associative learning, Seligman (1970) reviewed considerable evidence that prepared associations are not found only in taste-aversion learning. For example, Bolles (1970) proposed that animals exhibit a type of preparedness in avoidance learning. In this case, the preparedness does not involve a stimulus-stimulus association, but rather a propensity to perform certain behaviors in a potentially dangerous situation. Bolles was highly critical of traditional theories of avoidance learning, especially the popular two-factor theory discussed in Chapter 7. He suggested that a two-factor account of avoidance learning in the wild might go as follows: A small animal in the forest is attacked by a predator, and is hurt but manages to escape. Later, when the animal is again in this part of the forest, it encounters a CS—a sight, sound, or smell that preceded the previous attack. This CS produces the response of fear, and the animal runs away to escape from the CS, and it is reinforced by a feeling of relief. According to the two-factor account, then, avoidance behavior occurs because animals learn about signals for danger (CSs) and then avoid those signals. Bolles claimed, however, that this account is

utter nonsense....Thus, no real-life predator is going to present cues just before it attacks. No owl hoots or whistles 5 seconds before pouncing on a mouse. And no owl terminates its hoots or whistles just as the mouse gets away so as to reinforce the avoidance response. Nor will the owl give the mouse enough trials for the necessary learning to occur. What keeps our little friends alive in the forest has nothing to do with avoidance learning as we ordinarily conceive of it or investigate it in the laboratory....What keeps animals alive in the wild is that they have very effective *innate* defensive reactions which occur when they encounter any kind of new or sudden stimulus. (pp. 32- 33)

Bolles called these innate behavior patterns *species-specific defense reactions (SSDRs)*. As the name implies, SSDRs may be different for different animals, but Bolles suggested that they usually fall into one of three categories—freezing, fleeing, and fighting (adopting an aggressive posture and/or behaviors). Exactly which of these behaviors occurs may depend on how imminent the danger is. For instance, freezing may occur if a predator is in the general vicinity, and fighting

or fleeing are likely if the predator has attacked the animal (Fanselow & Lester, 1988).

Bolles proposed that in laboratory studies of avoidance, an avoidance response will be quickly learned if it is identical with or at least similar to one of the subject's SSDRs. If the required avoidance response is not similar to an SSDR, the response will be learned slowly, or not at all. To support this hypothesis, Bolles noted that rats can learn to avoid a shock by jumping or running out of a compartment in one or only a few trials. The rapid acquisition presumably reflects the fact that for rats, fleeing is a highly probable response to danger. In comparison, it may take a rat 100 trials to learn to avoid shock in a shuttle box. The greater difficulty may arise because this situation requires the rat to reenter a chamber where it was just shocked, and returning to a dangerous location is not something a rat is likely to do. It is even more difficult to train a rat to avoid shock by pressing a lever, presumably because this response is decidedly unlike any of the creature's typical responses to danger.

It is important to understand that the difficulty in learning new responses such as lever pressing depends on the nature of the reinforcer. When the reinforcer is avoidance of shock, lever pressing is a difficult response for rats to acquire, and some rats never learn it. Yet when the reinforcer is food or water, lever pressing is a relatively easy response for rats to learn. With other species, researchers have found similar variations in the difficulty of acquiring a response that depend on what reinforcer is used. We have seen that key pecking is an operant response that is frequently used with pigeons, partly because it is fairly easy to shape a pigeon to peck a key when food is the reinforcer. In comparison, it is very difficult to train a pigeon to peck a key to avoid a shock. The problem is apparently that a pigeon's most usual response to an intense aversive stimulus is to fly away, a response that has almost nothing in common with standing in place and pecking. When shock is less intense, however, a pigeon may exhibit SSDRs from the "fighting" category, including flapping its wings. Beginning with this response of wing flapping, Rachlin (1969) trained pigeons to operate a "key" that protruded into the chamber in order to avoid the shock.

This study provides another example consistent with Bolles's claim that the ease of learning an avoidance response depends on the similarity between that response and one of the subject's SSDRs.

Preparedness with Positive Reinforcement and Punishment

Shettleworth has conducted a series of experiments with golden hamsters which show that different classes of responses vary considerably in the degree to which they can be modified by reinforcement or punishment. In one study, Shettleworth (1975) began by measuring six different behaviors in a baseline situation. The behaviors were face washing, digging, scent marking, scratching the body with the hind leg,

rearing (standing on the rear legs with the front legs off the floor), and scrabbling ("scraping with forepaws against a wall while standing erect"). Each of these behaviors occurred at a low frequency in baseline. Next, Shettleworth attempted to increase the duration of one of these behaviors (different behaviors for different subjects) by delivering a food pellet each time the behavior occurred for two seconds. Figure 9-2 shows the results. This reinforcement contingency produced very large increases in rearing, digging, and scrabbling, but only small increases in face washing, scratching, and scent marking. We might expect that the behaviors that were most frequent in baseline would be the easiest to reinforce, but this was not the case. For instance, face washing, which showed little increase when reinforced, was the second most frequent behavior in base-

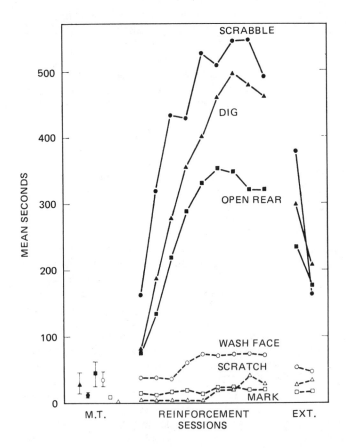

FIGURE 9-2. Results from six groups in Shettleworth's (1975) experiment in which six different behaviors were reinforced. The figure shows the durations of the different behaviors in baseline conditions (labelled "M.T.") where no behaviors were reinforced, in sessions where one of the six behaviors was reinforced, and in subsequent extinction conditions.

line. What Shettleworth did show, however, was that the three behaviors most affected by food reinforcement were each behaviors that tended to increase in frequency when the hamsters were food deprived. The other three behaviors decreased in frequency when subjects were food deprived. Shettleworth therefore proposed that food reinforcement is most effective for those behaviors that occur more frequently when an animal is motivated to obtain food.

The results from the foregoing experiment do not necessarily imply only that some responses are more modifiable by their consequences than others. It turns out that the modifiability of a response can differ depending on what the consequences are. In another study, Shettleworth (1978) found a different rank ordering of modifiability among three behaviors selected for punishment by electric shock. She observed that scrabbling was easily suppressed by punishment, but rearing (another behavior that was easy to increase with food reinforcement) was only slightly suppressed by shock. Face washing, which was difficult to reinforce, was suppressed to a moderate extent by shock. In short, the results from the first experiment on food reinforcement could not be used to predict the results of the later experiment on punishment. Furthermore, baseline response rates cannot be used to predict the effects of either reinforcement or punishment procedures.

Shettleworth and Juergensen (1980) discuss several possible explanations of why some behaviors are more readily reinforced or punished than others, but for the present purposes it is sufficient to understand that such differences exist. These results and those on avoidance learning described by Bolles represent a different type of preparedness than the studies on food aversions. The food-aversion studies showed that certain CS-US associations may be more prepared (more easily conditioned) than others. In contrast, the studies described in this section and the previous one deal with preparedness in associations between a response and a consequence. A response that is easy to increase with one reinforcer may be difficult to increase with another, and it might be either easy or difficult to decrease with punishment.

Preparedness in Discrimination Learning

Lawicka (1964) demonstrated another sort of preparedness, one that related the type of discriminative stimuli used and dogs' abilities to acquire a particular set of responses. In one situation, a dog was required to make a left response if one stimulus was presented and a right response for a second stimulus. If the two auditory stimuli differed in their location (coming from a speaker either above or below the dog), the dog was able to learn to turn in the correct direction for each stimulus. However, if the sounds came from a single speaker but differed in frequency (a high pitch or a low pitch), the subject had a difficult time learning to turn left or right. The second half of this experiment showed that this was not because the pitches were simply more difficult for the dogs to discriminate than location. This time the task was a *go/no-go* choice: Depending on the stimulus, the correct response was either leaving the compartment or staying. In this case, the dogs mastered the task more easily when the sounds differed in frequency than when they differed in location. In discussing these results, Seligman (1970) proposed that dogs are prepared to learn directional responses when the directions of the discriminative stimuli differ, but are counterprepared to learn directional responses when auditory stimuli differ in frequency. The reverse is the case in a go/no-go situation.

Summary

The preceding examples dealt with three different types of associations: stimulus-stimulus associations, response-reinforcer associations, and stimulus-response associations. In all three cases, we have found evidence for Seligman's concept of preparedness, and therefore evidence against the equipotentiality premise. We have seen that animals have an easy time associating certain pairs of events and a difficult time associating others. Furthermore, exactly which pairs of events are easy or difficult can vary from species to species. Critics of the general-principle approach used this evidence to bolster their arguments that the strategy of studying a small number of responses, stimuli, and reinforcers with only a few species in an artificial environment has serious shortcomings. Some proposed that a better understanding of an animal's learning abilities would come from studying its biological makeup, its inherited behavior patterns, and its behavior in a natural environment. The next section presents further evidence that an animal's hereditary endowment can have an important influence on its learned behaviors.

INTRUSIONS OF HEREDITY IN OPERANT CONDITIONING

Instinctive Drift

Learning theorists, especially those who favor one-factor theory, have generally held the belief that reinforcement exerts a simple but powerful influence on behavior: Behaviors that are reinforced will increase in frequency, and those that are not will decrease and eventually disappear. When the techniques of shaping, prompting, fading, and chaining are added to this basic idea, it should be possible to teach a typical animal complex and intricate sequences of behavior. Two psychologists who attempted to apply the principles of operant conditioning outside the laboratory were Keller and Marian Breland. After studying with B. F. Skinner, the Brelands became animal trainers who worked with many different species, teaching them complex and frequently amusing patterns of behavior. Their animals were trained for zoos, fairs, television commercials, and other public performances.

The Brelands' business was successful, and over the years they trained several thousand animals. On the surface, at least, it appeared that they had demonstrated that principles from the laboratory were usable in less controlled settings and applicable to creatures ranging from whales to reindeer. Despite the success of their business, however, the Brelands began to notice certain recurrent problems in their use of reinforcement techniques. They referred to these problems as "breakdowns of conditioned operant behavior."

In a frequently cited article entitled "The Misbehavior of Organisms" (Breland and Breland, 1961), they described several of their "failures" in the use of reinforcement. The following is one of their examples:

Here a pig was conditioned to pick up large wooden coins and deposit them in a large "piggy bank." The coins were placed several feet from the bank and the pig required to carry them to the bank and deposit them, usually four or five coins for one reinforcement. (Of course, we started out with one coin, near the bank.)

Pigs condition very rapidly, they have no trouble taking ratios, they have ravenous appetites (naturally), and in many ways are among the most tractable animals we have worked with. However, this particular problem behavior developed in pig after pig, usually after a period of weeks or months, getting worse every day. At first the pig would eagerly pick up one dollar, carry it to the bank, run back, get another, carry it rapidly and neatly, and so on, until the ratio was complete. Thereafter, over a period of weeks the behavior would become slower and slower. He might run over eagerly for each dollar, but on the way back, instead of carrying the dollar and depositing it simply and cleanly, he would repeatedly drop it, root it, drop it again, root it along the way, pick it up, toss it up in the air, drop it, root it some more, and so on.

We thought this behavior might simply be the dilly-dallying of an animal on a low drive. However, the behavior persisted and gained in strength in spite of a severely increased drive—he finally went through the ratios so slowly that he did not get enough to eat in the course of a day. Finally it would take the pig about 10 minutes to transport four coins a distance of about 6 feet. This problem behavior developed repeatedly in successive pigs. (p. 683)

This example differs from the instances of contraprepared associations discussed earlier. Here, the problem was not that pigs had difficulty learning the required response: At first, a pig would carry the coins to the bank without hesitation. It was only later that new, unreinforced behaviors—dropping and rooting the coins—appeared and increased in frequency. The Brelands noted that the intruding behaviors were those that pigs normally perform as part of their food-gathering repertoires. Because these behaviors appeared to be related to the subject's innate responses, they called them examples of *instinc-*

tive drift: With extensive experience, the subject's performance drifted away from the reinforced behaviors and toward instinctive behaviors that occur when the animal is seeking the reinforcer (in this case, food) in a natural environment.

It is interesting to compare the behavior of pigs with that of a raccoon in a similar situation. The task was to pick up coins and place them in a small container. With just one coin, the raccoon learned, with a little difficulty, to pick it up and drop it in the container, after which it received food as a reinforcer. When the raccoon was given two coins simultaneously, however, its behavior deteriorated markedly. Instead of picking up the coins and depositing them quickly (which would provide the most immediate reinforcement), the raccoon would hold on to the coins for several minutes, frequently rubbing them together, and occasionally dipping them into the container and pulling them out again. Although these behaviors were not reinforced, they became more and more prevalent over time, and the swift sequence of depositing the coins that the Brelands desired was never achieved.

You may recognize a similarity between this raccoon's behaviors and those of the pigs. The raccoon's intruding behaviors resemble those that are part of its food-gathering repertoire. A raccoon may repeatedly dip a piece of food in a stream before eating it, and the rubbing motions are similar to those it might use in removing the shell from a crustacean. Notice, however, that in the present context these behaviors were inappropriate in two respects: (1) the coins were not food, the container was not a stream, and there was no shell to be removed by rubbing the coins together, and (2) the intruding behaviors did not produce food reinforcement, and indeed they actually postponed its delivery.

The Brelands reported that they had found numerous other examples of this sort of instinctive drift, and they claimed that these examples constituted "a clear and utter failure of conditioning theory" (1961, p. 683). The problem was perfectly clear: Animals exhibited behaviors that the trainers did not reinforce in place of behaviors the trainers had reinforced.

Autoshaping

Whereas the Brelands were acutely aware of the importance of their findings for reinforcement theory, the authors of another influential article apparently did not recognize the far-reaching implications of their experiment at first. In 1968, Brown and Jenkins published an article entitled "Auto-shaping of the pigeon's key-peck." They presented their findings as simply a method for training pigeons to peck a key that was easier and less time-consuming than manual shaping. Naive pigeons were deprived of food and taught to eat from the grain dispenser. After this, a bird was exposed to the following contingencies: At irregular intervals averaging 60 seconds, the response key was illuminated with white light for eight seconds, and then the key was darkened and food was presented. Despite the fact that no response was necessary for the delivery of food, all 36 of the pigeons began to peck at the lighted key. The trial on which the first keypeck was recorded ranged from trial 6 for the fastest bird to trial 119 for the slowest.

Whereas autoshaping did seem to be an easier way to train the response of key pecking, psychologists soon realized the more important theoretical significance of the Brown and Jenkins result. Key pecking had been used in countless experiments because it was considered to be a "typical" operant response—a response that is controlled by its consequences. Yet here was an experiment in which the key-peck response was not necessary for reinforcement yet it occurred anyway. Why did the pigeons peck at the key? A number of different explanations have been proposed.

Superstitious Behavior, Automaintenance, and Negative Automaintenance. Brown and Jenkins suggested that autoshaping might be an example of a superstitious behavior, as discussed in Chapter 6. Consider the following scenario: At first, when the key is lit, the pigeon simply *looks toward* the key, and a reinforcer is delivered a few seconds later. This might accidentally strengthen the behavior of looking at the key. On the next trial, the bird might again look up when the key is lit, and when this behavior does not immediately produce the reinforcer, the bird might *approach* the key, and at this moment the reinforcer might occur. On later trials, a bird might *get closer* to the key, *make contact* with the key, and eventually *peck* at the key, and all of these behaviors might be adventitiously reinforced by the food. This scenario depicts a process by which the bird's behavior is gradually shaped into a keypeck through the presentation of a reinforcer that is not actually contingent on any response.

Although this hypothesis is ingenious, an experiment by Rachlin (1969) suggested that it is wrong. Using a procedure similar to that of Brown and Jenkins, Rachlin photographed pigeons on each trial at the moment reinforcement was delivered. The photographs revealed no tendency for the birds to get progressively closer to the key and finally peck it. On the trial immediately preceding the trial of the first keypeck, a pigeon might be far from the key, looking in another direction, at the moment of reinforcement. There was no hint of a gradual shaping process at work.

Whereas Rachlin's study showed that the first key peck in an autoshaping procedure is probably not the result of an inadvertent shaping process, could subsequent responses be superstitious behaviors that are maintained by the contiguity between a key peck and food? Many studies (Gamzu & Schwartz, 1973; Gamzu & Williams, 1973) showed that pigeons will continue to peck indefinitely at a lighted key that precedes food. This continued responding has been called *automaintenance* to distinguish it from *autoshaping* (which in its strictest sense refers only to the occurrence of the first key peck). To determine whether responses during automaintenance might be superstitious behaviors, Williams and Williams (1969) made a small change in the Brown and Jenkins procedure. If a key peck occurred while the key light was lit, the food reinforcer was eliminated on that trial. In other words, keypecks were punished by the omission of food. This procedure is sometimes called *negative automaintenance* because it incorporates a negative punishment contingency into the automaintenance procedure. The results of this experiment were quite remarkable: Even though no food ever

followed a key peck, pigeons still acquired the key-peck response and persisted in pecking at the lighted key on about one third of the trials for as long as the experiment continued (for several hundred trials). This finding was very surprising, because it showed that whatever factors produced the key pecking were strong enough to exert their influence despite the punishment contingency. This experiment showed quite convincingly that key pecking in an automaintenance procedure is not an instance of superstitious behavior.

Autoshaping as Classical Conditioning. A number of writers (Mackintosh, 1983; Moore, 1973; Schwartz & Gamzu, 1977) have proposed that autoshaping is simply an example of classical conditioning intruding into what the experimenter might view as an operant conditioning situation. Several types of evidence support this idea. As most people know, pigeons eat grain by pecking at the kernels with jerky head movements. We might say that pecking is the pigeon's unconditioned response to the stimulus of grain. According to the classical conditioning interpretation, this response of pecking is transferred from the grain to the key because the lighted key is repeatedly paired with food.

Further support for this interpretation comes from studies in which food can be delivered at any time during a session, but the probability of food might be either higher when the key light is on than when it is off, lower when the key light is on, or the same when the key light is on as when it is off. Pigeons will peck at the lighted key in the first condition but not in the other two (Durlach, 1986; Gamzu & Williams, 1973). These results parallel Rescorla's (1966, 1968) findings from classical conditioning experiments that showed that excitatory conditioning will occur when there is a positive CS-US correlation, but not when there is a zero or negative correlation between CS and US (Chapter 4). Other researchers have found that autoshaping occurs when the lighted key provides information about the upcoming food, but it is reduced or eliminated when the lighted key is redundant with other signals for food (Allaway, 1971; Wasserman, 1973). In short, the data show that autoshaping is successful when the lighted key is predictive of food, but not otherwise. This same general rule applies to the relationship between CS and US in traditional classical conditioning preparations.

Some intriguing evidence that also favors the classical conditioning interpretation of autoshaping comes from experiments in which the researchers either photographed or closely observed the behaviors of their subjects. In an important series of experiments by Jenkins and Moore (1973), illumination of a response key was regularly followed by the presentation of food for some pigeons and by the presentation of water for other pigeons. In both cases the pigeons began to peck at the lighted key. However, by filming the pigeons' responses, Jenkins and Moore were able to demonstrate that the pigeons' movements toward the key differed depending on which reinforcer was used. When the reinforcer was food, a pigeon's response involved an abrupt, forceful pecking motion made with the beak open wide. These movements are similar to those a pigeon makes when eating. When the re-

inforcer was water, the response was a slower approach to the key with the beak closed or nearly closed. On some trials, swallowing movements and a rhythmic opening and closing of the beak were observed. All of these movements are part of the pigeon's characteristic drinking pattern.

Jenkins and Moore proposed that these behaviors were clear examples of Pavlov's concept of stimulus substitution. The lighted key served as a substitute for either food or water, and responses appropriate for either food or water were directed at the key. In one experiment they observed these two response styles with a single pigeon in a single session when illumination of the left key signaled food and illumination of the right key signaled water. Figure 9-3 shows some representative responses on the left key (top row) and on the right key (bottom row). Notice the different beak and eyelid positions in the two sets of photographs.

Although Brown and Jenkins (1968) used the term *autoshaping* to refer to their specific experiment, in which pigeons pecked a lighted key that

FIGURE 9-3. Photographs of a pigeon's key pecks when the reinforcer was water (top row) and when the reinforcer was grain (bottom row). Notice the different beak and eyelid movements with the two different reinforcers. (From Jenkins & Moore, 1973)

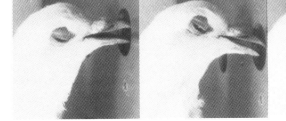

preceded food, later writers have used the term to refer to any situation in which an organism produces some behavior in response to a signal that precedes and predicts an upcoming reinforcer. In this broader sense, autoshaping has been observed in many species, and in many cases the results are consistent with the stimulus substitution theory of classical conditioning. For example, Peterson, Ackil, Frommer, and Hearst (1972) videotaped the behavior of rats to a retractable lever that was inserted into the chamber and illuminated 15 seconds before the delivery of each reinforcer. For some rats, the reinforcer was food, and for others it was electrical stimulation of the brain. Both groups of rats made frequent contact with the lever, but the topographies of their responses were distinctly different. Rats with the food reinforcer were observed to gnaw and lick the lever, whereas those with brain stimulation as a reinforcer would touch the lever lightly with paws or whiskers, or they might sniff and "explore" the lever. The gnawing and licking behaviors were, of course, similar to the rats' responses to the food itself. Peterson et al. also reported that the behaviors and postures of individual rats in response to the lever when it signaled brain stimulation were frequently similar to their behaviors and postures during the delivery of brain stimulation. Thus the two different reinforcers elicited two different behavior patterns, and these patterns were mirrored in the rats' responses to the lever that was paired with reinforcement.

An experiment on autoshaping in two species of fish (Squier, 1969) provided additional evidence consistent with the stimulus substitution account of autoshaping. A response key on one wall of an aquarium was illuminated on a VI 40-second schedule, and on each trial food was presented 8 seconds after the light came on. After several such pairings of key-light illumination and food, a fish would begin to make contact with the response key when it was lit. Squier reported that in both species, the manner of contacting the key was similar to the fish's normal feeding movements. Mullet were observed to swing their heads from side to side against the response key, making gobbling movements similar

to those they make while eating. Subjects of the species *Tilapia,* which maintain their bodies in a vertical (head above tail) position while eating food on the water surface, assumed this vertical position when contacting the response key. Here again, the response to the signal for a reinforcer resembled the response to the reinforcer itself.

Autoshaping as the Intrusion of Instinctive Behavior Patterns. Whereas the studies described in the preceding paragraphs provide support for the stimulus substitution interpretation of autoshaping, other studies do not. Wasserman (1973) observed the responses of 3-day-old chicks to a key light paired with warmth. In an uncomfortably cool chamber, a heat lamp was turned on briefly at irregular intervals, with each activation of the heat lamp being preceded by the illumination of a green key light. All chicks soon began to peck the key when it was green, but their manner of responding was unusual—a chick would typically move very close to the key, push its beak into the key and rub its beak from side to side in what Wasserman called a "snuggling" behavior. Similar responses were observed in chicks exposed to a negative automaintenance procedure, in which any contact with the key cancelled the activation of the heat lamp on that trial. These snuggling responses resembled behaviors a newborn chick normally makes to obtain warmth from a mother hen: The chick pecks at the feathers on the lower part of the hen's body, then rubs its beak and pushes its head into the feathers.

On the surface, this study seems to provide another example of stimulus substitution—a warmth-seeking behavior pattern is displayed to a signal for warmth. The problem, however, is that the chicks in the experiment exhibited a very different set of behaviors in response to the heat lamp itself. When the heat lamp was turned on, there was no pecking or snuggling; instead, a chick would extend its wings (which allowed it to absorb more of the heat) and stand motionless. On other trials, a chick might extend its wings, lower its body, and rub its chest against the floor. Thus although both snuggling and wing extension are warmth-related behaviors for a young chick, there was essentially no overlap between a chick's responses to the key light and its responses to the heat lamp. For this reason, Wasserman concluded that the stimulus substitution account of autoshaping is inadequate, and that the physical properties of the signal also determine the form of autoshaped responses.

Other experiments support Wasserman's conclusions. Jenkins, Barrera, Ireland, and Woodside (1978) observed the responses of dogs to an auditory-visual stimulus that preceded the delivery of food. The dogs exhibited a variety of responses to the signal, including approach, pointing, nuzzling, licking, barking, pawing, and tail wagging. These behaviors persisted, though at a lower level, in a negative automaintenance procedure in which food was omitted if a dog approached the signal. Some of these behaviors (for instance, approach, licking) are clearly related to eating, and others might be involved in obtaining food, for Jenkins and colleagues suggested that they resembled behaviors a dog performs when begging for food. As in Wasserman's experiment, however, the behaviors elicited by the reinforcer were quite different—a dog usually snatched the chunk of food with its teeth and swallowed it in one rapid motion.

One additional study of a similar nature is worth mentioning because it involves a situation where the predictions of stimulus substitution theory are not only incorrect but extremely implausible. Timberlake and Grant (1975) observed the behaviors of rats when the signal preceding the delivery of a food pellet was the entry of another rat (restrained on a small moving platform) into the experimental chamber. Since a food pellet elicits biting and chewing responses, the stimulus substitution interpretation of autoshaping predicts that a subject should perform these same biting and chewing responses to the restrained rat since it is a signal for food. Not surprisingly, Timberlake and Grant observed no instances of biting or chewing responses directed toward the restrained rat. However, they did observe a high frequency of other behaviors directed toward the restrained rat, including approach, sniffing, and social contact (pawing, grooming, and climbing over the other rat). The incidence of such behaviors toward the restrained rat was much higher in the autoshaping group than in a control group in which the restrained rat and food pellets were presented at random and unrelated times.

You may recognize a pattern in the types of responses that are directed toward a signal that precedes a reinforcer. In some cases, the signal elicits behaviors that resemble the behaviors produced by the reinforcer, as the stimulus-substitution approach would predict. In other cases the behaviors elicited by the signal are different from those elicited by the reinforcer, but they seem to be behaviors that are involved in obtaining that type of reinforcer in the animal's natural environment. Thus with rats, which usually feed in groups, the presence of a restrained rat predicting food elicited approach, exploration, and social behaviors—all behaviors that might occur during the course of a food-seeking expedition. With dogs, a signal for food elicited approach and begging responses. With young chicks, a signal preceding the activation of a heat lamp elicited some of these birds' normal warmth-seeking behaviors. Timberlake and Grant (1975) interpreted the results as follows:

As an alternative to stimulus substitution, we offer the hypothesis that auto-shaped behavior reflects the conditioning of a system of species-typical behaviors commonly related to the reward. The form of the behavior in the presence of the predictive stimulus will depend on which behaviors in the conditioned system are elicited and supported by the predictive stimulus. (p. 692)

In subsequent writings, Timberlake (1983, 1984) has called this interpretation of autoshaped behaviors a *behavior-systems analysis* to reflect the idea that different reinforcers evoke different systems or collections of behaviors. An animal may have a system of food-related behaviors, a system of water-related behaviors, a system of warmth-seeking behaviors, a system of mating behaviors, and so on. Exactly which behavior from a given system will be elicited by a signal depends in part on the physical properties of that signal. For instance, in Wasserman's study, the characteristics of the response key (such as a distinctive visual stimulus about head high) evidently lent themselves more readily to snuggling than to wing extension, so that the former was observed rather than the latter. Notice that the predictions of Timberlake's behavior-systems approach are more ambiguous than those of the stimulus substitution approach. It would be difficult (at least for me) to predict in advance whether a green key light would be more likely to elicit wing extension, snuggling, or some other warmth-related behavior. Nevertheless, the behavior systems approach is not totally devoid of predictive power, because it states that the behaviors provoked by signal will depend on the type of reinforcer it predicts. The theory predicts quite clearly that a signal for warmth should elicit behaviors that are part of the animal's warmth-seeking behavior system, not those that are part of its feeding system or its drinking system. Although these predictions are less specific than those of stimulus substitution theory, they are certainly in closer agreement with the evidence on the form of autoshaped behaviors.

Summary. Because autoshaped responses are observed under conditions that are similar to those in which CRs are observed, some writers have proposed that autoshaping is nothing more than an example of classical conditioning. However, in many cases autoshaped behaviors are neither similar to behaviors elicited by the reinforcer (as stimulus substitution theory would predict) nor the opposite of the behaviors elicited by the reinforcer (as conditioned opponent theories would predict). For these reasons, Timberlake and others (such as Woodruff and Williams, 1976) have chosen to treat autoshaped responses as an intrusion of species-typical, inherited behavior patterns into a learning situation. Regardless of whether one chooses to emphasize the hereditary aspects of autoshaped behaviors or their similarity to classically conditioned CRs, autoshaped behaviors and examples of instinctive drift pose difficulties for operant conditioners and especially one-factor theorists. Breland and Breland (1961) stated the problem succinctly: "The examples listed we feel represent clear and utter failure of conditioning theory.... the animal simply does not do what it has been conditioned to do" (p. 683). In their examples of instinctive drift, previously reinforced behaviors were grad-

ually replaced by unreinforced behaviors. In autoshaping and automaintenance, animals make responses on a key, a lever, or some other device although these responses have no effect on the delivery of reinforcement. In negative automaintenance, such responses persist despite the fact that each response cancels the delivery of a reinforcer.

By now it should be clear why some critics concluded that these data signaled the demise of the general-principle approach to learning. Before we accept this conclusion, however, let us take another look at the evidence and see how learning theorists might respond to their critics.

A DEFENSE OF THE GENERAL-PRINCIPLE APPROACH TO LEARNING

This section will reexamine, in turn, each of the three major categories of evidence against the general-principle approach.

Long-Delay Learning of Taste Aversions

There is no doubt that the findings of Garcia and his colleagues were a surprise to traditional learning theorists—few would have predicted that associative learning could occur with such long delays between stimuli, at least with animal subjects. It should be noted, however, that long-delay learning is not found only in taste-aversion paradigms. In a series of experiments, Lett (1973, 1975, 1979) inserted delays of various lengths between a rat's choice response in a T-maze and the animal's subsequent receipt of a reinforcer (if the response was correct). During the delay, a rat was returned to its home cage so that no cues in the end of the maze could be used to bridge the delay between choice response and reinforcer. Lett found that rats' choices of the correct arm of the maze increased over trials even when the delay interval was 60 minutes.

In a different sort of study, Capaldi (1967) reinforced rats at the end of a runway, but only every other trial. Thus the presence or absence of a reinforcer on one trial could serve as a signal about whether or not there would be a reinforcer on the next trial, provided the rat could remember what happened on the previous trial. Although there was a 24-hour delay between trials, the rats showed evidence of learning, running faster on trials when a reinforcer was due. Studies like these show that, at least in certain circumstances, animals can associate events separated by long delays in situations that do not involve taste aversions.

Besides showing that long-delay learning is not unique to taste aversions, we can also dispute the claim that taste-aversion learning violates the principle of contiguity. In essence, this principle states that individuals will more readily associate two events the more closely the events occur in time. Figure 9-4a shows the results from a fairly typical operant conditioning experiment involving delay of punishment, which used rats in a lever pressing procedure and shock as punishment (Baron, Kaufman, & Fazzini, 1969). As the delay between a response and shock increased, there was less and less suppression of responding, as compared to the rats' baseline response rates. Figure 9-4b shows the results from a study on taste-aversion learning, in which different groups of rats experienced different delays between their initial exposure to a saccharin solution and a poison injection (Andrews & Braveman, 1975). The graph shows the amount of saccharin consumed in a later test. Observe the similarity in the shapes of the functions in Figures 9-4a and 9-4b. Both sets of results are consistent with the principle of contiguity—the shorter the interval between a response and an aversive event, the stronger is the responding. The only major difference between the two experiments is the scale on the x-axis (seconds in Figure 9-4a, hours in Figure 9-4b). Taste aversions were conditioned with considerably longer delays, but this is merely a quantitative difference, not a qualitative one. That is, the results in Figure 9-4b do not require the postulation of a different law to replace the principle of contiguity; they merely require the use of different numbers in describing the relationship between contiguity and learning.

Preparedness in Taste Aversions and Elsewhere

The abundant evidence on preparedness in taste-aversion learning, avoidance learning, in discrimination learning, and in operant condition-

FIGURE 9-4.   (a) The effects of delay between a lever press and shock in an experiment on punishment (Baron, Kaufman, & Fazzini, 1969). With increasing delays, the punishment caused less suppression of lever pressing. (b) The effect of delay between saccharin consumption and poison administration in an experiment on taste-aversion learning (Andrews & Braveman, 1975). With increasing delays, the poisoning caused less suppression of saccharin consumption.

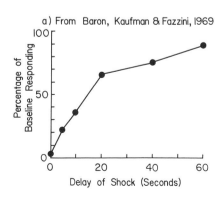

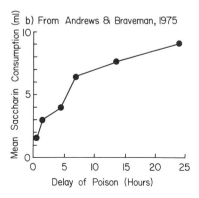

ing clearly shows that some associations are more easily formed than others. Furthermore, an association (for example, between the visual appearance of a food and illness) that is difficult for one species to learn may be easy for another. Notice, however, that Seligman's continuum of preparedness deals with differences in the *speed* of learning or the *amount* of learning, not in the *kind* of learning that takes place. It is not impossible for rats to develop an association between a visual stimulus and illness, it simply requires more conditioning trials than does a taste-illness association. It is not impossible for rats to learn to press a lever to avoid a shock, or for pigeons to learn to peck a key to avoid a shock—these responses are simply more difficult to learn when the reinforcer is shock avoidance than when it is food. Once again, this alleged evidence against general principles of learning merely amounts to a quantitative difference, not a qualitative one. A description of the learning of prepared, unprepared, and contraprepared associations would require different numbers, but not necessarily different laws.

What sorts of findings would demand a qualitatively different principle of learning rather than a quantitative adjustment in an established principle? Since taste-aversion learning has been heralded by some as a qualitatively different kind of learning, one that does not obey the principles of traditional learning theory, let us examine exactly how it might be different. In a review of the findings on taste-aversion learning, Logue (1979) discussed several ways in which taste-aversion learning might be unusual. Seligman and Hager (1972) had proposed that extinction of taste aversions was exceedingly slow, but Logue summarized evidence showing that extinction does occur if the food or liquid is repeatedly presented, especially if the subject is given no alternative source of food or water. The apparent slowness of extinction of taste aversions may be due to the same factors that make avoidance learning of all types difficult to extinguish: If the subject avoids the CS, it cannot learn that the CS is no longer followed by aversive consequences. Logue concluded that resistance to extinction in taste aversions is no greater than in many more traditional learning situations.

As another possible unique characteristic, Seligman and Hager proposed that it might not be possible to observe typical generalization gradients in taste-aversion learning. However, Logue cited evidence showing that generalization gradients in taste-aversion learning are not unusual: When illness follows ingestion of a particular food, animals will later show strong aversions to similar foods, but weaker aversions to more dissimilar foods.

To further strengthen her argument that taste-aversion learning fits into the framework of traditional learning theory without difficulty, Logue noted that many of the most familiar phenomena of classical conditioning, including conditioned inhibition, blocking, stimulus preexposure effects, and second-order conditioning, have been observed in taste-aversion learning. Logue concluded that taste-aversion learning violates no traditional principles of learning and requires no new principles of learning. This viewpoint is now shared by many researchers on classical conditioning (see Domjan, 1983; Shettleworth, 1983; Revusky, 1977). In fact, the taste-aversion paradigm has become an increasingly popular procedure for studying classical conditioning (Best, 1984; Holland, 1983; Rudy, 1984). Taste-aversion learning has joined the conditioned suppression and eyeblink paradigms as a commonly used classical conditioning procedure. There is considerable irony in the fact that a phenomenon that was once offered as a prime example of the weaknesses of the general-principle approach to learning is now utilized in research designed to investigate general principles of conditioning. This fact, perhaps more than any other, should put to rest the notion that taste-aversion learning is inconsistent with traditional learning theory.

Autoshaping and Instinctive Drift

A similar turn of events has surrounded the research on autoshaping. As we have seen, early discussions of autoshaped behavior suggested that it posed major problems for the general-principle approach because it seemed to defy the rules of operant conditioning. Later analyses suggested that autoshaping is simply an instance of classical conditioning. Although there may be aspects of autoshaped responses that distinguish them from other types of conditioned responses (Swan & Pearce, 1987; Wasserman, 1973), it is now commonly believed that autoshaping is in fact a good example of classical conditioning. And like taste-aversion learning, autoshaping is now widely used as a procedure for studying basic principles of classical conditioning (Kaplan, 1985; Locurto, Terrace, & Gibbon, 1981; Rescorla, 1986). Autoshaping therefore seems to be a type of behavior that is quite consistent with the general-principle approach to learning after all.

The evidence on instinctive drift in operant conditioning cannot be dealt with so easily. Here, it is not that reinforced behaviors are simply slow to be learned as might be the case with unprepared associations. What happens is that totally different, unreinforced behaviors appear and gradually become more persistent. These behaviors are presumably part of the animal's inherited behavioral repertoire, and their exact form depends on both the type of reinforcer that is being delivered and on the characteristics of the signal that predicts the reinforcer. Yet since these behaviors often cannot be eliminated by the selective use of reinforcement and punishment (such as the negative automaintenance procedure), it might appear that the principle of reinforcement is simply incorrect—it cannot explain why these behaviors arise and are maintained. Indeed, some writers have asserted that the concept of reinforcement is inadequate and should be abandoned (Timberlake, 1983, 1984).

How might a psychologist who relies heavily on the concept of reinforcement react to this empirical evidence and the theoretical challenges it poses? The reactions of B. F. Skinner are worth examining. First of all, it is important to realize that Skinner has always maintained that an organism's behavior is determined by both learning experiences and heredity. Well before "biological constraints on learning" became a popular topic, Skinner had written about the hereditary influences on behavior in several places (Heron and Skinner, 1940; Skinner, 1956b, 1966). Later, Skinner (1977) stated that he was neither surprised nor disturbed by phenomena such as instinctive drift or autoshaping. He asserted that these are simply cases where phylogenetic (he-

reditary) and ontogenetic (learned) influences on behavior are operating simultaneously: "Phylogeny and ontogeny are friendly rivals and neither one always wins" (p. 1009).

In other words, we should not be surprised that hereditary factors can compete with and sometimes overshadow the reinforcement contingencies as determinants of behavior. This does not mean that the principle of reinforcement is flawed; it simply means that reinforcement is not the sole determinant of a creature's behavior. Critics who use these data to claim that the principle of reinforcement should be abandoned appear to be making a serious logical mistake —they conclude that because a theoretical concept cannot explain everything, it is deficient and should be abandoned. This conclusion does not follow from the premises. It is just as incorrect as the claim of some radical environmentalists (such as Kuo, 1921) that all behaviors are learned, none innate. The past several chapters have provided ample evidence that the delivery of reinforcement contingent upon a response is a powerful means of controlling behavior. No amount of evidence on the hereditary influences on behavior can contradict these findings.

There is a growing consensus in the field of learning that the research on biological constraints does not forecast the end of the general-principle approach, but rather that it has provided the field with a valuable lesson (see, for example, Domjan, 1983; Domjan & Galef, 1983; Herrnstein, 1977; Logue, 1988). This research shows that an animal's hereditary endowment plays an important part in many learning situations, and the influence of heredity cannot be ignored. As we learn more about how these biological factors exert their influence, we will be better able to understand and predict a creature's behavior.

THE ADAPTATIONIST APPROACH TO LEARNING

Many psychologists now believe that there is no necessary conflict between the general-principle approach to learning and the biological limitations on learning that have been described in this chapter. In an effort to reconcile these two "friendly rivals"—general learning principles and hereditary predispositions—some researchers have taken an *adaptationist* approach to learning (for example, Beecher, 1988; Domjan & Hollis, 1988; Sherry, 1988; Staddon, 1983). The adaptationist approach is closely related to the theory of evolution. It assumes that if a creature displays some hereditary characteristic or ability, this is probably because this characteristic or ability has aided the survival of the creature's ancestors over the generations. General principles of learning that are shared by a wide range of species may exist because certain learning abilities are adaptive in almost any conceivable environment. For instance, it is hard to imagine an environment where it would *not* be advantageous to be able to use a neutral stimulus as a signal for some important upcoming event (as in classical conditioning) or to be responsive to the positive or negative consequences of one's actions (as in operant conditioning). So many different species may exhibit these learning abilities precisely because they are useful in so many different environments.

Staddon (1988) has argued that both general learning principles and species-specific learning abilities can be understood from the adaptationist perspective. He proposed that all types of learning are methods for making inferences about the future. These inferences can sometimes be wrong, but they will usually be right. For example, consider habituation, in which an animal learns to ignore an oft-repeated stimulus. The inference the animal seems to be making is that the stimulus is probably harmless, since it has never signaled anything important in the past. Similarly, in classical conditioning, an animal seems to be making inferences, based on past experience, about what important events will follow the CS.

More specialized learning abilities can be analyzed in similar ways. For example, *imprinting* is a special type of learning exhibited by newborn geese, whereby they learn to follow any moving object they see soon after birth. Once imprinted, the gosling will continue to follow this particular object, but not any other moving objects it may later encounter. This behavior is adaptive be-

cause in practice, the first moving object the gosling sees is almost always its mother. In some cases, however, the strategy can fail, as when the gosling becomes imprinted on a human caretaker (Lorenz, 1937). As with more general types of learning, imprinting is not fail-safe, but because it is successful most of the time, it is advantageous for goslings to have this special learning ability.

Others have used the adaptationist approach to try to account for differences in learning abilities among different species. For instance, Beecher, Medvin, Studdard and Loesche (1986) found that cliff swallows can discriminate between their own offspring and other young of the same species, whereas barn swallows cannot. We might say that cliff swallows are "prepared" to recognize their own infants, whereas barn swallows are "unprepared." Why do the abilities of these two species differ? Beecher (1988) proposed that the difference in abilities is a result of the different environments in which the two species raise their young. Young cliff swallows of different parents intermingle while their parents are foraging for food, so it is important for the parents to be able to identify their own youngsters when they return. Young barn swallows do not intermingle in this way. A keen ability to recognize one's offspring presumably did not evolve in barn swallows because it was not necessary. In short, these different recognition abilities seem to reflect the different lifestyles of the two species.

From the adaptationist perspective, it is incorrect to treat a biological constraint on some learning ability as a weakness. To illustrate this point, Beecher (1988) discusses the difficulty hummingbirds have in learning a *win-stay* strategy (in which the bird must choose whichever of two options was reinforced on the previous trial). We could take this as evidence that hummingbirds are slow learners, but they learn quickly on tasks that require a *win-shift* strategy (shifting to a new option after the first has delivered a reinforcer). According to Beecher, this predisposition toward a win-shift strategy is perfectly suited to the hummingbird's environment: In foraging for food, it is logical to move on to another flower after the nectar from one flower has been depleted.

Although the hummingbird's tendency to adopt a win-shift strategy is fine for its usual environment, this bird would have difficulty if the environment changed to one in which a win-stay strategy was needed. At least in this sense, biological constraints are indeed limitations: They restrict the animal's ability to adapt to a changing environment.

10

STIMULUS CONTROL
AND CONCEPT FORMATION

For John B. Watson, the first behaviorist, the goals of psychology were "the ascertaining of such data and laws that, given the stimulus, psychology can predict what the response will be; or, on the other hand, given the response, it can specify the nature of the effective stimulus" (1919, p. 10). Most psychologists now believe that Watson's stimulus-response approach to psychology was too simplistic. For one thing, it neglected the importance of the reinforcers or punishers that follow a behavior. Nevertheless, Watson's emphasis on antecedent stimuli was not completely misguided; these stimuli play a major role in determining if and when a behavior will occur, regardless of whether that behavior is learned or innate. The sign stimulus in ethological research, the conditioned stimulus in classical conditioning, and the discriminative stimulus in operant conditioning are three names for antecedent stimuli that psychologists must consider when attempting to "predict what the response will be."

The relationship between antecedent stimuli and the behaviors that follow them is the topic of this chapter, a topic frequently called *stimulus control*. As we have seen throughout this book, predicting what behavior will occur in the presence of a given stimulus, and predicting the behavior's vigor, its rate of occurrence, and its temporal patterning are challenging tasks. This is true even when the same stimulus is presented to the subject again and again in a controlled setting. But in the real world, all creatures are repeatedly confronted with stimuli and events they have never experienced before, and their survival may depend on an adaptive response. The topic of stimulus control also encompasses research on how creatures respond to such novel stimuli. In previous chapters, we have used the term *generalization* to describe a subject's tendency to respond to novel stimuli in much the same way that it has previously responded to similar, familiar stimuli. It is now time to examine the process of generalization more closely.

In its overall organization, this chapter progresses from simple to increasingly complex relations among stimuli. We will begin with analyses of generalization among stimuli that differ only in their location on a single physical continuum such as size or wavelength of light. Next, we will examine a more abstract sort of generalization in which the stimuli presented in two tasks are completely different and it is only the structures of the tasks that are similar. For instance, if a subject first masters a task in which one color signals reinforcement and another color signals extinction, will this facilitate the learning of a subsequent discrimination task involving not colors but lines of different orientations? Finally, we will consider the topic of concept formation, which involves the classification of different objects into a single category (for instance, "trees") even though their visual appearances may sometimes have little in common.

GENERALIZATION GRADIENTS

Measuring Generalization Gradients

Suppose that we have trained a pigeon to peck at a yellow key by reinforcing pecks with food on a VI 1-minute schedule. Our subject responds at a fairly steady rate of about 30 responses per minute when the key is illuminated with yellow light. Now we wish to determine how much generalization there will be to other key colors, such as blue, green, orange, and red. How can we collect this information? This answer is not as simple as it may seem. Suppose we switch to a red key light, intending to measure the pigeon's response rate over a five-minute period. The animal may start to respond, but do we reinforce the animal on the same VI 1-minute schedule or not? If we do, then after the first reinforcer we will not be able to determine how much of the animal's responding is due to generalization and how much is due to the previous reinforcement for pecking the red key. If we deliver no reinforcers, then pecking will start to extinguish and it will be difficult to compare response rates to the red and yellow keys in a meaningful way. The rate of pecking will probably get slower and slower if

we proceed to test the other colors in extinction. The shape of our generalization gradient will depend heavily on the order in which the stimuli are presented, which is not what we want.

In order to overcome such problems as much as possible, researchers have relied on two major techniques for obtaining generalization gradients. In both, the test stimuli are always presented under extinction conditions. In the first technique, test trials or *probe trials* with the unreinforced stimuli are occasionally inserted among reinforced trials with the training stimulus. For instance, each trial might consist of 10 seconds of exposure to one of the key colors, with successive trials being separated by a 5-second intertrial interval in which the key is dark. Ninety percent of the trials might involve the yellow key light and the VI 1-minute schedule, and the other 10 percent of the trials would include different key colors and an extinction schedule. The advantage of embedding probe trials among reinforced trials with the training stimulus is that the procedure can continue indefinitely without the threat of extinction until sufficient data are collected. The main disadvantage of this procedure is that the subject may begin to form a discrimination between the yellow key and all other key colors, so that there will be progressively less generalization as the training proceeds.

The other main technique for obtaining generalization gradients is exemplified by an experiment conducted by Guttman and Kalish (1956). For the group of pigeons we will consider, the training stimulus was a yellow key light of a wavelength of 580 nanometers. (One nanometer, abbreviated nm, equals one billionth of a meter.) After the pigeons had learned to respond steadily to the yellow key light, a series of extinction trials began that included the yellow light and ten other colors of both shorter wavelengths (the blue end of the spectrum) and longer wavelengths (the red end of the spectrum). The trick was to obtain enough trials with each wavelength before responding extinguished. Guttman and Kalish accomplished this by limiting the duration of each trial to 30 seconds. The first block of 11 trials included one trial with each color, presented in a random order. The second block of trials also presented these 11 colors, but in a different random order. This procedure continued for 12 blocks, so that each color was presented 12 times. Response rates declined across the 12 blocks, but because each stimulus was presented throughout the extinction period, the effects of extinction were approximately balanced across colors. The results of Guttman and Kalish are shown in Figure 10-1. They obtained a fairly symmetrical generalization gradient, with the most responding to the yellow training stimulus and less responding to colors of shorter or longer wavelengths.

What Causes Generalization Gradients?

Having examined two techniques for obtaining generalization gradients, we can now ask why such gradients occur in the first place. Why should reinforcement of a behavior in the presence of one stimulus cause this behavior to occur to similar stimuli which have never been used in training? Pavlov's (1927) answer was that generalization is an automatic by-product of the conditioning process. His explanation was based on his physiological theory about the "spread of excitation" across neurons in the cerebral cortex, a theory now known to be incorrect. Nevertheless, Pavlov's more general view that generalization is an inherent property of the nervous system cannot be so easily dismissed. Chapter 2 described the work of Hubel and Wiesel, some of which in-

volved recording the electrical responsiveness of single neurons in a cat's visual cortex. Hubel and Wiesel found that different cells were responsive to different features in the visual environment. For instance, one cell might fire most rapidly when a line at a 45-degree angle was presented. The cell would fire more slowly if the orientation of the line was 35 degrees or 55 degrees, and still more slowly if it was 25 degrees or 65 degrees. Notice that if Hubel and Wiesel plotted the cell's responsiveness as a function of line orientation, they would obtain a function quite similar to the typical generalization gradient.

Now let us imagine that the appropriate conditioning experience, such as reinforcing the cat for a lever press in the presence of a 45-degree line, were somehow to strengthen a chain of associations between this cell (and perhaps many others like it) and the motor neurons involved in a lever press (through physiological mechanisms that are at best only dimly understood). Because of the properties of the "45-degree angle detector" in the cat's visual cortex, we might expect some generalization of lever pressing to lines of similar orientations. Of course, we should not take this simplistic physiological hypothesis very seriously, because it is a far cry from the responsiveness of a single cortical cell to an animal's overt behavior. There is no reason why a behavioral generalization gradient should bear any resemblance to the response characteristics of any single neuron.

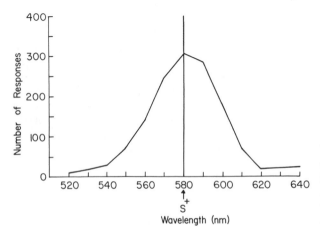

FIGURE 10-1. A generalization gradient for wavelength of light from the Guttman and Kalish (1956) experiment with pigeons. After training in which pecks at a 580 nm key light were reinforced, this and ten other wavelengths were tested under extinction conditions.

A hypothesis that is quite different from Pavlov's was proposed by Lashley and Wade (1946). They theorized that some explicit discrimination training along the dimension in question (such as wavelength of light, or frequency of tone) is necessary before the typical peaked generalization gradient is obtained. For instance, if the dimension of interest is color, they would claim that subjects must receive experience in which reinforcement occurs in the presence of one or more colors but not in their absence. Without such discrimination training, Lashley and Wade proposed that the generalization gradient would be flat—the subject would respond just as strongly to all the novel test stimuli as to the training stimulus. Thus whereas Pavlov proposed that generalization gradients are innate, Lashley and Wade proposed that they are dependent upon learning experiences.

How Experience Affects the Shape of Generalization Gradients. An experiment that provides some support for the position of Lashley and Wade was conducted by Jenkins and Harrison (1960). Two groups of pigeons responded on a VI schedule in the presence of a 1000 Hz tone. Three pigeons received *nondifferential training,* in which every trial was the same—the key light was lit, the 1000 Hz tone was on, and the VI schedule was in effect. Five other pigeons received *presence-absence training,* which included two types of trials: (1) trials with the 1000 Hz tone that were exactly like those of the other group, and (2) trials without the tone, during which the key light was lit as usual, but no reinforcers were delivered. In other words, the second group received discrimination training in which the presence or absence of the tone was the only signal indicating whether or not reinforcement was available.

After training, both groups received a series of extinction trials similar to those of Guttman and Kalish, where the different trials included different tone frequencies, and some trials included no tone at all. The results are presented in Figure 10-2. As Lashley and Wade predicted, the nondifferential training produced generalization gradients that were basically flat: Response rates were roughly the same at all tone frequencies. On the other hand, the presence-absence training with the 1000 Hz tone was sufficient to produce typical generalization gradients with sharp peaks at 1000 Hz.

In attempting to explain their results, Jenkins and Harrison suggested that it is useful to consider what discriminative stimuli might be expected to control responding in each condition. As we saw in Chapters 4 and 5, a general rule of classical conditioning is that the stimulus that is the best predictor of the US is likely to become the most effective CS. Extrapolating to an operant conditioning situation, we might expect that the discriminative stimulus that is the best predictor of reinforcement will exert the strongest control over responding. For the pigeons that received nondifferential training, many stimuli were equally good predictors of the reinforcer— the tone, the illuminated key light, and the many other sights, sounds, and smells of the experimental chamber. If all of these stimuli shared in the control of key pecking, then changing or removing one of them (the tone) should have little effect. In addition, if one of these stimuli (such as the key light) happened to be particularly salient, it might overshadow the other stimuli, just as one CS may overshadow another in classical conditioning. Perhaps the illuminated key light did indeed overshadow the tone in the nondifferential group, for the tone exerted no control over responding—the pigeons pecked just as rapidly when the frequency of the tone was changed, or when there was no tone at all.

On the other hand, for the pigeons that received presence-absence training, the tone was the only stimulus reliably correlated with reinforcement. The tone could not be overshadowed by the key light or by any other stimulus, because all these other stimuli were only weakly associated with reinforcement: Sometimes reinforcement was available in their presence, and sometimes it was not. Because it was the best signal for the availability of reinforcement, the tone came to exert control over the subject's responding, as witnessed by the sharp declines in response rate that occurred when one feature of the tone (its frequency) was altered.

A subsequent experiment by Jenkins and Harrison (1962) provided further information about

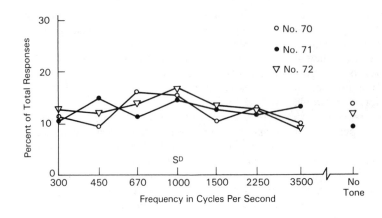

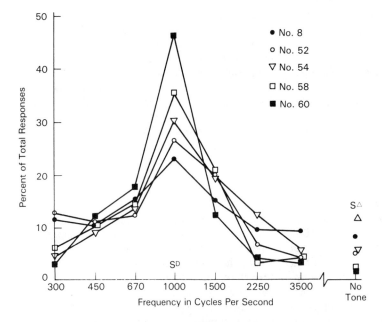

FIGURE 10-2.
Generalization gradients for tone frequency in the Jenkins and Harrison (1960) experiment after nondifferential training (top panel) and presence-absence training (bottom panel) with a 1000 Hz tone.

the effects of experience on generalization gradients. Two pigeons received discrimination training in which the 1000 Hz tone was an S^+ (a discriminative stimulus for reinforcement) and a 950 Hz tone was an S^- (a discriminative stimulus for the absence of reinforcement). In other words, nonreinforced trials with the 950 Hz tone replaced the no-tone trials of the presence-absence group in the previous experiment. The term *intradimensional training* has been used to label

discrimination training in which S^+ and S^- come from the same stimulus continuum (tone frequency in this case). In a subsequent extinction test, these two pigeons produced much narrower generalization gradients than those from the presence-absence training. There was little responding to the 950 Hz tone or to those of lower frequency, a sharp increase in responding to tones in the vicinity of 1000 Hz, and little responding to tones above 1100 Hz. These gradients were at least five times narrower than those from the differential group in the bottom of Figure 10-2.

These results provided further evidence on the effects of experience on generalization gradients, and once again Jenkins and Harrison (1962) interpreted the results in terms of the different stimuli that might compete for control of the pigeon's responding. After presence-absence training, the 1000 Hz tone was the only stimulus reliably correlated with reinforcement, but Jenkins and Harrison pointed out that this tone had many separate features—its frequency, its loudness, its location, and so on. To the extent that responding was controlled by features of the tone other than its frequency, we should expect responding to persist at other frequencies, as it did after presence-absence training. When the S⁻ was a tone of slightly different frequency, however, the only reliable predictor of reinforcement was the frequency of the 1000 Hz tone, so the other features of this tone, such as loudness and location, should lose their control over responding. The sharper gradients from the pigeons that received intradimensional training are consistent with this analysis.

In summary, the Jenkins and Harrison results support Lashley and Wade's hypothesis that generalization gradients are dependent on experience. With nondifferential training, tone frequency exerted no control over responding. After presence-absence training, tone frequency exerted modest control, and typical peaked generalization gradients were obtained. With intradimensional training, very sharply peaked gradients were obtained. Unfortunately for the Lashley and Wade theory, however, other studies have shown that peaked generalization gradients can sometimes be obtained with nondifferential training. We have already encountered one study of this type: In the Guttman and Kalish (1956) experiment, peaked gradients along the dimension of wavelength were obtained after nondifferential training with a 580 nm key light. These results seem to support Pavlov's theory that no special training is necessary for generalization gradients to appear.

It is not difficult to think of ways to reconcile the results of Guttman and Kalish (and others like them) with the Lashley and Wade theory. As Lashley and Wade themselves suggested, although subjects might receive only nondifferential training within an experiment, they may have learned from their everyday experiences prior to the experiment that different stimuli along the dimension in question can signal different consequences. Thus the pigeons in the Guttman and Kalish experiment might have learned from their everyday experiences that color is frequently an informative characteristic of a stimulus, and as a result they were predisposed to "pay attention to" the color of the key in the experimental chamber.

How Sensory Deprivation Affects the Shape of Generalization Gradients. Once the possibility of preexperiment learning is entertained, the Lashley and Wade theory becomes quite difficult to test: It becomes necessary to prevent the possibility of discrimination learning along the dimension in question from the moment a subject is born. Peterson (1962) conducted such an ambitious experiment by raising four ducklings in an environment that was illuminated with a monochromatic yellow light of 589 nm. Because this special light emitted only a single wavelength, all objects appeared yellow regardless of their actual color in white light. (To envision what this visual experience is like, imagine watching a black and white movie while wearing yellow-tinted glasses: Everything on the screen would appear as a mixture of yellow and black.) After training the ducklings to peck at a yellow key for water reinforcement, Peterson conducted a generalization test with key lights of different colors. These ducklings produced flat generalization gradients, indicating that color exerted no control over their behavior. Two ducklings reared in white light produced more normal, peaked generalization gradients.

It might seem that this study provides strong support for the position of Lashley and Wade, but there are two problems. First, it is always possible that this type of sensory restriction caused deterioration of the ducklings' visual systems, making them color-blind. Recall that Hubel and Wiesel found that sensory deprivation during certain critical periods made kittens functionally blind, at least in their perception of shapes (Chapter 2). The second problem is still more serious. Several attempts to replicate Peterson's experiment have been unsuccessful (Malott, 1968; Rudolf, Honig, and Gerry, 1969; Terrace, 1975; Tracy, 1970). For instance, Rudolf, Honig and Gerry (1969) raised chickens and quail under monochromatic light and found more sharply peaked generalization gradients than in a control group reared under ordinary white light. There seems to be no way to reconcile these results with the Lashley and Wade theory.

To summarize, research on the relationship between experience and generalization gradients has yielded a variety of findings. The experiments employing sensory restriction showed that, at least with birds, stimulus control by wavelength of light can occur even when a subject has had no previous exposure to more than one color. These studies contradict the extreme form of the Lashley and Wade theory, which states that no stimulus control will occur without some discrimination training involving the relevant stimulus dimension. At the other extreme is Pavlov's theory that peaked generalization gradients are derived from an inherent characteristic of the nervous system, and this theory is also incorrect. Jenkins and Harrison found no stimulus control along the dimension of tone frequency without some form of prior discrimination training (presence-absence training, intradimensional training) with tone frequency. The results suggest a compromise position: In some cases, discrimination learning may be necessary before stimulus control is obtained, and in other cases no experience may be necessary. The evidence that, for birds, such experience is necessary for tones but not for colors is consistent with the idea that vision is a dominant sensory modality for these creatures (see Chapter 9). Perhaps we might say that birds are "prepared" to associate the color of a stimulus with the consequences that follow, but are "unprepared" to associate the pitch of a tone with subsequent events.

Whether or not experience is necessary before a particular creature exhibits stimulus control along a particular stimulus dimension, one certainty is that explicit discrimination training can change the shape of a generalization gradient. We have already seen how intradimensional training can sharpen stimulus control. The next section explores some theories and evidence about exactly what a subject learns when it receives intradimensional discrimination training.

IS STIMULUS CONTROL ABSOLUTE OR RELATIONAL?

Consider a simple experiment on discrimination learning in which a chicken is presented with two discriminative stimuli, a light gray card and a dark gray card. If the chicken approaches the light gray card it is reinforced, but if it approaches the dark gray card it is not. This procedure is called *simultaneous discrimination* training because the two stimuli are presented together and the subject must choose between them. With sufficient training, the chicken will learn to choose the light gray card. But exactly what has the animal learned? According to the *absolute* theory of stimulus control, the animal has simply learned about the two stimuli separately: It has learned that choosing the light gray color produces food, and choosing the dark gray color produces no food. On the other hand, according to the *relational* theory of stimulus control, the animal has learned something about the *relationship* between the two stimuli—it has learned that the *lighter* gray is associated with food. The absolute position assumes that the animal responds to each stimulus without reference to the other; the relational position assumes that the animal responds to the *relationship* between the two. C. Lloyd Morgan (1894), an early writer on animal behavior, favored the absolute position because he believed that nonhumans are simply not capable of understanding relationships such as lighter, darker, larger, or redder. These relationships are abstract concepts that are not part of any single stimulus, and he felt that animals do not have the capacity to form such abstractions. A major advocate of the relational position was the German psychologist Wolfgang Kohler (1939). Let us look at the evidence on both sides of this debate and attempt to come to some resolution.

Transposition and Peak Shift

In support of the relational position, Kohler (1939) presented evidence for a phenomenon he called *transposition*. After training several chickens on the simultaneous discrimination task just described, he gave the chickens several trials on which the two stimuli were (1) the light gray card that had previously served as the S$^+$, and (2) a card with a still lighter gray (which we can call the "very light gray stimulus"). Which stimulus would a chicken choose? If the absolute position is correct, the chicken should choose the gray that had been the S$^+$, since the animal had been reinforced for choosing this stimulus, but it had never been reinforced for choosing the very light gray card (since it had never seen this stimulus before). On the other hand, if the animal had learned to respond to the relation between the two training stimuli (choosing the lighter gray), it should choose the novel, very light gray stimulus. Across several extinction trials, all of Kohler's subjects showed a preference for the novel stimulus over the previously reinforced stimulus. The term *transposition* is meant to convey the idea that the subject has transferred the relational rule ("Choose the lighter gray") to a new pair of stimuli (one of which happens to be the previous S$^+$).

Kohler also found evidence for transposition with chimpanzees, and other studies have found such evidence with rats (Lawrence and DeRivera, 1954) and with children (Alberts and Ehrenfreund, 1951). Besides the brightness of different grays, transposition has also been found when the different discriminative stimuli varied along the dimension of size (Gulliksen, 1932). These results constitute one of the main pieces of evidence for the relational theory.

In research on generalization gradients, a phenomenon that is in some ways similar to transposition was first reported by Hanson (1959), who referred to it as *peak shift*. Notice that whereas transposition is found in simultaneous discrimination tasks, generalization gradients are usually obtained by presenting the various stimuli one at a time, in what is called a *successive discrimination* procedure. In Hanson's experiment, pigeons in the control group received several sessions of training in which pecking at a 550 nm key light

occasionally produced food on a VI schedule. These pigeons had no training with any other key color until the generalization test. In an experimental group, pigeons received intradimensional training with the 550 nm key light as S$^+$ and a 555 nm key light as S$^-$. After this training, Hanson measured the birds' responses to a range of different key colors during extinction so as to obtain generalization gradients.

The results from both groups are shown in Figure 10-3. The control group produced a typical generalization gradient with a peak at 550 nm, as expected. In contrast, the group that received intradimensional training produced a peak around 530 to 540 nm rather than at the previously reinforced wavelength. In fact, there was very little responding to the 550 nm key light in the generalization test. The term *peak shift* thus refers to a shift in the generalization gradient in a direction away from the S$^-$.

Let us try to decide how these results relate to the absolute and relational views of stimulus control. The absolute position would seem to predict a peak at 550 nm for both groups, since this was the stimulus that had previously signaled the availability of reinforcement. On the other hand, the peak shift might provide some support for the relational position, for the following reason. Lights of both 550 nm and 555 nm are greenish-yellow, but the shorter wavelength is a bit greener. Thus according to the relational position, the pigeons that received intradimensional training might have learned that the *greener* of the two stimuli was a signal for reinforcement. This would explain why they responded more to the 530 and 540 nm stimuli, which are greener still. Unfortunately, the relational position cannot explain why responding was markedly lower to wavelengths between 500 and 520 nm, which are the purest greens. In summary, at this point in our discussion, Hanson's results do not seem to be completely consistent with either the absolute or relational positions.

Spence's Theory of Excitatory and Inhibitory Gradients

A clever version of the absolute theory developed by Kenneth Spence (1937) can account

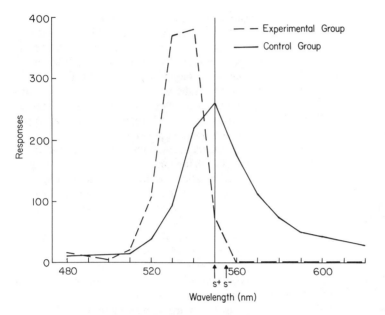

FIGURE 10-3.
Generalization gradients for wavelength of light in the experiment of Hanson (1959). The control group was trained only with a 550 nm key light as S⁺, whereas the experimental group was trained with a 550 nm key light as S⁺ and a 555 nm key light as S⁻.

quite nicely for both transposition and peak shift. The essence of the absolute position is that the subject learns only about the two stimuli individually, and learns nothing about the relation between the two. Beginning with this assumption, Spence proposed that in intradimensional training, an excitatory generalization gradient develops around the S⁺, and an inhibitory gradient develops around the S⁻. Let us see how this process might apply to Hanson's experiment. Figure 10-4a depicts an excitatory generalization gradient around 550 nm and an inhibitory gradient centered around 555 nm. We have borrowed the term *associative strength* from Rescorla and Wagner (Chapter 5) to represent the ability of each stimulus to elicit a response. Spence proposed that the net associative strength of any stimulus can be determined by subtracting its inhibitory strength from its excitatory strength. For each wavelength, the result of this subtraction is shown in Figure 10-4b.

Notice that the S⁺, 550 nm, has the highest excitatory strength, but it also has a good deal of inhibitory strength because of its proximity to the S⁻. On the other hand, a stimulus in the vicinity of 530 to 540 nm has considerable excitatory strength (by virtue of generalization from the S⁺)

but relatively little inhibitory strength (because it is further away from the S⁻). The result is that stimuli around 530 to 540 nm actually have a higher net associative strength than the S⁺ of 550 nm. If we assume (as Spence did) that the strength of responding in the presence of any stimulus depends on its associative strength, then Figure 10-4b predicts the type of peak shift that Hanson actually obtained.

Recall that the relational theory cannot explain why responding was so low with stimuli of 500 to 520 nm. Spence's theory has no problem explaining these results, however. As Figure 10-4 shows, we need only assume that these wavelengths are so far from both S⁺ and S⁻ that they acquired little excitatory or inhibitory strength. In short, Spence's theory can explain both the peak shift and the decreased responding with stimuli further away from S⁺. It does a very good job of accounting for the results from successive discrimination experiments.

Spence actually developed his theory to account for the transposition effect found in simultaneous discrimination tasks, and the reasoning is similar. If two stimuli are presented simultaneously, excitatory and inhibitory gradients will still develop around S⁺ and S⁻, respectively. If we

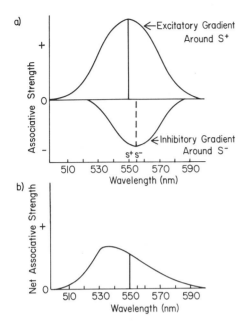

a)

b)

FIGURE 10-4. An analysis of peak shift based on Spence's (1937) theory. (a) Intradimensional training is assumed to produce an excitatory gradient around S$^+$ (550 nm) and an inhibitory gradient around S$^-$ (555 nm). (b) The net associative strength of each wavelength equals the difference between its excitatory strength and inhibitory strength. Because of the inhibitory gradient around S$^-$, the peak of this gradient is shifted from S$^+$ in a direction away from S$^-$

imagine an experiment in which Hanson's S$^+$ and S$^-$ were presented in a simultaneous discrimination task, we can use Figure 10-4 to explain the transposition effect. After the subjects had learned the discrimination, they might be presented with the former S$^+$ (550 nm) and a 540 nm stimulus. According to the gradient in Figure 10-4b, the subject should choose the novel stimulus of 540 nm, because its net strength is higher. Similar reasoning can account for the transposition effect found when the stimuli vary along other dimensions, such as brightness or size.

The predictions of the relational theory and of Spence's theory for simultaneous discrimination tasks differ in one important respect. Spence's theory predicts that if the two test stimuli are suf-

ficiently different from the training S$^+$ and S$^-$, there should be no transposition effect, and in fact the subject should choose the stimulus that is closer to the S$^+$. Referring once again to Figure 10-4, suppose the test stimuli were lights of 510 and 530 nm. Because the net associative strength of the 530 nm stimulus is larger, Spence's theory would predict a choice of this stimulus. On the other hand, the relational theory, which assumes that the subject has learned a rule something like "choose the greener stimulus," would predict a choice of the greener, 510 nm stimulus.

The results of several experiments in which the test stimuli were both far removed from S$^+$ and S$^-$ are, unfortunately, ambiguous. The general finding is that the transposition effect grows weaker when the test stimuli are very different from the S$^+$ and S$^-$, but the reversal in preference predicted by Spence's theory has not been found. Instead, subjects choose both stimuli about equally often, as if they are indifferent between the two (Ehrenfreund, 1952; Kendler, 1950). These results are not exactly what the relational theory predicts, but they are not that damaging to this theory either. Perhaps the animals simply become confused when the test stimuli are very different from the training stimuli. As an analogy, suppose you are out picking blackberries, and your companions have advised you to pick the larger ones, both because they are sweeter and because they fill your basket faster. You would probably have no difficulty following this rule when choosing between 0.4-inch and 0.3-inch blackberries or between 0.5-inch and 0.4-inch blackberries. Imagine your confusion, however, if you encountered some berries that were 2 to 3 inches in diameter: Are they really blackberries? Are they some sort of poisonous mutation? Just as you might wonder whether the "larger is better" rule still applies, animal subjects may abandon a relational rule and simply choose randomly when the test stimuli are very different from the training stimuli.

The Intermediate Size Problem

Except for the results discussed in the last paragraph, Spence's theory does a good job of accounting for the results from experiments on transposition and peak shift. However, a test known as the *intermediate size problem* poses a problem of major size for Spence's theory. Gonzalez, Gentry, and Bitterman (1954) conducted an experiment on the intermediate size problem with chimpanzees. Their stimuli were nine squares of different sizes. Their smallest square (which they called Square 1) had an area of 9 square inches, and their largest square (Square 9) had an area of about 27 square inches. During training, the chimpanzees were always presented with Squares 1, 5, and 9, and they were reinforced if they chose the intermediate square, Square 5. (Of course, the left-to-right locations of the squares varied randomly from trial to trial so that a subject could not use position as a discriminative stimulus.)

On test trials, the chimpanzees were presented with different sets of three squares, and they were reinforced no matter which they chose. As an example, suppose the three squares on one trial were Squares 4, 7, and 9. The predictions of the relational position are straightforward: If the chimps had learned to choose the square of intermediate size, they should choose Square 7. Figure 10-5 helps to explain the predictions of Spence's theory. The initial training should have produced an excitatory gradient around Square 5 and inhibitory gradients around Squares 1 and 9. Because Square 5 is flanked on each side by an inhibitory gradient, there is no peak shift in this case; instead, the inhibitory gradients simply sharpen the gradient of net associative strength around Square 5. Thus a subject should choose whichever stimulus is closer to Square 5 (Square 4 in the above example).

The actual results of Gonzalez et al. favored the relational theory over Spence's theory. To summarize the results briefly, the chimps usually chose the square of intermediate size on test trials regardless of which three squares were presented. In short, they behaved as if they were responding to the relationships among the stimuli, not their absolute sizes.

A Compromise Position

The intermediate size problem tells us that the most extreme version of the absolute position—

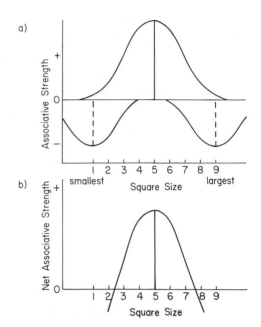

FIGURE 10-5. An application of Spence's (1937) theory to the intermediate size problem. (a) In initial training, an excitatory gradient develops around S$^+$ (Square 5) and inhibitory gradients develop around the two S$^-$s (Squares 1 and 9). (b) Because of the two symmetrical inhibitory gradients, there is no peak shift in the gradient of net associative strength. There is only a sharpening of the generalization gradient.

that animals *never* respond to the relationship between stimuli—is incorrect. On the other hand, studies on the peak shift such as Hanson's seem to favor Spence's theory over the relational position. As discussed above, the relational position cannot explain why responding decreases with stimuli that are far removed from S$^+$ in a direction away from S$^-$. Further support for Spence's theory comes from studies that show that an inhibitory generalization gradient does indeed develop around the S$^-$ (see Rilling, 1977, for a review of the abundant evidence for inhibitory stimulus control). For example, Honig, Boneau, Burstein, and Pennypacker (1963) obtained a good example of an inhibitory generalization gradient with pigeons. In the training for one group of pigeons, the S$^+$ was a plain white key, and the

S⁻ was a white key with a black vertical line down the middle. For a second group, the stimuli serving as S⁺ and S⁻ were reversed. In a subsequent extinction test, the responses of both groups were measured to black lines that had different orientations ranging from vertical to horizontal. Figure 10-6 shows the results for each group. The group for which the vertical line was S⁺ produced a typical peaked gradient centered around this stimulus. The group for which the vertical line was S⁻ produced a gradient of the opposite shape: Responses were fewest to the vertical line, and they became more numerous to lines whose orientations were further and further from vertical (even though the pigeons had never been reinforced for pecking at white keys with lines on them). Honig et al. concluded that the more similar a test stimulus was to the S⁻, the greater was its capacity to inhibit responding.

We have found that both Spence's theory and the relational theory have their strengths and weaknesses. It is important to see that the successes and failures follow a consistent pattern: Spence's theory does a better job of predicting the results from successive discrimination experiments, where the test stimuli are presented one at a time. The relational theory is superior in predicting the results from simultaneous discrimination tasks, where a subject must choose from two or three stimuli. Why is each theory superior for a particular class of experiments? Let us try to develop an explanation.

We can begin with the idea that both absolute cues and relational cues are "features" of the stimuli in a discrimination task. Contrary to the predictions of Morgan and Spence, the data suggest that the behavior of animals can be controlled by both types of cues. However, in a simultaneous discrimination task, where the stimuli are presented side by side, it is likely that relational cues will be more salient than absolute cues. For instance, imagine a simultaneous discrimination task in which the S⁺ is a 4-inch square and the S⁻ is a 3.8-inch square. The slight difference in size should be obvious when the stimuli are placed side by side, and it is not surprising that an animal learns to respond on the basis of this relationship. On the other hand, sup-

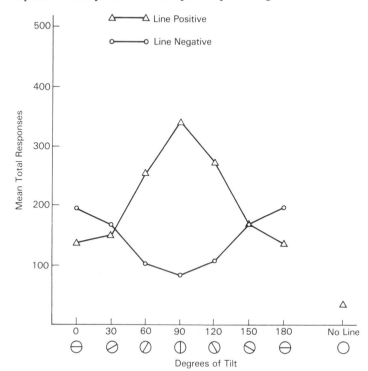

FIGURE 10-6. Generalization gradients along the dimension of line orientation from the experiment of Honig et al. (1963). The triangles show the results from the group with a vertical line on the response key as S⁺ and a blank key as S⁻. The circles show the results from the group with a blank key as S⁺ and a vertical line as S⁻.

pose these two squares were presented in a successive discrimination task. Here, the relational cues (the difference between the two squares) would be much less salient: To compare the two stimuli the subject would have to rely on its memory of one stimulus while viewing the other. In short, relational cues are more salient in a simultaneous discrimination task than in a successive discrimination task.

The simultaneous discrimination task may simply be one more example of a situation where a salient feature of the stimulus environment (for instance, a difference in the sizes of two adjacent squares) overshadows a less salient feature (the absolute sizes of the two squares). Because of their salience, the subject may learn about the relational cues at the expense of absolute cues. This would account for the results of the transposition and intermediate size experiments. In contrast, because relational cues are much less salient when the discriminative stimuli are presented one at a time, the subject may be forced to rely on absolute cues in a successive discrimination task. This analysis is consistent with the evidence that supports Spence's absolute theory in successive discrimination tasks. In summary, it appears that animals learn discriminations by using relational cues when the situation makes it easy to do so, and by using absolute cues when it does not.

BEHAVIORAL CONTRAST

The existence of peak shift shows that it is often impossible to predict how a subject will respond in the presence of one stimulus simply by knowing the reinforcement schedule associated with that stimulus. It is often essential to know what other stimuli have been presented and what reinforcement contingencies were associated with them. Thus in Figure 10-3, a 550 nm key light produced substantial responding in one group but only minimal responding in a second group (for which a 555 nm key light served as an S⁻). The phenomenon of *behavioral contrast* (Reynolds, 1961) offers another example of how the reinforcement contingencies operating in the presence of one stimulus can affect responding in the presence of a different stimulus.

An experiment by Gutman (1977) provides a convenient example of behavioral contrast. Like many experiments on behavioral contrast, Gutman's study used a special type of successive discrimination procedure otherwise known as a multiple schedule. As discussed in Chapter 6, in a multiple schedule two or more reinforcement schedules are presented one at a time, in an alternating pattern, and each schedule is associated with a different discriminative stimulus. The different reinforcement schedules that comprise a multiple schedule are sometimes called the *components* of the multiple schedule. In Phase 1 of Gutman's experiment, rats were exposed to a two-component multiple schedule in which the component schedules were identical: One VI 30-second schedule was signaled by a noise, and a separate VI 30-second schedule was signaled by a light. The light and noise were alternately presented every three minutes throughout a session. Not surprisingly, response rates to the noise and light were about the same in this first condition, as shown in Figure 10-7. In Phase 2, the only change was that the schedule operating during the noise was switched from VI 30 seconds to extinction. Figure 10-7 shows that, as expected, responding became slower and slower during the noise. What was more surprising, however, was that response rates increased dramatically in the presence of the light, even though the reinforcement schedule for the light was exactly the same as in the first condition. This phenomenon, in which responding to one stimulus changes as a result of a change in the reinforcement conditions for *another* stimulus, is called *behavioral contrast*.

To be more specific, Gutman's study provided an example of *positive contrast*, because it involved an increase in responding during the unchanged, light component. The opposite effect has also been observed. For example, suppose the noise schedule was switched, and now three times as many reinforcers were delivered in the presence of the noise. The likely result would be an increase in response rate during the noise and a decrease in response rate during the light. This decrease in response rate during the unchanged, light component would be called *negative contrast*.

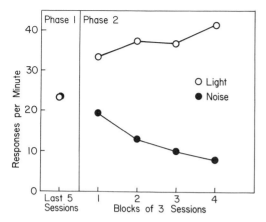

FIGURE 10-7. Results from Gutman's (1977) experiment on behavioral contrasts in rats. When both the light and the noise signaled VI 30-second schedules (Phase 1), response rates were about the same for both stimuli. When the noise signaled a period of extinction (Phase 2), response rates declined toward zero when the noise was present but increased substantially above those of Phase 1 when the light was present.

There are plenty of theories about why behavioral contrast occurs (see, for example, Nevin & Shettleworth, 1966; Schwartz & Gamzu, 1977). We will consider three distinctly different theories. One possibility is that positive contrast is due to the slower responding that occurs in the component that is changed to extinction. Perhaps this slower responding allows the animal to respond faster in the changed component. The slower responding in the extinction component might allow the subject to recover from fatigue, so the "well rested" animal can respond faster in the unchanged component. In addition, during the extinction component the animal may be able to spend more time performing various activities that would normally compete for its time in the unchanged component (for instance, grooming, exploring the chamber). That is, the animal may pack more of these extraneous behaviors into the extinction component, so it has more time to perform the operant response in the unchanged component (Ettinger & Staddon, 1982). Although

there is some evidence supporting this theory (Dougan, McSweeney, & Farmer-Dougan, 1986), response-rate changes in adjacent components do not seem to be the primary cause of behavioral contrast. This has been shown, for example, by switching the adjacent component from a VI schedule to one that delivers free reinforcers at the same rate. Naturally, response rates decline dramatically under the free-reinforcer schedule, but behavioral contrast is not observed in the unchanged component (Halliday & Boakes, 1971).

A second theory of behavioral contrast is *additivity theory* (Gamzu and Schwartz, 1973). In essence, this theory states that positive contrast occurs when autoshaped or classically conditioned responses are added to the subject's normal operant responses on the VI schedule. In their famous experiment on autoshaping, Brown and Jenkins (1968) found that pigeons would peck at a lighted key that signaled an upcoming reinforcer (Chapter 9). According to additivity theory, during the second phase of Gutman's experiment, the light had the same status as the illuminated key in the Brown and Jenkins experiment. That is, the light signaled that reinforcers were available, and the absence of the light (when the noise was on instead) signaled that no reinforcers were available. Because the light was positively correlated with the availability of food, we might expect it to elicit "autoshaped" lever presses, and when added to the rat's operant responses this would produce an increased response rate.

A third theory of behavioral contrast focuses on the decrease in reinforcement in the changed component (Herrnstein, 1970). According to this account, an animal's rate of response in one component of a multiple schedule depends not only on the reinforcement available during that component, but also on the rate of reinforcement in the adjacent components. To speak loosely, it is as if the subject judges the value of one component by comparing it to its neighbors. In the first phase of Gutman's experiment, the schedule during the light component was "nothing special", since the same schedule was available during the noise component. The light therefore produced only a moderate rate of response. On the other hand, during the second phase of the experiment, the light component was quite attractive compared to the extinction schedule of the noise component, so the light produced a high response rate.

In a review of the substantial body of research on behavioral contrast, Williams (1983) concluded that there may be more than one cause of contrast. It is not possible to review all the evidence here, but there is support for both the additivity theory and for view that the rate of reinforcement in adjacent components is important. In addition, Williams (1981) has obtained convincing evidence that behavior contrast is determined mostly by a change in the reinforcement rate of the upcoming component, not by a change in the preceding component. For example suppose a multiple schedule has three components that are signaled by red, white, and blue key lights, respectively. At first, each color is associated with a VI 1-minute schedule. If the schedule for the red component switches to extinction, little behavioral contrast will be observed in the unchanged, white component that follows it. However, if the schedule for the blue component switches to extinction, an increase in responding (positive contrast) will be observed in the white component that precedes it.

Although its causes are not completely understood, the phenomenon of behavioral contrast demonstrates once again that it can be dangerous to study reinforcement schedules as if they were isolated entities. A subject's behavior on one schedule may be greatly influenced by events occurring before and after the schedule is in effect.

"ERRORLESS" DISCRIMINATION LEARNING

Given what you have learned so far about operant conditioning and discrimination learning, consider the following problem. Suppose that as a laboratory exercise for a course on learning, your assignment was to teach a pigeon a strong discrimination between red and green key colors. The red key will signal a VI 1-minute schedule, and you would like moderate, steady responding to this key color. The green key will signal ex-

tinction, so you would like no responding during the green key. You might begin by training the bird to eat from the food hopper when it was presented, and then you might use a shaping procedure to train the bird to peck the red key. At first, you would reinforce every response, and then gradually shift to longer and longer VI schedules (such as VI 15 seconds, then VI 30 seconds, and finally VI 1 minute). After several sessions with a VI 1- minute schedule on the red key, the pigeon would probably respond steadily throughout the session, and you could then introduce the green key color and its extinction schedule. From now on, sessions might alternate between 3-minute red components and 3-minute green components. At first, we would expect the pigeon to respond when the key was green because of generalization, but eventually responses to this color should decrease to a low level.

This might sound like a sensible plan for developing a good red/green discrimination, but Terrace (1966) has enumerated several reasons why it is not ideal. One major problem is that this method of discrimination training takes a long time, and along the way the subject makes many "errors" (unreinforced responses to the green key). Because the training must continue for several sessions before a good discrimination is achieved, there are likely to be many setbacks, due to the spontaneous recovery of responding to the green key at the start of each session. Perhaps because of the numerous errors, it appears that this type of discrimination training is aversive for the subject. For one thing, the pigeon may exhibit aggressive behavior, such as wing flapping. If another pigeon is present in an adjacent compartment, the subject may engage in an aggressive display and eventually attack the other animal. Such attacks typically occur soon after the transition from S^+ to S^-. Further evidence that the procedure is aversive comes from the finding that if the pigeon can turn off the S^- by pecking at another key, it will do so. A final problem with this procedure is that even after months of training, the animal's performance is usually not perfect—there are occasional bursts of responding to the S^-.

The criticisms of this method of discrimination training would be of little use if there were no better method of discrimination training, but Terrace (1963) showed that there is one. He named this alternative *errorless discrimination learning* because the subject typically makes few or no responses to the S⁻. The errorless discrimination procedure differs from the traditional procedure in two major ways. First, rather than waiting for strong, steady responding to the S⁺, the experimenter introduces the S⁻ early in the training procedure. Terrace first presented the S⁻ within 30 seconds of the pigeon's first peck at the red key. Second, a fading procedure is used to make it unlikely that the subject will respond to the S⁻. Notice that in the procedure described above, the green key would remain on for three minutes the first time it was presented. This would give the subject ample time to respond to this key color. In Terrace's procedure, however, the S⁻ was presented for only five seconds at a time at first, which gave the pigeon little chance to respond in its presence. In addition, Terrace made use of the fact the pigeons are unlikely to peck at a dark response key: At first, the S⁻ was not an illuminated green key but a dark key. Using a fading procedure, Terrace gradually progressed from a dark key to a dimly lit green key, and over trials the intensity of the green light was increased. In summary, in Terrace's procedure the S⁻ was introduced early in training, it was presented very briefly at first, and it was initially a stimulus that was unlikely to elicit responding.

Terrace's errorless discrimination procedure is effective in decreasing the number of responses to the S⁻ and improving the subject's long-term discrimination performance. In one experiment, subjects trained with a conventional discrimination procedure made an average of more than 3000 responses to the S⁻ during 28 sessions. Subjects trained with the errorless procedure averaged only about 25 responses in the same number of sessions. In addition to enormous differences in responding to the S⁻, Terrace (1972) proposed that his errorless procedure produces several other performance differences compared to traditional procedures. He claimed that with the errorless procedure, the S⁻ does not become aversive, and so aggressive behaviors and responses to escape from the S⁻ do not occur. He also claimed that the S⁻ does not develop inhibitory properties,

so after errorless discrimination training there is no peak shift in the generalization gradient. Finally, he claimed that positive behavioral contrast to the S⁺ does not occur if the S⁻ never elicits responses. In short, Terrace proposed that none of the "by-products" of traditional discrimination learning occur with his errorless discrimination procedure.

Rilling (1977) has disputed each of Terrace's claims about the "by-products" of discrimination learning. Rilling and his colleagues have conducted a series of experiments which show that after errorless discrimination learning, subjects may exhibit aggressive responses during the S⁻, responses to escape from the S⁻, peak shift in their generalization gradients, and positive behavioral contrast. Based on these results, Rilling concluded that Terrace's claim that the errorless procedure produces a qualitatively different type of discrimination learning is unfounded. Nevertheless, Rilling conceded that Terrace's procedure does produce some quantitative differences in performance: With this procedure there is generally *less* aggressive behavior, *less* behavioral contrast, and perhaps less inhibition to the S⁻. Rilling's evidence suggests that these differences are due mainly to the early introduction of the S⁻, and that the fading procedure Terrace used is less important.

Although Terrace's assertion about the by-products of errorless discrimination learning may have been exaggerated, it is certainly true that his procedure generates excellent stimulus control in a minimum amount of time. Some might claim that errorless performance is advantageous, and that behavior therapists and educators should use Terrace's techniques whenever a discrimination must be learned. For instance, Skinner has maintained that classroom curricula should be designed so that the student almost never makes a mistake. His reasoning is that if we do not want children to avoid learning experiences, and if making an incorrect response (and thereby failing to receive reinforcement) is aversive, then we should try to eliminate these aversive episodes as much as possible. While this reasoning may be correct, errorless discrimination learning is not without its disadvantages. Marsh and Johnson (1968) found that if subjects are trained using an errorless procedure and then the stimuli serving as S$^+$ and S$^-$ switch their roles, these subjects are very slow to alter their behavior accordingly. Errorless discrimination performance may hinder an organism's ability to adapt to a changing stimulus environment.

TRANSFER OF LEARNING AFTER DISCRIMINATION TRAINING

In the examples of generalization and discrimination discussed so far in this chapter, the S$^+$, S$^-$, and all test stimuli varied along some simple physical dimension such as color, tone frequency, or size. We will now begin to turn to situations where the physical characteristics of the training stimuli and test stimuli may be totally different, and where the similarity between the training phase and the testing phase is more abstract. Therefore, if a subject exhibits "savings" from one task to the next, this will be evidence for a more sophisticated capacity to generalize from previous learning experiences.

Intradimensional and Extradimensional Transfer

Imagine an experiment on simultaneous discrimination in which pigeons must choose between two response keys that have lines of different colors and different orientations projected on them. In the first phase of the experiment, one stimulus is always a red line and the other a yellow line. One of the two lines (sometimes the red one and sometimes the yellow one) is horizontal, and the other is vertical. For one group of pigeons, the relevant dimension is color: The red line is the S$^+$ and the yellow line is the S$^-$, regardless of their orientations. After a sufficient number of trials, the pigeons in this group always choose the red line, regardless of its orientation, and regardless of whether it is projected on the left or right key. For a second group of pigeons, the relevant dimension is orientation: The horizontal line is the S$^+$ and the vertical line is the S$^-$, regardless of their colors or positions. Pigeons in this group eventually learn to choose the horizontal line on every trial.

After pigeons in both groups have mastered their tasks, they are presented with a new problem to see how their previous experience will affect their ability to learn a new discrimination. In this phase, the lines are two different colors, blue and green, and they have two new orientations, diagonal sloping to the left and diagonal sloping to the right. For both groups, the blue line is the S$^+$, the green line is the S$^-$, and the orientations and positions of the line are irrelevant. For the first group, the change from Phase 1 to Phase 2 is called an *intradimensional shift,* because color is the relevant dimension in both phases but the colors of S$^+$ and S$^-$ have changed. For the second group, the change is called an *extradimensional shift* because orientation is the relevant dimension in Phase 1 and color is the relevant dimension in Phase 2.

Mackintosh and Little (1969) conducted an experiment much like the one just described, and they found that their pigeons mastered the new discrimination more quickly after an intradimensional shift than after an extradimensional shift. Faster learning after an intradimensional shift has been obtained in a number of studies where the subjects ranged from rats to humans (Durlach & Mackintosh, 1986; Kemler & Shepp, 1971; Shepp & Eimas, 1964; Wolff, 1967), although some studies have found no difference between intradimensional and extradimensional shifts (Hall & Channell, 1985). For those studies in which an advantage for intradimensional shifts has been found, a common interpretation of these results makes use of the concept of attention. According to this reasoning, there are several stimulus dimensions to which a subject might attend in this type of experiment (for instance, left-right location, color, orientation). One theory says that part of what a subject learns in a discrimination task is which stimulus dimension is relevant. A slightly different theory states that a subject learns which stimulus dimensions are irrelevant and can be ignored. Either way, an extradimensional shift should cause problems for the subject, because the previously relevant dimension is now irrelevant, and vice versa. The important point of this research is similar to that of studies on relational learning: Subjects often learn more in a discrimination task than simply which stimulus is the S⁺ and which is the S⁻, and this additional learning can help (or hinder) their performance on subsequent discrimination tasks.

Learning Sets

Harry Harlow (1949) was the first to demonstrate that animals can learn much more in a discrimination task than which stimulus dimension they should attend to. Harlow's subjects were primates, who were typically tested on many different discrimination problems. For instance, in a famous experiment, Harlow presented two monkeys with over 300 different discrimination problems. Two different stimulus objects were presented on a trial. The choice of one stimulus led to food, and the choice of the other did not. The same objects were used as S⁺ and S⁻ for six

trials, which constituted one discrimination problem. Then another two objects served as S⁺ and S⁻ for the second discrimination problem (another six trials), then another two objects for the third problem, and so on. The results of Harlow's experiment are presented in Figure 10-8. The x-axis marks the six trials of a single discrimination problem, and the y-axis shows the percentage of correct responses (with 50 percent being the level of chance performance). As can be seen, on the first eight discrimination problems, the monkeys' performance improved gradually over trials, reaching a level of about 75 percent correct by the sixth and final trial. This shows that six trials were not enough to produce high levels of performance on the early discrimination problems. Figure 10-8 shows, however, that on later problems the monkeys acquired each new discrimination more and more quickly. The highest curve shows

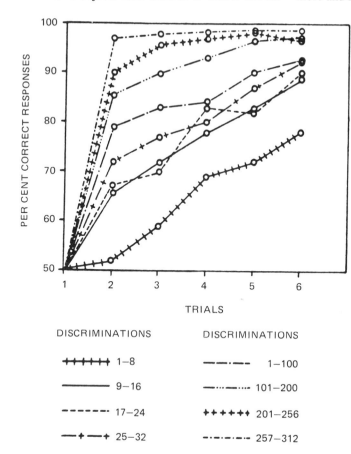

DISCRIMINATIONS
+++++ 1–8
———— 9–16
- - - - - 17–24
—+—+— 25–32

DISCRIMINATIONS
—·—·— 1–100
—···—···— 101–200
++++++ 201–256
—·—·—·— 257–312

FIGURE 10-8. Results from Harlow's (1949) experiment on learning sets, in which new stimuli were introduced as S⁺ and S⁻ every six trials. The x-axis shows the six trials with a given pair of stimuli, and the y-axis show the percentage of trials on which S⁺ was chosen. In the early discrimination problems, the monkeys' performances improved gradually across the six trials with the same two stimuli. Later in the experiment, the monkeys' performances were close to perfect on the second trial with each new discrimination problem.

that after over 250 discrimination problems, they were able to master each new discrimination by trial 2 (that is, after only one trial of learning).

Harlow called this improvement in the rate of learning across several different discrimination problems by several different names, including a *learning set, learning to learn,* and *transfer from problem to problem.* It is important to see that although the S⁺ and S⁻ were different from one problem to the next, each of the several hundred discrimination problems had a number of features in common: One and only one choice was correct on each trial, the same object was correct for all six trials of each problem, the positions of the objects were irrelevant, and so on. Evidently, the monkeys were able to learn that each problem had these similar properties, because by the end of the experiment their performance was nearly optimal: They needed only one trial to determine which stimulus object was the S⁺, and starting with trial 2 they chose this object nearly 100 percent of the time. This performance suggests that the monkeys had learned a "strategy" which they could apply to each new problem: If your choice is reinforced on trial 1, choose this same object on the next five trials; if not, choose the other object on the remaining trials.

Some evidence suggests that different species vary considerably in their ability to develop learning sets. Warren (1965) compared the results of learning-set experiments with several different species (conducted by a number of different researchers), and his findings are shown in Figure 10-9. After a few hundred discrimination problems, rhesus monkeys chose the correct stimulus on trial 2 almost 90 percent of the time. Other animals such as cats develop learning sets more slowly, and rats and squirrels showed only modest transfer from problem to problem even after more than one thousand discrimination tasks. Warren noted that there is clear tendency for animals higher on the phylogenetic scale to develop stronger learning sets. It seems that one noteworthy characteristic of higher species is the ability to acquire more abstract information from a learning situation. That is, besides learning which specific stimuli are S⁺ and S⁻ in each discrimination problem, the higher species may be better at recognizing the similarities between problems and at developing a behavioral strategy that improves performance on subsequent problems.

Such cross-species comparisons must be viewed with caution, however, because the success or failure of one species may depend on exactly how the experiment was conducted. Although Figure 10-9 suggests that rats show little transfer even after extended training, more recent studies with rats found substantial transfer after only a few dozen problems when olfactory cues or spatial locations were used instead of visual stimuli (Eichenbaum, Fagan, & Cohen,

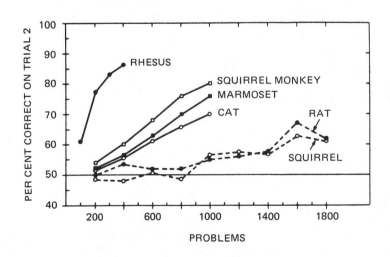

FIGURE 10-9. Warren's (1965) comparison of the performances of several different species in experiments on learning sets. If subjects learn that the structure of each new discrimination problem is similar to that of previous problems, they should begin to perform above chance level on the second trial of a new problem. The speed and amount of improvement varied considerably across species.

1987; Zeldin & Olton, 1986). These results show that with stimuli of the right modality, rats can develop substantial learning sets after all.

Harlow's (1949) procedure of repeated discrimination problems provides just one example of a learning set. Another situation in which a learning set can develop is the *discrimination reversal* procedure. In this procedure, a subject first acquires one discrimination, and then the roles of S^+ and S^- are periodically switched. For example, Harlow studied the behavior of eight monkeys in an experiment where S^+ and S^- were switched every 7, 9, or 11 trials. The experiment included over 100 discrimination reversals, and the results were similar to those shown in Figure 10-8. That is, early in the experiment the monkeys performed incorrectly for several trials after each reversal (which is not surprising since they had previously been reinforced for choosing the now-incorrect stimulus). However, after many reversals, they needed only one trial to correct their behavior—after one unreinforced choice, they would switch to the other stimulus. In short, they had learned how to perform this task with a minimum number of errors.

Researchers have investigated a number of other discrimination tasks in which animals appear to learn something more abstract than simply which stimulus is S^+ and which is S^-. For example, in an *alternation* task, the stimuli serving as S^+ and S^- switch roles each trial, so the subject must learn to choose the stimulus that was incorrect on the previous trial (Hunter, 1920). In a *double alternation* task, S^+ and S^- are switched every *two* trials. For example, Schlosberg and Katz (1943) studied rats in discrimination tasks where the left lever was S^+ for two trials, then the right lever was S^+ for two trials, and so on. The rats learned to perform quite well on this task, thus exhibiting a rudimentary ability to count trials. More recent studies on animals' abilities to learn such abstract relations will be discussed in Chapter 11.

CONCEPT FORMATION

Many of the discrimination tasks we have considered in this chapter might seem quite artificial, for three reasons: (1) The stimuli involved were simple, idealized images that an animal would be unlikely to encounter in the natural environment (such as a perfect square, uniformly red, on a plain white background). (2) Only a small number of stimuli were used. The simplest of discrimination tasks involves only two stimuli, S^+ and S^-. (3) From an objective point of view, the distinction between positive and negative instances was well defined and unambiguous. For instance, the S^+ might be a red square and the S^- a green square, and the subject would not be presented with any objects other than squares nor with any squares that were a mixture of red and green. In more recent work on the topic of *concept formation* or *categorization,* all three of these restrictions have been removed. This research is designed to mimic more closely the types of discrimination an animal must learn in the natural environment. For example, when an animal learns to discriminate between predators and non-predators or between edible plants and poisonous plants, there may be countless examples from each category, they will generally not be simple, idealized forms, and the distinction between positive and negative instances of a category may not always be easy to make. Research on concept formation is designed to investigate how individuals learn to make such complex discriminations.

This distinction between discrimination learning and concept formation is not always clear-cut, but the single most important difference is the number of stimuli used in training. Instead of using just one S^+ and one S^- during discrimination training, experiments on concept formation make use of many stimuli, which are divided into two categories—a set of *positive instances* (which are followed by reinforcement) and a set of *negative instances* (which are not followed by reinforcement). To perform well on such a task, a subject must learn what characteristics distinguish the members of the two categories. The following sections examine research on concept formation involving both human and nonhuman subjects.

The Structure of Natural Categories

Eleanor Rosch (1973, 1975, 1977) has conducted a series of experiments on how people respond to different members of "natural" categories—categories of objects found in the real world, such as *birds, vegetables,* or *vehicles.* Two of her most important conclusions are that the boundaries of these categories are not distinct, and that people tend to judge some members of a category as "good" or "typical" examples of the category and others as "bad" or "atypical" examples. Rosch used the terms *central* and *peripheral* to refer to typical and atypical instances, respectively. In one experiment, Rosch (1973) simply asked subjects to estimate the typicality of different examples of various categories. A seven-point rating scale was used, with 1 signifying a very typical instance and 7 a very atypical example. Rosch reported that subjects found this an easy task, and different instances received very different rankings. For example, in the category of birds, *robin* received a mean ranking of 1.1, *chicken* a mean ranking of 3.8, and *bat* a mean ranking of 5.8. Thus robins were judged to be typical birds, chickens much less typical, and bats were treated as very marginal examples of birds. The example of bats illustrates how the boundaries of a natural category may be indistinct. Whereas taxonomically speaking bats are not birds, many people probably do not know this, and they may consider bats as (atypical) members of the bird category. Conversely, whereas an *olive* is a fruit, many people do not classify it as such, and in Rosch's study it received a mean rating of 6.2.

Rosch described three important characteristics of natural categories. First, people tend to agree on which examples are central and which are peripheral. A second characteristic, related to the first, is that when people are asked to list the members of various categories, they list central instances more frequently. For instance, when Battig and Montague (1969) asked people to make lists of birds, *robins* was listed by 377 subjects, *chicken* by 40 subjects, and *bat* by only 3 subjects. A third characteristic is that in reaction time tests, subjects take longer to decide that peripheral examples are members of the category.

It is interesting to speculate about how children learn to identify members and nonmembers of various natural categories. Language presumably plays an important role: A parent may point

to a robin and say "That is a bird." Later, the parent may tell the child that it is a robin, and that robins are one type of bird. Yet whereas language is certainly important for human concept formation, it cannot explain why natural categories have the structure they do (with central instances, peripheral instances, and ambiguous boundaries). Consider the fact that a child may be repeatedly taught "A robin is a bird" and "A chicken is a bird," yet the child will still judge the latter to be an atypical bird, and will be a bit slower to agree that a chicken is a bird. How can we explain this behavior? Some theories of human concept formation (Franks & Bransford, 1971) propose that people judge whether a given instance is a member of a category by comparing its features to those of an idealized category member. For instance, through our numerous experiences with birds, we may decide that the "ideal" bird has the following characteristics, among others: It has wings, feathers, a beak, and two legs, it sings, it flies, it perches in trees. A robin has all of these features, so it is judged to be a typical bird; a chicken does not, so it is judged to be less typical.

Regardless of how people manage to classify natural objects, the task is a complex one. Consider the natural concept of *tree.* For many people, the ideal tree might be something like a full-grown maple tree, with a sturdy brown trunk and a full canopy of large green leaves. Yet people can correctly identify objects as trees even when they have none of the characteristics of this ideal tree (for example, a small sapling with no leaves, half-buried in snow). The human ability to categorize natural objects is remarkable, and scientists have not yet been able to build a machine that even approximates this ability. Recognizing the impressive concept formation abilities people possess, some psychologists wondered whether other animals (who do not use language and therefore cannot label objects as "bird" or "vegetable") have the ability to learn natural concepts.

Animal Studies on Natural Concept Formation

Quite a few experiments have examined natural concept learning by animals. Herrnstein and his colleagues have conducted several such experiments with pigeons as subjects (Herrnstein & Loveland, 1964; Herrnstein, Loveland, & Cable, 1976). In Herrnstein's procedure, a pigeon would perform in an ordinary experimental chamber containing a translucent screen onto which slides could be projected from behind. In one experiment, Herrnstein (1979) chose to study the natural concept of *tree*: If a slide contained one tree, several trees, or any portion of a tree (such as a branch, a part of the trunk), it was a positive instance, and pecking at the response key was reinforced on a VI schedule. If the slide contained no tree or portion of a tree, it was a negative instance, and extinction conditions were in effect. To avoid indiscriminate pecking in the presence of both positive and negative slides, there was a further restriction that a negative slide would remain on the screen until two seconds elapsed without a peck.

In each session, a pigeon saw 80 different slides, half positive instances and half negative. In most sessions, the same 80 slides were presented, but in several generalization tests some completely new slides were used. The first thing Herrnstein found was that the pigeons quickly learned to discriminate between positive and negative instances. After only a few sessions, the pigeons were responding significantly faster to the positive slides than to negative slides.

Let us consider how the pigeons might have mastered this task. One possibility is that the pigeons did not learn anything about the general category of *tree,* but simply learned about the 80 stimuli individually. This possibility is not inconceivable, since Vaughan and Greene (1984) have shown that with sufficient training pigeons can discriminate between over one hundred positive and negative slides when the stimuli are designated as positive or negative on a purely random basis. However, the results of generalization tests showed that the pigeons' accurate discrimination was not limited to the 80 slides used in training. When presented with slides they had never seen before, the pigeons responded about as rapidly to the positive slides and about as slowly to the negative slides as they did to old positive and negative slides, respectively. In other words, they

were able to classify new slides as trees or nontrees about as well as the old slides.

Similar concept formation experiments with pigeons have used a variety of categories besides trees. Among the concepts pigeons have successfully learned are *people* (Herrnstein and Loveland, 1964), *water,* a particular woman (Herrnstein, Loveland, and Cable, 1976), *fish* (Herrnstein & de Villiers, 1980), and *man-made objects* (Lubow, 1974). They have also been trained to distinguish among the different letters of the alphabet (Blough, 1982), and between triangles and squares (Towe, 1954). Although pigeons have been used in much of this research, the ability to form natural concepts has also been observed in other species, including the parrot (Pepperberg, 1981), the mynah (Turney, 1982), and the monkey (Schreir & Brady, 1987; Yoshikubo, 1985).

What makes natural concept learning so difficult for psychologists to analyze is the lack of a simple way to characterize the distinction between positive and negative instances. It would be easy to relate natural concept learning to traditional discrimination experiments if some simple feature or set of features was present in all positive slides but not in any negative slides. For instance, if all slides of trees included the color green, or some leaves, or a brown trunk, we might conclude that pigeons mastered the problem by attending to the relevant features. In Herrnstein's experiments, however, there were no features common to all positive slides. Some slides of trees included green leaves, but some slides of nontrees also included large green patches (such as a large grassy area). Some negative slides actually included green, leafy objects such as a stalk of celery. In positive slides taken during the fall, the leaves were red and orange, and in some taken during the winter there were no leaves. In some positive slides a large tree filled the center of the picture, and still others showed only distant treetops across a large body of water. Because of this great variability, Herrnstein concluded that there were no "common elements" in either the positive or negative slides.

How, then, did the pigeons manage to discriminate between pictures with trees and pictures without them (or between the presence and absence of water, or people, or man-made objects)? Herrnstein, Loveland, and Cable (1976) suggested one alternative to the common elements approach:

Pigeons respond to clusters of features more or less isomorphic with the clusters we respond to ourselves. The green should be on the leaves, if either green or leaves are present. However, neither is necessary or sufficient. The vertical or branching parts should be the woody parts, although neither of these features is necessary or sufficient either. What we see as trees comprises a complex list of probabilistic conjunctions and disjunctions, the discovery of which would require far more effort than seems justified by any possible benefit. Insofar as no visual element or configuration of them is either necessary or sufficient, there can be no single prototype or schema defined at the level of visual arrays...(pp. 298-299)

In short, Herrnstein et al. are saying that when people sort pictures into the categories of tree or nontree, they are responding to complex configurations of stimuli which allow them to treat the pictures as if they represented three-dimensional objects. Herrnstein et al. proposed that their pigeons did much the same thing: They responded to these complex visual patterns as if they represented objects in a three-dimensional world. By doing so, they were able to classify the visual patterns into the positive or negative categories depending on whether or not a particular real world object (such as a tree, a person) was represented in a picture.

Not everyone accepts this conclusion. Some psychologists still doubt that the animals in these studies actually treated the two-dimensional slides as representations of three-dimensional objects (Cerella, 1982). As an alternative hypothesis, some have suggested that the animals were simply responding to a complex set of features, both positive and negative, and that they were able to generalize to new slides because they shared some of these features (colors, shapes, patterns) with the training slides (see D'Amato & Van Sant, 1988). The issue of whether animals can form a coherent concept like *tree* or whether they merely respond to simpler visual features may be difficult to settle, because it is not clear

what sort of experiment could decisively distinguish between these two positions. But, if animals do have the ability to respond to two-dimensional images as if they were three-dimensional objects, then there is a parallel between this ability and the adaptability of movement discussed in Chapter 6 in the section on "Problems with the Stop-Action Principle." There we saw that when a particular sequence of movements is reinforced, the future likelihood of different movements that have the same effect on the environment is increased. To put it another way, as far as responses are concerned, animals tend to use interchangeably all responses that have the same effect in their three-dimensional environment. As far as stimuli are concerned, animals may have the ability to group together all visual images that represent the same type of object in their three-dimensional environment. In both cases, how these impressive feats might be accomplished is not well understood. In both cases, it has proven difficult to develop machines with similar abilities.

STIMULUS CONTROL IN BEHAVIOR MODIFICATION

Previous chapters have presented several illustrations of the importance of stimulus control in behavior modification. For instance, the treatment of a phobia is designed to eliminate a response (a fear reaction) that is under the control of a certain class of stimuli (the phobic objects or situations). When a therapist attempts to teach an autistic child to speak, the child must be taught numerous discriminations, each involving some discriminative stimulus in the environment (for instance, an object, event, or situation) and the appropriate verbal response. The task of ensuring that the child's new verbal behavior generalizes to other adults besides the teacher is also a problem of stimulus control. In fact, almost every instance of behavior modification involves generalization and/or discrimination in one way or another. What is special about the following examples, however, is that one of the main features of the behavioral treatment is the development of appropriate stimulus control.

Study Behavior

There are many different reasons why some students do poorly in school, but one frequent problem among poor students is that no matter where they are, studying is a low-probability behavior. Such a student may intend to study regularly but may actually succeed in doing productive work only rarely. The problem is simply that there are no stimuli that reliably occasion study behavior. A student may go to her room after dinner planning to study, but may turn on the television or stereo instead. She may go to the library with her reading assignments but may find herself socializing with friends or taking a nap instead of reading.

Recognizing that poor study habits are frequently the result of ineffective stimulus control, Fox (1962) devised the following program for a group of college students who were having difficulty. Each student gave the therapist a detailed weekly schedule, and the therapist found one hour that the student was free each day. The student was instructed to spend at least a part of this hour studying his most difficult course every day. Furthermore, this studying was to be done in the same place every day (usually in a small room of a library or a classroom building). The student was told to take only materials related to the course into that room, and not to use that room on other occasions. A student was not necessarily expected to spend the entire hour in that room: If he began to daydream or became bored or restless, he was to read one more page and then leave immediately. The importance of leaving the room promptly if he was not studying was emphasized to the student. The purpose of this procedure was to establish a particular time and place as a strong stimulus for studying a particular subject by repeatedly pairing this time and place with nothing but study behavior. Fox's reasoning was that other stimuli did not lead to study behavior because they were associated with competing activities (watching television, talking with friends), so it was best to select a new setting where it would be difficult for competing activities to occur.

Not surprisingly, at first students found it difficult to study for long in this new setting, and

they would leave the room well before the hour was over. Gradually, however, their study periods grew longer, and eventually they could spend the entire hour in productive study. At this point, the therapist chose the student's second most difficult course, and the stimulus control procedure was repeated. That is, the student was told to study this subject at a specific time of day in a *different* special location. Before long, each student was studying each of his courses for one hour a day at a specific time and place. If the student needed to spend more time on any course, he could do this whenever he wished, but not in the special room.

All of Fox's students exhibited considerable improvement in their grades. The smallest gain in semester grades was one full grade above those of the previous semester. It is impossible to tell how much of this improvement was due to better stimulus control, because the students were also given training in other techniques, including the SQ3R method (survey, question, read, recite, and review) of reading new material. Other evidence suggests that teaching students only stimulus control techniques may not be particularly effective, but combining these with other behavioral methods such as self-reinforcement can lead to improved academic performance (Richards, 1980).

Insomnia

Most people have experienced occasional insomnia, but persistent, severe insomnia can be a serious problem. A person who lies in bed awake most of the night is unlikely to function well the next day. Although some cases of chronic insomnia are due to medical problems, many are the result of inappropriate stimulus control. That is, the stimulus of one's bed does not reliably produce the behavior of sleeping. The role of stimulus control becomes apparent if we compare the behavior of insomniacs with those of people without sleeping problems. A normal person exhibits one sort of stimulus control—she is able to sleep well in her own bed, but may have some difficulty falling asleep in a different place, such as on a couch or in a hotel room. An insomniac may exhibit exactly the opposite pattern—he may have difficulty falling asleep in his own bed, but may fall asleep on a couch, in front of the television, or in a different bed. This pattern shows that insomnia is often not a general inability to fall asleep, but a failure to fall asleep in the presence of a particular stimulus, one's own bed.

The reason a person's own bed may fail to serve as a stimulus for sleeping is fairly clear: The bed may become associated with many activities that are incompatible with sleeping, including reading, watching television, eating, and thinking about the day's events or one's problems. To make one's bed a more effective stimulus for sleeping, some behavior therapists recommend that the client never do anything but sleep there. Bootzin (1972) described the case of a man who would lie in bed for several hours each night worrying about everyday problems before falling asleep with the television on. The man was instructed to go to bed each night when he felt sleepy, but not to watch television or do anything else in bed. If he could not get to sleep after a few minutes, he was to get out of bed and go into another room. He could then do whatever he liked, and he was not to go back to bed until he felt sleepy. Each time he went to bed, the same instructions were to be followed: Get up and leave the room if you do not fall asleep within a few minutes. At first, the client had to get up many times each night before falling asleep, but after a few weeks he would usually fall asleep within a few minutes the first time he got in bed.

This treatment has been used with many insomniac patients with good results (Bootzin & Nicassio, 1978; Ladouceur & Gros-Louis, 1986; Morin & Azrin, 1987). The procedure is effective for at least two reasons. First, since the clients are instructed to remain out of bed when they cannot sleep, their need for sleep increases early in the program, when they spend a good portion of the night out of bed. Thus when they go to bed, their chances of falling asleep are greater. Second, since the bed is used only for sleeping, its associations with other behaviors gradually decrease and at the same time its association with sleep increases.

The usefulness of these procedures for training stimulus control may hinge on the reduction of incompatible behaviors. The student in a quiet room of the library will have little to do but study. In addition, those few behaviors other than studying that can occur (such as daydreaming) are prevented because the student is instructed to leave the room immediately if he stops studying. Similarly, the therapy for insomnia involves preventing the client from engaging in any behavior other than sleeping in one's bed. In a sense, then, these stimulus-control techniques are the opposite of the procedure of reinforcing incompatible behaviors so as to eliminate an undesirable behavior. In the former, incompatible behaviors are prevented, and in the latter they are reinforced.

CHAPTER

11

ANIMAL COGNITION

Considering the current popularity of cognitive psychology, the title of this chapter should come as little surprise. In recent years, there has been increasing interest in applying concepts from cognitive psychology (which in the past has employed human subjects almost exclusively) to animals. Through this interest a new field has emerged, and it has been called *animal cognition* (Mellgren, 1983; Roitblat, Bever, & Terrace, 1984) or *comparative cognition* (Roitblat, 1987). The word *comparative* is especially revealing, because a major purpose of research in this field is to compare the cognitive processes of different species, including humans. By making such comparisons, researchers hope to find commonalities in the ways different species receive, process, store, and use information about their world (Rilling & Neiworth, 1986). Thus although the cognitive and behavioral approaches to animal learning differ in some significant ways, they share one very fundamental goal: To discover general principles that are applicable to many different species. Of course, when psychologists compare species as different as humans, chimps, rodents, and birds, differences in learning abilities are likely to emerge as well, and these differences can be just as informative as the similarities. The comparative approach can give us a better perspective on those abilities that we have in common with other species, and it can also help us understand what makes the human species unique.

We have already encountered the cognitive approach in several different places in this book. Chapter 1 described the major differences between the behavioral and cognitive approaches to learning. One important difference is that strict behaviorists believe that psychology should focus on observable stimuli and responses, whereas cognitive psychologists are interested in developing theories about what is going on inside the individual's head. In other chapters, we have examined the cognitive approach to maze learning (Chapter 8) and avoidance learning (Chapter

7). In addition, much of the modern research on classical conditioning (Chapter 5) and concept formation (Chapter 10) has a cognitive flavor. Later chapters will discuss the cognitive approach to observational learning and motor-skill learning. The present chapter, however, is entirely devoted to the topic of comparative cognition. We will survey some of the major topic areas of traditional cognitive psychology, including memory, problem-solving, reasoning, and language. We will try to determine how animals' abilities in each of these domains compare to those of people.

MEMORY

The topics of learning and memory are closely interrelated. Think of a pigeon whose pecks at a lighted key are reinforced one day, and who then pecks the key repeatedly when tested the next day. We can talk about this behavior as an instance of learning, and say that the pigeon has learned to make a certain operant response in the presence of a certain discriminative stimulus. We can also talk about the animal's memory, and say that the animal remembers that yesterday it received food whenever it pecked the key. Although these two statements may sound similar, once the term "memory" is introduced, a number of new questions arise: How is this memory stored? How is it retrieved? Which details of the learning experience are part of the memory, and which are not? For example, in Chapter 8 we considered the question of whether animals simply learn stimulus-response associations during operant conditioning, or whether some "expectation" of the reinforcer is also involved. The evidence suggested that an expectation of a specific type of reinforcer is indeed part of what is learned in operant conditioning. In other words, there is evidence that the animal's memory contains information about the discriminative stimulus, the response, *and* the reinforcer. The point is that this sort of question is unlikely to be asked if one adopts the behavioral approach, since expectations, representations, and memories are not directly observable. The question arises quite naturally from the cognitive approach, however.

A prevalent view about human memory is that it is important to distinguish between *long-term memory,* which can retain information for months or years, and *short-term memory,* which can only hold information for a matter of seconds. The facts in your long-term memory include such items as your birthday, the names of your friends, the fact that 4+5=9, the meaning of the word *rectangle,* and thousands of other pieces of information. On the other hand, an example of an item in short-term memory is a phone number you have just looked up for the first time. If someone distracts your attention for a few seconds after you have looked up the number, you will probably forget the number and have to look it up again.

Researchers who study animal memory have also found it important to distinguish between long-term and short-term memory, so it will be convenient for us to examine these two types of memory separately in the following sections. We will also examine animal research on rehearsal, a process that is important for both types of memory.

Short-Term Memory, or Working Memory

Besides being short-lived, short-term memory is also said to have a very limited capacity compared to the large capacity of long-term memory. Although your short-term memory is large enough to hold a seven-digit phone number long enough to dial it, you would probably have great difficulty remembering two new phone numbers at once. (If you do not believe this, look up two phone numbers at random and try to recall them ten seconds later.) According to cognitive psychologists, because of the brevity and limited capacity of short-term memory, information must be transferred to long-term memory if it is to have any permanence.

In both human and animal research, the term *working memory* is now frequently used instead of *short-term memory* (Bower, 1975; Honig & Dodd, 1986). This change in terminology reflects the view that the information in working memory is used to guide whatever tasks the individual is currently performing. For example, suppose you are working on a series of simple addition problems, without the aid of a calculator. At any given moment, your working memory would contain several different pieces of information: that you are adding the hundreds column, that the total so far is 26, that the next number to be added is 8, and so on. Notice that the information must continually be updated: Your answers would be incorrect if you remembered the previous total rather than the present one, or if you failed to add the hundreds column because you confused it with the hundreds column of the *previous* problem. In many tasks like this, people need to remember important details about their current task and to ignore similar details from already-completed tasks. In a similar way, a butterfly searching for nectar may need to remember which patches of flowers it has already visited today, and it must not confuse today's visits with yesterday's. The following sections describe two techniques that are frequently used to study this type of working memory in animals.

Delayed Matching to Sample. As an introduction to this procedure, Figure 11-1a diagrams the simpler task of *matching to sample* as it has been used in experiments with pigeons. A suitable experimental chamber is one with three response keys mounted in one wall. Before each trial, the center key is lit with one of two colors (for instance, red or green). This color is called the *sample stimulus*. Typically, the subject must peck at this key to light the two side keys: The left key will then become green and the right key red, or vice versa. These two colors are called *comparison stimuli*. The pigeon's task is to peck at the side key that has the same color as the center key. A correct response produces a food reinforcer; an incorrect response produces no food. Matching to sample is an easy task for pigeons and other animals, and at asymptote they make the correct choice on nearly 100 percent of the trials (Blough, 1959).

Figure 11-1b diagrams the slightly more complex procedure of *delayed matching to sample* (DMTS). In this case, the sample is presented for a certain period of time, then there is a delay during which the keys are dark, and finally the two side keys are lit. Once again, the correct response

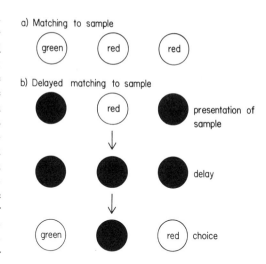

FIGURE 11-1. (a) The procedure of simple matching to sample. The right key matches the center key, so a peck at the right key is the correct response. (b) Delayed matching to sample. A peck at the right key is again the correct response, but now the pigeon must remember the sample color through the delay interval.

is a peck at the comparison stimulus that matches the sample, but because the sample is no longer present, the pigeon must remember its color through the delay if it is to perform better than chance. Since one of the two keys is correct, chance performance is 50 percent. If the animal is correct more than 50 percent of the time, this means it has remembered something about the sample through the delay interval.

By using delays of different durations in the DMTS procedure, we can measure how long information about the sample is retained in working memory. The answer is different for different species. For example, the filled circles in Figure 11-2a show the accuracy of pigeons in an experiment by Grant (1975), in which the delay was varied from 0 seconds to 10 seconds. The average percentage of correct choices decreased steadily with longer delays, and with the 10-second delay the pigeons made the correct choice about 66 percent of the time. The results from a similar study with three capuchin monkeys

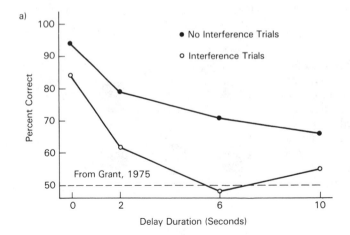

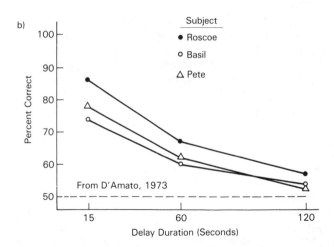

FIGURE 11-2. (a) Performance of pigeons in a delayed matching to sample task, where the delay between sample and choice stimuli was varied. (b) Performance of three capuchin monkeys in a delayed matching to sample task. Note that the scale on the x-axis is different in the two panels.

(D'Amato, 1973) are shown in Figure 11-2b. These monkeys were able to perform well with much longer delays, maintaining about a 66 percent success rate with delays of 60 seconds. Like monkeys, dolphins can perform at better-than-chance levels with delays of a minute or more (Herman & Thompson, 1982).

It is important to realize that functions like those in Figure 11-2 do not depict a fixed or immutable time course of working memory for these species, because many factors can significantly alter the rate at which performance deteriorates as a function of delay. For example, the performance of pigeons on DMTS improves if

the sample is presented for a longer duration (Roberts & Grant, 1978). This improvement may occur because the subject has more time to study the sample and thereby strengthen its representation in working memory.

Performance on this task can also be affected by the presence of other stimuli that interfere with the memory of the sample. In human memory tasks, two types of interference have long been recognized—*retroactive interference* and *proactive interference*. Retroactive interference occurs when the presentation of some new material interferes with the memory of something that was learned earlier. (That is, the interfering material works backward in time—retroactively—to disrupt previously learned material.) For example, suppose that in a list-learning task like the one used by Ebbinghaus (Chapter 2), a subject memorizes List A, then List B, and then is tested on List A. The memorization of List B will impair the subject's memory of List A and lead to poorer performance than if the subject simply rested instead of learning List B. *Proactive interference* occurs when previously learned material impairs the learning of new material. (In this case, the interfering material works forward in time—proactively—to disrupt subsequent learning.) For example, it might be easy to memorize one list, List D, in isolation, but this list may be much harder to learn if it is preceded by the memorization of Lists A, B, and C.

Both types of interference have been found with animals in DMTS. Retroactive interference can be demonstrated by presenting various sorts of stimuli during the delay interval. Not surprisingly, when the sample and comparison stimuli are different colors, matching performance is impaired if colored lights are presented during the delay interval (Jarvik, Goldfarb, & Carley, 1969; Kendrick & Rilling, 1984). Performance is also impaired if the chamber lights are turned either on or off during the delay interval (Cook, 1980; Kendrick, Tranberg, & Rilling, 1981), especially if these changes in illumination occur near the end of the interval. It would be easy to conclude that these effects occur because a visual stimulus presented during the delay interferes with the decaying memory of another visual stimulus (the sample), but this would be an oversimplification. For one thing, some of these interfering stimuli (for instance, changes in illumination) become less disruptive of matching performance after the animals are given sufficient training (Tranberg & Rilling, 1980). It is probably more accurate to say that any sort of surprising or unexpected stimulus presented during the delay interval is likely to impair performance on the matching task. This type of interference supports the idea that the capacity of an animal's working memory is very small—the occurrence of just one unexpected stimulus is enough to interfere with the animal's memory for the sample.

To demonstrate the existence of proactive in-

terference in DMTS, one must show that stimuli presented *before* the sample can impair performance. Grant's (1975) experiment with pigeons, discussed above, provides one such demonstration. This study included a condition in which each test trial was immediately preceded by one or more interference trials, on which the opposite color was correct. The open circles in Figure 11-2a show the results from this condition. As can be seen, performance was considerably worse when these interference trials were added, and the percent correct was no better than chance with a delay of only six seconds. Other researchers have studied proactive interference by varying the intertrial interval (the time between the end of one trial and the start of the next). With short intertrial intervals, the animal might easily confuse the memory of the sample stimulus with the stimuli from the preceding trial. With long intertrial intervals, the animal's memory for the events of the preceding trial should fade before the next trial begins, so there should be less proactive interference and performance should improve. Just such an effect has been found in several studies (for example, Jarrad & Moise, 1971; Roberts, 1980).

So far, we have examined some factors that affect performance on DMTS, but we have not discussed exactly what strategy the animal uses when performing on this task. For a human observer, it is tempting to conclude that the animal follows a simple rule: "Choose the comparison stimulus that matches the sample." Notice that this is a general rule, which could be applied to any sample and comparison stimuli the animal might encounter. However, it is also possible that the animal has learned two more specific rules: "After a red sample, choose red," and "After a green sample, choose green." If the animal has learned the general rule, it should be able to transfer this learning to a new set of stimuli (for example, blue and yellow keys instead of red and green). If it has only learned the two specific rules, such transfer to new stimuli should not occur. When tested for transfer to new stimuli, pigeons generally show some degree of savings—they learn the new task more quickly—but not the immediate and complete success with new stimuli that we would expect if they had developed a general rule for responding to "sameness" (Edwards, Jagielo, & Zentall, 1983; Wilkie, 1983; Zentall & Hogan, 1978). Even monkeys have difficulty in transfer tests if the new stimuli are very different from the original stimuli (D'Amato, Salmon, & Colombo, 1985). For example, after DMTS training with different shapes as stimuli, some monkeys showed immediate transfer when the new stimuli were other shapes, but not when they were a steady green light and a flashing green light (Iverson, Sidman, & Carrigan, 1986). If these monkeys had developed a rule about responding to sameness, it was general enough to apply to new shapes but not to stimuli that differed along another dimension.

A slightly different procedure, in which it is not possible to follow a general rule about sameness, is called either *conditional discrimination* or *symbolic DMTS*. The latter name, though widely used, is not really appropriate, because the sample and comparison stimuli are completely different in this task, so no "matching" is involved. For example, the sample stimuli might be red and green, and the comparison stimuli might be a horizontal black line and a vertical black line, each on a white background. The correct response rules might be: "If red, choose horizontal" and "If green, choose vertical." In analyzing performance on this task, psychologists have tried to determine whether animals use *retrospective* or *prospective coding* to retain information in working memory. *Retrospective coding* involves "looking backward" and remembering what has already happened (for example, "The sample was red"). *Prospective coding* involves "looking forward" and remembering what response should be made next (for example, "Peck the key with the horizontal line").

An experiment by Roitblat (1980) found evidence that pigeons use a prospective strategy on a conditional discrimination task. In this experiment, there were three possible sample stimuli (red, orange, and blue) and three comparison stimuli (black lines that were horizontal, vertical, and almost vertical). The correct response rules were: if red, choose horizontal; if orange, choose almost vertical; and if blue, choose vertical. A pigeon using a retrospective strategy (looking back and remembering the sample color through the

delay interval) would be expected to make more errors with the red and orange samples, since these colors are more similar to each other than either is to blue. On the other hand, a pigeon using a prospective strategy (looking ahead and remembering which line orientation to choose) would tend to make more errors when the correct comparison stimulus was either vertical or almost vertical, since these are more similar to each other than either is to horizontal. Roitblat found greater confusion with the similar line orientations than with the similar colors, which suggested that his pigeons were using a prospective strategy. To put it simply, the animals appeared to be remembering which response to make, not which color they had seen.

A number of other studies have found further evidence for prospective coding (for example, Edwards, Jagielo, Zentall, & Hogan, 1982; Honig & Dodd, 1983). However, it would be a mistake to conclude that pigeons always use prospective coding in conditional discrimination procedures. Urcuioli and Zentall (1986) obtained strong evidence for retrospective coding when the sample stimuli were easy to discriminate and the comparison stimuli were not. These experimenters concluded that pigeons are capable of both prospective and retrospective coding, and that they may rely more heavily on one or the other depending on which is more useful in a particular task.

The Radial-Arm Maze. The DMTS task is quite different from anything an animal is likely to encounter in its natural environment. A somewhat more realistic task that involves working memory is provided by the *radial-arm maze*: It simulates a situation in which an animal explores a territory in search of food. Figure 11-3 shows the floor plan of an eight-arm maze for rats used by Olton and his associates. The entire maze is a platform that rests a few feet above the floor, and the maze has no walls, so the rat can see any objects that may be in the room (windows, doors, desks, and so on). At the end of each arm is a cup in which a bit of food can be stored. In a typical experiment, some food is deposited at the end of each arm. The rat is placed in the center area to start a trial and is given time to explore the maze

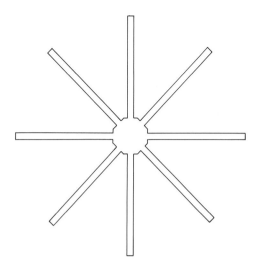

FIGURE 11-3. The floor plan of an eight-arm maze for rats.

and collect whatever food it can find. Once the rat collects the food in one arm, it will find no more food in that arm if it returns later during the same trial. The most efficient strategy for obtaining food is therefore to visit each arm once and only once.

The role of working memory in this situation should be obvious: To collect food efficiently, the rat must remember either which arms it has already visited on the current trial (if it is using retrospective coding) or which arms it has not yet visited (if it is using prospective coding). This information must be continually updated, and visits on the current trial must not be confused with visits on a previous trial. Perhaps the most remarkable feature of an average rat's performance on this task is its accuracy. Let us call the first visit to any arm a correct response and any repeat visit an error. If a trial is ended after the rat visits eight arms (including any repeat visits), it will usually make seven or eight correct responses (Olton, 1978). This performance means that the rat is very skillful at avoiding the arms that it has already visited on the current trial. With a larger, 17-arm maze, rats still average about 15 correct responses out of 17 visits (Olton, Collison, & Werz, 1977), and similar performance has been obtained from gerbils (Wilkie & Slobin, 1983).

The first question we must ask about this exceptional performance is whether the animals rely on some external cues or special strategies to make the task easier. For instance, if a rat simply started at one arm and then went around the maze in a clockwise pattern, it could visit all the arms and make no errors, but this strategy would place few demands on working memory. However, there is good evidence that rats do not follow this type of strategy. Instead, they seem to select successive arms in a haphazard manner (Olton, 1978; Olton et al., 1977). Other studies have shown that rats do not use the smell of food to guide them, and that they do not use scent markings to avoid repeat visits. What they do use to orient their travels within the maze are visual landmarks in the room surrounding the maze (Mazmanian & Roberts, 1983; Olton & Samuelson, 1976).

Experiments with the radial-arm maze have provided considerable information about the capacity and duration of animals' working memory for spatial locations. It is commonly said that human working memory can retain only about seven unrelated items at once (for example, seven words, or seven random digits). With this number as a point of comparison, the nearly flawless performance of rats in a 17-arm maze is especially impressive. Equally impressive are the time intervals over which rats can remember which arms they have visited. Beatty and Shavalia (1980) allowed rats to visit four arms of an eight-arm maze, after which they were removed from the maze for durations ranging from a few minutes to 24 hours. When a rat was returned to the maze, it was allowed to make four more visits to see if it would remember which arms it had already entered and avoid them. Beatty and Shavalia found that the rats were almost perfect in their selection of previously unvisited arms with delays of up to four hours, but with longer delays their performances gradually deteriorated. This experiment, and others like it, show why working memory is probably a more appropriate term than short-term memory. In research with people, short-term memory has generally referred to information that is lost in a matter of seconds (Peterson & Peterson, 1959), but an animal's memory for its travels in the radial-arm maze can last 100 times longer.

Do rats use retrospective or prospective coding in the radial-arm maze? One way to answer this question is to look at the occasional errors a subject makes in the maze. If the animal is using retrospective coding (remembering which arms it has already visited), it is more likely to forget (and therefore revisit) an arm that was visited early in the trial than one that was recently visited. On the other hand, if the animal is using prospective coding (remembering which arms are still to be visited), the order of previous visits should have nothing to do with the errors it makes. Several studies have shown that early visits are most likely to be forgotten, as would be expected with retrospective coding (Olton, 1978; Olton & Samuelson, 1976). However, Cook, Brown, and Riley (1985) found evidence for both types of coding using a 12-arm maze for rats. Each 12-visit trial was interrupted for 15 minutes after either 2, 4, 6, 8, or 10 visits. An interruption after 6 visits produced more errors than interruptions either earlier or later in a trial. In addition, the pattern of errors suggested that the rats used primarily retrospective coding during the first 6 visits or so, and then switched to primarily prospective coding. Notice how this switch in coding strategies can serve to lessen the demands on working memory. For example, after 2 visits, a rat could either use retrospective coding to remember these 2 arms, or it could use prospective coding to list the 10 yet-to-be-visited arms. Obviously, the retrospective strategy is easier. But later in the trial, when faced with the choice of remembering, say, 9 visited arms or 3 to-be-visited arms, the prospective strategy of remembering the to-be-visited arms is easier. This analysis also explains why the most errors occurred when a trial was interrupted after 6 visits. The demands on working memory were greatest half-way through a trial, because with either a retrospective or prospective strategy, 6 arms had to be remembered during the 15-minute interruption. At other points in the trial, however, the rats tended to use whichever coding strategy placed fewer demands on working memory.

Summary.   Research with DMTS and the radial-arm maze has substantially increased our understanding animal working memory, which turns out to have many of the same properties as human working memory. Depending on the species and the task at hand, information in working memory may last only a few seconds or as long as several hours. Because the amount of information that can be stored in working memory is quite small, this information is very susceptible to disruption by either proactive or retroactive interference. Many studies have investigated exactly what type of information is stored in working memory, and these studies have provided evidence for both retrospective coding (remembering what has just happened) and prospective coding (remembering what remains to be done). Which type of coding dominates in a particular situation often seems to depend on which is easier to use in that situation.

Rehearsal

The concept of *rehearsal* is easy to understand when thinking about human learning. We can rehearse a speech by reading it aloud, or by reading it silently. It seems natural to think of rehearsal as overt or silent speech in which we repeatedly recite whatever we wish to remember. Theories of human memory state that rehearsal has two main functions: It keeps information active in short-term memory, and it promotes the transfer of this information into long-term memory.

Because we tend to equate rehearsal with speech, it may surprise you to learn that psychologists have found strong evidence for rehearsal in animals. Since animals do not use language, what does it mean to say that they can engage in rehearsal? With animals, rehearsal is more difficult to define, but it refers to an active processing of stimuli or events after they have occurred. Rehearsal cannot be observed directly; its existence can only be inferred from an animal's behavior on tasks that make use of short- or long-term memory. To demonstrate its existence in animals, researchers have tried to show (1) that animals can choose whether or not to engage in rehearsal, just as they can choose whether or not to perform any operant behavior, and (2) that rehearsal can be disrupted by distracting the animal.

Rehearsal seems to serve the same two functions for animals as it does for people. For this reason, Grant (1984) has suggested that we should distinguish between *maintenance rehearsal,* which serves to retain information in short-term memory, and *associative rehearsal,* which promotes long-term associative learning (as when an animal learns to associate a CS and US in classical conditioning). The evidence for rehearsal in animals can be divided into these two categories.

Evidence for Maintenance Rehearsal. We have already examined evidence that information is retained in working memory for a short period of time and then is lost. Some researchers have attempted to show that animals have at least partial control over how long information is retained in working memory. Their purpose is to demonstrate that working memory involves more than a passive memory trace that decays over time; rather, by using rehearsal an animal can actively maintain information in working memory (Grant, 1981; Maki, 1981). This process of rehearsal can be thought of as a sort of covert behavior that an animal can learn to use or not use as the situation demands.

One line of evidence that animals use rehearsal to keep information in working memory is the observation that with extensive practice, performance on DMTS improves, even with fairly long delays. Such improvement has been found with both monkeys (D'Amato, 1973) and pigeons (Grant, 1976). This improvement might occur because, with practice, animals learn to use rehearsal as a strategy for improving their memory of the sample stimulus. The weakness of this type of evidence, however, is that many other factors besides rehearsal could also explain the improvement (for instance, simply increased familiarity with the task).

A second type of evidence for maintenance rehearsal comes from experiments showing that animals can remember "surprising" stimuli is better than "expected" stimuli (Maki, 1981; Terry & Wagner, 1975). The premises underlying these experiments are that (1) rehearsal helps refresh the animal's short-term memory for recent events, and (2) surprising events receive more rehearsal than expected events. For example, Grant, Brewster, and Stierhoff (1983) trained pi-

geons in a fairly complicated conditional discrimination procedure to set up a situation in which either of two sample stimuli would be expected on some trials (because each was usually preceded by a certain stimulus) and surprising on other trials (because the sample was not preceded by the usual stimulus). As in the typical conditional discrimination task, the sample stimulus was followed by a delay, and then the animal had to choose between the two comparison stimuli. Performance was substantially better when the sample was surprising, especially when the delay interval was long. In fact, choice accuracy with surprising sample stimuli was just as high with a delay of 10 seconds as with a delay of 0 seconds. These results are consistent with the hypothesis that surprising stimuli receive more rehearsal, which strengthens the animal's short-term memory for these stimuli.

Perhaps the best evidence for maintenance rehearsal comes from a technique called *directed forgetting,* which can be demonstrated with the conditional discrimination procedure. The purpose of this technique is to teach the animal that on some trials it is important to remember the sample stimulus, and on other trials it is safe to forget the sample. To accomplish this, either a "remember cue" or a "forget cue" is presented during the delay that follows the sample stimulus. The remember cue tells the animal that it is important to remember the sample because a test is coming up (that is, the comparison stimuli will soon follow). The forget cue tells the animal that it is safe to forget the sample because there will be no test on this trial. Thus the animal is "directed" either to remember or to forget the sample. If an animal can choose whether or not to engage in rehearsal, it should eventually learn to follow the directions and rehearse the sample when it sees the remember cue but not when it sees the forget cue. For the experimenter, the trick is to find a way to show that the animal is indeed rehearsing in one case but not the other.

An experiment with pigeons by Maki and Hegvik (1980) illustrates how this can be done. Figure 11-4 diagrams the procedure. The two sample stimuli in this experiment were not key colors but rather the presence or absence of food. Each trial started with the presentation of the

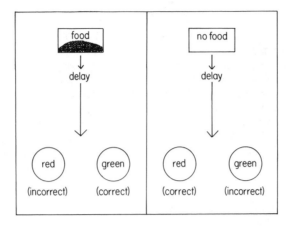

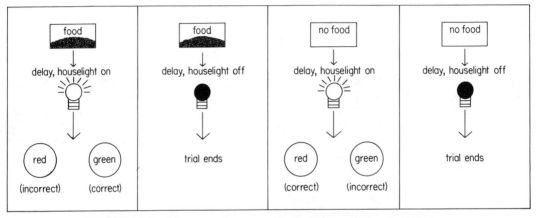

FIGURE 11-4. The procedures used in the Maki and Hegvik (1980) experiment on directed forgetting. The top row shows the two types of trials used in the initial training. The bottom row shows the four types of trials used in the second phase, which taught the pigeons to "forget" on trials with the houselight off.

sample, then there was a delay of a few seconds, and finally the comparison stimuli (red and green keys) were presented. The response rules for reinforcement were: After a food sample, peck red; and after a no-food sample, peck green. Once the pigeons had mastered this task, remember and forget cues were introduced during the delays. For half the birds, the remember cue was houselight-on, and the forget cue was houselight-off. For the other birds, these two cues were reversed. As Figure 11-4 shows, the red and green comparison stimuli were presented after the remember cue, and a correct choice was reinforced. After

the forget cue, no comparison stimuli were presented, and the trial simply terminated with no possibility of reinforcement. After several sessions of training with this procedure, occasional "probe trials" were included, during which the comparison stimuli *did* follow the forget cue, and a correct choice was reinforced. Maki and Hegvik reasoned that if the animals had learned not to bother rehearsing on trials with the forget cue, they should perform poorly on these occasional surprise quizzes. This is just what they found: On probe trials that followed the forget cues, the pigeons averaged about 70 percent correct choices, compared to about 90 percent on trials with the remember cue.

Evidence for directed forgetting has been obtained in a number of experiments with pigeons and several other species (Grant, 1982; Kendrick, Rilling, & Stonebraker, 1981; Roberts, Mazmanian, & Kraemer, 1984). Nevertheless, the poor performance that follows a forget cue could be caused by factors that have nothing to do with rehearsal. For example, the poor performance could occur because the forget cue is distracting, or because the animals do not expect to receive reinforcement and therefore are not motivated to respond accurately. Studies designed to test these other possibilities have found, however, that they cannot account for the inaccurate performance that follows a forget cue (Maki, Olson, & Rego, 1981). For this reason, researchers who have studied this phenomenon have concluded that the inaccurate performance that follows a forget cue is due to an absence of, or decrease in, rehearsal (Kendrick & Rilling, 1984; Maki, 1984).

Evidence for Associative Rehearsal. Research on human memory has shown that rehearsal increases the strength of long-term memory. If a person is first presented with a list of items to remember and is then given a distraction-free period (in which the subject presumably recites or rehearses the material in some way), this person's ability to recall the list items at a later time will be improved. In a clever series of experiments, Wagner, Rudy, and Whitlow (1973) demonstrated that rehearsal also contributes to the strength of long-term learning in classical conditioning with rabbits. They demonstrated that the acquisition of a CR proceeds more slowly if some *post-trial episode* (PTE) that "distracts" the animal occurs shortly after each conditioning trial. They also showed that surprising PTEs are more distracting (have a greater decremental effect on learning) than expected PTEs.

In one experiment, Wagner et al. developed surprising and expected stimuli by first giving rabbits training with two CSs that they labeled A and B, stimuli that would later serve as components of the PTEs. Trials with A and B were randomly intermixed, but while A was always followed by the US (a mild shock in the vicinity of the eye), B was never followed by the US. After many trials, the rabbits demonstrated that they had developed a strong discrimination between A and B: A elicited a CR about 90 percent of the time, and B elicited a CR less than 10 percent of the time. Wagner et al. reasoned that the events A^+ and B^o were now expected by the subjects, and these two events were used as expected PTEs in the next phase of the experiment. In addition, it seemed plausible that two events the rabbits had never experienced before, A^o and B^+, would be unexpected, and these two events were used as surprising PTEs. In the test phase, the rabbits were divided into four groups, and all groups received a series of conditioning trials with a new CS, C, consistently followed by the US. In all groups, a PTE occurred 10 seconds after each conditioning trial. What differed across groups was the nature of the PTE: In two groups, the PTE was an expected sequence of stimuli (either A^+ or B^o), whereas in the other two groups the PTE was surprising (either A^o or B^+). Wagner et al. found that conditioning to stimulus C developed much more slowly in the two groups that received surprising PTEs. For example, after 10 trials the probability of a CR to stimulus C was about 85 percent in the groups with the expected PTEs but only about 50 percent in the groups with the surprising PTEs.

Wagner et al. used the following reasoning to interpret their findings: (1) In order for a long-term CS-US association to develop, an animal needs a distraction-free period after each conditioning trial, during which rehearsal takes place; (2) this rehearsal process utilizes the animal's working memory, which has a limited capacity; (3) attending to an event such as a PTE also utilizes the animal's working memory, and so the processing of a PTE competes with the rehearsal of the previous conditioning trial; and (4) surprising events attract more attention than do expected events, so they have a greater disruptive effect on the animal's rehearsal of the previous conditioning trial. Thus the subjects' greater attention to a surprising PTE presumably decreased the amount of rehearsal that was devoted to the events of the previous conditioning trial, and so acquisition was slower.

Another experiment by Wagner et al. provided

further support for this interpretation. If rehearsal is necessary for conditioning, and if a surprising PTE interferes with this rehearsal to some extent, then the sooner the PTE occurs after the conditioning trial, the greater should be the disruption of conditioning. To test this prediction, Wagner et al. varied the time between the trial and the surprising PTE from 3 to 300 seconds for different groups of subjects. Figure 11-5 shows the median percentages of CRs to the new CS over the first ten conditioning trials. As can be seen, the PTEs had their greatest disruptive effects when they closely followed each conditioning trial, and thereby kept rehearsal to a minimum.

Two common ideas about rehearsal—that rehearsal is necessary for long-term learning, and that surprising events elicit more rehearsal than expected events—can give us a fresh perspective on some of the phenomena of classical conditioning discussed in Chapter 5. For instance, the blocking effect may occur because a US that is already predicted by one CS will not be surprising, and therefore will not provoke further associative rehearsal. The stimulus preexposure effect (in which slow acquisition is found with a stimulus that has been previously presented many times by itself) may occur because this stimulus receives little rehearsal, since its occurrence in the experimental chamber is no longer surprising. Based on reasoning like this, Wagner's (1981) sometimes-opponent-process theory (described

briefly in Chapter 5) proposes that rehearsal plays an essential role in the development of long-term associations in all instances of classical conditioning.

Long-term Memory, or Reference Memory

Nearly all of the experiments described in this book relate to long-term memory. Whether behavior is modified through habituation, classical or operant conditioning, or observational learning, a cognitive psychologist would attribute a long-term change in behavior to a change in the individual's long-term memory. Long-term memory has also been called *reference memory,* because an individual must refer to the information in long-term memory when performing almost any task (Honig, 1984; Roitblat, 1987). Consider once again the task of performing a series of addition problems. Whereas you use working memory to keep track of which steps you have completed, you must refer to long-term memory to know what the sum of any two digits is, how to carry digits from one column to the next, and so on.

Within the field of animal cognition, much of the research on long-term memory has been concerned with discovering exactly what information is stored as a result of simple learning experiences. We have already examined some of

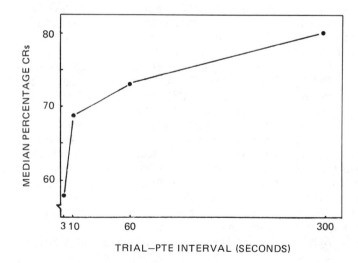

FIGURE 11-5. The four data points show the percentage of conditioned eyeblink responses in four different groups of rabbits in the Wagner, Rudy, and Whitlow (1973) experiment. For each group, the x-axis shows the amount of time that elapsed between each conditioning trial and a surprising posttrial episode (PTE).

the research on the types of associations that are formed during classical conditioning (Chapter 5) and operant conditioning (Chapter 6). To conclude this section, we will briefly examine some other questions about long-term memory: How large is its capacity? How permanent are its contents? What factors affect success or failure in retrieving information from long-term memory?

Besides their different durations, probably the biggest distinction between short- and long-term memory is their different storage capacities. In contrast to the very limited size of short-term memory, the storage capacity of long-term memory is very large. It is probably safe to say that no one has yet found a way to measure and quantify this capacity for either animals or people (as can be easily done for a computer, which might have the capacity to store, for instance, 64,000 bytes of information). Although we do not know how much information can be stored in an animal's long-term memory, some studies have demonstrated impressive feats of learning and remembering. For example, Vaughan and Greene (1983, 1984) trained pigeons to classify slides of everyday scenes as either "positive" (because responses to these slides were reinforced with food) or "negative" (because responses to these slides were never reinforced). The procedures were similar to those used by Herrnstein and his associates to examine visual concept formation in pigeons (Chapter 10), with one major difference: There was no concept such as *tree* or *water* that specified which slides were positive and which were negative. Instead, Vaughan and Greene decided whether each slide would be positive or negative simply by flipping a coin. Therefore, the first time a pigeon saw a slide it had no way of knowing whether it was positive or negative, and on subsequent presentations the bird could respond correctly only if it remembered that specific slide.

In one study, Vaughan and Greene started with 80 slides, randomly divided into 40 positive and 40 negative instances. After about ten sessions (with each slide appearing twice a session), the birds were discriminating between positive and negative instances with better than 90 percent accuracy. Then the birds were presented with a new set of 80 slides, which they learned

even faster. The procedure was successfully repeated with two more sets of 80 slides, which were learned in just a few sessions each. Finally, the birds were tested with all 320 slides, and their accuracy was still above 90 percent. Since there was no way to succeed on this task without remembering the individual slides, the experiment showed that pigeons can remember at least several hundred visual stimuli. Equally impressive memory for pictorial materials has been found with human subjects (Shepard, 1967).

Studies with other species of birds have demonstrated similar feats of memory, often involving memory for *caches*—sites where the birds have stored food (Sherry, 1984, 1987; Shettleworth & Krebs, 1982, 1986). For example, a bird known as Clark's nutcracker gathers over 20,000 pine seeds each fall and stores them in the ground in several thousand different locations. To survive the winter, the bird must recover a good portion of these seeds. Field observations and laboratory experiments have shown that nutcrackers do not use random searching or olfactory cues in recovering their caches. Although they may use certain characteristics of cache sites to aid their searches (such as the appearance of the soil above a cache), the birds' memories of specific visual landmarks are much more important (Kamil & Balda, 1985; Vander Wall, 1982).

The experiments of Vaughan and Greene (1984) also showed that information in an animal's long-term memory can last for extended periods of time. After their pigeons were tested with the full set of 320 slides, the birds saw no slides for two years, and then they were tested again. Their performance was not as good as before, but they still responded with over 70 percent accuracy, which was significantly better than the chance level of 50 percent. The birds therefore showed that they remembered many of the slides (and whether they were positive or negative) even after an interval of two years. Other studies have investigated the time course of forgetting from long-term memory, just as Hermann Ebbinghaus tested his recall of nonsense syllables after different intervals to construct a forgetting curve (see Chapter 2 and Figure 2-2). The general shape of forgetting curves for animals is similar to that of

Ebbinghaus: Forgetting is rapid at first, with a substantial loss during the first 24 hours, but subsequent forgetting proceeds at a much slower rate (Gleitman, 1971; Thomas & Lopez, 1962).

What causes the forgetting of information in long-term memory? For humans, a prevalent view is that interference from similar stimuli or events is a major cause of forgetting (Keppel, 1968), and this view has substantial empirical support. It is therefore of interest to note that both proactive and retroactive interference have been observed in studies of animal long-term memory (Honig, 1974; Thomas, 1981). As an example of proactive interference, suppose that a pigeon receives several days of training on a discrimination task in which S⁺ is a pure green and S⁻ is a slightly bluer green. Then the roles of S⁺ and S⁻ are reversed for one session, and the bird learns to respond to the blue-green stimulus. If the bird is then tested on the following day, the early training with green as the S⁺ is likely to interfere with the bird's memory of the more recent training, and it may respond more to green and less to blue-green. This is an instance of proactive interference because the memory of prior training impairs the memory of subsequent training.

If an individual forgets something that was learned long ago, is this because the memory has been lost forever, or is the problem one of retrieval failure (the memory is still there but it is difficult to find)? In research on human memory, there is evidence that many instances of forgetting are really cases of retrieval failure. Although you may not be able to recall some information on your first attempt (for instance, the Republican nominee for president in 1964), you may succeed if you are given a hint (for instance, a conservative Senator from Arizona). There is similar evidence from animal studies that forgetting is often a problem of retrieval failure, and that "forgotten" memories can be recovered if the animal is given an appropriate clue or reminder (Gordon, 1983; Spear, 1971). For example, Gordon, Smith, and Katz (1979) trained rats on an avoidance task in which a subject had to go from a white room to a black room to avoid a shock. Three days after training, rats in one group were given a reminder of their previous avoidance

learning: They were simply confined in the white compartment for 15 seconds, with no shock. Rats in a control group were not returned to the test chamber. Twenty-four hours later, both groups were tested in extinction to see how quickly they would move into the black chamber. The rats that had received the reminder treatment entered the black room significantly faster, presumably because the reminder served to revive their memories of their earlier avoidance training. Similar effects of reminder treatments have been obtained in classical conditioning situations (Gordon, McGinnis, & Weaver, 1985). The general conclusion from this line of research is that any stimulus that is present during a learning experience (such as the room or chamber in which the learning takes place) can later serve as a reminder and make it more likely that the experience will be remembered.

Although our survey of animal memory is now finished, both short- and long-term memory are important for many of the other cognitive tasks we will now consider. Whether an animal is solving a problem, learning an abstract concept, or counting stimuli, it must rely on long-term memory for background information about the current task, and on short-term memory for information about what has already happened and what is likely to happen next.

TIME, NUMBER, AND SERIAL PATTERNS

Can animals sense the passage of time and estimate the duration of an event? Can they count objects, and if so, how many and how accurately? Can they detect orderly sequences of events in their environment? These questions are interesting because they all deal with abstract properties of stimuli. A 30-second television commercial may have nothing in common with a 30-second traffic light, yet a person can easily understand the abstract feature (duration) that makes these two events similar. In the same way, even young children can recognize what four blocks, four cookies, and four crayons have in common, even though the physical properties of these objects are very different. Determining whether animals can also recognize and respond to such abstract dimensions as time and number is not an easy task, but substantial progress has been made in recent years.

Experiments on an "Internal Clock"

On a fixed-interval schedule, responding typically gets faster and faster as the time for reinforcement approaches (see Chapter 6). Research by Dews (1962) has shown that, for pigeons, the passage of time serves as a discriminative stimulus that controls this response pattern. More recent studies have provided additional information about animals' timing abilities. Try to imagine what would happen in the following experiment. A rat is first trained on an FI 40-second schedule. A light is turned on to signal the start of each 40-second interval, and after the reinforcer the light is turned off during an intertrial interval, and then the next trial begins. Training on this schedule continues until the animal's response rate in each

interval consistently shows the accelerating pattern that is typical of FI performance. Now the procedure is changed so that on occasional trials no reinforcer is delivered—the light remains on for about 80 seconds, and then the trial ends in darkness. With further training, the animal will learn that a reinforcer is available after 40 seconds on some trials, but not on others. For the first 40 seconds, however, both types of trials look exactly alike, and there is no way to tell whether a reinforcer will be available or not. How do you think the animal will respond on nonreinforced trials? Will it respond faster and faster throughout the 80-second period? Will it cease responding after 40 seconds have elapsed without reinforcement?

Figure 11-6 presents the results from an experiment like the one just described (Roberts, 1981). The open circles show that on trials without reinforcement, response rates started low, increased for a while, reached a maximum at about 40 seconds, and then declined. The location of

FIGURE 11-6. Pigeons' response rates in Roberts's (1981) experiment using the peak procedure. The filled circles show the results from trials with a tone that usually signaled an FI 20-second schedule. The open circles show the results from trials with a light that usually signaled an FI 40-second schedule. (From Roberts, 1981)

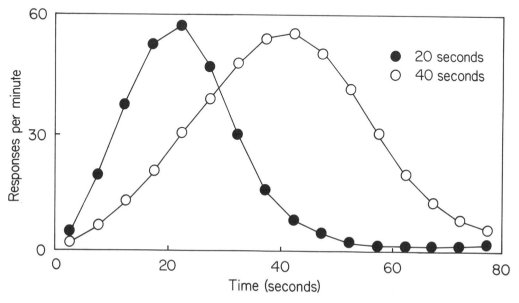

the peak indicates that the rats were able to estimate the passage of time fairly accurately, since they responded the fastest at just about the time a response might be reinforced. It was no coincidence that the peak occurred at about 40 seconds. On other trials, a tone was presented instead of the light, and the tone usually meant that a reinforcer was available on a FI 20-second schedule. The filled circles in Figure 11-6 show the results from nonreinforced test trials with the tone, which also lasted for about 80 seconds. Again, response rates first increased and then decreased, but on these trials the peak response rate occurred at about 20 seconds. These results show that the rats had learned that the tone signaled a 20-second interval and the light signaled a 40-second interval, and in both cases they could estimate these intervals fairly well. This procedure for studying animal timing abilities is called the *peak procedure* because the peak of the response-rate function tells us how accurately the animals could time the intervals.

How accurately can animals distinguish between two events that have different durations? A conditional discrimination procedure can be used to answer this question. Suppose a rat is reinforced for pressing the left lever after a five-second tone and for pressing the right lever after an eight-second tone. Even a well-trained rat will make some errors on this task, but if the animal makes the correct response most of the time (for instance, on 75 percent of the trials), we can conclude that the rat can discriminate between the two different durations. Experiments using this type of procedure with both rats and pigeons have shown that they can discriminate between two stimuli if their durations differ by roughly 25 percent (Church, Getty, & Lerner, 1976; Stubbs, 1968). This finding illustrates a principle of perception called *Weber's Law,* which says that the amount a stimulus must be changed before the change is detectable is proportional to the size of the stimulus. Thus an animal may be able to discriminate between a 4-second tone and a 5-second tone (which differ by 25 percent), but not between a 10-second tone and an 11-second tone (which differ by only 10 percent), even though there is a 1-second difference in both cases. Thus an animal's timing ability (like a person's) becomes less and less accurate with increasingly long durations.

Based on findings like these, some psychologists have proposed that every animal has an "internal clock" that it can use to time the duration of events in its environment (Church, 1978; Roberts, 1983). Behaviorists may object to this concept because the internal clock, whatever it is, is unobservable. As with other disputes between behavioral and cognitive psychologists, however, the disagreement may be partly one of semantics. We have plenty of evidence that animals can estimate the passage of time and discriminate between events of different durations. Cognitive psychologists may say that the animal has an internal clock; behaviorists may say that the animal has the ability to respond to duration as a discriminative stimulus.

Church (1984) and Roberts (1983) have proposed that in some respects an animal's internal clock is analogous to a stopwatch. Like a stopwatch, the internal clock can be used to time different types of stimuli. Roberts (1982) trained rats to press one lever after a one-second tone and another after a four-second tone. When the stimuli were then changed to one- and four-second *lights,* the rats continued to choose correctly without additional training. Like a stopwatch, the internal clock can be stopped and then restarted. Roberts (1981) demonstrated this point with his peak procedure. Recall that on most trials a light signaled an FI 40-second schedule, but on a few trials the light stayed on for 80 seconds or more and no reinforcer was available. In one experiment, Roberts included occasional nonreinforced trials in which the light was turned on for 10 or 15 seconds, then turned off for 5 or 10 seconds, then turned back on for the remainder of the 80-second trial. The rats' response patterns indicated that they stopped timing the 40-second interval during the blackout and then picked up where they left off when the light was turned back on.

These experiments show that animals have fairly versatile timing abilities. They can discriminate between stimuli of slightly different durations, and they can transfer this skill from a visual stimulus to an auditory stimulus. They can time the total duration of a stimulus that is temporarily interrupted. They can time the total duration of a compound stimulus that begins as a light and then changes to a tone (Roberts, 1981). An animal's ability to time events is certainly far less accurate than an ordinary wristwatch, but then so is a person's.

Counting

Many of the techniques used to study animals' counting abilities are similar to those used to study timing, and the results are similar as well. A conditional discrimination procedure can be used to determine whether an animal can discriminate between two different quantities (for example, five light pulses versus eight light pulses). As with the discrimination of durations, animals can generally discriminate between two quantities if they differ by about 25 percent or more, although Weber's law is only approximately supported, because this percentage decreases slightly with large numbers. That is, it may be easier for an animal to discriminate between 40 and 50 than between 4 and 5 (Hobson & Newman, 1981).

Procedures that require animals to count their own responses have shown that they can do so in an approximate way, just as the peak procedure showed that animals can roughly time the absolute durations of stimuli. In one procedure, Mechner (1958) used a variation of a fixed-ratio schedule in which a rat had to switch from one lever to another after completing the ratio requirement. For example, if 16 responses were required, on half of the trials the sixteenth consecutive response on lever A was reinforced. On the other half of the trials, the rat had to make 16 or more consecutive responses on lever A and then one response on lever B to collect the reinforcer. If the rat switched too early (say, after 14 responses), there was no reinforcer, and the rat had to start from the beginning and make another 16 responses on key A before a reinforcer was available. In four different conditions, either 4, 8, 12, or 16 consecutive responses were required. For these four conditions, Figure 11-7 shows one rat's probability of switching to lever B after different run lengths (where a run is a string of consecutive responses on lever A). We can see that as the ratio requirement increased, the average

run length also increased in a systematic way. When 4 responses were required, the most common run length was 5; when 16 responses were required, the most common run length was 18. Producing run lengths that were, on the average, slightly longer than required was a sensible strategy because the penalty for switching too early was severe.

Because of the many similarities between animals' timing and counting abilities, Church and Meck (1984) proposed that these two skills may be different manifestations of the same cognitive mechanism. That is, they suggested that an animal's internal clock may operate in a "continuous" mode to measure the duration of a single stimulus, or it may operate in a "discrete" mode to count the number of stimuli. Besides the parallels already mentioned, Meck and Church (1983) noted that timing and counting are similarly affected by the drug metamphetamine. Judging by their responses in a choice situation, rats' estimates of both duration and number were about 10 percent longer after an injection of metamphetamine. And as with timing, rats show crossmodal transfer in a counting task. After rats learned to discriminate between two and four sounds, they needed no additional training to respond correctly when the stimuli were switched to two or four light pulses (Church & Meck, 1984).

This cross-modal transfer of a counting skill has important theoretical implications. It shows that the rats had formed, at least in a rudimentary way, an abstract concept of number— one that was not tied to the physical characteristics of the stimuli being counted. To put it simply, the rats were able to respond to the abstract feature that four sounds and four lights had in common—the attribute of "fourness." Nevertheless, in some ways this ability to respond to the number of stimuli is quite primitive compared to the counting abilities of people, even young children. For one thing, the counting abilities we have examined so far are not exact: The rats in Mechner's research did not switch to lever B after they had made exactly the right number of responses on lever A. On some trials they switched too early, and on others they made more responses on lever A than necessary. In contrast, a person could

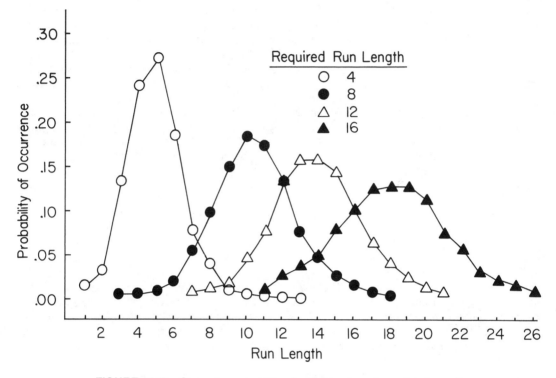

FIGURE 11-7. One rat's probability of switching from lever A to lever B after different run lengths in Mechner's (1958) experiment. The required run length is the number of consecutive responses required on lever A before a switch to lever B would be reinforced. (From Mechner, 1958)

learn to switch after exactly the right number of responses each time by simply counting responses.

Can animals learn to count objects in an exact rather than approximate way? A few studies suggest that they can, at least with small numbers. Davis and Albert (1986) used a procedure in which rats' responses were reinforced on trials that included repeating cycles of three bursts of noise, but not on trials with cycles of two or four bursts. After considerable training, the rats learned to respond significantly more rapidly on trials with three bursts, but responding on trials with two or four bursts was not completely eliminated. More convincing evidence for an exact counting ability was presented by Pepperberg

(1987), who trained a parrot, Alex, to respond to any number of objects from two through six by actually saying the appropriate number. In training, a number of objects (such as keys, small pieces of paper or wood, corks) would be placed on a tray, and Alex was reinforced if he said the correct number. For instance, the experimenter might present three corks and ask, "What's this?", and the correct response would be "Three corks." Different objects were used on different trials so that Alex would not simply learn to say "three" whenever he saw corks. After a few months of training, Alex was responding correctly on about 80 percent of the trials. Since Alex had learned names for five different numbers, he would have been correct on only about

20 percent of the trials if he was picking one of these numbers at random.

To show that Alex's counting ability was not limited to the training stimuli, new objects were presented on test trials. In some cases, Alex did not even know the names of the objects (such as wooden beads or small bottles), but he was able to give the correct number of objects on about 75 percent of the test trials with new stimuli. With somewhat less accuracy, Alex could count subsets of heterogeneous objects (for instance, with three keys and two corks, he would be asked either "How many keys?" or "How many corks?"). By arranging the objects on the tray in many different ways, Pepperberg was able to show that Alex was not responding to other cues such as the length of a row of objects or the overall shape of the group (such as a diamond shape that might be formed by four objects). All in all, Pepperberg has made a convincing case that Alex can count up to six objects, whether familiar or novel, with a high degree of accuracy. Matsuzawa (1985) has reported a similar counting skill in a chimpanzee (although naturally the chimp did not speak, but rather pressed response keys with the numbers 1 through 6 on them). These studies provide the best evidence available for accurate counting by animals.

Serial Pattern Learning

Suppose you are taking a calculus course with an eccentric professor who assigns a certain number of homework problems at the end of each class. He assigns 14 problems in the first class, 7 in the second class, 3 in the third, 1 in the fourth, and 0 in the fifth. In the next ten classes, the numbers of problems assigned are 14, 7, 3, 1, 0, 14, 7, 3, 1, and 0. After 10 or 15 classes, you may detect the repeating pattern of five numbers and thereby be able to predict how many problems will be assigned in each future class.

Hulse and Campbell (1975) wanted to know whether rats can detect such repeating serial patterns. They trained rats to run down a long runway that had food at the end. (The food could not be seen until a rat reached the end of the runway.) For one group of rats, the number of pellets

available on each trial in the runway followed the repeating pattern described in the previous paragraph (14 pellets on the first trial, 7 on the second, and so on). With enough training, these rats showed that they had learned something about the cyclical pattern: They ran fast on trials with 14, 7, or 3 pellets, more slowly on trials with 1 pellet, and very slowly on trials with no pellets. The same was true for a second group of rats that was trained with the reverse pattern (0, 1, 3, 7, and 14 pellets). For a third group, the number of pellets on each trial was chosen randomly (that is, there was no pattern to be learned), and these rats ran at about the same rate on every trial.

It is clear that the rats in the first two groups had learned something about the serial pattern, but exactly what had they learned? One possibility (Capaldi, Verry, & Davison, 1980) is that they simply learned associations between adjacent items (that is, that 14 pellets were followed by 7 pellets, 7 pellets by 3 pellets, and so on). Another possibility is that they learned a more abstract rule, such as "The number of pellets steadily decreases over trials until there are none." To support this possibility, Hulse and Dorsky (1979) showed that rats were able to learn a steadily increasing or decreasing sequence in fewer trials than a sequence that decreased, increased, and decreased again—14, 1, 3, 7, and 0 pellets. Their explanation is that the learning was slower with this pattern because a more complex rule is needed to describe it.

A third possibility is that besides learning a rule about a decreasing or increasing pattern, the rats learned something about the overall structure of the sequence—that it is five trials long, that three pellets occur in the exact middle of the sequence, and so on. Roitblat, Pologe, and Scopatz (1983) provided evidence for this idea by first training rats with the steadily decreasing sequence (14, 7, 3, 1, 0) and then occasionally presenting test trials on which one trial somewhere in the middle of the sequence delivered no pellets (for example, 14, 0, 3, 1, 0). The experimenters reasoned that if the rats had learned only associations between adjacent items or a simple rule about decreasing pellets, then a trial with no pellets in the middle of the sequence should disrupt the rats' performance for the rest of the sequence. What they found, however, was that the no-pellet trials had no detectable effect—running rates on the remaining trials of the sequence were the same as on normal trials. They concluded that in addition to any learning of trial- to-trial associations or a rule about decreasing numbers of pellets, the rats had some understanding of the overall structure of the sequence, so that an occasional odd trial did not disrupt their performance during the rest of the sequence.

Another way to determine what animals can learn about sequences of stimuli is to ask whether they can discriminate between different sequences composed of the same stimuli (Weisman, Wasserman, Dodd, & Larew, 1980). In one experiment with pigeons, Roitblat, Scopatz, & Bever (1987) used a discrimination procedure in which the positive stimulus was three colors presented in a particular order, and all other combinations of the same three colors were negative stimuli. By carefully analyzing the birds' responses over trials, Roitblat et al. found that the stimuli controlling the birds' responses changed as they learned this task. Different sequences of colors were used for different birds, but let us call the positive sequence A-B-C. One bird began by responding to all sequences ending with C, regardless of what the first two colors were. At this point, the bird's behavior was controlled only by the most recent color it had seen. A bit later in training, the bird responded to all sequences that started with A and ended with C (which included the positive sequence and two negative sequences, A-A-C and A-C-C). Finally, the bird responded almost exclusively to the positive sequence. Thus with practice, the stimuli that controlled the bird's responses became increasingly more sophisticated.

Still another way to detect an animal's ability to learn about sequences of events is to ask whether it can be taught to make a series of responses in a specific order, even when the environment provides no information about which responses have been made and which should be made next. Research on this topic will be discussed in Chapter 13 under the heading, "Simultaneous Chaining."

PROBLEM SOLVING, LANGUAGE, AND REASONING

Finding a creative solution to a difficult problem, communicating with language, and engaging in logical reasoning are among the most sophisticated learned behaviors that people can perform. Cognitive psychologists have studied these classes of behavior extensively, almost always with human subjects. Over the years, however, a few psychologists have attempted to determine whether animals are capable of these complex behaviors. Regardless of how this question is ultimately answered, the research with animals should give us a better perspective on the most advanced of human cognitive skills.

Problem Solving

In a text on human cognitive psychology, Anderson (1985) proposed that problem solving has three main characteristics. First, it is goal-directed. This characteristic is certainly not unique to problem solving, because as we have seen throughout this book, most behaviors, even reflexive movements, are goal-directed. Second, a problem-solving task can be broken down into a series of subgoals—a problem cannot usually be solved in one step. This characteristic is also found in other behaviors, such as innate reaction chains (Figure 3-5) and learned response chains (Figure 6-7). The third characteristic of problem solving, according to Anderson, is that it involves "operator selection"—the individual must select a series of operators (actions) that will achieve each subgoal. This, of course, is also true of reaction chains and response chains. To these three characteristics, I would add a fourth—novelty. Usually, when we speak of problem solving, we mean that a person must select a sequence of actions he or she has never performed before in exactly the same way. The first time you work on an exercise from an algebra text, you are indeed solving a problem. If you repeat the same exercise the next day, you might simply rely on your memory for the correct sequence of steps.

What do behavioral psychologists have to say about problem solving? Where do novel behaviors and novel sequences of behaviors come from? Well-known behavioral principles suggest at least three answers to this question. First, some novel behaviors are the result of random variability, or trial and error. Remember the cats in Thorndike's puzzle box, who eventually managed to escape simply by persisting with their seemingly haphazard movements until one of them, by chance, opened the door. With enough trials, the cats learned to produce the escape response fairly quickly. They had solved the puzzle by trial and error. A second behavioral principle that can lead to novel problem-solving behavior is generalization. A new problem may be similar enough to other problems you have solved to allow you to transfer the techniques that produce a solution. A third source of novel behaviors is imitation. As we will see in Chapter 12, even monkeys can learn to solve a problem by watching a peer who already knows how to solve it.

Together, these three sources of novel behavior—random variation, generalization, and imitation—can undoubtedly account for many instances of "creative" problem solving. Still, some examples of problem solving by both animals and people seem hard to explain with these behavioral principles. Consider the findings of Wolfgang Kohler (1927), who studied problem solving in chimpanzees. One of his favorite test situations involved hanging a banana from the ceiling of a large cage, well above a chimp's reach. In the cage were large wooden crates and a few long sticks. The chimp's problem was, of course, to find a way to reach the banana. Kohler claimed that in many cases, a chimp would solve the problem, not by trial and error, but through a burst of *insight*. In the following description, the behavior of a chimp named Sultan provides a clear example of what Kohler meant by insight:

Sultan was alone. At first he took no notice of the boxes, but tried to knock down the objective, first with a short stick and then with one of more appropriate length. The heavy sticks wobbled helplessly in his grasp. He became angry, kicked and drummed against the wall and hurled the sticks from him. Then he sat down on a table, in the neighborhood of the boxes, with an air of fatigue; when he had recovered a little, he gazed about him and scratched his head. He caught

sight of the boxes—stared at them, and in the same instant was off the table, and had seized the nearer one of them, which he dragged under the objective and climbed upon, having first re-captured his stick, with which he easily secured the prize. (1927, p. 46).

This example illustrates the characteristics of an insightful solution: an initial period of confusion, unsuccessful attempts, and no apparent progress; evidence of planning, thinking; and the sudden appearance of a solution, in which the successful sequence of behaviors is performed quickly and smoothly from beginning to end. This is surely quite different from the random behavior of Thorndike's cats.

Over the years, much has been written about methods to help people improve their problem-solving skills, to increase the chances that they will experience such bursts of insight. We will not examine these techniques here (for several different approaches to human problem solving, see Berger, Pezdek & Banks, 1987; Hayes, 1984; Polya, 1957). We will, however, examine the efforts of one researcher, Robert Epstein, to apply a strict behavioral approach to the domain of problem solving.

In his analysis of problem solving, Epstein has relied on a mixture of well-established and newly-identified behavioral principles, and he has stressed the importance of past experience as a crucial determinant of success or failure. In one series of experiments, Epstein, Kirshnit, Lanza and Rubin (1984) sought to determine whether pigeons could solve Kohler's banana problem. More specifically, they wanted to discover what types of experience a pigeon needed before it could succeed on this problem. From Kohler's writings, it is clear that his chimpanzees had extensive experience in pushing, manipulating, and climbing on boxes and other objects. Pigeons, on the other hand, have little experience in either climbing (since they can fly) or pushing objects (since their wings are ill-suited for this). The experimenters therefore used painstaking shaping procedures to train pigeons to push a cardboard box around, and to climb on top of it. Pushing and climbing were always taught in separate sessions: In some sessions, the cardboard box was attached to one spot on the floor of the chamber, and directly above this spot, a plastic banana hung from the ceiling. A pigeon was taught to climb on top of the box and peck at the banana, using grain as the reinforcer (since pigeons do not eat bananas, especially plastic ones). In other sessions, the plastic banana was absent, the cardboard box was movable, and the bird was trained to use its beak to push the box toward a small green spot that appeared at different points along the edge of the circular chamber.

At the end of this training, the pigeons had learned (1) to push the box around when the banana was not present, and (2) to climb and peck at the banana when it was present. In the test phase, each bird faced a situation it had never encountered before: The banana was hanging from the ceiling, but the box was in the center of the chamber, far from the banana. Would the birds solve this problem by first pushing the box below the banana and then climbing and pecking? Each bird's performance (which was videotaped so it could be carefully analyzed) followed a similar pattern: The bird first stood below the banana and stretched toward it. Then the bird looked around the chamber, and suddenly started to push the box in the direction of the banana. When the box was below the banana, the bird climbed, pecked at the banana, and was reinforced—it had solved the problem. Each of the three birds solved the problem in less than two minutes from when it entered the chamber.

By giving other birds different types of training, Epstein and his colleagues could determine what experiences were necessary for a bird to solve this problem. Experience in pushing the box was essential: Two birds were taught to climb on the box and peck the banana but not to push the box, and in the test situation these birds never pushed the box and therefore failed to solve the problem. Two other birds were trained to climb and peck, and to push the box around randomly, but they were not trained to push the box toward the green spot. In the test situation, these birds pushed the box around the chamber, and it occasionally stopped beneath the banana, but the birds never climbed on the box—they just kept pushing. The experimenters therefore concluded that learning to push the box around was

not enough, and that learning to push the box toward a target was necessary.

Instead of simply attributing the successful pigeons' performances to insight, Epstein (1985a) offered a moment-to-moment explanation of the their actions, based on behavioral principles. For simplicity, we can divide this explanation into five steps:

1. An initial conflict between two responses. In their previous training, the birds had learned about two different discriminative stimuli: "Box below banana" was a stimulus for climbing and pecking, and "Banana not present" was a stimulus for pushing. On the test day, the stimulus was a kind of mixture of the two: The banana was present, but the box was not below it. This stimulus therefore tended to evoke both behaviors to some extent, and a bird would stretch toward the banana, look toward the box, look back at the banana, and so on.

2. Extinction of banana-directed responses. Attempts to peck at the banana were not successful, and they were not reinforced, so these responses began to extinguish.

3. Resurgence of pushing responses. In earlier work, Epstein (1983, 1985b) studied the phenomenon of *resurgence,* which is the reappearance of a previously learned response when alternative responses become ineffective (that is, when they are no longer reinforced). In this case, as behavior directed toward the banana declined through extinction, box-pushing (a different behavior that had been previously reinforced) took its place.

4. Functional generalization. When a bird started to push the box, why did it push in the direction of the banana? The bird was taught to push the box toward a green spot, never toward the banana. Epstein suggested that this was an example of *functional generalization,* or generalization based on similarity of function (as opposed to physical similarity). Although the banana and the green spot were not physically similar, they did have something in common: Responses directed toward each (pecking in one case, and box-pushing in the other) had been reinforced with food. As a result, when the green spot was not present, the banana served as a substitute target. Consistent with this hypothesis, birds that had been reinforced for pushing the box toward the green spot but not for pecking at the banana did not push the box toward the banana in the test situation (Epstein et al., 1984).

5. Automatic chaining. When the box was finally located beneath the banana, it became the perfect discriminative stimulus for climbing and pecking (that is, climbing and pecking had previously been reinforced in the presence of precisely this stimulus). The switch from pushing to climbing therefore matched the usual characteristics of a response chain, in which performing one response eventually produces the discriminative stimulus for the next response. In this case, however, Epstein called the process *automatic chaining,* because the bird produced the complete sequence of responses (pushing followed by climbing and pecking) without ever having been taught to do so.

With this collection of behavioral concepts—discriminative stimuli, behavioral competition, extinction, resurgence, generalization, response chains, and reinforcement—Epstein could account very well for the sequence of behaviors each bird displayed in its test session. He argued that the "insightful" behaviors of Kohler's chimpanzees could probably have been explained with these same principles if the animals' past experiences with boxes, sticks, and bananas had been carefully studied. In subsequent work, Epstein has studied pigeons' problem solving with more complex tasks that required the automatic chaining of three or four separately-learned behaviors (Epstein, 1985c, 1987). In the four-response chain, a pigeon was trained to perform four separate behaviors: to peck at the plastic banana while standing on the floor, to climb onto a box, to push the box toward the green spot, and to open a clear plastic door with its beak. In the test situation, the box was placed behind the closed door, and for the first time, the banana was too high for the bird to reach while standing on the floor. Within four minutes, the bird managed to open the door, pull out the box and push it under the banana, climb onto the box, and peck at the banana, thereby earning a well-deserved reinforcer. This performance was especially impressive because no two of the behaviors were ever taught at the same time.

Epstein (1985a) has also applied the behavioral approach to human problem solving, using Maier's (1931) well-known "two-string problem." In a large room, two strings hang from a high ceiling, about 15 feet apart, and the subject's task is to tie the two strings together. The subject can use any of the objects in the room, including a cylindrical rod with a large hook on one end. The two strings cannot be reached at the same time, even if the subject pulls one string as far as possible with one hand and reaches with the rod and hook with the other. The solution is to tie the hooked rod to one of the strings to make a pendulum, start the pendulum swinging, take the other string in one hand, stretch, and catch the rod as it swings toward you. The solution may seem obvious once you know it (as is true with many problems), but when college students try this problem for the first time, they usually require several minutes to find the solution, and some never find it.

To predict the behavior of an average subject working on this problem, Epstein developed a simple mathematical model that involved only four behavioral principles—reinforcement, extinction, resurgence, and automatic chaining. The model predicted that pulling the strings together would occur first but extinguish, tying the rod to a string would then emerge, eventually the subject would start the rod and string swinging (perhaps accidentally), and then the solution would appear quickly (because this stimulus would make the solution obvious). The actual performance of Epstein's subjects supported these predictions reasonably well.

Cognitive psychologists have long had an interest in problem solving, and some have made careful observations of subjects' moment-to-moment performance (for example, Newell & Simon, 1972). What makes Epstein's approach different is its heavy emphasis on past experience, discriminative stimuli, and basic behavioral principles. Like other behavioral research, it emphasizes general principles that are applicable to both animal and human problem solving. Whether this approach can be successfully applied to more complex and abstract problems (such as problems in mathematics or physics, where much of the problem-solving activity is unobservable) remains to be seen.

Teaching Language to Animals

Most people would probably credit animals with at least some rudimentary problem-solving abilities, since the challenge of surviving in the wild frequently poses obstacles that demand creative solutions. On the other hand, many have claimed that the ability to use language is one skill that only human beings possess (for example, Chomsky, 1972). For this reason, attempts to teach language to chimpanzees and other animals have received tremendous attention. A number of different questions can be asked about the linguistic abilities of animals: Can they learn to use words or other symbols to represent objects or events? Can they learn grammatical rules, which make it possible to combine words into organized sentences and to produce novel yet understandable sentences? Can they use language to communicate information about objects not currently visible and about events not currently taking place? If and when an animal acquires such skills, will it use them spontaneously to communicate with others? Research on animal language learning has provided insights into all of these issues, but the final answers to these questions are still far from certain.

Some Representative Studies.   In the earliest attempts to teach language to chimpanzees, researchers tried to get the animals to speak (Hayes, 1951; Kellogg & Kellogg, 1933). For the most part, these studies were unsuccessful, although the chimps eventually learned to say a few words. The main problem was that a chimpanzee's vocal apparatus does not permit it to make many human speech sounds. To avoid this problem, Allen and Beatrice Gardner (1969, 1975) decided to try to teach their chimpanzee, Washoe, to use American Sign Language (ASL). Washoe was about one year old when the Gardners obtained her, and she lived in an enclosed yard and a small trailer. She was trained by a number of different people, all of whom were moderately proficient in ASL. The trainers tried to teach Washoe signs, but they also played games with her and got her to participate in a variety of activities. During Washoe's waking hours, a trainer was always with her. By relying on a mixture of modeling, manual guidance, and a good deal of patience, the trainers were able to teach Washoe to produce signs for quite a few different words, including nouns (such as *flower, toothbrush, hat*), verbs (*go, listen, tickle*), adjectives (*sweet, funny, more*), pronouns (*you, me*) and prepositions (*in, out*). To make sure that the trainers were not seeing more in Washoe's signs than was really there, the Gardners conducted tests in which one person showed Washoe a picture of some object while another person, who could not see the picture, watched and interpreted Washoe's response. On these tests, Washoe was often correct on better than 70 percent of the trials. After four years with the Gardners, Washoe had learned about 130 signs. This was quite an impressive vocabulary (though still small compared to that of the average four-year-old child, who knows several thousand words).

After being taught a sign in a few contexts, Washoe sometimes used it in a new context without further training. For instance, she was taught the sign for *more* in combination with a few different signs (including *more tickle* and *more swinging*), and she later began to use the sign to ask for more food and for more of other activities. The Gardners reported that Washoe occasionally used creative combinations of words, as when she signed *water bird* upon seeing a swan (for which she had learned no sign). We cannot assume, however, that Washoe was using this novel phrase to describe the swan, because she was looking at a scene in which both water and a bird were present.

Although Washoe's vocabulary of signs was substantial, and although she frequently used signs in various combinations, the order in which she used the signs in a "sentence" was quite inconsistent. For example, she might sign the phrase *food eat* on some occasions and *eat food* on others, with no apparent reason for the different word orders. In contrast, both children and adults tend to use consistent word orders whether they are using spoken or sign language. In short, Washoe had a good vocabulary but poor (perhaps nonexistent) grammar.

Using a very different training situation, David Premack (1971, 1983) obtained much more encouraging evidence that chimpanzees can learn at least some rules about grammar and word order. Instead of using ASL, Premack constructed a language consisting of different plastic shapes that represented different words. Sentences were created by placing the shapes (which had metal backings) on a magnetic board in a specific order. Premack's pupil, a six-year-old chimpanzee named Sarah, learned to respond appropriately to many different configurations of these symbols. Unlike Washoe, who learned ASL in an informal outdoor setting from trainers who were also playmates and companions, Sarah lived in a cage and received more rigorous and systematic training. Sarah's trainers started by teaching her to associate symbols with different objects or events, and they progressed slowly to short sentences and then to longer and more complex ones.

The order of symbols was a critical part of the language Sarah learned, and she demonstrated an impressive ability to respond on the basis of symbol order. For instance, after Sarah learned the symbols for several different colors, her trainer introduced a symbol for *on*. Symbols for *green on red* were put on the board, and then the trainer gave Sarah a green card and got her to place it on top of a red card. Sarah was then taught to produce the opposite response to the symbol sequence *red on green*. Eventually, she learned to respond appropriately to either sequence when given the red and green cards at once. This performance in itself shows that her responses were controlled by the order of the symbols, not just by the symbols themselves. Having succeeded at this task, Sarah was then able to respond correctly to new symbol strings such as *blue on yellow* with no further training. Sarah had learned not only that the order of symbols was important, but that this same order could be applied to other symbols. In a simple way, this example illustrates an understanding of a grammatical rule—an abstract rule about sentence structure that applies to entire classes of words.

In another case where word order was important, Sarah learned to respond to a complex sentence of symbols, *Sarah insert banana pail apple dish,* by putting a banana in a pail and an apple in a dish. To respond correctly, Sarah had to pay attention to word order; otherwise, she would not know what to insert into what. It is instructive to examine some of the training steps that were used to achieve this level of complexity. Once Sarah had learned the relevant symbols, her trainers started with the simpler sentence *Sarah insert banana pail,* and the appropriate response was reinforced. On different trials, symbols for *apple* and *pail* were also used, in different combinations (*banana in dish, apple in pail,* and so on). Later, Sarah was presented with two sentences side by side—*Sarah insert banana pail* and *Sarah insert apple dish*—and she learned to respond to each in turn. Then the two sentences were combined into one long one, *Sarah insert banana pail Sarah insert apple dish,* and in successive steps the symbols we would consider redundant (the second occurrences of *Sarah* and *insert*) were removed.

This example illustrates the type of procedure Premack used to train Sarah to respond appropriately to long and difficult sentences. You may have noticed that this technique is really an advanced version of the familiar operant procedure of successive approximations— each change is just a small step harder than something the subject has already mastered. Premack (1971) explained that his procedure involved "one-to-one substitution"—each new type of sentence would differ in only one way from sentence forms Sarah had already learned. Using this technique, Premack and his associates trained Sarah to respond appropriately to a wide range of grammatical forms and concepts, including plurals, yes-no questions, and quantifiers (*all, some, none,* and *several*). One disappointing feature of Sarah's performance, however, was that she seldom initiated a conversation. Her use of the symbol language was almost exclusively confined to answering questions posed by the experimenters. Furthermore, if one of her trainers placed a question on the board and then left the room, Sarah would usually either give an incorrect response or none at all. She was hardly bursting with enthusiasm about the power of her newly acquired communication skills, eager to use them wherever she could. This behavior contrasts quite starkly with that of young children, who spontaneously practice and use the words they have learned, whether anyone is listening or not.

In addition to the work of the Gardners and Premack, there have been several other attempts to teach language to chimpanzees and other primates, including a gorilla and an orangutan (for example, Miles, 1983; Patterson, 1978; Rumbaugh, 1977; Savage-Rumbaugh, 1984; Terrace, 1979). ASL has been used in some cases, and pictorial symbols in others. In many of these studies, the animals were able to learn well over one hundred signs. Patterson and Linden (1981) reported that a gorilla named Koko had mastered over 400 signs. There have also been some studies with nonprimates. Herman, Richards, & Wolz (1984) trained two bottlenosed dolphins to respond to about two dozen manual gestures by engaging in the appropriate activities. For example, a trainer might make the gestures for *frisbee fetch basket,* and the dolphin would then find the frisbee and put it in the basket. The dolphins could also answer questions about whether a particular object was or was not present in the tank (Herman & Forestell, 1985). Similar work has been done with sea lions (Schusterman & Krieger (1984). And the parrot Alex, whose counting abilities have already been described, learned to say about 50 English words and use them appropriately to make requests ("Gimme tickle") and answer questions (Trainer: "What's this?"; Alex: "clothespin"). Alex could also answer questions about the physical properties of objects, describing either an object's shape or color depending on what question his trainer asked (Pepperberg, 1983).

Criticisms. Despite these accomplishments, some have argued that the ways these animals learned to use signs are not really comparable to human language. One researcher who has articulated this view quite forcefully is Herbert Terrace (1979, 1985). Over a four-year period, Terrace and his associates taught ASL to a chimpanzee who was called Nim Chimpsky (a name with a curious resemblance to that of Noam Chomsky, the linguist who claimed that only people can learn language). Nim's training sessions were frequently videotaped so that his signs and the context in which they occurred could later be carefully analyzed. In many respects, Nim's performance was impressive. He learned about 125 signs for nouns, verbs, adjectives, pronouns, and prepositions. He frequently used these signs in combinations of two or more, and Terrace's analysis revealed that he had learned to use some primitive grammatical rules. The evidence for grammatical rules was the consistency of sign order in Nim's two-sign "sentences". For example, of all the two-sign sentences that included the sign for *more,* this sign occurred first in 85 percent of the cases (*more drink, more tickle,* and so on). Similarly, when Nim used the sign for *me* in combination with a transitive verb (*hug, give*), *me* occurred in the second position 83 percent of the time. This consistency of sign order also occurred at a more general level involving whole classes of words of similar grammatical categories. For instance, when Nim made a two-sign sentence including an action and an agent, the sign for the action usually came first, whereas in sentences involving an action and a place, the sign for the action usually came second. This consistency of sign order suggested that Nim was following certain grammatical rules (though not necessarily those used in the English language) in his two-sign sentences.

Unfortunately, in Nim's sequences of three or more signs, inconsistency was the rule. For example, in three-sign sequences involving *eat, me, Nim,* and *more,* these signs occurred in almost every possible order. Out of a large sample of Nim's behavior, *me more eat* and *more eat Nim* both occurred 19 times, *eat me Nim* 48 times, *Nim me eat* 27 times, *eat Nim eat* 46 times, and *me Nim eat* 21 times. As Terrace pointed out, Nim's sequences of signs were different from the short sentences spoken by a typical two- or three-year-old child in several ways. First, there was no consistency of word order. Second, there were pointless repetitions of signs, and redundant signs (*me* and *Nim* used in a single sequence). Third, the *average* length of Nim's sign sequences (corresponding to what psycholinguists call the *mean length of utterance*) leveled off at about 1.5 signs per sequence and never increased again. In contrast, a child's mean length of utterance steadily increases with age. Fourth, when a child's sentences increase in length, the amount of information conveyed by each sentence also increases, but this was not the case with Nim. When Nim did produce a longer sequence of signs, it tended to include only repetitions of a few signs, in no particular order. An extreme example is the longest string the experimenters recorded, involving 16 signs: *give orange me give eat orange me eat orange give me eat orange give me you.* No ordinary child, whether speaking or using ASL, would ever produce such a redundant and chaotic string of words.

Terrace (1979) also reported that Nim's performance differed from a typical child's in other ways. The proportion of a child's utterances that are full or partial repetitions of what an adult just said decreases with age. Nim's repetitions, however, increased from an already high 38 percent when he was 26 months old to 54 percent at 44 months. In addition, only a small percentage of Nim's utterances were spontaneous; most were immediately preceded by a sign from his trainer. In fact, Nim frequently interrupted his trainer by starting to gesture while the trainer was in the middle of a sequence of signs. This suggests that Nim did not understand the turn-taking character of most human conversation.

Based on his analyses of Nim's behavior, as well as those of Washoe, Sarah, and other chimps, Terrace (1979) concluded that the "language" these animals had learned lacked many of the essential characteristics of human language. He asserted that the chimps had learned only the most primitive grammatical rules, and that for the most part they would string together signs in a random order. They relied heavily on imitation and on prompting by their trainers, and showed little spontaneous use of language. The complexity of their utterances did not increase with additional training. Not surprisingly, some have agreed with the general tone of Terrace's evaluation of the chimp language projects (Brown, 1985), whereas others have disputed its validity (Premack, 1986).

Some Tentative Conclusions. Terrace was almost surely correct in saying that, so far, the linguistic capacities that animals have demonstrated are quite limited compared to those of humans. On the positive side, however, two points can be made. First, this research has shown that animals have at least some measure of linguistic

ability. Animals of several species have demonstrated the ability to use words, signs, or symbols to represent objects, actions, and descriptions. Second, the limitations of the initial research could prove to be more the fault of the training and testing procedures used than of the animals themselves. Even if it is correct to say that no ape has yet generated a "true sentence" (Terrace, Petitto, Sanders, & Bever, 1979), it would be foolhardy to claim that no ape can ever be taught to do so.

Evidence is already starting to accumulate that Terrace's assessment of animal language abilities may have been too pessimistic. Although Nim and some of the other chimpanzees may have relied heavily on imitation, Miles (1983) has reported that an orangutan named Chantek, who had learned a few dozen signs, almost never engaged in direct imitation. Although Nim and other chimps seldom initiated a conversation, over one-third of Chantek's utterances were classified as "spontaneous"—not immediately preceded by a trainer's utterance. In addition, the mean length of Chantek's utterances, unlike those of Nim, steadily increased over a period of about 16 months. In another example of the spontaneous use of symbols, two pygmy chimpanzees (not the same species as ordinary chimpanzees) learned to use several dozen pictorial symbols on a keyboard without any explicit training by humans. These animals learned by watching others use these symbols, and they could use the symbols to refer to objects and events not present (Savage-Rumbaugh, McDonald, Sevcik, Hopkins, & Rubert, 1986).

Terrace (1979) has claimed that language-trained animals used their language only to obtain reinforcers, not to communicate information. However, a number of subsequent findings suggest that these animals do sometimes use their signs to communicate with other animals or with people. Fouts, Hirsch, and Fouts (1982) reported that the chimp Washoe appeared to teach ASL signs to her adopted infant. The infant did imitate some of the signs, but whether he understood their meanings was not known. Two other studies found that chimpanzees can use their signs to describe behaviors they have just performed, or are about to perform (Premack, 1986; Savage-

Rumbaugh, 1984). It therefore seems that some features of language that may have been absent from the early chimpanzee studies—spontaneity, use of signs purely for the sake of communication, and reference to objects and events not present—have in fact been found in subsequent studies. Given this trend, it seems likely that future research will find additional similarities in the ways people and animals can learn to use language.

Reasoning by Animals

This topic follows naturally from the preceding discussion, because many of the tests of animals' reasoning abilities have been conducted with animals who have first been given some training in language. Premack (1983) has found that language-trained chimpanzees can succeed on some reasoning tasks that non-language-trained chimpanzees cannot. On other tasks, however, language-trained and non-language-trained animals perform identically. Premack attempted to explain these differences by proposing that language training, with its use of abstract symbols, gives chimpanzees a vocabulary for describing relations among objects rather than simply responding to the physical properties of objects. In Premack's terms, non-language-trained chimpanzees use only an *imaginal code* (one related to the visual properties of objects), whereas language-trained chimpanzees learn to use an *abstract code*. On tasks that can be solved with an imaginal code, chimps with and without language training can perform equally well. If the task requires an understanding of abstract relations, however, only language-trained animals will succeed. Premack's theory is controversial, but it is certainly worth examining in more detail. We will look at some reasoning tasks for which language training makes a difference, and some for which it does not.

Reasoning about the Locations of Objects. Premack (1983) described an experiment in which chimpanzees faced the following situation. A chimp was shown two containers at opposite ends of a room, and the chimp watched as a trainer placed an apple in one container and a ba-

nana in the other. The chimp was then briefly taken out of the room, and when she returned she saw the trainer standing in the middle of the room, eating either an apple or a banana. The trainer then left, and the chimp was allowed to go to either of the two containers. Would the chimp infer that the fruit the trainer was eating was from one of containers, and would she therefore go to the other container?

Premack's chimps (all of whom were at least six years old) made the correct choice on this type of problem, both those that had received language training and those that had not. Premack argued that all chimps were able to solve this problem because, even without language training, they have the ability to reason about physical similarity and object locations: They could infer that the fruit the trainer was eating was the same as the fruit that had been placed in one of the containers. Although this problem may not require an understanding of abstract relations, it is not trivially easy. As a point of comparison, Premack found that five-year-old children also succeed on this task, whereas some children who are four or younger do not—they are just as likely to go to either container.

Analogies. An analogy is a statement of the form "A is to B as C is to D." To test someone's ability to understand analogies, we can give him two or more choices for D and ask him which is correct. For example, consider the analogy, "Lock is to key as can is to ____." Is *paint brush* or *can opener* a more appropriate answer? On this type of problem, the ability to make judgments about physical similarity is usually not enough. In physical terms, a can opener is not especially similar to a key, a lock, or a can. To solve this analogy, one must understand (1) the relation between lock and key, (2) the relation between can opener and can, and (3) the similarity of the two relations (that is, that the second item of each pair is used to open the first). In other words, to understand an analogy, one must be able to understand a relation (similarity) between two relations.

Gillan, Premack, and Woodruff (1981) tested Sarah, the language-trained chimpanzee, with analogies that involved either perceptual relations or functional relations between objects. The analogy in the previous paragraph involves functional relations because it requires an understanding of the functions the different objects serve, and it was one of the analogies given to Sarah (see Figure 11-8). An example of a perceptual analogy is the following: Large yellow triangle is to small yellow triangle as large red crescent is to (small red crescent, or small yellow crescent)? This analogy also requires an understanding of the relations between objects, but in this case the relations pertain only to the perceptual properties of the objects (their relative sizes).

Sarah was fairly successful at solving both types of analogies. In contrast, non-language-trained chimpanzees were never significantly better than chance (50 percent correct), even though they were tested on very simple perceptual analogies. This finding is consistent with

FIGURE 11-8. Pictures presented to the chimpanzee Sarah, which represent the analogy, "Lock is to key as can is to what?" Two possible answers, can opener and paint brush, were presented below the line, and Sarah chose the correct answer. (From Gillan, Premack, & Woodruff, 1981)

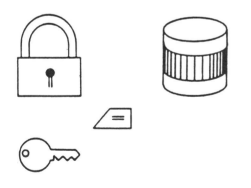

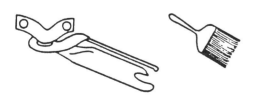

Premack's hypothesis that without language, an animal cannot understand abstract relations between objects.

Transitive Inference. If Alex is shorter than Bill, and if Bill is shorter than Carl, then it follows that Alex is shorter than Carl. This conclusion is justified because inequalities of size are *transitive*. That is, they conform to the following general rule: if $A < B$, and if $B < C$, then $A < C$. If we draw the correct conclusion about the heights of Alex and Carl without ever having seen them side by side, we are displaying the capacity for *transitive inference*.

Gillan (1981) tested whether three non-language-trained chimpanzees were capable of transitive inference by first training them with containers of different colors, which had food in some situations but not others. For instance, one chimp was taught that blue was better than black, black was better than red, and so on. In the test for transitive inference, a chimp had to choose between two containers that had never been paired before. For instance, when given a choice between blue and red, would the chimp choose blue? Gillan found that the chimps were capable of making such inferences. Premack claimed that this result is neither evidence for or against his theory, because this type of problem can be solved by using either abstract reasoning or visual imagery (for instance, by imagining the different colored containers in a row, and choosing the container closest to the "better" end of the row). Premack's view is that whereas only language-trained chimps are capable of abstract reasoning, those without language training can solve this problem using the simpler visual strategy. In any case, it is interesting to know that at least one species besides *homo sapiens* is capable of this type of reasoning.

Judgments about "Sameness." Can animals judge whether two objects are the same or different? At first glance, this seems like a very easy problem, and one that is accomplished every time an animal succeeds on the matching-to-sample task (an easy task even for pigeons). Premack has argued, however, that there is a subtle yet important distinction between responding on the basis of visual similarity (which is all that the matching-to-sample task requires) and learning the abstract concepts of *same* and *different*. In the matching-to-sample task, the subject only needs to choose the comparison stimulus that matches the sample, and this can be done on the basis of visual similarity (which requires only an imaginal code). In a same/different task, two stimuli are presented simultaneously, and the subject must make one response if the stimuli are the same and another response if they are different. Premack reported that only language-trained chimpanzees are successful on the same/different task. He claimed that this is because this task requires the subject to respond to the relation between stimuli (*same* or *different*), which necessitates the use of an abstract code.

Not everyone agrees with Premack's analysis of the same/different task. For instance, Zentall (1983) argued that both matching-to-sample and same/different tasks can be performed on the basis of visual similarity. In both cases, however, if the animal can successfully generalize to new stimuli, it has learned the general concept of *same,* at least at some level. Zentall proposed that certain procedural problems may explain why Premack's non-language-trained chimpanzees could not solve the same/different task with novel stimuli. Zentall, Hogan, and Edwards (1984) found that pigeons could learn the same/different task and exhibited substantial transfer to new stimuli. Based on these and similar results, Zentall concluded that language training is not necessary for success on the same/different task, and that animals besides primates are capable of generalized same/different judgments.

Conclusions. Chimpanzees with language training seem to be capable of solving at least some reasoning tasks that chimpanzees without language training cannot. It is not yet clear exactly why this is so. Premack has argued that language training teaches chimpanzees to use an abstract code instead of (or in addition to) an imaginal code. Others have concluded, however, that language training simply makes the chimps better test-takers, since this training involves extensive experience with answering questions, following instructions, and so on. Premack has also proposed that only primates are capable of using an abstract code, and that therefore only primates are capable of abstract reasoning. This claim has met even more strenuous opposition. Many lines of evidence suggest that nonprimates can learn a variety of tasks that involve abstract reasoning. These include the learning of natural concepts by several species of birds (Chapter 10), judgments of same/different by pigeons, accurate counting of objects by a parrot, and language learning by dolphins and sea lions. It seems likely that more species of animals are capable of more types of abstract reasoning than Premack and many others have assumed.

Perhaps the moral is that it is always risky to claim, "Here is a problem in abstract reasoning that only humans (or only primates) can solve." The danger is that some clever researcher will find a way to teach a bird or rodent to solve exactly that problem. Although no one would seriously question the vast differences between human and nonhuman intellectual abilities, some of the apparent limitations of animals' reasoning abilities might be attributed to deficiencies in current training or testing procedures, not to the animals.

CHAPTER
12
LEARNING BY OBSERVATION

Let there be no mistake about it: A large proportion of human learning occurs, not through classical conditioning or as a result of reinforcement or punishment, but through observation. Two psychologists whose writings and experiments repeatedly emphasized this fact are Albert Bandura and Richard H. Walters. In their classic book, *Social Learning and Personality Development* (1963), Bandura and Walters argued that traditional learning theory was grossly incomplete because it neglected the role of observational learning. As we have seen, traditional learning theory emphasizes the importance of individual experience: An individual performs some behavior and experiences the consequences that follow. The point of Bandura and Walters is that a good deal of learning occurs through vicarious rather than personal experience: We observe the behavior of others, observe the consequences, and later we may imitate their behavior. In short, Bandura and Walters claim that the traditional approach to learning, which stresses personal ex-

perience and practice, is insufficient—it can account for some types of learning but not all.

As the title of their book implies, Bandura and Walters were interested in how people develop different personalities (for instance, why some people are extroverted and others introverted, some peaceful and others aggressive, some industrious and others lazy). They suggested that while some personality differences have a hereditary basis, most are due to an individual's learning experiences. They rejected the Freudian or psychodynamic approach to personality, which emphasizes the interactions of unconscious psychic forces in determining an adult's personality. Like Freud, Bandura and Walters believed that early childhood experiences can have a profound influence on adult personality, but they proposed that these experiences exerted their influence through the principles of *social learning theory*. By social learning theory, Bandura and Walters meant a combination of (1) the traditional principles of classical and operant conditioning, plus

(2) the principles of *observational learning* or *imitation*. Thus they felt that they were not rejecting the principles of traditional learning theory but rather were adding one more important principle of learning to the list.

Later in this chapter, we will examine some of a large body of evidence collected by Bandura and Walters and others that shows that observational learning is indeed an important contributor to personality differences among individuals. To begin, however, we will survey a number of different theories about why imitation occurs in the first place, and we will examine Bandura's analysis of the factors that determine when imitative behavior will and will not be observed.

THEORIES OF IMITATION

Imitation as an Instinct

A number of early psychologists (Baldwin, 1906; Morgan, 1896; McDougall, 1908) suggested that people and other animals have an innate propensity to imitate behaviors they see others perform. In discussing a child's tendency to imitate the speech and gestures of adults, and of adults' tendencies to "speak, walk, and behave like others," William James (1890) stated: "This sort of imitativeness is possessed by man in common with other gregarious animals, and is an instinct in the fullest sense of the term..." (p. 408). This belief that imitation was an innate tendency stemmed in part from evidence that young infants may imitate the movements of an adult. For instance, McDougall (1908) reported that his four-month-old child would stick out his tongue when an adult in front of the child did the same. Of course, the possibility that the infant might have learned this response because it was reinforced (with the smiles and laughter of adults) cannot be entirely ruled out. A more recent line of research provides much stronger evidence for an innate tendency to imitate.

In some carefully controlled experiments, Meltzoff and Moore (1977; 1983) sought to determine whether twelve- to twenty-one- day-old infants would imitate any of four gestures made by an adult tester—lip protrusion, mouth opening, tongue protrusion, and sequential finger movement. The tester made one of these gestures at a time, then waited to see whether the infant would copy it. The infant's behavior was videotaped and subsequently scored by people who did not know which of the four gestures the infant had observed on a given trial. Meltzoff and Moore found a reliable tendency for the infants to imitate the specific behavior that they had just seen. Because of the young ages of these infants, it seems very unlikely that such imitative behaviors had been reinforced by their parents. In fact, all of the parents claimed that they had never seen imitative behavior in their infants, and most felt that it was not possible at such a young age.

The results of Meltzoff and Moore are still controversial (Hayes & Watson, 1981), but they have been replicated several times (Field, Woodson, Greenberg, & Cohen, 1982; Jacobson, 1979). Other research suggests that infants' imitation of facial expressions decreases between the ages of two and six months (Field, Goldstein, Vega-Lahr, & Porter, 1986). Nevertheless, this ability of newborn infants to imitate a variety of gestures is remarkable, because it suggests that humans are born with the capacity to associate a visual input (the sight of an adult making a certain gesture) with a set of muscle movements that allows the infant to mimic that visual input. Notice that the infant cannot see its own face when it opens its mouth or sticks out its tongue. Indeed it was probably the case that most of the infants studied by Meltzoff and Moore had never seen their own face in a mirror or other reflecting surface. It is even less likely that any of these infants had the opportunity to practice making different facial movements in front of a mirror and systematically associate different muscular movements with different visual images. Although it is not clear why human infants are born with this capacity, the Meltzoff and Moore experiments make a convincing case that they are.

As the quotation from William James showed, he believed that other animals were also capable of learning by imitation. The earliest controlled experiments on this topic did not support James's claim. Thorndike (1911) attempted to determine whether animals could learn the appropriate response in a puzzle box through observation. For instance, an inexperienced cat might be placed in a cage where it could watch a well-trained cat escape from the puzzle box and receive some fish outside. Regardless of the number of trials of such observational learning, Thorndike found no evidence whatsoever that the observing cat had learned anything. When placed in the puzzle box, such a cat did no better than a naive cat. Thorndike obtained similar negative results with chicks, dogs, and monkeys, and he concluded that nonhuman animals cannot learn by observation. These results strengthened his belief in the Law of Effect, which states that animals learn by actively responding and experiencing the consequences that follow.

Quite a few later studies on imitation in animals have shown that Thorndike's conclusion was incorrect. The learning tasks in these studies span quite a large range of complexity, and it will be helpful to consider three categories of observational learning proposed by Thorpe (1963). The simplest is called *social facilitation,* in which the behavior of one individual prompts a similar behavior from another individual, but the behavior is one that is *already in the repertoire* of the imitator. For instance, Turner (1964) exposed newly hatched chicks to a mechanical "hen" that pecked at a piece of grain that was orange for some chicks and green for others. Turner found that the chicks pecked at grain of the same color about twice as frequently as grain of the other color. (The kernels were glued to the floor, so that the chicks' pecking responses would not be reinforced by the ingestion of food.) This example of imitation is labeled social facilitation because the chicks already knew how to peck. Similarly, Wyrwicka (1978) trained mother cats to eat some unusual foods (bananas and mashed potatoes), and their kittens also began to eat these foods.

Thorpe's second category of observational learning is *local enhancement,* in which the behavior of a model directs the attention of the learner to a particular object or place in the environment. As a result, a response that might otherwise have been learned through trial and error is acquired more rapidly. For instance, Warden, Fjeld, and Koch (1940) trained some monkeys to earn food reinforcers by making responses such as pulling a chain. An untrained monkey was then placed in an identical test chamber adjacent to the chamber with a trained monkey. These investigators recorded numerous instances in which the untrained monkey would observe the other monkey make the required response and immediately imitate it. Since the reinforced responses were similar to those studied by Thorndike in his puzzle box, the untrained monkeys would probably have eventually learned the responses by trial and error, but their learning was accelerated by watching the behavior of another, more experienced individual. Local enhancement has also been observed in birds (for example, Hogan, 1986; Johnson, Hamm, & Leahey, 1986). It is not necessary for the model to be the same species as the learner. Bullock and Neuringer (1977) found that pigeons could learn to produce a two- response chain (pecking two keys in a specific order) by observing a human hand demonstrate the appropriate sequence.

Thorpe's third category of imitation, which he called *true imitation,* is not clearly distinguishable from local enhancement, but it refers to the imitation of a behavior pattern that is very unusual or improbable for the species, so that it would seldom be learned through trial and error. Kawai (1965) described several examples of true imitation that have been observed in a troop of monkeys living on an island off the coast of Japan. For example, when grains of wheat were spread along the beach, the monkeys would pick them out of the sand one by one and eat them. However, one monkey learned to separate the wheat from the sand more efficiently by picking up a handful of the mixture and throwing it in the water. The sand would sink and the wheat would float, so it could be collected easily. Soon many of the other monkeys of the troop were imitating this behavior. Kawai reported that several other novel behaviors spread quickly through the troop as a result of observational learning, including washing the sand off sweet potatoes, and bathing in the ocean (which the monkeys had never done until one pioneer took up this activity).

Well-documented examples of true imitation in animals other than primates are rare, but some anecdotal evidence reported by Fisher and Hinde (1949) seems quite convincing. In 1921, residents of a village in southern England first reported that some birds had begun to obtain milk by piercing the covers of milk bottles left out on doorsteps. Over several years, this behavior spread through parts of England, Ireland, Wales, and Scotland, and it was observed in several different species of birds. Since it makes little sense to propose that all of these birds suddenly learned this behavior on their own, the behavior must have been acquired and transmitted through observational learning.

We have seen that the ability to learn through observation is by no means unique to human beings, and that the tendency to imitate the behavior of others can be seen at a very young age in many species. Thus there seems to be some truth to the claims of early psychologists that the tendency to imitate is instinctive. The problem with this account, however, is that it tells us nothing about when imitation will occur and when it will not. More recent theories of imitation have tried to answer this question.

Imitation as an Operant Response

In a well-known book, Miller and Dollard (1941) claimed that observational learning is not an additional type of learning (beside classical and operant conditioning) but rather that it is simply a special case of operant conditioning. We have already seen that discriminative stimuli play a crucial role in operant conditioning both inside and outside the laboratory. For instance, a laboratory animal may learn to make one response in the presence of a red light, another response in the presence of a green light, and yet another response in the presence of a yellow light. (A person driving a car has also learned different responses to these three stimuli.) According to Miller and Dollard, observational learning involves situations where the discriminative stimulus is the behavior of another person, and the appropriate response just happens to be a similar behavior on the part of the observer.

One of Miller and Dollard's many experiments will illustrate their approach. First-grade children participated in this experiment in pairs, with one child being the "leader" and the other the "learner." On each of several trials, the two

children would enter a room in which there were two chairs with a large box on top of each. The leader was instructed in advance to go to one of the two boxes, where there might be a piece of candy. The learner could see where the leader went, but not whether the leader obtained any candy. Next, it was the learner's turn to go to one of the two boxes, where he might or might not find a piece of candy. Half of the learners were in an *imitation group*—they were reinforced for making the same choice as the leader. The other learners were in the *nonimitation group*—they obtained reinforcement if their choice was opposite that of the leader.

The result of this simple experiment was not surprising: After a few trials, children in the imitation group always copied the response of the leader, and those in the nonimitation group always made the opposite response. Miller and Dollard concluded that, like any other operant response, imitation will occur if an individual is reinforced for imitating. Conversely, nonimitation will occur if nonimitation is reinforced. In both cases, the behavior of some other person is the discriminative stimulus that indicates what response is appropriate. Similar follow-the-leader behavior has been observed in rats and other animals (see Hake, Donaldson, & Hyten, 1983). According to Miller and Dollard, then, imitative learning fits nicely into the Skinnerian three-term contingency of discriminative stimulus, response, and reinforcement. There is no need to claim that observational learning is a separate class of learning that is different from operant conditioning.

Imitation as a Generalized Operant Response

As Bandura (1969) has pointed out, Miller and Dollard's analysis of imitation applies only to those instances in which a learner (1) observes the behavior of a model, (2) immediately copies the response, and (3) receives reinforcement. Many everyday examples of imitation do not follow this pattern. For instance, suppose a little girl watches her mother make herself a bowl of cereal: The mother takes a bowl out of the cabinet, pours in the cereal, and then adds milk and sugar. The next day, when the mother is not in the kitchen, the girl may decide to make herself a bowl of cereal, and she may do so successfully. Here we have an example of imitation, of learning by observation, but notice that if the girl had never performed this sequence of behaviors before, she obviously could not have been reinforced for these behaviors. This example therefore illustrates a case of learning without prior practice of the response, and without prior reinforcement. Just as the principle of reinforcement cannot explain why a rat makes its first lever press (before receiving any reinforcers for that behavior), it cannot explain the first occurrence of any response learned by observation.

Actually, the last sentence is not quite correct, so let us quickly qualify it. Although the principle of reinforcement *by itself* cannot account for the first occurrence of any response, it can account for some instances of novel behavior if we now include the concept of generalization. That is, some novel responses may be nothing more than variations of similar responses that have been reinforced in the past. Chapter 6 showed that reinforcing one response can serve to strengthen an entire class of similar responses. In Lashley's (1924) experiment, after rats had been reinforced for wading correctly through a water maze, they were able to swim through the same maze with deeper water without further training. We might say that the correct swimming responses were the result of generalization from previously learned wading responses. In a similar fashion, we could propose that the young girl had been previously reinforced for imitating the behavior of her parents, and so her imitation of the behaviors involved in making a bowl of cereal is nothing more than an example of generalization. This explanation seems plausible considering that most parents frequently reinforce their children for imitation. Imitating a parent's behavior of speaking a word or phrase, of solving a puzzle, of holding a spoon correctly, and the like, may be reinforced with smiles, hugs, and praise. It would not be surprising if this history of reinforcement led to the imitation of other behaviors.

This concept of generalized imitation has some experimental evidence to support it. For example, Baer, Peterson, and Sherman (1967) reinforced several profoundly retarded children for

imitating a variety of behaviors performed by the teacher (standing up, nodding yes, opening a door). After establishing imitative responses (which required several sessions), the teacher occasionally performed various new behaviors, and the children would also imitate these behaviors although they were never reinforced for doing so. Other studies have demonstrated a similar generalization of imitative behavior (Martin, 1971; Weisberg, Stout, & Hendler, 1986).

Bandura's Theory of Imitation

Bandura has maintained that the theory of generalized imitation, like the other theories of imitation, is inadequate. His reasons can be nicely illustrated by considering a famous experiment on the imitation of aggressive behaviors by four-year-old children (Bandura, 1965). The children participated in the experiment individually. Each child first watched a short film (projected onto a TV screen) in which an adult performed four distinctive aggressive behaviors against a large Bobo doll. Each behavior was accompanied by a specific verbalization. The behaviors were:

1. Sitting on the doll and punching it in the face, while saying, "Pow, right in the nose, boom, boom."
2. Hitting the doll's head with a mallet, while saying, "Sockeroo, stay down."
3. Kicking the doll, while saying, "Fly away."
4. Throwing rubber balls at the doll, while saying, "Bang."

Some of the children subsequently saw the aggressor being reinforced by another adult: He was given soda, candies, and other snacks and was called a "strong champion." Other children saw the model being punished for his aggressive behavior: The model was scolded for "picking on that clown," was spanked by another adult, and was warned not to act that way again. For children in a third group, the film contained no consequences for the model's aggressive behavior.

Immediately after viewing the film, a child was brought into a room that contained a Bobo doll and many other toys. The child was encouraged to play with the toys and was left alone in the room, but was observed through a one-way mirror. Many instances of aggressive behaviors against the Bobo doll were recorded, and most of these resembled those of the adult model in the film (see Figure 12-1). In many cases, the children's utterances were similar to those made by the model. Boys exhibited significantly more aggression than girls.

So far, these results do not contradict the theory of generalized imitation, but Bandura claimed that two additional findings cannot be explained by this theory. First, the consequences to the model made a difference—children who saw the model being punished exhibited less imitation than children in the other two groups. According to Bandura, the theory of generalized imitation states that children (or adults) imitate others *because imitation has been reinforced* in the past, but it says nothing about how reinforcement or punishment *of the model* should affect the learner. Second, in the final phase of Bandura's study, the experimenter offered to re-

ward the child if he or she would imitate the behavior of the model in the film. With this incentive, children in all three groups produced large and equal amounts of aggressive behavior. Bandura concluded that reinforcement is not necessary for the *learning* of new behaviors through observation, but that the expectancy of reinforcement is essential for the *performance* of these new behaviors. Bandura claimed that the theory of generalized imitation makes no provisions for distinguishing between the learning and the performance of imitative behaviors.

Before trying to decide whether Bandura's criticisms of the generalized imitation theory are justified, let us examine the theory he proposes as an alternative. Bandura's (1969; 1986) theory can definitely be called a cognitive theory, for it proposes several processes that can never be observed in an individual's behavior. It states that there are four factors that determine whether imitative behavior will occur:

1. *Attentional Processes.* The learner must pay

FIGURE 12-1.   The top row shows frames from a film in which an adult model exhibits a number of different aggressive behaviors toward a Bobo doll. The two bottom rows show children imitating the model after having watched the film. (From Bandura, Ross, & Ross, 1963)

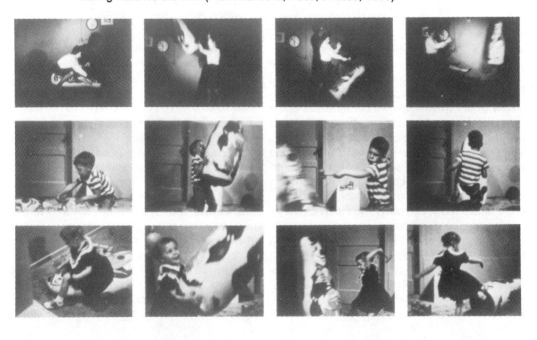

attention to the appropriate features of the model's behavior if imitation is to occur. A young girl may watch her mother make a bowl of cereal, but if she did not pay attention to where the sugar came from and how much to put in, she may be quite unsuccessful in her attempt at imitation.

2. *Retentional Processes*. It is obvious that an individual must retain some of the information that is gained through observation if imitation is to occur at a later time. Bandura states that rehearsal can be important here. Thus the little girl may say to herself, "First the cereal, then the milk, then the sugar." Notice that this information is stated in a fairly abstract way, and Bandura assumes that some abstraction of this type is indeed all that is remembered. Thus the child may not remember exactly where in the refrigerator the milk was, or exactly where on the table her mother placed the bowl, but such specific information is not usually necessary for successful imitation.

3. *Motor Reproductive Processes*. Bandura's assumptions about what is retained in memory after a period of observational learning are consistent with studies demonstrating that a similar sort of "abstract" learning takes place during operant conditioning. In Chapter 6, we saw that reinforcement does more than strengthen a particular set of muscle movements—it strengthens an entire class of responses that have a similar effect (such as depressing a lever, bringing the subject closer to the goal box). Whereas it seems likely that a similar class of responses can be learned through observation, it is nevertheless true that *some* specific muscular responses must occur during the course of an imitative response. In other words, the individual must be able to translate some general knowledge ("Put a bowl on the table", "Pour in some cereal") into a coordinated pattern of muscle movements. In the examples of children making cereal or hitting a Bobo doll, this translation of knowledge into action poses no problem, because the children already possessed the required motor skills (handling objects, pouring, kicking, punching, and so on). In other cases of observational learning, however, the motor reproductive processes must not be taken for granted. For example, a

model may demonstrate slowly and in a step-by-step manner the sequence of movements involved in juggling three balls, and the learner may retain this information in an abstract form (that is, he or she may be able to recite the necessary sequences), but may still be unable to produce the appropriate movements without extensive practice. Similarly, imitating such behaviors as doing a cartwheel, landing an airplane, or smoothly plastering a wall may be impossible because the observer lacks the necessary motor skills. Chapter 13 will have more to say about how these skills are learned.

4. *Incentive and Motivational Processes*. According to Bandura, the first three processes are all that are necessary for an individual to acquire the *capability* to perform some new behavior, but this capability will not be reflected in the learner's behavior without the appropriate incentive. Bandura states that the individual must have an expectation that the performance of this new behavior will produce some type of reinforcement. Bandura's (1965) study on aggressive behavior provided a clear example of the role of incentive. Children who saw the adult model being punished for his aggressive play with the Bobo doll presumably developed the expectation that such behavior would lead to unpleasant consequences, so they exhibited less imitation than the other groups of children. When the experimenter changed their expectations by offering reinforcement if the children imitated the model, these children exhibited just as much imitation as the other two groups. These results should not seem surprising, because they are similar to those of the Tolman and Honzik (1930) latent learning experiment (Chapter 8), in which rats displayed their ability to travel through a maze without errors only after food became available in the goal box.

Evaluation of the Theories of Imitation

As we have seen, Bandura has claimed that two problems with the theory of generalized imitation are (1) that it does not explain why observers will imitate a reinforced model more readily than a punished model, and (2) that it does not distinguish between the learning and performance of an imitative behavior. In my opinion, both of these criticisms are weak. It is true that in its simplest form the theory of generalized imitation states only that new imitative responses occur because similar imitative responses have been reinforced in the past. But this theory certainly needs more details before it can make any specific predictions. Neither children nor adults nor animals, all of whom may have been reinforced for imitating others in the past, will subsequently imitate any behavior of any organism they see. When will the observer imitate the model, and when not? Based on what we know about generalization, it seems reasonable to make the following, more specific prediction: Imitation will be most likely when the current situation is similar to situations in which the observer has been reinforced for imitation in the past. Conversely, imitation will be least likely when the current situation is similar to situations in which the observer has been punished in the past.

Let us try to apply these two principles to the results of Bandura's (1965) experiment. Why did children frequently fail to imitate the adult model who was punished? A plausible answer from the theory of generalized imitation is that children have been punished for imitation in similar situations in the past. For instance, a boy might watch his older sister take some ice cream out of the refrigerator without permission, and get punished for doing so. Later, the boy might try the same behavior, and get the same result. After a number of such learning experiences, it would not be surprising if the boy learned to avoid imitation after seeing the model get punished. Similarly, the boy might learn that he is frequently reinforced for imitation when the model is also reinforced. For example, his sister cleans up her room and is rewarded by her parents; the boy cleans up his room and is similarly rewarded.

In short, the theory of generalized imitation can easily explain why children imitate models that are reinforced but not models that are punished. What makes Bandura's theory different (and what gives his theory its cognitive tone) is its speculation about the abstract propositions an individual supposedly forms as a result of a learning experience. Thus Bandura might suggest that the children in his 1965 experiment had learned the general rules "If you imitate someone who is rewarded, you are also likely to be rewarded" and "If you imitate someone who is punished, you are also likely to be punished." Having already developed these expectations, the children in the different groups behaved appropriately. On the other hand, a behaviorist might say that the children had learned a complex set of contingencies concerning imitation and were simply generalizing to a new situation. The behaviorist might go so far as to say that the children were *acting as if* they were following the general rules just quoted, but that since we cannot actually see how information is retained in their memories there is no point in speculating about this.

The fact that children in all groups exhibited large amounts of imitation when offered rewards poses no real problem for a behavioral analysis either. At least since the Tolman and Honzik (1930) experiment, behaviorists have recognized the distinction between learning and performance, and some have concluded that reinforcement is not essential for learning but it is essential for the performance of learned behaviors. Although the children were not actually reinforced until after they had displayed their imitative responses, this is another instance in which generalization from past experiences may have been at work. The children may have learned that when a responsible adult promises you a reward for certain behaviors, she frequently keeps her promise. Bandura would say the children had an "expectation of reinforcement"; behaviorists would say that the children were generalizing from similar experiences in the past. Thus Bandura's claim that the theory of generalized imitation cannot explain his results is incorrect. Both theories can account for the results, but they do so in slightly different ways. As in other debates between the cognitive and behavioral approaches, the debate over explanations of imitative behavior is partly about semantics, and partly about how much we should speculate about processes that we cannot observe directly.

FACTORS THAT AFFECT
THE LIKELIHOOD OF IMITATION

A good deal of Bandura's early work examined different factors that make it more or less likely that an observer will imitate a model. We have already seen two important and obvious factors: the consequences to the model, and the consequences to the learner. Children are more prone to imitate a model whose behaviors are reinforced, and they are more likely to imitate a model when the children themselves have been reinforced for imitation. Some of the many other factors known to affect imitation are discussed next.

Characteristics of the Model

As Mischel (1971) has noted, young children generally have more contact with their parents than with anyone else, but they are also exposed to a wide range of other potential models, including siblings, classmates, teachers, grandparents, television personalities, cartoon characters, and sports stars. It is obvious that children do not imitate everyone to an equal degree. What characteristics of these potential models make a difference?

Mischel (1971) has summarized some of the most extensively studied factors. Many theorists have suggested that a model's "rewardingness" plays an important role in imitation (Mowrer, 1960). To be more specific, the idea was that children receive many reinforcers from their parents, and this is why they tend to imitate their parents. Bandura and Huston (1961) tested this idea in an experimental setting. Nursery-school children had individual meetings with a woman who acted either in a "nurturant" manner (for some children) or a "nonnurturant" manner (for other children). In the nurturant condition, the woman was affectionate and attentive to the child, but in the nonnurturant condition she was aloof. Several days later, each child was asked to participate in a game with the same woman, and during the game the woman made a number of distinctive gestures and verbalizations. Bandura and Huston found that children in the nurturant condition imitated the women's behaviors significantly more often. Subsequent research has substantiated Bandura and Huston's conclusions that models who are more affectionate or more rewarding in other ways are more frequently imitated (Zimmerman & Koussa, 1979).

Besides delivering many reinforcers to their children, parents also exert a good deal of control over them: In many matters, parents determine what a child may or may not do. It has been suggested that children tend to imitate their parents because they are powerful figures in their lives, and Mischel and Grusec (1966) put this idea to a test. Some nursery-school children met a woman who was introduced as their "new teacher," and this woman emphasized the fact that they would be seeing a lot of her in the future. In another condition, different children were introduced to the same woman as a "visiting teacher from out of town" whom they would not see again. In both cases, the woman played a game with the children, and later the children were observed at play when the woman was absent. Those children who were told that the woman was their new teacher (and would therefore have considerable control over them) imitated the woman's behaviors and mannerisms considerably more.

The concept of control or power is closely related to the concept of dominance within a social group. Abramovitch and Grusec (1978) found a high correlation between the teacher's ranking of a child's dominance and the number of times that child was imitated by other children in a free play situation. The social status of the model is another important factor. In one study, ten- to fourteen-year-old girls were more imitative of a young woman when she was introduced as a college cheerleader (a high-status position for these girls) than when she was introduced as an ordinary college student (McCullagh, 1986).

Besides rewardingness and dominance, another important variable is the model's similarity to the learner. For instance, it has been shown that a child is more likely to imitate a model who is the same sex, the same age, or who seems to have similar interests (Burnstein, Strotland, and Zander, 1961; Davidson and Smith, 1982). Yet another variable is the model's sincerity—in one study, children imitated a model who appeared sincere more than one who appeared insincere (Klass, 1979).

This brief review of characteristics of the model that influence imitation is by no means exhaustive, but it is easy to see how these variables can be explained by both Bandura's theory and by the generalized imitation theory. For instance, if a child has dealt with a dominant parent or peer, the child may have learned that this dominant individual will reinforce imitation (or punish nonimitation). It is also plausible to assume that in the past the child may have been reinforced for imitating children of the same sex or the same age, but punished for imitating some behaviors of individuals of the opposite sex or of very different ages. Finally, a child may have learned that it is unwise to imitate people who appear insincere. According to the generalized imitation theory, each of these variables reflects the effects of a child's past experiences; according to Bandura's theory, they reflect the child's expectations of future reinforcement.

Characteristics of the Learner

Beginning with Bandura's early work, there have been numerous attempts to discover individual differences that are correlated with a person's tendency to imitate others. Many of the variables discovered seem to be specific to certain situations, and while some are fairly obvious, others are not. Bandura (1965) found a strong tendency for boys to imitate aggressive behaviors more than girls. In their study of peer imitation during unstructured play periods, Abramovitch and Grusec (1978) found more imitation by younger children (four-year-olds) than by older children (nine-year-olds). More surprisingly, they found that dominant children (who were themselves more frequently imitated) also tended to engage in more imitative behavior.

Although many of these characteristics associated with imitation may be situation-specific, one general and intuitively reasonable statement that can be made is that individuals who are uncertain of their own behaviors are more likely to imitate the behaviors of others (Thelen, Dollinger, & Kirkland, 1979). Beginning with the work of

Kanareff and Lanzetta (1960), numerous studies have shown that people who are unconfident of their own abilities are more prone to imitation. Many studies experimentally manipulated subjects' levels of confidence by giving them initial tasks on which they either failed or succeeded (Roberts, Boone, & Wurtele, 1982; Turner & Forehand, 1976; Turnure & Zigler, 1964). For example, in the study of Roberts et al. (1982), elementary school children were first given either positive or negative feedback on a commodity-selection task, and those given negative feedback exhibited more imitation of a videotaped model on a subsequent task. Abelson and Lesser (1959) found that children who were judged to be low in self-esteem were also more prone to imitation. In a related experiment, Jakubczak and Walters (1959) found that children who exhibited independence on a separate task (that is, children who did not accept help although they were having difficulty) were less likely to imitate a model than highly dependent children (who accepted help even when they did not need it).

Characteristics of the Situation

If it is true that people are more likely to imitate when they are uncertain about the correct behavior, it follows that some situations by their very nature will elicit more uncertainty and therefore more imitation. For example, in the study of Jakubczak and Walters just mentioned, the task was a very ambiguous one—to estimate how much a pinpoint of light moved in a completely dark room. Actually, the light was always stationary, but because of the subject's random eye movements the light appeared to move. Considering the ambiguity of this situation, it is not surprising that subjects imitated a model. Thelen, Paul, and Dollinger (1978) tried to control the degree of task uncertainty by presenting preadolescent subjects with tasks that had 2 possible options (low uncertainty condition) or 10 possible options (high uncertainty condition). They found more imitation of a model by children in the high uncertainty condition.

The difficulty of a task has an effect on imitation even in fairly young children. Harnick

(1978) had toddlers (ages 14 to 28 months) attempt three tasks of varying difficulty with the aid of an adult female as a model. Harnick found the most imitation with tasks of intermediate difficulty. If a task was very easy for the toddlers, they did not bother to imitate the model; if it was too difficult, they did not attempt to perform it even with the aid of the model. The youngsters' strategy is adaptive, because one is likely to learn the most through observation and imitation when the task is neither so easy that one has nothing to learn by watching nor so difficult that watching a model will not help.

Another situational factor that might be important is the manner in which the model is presented. In one study by Bandura (1962), children in one group watched a live model perform aggressive behaviors, children in a second group watched a film of the model, and children in a third group watched a cartoon character who exhibited the same behaviors. Although we might expect the mode of presentation to have a large effect, Bandura found no significant differences among these three groups, all of which showed much more aggressive behavior in a subsequent test than control subjects who observed no model at all. A very different study which also found no difference between a live model and a videotaped model was conducted by O'Dell, O'Quin, Alford, O'Briant, Bradlyn, and Giebenhain (1982). These researchers tried several different methods for training parents to use reinforcement procedures with their children. Different groups of parents received information via a live model, a videotaped model, a written manual, or an audiotape. Several days later, the parents were observed interacting with their children in their homes. All groups of parents learned something about the use of reinforcement techniques, but those in the audiotape group learned less than those in the other three groups, which were not significantly different. Of course, these two studies do not imply that a filmed model will always be as effective as a live model. But because they can be very effective in certain situations, behavior therapists frequently rely on filmed or videotaped models in attempting to teach new skills to their clients, as we will see at the end of this chapter.

INTERACTIONS BETWEEN OBSERVATIONAL LEARNING AND OPERANT CONDITIONING

In much of their book, Bandura and Walters (1963) surveyed research findings that showed how the behavior of parents affects a child's personality development. They presented research on such characteristics as dependency, aggressiveness, sexual preferences and behaviors, delinquency, and industriousness. They suggested that there are two main ways a parent can shape a child's personality—by the control of rewards and punishments, and by serving as a model whom the child can imitate. Bandura and Walters contended that in order to predict how upbringing will affect a child's personality, it is necessary to take both of these factors into account. They maintained that in some cases direct reinforcement and observational learning can work in concert, and in other cases they may work in opposite directions. We will briefly consider one case of each type.

Achievement Motivation

Bandura and Walters claimed that these two factors work together in shaping what we might call self-discipline and a high achievement motivation. These terms encompass such characteristics as an individual's willingness to work and make sacrifices so as to obtain long-term goals, to set high standards for oneself and attempt to achieve them, and to be independent and self-reliant. Bandura and Kupers (1964) conducted an experiment that illustrates how an adult model can influence a child's self-discipline in a situation that allowed the child to reinforce herself for good (or perhaps not so good) behavior. First, a child watched an adult play a bowling game in which the scores could range between 5 and 30. For children in one group, the adult would reward himself by taking a candy from a bowl for every score of 20 or better. For a second group, the adult was more lenient, rewarding himself for any score above 10. As in most studies of this type, the adult left the room before the child began to play the game, and the child was secretly observed. The children tended to use the same criteria for rewarding themselves as those they had observed the adult use. Children in a third group, who observed no model, tended to reward themselves no matter what score they obtained.

This study showed that children can learn to apply either strict or lenient standards of self-discipline by observing a model, and Bandura and Walters speculate that numerous learning experiences of a similar type must occur as children observe their parents' behaviors over a period of many years. Of course, besides serving as models, parents may directly reinforce either strict or lenient standards of achievement and self-discipline in their children. A study by Rosen and D'Andrade (1959) is instructive. These researchers measured the achievement orientation of nine- to eleven-year-old boys by administering a type of questionnaire, and then they observed the boys perform on several tasks in the presence of their parents. For example, in one task, a boy was blindfolded and asked to build a tower by stacking as many blocks as he could. As partial validation of the questionnaire results, Rosen and D'Andrade found that boys with a higher achievement-motivation score built higher towers. There were several significant correlations between a boy's level of achievement motivation and his parents' behaviors. The first related to the parents' level of aspiration for their son. They were told that an average boy of their son's age could build a tower of eight blocks, and were then asked to guess how many blocks their son would use. Parents of the boys with higher achievement motivation made higher estimates. Second, there were differences in the way the parents of high-achievement boys acted during the tasks. They appeared to be more concerned with their son's performance, and gave more encouragement as the boy worked on the tasks. When the boy did well, they responded with more approval and affection, and they showed more irritation and disapproval if the boy did poorly (especially the mother). In short, the parents of boys with high achievement motivation made more use of reinforcers and punishers to encourage high standards of performance in their sons.

The combined influences of reinforcement and modeling on achievement motivation may operate not only within families but across entire societies. McClelland (1961) noted that folktales and stories in children's readers from some societies emphasize the achievement of excellence, whereas those from other societies do not. In an ingenious and extensive piece of research, McClelland had readers score the stories of different countries (which were disguised so that the country could not be identified) for achievement-related themes. These stories had all been published during the 1920s. He also developed measures of economic growth in these countries that were based on increases in per capita income and per capita electrical use between the years of 1925 and 1950. McClelland found a significant correlation between the average level of achievement motivation depicted in a country's children's stories and its rate of economic growth over the next 25 years.

Of course, there is nothing in McClelland's research that implies that either achievement motivation or economic growth is desirable. The rapid economic growth of industrialized countries over the past century or so has brought with it the problems of toxic waste, acid rain, nuclear weapons, and others. What the results do suggest, however, is that the values a society emphasizes via its stories, legends, and heroes can have a substantial influence on the level of achievement motivation (and probably other characteristics) in its next generation. It is interesting (and not particularly reassuring) to consider what values are being modeled for our present generation of children via the most prolific dispenser of stories, legends, and heroes yet invented—the television set.

Aggression

As is probably already apparent, a large portion of the work of Bandura and his associates has examined how aggressive behavior could be encouraged through the actions of a model. This research set the stage for the continuing debate over whether violence on television makes the people who watch it more violent. (For some differing views on this controversy, see Freedman, 1986; Friedrich-Cofer & Huston, 1986.) TV viewing may affect the attitudes of both children and adults. Gerbner and his colleagues (Gerbner, Gross, Eleey, Jackson-Beeck, Jeffreys-Fox, & Signorielli, 1977) found that heavy viewers (those who average over six hours of TV viewing a day) have different perceptions of the world than less frequent viewers. Based on their responses to questionnaires, it seems that heavy viewers see the world as a meaner place, inhabited by more violent and selfish people. They are also more likely to own a gun and to say that it is all right to hit people when you are angry at them.

Regardless of the relationship between television and violence, Bandura and Walters (1963) have shown that parents' behaviors can influence the aggressiveness of their children in conflicting and seemingly paradoxical ways. The apparent paradox is that parents who use the most severe punishment for aggressive behaviors tend to produce more aggressive children. This result has been obtained in many different studies (Sears, Maccoby, and Levin, 1957; Vienero & Lagerspetz, 1984). Glueck and Glueck (1950) found that the use of severe punishment was correlated with juvenile delinquency in young boys. On the surface, this seemed to suggest that punishment is ineffective as a deterrent for aggressive behaviors, a finding that conflicts with the ample evidence showing that punishment is an effective procedure for eliminating unwanted behaviors (see Chapter 7).

Bandura and Walters pointed out that this apparent paradox is resolved when we realize that parents who use physical punishment with their children are providing their children with models of aggressive behavior. They supported this theory by showing that children whose parents punished aggressive behaviors usually avoided aggressive behaviors when their parents were present, but they were aggressive in their interactions outside the home (Bandura & Walters, 1959). As Brown (1965) has put it, these children apparently learned a fairly sophisticated distinction by observing their parents: "Do not be aggressive to parents, since that is punished, but do be aggressive to those smaller or subordinate to yourself as your parents successfully do" (p. 388). This analysis is supported by findings

showing that when parents use threats and physical force to discipline their children, the children use these same techniques in dealing with peers (Hoffman, 1960). In addition, the children of parents who make use of force so severe it must be termed "child abuse" are more likely to resort to physical punishment and child abuse when they become parents (Lefkowitz, Huesman, & Eron, 1978; Silver, Dublin, & Lourie, 1969). All of these results are consistent with the view that when they discipline their children, parents are serving as models as well as controlling agents (see Eron, 1987).

These findings do not imply, however, that parents have no recourse when they observe aggressive behaviors in their children. Chapter 7 described several procedures for reducing unwanted behaviors that do not make use of physical punishment or other aversive stimuli, including differential reinforcement for incompatible behaviors, response cost, and time-out. Research has shown that such techniques can successfully reduce aggressive behaviors, and that parents of unusually aggressive children can be trained to use those techniques (Patterson, Chamberlain, & Reid, 1982; Patterson & Reid, 1973). The advantage of these techniques is that besides reducing unwanted behaviors, they provide the child with a model whose reaction is firm yet moderate and nonviolent when displeased with someone else's behavior.

WHAT CAN BE LEARNED THROUGH OBSERVATION?

It is the contention of social learning theorists like Bandura and Walters that an individual's characteristic ways of responding to different situations, which some call the individual's "personality," is developed to a large extent during childhood through the interacting influences of operant conditioning and observational learning. Since Bandura and Walters's influential book was published, there have been hundreds of studies attempting to demonstrate the effects of observational learning on a person's personality traits, probem-solving skills, aesthetic preferences, and so on. In many of these studies, the evidence consists of a correlation between some behavior or characteristic of a model (usually a parent) and some behavior of the learner (a child). However, there is an inherent weakness in results that consist of correlations between two measures, because as all psychologists know, correlation does not imply causation. That is, a correlation between two variables does not necessarily mean that the first variable is the cause of the second. As a concrete example, consider the findings that show a correlation between a parent's use of physical punishment and the child's aggressiveness. The usual interpretation of these data is that the first variable (physical punishment) is the cause of the second (aggressiveness in the punished individual). It is also possible, however, that the causation works in the opposite direction. Perhaps some children develop aggressive tendencies for reasons totally unrelated to the parent's disciplinary techniques, but when parents see this aggression they feel they must punish it severely. Thus it could be the case that a child's aggressive behavior is the cause, not the result, of a parent's use of physical punishment. Another possibility is that both variables, physical punishment and aggressiveness, are caused by some third factor, such as extreme poverty (the stresses of which might produce aggression in both parent and child).

So as to partially overcome the weaknesses of correlational evidence, psychologists can make use of a number of strategies. First, they can attempt to control for as many potential "third factors" as possible (for example, by comparing aggressive and nonaggressive children with approximately equal ages, income levels, school grades, numbers of siblings, and so on). A second strategy is to examine two events that occur at different times. This was done in McClelland's (1961) study of the correlation between achievement themes in children's stories and economic growth. It makes no sense to say that the higher rates of economic growth somehow caused the achievement themes to appear in a country's children's stories, because the economic growth took place after the stories were written. Of course, it is still possible that some other factors, such as parents' attitudes towards achievement, were the primary causes of an achievement orientation in their children, and that the stories of each country simply reflected the attitudes of parents.

A third strategy is to form a hypothesis on the basis of correlational evidence and then proceed to test it by conducting a controlled experiment. As we have already seen, some of the support for the social-learning analyses of achievement motivation and of aggressive behavior comes from correlational evidence and some comes from experiments in which different groups were exposed to different modeling episodes. For instance, Bandura's experiments on aggressive behavior certainly show that such behaviors can be acquired through observational learning. They make a stronger case for the idea that these behaviors can also be learned through observation outside the laboratory. A fourth strategy (and probably the strongest) for demonstrating that observational learning can affect a given personality characteristic or behavioral tendency is to give the individual some fairly brief exposure to a model in a controlled setting and show that this exposure has long-term effects on the individual's day-to-day behavior. This type of evidence is provided mainly by behavior therapists who use modeling in an effort to solve some behavioral problem for which the client seeks help.

Keeping in mind the relative strengths and weaknesses of the different types of evidence, let us examine a few areas in which the effects of observation and imitation have been investigated.

Phobias

Rachman (1977) has summarized several pieces of evidence that suggest that phobias can be acquired vicariously, most of which demonstrate that members of the same family frequently have similar fears. Several studies have found high correlations between the fears of a mother and her children, or among the children of one family (May, 1950). During World War II, Lewis (1942) investigated what long-term psychological effects might result from the repeated bombings and air raids that occurred in various parts of England. Overall, he found that the incidence of phobias or anxiety attacks after such traumatic events was surprisingly low, but about 4 percent of the schoolchildren in Bristol exhibited some sort of anxiety reaction. Lewis reported that for some children, the problem resulted from traumatic personal experience during an air raid, but in other cases children seemed to be reacting to the excessive fears exhibited by their mothers. Along these same lines, Grinker and Spiegel (1945) reported a number of case studies of fighter pilots who developed phobias after observing a crewmate's fear reaction during or after a mission. As can be seen, the evidence for the vicarious acquisition of phobias is based on correlational evidence and case studies, and this is not the strongest type of evidence. However, several experiments with animals have obtained more convincing evidence. For example, Mineka, Davidson, Cook, and Kerr (1984) reported that monkeys rapidly developed a long-lasting fear of snakes through observing another monkey's fearful reactions to a snake. Thus in this case, the evidence for observational learning is stronger for animals than for people.

Addictions

Many types of evidence suggest that Bandura's social-learning theory can help to account for the acquisition of various addictive behaviors, including smoking, alcoholism, and drug abuse. Notice that simple principles of reinforcement and punishment are in themselves sufficient to explain why an addiction is maintained once it has been established. As described in Chapter 3 during the discussion of the Solomon and Corbit theory, cessation of smoking or drug use after an addiction has been established frequently causes aversive withdrawal symptoms that can be escaped (all too conveniently) by further intake of the addictive substance. On the other hand, observational learning and social reinforcement can help to explain why such addictions are developed in the first place. For example, consider the fact that smoking one's first cigarette is usually an aversive event, involving harsh and burning sensations. Why then does a person ever smoke again? One answer is based on observational learning: Even when very young, many children are exposed to parents, older siblings, television

personalities, and others who smoke. The consequences of this behavior may appear to be positive: Some people say they started smoking because smokers seemed to be more mature, sophisticated, or attractive. Perhaps these advantages outweigh a little burning in the throat for the beginning smoker. In addition, among teenagers, peers often deliver strong social reinforcers for smoking: They may encourage nonsmokers to begin and ridicule those who do not. These joint factors of observational learning and social reinforcement are frequently cited as major contributors to the onset of smoking (Kozlowski, 1979; Leventhal & Cleary, 1980), since it has repeatedly been found that the tendency to smoke is correlated with the smoking habits of one's parents, spouse, and peers.

The principles of social-learning theory also appear to be important in the development of alcoholism and drug abuse. For instance, it has been found that about 20 percent of all heroin addicts have one or more family members who are also addicted (Hekimian & Gershon, 1968). In a study of the family backgrounds of alcoholics, O'Leary, O'Leary, and Donovan (1976) found an interesting pattern. There was a tendency for the parents of alcoholics to fall into one of two classes: They were often either heavy drinkers themselves or rigid abstainers. O'Leary et al. suggested that in both cases, the parents failed to provide their children with a model of moderate drinking. If a parent is a heavy drinker, the child may imitate this behavior. If a parent is strictly abstinent, the child might also imitate this behavior, but suppose that at some point the child decides to begin drinking. The parents have not demonstrated the habits that prevent most social drinkers from becoming alcoholics (such as drinking only on special occasions, never drinking before work, stopping after one or two drinks). Unless the new drinker has learned these guidelines elsewhere, he or she may inadvertently progress into a pattern of heavy drinking.

Cognitive Development

Many developmental psychologists, such as Jean Piaget (1926, 1929) have suggested that as children grow, they pass through a number of stages of cognitive ability, and that the passage from one stage to the next depends heavily on growth, maturation, and personal experience. In contrast, social-learning theorists such as Rosenthal and Zimmerman (1972, 1978) claim that observational learning plays a major role in the development and refinement of cognitive skills. As a representative test of cognitive development, let us consider the well-known *conservation task*. In one version of this task, a child is shown three clear cylindrical beakers, as illustrated in Figure 12-2. Beakers A and B are identical, and they have the same amount of water in them. The test begins by asking the child which has more water, and the child usually says that A and B have the same amount. Then, as the child watches, the contents of B are poured into beaker C, a taller and thinner beaker. The child is then asked whether A or C has more water. Children are said to have mastered the concept of conservation of volume if they say that A and C have the same amount of water. However, children who are younger than about age seven usually say there is more water in C. They are apparently misled by the higher water level in C. These children are called *nonconservers* because they have not yet learned that liquids retain a constant volume regardless of the shape of the container they are in.

Rosenthal and Zimmerman have tried to demonstrate that a child's mastery of the conservation task depends on more than simply maturation and personal experience. They maintain that observational learning is a major determinant of a child's ability to perform well on the conservation task and others like it. To demonstrate the potential of observational learning, they had children who were nonconservers observe a model (an adult female) perform correctly on the conservation task. In one group, the model gave an explanation for her answer that A and C had the same amount of water (for instance, "Because they were the same in the first place"), and in another group she gave no explanation. In a subsequent test, children in both groups showed improved performance on conservation tasks, and those who heard the model explain her choices improved the most. In one of the Rosenthal and Zimmerman studies, the children were only four to five years old, well below the age at which children typically master the conservation task.

In a critique of this and other studies that involve "training" on the conservation task, Kuhn (1974) argued that the children may have simply changed their answers, not their understanding of the situation. However, several lines of evidence suggest that this criticism is unjustified. For one thing, Rosenthal and Zimmerman found that the children's improved performances generalized to other types of conservation tasks on which the model had not worked (for example, a conserva-

A and B begin with equal amounts of water:

B is poured into C:

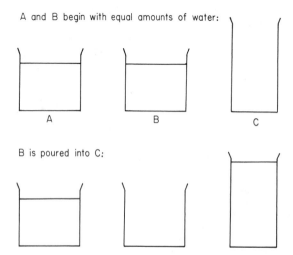

FIGURE 12-2. The steps of a test for conservation of volume. After seeing the contents of B poured into C, the child is asked which container, A or C, has more water.

tion-of-number task, which involves an understanding that the number of objects in a row does not change if the row is made longer by spacing the objects further apart). Furthermore, this improved performance is maintained in follow-up tests given several months later (Charbonneau, Robert, Bourassa, & Gladu-Bisonnette, 1976). Given such results, it becomes difficult to maintain that there is a difference between what these children say and what they understand about the conservation tasks. Murray (1983) has summarized the evidence as follows: "There is really no longer any question that nonconservers can be trained to give conservation judgments which meet the most stringent tests of authenticity" (p. 58). In addition, there is considerable evidence that many other cognitive skills besides conservation can be improved through observational learning. Numerous studies have shown that children can learn grammatical rules, abstract concepts, and problem-solving skills by observing a model (Rivera & Smith, 1987; Zimmerman & Blom, 1983).

Moral Judgments and Moral Behavior

Bandura has proposed that a child's judgments about what behaviors are good and what ones are bad are largely learned by observation. Thus a child whose parents are impeccably honest in all financial matters may learn to behave the same way. A child who sees and hears his parents cheat on their taxes, steal from their employers, and ignore their bills wherever possible may decide that these are acceptable or even desirable activities. To demonstrate that a child's moral judgments can be influenced by the behavior of a model, Bandura and McDonald (1963) conducted the following experiment, which employed a moral reasoning task developed by Piaget (1932). Children were asked to judge which of two behaviors was "naughtier" in a series of hypothetical stories, both before and after observing an adult model make similar judgments. In each pair of stories, one protagonist caused a greater amount of damage than the other, but this protagonist had better intentions. For example, in one story a child responded to his mother's call to come to dinner, opened the

door, knocked down a chair behind the door and broke many coffee cups that had been resting on the chair. This child unwittingly caused a good deal of damage while being obedient to his mother. In a second story, a child was climbing on a chair to reach a cookie jar when his mother was out, and he accidentally broke one cup. This child caused less damage, but he did so while engaging in mischievous behavior. It is known that younger children tend to judge the "naughtiness" of an act in terms of the amount of damage done, whereas older children consider the person's intentions in making such a judgment. After making some initial judgments, each child observed the adult model come to the opposite conclusion (regardless of which type of decision the child had reached). Bandura and McDonald found that the children's judgments could be shifted in either direction by having them observe the model. Since their final judgments were made about new stories, it is clear that they had learned a general rule about moral judgments, not simply specific instances. Other studies (Dorr and Fey, 1974) found that such changes in moral judgment were maintained after several weeks.

It is important to distinguish between moral judgments and moral behavior, for people certainly do not always choose to perform the behavior that they judge to be the morally correct one. Several studies have shown that the behavior of a model can influence the behavior of observers in situations where morally laudable or deplorable behaviors are involved. For instance, it has been found that children are more altruistic after observing an altruistic model (Israely & Guttman, 1983), and that both children and adults are more likely to break rules or laws after observing a model do so (Lefkowitz, Blake, & Mouton, 1955; Walters, Leat, & Mezei, 1963).

Research by Phillips (1982) provides a striking example of how observing a model can increase a person's likelihood of performing an action that many consider to be both gravely immoral and irrational. Using statistics from the year 1977, Phillips found a significant increase in the number of suicides, motor vehicle deaths, and serious motor vehicle injuries in the several days that followed the suicide of a character in a nationally broadcast soap opera. For each instance of a soap opera suicide, Phillips used the preceding week as a baseline period, and he was careful to correct his data for seasonal fluctuations, to exclude data from holiday periods, and so on. Phillips's explanation of his results is that soap operas are widely watched, that many viewers identify themselves with the characters, and that the suicide of a character leads some (admittedly few) viewers to attempt to imitate this behavior. He interprets the increased motor vehicle accidents as disguised suicides or attempted suicides. The largest increases in suicides and motor vehicle accidents occurred among females living in urban environments, who were also the heaviest viewers of soap operas. Similar increases in teenage suicides and suicide attempts have been found in the days that follow TV movies or news stories about suicide (Gould & Shaffer, 1986; Phillips & Carstensen, 1986). This research supports the position that there is virtually no limit to the variety and importance of behaviors that can be influenced through observational learning. It also raises some serious policy issues for the producers of television dramas.

MODELING IN BEHAVIOR THERAPY

Largely because of Bandura's influential work, modeling has assumed its place as one of the major tools available to the behavior therapist. Bandura and Walters suggested that a model can influence an observer's behavior in three main ways, and each of these is utilized by behavior therapists. First, a model's behavior can facilitate responses the observer already knows how to perform. This category is similar to Thorpe's (1963) concept of social facilitation, mentioned earlier. Second, an observer may learn how to produce totally new behaviors (as in Thorpe's local enhancement and true imitation). Finally, undesired responses, such as fear reactions to harmless objects or situations (phobias) can be reduced or eliminated through observational learning. Although the boundaries among these categories are not always distinct, the three categories provide a convenient way to organize the large and growing literature on the therapeutic applications of modeling.

Facilitation of Low-Probability Behaviors

O'Connor (1969) used filmed models in an attempt to increase the sociability of nursery school children who were characterized as being socially withdrawn. In a classroom setting, the children would keep to themselves and only rarely interact with other children or adults. Children in the experimental group saw a 23-minute film depicting a child of similar age engaging in a series of social interactions. The film began with relatively calm activities, such as two children sharing a book or toy while seated at a table. It progressed through more involved and energetic social interactions, eventually ending with a scene in which six children were shown throwing toys around the room with obvious enjoyment. This method of progressing from simple to more demanding behaviors is called *graduated modeling*, and it is a frequent component in many modeling programs. Of course, every scene depicted a situation in which the model experienced favorable consequences during the social interaction. Children in a control group saw a film of equal length about dolphins at Marineland that contained no human characters. Immediately after viewing one of the films, the children returned to their classrooms, where observers recorded their behaviors. There was a five-fold increase in the number of social interactions for children in the experimental group, and no increase in the control group. Similar studies by Evers and Schwarz (1973) and Keller and Carlson (1974) found that children's increased social interactions were maintained after three or four weeks, which is an impressive result considering that the treatment took less than half an hour.

This example was classified as facilitation because these children did engage in some social interactions before the treatment began. Nevertheless, elements of the other two categories may have been involved. First, the children may have been deficient in certain skills used in initiating a social interaction, and they could have learned some of these skills from the film. Second, the film, with its consistently pleasant interactions, may have reduced the children's fears of social interactions. The next example of facilitation, in which the clients are adults, may also incorporate elements of skills acquisition and fear reduction.

In recent years, interest in a type of therapy known as *assertiveness training* has grown rapidly. Assertiveness training is designed for people who behave in an overly submissive manner in certain contexts or with certain people, and who wish to develop the ability to stand up for their rights. For example, some wives (or husbands) may do whatever their spouses decide is best regardless of what they think about a decision. Some young adults may be bullied by their parents into occupations or life-styles they do not really like. Some people have difficulty refusing unreasonable requests made by friends, employers, coworkers, relatives, or strangers. The goal of assertiveness training is to help people deal with these situations more effectively. It frequently consists of a combination of modeling, role playing, and behavioral rehearsal, in which the therapist describes a hypothetical situation, models an appropriate response, asks the client to imitate this response, and evaluates the client's performance. Many case studies and controlled experiments suggest that a few sessions of such assertiveness training can have long-term benefits (Edelstein & Eisler, 1976; Goldsmith & McFall, 1975; Wolpe & Lazarus, 1966). In one study, Kirkland and Caughlin-Carver (1982) found that mentally retarded adults who received 14 sessions of training showed significant improvement in their ability to refuse unreasonable requests politely, and these improvements were maintained in observations made 12 weeks after the end of training. Assertiveness training also seems to be an effective method for training juveniles and adults in correctional institutions, who need to learn how to be assertive without being aggressive (Beidleman, 1981).

Acquisition of New Behaviors

Perhaps the best therapeutic example of the training of totally new behaviors through modeling comes from the work of Lovaas (1967) and others who have taught autistic children to speak, as described in Chapter 6. This therapy makes use of a large number of behavioral techniques such as shaping, prompting, fading, and discrimination training, but the teacher's modeling of speech is indispensable at every stage of therapy. The teacher repeatedly models the desired words and the child is reinforced for successful imitation. To obtain an appreciation for the importance of modeling in this training, imagine how much more difficult it would be to train an autistic child to say "My name is Billy" if the teacher were required to remain completely quiet and rely only on reinforcers and the process of successive approximations. Even when training a simple response such as a lever press, shaping can be a time-consuming process; shaping language skills would be a virtual impossibility without the opportunity to model the appropriate speech patterns. Of course, many new behaviors besides speech can be taught through modeling, and Lovaas, Freitag, Nelson, and Whalen (1967) described how they used modeling (along with manual prompting) to teach autistic children such nonverbal behaviors as playing games, washing, brushing their hair, making their beds, and preparing snacks.

Elimination of Fears and Unwanted Behaviors

Chapter 4 described one fairly successful treatment for phobias, systematic desensitization. In Chapter 7, we examined an alternative treatment, flooding, which can be effective but which is less pleasant for the patient. Various modeling procedures comprise a third major treatment alternative. Modeling sometimes offers several advantages over systematic desensitization: It can be used with very young patients, who may not be able to follow the therapist's instructions during deep-muscle relaxation training. It can be a more rapid procedure and require less of the therapist's time, especially when films or videotapes are used. Because of the realistic nature of some modeling procedures (as described below), there may be better generalization to real-world situations.

Bandura and his colleagues conducted some of the earliest experiments assessing the therapeutic potential of modeling. Bandura, Grusec, and Menlove (1967) attempted to reduce excessive fears of dogs in young children. The children were divided into four groups. The first group received eight three-minute sessions of graduated modeling in which they observed a child of their age engage in more and more demanding interactions with a friendly dog. The child approached the dog, petted it, fed it biscuits, walked around with the dog on a leash, and finally climbed into the dog's pen and played with it. In this group, the modeling sequences took place in a party context (with party hats, balloons, cookies, and prizes) to reduce anxiety. A second group of children observed the same modeling sequences without the party context. A third group experienced the party context with the dog present but with no model (to control for exposure to the dog). A fourth group experienced the party context but without the dog and the model. All children then received two posttreatment behavioral tests in which they were asked to imitate the model, one immediately and a second a month later. Figure 12-3 shows the results. Both groups with the model were superior to the two groups without a model, and there was no significant difference between the party context and the neutral context. For the two groups that watched the model, these improvements remained essentially

unchanged a month later. Similar results were obtained when children watched a film of different children interacting with dogs (Bandura & Menlove, 1968). The term *symbolic modeling* has been used to refer to procedures that do not include a live model but rather a model on film or simply a verbal or written description of the model's behavior.

Modeling has also been used to eliminate phobias in adults. In a variation called *participant modeling,* the patient imitates the behavior of the model in each step of the treatment, and the patient's involvement with the object of the phobia becomes more demanding each time. For example, Bandura, Blanchard, and Ritter (1969) used this procedure with snake phobics. During the treatment, the therapist fearlessly handled a large king snake. The patient was first asked to touch the therapist's arm as he held the snake, then to touch his hand, then to touch the snake itself, and so on, until the patient took over the handling of the snake, and held the snake in his or her lap. Bandura et al. reasoned that participant modeling should be especially effective because of the realistic experience it gives the patient. In fact, they found that participant mod-

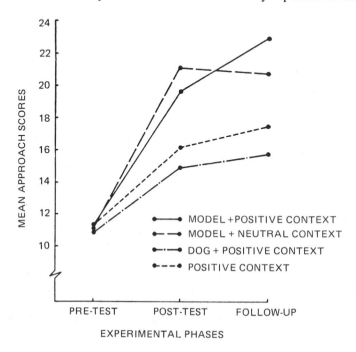

FIGURE 12-3. Results from the four groups in the Bandura, Grusec, and Menlove (1967) study on the use of modeling in the treatment of children's fears of dogs.

eling produced about twice the improvement of both a symbolic modeling treatment and a systematic desensitization treatment. Participant modeling has been successful when used to treat other types of phobias, such as fears of heights, needles, or dentists (Bernstein & Kleinknecht, 1982; Ferguson, Taylor, & Wermuth, 1978).

Although it has not been frequently employed for this purpose, modeling can also be used to eliminate responses other than fear reactions. One example comes from the work of Meichenbaum and Goodman (1971), who have attempted to improve the academic performance of first-grade children who might be described as "impulsive" or "hyperactive." These children often do poorly in school, partly because they tend to behave erratically or carelessly when working on a challenging task. The goal of Meichenbaum and Goodman was to reduce or eliminate such reckless and error-prone behaviors. They noted that hyperactive children exhibit less self-instruction than average children of their age. For instance, when painting a picture, a typical first grader might be heard to utter self-instructions such as "Don't spill the paint" or "I want to make a nice, straight line." Meichenbaum and Goodman observed that in hyperactive children, either such self-instructions are absent, or if present they are nevertheless followed by the wrong behavior. Their treatment therefore consisted of having a child watch an adult model who gave himself overt self-instructions while performing various tasks. The following self-instructions were used by a model during a simple task of copying a line drawing:

Okay, what is it I have to do? You want me to copy the picture with the different lines. I have to go slowly and carefully. Okay, draw the line down, down, good; then to the right, that's it; now down some more and to the left. Good, I'm doing fine so far. Remember, go slowly. Now back up again. No, I was supposed to go down. That's okay. Just erase the line carefully....Good. Even if I make an error I can go on slowly and carefully. I have to go down now. Finished. I did it! (Meichenbaum & Goodman, 1971, p. 117)

Later, the adult would give the child similar instructions as the child worked on the task, and eventually the child was trained to give himself such instructions as he worked. The modeling of self-instruction was also given for more complex tasks. After this training, Meichenbaum and Goodman found that these children showed significant improvements on a number of standardized tests, and this improvement was maintained in a one-month follow-up. As with most cases in which a behavior therapist wishes to eliminate one behavior pattern (careless performance in this case), the modeling treatment involved teaching an alternative behavior pattern (following one's self-instructions to work carefully) that is incompatible with the unwanted behavior.

CONCLUSIONS: THE SOPHISTICATED SKILL OF LEARNING BY OBSERVATION

The increasing popularity of modeling as a technique of behavior modification is a reflection of the power of this method of inducing change in behavior. Learning by observation is the most sophisticated type of learning we have considered in this book. Its relative advantages can be appreciated by reviewing the major categories of learning we have examined. We began with habituation, a form of learning so primitive it is found in one-celled organisms. It consists of nothing more than a decrease in the probability of a reflexive response after repeated presentations of the eliciting stimulus. Classical conditioning is considerably more complex, for it typically consists of the transfer of an old response to a new (conditioned) stimulus. Still, no new responses can be taught using classical conditioning, because the form of the response is determined by the learner, not the teacher. With operant conditioning, we finally have a mode of learning in which the teacher can select the response: Any arbitrary response the learner makes can be reinforced, and its probability should increase. And when the techniques of successive approximations and response chaining are added to the principle of reinforcement, the teacher can gradually build up complex behavior patterns that the learner would probably never produce on his or her own. In Chapter 6, it was stated that, in principle, any behavior a learner is capable of performing can be taught using the technique of successive approximations.

What is possible in principle is not always feasible in practice, however. Teaching a child how to speak, a college student how to write a computer program, or a figure skater how to do a triple jump would be next to impossible if the teacher's intervention were limited to the delivery of reinforcers for successive approximations to the desired goal. However, if the learner is capable of learning through observation, as people and many animals are, the task of teaching such complex behaviors becomes many times easier. The beauty of observational learning is that the learner can develop some understanding of the desired behavior well before he actually produces this behavior himself. To modify a cliché, it is probably not an exaggeration to say that one model is worth a thousand successive approximations.

Closely related to observational learning, though still more advanced, is the human ability to learn new behavior patterns through the spo-

ken or written word. Since most types of formal education rely heavily on these modes of learning, enormous amounts of research have been directed toward the goal of making them more effective. Treatment of this vast topic is well beyond the scope of this book, but the relationship between these types of learning and observational learning should be clear. We have seen that the behavior of even young children can be altered if they (1) watch a live model, (2) watch a filmed model, or (3) listen to a verbal account of the model's behavior. When they are a bit older, children can learn by reading about the behavior of a model and the consequences that followed. In each case the children are presumably learning about the contingencies of reinforcement—the stimulus-response-reinforcer relationships—that are found in their world. The advantage of education via observation or the spoken or written word is that the individual can learn about these relationships without having to experience them firsthand.

13
LEARNING MOTOR SKILLS

As discussed in the previous chapter, Bandura's (1969) theory states that motor reproductive processes are essential for successful imitative behavior. Unless a learner possesses or acquires the skills needed to mimic the actions of a model, imitation is impossible. It should be clear that motor skills are an essential ingredient for all other types of learned behaviors as well. Classical eyeblink conditioning will fail if a neurological deficit prevents a rabbit from blinking its eye. Reinforcement for correct turns in a water maze will be ineffective if the subject cannot swim. These points are obvious, but people often take for granted their abilities to perform complex sequences of movement. The bicyclist seldom marvels at her ability to remain upright on two thin wheels. The typist seldom wonders how he can coordinate ten fingers to produce five or more keystrokes a second, usually in the correct order. Likewise, in previous chapters we have generally taken for granted a subject's response-production

abilities. This chapter will examine these abilities in some detail.

Scientists have used a variety of strategies to study motor-skill learning, and we can group these strategies into three categories that parallel the three major approaches to the study of learning in general—the behavioral, cognitive, and physiological approaches. Much of the early research on motor-skill learning (beginning with the work of E. L. Thorndike and continuing through the first half of the twentieth century) had a behavioral character. Researchers were interested in discovering the relationships between various independent variables (such as the amount of practice, the distribution of practice) and dependent variables (speed of learning, quality of asymptotic performance). They had relatively little interest in speculating about what internal, unobserved processes were involved in the learning and performance of a new skill. There were also, however, physiologists who were interested in the neural mechanisms of movement. They tried to discover what brain, spinal-cord, and bodily structures were involved in movement. Lastly, with the rise of cognitive psychology in the second half of this century, many theorists have adopted the information-processing approach in analyzing motor skills. There has been much discussion of processes that are not directly observable, such as attention, short-term memory, sensory processing, and response sequencing mechanisms. All three approaches to motor-skill learning have produced many interesting findings, and this chapter will sample some from each category.

THE VARIETY OF MOTOR SKILLS

The skilled movements that people are capable of learning are indeed diverse. Consider the following examples of motor skills: balancing—on a bicycle, on a log, or on an icy sidewalk; shooting a foul shot in basketball; putting a golf ball; pressing a stopwatch as a runner crosses the finish line; slamming on the brakes of an automobile during an emergency; typing; playing the piano or some other musical instrument. Before reading further, pause for a moment and think about these different skills. What features do some of these movements have in common? Along what dimensions do they differ?

One obvious characteristic of a movement is its duration. Some motor skills are called *discrete* because they are completed shortly after they have begun (pressing a stopwatch, slamming on the brakes). Others are called *continuous* because they extend for an indefinitely long period of time (balancing). The terms *discrete* and *continuous* represent two ends of a continuum, and many behaviors fall between these two extremes. Another dimension that is closely related to a movement's duration deals with whether or not the individual receives feedback from the environment while the movement is in progress. Chapter 3 described the basic concepts of feedback theory, and it may be helpful to review that section now. Recall that behaviors such as the wood louse's humidity-seeking behavior are called *closed-loop* feedback systems because the organism continuously receives feedback from

the environment about whether its movements are bringing it closer to or further from its goal. Similarly, most (but not all) movements other than discrete movements can be called closed-loop movements because the individual continually receives and can react to feedback about whether the movement is proceeding correctly. Balancing on a log is a good example: If you feel yourself tipping to the right, you can immediately compensate by shifting your weight to the left. In contrast, many discrete movements (such as slamming on the brakes) occur so rapidly that a person has no time to react to any possible error. In the terminology of feedback theory, these are called *open-loop movements,* and they are characterized by the fact that once the movement begins, it is too late to make any corrections.

One further difference among motor skills is that some require exactly the same movement every time, whereas others demand that the movement be modified to suit the situation. Compare the skills of shooting a foul shot and putting a golf ball. The movements required in a foul shot are always the same, for the player always stands 15 feet from the basket, which is 10 feet above the floor. If one motion is successful on one foul shot, an exact replica of this movement will be successful on any future foul shot. On the other hand, the movements required to sink a putt can vary considerably from one putt to the next. The ball may be a different distance from the hole, at a different angle, and the slope of the green may be different. The golfer must take all of these factors into account and then produce a stroke that has the appropriate force and direction. Motor-skill researchers have studied both types of tasks—those that require accuracy on a single, repetitive movement, and those that demand the flexibility to adapt the movement to fit the occasion.

One additional dimension that distinguishes among different motor skills is whether they involve basically one motion (for example, pressing a stopwatch) or a sequence of distinct movements that must be carried out in the appropriate order (typing, playing the piano). We will examine the research on both single movements and sequences of movements, beginning with the former and concluding with the latter.

The motor skills mentioned so far all have practical utility in one real-world activity or another, but such everyday movements are not usually the ones that are studied in the laboratory. Instead, researchers frequently choose to study more artificial tasks, such as turning a knob 90 degrees in 150 milliseconds, or tracking a dot on a rotating turntable with a pointer. The reasons motor-skill researchers study these unusual tasks are similar to the reasons operant conditioners study simple responses in a barren Skinner box. First, these tasks are selected to be *representative* of a wide range of everyday movements—the knob turning task involves a discrete, open-loop movement, and the tracking task involves a continuous, closed-loop movement. Second, these tasks are selected to be as simple as possible, so that unnecessary complexities will not make the results difficult to interpret. Third, since it is unlikely that subjects will have encountered these tasks outside the laboratory, the researcher can witness the acquisition of a new motor skill. If a researcher chose to study a more familiar task such as steering a car, it could be difficult to sort out the contribution of innate ability, previous driving experience, and practice during the experiment itself.

VARIABLES AFFECTING MOTOR LEARNING AND PERFORMANCE

We will begin our survey of motor-skill research with what can be characterized as the behavioral approach. We will examine some factors that determine how quickly a motor skill is learned and how adroitly it is performed.

Reinforcement and Knowledge of Results

The Law of Effect and Motor Learning. E. L. Thorndike, who is best known for his experiments with the puzzle box (Chapter 6), also conducted some of the earliest research on human motor learning (Thorndike, 1927). In one experiment, subjects were blindfolded, and their goal was to draw a line exactly three inches long. Thorndike wanted to see how the accuracy of

two groups of subjects changed over trials. One group received reinforcement for each line whose length was within one-eighth of an inch of three inches, plus or minus: Immediately after a subject drew such a line, the experimenter said, "Right." If the line did not meet this criterion, the experimenter said, "Wrong." Subjects in the second group received no consequences for accurate or inaccurate lines. They received as many trials as the first group, but they had no way of knowing which lines were close to three inches and which were not.

Thorndike viewed this experiment as a test of two principles: the Law of Effect (with which we are already familiar) and the "Law of Practice." Although it is often said that "practice makes perfect," Thorndike found that practice without verbal reinforcement was completely ineffective: Subjects in the second group showed no improvement over trials. On the other hand, subjects in the reinforcement group showed a substantial increase in accuracy over trials. Thorndike's conclusion was that the Law of Effect is just as important in human motor learning as it was for his animals in the puzzle box. In both cases, reinforcement "stamps in" or strengthens the correct response, so this response is more likely to be repeated in the future.

What Can Be Better Than Reinforcement? In a frequently cited experiment, Trowbridge and Cason (1932) challenged Thorndike's conclusion that reinforcement is the crucial variable in the acquisition of a motor skill. They argued that although saying "Right" after a response might serve as a reinforcer in some circumstances, in Thorndike's experiment it was important because it gave the subject information or *feedback* about the accuracy of each response. In the literature on motor-skill learning, this type of feedback is usually called *knowledge of results* (often abbreviated *KR*). In short, Trowbridge and Cason proposed that the information provided by the words "Right" and "Wrong" was what produced the subjects' improved accuracy, not the reinforcing and punishing aspects of the words.

In Thorndike's experiment, the informational and reinforcing properties of the experimenter's words could not be separated, but Trowbridge and Cason devised an ingenious way to distinguish between these two variables. In their experiment, the task was the same as in Thorndike's —to draw a three-inch line while blindfolded. Two of their groups were the same as Thorndike's: The group that received practice only was called the *No KR* Group, and the group that was told "Right" or "Wrong" was called the *Qualitative KR* Group (because they received no quantitative feedback on the size of their errors). In addition, Trowbridge and Cason included a *Quantitative KR* Group, in which the subjects were told the direction and magnitude of each error, to the nearest eighth of an inch. For instance, if a line was seven-eighths inches longer than three inches, the experimenter would say "Plus seven." If a line was five-eighths inches shorter than three inches, the experimenter would say "Minus five." Trowbridge and Cason reasoned that the Quantitative KR Group received more information than the Qualitative KR Group, but not more reinforcement. Finally, a fourth group, the *Irrelevant KR* Group, received useless "feedback" after each trial—a meaningless nonsense syllable.

Each group received 100 trials, and the results are shown in Figure 13-1. Neither the No KR nor the Irrelevant KR Groups showed any improvement over trials. In the Qualitative KR Group, there was clear improvement: The size of the average error decreased from about one inch at the start of the experiment to about half an inch at the end. Figure 13-1 shows, however, that the performance of the Quantitative KR Group was vastly superior to that of the Qualitative KR Group. With Quantitative KR, the average error dropped to just over an eighth of an inch after about 40 trials and remained there for the rest of the experiment. From this pattern of results, we can conclude that information, not reinforcement, is the crucial variable in motor-skill learning, and the more detailed the information the better.

To be completely accurate, this last statement needs to be qualified a bit. You might expect that as quantitative KR becomes increasingly accurate, there will come a point where the person cannot make use of this additional accuracy. For instance, if the quantitative KR in the Trowbridge and Cason experiment were in thousandths of an inch instead of eighths of an inch (so that, for example, "Plus 576" meant the line was 3.576 inches long), performance might be no better than with feedback to the nearest hundredth or even eighth of an inch. A number of experiments with adults have indeed shown that there are limits beyond which additional accu-

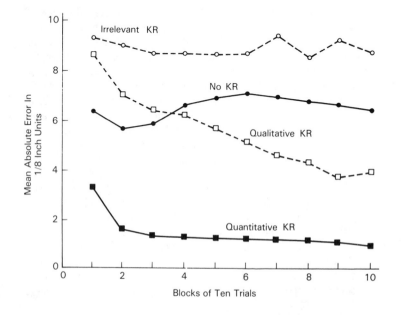

FIGURE 13-1. Results from the four groups of the Trowbridge and Cason (1932) experiment.

racy in quantitative KR does no good (Rogers, 1974). With young children, increasing the accuracy of quantitative KR can actually have detrimental effects on performance (Newell and Kennedy, 1978). The children evidently become confused when the KR becomes absurdly precise compared to the trial-to-trial variability in their movements.

It is often possible to give a subject many types of feedback besides information on how close the movement came to some goal. Consider, for example, the many useful pieces of information a coach might be able to give a pole-vaulter after each vault in practice. The coach might discuss various details related to the athlete's take-off, approach, pole placement, ascent, limb positions, and the like, and each piece of information might help to improve the athlete's future performances. The delivery of such information about the sequence of components of a complex movement is called *kinematic KR* (Adams, 1987). Hatze (1976) provided one illustration of the usefulness of detailed feedback during the acquisition of a motor skill in a laboratory setting. The subject's task was to stand in front of a target, and then to raise his right foot and kick the target as rapidly as possible. For the

first 120 trials, the subject received quantitative KR—he was told his time after each trial. As Figure 13-2 shows, the subject's movement time decreased over these trials and leveled off at about 800 milliseconds. After trial 120, the subject was shown a videotape of his performance, and his motions were compared to a stick figure performing the response in the best possible way. After receiving this feedback, the subject began a new phase of improvement, and as Figure 13-2 shows, his movement times decreased to about 500 milliseconds. These results suggest that a comparison between the individual's movements and those of an ideal performer is a particularly effective form of feedback.

This type of feedback is now being used in conjunction with the training of Olympic athletes. For instance, a discus thrower might be videotaped as he practices, and later his performance can be reviewed and compared to the motions of a computer-generated figure which demonstrates the movements that would maximize the distance the discus is thrown. In addition, there has been an increasing interest in providing athletes with various types of special feedback to determine which are the most effective (for example, den Brinker, Stabler, Whiting,

FIGURE 13-2. Results from the experiment of Hatze (1976) before and after the subject viewed a videotape comparing his leg movements with the best possible movements.

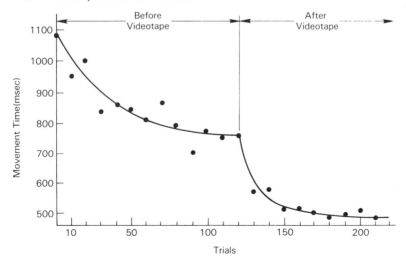

& Van Wieringen, 1986). In some cases, techniques similar to biofeedback (in which the learner is given amplified or quantitative feedback about his movements; see Chapter 8) can assist the acquisition of a novel motor skill (Mulder & Hulstijn, 1985b).

Delaying Knowledge of Results. Since receiving KR seems to be such an important part of learning a new motor skill, we might expect that acquisition will be impaired if there is a delay between the performance of a response and the delivery of KR. After all, we have seen that a delay between CS and US in classical conditioning or between response and reinforcement in operant conditioning can be very detrimental to learning. The topic of delayed KR has been extensively researched, and some of the results are quite surprising. Before looking at them, however, we should distinguish between two types of feedback a subject might receive—feedback that is delivered after a response is completed (as in the Trowbridge and Cason experiment), and feedback that is delivered constantly during the performance of a continuous movement. The effects of delaying these two types of feedback are very different.

In most tasks where continuous immediate feedback is the norm, slight delays in this feedback can produce marked deterioration in performance. A number of studies have examined how a subject's speech is affected when auditory feedback from the subject's voice is delayed by a fraction of a second. (The subject listens to his own voice through headphones that delay the transmission of his speech.) The typical result is that subjects begin to stutter, and to speak more slowly and in a halting manner (Lee, 1950; Smith, 1962). In addition, subjects show little improvement with practice, and when they do improve it is because they have learned to ignore the feedback from the headphones and to rely on other sources of feedback (Goldiamond, Atkinson, and Bilger, 1962). Smith (1962, 1966) has examined subjects' performances on various tracking tasks with delayed feedback. For instance, a subject might have to trace a curving figure with a pencil while watching his performance on a television screen that delays the vi-

sual feedback of his movements. Not surprisingly, Smith found that performance worsened as delays in feedback got longer. As in the studies of speech with delayed feedback, there was little improvement with practice.

In contrast to the above results, there is little or no impairment of learning when a delay is imposed between a response and feedback that normally comes after the response (which we have been calling KR). In an early experiment by Lorge and Thorndike (1935), subjects had to toss a ring at a target behind their backs, and information on the accuracy of each toss was delivered either immediately or after delays of up to six seconds (with different delays for different subjects). Lorge and Thorndike found no detrimental effects of the delayed KR. Other studies have generally found similar results with considerably longer delays (see Bilodeau, 1966; Mulder & Hulstijn, 1985a). Many of these experiments have employed what are called *slow positioning tasks,* in which the subject must move a sliding knob or pointer a certain distance, with no time limit. The knob or pointer is usually out of the subject's sight, so she must rely on tactile or kinesthetic cues rather than visual ones. Bilodeau and Bilodeau (1958) found no differences in the degree of improvement on such tasks when KR delays varied from 20 seconds to 7 days!

In order to benefit from delayed KR, the subject must remember what the previous response was like (for instance, how one's hand, arm, and wrist felt at the completion of the movement). The predominant finding that delaying KR has no adverse effects suggests that this sort of information can be retained over fairly long periods of time. This conclusion does not hold, however, if the subject is required to make other responses during the delay interval. Using what has been called a *trials delay procedure* and a slow positioning task, Bilodeau (1956) gave subjects feedback for one trial only after one or more additional trials had occurred. For example, in the group with a two-trial delay of KR, a subject received KR for trial 1 after trial 3, for trial 2 after trial 4, and so on. (The subjects were aware that the KR applied to an earlier trial, not the immediately preceding one.) For different groups of subjects, Bilodeau used delays of from zero to six trials, and she found that performance decreased markedly as the number of intervening trials increased.

The different effects of the trials delay procedure and simple delayed KR suggest the following interpretation: If the delay between a motor response and the delivery of KR is relatively free of distractions, a person can remember how the previous response felt and can therefore use the KR to "learn from his or her mistakes." On the other hand, if additional motor responses fill the delay interval, they evidently interfere with the subject's memory of the earlier response, so it becomes difficult for the subject to associate the KR with that response. And unless the subject can compare the tactile and kinesthetic stimuli that accompany a response with information about the accuracy of that response, no learning is possible.

Distribution of Practice

One of the most heavily researched areas in motor learning from the turn of the century through the 1950s was how the temporal distribution of practice affects learning. One reason for the interest in this topic was strictly pragmatic: Researchers wanted to find the most efficient method of learning a new skill. For example, suppose a foreman has four hours in which to teach a new employee to operate a semiautomatic machine. Will the employee's performance be best if he practices steadily for the four hours, or if he alternates between 30-minute practice periods and 30-minute rest periods, or with some other distribution of practice and rest? As a general rule, the laboratory studies found that performance is better if rest periods are interspersed among fairly brief practice periods than if practice occurs in one continuous block. In short, *distributed practice* is better than *massed practice*. It is interesting to note that Ebbinghaus (1885) obtained a similar result in his research on the memorization of lists of nonsense syllables, a very different type of task.

An experiment by Dore and Hilgard (1937) shows what a big difference the distribution of practice and rest can make. These researchers used the *pursuit rotor* task, which has been al-

luded to earlier—the subject tries to keep a pointer in contact with a small circular target that is spinning on a turntable at a rate of one revolution per second. The measure of performance is the amount of time the pointer is touching the target. Figure 13-3 shows the results from three groups in the experiment of Dore and Hilgard. For the first three trials, all groups received the same treatment—three one-minute trials separated by one-minute rest periods. Immediately after the third trial, the groups began to receive different durations of rest. In Group A, the one-minute practice trials were separated by 11-minute rest periods. In Group B, the rest periods lasted for three minutes, and in Group C they lasted for only one minute. As Figure 13-3 shows, the performances of the three groups diverged immediately, with the longer rest periods producing superior performance.

To explain the effects of distributed practice, Clark Hull (1943) developed the concept of *reactive inhibition,* which is in fact very similar to the average person's concept of *fatigue.* Hull proposed that as a person continues to practice at some task without a break, reactive inhibition steadily builds up and artificially depresses performance. However, reactive inhibition was said to dissipate spontaneously during any rest period (again, notice the similarity to fatigue), so that overall performance will be better if frequent rest periods are allowed. One of the strongest pieces of evidence for Hull's concept of reactive inhibition comes from studies on a phenomenon with a misleading name—the *reminiscence effect* (Ammons, 1947; Kimble, 1949). In a learning task, reminiscence refers to an improvement in performance that is observed immediately after a rest period. That is, the subject shows a sudden increment in performance that occurs without additional practice. Although the term reminiscence suggests that the improvement occurs because the subject has time to contemplate her past performances during the rest period, it is now generally accepted that the effect is due to the dissipation of fatigue.

The experiments on the distribution of practice would have important implications for people learning new motor skills were it not for one major qualification: The disadvantages of massed

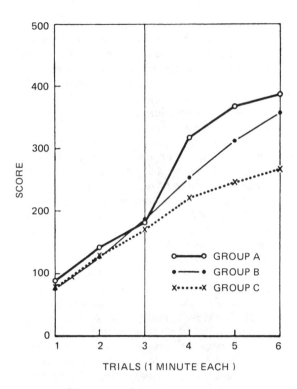

TRIALS (1 MINUTE EACH)

FIGURE 13-3. Results from three groups in the experiment of Dore and Hilgard (1937) on the pursuit rotor apparatus. The distribution of practice and rest was the same for all groups on the first three trials and different thereafter, as described in the text.

practice appear to be in large part transitory. Subjects who receive massed practice do substantially worse *during that practice,* but after a sufficient rest period their performance is usually about as good as that of subjects who initially received distributed practice. Adams and Reynolds (1954) provided a clear demonstration of this phenomenon. One group of subjects received distributed practice on the pursuit rotor task, and Figure 13-4 shows the relatively smooth learning curve produced by this group. Four other groups received massed practice for 5, 10, 15, or 20 trials, respectively, and then they were shifted (after a ten-minute rest) to distributed practice for the remainder of the experiment. The lower left portion of Figure 13-4 shows that as long as the massed practice continued, the performance of these four groups was much lower than that of the distributed-practice group. Once they switched to distributed practice, however, all groups required only a few trials to reach roughly the same performance level as the distributed-practice group. Over the last ten trials, the perfor-

mance levels of the five groups were indistinguishable. Thus the early massed practice had no long-term adverse effects. Similar results have been obtained in several other studies employing different tasks (Bilodeau, 1954; Stelmach, 1969). In summary, the distribution of practice and rest periods has a large temporary effect, but it seems to have little or no effect on long-term performance.

Transfer from Previous Training

In motor-skill research, the topic of *transfer of training* is similar to the topic of generalization in animal-learning research. In both cases, the question is how experience with one set of stimuli will affect performance with a new set of stimuli. Early theorists (Osgood, 1949) believed that it should be possible to observe *positive transfer* (in which practice in one task aids the acquisition of a similar task) in some situations, and *negative transfer* (in which practice on one task interferes with the acquisition of a similar

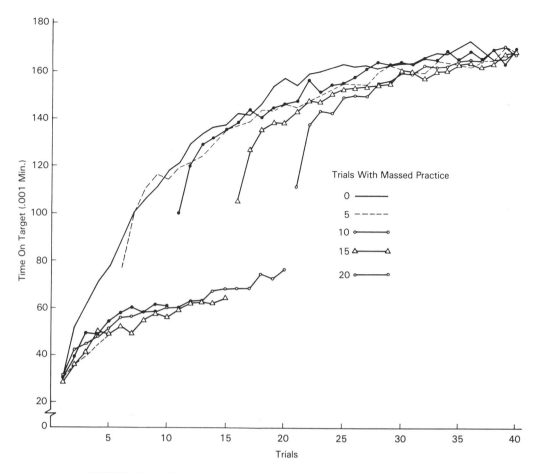

FIGURE 13-4. Results from the five groups in the experiment of Adams and Reynolds (1954). The four groups with massed practice exhibited poor performance as long as this massed practice continued, but they each displayed sudden improvement when shifted to distributed practice conditions.

task) in other situations. From an intuitive standpoint, both possibilities seem reasonable. For instance, it seems likely that learning to drive a car with a three-speed manual transmission should make it easier to learn to drive a car with a four-speed transmission. The topic of negative transfer reminds me of the discussions I had with friends when I was young about how playing baseball early in the day would be detrimental to a golf game later in the day. Our theory was that the flat swing of a baseball bat would interfere with

one's ability to produce the relatively upright golf swing shortly afterward. (Of course, we had only anecdotal evidence to support our theory.)

Despite the intuitive appeal of these ideas, it has proven to be quite difficult to find experimental evidence for negative transfer in motor-skill tasks. On the other hand, evidence for positive transfer is abundant, but the effects are usually not very large (see Schmidt, 1982, pp. 506-511). As we might expect, the amount of positive transfer from one task to another depends on the similarity of the two tasks. An experiment demonstrating this point was conducted by Baker, Wylie, and Gagne (1950). The subject's task was to turn a crank at a speed that kept a pointer in contact with a target. For each subject, the number of crank revolutions that were needed to move the pointer a certain distance varied from the training phase to the test phase. In all, there were four different test speeds, which can be numbered 1 (very slow) to 4 (very fast). Baker et al. found that a subject trained with speed 4 would exhibit substantial transfer if tested at speed 3, less transfer if tested at speed 2, and still less at speed 1. In short, the amount of transfer depended on the similarity of the two tasks. This study also showed that transfer can be minimal even when two tasks have a good deal in common. The trials with speed 1 and those with speed 4 were identical in all respects except that the crank had to be turned much more slowly with speed 1. Yet Baker et al. found a "savings" of only 6 percent when a subject was transferred from speed 4 to speed 1, and no savings at all in transfers from speed 1 to speed 4.

Although experimental demonstrations of negative transfer are rare, one such demonstration was provided by Lewis, McAllister, and Adams (1951). The subject's task in this experiment was to use a joystick to move several green lights on a display toward different targets. In the initial phase of the experiment, moving a joystick in one direction caused a green light to move in the same direction (for instance, moving the joystick to the upper left made the light move toward the upper left). With practice, subjects became faster at moving the lights toward their targets. In the second (interference) phase, subjects in several experimental groups received a number of trials in which the action of the joystick was reversed (moving the joystick to the upper left made the light move to the lower right). Here too, subjects' performances improved with practice. Subjects in a control group received no trials with the controls reversed. The test of negative transfer came in the third phase of the experiment, in which the original operation of the joystick was restored. Subjects in the experimental groups performed more poorly than

they had at the end of the first phase, and they required several trials to regain their previous performance levels. There was no such drop in the performance of control subjects, which shows that the decrements were not simply due to the passage of time without practice. Rather, the deterioration in performance was caused by the practice with the reversed controls.

Although it is difficult to make any definitive statements about when positive and negative transfer effects will be observed, the following principles may be useful rules of thumb: Positive transfer is most likely to be found when two tasks involve similar or identical movements in response to a similar stimulus situation. In the Baker et al. experiment, for example, the stimulus was identical in both tasks (a moving target), and the required motions were similar (turning the same crank in the same direction, only at different speeds). On the other hand, negative transfer is most likely to be observed when two tasks demand antagonistic or incompatible responses to a similar stimulus situation. Thus the strong negative transfer found by Lewis et al. probably occurred because a particular stimulus (such as a green light below its target) required one response in the original task and the opposite response in the interfering task. The difficulty in applying these rules, however, is that it is often not obvious whether two movements (for example, swinging a baseball bat and swinging a golf club) should be considered similar or antagonistic.

THEORIES OF MOTOR-SKILL LEARNING

So far we have considered some factors that determine how quickly and how well a new skill will be learned, but we have entertained few hypotheses about what takes place inside the individual during such learning episodes. We will now turn to some theories that deal with this question. As mentioned earlier, the emergence of cognitive psychology has had a large impact on the field of motor skills. Many modern theories of motor behavior treat the organism as an information-processing system, and they speculate about the stages and possible internal mechanisms involved in the execution of skilled movements. Of course, various theories differ in the extent to which they rely on the terminology and concepts of cognitive psychology. As we examine a few important theories of motor-skill learning, try to decide where you would locate them on a continuum that extends from strict behavioral analyses at one extreme to distinctly cognitive theories at the other.

Adams's Two-Stage Theory

Jack Adams (1971) proposed what is probably the most influential theory of motor learning to date. It has generated both numerous experiments and substantial theoretical debate. To make the discussion of Adams's theory more understandable, it will be helpful to relate some of Adams's terms to the terminology of control systems theory that was introduced in Chapter 3. One important concept of Adams's theory is the *perceptual trace,* which corresponds to the reference input of control systems theory. According to Adams, when a person begins to learn a new motor skill, the perceptual trace or reference input is weak or nonexistent. Consider any simple task in which KR is delivered after the movement is completed, such as Thorndike's line drawing task. The blindfolded subject knows that the task is to draw a three-inch line, but does not yet know what it "feels like" to draw a line of this length. Adams proposed that an important part of the learning of such a skill is the development of an appropriate perceptual trace. In the line-drawing task, the perceptual trace is presumably a memory of the sensations that were produced by the sensory neurons of the hand and arm when a line of the appropriate length was drawn. After a number of trials with KR, the subject begins to develop an appropriate perceptual trace. On subsequent trials, the subject will continue to move the pencil until the actual input (the current sensations in the hand and arm) matches the reference input (the subject's memory, albeit imperfect, of the sensations that accompany the drawing of a three-inch line).

A second important concept in Adams's theory is the *motor trace* (which Adams actually called the *memory trace*). The motor trace relates to the workings of the action system of control systems theory. The basic idea is that in addition to learning what it feels like to produce the correct movement, a person must also learn to coordinate his muscles so that the movement is indeed produced. For instance, in the line-drawing task, the subject must learn to move the pencil so as to reduce the discrepancy between actual input and reference input without overshooting the reference input. It will do the subject little good to say, "I know what it feels like to draw a three-inch line, but I accidentally moved the pencil about an inch too far." If this statement were true, though, it would suggest that the subject had developed a good perceptual trace but needed to improve the movements of his action system, the hand and arm.

Other motor skills provide much clearer illustrations of how an individual may have an accurate perceptual trace but a poorly functioning action system. A beginning pianist may listen to a recording of a difficult piece again and again, until she has a firm idea of what an excellent rendition sounds like. (That is, she develops the ability to discriminate between a very good rendition and an excellent rendition, much as the judges in a competition attempt to do.) Having reached this point, however, it may take long hours of painstaking practice before she can even approximate a good rendition on her own. As another example, having hit thousands of golf balls over the years, I believe I can distinguish between the sensations that accompany a good golf swing and those that accompany a bad swing. A good swing involves a certain rhythm of the wrists, arms, hips, and knees that causes the clubhead to "snap" at the ball, and I can tell the shot is a good one before looking up to see where the ball has gone. My problem is that although I can recognize a good swing when I feel one, my action system does not produce one every time. In fact, I sometimes go through an entire round without ever experiencing the sensations of a good swing.

According to Adams's theory, there are two stages in the learning of a typical motor skill. The first stage is called the *verbal-motor* stage, because in this stage improvement depends on the delivery of feedback, usually in a verbal form.

That is, the experimenter must supply the subject with KR, because the subject does not have an accurate perceptual trace, and therefore cannot discriminate a good trial from a bad one. The name *verbal-motor* should not be taken literally, because KR could be delivered in many ways other than verbally (through a computer printout, an oscilloscope, and so on). Outside the laboratory, the verbal-motor stage is the time when improvement depends on constant feedback from the piano teacher, the pitching coach, or the gymnastics instructor. Without this feedback, the learner cannot tell whether the movement was good, or what was wrong with it.

Adams (1976) described the end of the verbal-motor stage in this way:

The Verbal-Motor Stage has a somewhat indefinite end point, and it will vary from subject to subject, but it comes to an end when knowledge of results has been signifying trivial error for some time and that the response is being successfully made. At this point the subject can switch wholly to the perceptual trace as a reference for responding because it now defines the correct response. The subject can now behave without knowledge of results...(p. 205)

Adams calls this second stage the *motor stage*. At this point the individual can rely on an internal perceptual trace to judge the accuracy of a movement in the absence of external KR. Adams goes on to say that in addition to maintaining his current performance level in the absence of KR, the learner can actually improve his performance by refining the precision of the motor trace (that is, by becoming more skillful in producing the desired movement).

We have already seen that KR is essential when a new motor skill is first being learned, but there is also solid evidence that KR becomes unnecessary later in training. The best evidence comes from studies in which KR is withdrawn at some point in the middle of the experiment. For example, Newell (1974) had subjects practice a discrete movement—moving a slide 9.5 inches in 150 milliseconds—for 77 trials. One group of subjects received quantitative KR on all trials, whereas in five other groups quantitative KR was withdrawn after either 2, 7, 17, 32, or 52 trials. Figure 13-5 shows that in the group with uninter-

rupted KR, errors steadily decreased to a low level. At the other extreme, two trials with KR were clearly not enough to establish a perceptual trace. This group showed some improvement at first, but then performance deteriorated after many trials without KR. This pattern suggests that the subjects began to establish a perceptual trace, but it was later "forgotten." The results from the groups with 7, 17, or 32 trials with KR suggest that these groups derived some permanent benefits from this initial KR. There was some deterioration in performance when the KR was removed, but these groups continued to perform better than the 2-trial group. The results from the group with 52 trials with KR are probably the most interesting. This group showed no decreases in accuracy when KR was removed, and its performance equaled that of the group with uninterrupted KR throughout the experiment. Adams's interpretation is that subjects in this group had progressed to the motor stage, where an internal perceptual trace replaced external KR as a means of evaluating their performances on each trial.

Adams's theory predicts that if an individual has reached the motor stage in some skill, she should be able to do more than simply maintain her current performance level if KR is withdrawn—she should be able to exhibit further improvement with continued practice without KR. There is little laboratory evidence demonstrating actual improvements in performance without KR, but one such study was conducted by Newell (1976). As in Newell's earlier study, the task involved the rapid movement of a slide, and the subject's goal was to move the slide at the correct speed. The apparatus made distinctive sounds at the beginning and end of the movement, so the sounds could provide cues concerning the duration of a trial. In several "demonstration" trials, the subjects were told to listen to the sound made when the experimenter moved the slide at the correct speed. They then received a series of learning trials in which they tried to produce the response at the appropriate speed, but no KR was ever given. That is, the subjects simply made one response after another, and the experimenter told them nothing about their accuracy. Yet despite the absence of KR, the subjects' responses be-

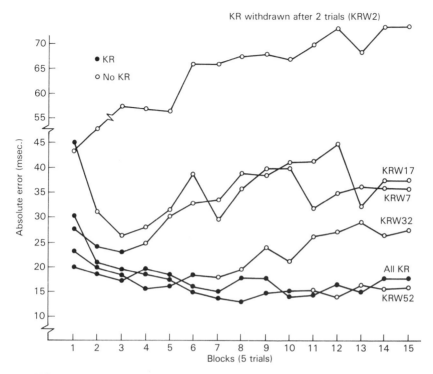

FIGURE 13-5. Results from the six groups of the Newell (1974) experiment. Each group received a different number of trials with KR.

came more accurate with practice. According to Adams's theory, the demonstration trials provided the subjects with an auditory perceptual trace, and their subsequent improvements without KR occurred as they learned how to generate movements that produced approximately the correct sound.

Less direct but still suggestive evidence for Adams's theory comes from studies in which KR is provided to subjects on only a certain fraction of the trials. Not surprisingly, one finding is that subjects learn more rapidly when KR is presented on every trial than when it is intermittent (Annett, 1959; Taylor & Noble, 1962). This result simply reemphasizes the importance of KR for motor-skill learning. However, an interesting question is what happens when KR is completely withdrawn during the test phase. Using a simple positioning task, Baird and Hughes (1972) gave different groups of subjects KR on either 25 percent, 50 percent, 75 percent, or 100 percent of

their trials during acquisition. Each group received ten trials with KR, so the groups with less frequent KR had more trials altogether. In a subsequent test phase with no KR, the groups with *less* frequent KR during acquisition performed more accurately. These results can be interpreted using Adams's theory as follows. The training of the groups with less frequent KR presumably encouraged them to develop accurate perceptual traces (that is, to use sensory cues to judge their performances) since external KR was frequently unavailable. On the other hand, subjects who received KR on every trial may have had it too easy: They may have felt no need to develop the ability to judge the accuracy of their performance because the experimenter always provided them with external KR. The results suggest that intermittent KR may be desirable if the learner will eventually have to perform when no KR is available.

Once a person has reached the motor stage,

feedback from the piano teacher, the pitching coach, or the gymnastics instructor becomes less important. Of course, the instructor can continue to provide helpful feedback to correct minor flaws in one's technique or to make further refinements in one's style. At the same time, however, the learner can also improve through practice on his own by relying on internal feedback in place of the coach's feedback. Perhaps the most important contribution of Adams's theory is that it distinguishes between the two types of learning that take place during the acquisition of most motor skills—learning to recognize what it feels like to make an accurate response, and learning to produce such a response consistently. The strongest support for this theory comes from studies that separate these two types of learning (Newell, 1974, 1976).

Schmidt's Schema Theory

Adams's two-stage theory represented an important advance in the analysis of motor-skill learning. Yet all theories have their limitations, and a major limitation of Adams's theory is that it seems to be limited to the acquisition of single, repetitive movements (that is, to movements of the foul-shot type, where the stimulus conditions and the required movement are exactly the same, trial after trial). The theory says nothing about how people can acquire skills which involve the production of different responses on different trials so as to deal with different stimulus conditions. Consider the tennis player's response to an approaching ball, a bird's response to the diversionary tactics of a flying insect it is chasing, a hiker's response to the irregular terrain of a rocky hillside, or a driver's response to an unfamiliar winding road. In all of these cases and many others, the individual is confronted with new and different stimulus conditions and must generate a response to suit these conditions. It seems clear that more is involved in the acquisition of such skills than the development of a single perceptual trace and a single motor trace. In an effort to go beyond Adams's theory and deal with these more flexible motor skills, Richard Schmidt (1975) developed his schema theory of motor-skill learning.

Schmidt's theory retains the most novel part of Adams's theory—the idea that two types of learning take place during the acquisition of most motor skills (learning to recognize the correct response and learning to produce it). However, to deal with more flexible motor skills such as those discussed above, Schmidt proposed that people can acquire general rules (which he called *schemas*) as they practice. Schmidt borrowed the term *schema* from Bartlett (1932), an early writer on the topic of memory. Bartlett proposed that our memories consist to a large extent of abstractions and generalizations rather than specifics and details. Similarly, Schmidt proposed that people do not retain information about specific past movements and their consequences but rather that they develop what I will call *perceptual schemas* and *motor schemas*. (These are not the terms Schmidt used, but I will use them to be as consistent as possible with the terminology used in describing Adams's theory.)

To make these concepts more concrete, let us consider how a golfer learns to putt a ball the appropriate distance (ignoring the problem of moving the ball in the appropriate direction). The golfer must learn to stroke the ball with different amounts of effort depending on how far the ball is from the hole. In practice, the golfer may use different amounts of effort on different trials and observe the result (the distance the ball travels). This situation is illustrated in Figure 13-6a. Each point represents a single practice trial: The x-axis represents the golfer's estimate of the effort used in the stroke, and the y-axis represents her estimate of the distance the ball traveled. According to Schmidt, these individual data points are soon forgotten, but what the golfer develops and retains is a general rule or motor schema about the relationship between effort and the distance the ball moves (as signified by the solid line in Figure 13-6a). Furthermore, Schmidt states that motor schemas may consist of more than a single function, because other situational variables can affect the outcome of a particular movement. In the example of putting, one such variable is the slope of the green. Figure 13-6b shows a simplified illustration of the more complex motor schema a golfer might develop by practicing level, uphill, and downhill putts. A skillful

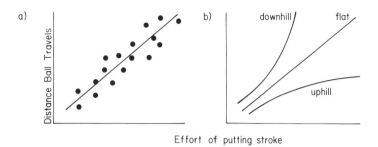

Effort of putting stroke

FIGURE 13-6.   (a) A hypothetical illustration of how, according to Schmidt's schema theory, a person might learn a general rule or schema about the relationship between the effort of a putting stroke and the distance the golf ball moves. Each data point represents the learner's estimates of effort and distance on one practice trial, and the line represents the general rule the learner supposedly retains from these trials. (b) This figure makes the point that a successful golfer's schema for putting would have to include different rules for downhill, flat, and uphill putts. In reality, the golfer's schema would have to be considerably more complex, so as to account for continuous variations in the slope of the putting surface.

golfer's motor schema would be much more complex than this, of course, because the slope of a green can vary continuously, and other factors such as the length of the grass and any moisture on the green must be taken into account. The advantage of such a schema is that it allows the individual to respond to new situations with a reasonable chance of success. Thus although a golfer may never have practiced a 22-foot putt on a moderately slow green with a downhill slope of 4 degrees, the motor schema allows her to generalize from similar past experiences, so as to produce a reasonably suitable response.

Schmidt's theory states that besides developing such a motor schema, learners also develop perceptual schemas that allow them to use sensory feedback to predict whether the appropriate movement was produced. The perceptual schema is simply a generalized version of the perceptual trace in Adams's theory that is applicable to more than one situation. Such a perceptual schema presumably allows a golfer to predict before seeing the result whether her stroke was too strong, too weak, or about right, regardless of

whether the distance to the hole was 5 feet, 10 feet, or 40 feet. Indeed, in professional golf tournaments one frequently sees a golfer stroke a putt and then immediately start walking toward the hole in disgust, knowing before the ball has traveled very far that the putt was not a good one. The development of a perceptual schema may not seem particularly important in putting because the golfer can always see the result as the ball approaches the hole anyway. In other situations, however, the ability to compare the immediate sensory feedback from a movement with some perceptual schema can be valuable. For example, basketball players frequently remark that the shooter is the first person to know whether or not a shot will go into the basket. All the players can watch the flight of the ball and try to estimate whether it will hit or miss, but only the shooter has the additional sensory feedback provided by the shooting motion itself. The shooter can take advantage of this information by moving in position to grab the rebound if he determines that the shot will bounce off the rim.

The ability to deal with open-ended classes of

movements such as putting golf balls and shooting baskets from different parts of the court makes Schmidt's theory more versatile than that of Adams. Besides its broader applicability, Schmidt's theory makes several predictions that are different from those of Adams's theory. One difference concerns the possibility of "learning from one's mistakes." The question is whether a person can benefit from practice trials on which the person makes a response that is far off target and then receives KR indicating the size of the error. As a concrete example, let us think of a slow positioning task where the subject moves a slide 18 inches instead of the goal of 10 inches. According to schema theory, this trial can be a beneficial learning experience despite the magnitude of the error, because it still contributes to the development of the subject's perceptual and motor schemas. On the other hand, Adams's theory suggests that such errant movements will be detrimental to learning because the sensory feedback from these trials will interfere with the subject's perceptual trace, which is nothing more than the memory of the sensations produced by a *correct* movement. Speaking loosely, we might say that according to Adams, errant movements are detrimental because they make the subject forget what it feels like to produce the correct movement. Shapiro and Schmidt (1982) reviewed the evidence on variability in practice and concluded that subjects benefit about as much from practicing a variety of different responses as from practicing the single correct response in a positioning task. These results are consistent with schema theory but not with Adams's theory.

Research with children has provided the most consistent support for schema theory's prediction that variable practice is beneficial. For example, in a study by Kerr and Booth (1978), children tossed bean bags at a target without visual feedback, and they were given quantitative KR by the experimenter. One group of children received *specific training,* in which they always aimed for a target that was three feet away. A second group received *variable training,* in which the target was sometimes two feet away and sometimes four feet away. Both groups later received test trials with the three-foot target distance, and the

group that had received variable training performed more accurately, even though they had never practiced with the three-foot distance. Kerr and Booth suggested that the variable training helped the children develop stronger schemas than did the specific training.

With adult subjects, the evidence on the effects of variable training has been mixed. Some studies have found variable training to be beneficial (Johnson & McCabe, 1982; Wrisberg & McLean, 1984), whereas others have not (Bird & Rikli, 1983). Lee, Magill, and Weeks (1985) suggested that the way variable training is scheduled may explain these different results. When the different variations of a behavior were practiced in separate blocks (for instance, a block of two-foot throws, then a block of four-foot throws), the benefits of this variable training were minimal. On the other hand, when the different variations were randomly intermixed (two-foot throws intermixed with four-foot throws), this variable training proved to be superior to specific training. This pattern suggests that if you want to reap the greatest benefits from variable practice (such as practicing different shots on a basketball court), you should randomly intermix the different behaviors you practice (changing your position on the court after each shot).

To recapitulate, a major strength of Schmidt's schema theory is that it provides a framework for understanding how people develop flexible motor skills that allow them to make successful responses when confronted with situations they have never experienced before. The theory states that this ability develops as a person acquires general rules or schemas that describe the relations between different stimulus conditions, possible movements, and their expected consequences.

Attention and Automatization

The idea that attention is essential for simple associative learning was briefly discussed in Chapter 5. With respect to learning motor skills, many theorists have made the similar claim that attention is necessary during the learning phase, but perhaps less so after a skill is well practiced. A theory presented by Fitts and Posner (1967) is representative of hypotheses about the role of attention in motor-skill learning. Like Adams (1971), Posner suggested that there are different stages in the acquisition of a complex skill, but their three stages are so different from Adams's two stages that it is not clear how to compare the two theories. Fitts and Posner proposed that in the early stage of skill learning, a person simply learns what the task demands and what components are involved. For instance, in the early stage of learning to fly an airplane, a student pilot learns what all the controls and instruments are for, and when they are used during a flight. In the intermediate or *associative* phase, the individual begins to strengthen stimulus-response associations, and learns to produce the correct response to a given situation (such as what to do when the airplane begins to tilt to the left). In any moderately complex task, the learner can perform adequately only by directing the fullest possible attention to the task during the intermediate phase. However, in the final or *autonomous* stage, the task becomes less demanding of one's attentional resources. Many of the component activities of the skill have become "automatic" and can be performed "without thinking about them."

It is difficult to define the autonomous stage or the process of automatization in a rigorous way. Nevertheless, I am sure that you can list many skills you possess that once demanded careful attention but which can now be performed with a minimum of attention. Some common skills of this type are driving a car, writing, tying a shoelace, or eating with chopsticks. If one activity demands a good deal of attention, a person will not be able to engage in other behaviors simultaneously. The behavior of driving a car is frequently used as an example. Whereas experienced drivers can often carry on a conversation while driving, beginning drivers cannot, because they must devote all of their attention to the task of keeping the car on the road.

This sort of anecdotal evidence about the changing roles of attention in skilled performance is supported by several experimental results. Allport, Antonis, and Reynolds (1972) found that experienced pianists could shadow (repeat word by word) tape-recorded passages while simultaneously playing unfamiliar piano pieces by sight-reading. It seems clear that less-experienced pianists would be unable to perform these tasks simultaneously. Spelke, Hirst, and Neisser (1976) trained two subjects to write words that were dictated to them while simultaneously reading for comprehension at their normal reading speeds. The subjects could not perform these two tasks simultaneously at first, but their performance gradually improved over many weeks of daily practice. The researchers concluded that with sufficient practice, two tasks that both seem to be demanding of attention can be performed at once.

Other research on the role of attention in motor skills has investigated exactly when during the course of a movement attention is needed. Posner and Keele (1969) developed a procedure in which a subject performed a rapid positioning task with one hand and a reaction-time task with the other. The positioning task involved turning a handle to move a pointer to a target 135 degrees away in 700 milliseconds. The reaction time task was simply to press a button as rapidly as possible when an auditory signal was presented. On different trials the signal was presented at different times during the course of the rapid movement. Figure 13-7 shows the mean reaction times on different types of trials. The first thing to observe is that reaction times were shortest when no positioning movement was required. Second, reaction times were longer when a smaller target was used in the positioning task. These findings suggest that the positioning task required some attention, and more attention was necessary when the target was smaller (thereby decreasing attention to the reaction-time task and slowing performance).

The x-axis in Figure 13-7 shows the different points during the positioning movement at which the signal was presented. As can be seen, reaction times were slow if the signal was presented near the beginning or near the end of the movement, but faster if it was presented in the middle of the movement. Posner and Keele concluded that more attention is required to initiate a positioning movement (perhaps because the appropriate commands must be sent to the muscles) and at the end (because accuracy depends on one's stopping at the right position). They obtained fur-

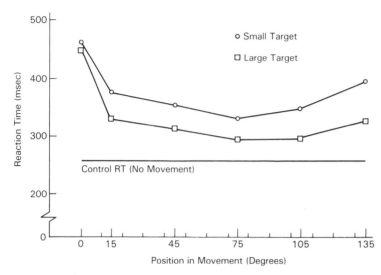

FIGURE 13-7. Results from the experiment of Posner and Keele (1969) showing how reaction times to respond to a signal with one hand varied as a function of when the signal was presented during the course of rapid-positioning task involving the other hand. The figure also shows that reaction times were slower when the positioning task had a smaller target.

ther support for this interpretation from an experiment that did not require accuracy at the end of the movement. A barrier was placed at the target so the movement would always stop at the correct point. In this case, responses on the reaction-time task were slower only at the beginning of the movement: Reaction times during the middle or end of the movement were just as fast as when no movement was required. This result suggests that once the movement was initiated, no further attention was needed.

A very different approach to the topic of automatization concerns what brain structures may be involved in the production of automatic learned behaviors. Whitaker (1983) has proposed that several aspects of adult speech have become automatic, and he has tried to determine what brain structures may be involved. Consider how easy it is for you to carry on a casual conversation with friends. Unlike a young child or a foreigner just learning the English language, you do not have to stop to think about how to pronounce each syllable or how to combine words into a grammatical sentence. By studying patients with localized brain damage due to illness or injury, Whitaker has attempted to determine what portions of the brain are involved in these abilities. He has found that different parts of the cerebral cortex seem to be necessary for different aspects of automatic speech production. As one unusual example, he reported the case

of a woman with a small brain lesion who had only one speech problem: She had difficulty adding suffixes such as "tion" or "ity" to words she already knew. For instance, she could not read aloud the words *degradation, femininity,* or *enthusiastic.* At the same time, however, she could correctly read nonwords with the same endings, such as *maygradation, ramininity,* and *anthusiastic.* Whitaker proposed that the addition of suffixes to ordinary words is an automatic behavior for most people, but because of her brain lesion the woman had lost this ability. On the other hand, nonwords require our attention to read correctly because we must examine each syllable in turn (since in a nonword we cannot predict what the next syllable will be). The brain lesion had evidently impaired the woman's automatic reading of familiar words with suffixes but not her attention-demanding, syllable-by-syllable reading of nonwords. This type of evidence suggests that anatomically distinct brain structures may be involved in automatic versus attention- demanding movements.

LEARNING MOVEMENT SEQUENCES

In this section, we will consider motor skills that involve sequences of movements that must be performed in a specific order. Some skills of this type are walking, swimming, typing, or playing a musical instrument. In the first two of these examples, the appropriate sequences of movement are cyclical or repetitive, whereas in the second two they are usually not. In all of these examples, however, successful performance depends on producing the sequence of movements in the correct order and with the correct timing. For instance, in performing the breast stroke, a swimmer must coordinate the movements of the arms and legs in order to move through the water efficiently. A pianist will not get much credit for playing all of the notes in a score if they are not played in the correct sequence, and with the correct tempo.

One of the most obvious characteristics of such skilled movements is that people become more proficient in performing them with practice. The learning curve in such tasks is similar in form to learning curves in classical and operant conditioning. For instance, in learning to type, a beginner's average number of words per minute increases rapidly at first and then more gradually as it approaches some asymptotic level of performance (Thurstone, 1919). The challenge for motor-skill researchers is to explain why people become more skillful in performing such sequences of movement with practice.

The Response Chain Approach

One major approach to the topic of movement sequences is based on the concept of a *response chain,* which was discussed in Chapter 6. The relationship should be clear, since a response chain was defined as a sequence of behaviors that must occur in a specific order, with a primary reinforcer following the completion of the last behavior of the chain. According to the standard analysis, what keeps the behaviors of the chain in their correct sequence is the fact that each response produces a distinctive stimulus that acts as a discriminative stimulus for the next response of the chain. For instance, the beginning of a maze may serve as a discriminative stimulus for running, and running may bring an animal to a choice point, which is a discriminative stimulus to turn left. If the animal is then reinforced with a bit of food, the entire sequence of behaviors is strengthened.

It is easy to see how this analysis could be applied to some skilled-movement sequences, such as walking. The sight or feeling of having one's right leg in front might serve as a discriminative stimulus to shift one's weight to this leg and bring the left leg forward. The opposite might be true when one's left leg is in front. Of course, the movements of walking could be broken down further into a complex sequence of muscle contractions. Nevertheless, the principles of a response chain analysis would remain the same: The visual, tactile, or kinesthetic feedback from one muscle contraction might serve as a discriminative stimulus for the next muscle contraction in the sequence. Why, according to this analysis, does a person's ability to perform a sequence of movements improve with practice? The answer is that the appropriate stimulus-response associations are strengthened by reinforcement. For instance, to achieve the maximum propulsion in the breast stroke, a swimmer must begin to move his hands forward at a particular point during each stroke. If we assume that swimming speed is the reinforcer, then through the process of successive approximations the swimmer should eventually learn exactly what cues signal that the forward movement of the hands should begin.

The response chain analysis of movement sequences is compatible with theories such as those of Adams and Schmidt, which emphasize the role of feedback in the control of movement. Chapter 3 (especially Figures 3-5 and 3-6) showed how a response chain can be viewed as a series of feedback loops, with the completion of one loop leading to the start of the next. Yet although the response chain approach provides a satisfactory analysis for many response sequences (as in Figure 6-7), there are now several types of evidence which suggest that it cannot account for all examples of behavior sequences. The next two sections describe two major lines of attack against the response chain approach.

Simultaneous Chaining

In the typical response chain, each response produces a new stimulus which can serve as a discriminative stimulus for the next response. However, Terrace and his colleagues have employed a procedure in which there is no change in stimuli as a pigeon progresses through a chain of several responses (Terrace, 1983). The bird's task is to peck four keys, each a different color, in a specific order (say, red, green, blue, yellow). The positions of the colors are varied randomly from one trial to the next. All four keys are lit at the start of a trial, and they remain lit until the bird has made four responses. If the pigeon pecks the keys in the correct order it is reinforced after the final response; otherwise it is not. Terrace has called this procedure *simultaneous chaining* because all four stimuli are presented simultaneously and remain on throughout the trial.

Although there is no change in stimuli as the subject responds on this task, Terrace, Straub, Bever and Seidenberg (1977) found that pigeons could learn to produce the correct sequence of responses (which we will call A→B→C→D) on a large majority of the trials. By itself, this result is not very damaging to the response chain approach. As discussed in Chapter 6 with regard to maze learning, although there are no changes in external stimuli after each response, sensory feedback from the animal's movements might provide the distinctive discriminative stimuli the animal needs to guide its responses. For instance, the onset of the four key lights might serve as the S^D for pecking color A, moving away from color A might serve as the S^D for pecking color B, and so on.

The big problem for a response chain analysis came from subsequent test trials in which only two or three keys were lit. For instance, suppose only colors A, C, and D were lit. A pigeon should begin by correctly pecking color A, but what response will it make next? According to a response chain analysis, pecking color A serves only as an S^D for pecking color B, but with color B unavailable the bird should exhibit no better than chance performance in choosing C or D next. The response chain approach makes this prediction because it assumes there is no association between A and either C or D. However, Terrace et al. found that their pigeons generally responded in the correct order when confronted with novel subsets of the colors such as A, C, and D. They

concluded that the response chain approach is incorrect in its assumption that subjects learn nothing more than associations between adjacent responses.

This conclusion seems undeniable, but exactly what a subject does learn in this type of task is still not clear. One possibility is that it learns something about the overall structure of the "list" of colors (such as that A is first, D is last, and B and C are in between). A slightly different possibility is that the animal develops associations between nonadjacent items on the list, in much the same way that Ebbinghaus (1885) learned to associate nonadjacent nonsense syllables in his list-learning experiments (Chapter 2). For instance, the animal might learn that on reinforced trials, C is pecked fairly soon after A, and D is not pecked so soon. This type of learning would allow the animal to respond correctly on the novel sequence A→C→D. In any case, it should be clear that the simple response chain approach cannot explain why the subjects of Terrace et al. performed so well on the test trials with novel subsets of the colors used in training.

Motor Programs

Another line of attack against the response chain approach to movement sequencing is based on evidence for the existence of *motor programs*. Those who favor the concept of motor programs suggest that the response chain approach is incorrect because some movement sequences do not depend on continual sensory feedback for their proper execution. After presenting evidence for the existence of movement sequences that do not rely on sensory feedback, Keele (1973) introduced the concept of a motor program as follows:

If neither visual nor kinesthetic feedback is needed for the execution of patterns of movement, then the movement patterns must be represented centrally in the brain, or perhaps in some cases in the spinal cord. Such representation is called a *motor program*. As a motor program is executed, neural impulses are sent to the appropriate muscles in proper sequence, timing, and force, as predetermined by the program, and the neural impulses are largely uninfluenced by the resultant feedback (p. 124).

To make the distinction between a response chain and a motor program clear, let us consider a concrete example of a movement sequence— the typing of the word *the*. A response chain analysis might proceed as follows: Upon seeing the word *the* in the text to be typed, a typist responds by striking the *t* key with his left forefinger. This movement produces sensory feedback (kinesthetic feedback from the finger and perhaps auditory feedback from the typewriter) that serve as a discriminative stimulus to make the next response—striking the *h* key with the right forefinger. Sensory feedback from this response serves as a stimulus for the final response of striking the *e* key with the left middle finger.

Advocates of the motor program approach might agree that this analysis is correct for a beginning typist, but that after typing *the* many, many times, a skilled typist may develop a motor program for producing this response sequence. The idea is that when the skilled typist sees the word *the,* this motor program is activated and sends a series of commands to the muscles of the left forefinger, the right forefinger, and the left middle finger. These commands are timed so that the three movements are performed in the correct sequence, but this timing does not depend on sensory feedback from each successive movement in the sequence. One obvious advantage of the motor program is an increase in speed: The typist can begin to produce the second keystroke before receiving sensory feedback from the first keystroke.

Evidence for Motor Programs. One of the first advocates of the concept of a motor program was Karl Lashley (1951), who described several types of evidence that a response chain analysis cannot explain all movement sequences. For one thing, Lashley argued that human reaction times are too slow to support the idea that sensory feedback from one response can serve as the stimulus for the next response in a rapid sequence. The minimum reaction time for a person to respond to kinesthetic stimulation is over 100 milliseconds (Glencross, 1977), and reaction times are no faster for other sensory modalities. Yet Lashley pointed out that musicians can produce as many as 16 finger movements per second. His point is

that this rate could never be achieved if the musician had to wait for sensory feedback from one movement before beginning the next. Similar arguments have been made for the skill of typing (Shaffer, 1978). Such arguments have been somewhat weakened by evidence that monkeys can react to certain types of kinesthetic feedback in 50 milliseconds or less (Evarts & Tanji, 1974). The relevance of this evidence for human skilled movements is uncertain, however, and the question of whether some movement sequences are simply too rapid to rely on sensory feedback is still a topic for debate.

A second argument made by Lashley was that skilled movements and sequences of movements are still possible for individuals who have lost sensory feedback. He reported the case of a man who had lost all sensation in the area of the knee as a result of a gunshot wound. Despite the loss of sensation, the man could move and position his leg as accurately as an uninjured person (Lashley, 1917). Other evidence that complex movements can continue in the absence of sensory feedback comes from animal studies in which sensory nerve fibers are severed before they enter the spinal cord. For example, Taub and Berman (1968) surgically removed all sensory feedback from both forelimbs of several monkeys. After this surgery, the monkeys were still able to use these limbs to walk and climb (even when blindfolded, which removed the possible influence of visual feedback). The monkeys could coordinate the movements of their senseless forelimbs with their normal hindlimbs. This research provides strong evidence that sensory feedback is not always necessary for skilled movements. However, it should be noted that the movements of the forelimbs were less fluid and clumsier than normal (Bossom, 1974) which suggests that kinesthetic feedback does contribute to the smoothness of movement.

Further evidence for movement sequencing without sensory feedback has involved lower animals. Wilson (1961) found that locusts can continue to produce coordinated, rhythmical wing beating when all sensory nerves in their wings are severed. He concluded that the timing of the wing-beating motions is controlled by a motor program. In research on various songbirds,

Nottebohn (1970) determined that young birds will not develop the normal song of their species unless they (1) have the opportunity to hear other members of their species sing, and (2) can hear themselves sing as they first learn the song. However, if the birds are deafened after they have learned the song, they can continue to sing the song with only minor deterioration of their performance. One interpretation is that auditory feedback is necessary while a motor program for the song is being developed, but once it is developed auditory feedback is no longer necessary.

Lashley's third argument for motor programs concerns the types of errors that are frequently found in rapid movement sequences. He noted that many typing mistakes are errors of anticipation or transposition. For instance, I sometimes type *hte* when I intend to type *the*. It is difficult to explain this sort of error with a response chain analysis. If the stimulus for striking the *h* key was the sensory feedback from the movement of striking the *t* key, the second movement should never precede the first. Instead, Lashley would argue that the separate movements were sequenced by a motor program, but that the synchronization of the movements became distorted somewhere along the line from command to execution. In short, Lashley suggested that any errors that indicate the individual was planning ahead support the notion of a motor program but are inconsistent with the response chain approach.

To summarize, Lashley presented three types of evidence for the existence of motor programs: (1) Some movement sequences appear to occur too rapidly to make use of sensory feedback to guide the movement, (2) Some movements and sequences of movements can occur when sensory feedback has been removed, and (3) Errors of anticipation or transposition in movement sequences suggest that the individual is planning ahead, and is not waiting for feedback from one movement as a stimulus to start the next. Although Lashley presented these ideas several decades ago, they are still the three most common lines of evidence used by motor-skill researchers to support the concept of motor programs. More recent conceptions of motor programs are a bit different from Lashley's, however, and the next section describes some of these differences.

A Modern View of Motor Programs. Early theorists described motor programs as sequences of movements that are produced without reference to any sensory feedback, but more recently there has been a recognition that feedback can play a role in motor programs in several different ways (Schmidt, 1982; Summers, 1981). First, sensory feedback is needed to give the individual information about the starting conditions—for example, about where the typist's fingers are before the typing of the next word begins. Second, we have seen that feedback after a movement is important for learning, and this is equally true for movement sequences. A typist can use either visual feedback (from the typed page) or tactile feedback (from the fingers) to determine whether the appropriate letters were typed in the correct order. If you know how to touch type, then you undoubtedly have a firsthand understanding of how it is possible to recognize from tactile stimuli alone that you have made an error. Third, sensory feedback during the execution of a motor program may let the individual know that the current movement will fail to meet its goal and that a correction will be needed. For example, Summers (1981) suggests that walking is usually controlled by a motor program, but when a person's foot unexpectedly strikes an object, sensory feedback tells the person he is about to fall. "To avoid falling the person must consciously attend to his movements and make a rapid correction to the motor program" (Summers, 1981, p. 49).

Because of the duration of human reaction times, it would typically take a person about 200 milliseconds to respond to a stimulus (such as the foot meeting an impediment while walking) and make the necessary correction in one's movement. However, there is evidence that feedback at the level of the spinal cord may allow an individual to make rapid adjustments in a motor program (in the order of 50 milliseconds) while the program is being executed. Marsden, Merton, and Morton (1972) had subjects move their thumbs back and forth rhythmically, while recording both the position of the thumb and EMG activity from the single muscle controlling this movement. At unpredictable points during this motion, the apparatus suddenly applied increased resistance to the thumb movement. Marsden et al. observed an increase in EMG activity about 50 milliseconds after the resistance was increased. In other words, the muscle began to compensate for the change in resistance very rapidly. This compensatory action was presumably controlled at the spinal level by the feedback loops such as those involved in the spinal reflex arc (Chapter 3). This muscular action has been characterized as a reflexive adjustment that does not depend on attention or voluntary movement.

In summary, sensory feedback is now thought to modulate the activity of motor programs in several ways. A second change in modern conceptions of motor programs has been based on attempts to apply the virtues of Schmidt's schema theory to motor programs. The problem that led to the synthesis of these concepts was similar to the problem that prompted Schmidt to propose his schema theory in the first place: Even in seemingly repetitive sequences of movements such as typing the word *the,* different movements will be required on different occasions. The spacing between keys and the force and amount of movement required to operate them can vary considerably from one typewriter to the next. Nevertheless, an experienced typist will have little difficulty transferring his skills from one keyboard to another. He can also adapt reasonably well to a keyboard that is six inches below the waist or twelve inches above the waist, although the relationships among forearms, wrists, and fingers will be considerably different. For a motor program to be useful in such variable conditions, it cannot simply specify one fixed pattern of muscle movements. Instead, theorists have suggested that motor programs provide a general framework (or schema) about the proper timing and sequencing of movements, but the details of the movement sequence can (and must) be adapted to suit the current situation.

This conception of adaptable motor programs is similar to the observation that in operant conditioning, animals can easily make substitutions among responses that have the same effect on the environment although they may involve very different muscle movements. Within the realm of motor skills, a good example of this adaptability is the observation that people's handwriting styles retain their individuality whether they are writing quarter-of-an-inch letters on a piece of paper or five-inch letters on a blackboard. The schema theory takes an initial step toward an understanding of how this adaptability is possible. It suggests that individuals can generalize from their past experience with different stimulus conditions, different movements, and the results of those movements so as to select a new movement to meet the requirements of a new situation. Thus in handwriting, an individual has presumably already learned what muscle movements are needed to draw a quarter-of-an-inch oval, a five-inch oval, or one of any other size (within limits). According to Schmidt, once these relationships are learned, the production of letters of any height requires only the selection of the appropriate parameters within an existing motor program.

Summary

The two lines of evidence against the response chain approach that we have considered, simultaneous chaining and motor programs, by no means imply that the response chain approach is completely wrong. Rather, they simply suggest that in some cases individuals learn more than is specified by a strict response chain analysis. The results from the simultaneous chaining procedure, like some of the research described in Chapter 11, show that organisms can learn something about the overall structure of a behavior sequence in addition to individual stimulus-response associations. The evidence for motor programs suggests that some well-practiced behavior sequences may no longer depend on continual sensory feedback.

CHAPTER

14
CHOICE

It is not much of an exaggeration to say that all behavior involves choice. Even in the most barren of experimental chambers, an animal can choose among performing the operant response, exploring, sitting, standing, grooming, sleeping, and so on. For creatures outside the laboratory, the choices are much more numerous. At any moment, an organism can choose either to continue with its current behavior or switch to another. The consequences of some choices (such as to pick up a piece of food with the left or right paw) may be fleeting and insignificant, whereas other choices (for instance, to flee or fight an opponent) can have important and irreversible consequences. In either case, however, it should be clear that an understanding of how creatures make choices is essential to an understanding of behavior itself.

Since about the 1960s, a large number of experiments on operant conditioning have dealt with choice behavior, as a quick perusal of titles in such periodicals as *Journal of the Experimen-*

tal Analysis of Behavior or *Animal Learning and Behavior* will demonstrate. Although it will not be possible to do justice to this large and growing body of knowledge, this chapter will attempt to present a representative sample of some of the important experiments, theories, and points of controversy in this area.

One of the most remarkable characteristics of the behavior of animals in choice situations is its orderliness and predictability. Much of my own research deals with choice behavior, and when I give students or visitors a tour of the laboratory, they frequently ask, "Can these pigeons and rats really understand the complex choices you present to them and respond in anything but a haphazard way?" The answer is that they certainly can (and research on choice behavior would not have flourished if animals did not behave in an orderly way). Perhaps the reason people ask this question so often is that the behavior of animals in the wild can appear to be haphazard and unpredictable to a casual observer. If you watch the behavior of a pigeon on a city sidewalk, it may be difficult to discern any order in its movements. It may walk forward, turn left, turn right, stop, turn around, and so on, in no obvious pattern. It may peck at various objects on the ground, it may approach or move away from another pigeon, it may fly away with no apparent provocation. Although the pigeon's selection of behaviors may seem to be random, this may be largely due to the complexity and randomness of its natural environment, because if this same pigeon were brought into the operant laboratory, its behavior in a simplified choice situation would almost certainly show some striking regularities.

One fairly simple mathematical expression that captures some of the regularities of behavior in many choice situations is the *matching law,* developed by Richard Herrnstein. The next several sections describe the matching law, illustrate how it has been applied to several types of experimental results, and discuss some theories about why matching behavior is such a prevalent result in experiments on choice.

THE MATCHING LAW

Herrnstein's (1961) Experiment

Herrnstein used a pigeon chamber with two response keys located on one wall, a few inches apart. Beneath and midway between the two keys was an opening in the wall where grain could be presented as a reinforcer. Each of three pigeons was first trained to peck at both the left key, which was red, and the right key, which was white, until the animals responded readily on both keys. After this initial training, the remainder of the experiment consisted of a series of conditions in which each key was associated with its own VI schedule of reinforcement. For example, two of the pigeons received one condition in which pecks at the left key were reinforced on a VI 135 seconds schedule, and pecks at the right key were reinforced on a VI 270 seconds schedule. (Technically, this schedule is called a *concurrent* VI 135 seconds VI 270 seconds schedule. In general, any situation in which two or more reinforcement schedules are presented simultaneously can be called a concurrent schedule.) The schedules on the two keys were completely independent—that is, each key had its own VI timer. As in a typical VI schedule, once a reinforcer was stored, the VI timer for that key would be stopped until that reinforcer was collected. If a bird pecked at each key every few seconds, it would collect each reinforcer soon after it became available, and it would obtain approximately 27 reinforcers per hour from the left key and 13 reinforcers per hour (half as many) from the right key (see Table 14-1). In this condition, the pigeons did in fact receive about two thirds of their reinforcers from the left key.

Herrnstein was less interested in the acquisition phase (during which the birds' behaviors changed as they became acquainted with the two schedules) than in the birds' "steady-state" performance (after many sessions with these same two schedules, when their behavior was roughly the same from day to day). In other words, Herrnstein's question was: After the birds have learned all that they can about this choice situation, how will they distribute their responses? For this reason, each separate condition lasted for at least 16 sessions, but Herrnstein only used the data from the last five sessions in his analysis (as measures of the subjects' stable choice behavior). Table 14-1 shows the results from one subject. As in most VI schedules, the bird made many re-

TABLE 14-1. Performance of a typical subject in two conditions of Herrnstein's (1961) experiment

VI 135 Seconds versus VI 270 Seconds	Left Key	Right Key
Approximate Reinforcements per Hour	27	13
Percent of Total Reinforcements	67	33
Approximate Responses per Hour	3100	1600
Percent of Total Responses	66	34

VI 720 Seconds versus VI 108 Seconds	Left Key	Right Key
Approximate Reinforcements per Hour	7	34
Percent of Total Reinforcements	17	83
Approximate Responses per Hour	900	3900
Percent of Total Responses	19	81

sponses for each reinforcer it received. What is of interest, however, is that in the condition described above, where about two thirds of the reinforcers came from the left key, the bird made approximately two thirds of its responses on the left key. That is, the proportion of responses that were directed at the left key equaled or *matched* the proportion of reinforcers that were delivered by the left key.

The bottom of Table 14-1 shows the results for this same subject from another condition, where the left key schedule was VI 720 seconds and the right key schedule was VI 108 seconds. In this condition, the bird received only about 17 percent of its reinforcers on the left key, and Table 14-1 shows that it made about 19 percent of its responses on this key. Once again, the percentage of left-key responses approximately matched the percentage of left-key reinforcers. Based on results like these, Herrnstein proposed the following general principle, now known as the *matching law:*

$$\frac{B_1}{B_1 + B_2} = \frac{R_1}{R_1 + R_2} \tag{14-1}$$

B_1 is the number of responses of type 1 (for instance, left-key responses), and B_2 is the number of responses of type 2 (for example, right-key responses). Similarly, R_1 is the number of reinforcers obtained by making response 1, and R_2 is the number of reinforcers obtained by making response 2. Equation 14-1 states that, in a two-choice situation, the proportion of responses directed toward one alternative should equal the proportion of reinforcers delivered by that alternative.

Figure 14-1 plots the results from all of the conditions of Herrnstein's experiment. The x-axis represents the proportion of left-key reinforcers and the y-axis the proportion of left-key responses. According to the matching law, the data points should fall along the diagonal line,

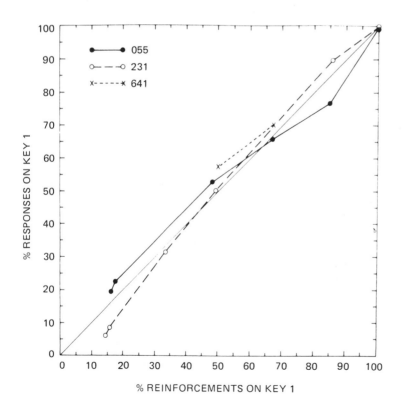

FIGURE 14-1. The results from three pigeons in Herrnstein's (1961) experiment on concurrent VI VI schedules. Each data point shows the results from a different condition. The diagonal line shows the predictions of the matching law (Equation 14-1), which predicts that response percentages will match reinforcement percentages.

since this is where these two proportions are equal. As can be seen, the data points do not lie exactly on the line, but all the points are close to the line. Furthermore, the deviations from the predictions of the matching law appear to be random rather than systematic. We can conclude, therefore, that the matching law provided a good description of the subjects' behavior, except for the sort of random variations that are found in any psychological experiment.

Other Experiments on Matching

One reason that many researchers have come to view the matching law as an important principle of choice behavior is that it has been applied with reasonable success in a wide range of experiments (see Davison & McCarthy, 1988). It has also been applied to species as different as rats (de Villiers, 1980), cows (Matthews & Temple, 1979), humans (Schroeder & Holland, 1969), and wagtails foraging in the natural environment (Houston, 1986). It has also been applied to situations where the two choice alternatives required topographically different responses, such as pecking a key and standing on a treadle (Hanson & Green, 1986). Although most of the experiments involved standard responses such as lever pressing and standard reinforcers such as food or money, a few have employed more unusual responses and reinforcers.

One such experiment was conducted by Conger and Killeen (1974). Groups of four college students sat around a table and had a 30-minute discussion about drug abuse. The discussants knew that the proceedings were being videotaped and would later be analyzed by the experimenters. However, three members of the group were not real subjects but confederates working for the experimenter. The task of the confederate sitting across from the subject was simply to keep the discussion going. The tasks of the confederates to the left and right of the subject were to deliver verbal reinforcers to the subject on two different VI schedules. For instance, whenever the confederate on the left received a signal (a light only he could see), he would reinforce the next statement of the subject by saying something like "That's a good point." The same was true for the confeder-

ate on the right. Conger and Killeen later had observers view the videotapes and measure the amount of time the subject spent talking to the confederate on the left, and the amount of time talking to the confederate on the right. This procedure was repeated with five different subjects.

In the first 15 minutes of the discussion, the confederate on the left delivered about 82 percent of the reinforcers. Would a subject spend more time talking to this confederate? This did not happen in the first five minutes: On the average, subjects talked about equally often to the left and right confederates. However, by the end of the 15 minutes, the different amounts of verbal reinforcement had clear effects on each subjects' behavior. In the last five minutes of this part of the experiment, subjects spent about 78 percent of the time talking to the confederate on the left. This percentage approximately matched the reinforcement percentage.

In the second 15 minutes, the confederate on the left now delivered fewer reinforcers than the confederate on the right (about 38 percent of the total). Once again, it took subjects a while to react to this change, but in the last five minutes of the session they spent an average of about 29 percent of the time talking to the confederate on the left. This approximate matching is impressive considering the brief duration of the experiment and the many possible confounding variables (for example, one confederate might have appeared inherently more friendly or more likeable than the other, excluding any consideration of the verbal reinforcers they delivered).

The idea that people tend to talk more with those who agree with them is not new (Homans, 1961). Nevertheless, the study of Conger and Killeen provides a nice demonstration of how such an idea can be rigorously tested in a controlled yet realistic setting. Furthermore, it shows that there may be a direct proportionality between verbal reinforcers received and verbal behavior delivered, as predicted by the matching law.

Deviations From Matching

It would certainly be wrong to conclude that all experiments on concurrent VI VI schedules have produced results that are consistent with

Equation 14-1. Baum (1974, 1979) listed three ways that the results of experiments have deviated from strict matching, and each of these is depicted graphically in Figure 14-2. The most common of these deviations is *undermatching,* in which response proportions are consistently less extreme (that is, closer to .5) than reinforcement proportions. In the idealized example of undermatching shown in Figure 14-2, when the proportion of left reinforcers is .8, the proportion of left responses is only .6. When the proportion of left reinforcers is .3, the proportion of left responses is .45. In other words, undermatching describes the case where a subject's preferences are closer to indifference than they should be according to the matching law.

To understand one common explanation of undermatching, it is necessary to consider one additional feature of Herrnstein's (1961) experiment that was not previously mentioned. Herrnstein included a 1.5 second *changeover delay,* which was, in effect, a penalty for switching between keys. Suppose a reinforcer was stored on the right key while a pigeon was pecking on the left key. If the bird then switched to the right key, it would not receive the reinforcer for its first peck. Because of the changeover delay, no reinforcer could be collected for 1.5 seconds after a

switch, but the first peck after 1.5 seconds had elapsed would produce the reinforcer.

Herrnstein included the changeover delay because he found that without it the birds tended to develop the habit of alternately pecking the left key, then the right key, then the left key, and so on, regardless of the sizes of the two VI schedules. Herrnstein suggested that this alternating pattern might be an example of a superstitious behavior. For instance, if a bird pecked left, then right, then received a reinforcer, the left- right sequence might be adventitiously reinforced even though only the right response was necessary for that particular reinforcer. Once the changeover delay was added, however, a subject had to make at least two consecutive responses on a key before collecting a reinforcer, thereby making the adventitious reinforcement of switching behavior less likely.

Another hypothesis about undermatching is that animals may occasionally attribute a reinforcer to the wrong response (Davison & Jenkins, 1985). For instance, in the short time between making a response and collecting the reinforcer, a pigeon may forget which key it pecked. This hypothesis is supported by the finding that undermatching becomes more pronounced when the visual appearances of the two response keys are more similar (Miller, Saunders, & Bourland,

FIGURE 14-2.   In each panel, the broken diagonal line shows where data points would fall if a subject's behavior conformed perfectly to the matching law (Equation 14-1). The solid curves illustrate three types of deviation from perfect matching.

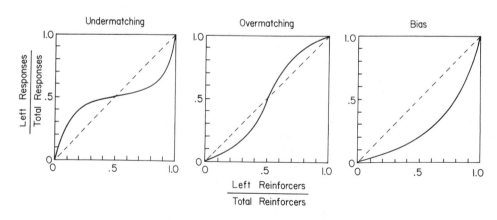

1980). Still other explanations of undermatching have been proposed, however (Baum, 1979; Myers & Myers, 1977), and there is no general agreement about why it occurs.

The opposite of undermatching is *overmatching,* in which a subject's response proportions are more extreme than the reinforcement proportions. For example, in the illustration of overmatching in Figure 14-2, a reinforcer proportion of .8 produces a response proportion of .9, and a reinforcer proportion of .3 produces a response proportion of .15. Overmatching has been observed much less frequently than either matching or undermatching, but it has been observed in situations where there is a substantial penalty for switching between schedules. For example, Baum (1982) found overmatching when pigeons had to walk around a barrier and over a hurdle to switch from one key to the other. As the effort involved in switching keys was increased, the pigeons switched between keys less and less, and spent most of their time responding on the better VI schedule, which resulted in overmatching.

In the third type of deviation from matching, *bias,* a subject consistently spends more time on one alternative than predicted by the matching equation. Figure 14-2 illustrates the sort of results that might be obtained if a subject has a bias for the right key. When 80 percent of the reinforcers come from the left key, the subject makes only 50 percent of its responses on the left key. When 30 percent of the reinforcers come from the left key, the subject makes only 10 percent of its responses on the left key. A similar preference for the right key is shown for all other reinforcer percentages except 0 percent and 100 percent, where exclusive preference for the only key that is providing reinforcers is predicted.

Many factors can produce a bias, such as a preference for a particular side of the chamber, for a particular response key (if one key requires a bit less effort than the other), or for a particular color (if the two response keys have different colors). In one study where substantial bias was observed, there were no response keys at all, but pigeons could earn reinforcers from two VI schedules simply by standing on one side of the chamber or the other (Baum & Rachlin, 1969). To signal which VI schedule was in effect, the chamber was lit with green light when the subject was on one side, and with red light when the subject was on the other side. Since there were no responses to count, Baum and Rachlin simply measured how much time the birds spent on each side of the chamber. They found a consistent bias for the right side of the chamber, which was illuminated with green light. Baum and Rachlin were not particularly interested in the cause of the bias, but if they wanted to distinguish between a position bias and a color bias they could have switched the green light to the left side of the chamber. If the subjects then showed a bias for the left side, this would suggest a preference for the green light. If the birds still showed a bias for the right side, this would suggest a position preference.

Varying the Quality and Amount of Reinforcement

All of the experiments described so far in this chapter have dealt with two alternatives that deliver exactly the same reinforcer (such as food or verbal approval), but at different rates. In such experiments, the presence of bias might be considered a nuisance that must be corrected for with appropriate counterbalancing. On the other hand, if bias is treated as an indication of preference for one alternative, the matching law can be used to measure a subject's preferences for different types of reinforcers. An interesting study by Harold Miller (1976) showed how this can be done. Like Herrnstein (1961), Miller used different pairs of VI schedules, but the two schedules offered the pigeons two different types of grain as reinforcers. In some conditions, the choice was between hemp and buckwheat, in others it was between wheat and buckwheat, and in others it was between hemp and wheat.

In choices between wheat and buckwheat, for example, Miller found a strong preference (bias) for the wheat, but he suggested that the matching equation could take this bias into account if it were modified in the following way:

$$\frac{B_1}{B_1 + B_2} = \frac{Q_1 R_1}{Q_1 R_1 + Q_2 R_2}, \qquad (14\text{-}2)$$

where Q_1 and Q_2 stand for the *qualities* of the reinforcers available on the two keys. This equation states that a subject's distribution of behavior is determined by both the rate of reinforcement and the quality of reinforcement delivered by the different schedules. Miller arbitrarily assigned a value of 10 to Q_b, the quality of buckwheat, and he found that Equation 14-2 provided a good description of the results if Q_w, the quality of wheat, was given a value of about 14. He interpreted this number as meaning that each wheat reinforcer was worth about 1.4 times as much as each buckwheat reinforcer. Miller made similar calculations for conditions where the alternatives were hemp and buckwheat, and he estimated that Q_h, the quality of hemp, was about 9.1, or slightly less than that of buckwheat.

Miller suggested that his estimates of Q_b, Q_w, and Q_h were measures of the strengths of these different grains as reinforcers, but how do we know they were not simply meaningless numbers? Miller's answer to this question was the same as the one discussed in Chapter 8 as a way of avoiding a tautological definition of reinforcement: The numbers become meaningful and useful if they lead to new predictions that would not be possible without them. The new predictions Miller made were for the third set of choices, those between hemp and wheat. For example, in one condition, both grains were delivered at a rate of 30 reinforcers per hour. With $Q_w = 14$ and $Q_h = 9.1$, Equation 14-2 predicts that subjects should allocate about 61 percent of their responses to the key delivering wheat. For this condition and four others with different VI schedules, the predictions of Equation 14-2 were very close to the subjects' actual behaviors. To recapitulate, Miller separately compared wheat and hemp to buckwheat so as to estimate the values of Q_w and Q_h, and he then used these values to predict pigeons' choices between wheat and hemp with considerable accuracy. This last phase of the experiment provided the strongest evidence for the validity of Equation 14-2.

Besides the rate of reinforcement and the quality of reinforcement, another variable that can affect preference is the amount or size of each reinforcer. If one key delivers two food pellets as a reinforcer and the other key delivers only one, this should certainly affect a subject's choices. Several writers (Baum & Rachlin, 1969; Killeen, 1972) have suggested that amount of reinforcement can be added to the matching equation in the same way that quality of reinforcement was:

$$\frac{B_1}{B_1 + B_2} = \frac{Q_1 R_1 A_1}{Q_1 R_1 A_1 + Q_2 R_2 A_2} , \quad (14\text{-}3)$$

where A_1 and A_2 are the amounts of reinforcement delivered by the two alternatives. In most experiments on choice, only one or two independent variables are studied, so only those need to be considered in the matching equation. For instance, if the two alternatives differed in amount of reinforcement but not in rate or quality, the following equation would be appropriate:

$$\frac{B_1}{B_1 + B_2} = \frac{A_1}{A_1 + A_2} \quad (14\text{-}4)$$

Catania (1963) found results that were quite consistent with Equation 14-4 in a study where pigeons' access to grain was varied between 3 and 6 seconds per reinforcer. Other studies, however, have found large deviations from the predictions of Equation 14-4: Substantial undermatching and overmatching have both been observed (Davison & Hogsden, 1984; Schneider, 1973). As with other deviations from matching, a number of explanations have been offered, but there is no consensus about why they occur (de Villiers, 1977; Dunn, 1982; Logue & Chavarro, 1987).

Punishment and the Matching Law

As discussed in Chapter 1, one important characteristic of a scientific theory is its generality. This is one reason why researchers have tried to determine whether the matching law can be extended to account for quality and amount of reinforcement as well as rate. Similarly, since choices in the real world can involve unpleasant as well as pleasant features, other researchers have attempted to incorporate punishment within the framework of the matching law. Besides providing more information about choice behavior, this research has yielded the added benefit of helping to distinguish between two theories of punishment that were discussed in Chapter 7: the avoidance theory of punishment and the one-factor theory of punishment.

You may recall that according to the avoidance theory of punishment, the effects of punishment are indirect: Punishing one behavior produces a reduction in this behavior only because the individual spends more time doing something else. The reason this other behavior increases is that it is reinforced by the reduction of fear. Let us see how this reasoning could be applied to a choice situation with which we are now well acquainted—the concurrent VI VI situation. Suppose a pigeon begins by receiving about 60 reinforcers per hour from key 1 and about 20 reinforcers per hour from key 2. As predicted by the matching law, the subject makes 75 percent of its responses on key 1. Now suppose a VI schedule that delivers 10 shocks per hour is added to key 1. According to the avoidance theory of punishment, the pigeon will shift more of its responses to key 2 because there are now two sources of reinforcement for pecking this key: (1) the food, and (2) avoiding the fear associated with pecking key 1. Deluty (1976) suggested that the following variation of the matching equation could account for such a situation:

$$\frac{B_1}{B_1 + B_2} = \frac{(R_1 + P_2)}{(R_1 + P_2) + (R_2 + P_1)}, \quad (14\text{-}5)$$

where P_1 and P_2 are the rates of punishment for the two alternatives.

Notice that in this equation, the rate of punishment for alternative 1 is added to the rate of reinforcement for alternative 2, and vice versa. This arrangement captures the basic assumption of the avoidance theory, that punishing one response actually results in additional reinforcement for the other response. In the above example, $P_1 = 10$ and $P_2 = 0$ (since there was no punishment on key 2). By solving Equation 14-5, you should see that it predicts the subject will make 66.7 percent of its responses on key 1 when the shocks are added. (For simplicity, Equation 14-5 gives equal weight to one food reinforcer and one shock, but it would be easy to give them different weights by multiplying P_1 and P_2 by some constant.)

The assumptions of the one-factor theory of punishment are quite different. This theory assumes that reinforcement and punishment are direct opposites, and whereas reinforcement strengthens behavior, punishment weakens behavior. De Villiers (1977, 1980) suggested that this weakening process should be represented in the matching equation by a subtraction operation:

$$\frac{B_1}{B_1 + B_2} = \frac{(R_1 - P_1)}{(R_1 - P_1) + (R_2 - P_2)} \quad (14\text{-}6)$$

Equation 14-6 assumes that just as each reinforcer adds to the value of an alternative, each punisher subtracts from the value of an alternative. For the example described above, where $P_1 = 10$ and $P_2 = 0$, you should be able to calculate that Equation 14-6 predicts 71.4 percent of the subject's responses will be on the left key.

For this example, both the avoidance theory and the one-factor theory predict that the punishment will make the subject's preference for the left key less extreme, and their respective predictions of 66.7 percent and 71.4 percent are so close that it would be difficult to decide between them, given the usual variability in pigeons' behavior. However, the advantage of stating these two theories of punishment in a mathematical form is that Equations 14-5 and 14-6 make clearly different predictions for slightly different choice situations. Suppose we start once again with 60 reinforcers per hour on key 1 and 20 on key 2, but this time we add an equal number of shocks to both keys—10 shocks per hour on each key. With $P_1 = P_2 = 10$, Equation 14-5 again predicts a shift toward indifference: A subject should now make 70 percent of its responses on key 1. In contrast, Equation 14-6 predicts that a subject will move toward exclusive preference, now making 83.3 percent of its responses on key 1. Intuitively, the reason for this prediction is that the shocks have a proportionally greater detrimental effect on key 2, which did not deliver many reinforcers in the first place.

De Villiers (1980) conducted an experiment that was quite similar to this hypothetical experiment, and he found that pigeons shifted toward exclusive preference of the better VI schedule when an equal number of shocks was added to each key. This result is consistent with Equation 14-6 but not with Equation 14-5. De Villiers therefore concluded that the avoidance theory is incorrect, and that the effects of punishment are subtractive, as predicted by the one-factor theory. Other tests of the two theories have been made by Farley (1980), whose results also favored the one-factor theory. On the basis of this evidence it is now possible to conclude with some confidence that the one-factor theory of punishment is correct. This research shows how two theories that seem to make similar predictions when stated verbally may become easy to distinguish when they are expressed mathematically.

An Application to Single Schedules

It may appear that the matching law, which makes predictions for choice situations, has nothing to say about cases where there is only one reinforcement schedule. However, Herrnstein (1970, 1974) developed a way to use the matching law to make predictions about behavior on single VI schedules. To see how Herrnstein's analysis works, let us start with a few arbitrary assumptions. Suppose that a particular pigeon pecks a key at a rate of 2 pecks per second whenever it is responding on a VI schedule. That is, if the bird pecked the key without pausing, it would make 120 pecks per minute. Second, let us assume that although the only way the pigeon can obtain food reinforcers is by pecking the key, there are "built-in" reinforcers (we might call them "Premackian reinforcers") for performing other behaviors such as grooming, exploring, resting, and so on. Herrnstein suggested that whereas the experimenter can control the number of food reinforcers, the built-in reinforcers for nonpecking behaviors are out of the experimenter's control, and they occur at a fairly constant rate.

Although these background reinforcers are not food, in order to perform the necessary calculations we need to measure them in the same units

as the food reinforcers. For this example, let us imagine that all behaviors other than pecking provide the pigeon with built-in reinforcers which have a value equivalent to 30 food reinforcers per hour. Similarly, although the pigeon's various behaviors such as grooming and exploring are quite different from key pecking, we need to measure them on a common scale. A useful strategy is to measure all behaviors in units of time, thereby translating Equation 14-1 to the following:

$$\frac{T_1}{T_1 + T_2} = \frac{R_1}{R_1 + R_2} \tag{14-7}$$

Let T_1 represent the time spent key pecking and T_2 the total time spent in all other behaviors, so that $T_1 + T_2$ equals the total session time. R_1 is the rate at which food reinforcers are delivered by the VI schedule, and R_2 is the equivalent reinforcing value of all the built-in reinforcers (which equals 30 in our example).

We are now ready to make predictions for different VI schedules. If the pigeon is exposed to a VI schedule that delivers 30 reinforcers per hour, Equation 14-7 predicts that the bird will spend half of its time pecking and half of its time engaging in other behaviors (because R_1 and R_2 both equal 30). Since we have assumed that the pigeon pecks at a rate of 2 responses per second, the bird should average about 60 responses per minute during the session. If the bird is now presented with a VI schedule that delivers 90 reinforcers per hour, Equation 14-7 states that it should spend 75 percent of its time pecking, which would result in an average response rate of 90 responses per minute. Similar predictions can be made for any size of VI schedule the experimenter might arrange. The solid curve in Figure 14-3 shows the predictions for our hypothetical example for all reinforcement rates between 0 and 500 food reinforcers per hour. It shows that as the rate of reinforcement increases, Equation 14-7 predicts that response rates will climb toward the animal's full-time rate of 120 pecks per hour. Of course, these predictions are based on specific assumptions about the pigeon's pecking rate and the values of all nonpecking behaviors.

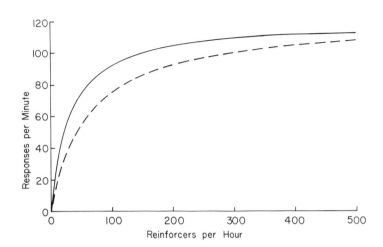

FIGURE 14-3. The two curves depict some representative predictions from Herrnstein's (1970) equation for single reinforcement schedules (Equation 14-7). This equation predicts how response rates should change as reinforcement rates are varied. The solid curve represents a case where there are relatively few reinforcers for behavior other than pecking ($R_2 = 30$ in Equation 14-7). The broken curve represents a case where there are more reinforcers for behaviors other than pecking ($R_2 = 60$), so the subject's rate of pecking should be slower.

Suppose we took this same pigeon and put it in a more interesting chamber where R_2 was equal to 60 (perhaps because this second chamber had a window through which the subject could watch another pigeon). With the increased value of non-pecking behaviors, Equation 14-7 now predicts that the bird will spend less time pecking on all VI schedules, as shown by the broken line in Figure 14-3.

Herrnstein (1970) applied this analysis to the results of an experiment by Catania and Reynolds (1968) in which six pigeons responded on several different VI schedules (presented one at a time, for several sessions each). Figure 14-4 shows the results of Catania and Reynolds (data points), and the curves are the predictions of Equation 14-7. Before these predictions could be made, Herrnstein had to estimate (1) each pigeon's full-time pecking rate, and (2) the value of R_2 for each pigeon. Herrnstein chose values that brought the predictions of Equation 14-7 as close as possible to the results from each pigeon, and these values are listed in the panel for each bird in Figure 14-4. These two numbers can be called *free parameters,* because the theorist is free to select whatever values bring the predictions closest to the data points. Theories that make use of free parameters have less predictive power than those that do not (with all else equal), because no precise predictions can be made before looking at the data. Thus although Herrnstein could predict that the general pattern of results should look something like the curves in Figure 14-3, obviously he could not predict in advance that Catania and Reynolds's first bird would have a higher response rate than any of the others.

Despite the use of two free parameters, the close correspondence between predictions and data points in Figure 14-4 is impressive. De Villiers and Herrnstein (1976) have performed similar analyses of the results from several dozen experiments involving single schedules of reinforcement. These experiments were conducted by many different researchers, and they featured a variety of species, operant responses, and reinforcers. In nearly all cases, the correspondence between the predictions of the matching law and the results was about as good as it was for the Catania and Reynolds (1968) experiment.

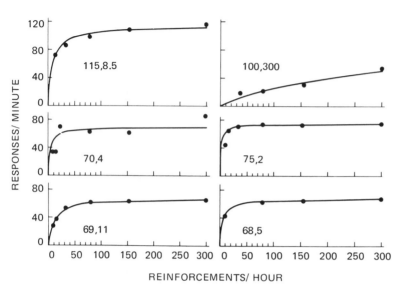

FIGURE 14-4. Each panel shows the results from one of six pigeons in the Catania and Reynolds (1968) experiment. Each point shows the reinforcement rate and response rate on one VI schedule. For each subject, the curve shows the predictions of Equation 14-7, using the best-fitting estimates of the bird's full-time pecking rate and of R_2. The numbers in each panel are the best-fitting estimates of these two quantities. The pattern of results for each subject is well described by Equation 14-7. (From Herrnstein, 1970)

Herrnstein's interpretation of these results can be stated simply: An operant response must compete with all other possible behaviors for the animal's time. As the reinforcement for the operant response increases, the animal will devote more and more of its time to this behavior. Thus Herrnstein suggests that responding on a single VI schedule can be explained using exactly the same principles that apply to choice in a concurrent VI VI situation. Not everyone agrees with Herrnstein's interpretation, however (see, for example, Catania, 1973; Killeen, 1982).

Heyman and Monaghan (1987) provided support for Herrnstein's analysis by showing that the best-fitting estimate of R_2 in Equation 14-7 could be changed by varying a subject's deprivation level. For rats pressing a lever for water reinforcers, estimates of R_2 decreased as the level of water deprivation increased. This is consistent with Herrnstein's interpretation of R_2, because the reinforcing power of nonwater reinforcers should decrease, relatively speaking, as the reinforcing power of water increased. Conversely, Heyman and Monaghan found that making the

lever more difficult to depress lowered the estimates of each animal's full-time response rate, but it produced no change in R_2. They therefore showed that R_2 and the full-time response rate—the two quantities that determine the shape of the response-rate function—could be independently controlled by manipulating the appropriate independent variables.

This distinction between R_2 and the full-time response rate has been put to practical use in the field of behavioral pharmacology, where researchers frequently want to determine the behavioral effects of some drug. By measuring an animal's response rate on a series of VI schedules both with and without the drug, a researcher can determine if the drug affects the hedonic value of the reinforcer, which would change R_2, or if it affects the animal's motor capabilities, which would change the full-time response rate (Hamilton, Stellar, & Hart, 1985; Heyman, Kinzie, & Seiden, 1986).

The matching law also has definite implications for real-world behavior. One important implication is that it is impossible to predict how a reinforcer will affect a behavior without taking into account the context—the other reinforcers that are simultaneously available for other behaviors. This principle is illustrated in Figure 14-3, which shows two different predictions for each VI schedule, depending on the amount of reinforcement available for nonpecking behaviors. As a real-world parallel, try to predict how a young child's behavior would be altered by giving him a new reinforcer—a yo-yo, for example. To make any sensible prediction, we need to know something about the context. If the yo-yo is given on an average rainy day in August, the child may play with the yo-yo for hours, because he may be bored with all his other toys and indoor activities. On the other hand, if the yo-yo is given on Christmas day and the context includes a host of new toys—trucks, video games, puzzles,—the amount of time spent playing with the yo-yo will probably be small. The rich supply of other reinforcers will attract most of his time.

Other examples where the total reinforcement context plays a major role are easy to think of. Many people claim that they tend to eat more when they are bored. This presumably happens not because the reinforcing value of food actually increases when one is bored, but rather because there are few reinforcers available to compete with eating. As another example of a situation where the reinforcement context is meager, imagine that you are sitting in a reception area, waiting for an appointment with someone who is running behind schedule (such as your mechanic or your optometrist). There is little to do but wait, and if you are like me you may find yourself reading magazines you would not ordinarily spend your time on, such as two-year-old issues of *Newsweek, Good Housekeeping,* or *Optometry Today.* What little reinforcement value these outdated magazines offer takes on added significance in the absence of any alternative sources of reinforcement.

THEORIES OF CHOICE BEHAVIOR

In many areas of science, it is important to distinguish between *descriptions* of a phenomenon and *explanations* about the mechanisms that underlie the phenomenon. For example, that statement that water increases in volume when it freezes is simply a description—it does not explain why this expansion occurs. Such descriptive statements can be extremely useful in their own right, for they can help us to predict and control future events (for instance, avoiding the bursting of outdoor water pipes by draining them before they freeze). On the other hand, a statement that attributes this expansion to the crystalline structure that hydrogen and oxygen molecules form when in a solid state can be called an explanation: It is a theory about the molecular events which underlie this phenomenon.

In principle, the matching equation can be viewed as either simply a description of choice behavior or as a theory about the mechanisms of choice behavior. We have seen that, as a description of behavior in certain choice situations, the matching equation is fairly accurate. We will now consider the possibility that the matching law is an explanatory theory, and we will compare it to a few other theories that have been presented as possible explanatory theories of choice.

Matching as an Explanatory Theory

In his earlier writings, Herrnstein (1970, 1974) suggested that the matching equation is also a general explanatory theory of choice behavior. The idea is quite simple: It is possible that animals exhibit matching behavior because they are built to do so. That is, in any choice situation, an animal might measure the value of the reinforcement it receives from each alternative (where "value" encompasses such factors as the rate, size, and quality of the reinforcers), and the animal then might distribute its behavior in proportion to the values of the various alternatives. According to such a theory, matching is not just a description of behavior in concurrent VI VI schedules. It is a general principle that explains how animals make choices in all situations, in the laboratory and in the wild.

Having put forward this theory of choice behavior, let us now examine one reason why Herrnstein later decided that it is incorrect (Herrnstein & Vaughan, 1980). Imagine that a pigeon is presented with a choice between two concurrent VR schedules instead of two VI schedules. Herrnstein and Loveland (1974) conducted such an experiment. For example, in one condition the schedule on the left key was VR 100 and the schedule on the right key was VR 20. After several sessions of experience with these two schedules, all subjects made nearly 100 percent of their responses on the right key. This behavior is certainly reasonable, because it would require, on the average, five times as many responses on the left key to obtain each reinforcer. And although it may not be obvious at first, this behavior is consistent with the matching equation. Remember that the right side of Equation 14-1 represents the number of reinforcers a subject actually receives, not the number of potential reinforcers. If a bird makes 100 percent of its responses on the VR 20 key, it will receive 100 percent of its reinforcers from that key, so the matching equation is satisfied (the percentage of responses matches the percentage of reinforcers). The problem is that the matching equation would also be satisfied if a subject made all of its responses on the VR 100 key: It would receive, for example, 15 reinforcers for 1500 responses on the VR 100 key, and 0 reinforcers for 0 responses on the VR 20 key, and this is also consistent with Equation 14-1.

In summary, the matching equation predicts that subjects will exhibit exclusive preference for one of the two alternatives on a concurrent VR VR schedule (when the ratios are unequal), but it does not specify which alternative. To deal with this problem, Herrnstein and Vaughan (1980; Vaughan, 1981, 1985) have developed a refinement of the matching law that they call *melioration.*

Melioration Theory

To meliorate is to "make better," and in essence the principle of melioration states that animals will invest increasing amounts of time and/or effort into whichever alternative is better. This principle sounds simple enough, but let us see how it can be put into practice.

It is easy to show that Equation 14-1 is equivalent to the following equation:

$$\frac{R_1}{B_1} = \frac{R_2}{B_2}. \tag{14-8}$$

This equation emphasizes the fact that at the point of matching, the ratio of reinforcers received to responses produced is equal for both alternatives. We might say that the "cost" of each reinforcer is the same for both alternatives. The principle of melioration states that if these ratios are not equal, the animal will shift its behavior toward whichever alternative currently has the higher reinforcer:response ratio. Suppose that a subject begins by making approximately equal numbers of responses on each key in a concurrent VI 30-seconds VI 120-seconds schedule. Let us say that the VI 30-seconds schedule delivers 118 reinforcers for 1000 responses in the first hour-long session, and the VI 120-seconds schedule delivers 30 reinforcers for 1000 responses. Since the reinforcer:response ratio is larger on the VI 30-seconds schedule, the principle of melioration predicts that the subject will subsequently make more of its responses on the VI 30-seconds key. You should be able to demonstrate for yourself that the animal's behavior will continue to shift toward the VI 30 seconds key until about 80 percent of the responses are made on this key. At that point, Equation 14-8 is satisfied, so there should be no further shifts in behavior (except for inevitable random variations). In short, the principle of melioration predicts that matching behavior will occur in concurrent VI VI schedules.

Now let us consider concurrent VR VR schedules, which posed problems for the matching law. If the two schedules are VR 30 and VR 120, for example, then their respective reinforcer:response ratios are 1:30 and 1:120. These ratios will not change no matter how the subject distributes its behavior, so the principle of melioration predicts that the subject's behavior will continue to shift toward the VR 30 key until there is no more behavior to shift (that is, until it is responding exclusively at that key). The predictions are the same for any pair of VR schedules: The subject should eventually respond exclusively on the schedule with the more favorable reinforcer:response ratio. In summary, the principle of melioration correctly predicts matching behavior in a choice between two VI schedules, and it predicts exclusive preference for the better of two VR schedules.

Optimization Theory as an Explanation of Matching

As discussed in Chapter 8, some psychologists have proposed that optimization theory is a general explanatory theory of choice for both humans and nonhumans. It is easy to see that optimization theory predicts exclusive preference for the better of two VR schedules—this behavior maximizes reinforcement and minimizes effort. Rachlin, Green, Kagel, and Battalio (1976) proposed that optimization theory can also explain why matching occurs on concurrent VI VI schedules. Before examining their reasoning, it is important to understand the implications of their position. Rachlin et al. proposed that although the matching law may provide a satisfactory description of behavior in these situations, optimization theory actually provides an explanation of matching behavior. They asserted that optimization is the basic mechanism of choice behavior, and the only reason matching occurs in some situations is that it is the optimal thing to do. For Rachlin et al., matching behavior is just one more example of the optimization process at work.

To examine the logic of Rachlin et al., imagine a pigeon on a concurrent VI 30-seconds (left-key) VI 120-seconds (right-key) schedule. Rachlin et al. conducted a series of computer simulations to determine how different ways of distributing responses between the two keys would affect the total rate of reinforcement. The results of these simulations are presented in Figure 14-5. To convince yourself that these simulations are at least approximately correct, first consider what would happen if a pigeon made all of its responses on the left key. The left key would provide about 120 reinforcers per hour, and no reinforcers would be collected from the right key, so the total from the two keys would be about 120 reinforcers per hour (the point at the extreme right in Figure 14-5). If the bird responded only on the right key, it would collect reinforcers only from the VI 120-seconds schedule, so its total reinforcement rate would be about 30 per hour (the point at the extreme left in Figure 14-5.) However, by making some responses on each key, the bird could collect many of the reinforcers from both schedules. The computer

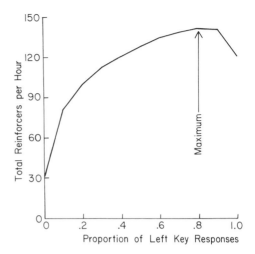

FIGURE 14-5. Predictions of the computer simulations of Rachlin, Green, Kagel, and Battalio (1976) for a concurrent VI 30-seconds (left-key) VI 120-seconds (right-key) schedule. If these predictions are correct, a subject on this schedule would maximize the rate of reinforcement by making 80 percent of its responses on the left key.

simulations of Rachlin et al. projected that the maximum total reinforcement rate would be obtained by allocating 80 percent of one's responses to the left key, which is also the point of matching behavior. The reason for the lower rates of reinforcement with other response proportions is that while responding on one key, the VI clock for the other key might be stopped (with a reinforcer available), and any stoppage of either clock will lower the total reinforcement rate. For instance, if a bird spent 90 percent of its time on the VI 120-seconds key, the clock for the VI 30-seconds key would frequently be stopped, so substantially fewer than 120 reinforcers would be obtained from the latter.

Speaking more generally, Rachlin and his colleagues have proposed that in any typical concurrent VI VI schedule, matching behavior will maximize the rate of reinforcement. Of course, it should take a pigeon some time (perhaps many daily sessions) to determine what manner of responding is optimal. According to optimization theory, an animal in this sort of situation will try different ways of distributing its behaviors (for instance, 50 percent left, 80 percent left, 90 percent left, and so on) and eventually stabilize around the distribution that maximizes the overall rate of reinforcement. Furthermore, just as the human consumer must weigh the costs and benefits of qualitatively different purchases (clothing, entertainment, and so forth), Rachlin assumed that animals must consider several factors such as the value of food, the effort involved in responding, and the value of "leisure time" (times when the animal is not performing the operant response). In discussing the concurrent VI VI situation we were able to ignore the cost of responding because the same response (a key peck) is required for both reinforcers. We ignored leisure time because its role should be neutralized when the choice is simply between pecking one key or another.

Not everyone agrees with the conclusions of Rachlin and his colleagues that matching behavior produces the optimal rate of reinforcement in concurrent VI VI situations. Heyman and Luce (1979) performed some elaborate calculations which suggested that, rather than matching, a slight amount of overmatching optimizes reinforcement rate. Nevertheless, the calculations of Heyman and Luce imply that an animal can achieve close to the maximum rate of reinforcement by matching.

A Test of Optimization Versus Matching. The standard concurrent VI VI situation is not a good one in which to contrast the predictions of the matching law and optimization theory because the two make very similar predictions— both predict matching behavior, or something close to it. To determine which of these principles is a more fundamental rule of choice, it would be best to arrange a choice situation in which the matching law makes one set of predictions and optimization theory makes a very different set of predictions. We could then observe the subjects' behaviors and determine which set of predictions were more accurate. A number of experiments of this type have been conducted (Herrnstein & Heyman, 1979; Herrnstein & Vaughan, 1980), but an experiment of my own (Mazur, 1981) is probably the easiest to describe.

This experiment was not very different in design from Herrnstein's (1961) experiment. Pigeons could peck at either of two keys, and occasionally a response produced a *dark-key period,* in which the red and green key lights were turned off, and food might or might not be presented. The major differences from Herrnstein's experiment were (1) food was not presented in some dark-key periods, and (2) the dark-key periods on both keys were controlled by a single VI timer, not by two separate VI timers as in Herrnstein's experiment. Figure 14-6 outlines the procedure of my experiment. Each time the VI 45-second timer reached the end of an interval, it would stop and assign a dark-key period to one of the two keys on a random basis. The VI timer would not run again until the subject pecked the appropriate key and collected the dark-key period. (The procedure also included a changeover delay of 3 seconds.) The only thing that was changed from condition to condition was the probability that dark-key periods would include a food reinforcer.

In the first condition, all dark-key periods included food. The subjects received about 32 reinforcers per hour on each key, and they made about 50 percent of their responses on each key. This result is not surprising, and it is consistent with both optimization theory and the matching law. The second condition was more revealing. In this condition, only 10 percent of the dark-key periods that followed a red-key response included food; the other 90 percent provided no reinforcer. All dark-key periods that followed a green-key response continued to include food. The matching law predicts that a bird should begin to make many more responses on the green key, since this key will now provide about ten times as many reinforcers. But if a bird shows a preference for the green key, this will lower the total rate of reinforcement. The reason is that if the bird spends long periods of time pecking at the green key, the VI timer will frequently be stopped because a dark-key period has been assigned to the red key. The optimal strategy in this condition (and in all conditions of the experiment) would therefore be to switch back and forth between the two keys frequently, making about 50 percent of one's responses on each key.

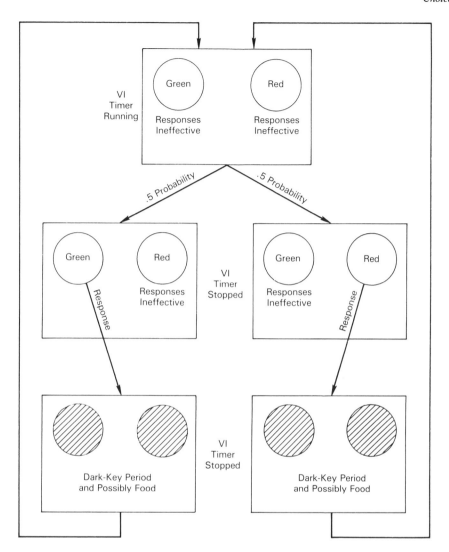

FIGURE 14-6. A schematic diagram of the procedure in Mazur's (1981) experiment.

This strategy would ensure that the VI timer would be running most of the time.

If subjects did not change their behavior between Conditions 1 and 2, they would have received about 32 green-key reinforcers and 3.2 red-key reinforcers per hour (since the only change was that now only 10 percent of the red dark-key periods would include food). However, the birds' behaviors did shift, and at the end of the condition they made an average of 86 percent of their responses on the green key (which delivered about 92 percent of the reinforcers). Because of this shift, the birds received only about 23 reinforcers per hour from the green key and 2 reinforcers from the red key. Thus by showing a strong preference for the green key (as predicted by the matching law), the birds lost about 29 percent of their reinforcers. In some other conditions of the experiment, the birds lost 75 percent or more of their potential reinforcers.

The procedure of this experiment was quite complex, but the results can be stated simply: Although optimization theory predicted that the birds would always allocate about 50 percent of their responses to each key, the birds consistently showed a preference for whichever key delivered more reinforcers, as predicted by the matching law. These preferences produced substantial decreases in the total rate of reinforcement.

As it turned out, the pigeons' performances were more nearly optimal in the first few sessions of a condition (when their response proportions were closer to 50 percent) than in the end of the condition (when they had learned which key delivered more reinforcers and a majority of their responses were directed at this key). For example, in the first six sessions of Condition 2 the birds averaged about 29 reinforcers per hour, as compared to about 25 reinforcers per hour in the last six sessions. Thus the pigeon's behavior shifted in a direction that decreased the rate of reinforcement, exactly the opposite of what optimization theory would predict. This shift brought the distribution of responses closer to matching behavior, however.

Other Tests of Optimization Theory. Using a variety of experimental procedures, psychologists have obtained other types of evidence favoring the matching law (and the related theory of melioration) over optimization theory. For example, in choice situations involving both a VI schedule and a VR schedule, optimization theory predicts that animals will make most of their responses on the VR schedule, since most of the responses on any VI schedule are wasted, whereas every response on a VR schedule brings the animal closer to reinforcement. The results of several experiments failed to support this prediction, but they were consistent with the predictions of the matching law (DeCarlo, 1985; Herrnstein & Heyman, 1979; Heyman & Herrnstein, 1986). Several other experiments, though not necessarily designed to test the matching law, have failed to support the predictions of optimization theory (Ettinger, Reid, & Staddon, 1987; Mazur & Vaughan, 1987; Tierney, Smith, & Gannon,

1987). Although there are still some who favor optimization theory, it has not fared well in experimental tests.

In contrast to these laboratory findings, behavioral ecologists have provided ample evidence that the choices made by many animals in numerous real-world situations are close to those predicted by optimization theory. How can these two sets of findings be reconciled? Staddon and Hinson (1983) offered an answer that relates to the distinction between description and explanation discussed earlier. They suggested that optimization theory provides an adequate description of choice behavior in some situations, but it does not offer the correct explanation of how animals arrive at these optimal choices. As a description of behavior, optimization theory is sometimes right and sometimes wrong, but either way it does not explain how an animal's moment-to-moment choices are made.

Because they deal with a subject's overall distribution of responses over long periods of time (such as over an entire experimental session), matching theory, melioration theory, and optimization theory can be classified as *molar* theories (see Chapter 6). Some researchers now believe that more complete explanations of choice behavior will be found in *molecular* theories, which attempt to predict moment-to-moment behavior, and which assume that short-term consequences have a large influence on choice. For example, after failing to find empirical support for optimization theory, Ettinger et al. (1987) concluded that "animals may not be sensitive to the molar rates of responding and reinforcement....Our animals were sensitive to the schedules at a molecular level, and it is to this molecular level that we should direct our attention" (p. 366). One molecular theory of choice is presented in the next section.

Momentary Maximization Theory

In its most general sense, momentary maximization theory states that at each moment, an organism will select whichever alternative has the highest value *at that moment*. The value of an alternative will usually depend on many factors: the size and quality of the reinforcer, the subject's state of deprivation, and so on. Although both momentary maximization theory and optimization theory state that animals attempt to maximize the value of their choices, the two theories frequently make different predictions because the best choice in the short run is not always the best choice in the long run. As a simple example, consider a dieter who must choose between jello or a strawberry sundae for dessert. The strawberry sundae may appear more attractive at the moment, but the jello might be the more beneficial alternative for the dieter in the long run. Choices that involve a conflict between short-term and long-term benefits will be examined in detail later in the chapter; this issue is raised now only to show that the strategies of momentary maximization and overall optimization may lead to very different decisions.

To understand what sorts of predictions the momentary maximization hypothesis makes for a concurrent VI VI situation, it will be helpful for you to take part in the following hypothetical gambling game. Imagine that you are allowed to play this game for nine trials. You are seated in front of a panel with two small doors, and on each trial you are allowed to open one of the two doors. There may be a dollar behind the door (which you win) or there may be no money. The following rules determine whether a dollar is deposited behind a door or not: There is a modified roulette wheel for each door, which is spun before each trial begins. The probability of winning is .1 on the roulette wheel behind door 1, and .2 on the wheel for door 2. Therefore, on trial 1 of the game, there may be a dollar behind *both* doors, behind *one* door, or behind *neither* door, depending on the outcome of the wheel for each door. Which door do you choose on trial 1?

Two additional rules apply for the next eight trials:

1. Once a dollar is deposited behind a door, it will remain there until you collect it. Thus if a dollar is deposited behind door 1 on trial 4, it will remain there until you choose door 1; say, on trial 7.

2. There will never be more than one dollar behind a door at one time. For instance, if a dollar is deposited behind door 1 on trial 4 and you do not collect it until trial 7, the spinning of the

wheel is irrelevant on trials 5, 6, and 7, since no more dollars will be deposited behind door 1. However, the spinning of the wheel for door 2 will continue to be important on these trials, since it might pay off on any trial. In other words, door 2 is not affected by what is happening at door 1, and vice versa. Before reading further, write down what door you would choose on each of the nine trials.

For a situation like this, momentary maximization theory predicts that a subject will choose whatever alternative has the higher probability of reinforcement on each trial. On trial 1, the probability of reinforcement for door 1 (which will be denoted as p_1) is .1, and the probability of reinforcement for door 2 (p_2) is .2, so momentary maximization theory predicts a choice of door 2. On the second trial, the situation is somewhat different. Assuming door 2 was chosen on trial 1, p_2 is still .2, regardless of whether a dollar was collected on trial 1 or not. But p_1 will be higher on trial 2 because there are two ways a dollar might be deposited—the roulette wheel for door 1 might have paid off on trial 1 (and waits to be collected) or it might have paid off on trial 2. It can be shown (using some elementary rules of probability theory that will not be explained here) that p_1 will be .19 on trial 2. This is still slightly less than p_2, so momentary maximization theory predicts that door 2 will again be chosen.

It can be shown that after two choices of door 2, p_1 will equal .271 and p_2 will equal .2 (because there are now three trials on which a dollar might be deposited at door 1). A momentary maximizer would therefore choose door 1 on trial 3. On trial 4, however, there are two ways to win at door 2 (from a payoff on either trial 3 or 4), so p_2 is again greater than p_1, and door 2 should be chosen. It turns out that the pattern followed by a momentary maximizer on the nine trials would be 2, 2, 1, 2, 2, 1, 2, 2, 1, and this cyclical pattern would be repeated on any additional trials. You can check to see whether your choices followed the momentary maximizing strategy.

This hypothetical gambling game is quite similar to a concurrent VI VI schedule. The two roulette wheels are similar to two independent VI timers, and like VI clocks the roulette wheels will only store one reinforcer at a time. You can therefore probably anticipate what momentary maximizing theory predicts about a subject's behavior on a concurrent VI VI schedule: It predicts that there should be an orderly and cyclical pattern to an animal's moment-by-moment choices. Of course, advocates of momentary maximizing theory (Shimp, 1966; 1969; Silberberg, Hamilton, Ziriax, & Casey, 1978) recognize that animals have limited memorial and decision-making capacities, and they do not expect perfect momentary maximizing behavior to occur. (After all, even people have difficulty determining the probabilities in situations like the gambling game described above.) What they do predict, however, is that animals will exhibit *some tendency* to choose the alternative that has the higher probability of reinforcement. For example, after an animal has made several consecutive responses on the better of two VI schedules, it should show a tendency to switch to the other VI (since a reinforcer may have been stored on this VI during the interim). According to momentary maximizing theory, matching behavior is simply an incidental byproduct of an animal's orderly moment-by-moment choices. In contrast, molar theories of choice do not predict that an animal's moment-to-moment behavior will exhibit any orderly patterns, because these theories assume that an animal's behavior is controlled by variables (for instance, total reinforcement rate) that do not change from moment to moment.

When animals exhibit matching behavior, are there orderly moment-by-moment patterns in their behavior, or are there not? It may seem that it should be easy to obtain an answer to this question, but the results of several experiments have been anything but clear-cut. Some studies have found such patterns (Shimp, 1966; Silberberg et al., 1978), but others have not (Heyman, 1979; Nevin, 1969, 1979). For example, Nevin (1979) analyzed his data in several different ways in search of orderly sequences of responses, but found none. At the molar level, however, the data were quite orderly: The pigeons' overall choice proportions were well described by the matching law. Nevin concluded that the momentary maximizing theory does not provide the correct explanation of why animals match, because matching behavior sometimes occurs even when animals'

choices appear to be random from moment to moment.

In a subsequent article, Hinson and Staddon (1983) used a different method of analysis and came to a different conclusion. Instead of looking at *sequences of responses,* as was done in all previous studies, Hinson and Staddon continually recorded the *time* since a pigeon sampled (pecked at) each of two VI keys. They reasoned that time is the critical independent variable, since on VI schedules it is the passage of time and not the number of responses that actually determines the availability of a reinforcer. They showed that their pigeons could follow a momentary maximizing strategy if they used a fairly simple rule: If schedule 1 delivers, for example, *three times* as many reinforcers as schedule 2, you should check schedule 2 if the time since you last checked it is more than *three times longer* than the time since you last checked schedule 1. Hinson and Staddon showed that their pigeons' behaviors were by no means perfect from the standpoint of momentary maximization theory, but a majority of their responses did follow this rule.

Momentary maximizing theory has been applied to other behaviors besides matching. For example, Silberberg, Warren-Boulton, and Asano (1988) proposed that the theory can explain why interresponse times (and response rates) on VI schedules are moderate, rather than very long or very short. An IRT can be thought of as a delay, during which the animal must wait before making a response and possibly collecting a reinforcer. With long IRTs, the delay is long but the probability of reinforcement is high. With short IRTs, the delay is short but the probability of reinforcement is low. Silberberg et al. suggested that animals maximize the "momentary value" of each response by producing IRTs of intermediate duration, which involve only a moderate delay yet have a reasonable probability of reinforcement.

Not all molecular theories of choice assume that animals follow the principle of momentary maximization. Although animals' choices may be influenced by how quickly the reinforcer is delivered, they may or may not always choose the alternative with the shorter delay or the higher momentary probability. As one example of an alternative molecular theory, Vaughan (1985; Vaughan & Miller, 1984) suggested that different choice responses are strengthened to different degrees by their short-term consequences. A choice response that is followed by a delayed reinforcer will be strengthened less than one followed by an immediate reinforcer, and as a result the first response will be chosen more often in the future. Yet unlike momentary maximizing theory, Vaughan's theory does not predict exclusive preference for the response with greater strength—as long as each has *some* strength, each will be chosen some of the time.

Regardless of whether or not the momentary maximization hypothesis is correct, no one can dispute the more general assertion of molecular theories that short-term factors have a large effect on choice behavior. This should come as no surprise, since previous chapters have shown that response-reinforcer contiguity is very important in operant conditioning. The next section shows that when a small but immediate reinforcer is pitted against a large but delayed reinforcer, the small, immediate reinforcer is frequently chosen.

SELF-CONTROL CHOICES

Every day, people make many choices that involve a conflict between their short-term and long-term interests. Consider the situation of a college student who has a class that meets early Monday morning, in a course where it is important to attend each lecture. On Sunday evening, the student sets her alarm clock so that she can awaken early enough to get to class on time. The student has chosen going to class (and the improved chances for a good grade this will bring) over an hour of extra sleep. This may sound like the prudent choice, but unfortunately the student has plenty of time to change her mind. When the alarm clock rings on Monday morning, the warmth and comfort of the bed seem more appealing than going to class, and the woman turns off the alarm and goes back to sleep. Later in the day, she will probably regret her choice and vow not to miss class again.

This example is a typical *self-control* situation, or one which involves a choice between a small, proximal reinforcer and a larger but more distant reinforcer. The small reinforcer is the extra hour of sleep, and the larger, delayed reinforcer is the better grade that will probably result from going to class. One noteworthy characteristic of self-control situations is that an individual's preferences may exhibit systematic changes over time. On Sunday evening, the woman in our example evidently preferred going to class (and its long-term benefits) over an extra hour of sleep, since she set the alarm for the appropriate time. The next morning, her preference had changed, and she chose the extra hour of sleep. Later that day she regrets this choice, and decides to make a different decision in the future.

In case you are not convinced that self-control situations are commonplace, consider the following everyday decisions. You should be able to identify the small, proximal reinforcer and larger, delayed reinforcer in each case:

1. To smoke a cigarette or not to smoke.
2. To keep the thermostat at 65° during the winter months, or set it at a higher temperature and face a larger fuel bill at the end of the month.
3. When on a diet, to choose between low-fat yogurt or ice cream for dessert.
4. To shout at your roommate in anger or control your temper and avoid saying something you do not really mean.
5. To save money for some big item you want (such as a car) or spend it on parties each weekend.

For each example, you should also be able to see how one's preference might change over time. It is easy to say you will begin a diet—tomorrow. On Monday or Tuesday, it is easy to decide you will have a frugal weekend and begin saving for that car. It is much harder, however, to keep these commitments when the time comes to make your final choice. Herrnstein and Mazur (1987) have argued that this tendency to switch preferences over time in self-control choices is one of the strongest pieces of evidence against optimization theory. If people followed the strategy that optimized their satisfaction in the long run, they would consistently choose one alternative or the other.

Why do people's preferences change over

time in such self-control situations? Is there anything people can do to improve their self-control, to make it less likely that they will make an "impulsive" decision (in favor of the small, proximal reinforcer)? In attempting to answer questions like these, Howard Rachlin (1970, 1974) and George Ainslie (1975) independently developed similar ideas about self-control. The *Ainslie-Rachlin theory,* as it is sometimes called, suggests that changes of preference in self-control situations are understandable if we consider how delay changes a reinforcer's effectiveness.

The Ainslie-Rachlin Theory

The example of the student who must choose between sleep and an important class can be used to illustrate the features of this theory. Its first assumption is that the value of a reinforcer decreases as the delay between making a choice and receiving the reinforcer increases. The upper panel of Figure 14-7 shows that the value of a good grade is high at the end of the term, but on the Sunday and Monday in question its value is much lower because it is so far in the future. In the lower panel, the value of an hour of extra sleep at different points in time is also shown, and the same rule applies to this reinforcer: With greater delays between choice and the delivery of the reinforcer, its value decreases. The second and (very reasonable) assumption of the theory is that a subject will choose whichever reinforcer has the higher value at the moment a choice is made. Notice that the way the curves are drawn in Figure 14-7, the value of the good grade is higher on Sunday evening, which explains why the student sets the alarm with the intention of going to class. On Monday morning, however, the value of an hour of extra sleep has increased substantially because of its proximity. Because it is now greater than that of the good grade, the student chooses the more immediate reinforcer.

If you find the curves in Figure 14-7 difficult to understand, it may help to draw an analogy between time and distance. Figure 14-8 shows a sketch of a long street with two buildings on the left. The buildings are analogous to the two reinforcers in a self-control situation. Building number 2 is clearly larger, but for a person standing at

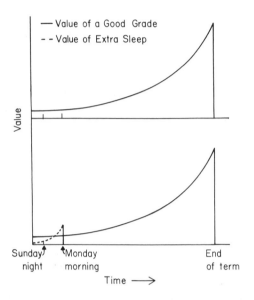

FIGURE 14-7. An application of the Ainslie-Rachlin model to the hypothetical example described in the text. The top panel shows how the subjective value of a good grade increases as the time of its delivery gets closer. The bottom panel shows that the value of a bit of extra sleep also increases as the time of its delivery gets closer. Because of these changes in value, a person may prefer the good grade at some times (such as Sunday evening) and the extra sleep at other times (say, Monday morning).

point A, building number 1 would subtend a greater visual angle. We might say that from the perspective of point A, building 1 appears larger (although people obviously have the ability to take their distances into consideration, and so would not be fooled by this illusion). On the other hand, if the person walked to point B, both buildings would appear smaller, but now the visual angle subtended by building 2 would be the larger of the two. Thus by stepping back from both buildings, a person can get a better perspective on their relative sizes. Similarly, by examining two reinforcers (say, an extra hour of sleep and a better grade) from a distance (for example, the night before a class), a person "gets a better perspective" on the values of the two reinforcers, and is more likely to choose the larger one.

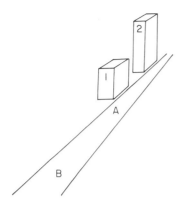

FIGURE 14-8. For a person standing at point A, building 1 subtends a larger visual angle than building 2. The opposite is true for a person standing at point B. This situation is somewhat analogous to a self-control situation if we replace physical distance with time and think of the large distant building as a large, delayed reinforcer and the small, closer building as a small, more immediate reinforcer.

As you can probably see, the student's problem is that she is free to change her mind on Monday morning, when the proximity of the extra hour of sleep gives her a distorted perspective on its value. If she had some way of making her decision of Sunday evening a binding one, she would have a better chance of obtaining the larger, delayed reinforcer. One technique that exploits this possibility is called *precommitment*— the individual makes a decision in advance, which is difficult or impossible to change at a later time. For example, on Sunday evening the student might ask a friend from the same class to come and get her on the way to class Monday morning, and not to take "no" for an answer. This would not make it impossible for the woman to change her mind, but would make it more difficult and more embarrassing to stay in bed. In short, the woman could make a precommitment to go to class by having a friend pick her up. The technique of precommitment is a useful way to avoid making an impulsive choice, and the next section shows that it can work for animals as well as people.

Animal Studies on Self-Control

A good deal of the research supporting the Ainslie-Rachlin theory has involved animal subjects, and this research shows how it is often possible to design simple laboratory analogs of complex real-world situations. Probably the major difference between the self-control situations described above and the following animal research is the time scale involved. With pigeons, rats, and other animals, a delay of a few seconds can often make the difference between self-control and impulsiveness.

A study by Green, Fisher, Perlow, and Sherman (1981) demonstrated the sort of preference reversals we would expect if the Ainslie- Rachlin theory is correct. Pigeons received many trials each day, and on each trial a bird made its choice by pecking just once at one of two keys. A peck at the red key delivered two seconds of grain, and a peck at the green key delivered six seconds of grain. There was, however, a short delay between a peck and the delivery of the reinforcer. For example, in one condition there was a two-second delay for the two-second reinforcer and a six-second delay for the six-second reinforcer. In this condition, the birds showed impulsive behavior on nearly every trial, choosing the two-second reinforcer. This choice did not speed up subsequent trials, because trials occurred every 40 seconds regardless of which choice was made. It should be clear that this behavior was inconsistent with optimization theory, since the optimal solution would have been to choose the six-second reinforcer on every trial. By consistently choosing the smaller but more immediate reinforcer, the birds lost about two-thirds of their potential access to grain.

In another condition, the experimenters simply added 18 seconds to the delay for *each* reinforcer, so the delays were now 20 seconds and 24 seconds. When they had to choose so far in advance, the birds' behaviors were more nearly optimal—they chose the six-second reinforcer on over 80 percent of the trials. This shift in preference when both reinforcers are further away is exactly what the Ainslie-Rachlin model predicts.

Ainslie (1974) conducted an ingenious experiment that showed that at least some pigeons can learn to make use of the strategy of precommitment to avoid impulsive choices. Ainslie's procedure is diagrammed in Figure 14-9. Each pigeon received 50 trials a day, and each trial lasted for exactly 19 seconds no matter what the pigeon did. The top of Figure 14-9 shows the sequence of events that would occur if the bird did not peck the response key at all. The key would first be lit green for a few seconds, then it would be dark for a few seconds, then it would be lit red for three seconds, and then the bird would receive four seconds of access to grain. Thus by doing nothing, the bird was certain to receive four seconds of food. The middle section of Figure 14-9 shows, however, that if the bird pecked at the key at any time when it was red, it would immediately receive two seconds of grain. Ainslie found that each pigeon would almost always peck the key when it was red, thereby exhibiting impulsive behavior—an immediate two seconds of food was evidently preferred over four seconds of food delivered after a delay of only three seconds. When the key turned red, the birds pecked it over 95 percent of the time.

As the bottom of Figure 14-9 shows, the purpose of the initial period when the key was green was to give a subject the chance to make a precommitment for the larger reinforcer. Notice that when the key was green, *both* reinforcers were several seconds away, so the two-second reinforcer should not be so tempting. By making one peck at the green key, a bird made an irreversible choice of the four-second reinforcer—the key never turned red, so there was no opportunity to peck the red key and get an immediate two seconds of food. Three of Ainslie's ten pigeons learned to use the precommitment option, pecking the green key on more than half of the trials. The other subjects did not peck the green at any substantial rate.

Part of the reason Ainslie's precommitment procedure was difficult for some birds to master was that making a precommitment required an active response (a peck at the green key), whereas failing to make a precommitment required nothing more than the passage of time. We might suspect that if pigeons had to make an active choice for or against precommitment before the trial would continue, they might use the precommitment strategy more often. An experiment by Rachlin and Green (1972) showed this to be the case. On each trial a bird had to either peck one key and make a precommitment for a large reinforcer, or peck a second key and later receive a choice between the large reinforcer and a smaller but more immediate reinforcer. In this

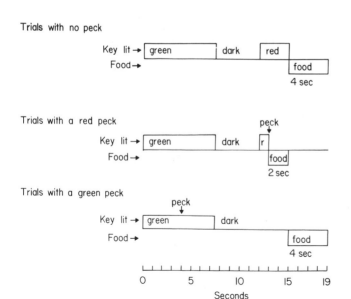

FIGURE 14-9. A diagram of Ainslie's (1974) procedure. The three sections show, from top to bottom, the events on trials with no pecks, with a peck at the red key, and with a peck at the green key.

procedure, four of five pigeons chose the pre-commitment key on a majority of trials, and the fifth subject also chose this key on occasional trials. In summary, the precommitment procedure seems to work because the individual can make an irreversible choice when neither reinforcer is immediately available—when the individual has "a better perspective" on their relative sizes (as illustrated in Figures 14-7 and 14-8).

When the alternatives in a self-control situation are punishers rather than reinforcers, they have the reverse effect on choice. In one study, rats tended to choose a large delayed shock over a smaller but more immediate one. However, when they could make a precommitment, a few seconds before the trial began, to the smaller but more immediate shock, they frequently did so (Deluty, Whitehouse, Mellitz, & Hineline, 1983). This study provides one more example of how reinforcers and punishers have symmetrical but opposite effects on behavior.

Other research with animals has examined factors that may make a subject more or less likely to choose a more preferred but delayed reinforcer. Grosch and Neuringer (1981) used a procedure similar to Ainslie's, except that there was no possibility of precommitment: A pigeon could either wait 15 seconds and then eat a preferred grain, or it could peck a key and receive a less preferred type of grain immediately. (Thus another difference was that the two reinforcers differed in their *quality* rather than their amount). The pigeons must have had a substantial preference for the delayed reinforcer, because Grosch and Neuringer found that they would wait for this reinforcer on about 80 percent of the trials. The experimenters then made one small change in the procedure: The two types of food were now placed where they were visible to the pigeons (behind a transparent barrier) throughout the waiting period. With the reinforcers in plain sight, the pigeons became much more impulsive, and they waited for the preferred reinforcer on only 10 or 15 percent of the trials. The sight of the food evidently provided too much of a temptation to resist. In another study, Grosch and Neuringer found that stimuli associated with the food reinforcers had a similar effect. In this case, no food was visible during the waiting interval,

but the food hoppers were lit with the same colored lights that normally accompanied the presentation of food. Like the presence of food itself, the colored lights made the pigeons more likely to choose the immediate, less desirable grain.

Grosch and Neuringer also found that their pigeons were more likely to wait for the delayed reinforcer if they had the opportunity to engage in some specific activity during the delay. We have seen that with the food in sight, the pigeons would wait for the preferred grain on only about 15 percent of the trials. Grosch and Neuringer then taught the birds to peck at a key in the rear of the chamber, which at first delivered food on a FR 20 schedule. Not surprisingly, the birds found it easier to wait for preferred grain when they could spend the delay working on the FR 20 schedule. More surprising was the fact that when the rear key no longer delivered any reinforcers, the birds continued to peck at it during the delays for the rest of the experiment with no signs of extinction.

These studies illustrate a few of the factors which have been found to affect the self-control choices of animal subjects. The next section shows that these same factors affect children's choices.

Factors Affecting Self-Control in Children

The experiments of Grosch and Neuringer were patterned after a series of experiments conducted by Walter Mischel and his colleagues with children (Mischel, 1966, 1974). In one experiment (Mischel & Ebbesen, 1970), preschool children (tested one at a time) were given a choice between waiting 15 minutes for a preferred reinforcer (such as pretzels) or receiving a less preferred reinforcer (such as cookies) immediately. During the 15-minute wait, a child could terminate the trial at any time and get the less preferred snack. Like the pigeons of Grosch and Neuringer, the children found it considerably more difficult to wait when the reinforcers were visible (in an open cake tin in front of the child). In another study with one different reinforcer, Mischel, Ebbesen, and Zeiss (1972) told some children that they could "think about the marsh-mallow and the pretzel for as long as you want." Other children were given no such instructions. The children who were encouraged to think about the reinforcers chose to terminate the trial and obtain the less preferred reinforcer more frequently. Mischel et al. also found that children were more likely to wait for the preferred reinforcer when given an activity to engage in during the delay (some children were given a slinky to play with).

Mischel's research has uncovered a number of other variables which are related to a child's choice in a self-control situation. For instance, he found that the tendency to wait for a large delayed reinforcer is correlated with age, IQ, the presence of the child's father in the home, and other factors (Mischel, 1961, 1981, 1983). He also showed that a child's behavior in a self-control situation can be greatly influenced by observational learning (Mischel, 1966). Fourth and fifth graders were asked to participate in a "study of consumer behavior." Each child first observed an adult make choices between such items as a set of plastic chess pieces versus wooden pieces, with the latter not available for two weeks. The child then made similar choices, but with items appropriate for children. The child was told to take his decisions seriously, because he would actually receive one of his choices. Some children observed an adult who consistently chose the immediate reinforcer, making such statements as, "Chess figures are chess figures. I can get much use out of the plastic ones right away." Other children observed an adult who chose the delayed reinforcers, noting their better quality and remarking "I usually find that life is more gratifying" when one is willing to wait for good things. Mischel found that children's choices were greatly affected by the adult model's behavior. Furthermore, the model's influence was long-lasting, for most children continued to follow the example of the model they observed when tested four weeks later in a different context. Like so many other behaviors, self-control choices are heavily influenced by observational learning.

Techniques for Improving Self-Control

Behavior therapists can give quite a few suggestions to clients who wish to avoid impulsive behaviors in such varied realms as dieting, maintaining an exercise program, studying regularly, saving money, and avoiding excessive drinking or smoking. Let us look at some of these strategies and see how they relate to the Ainslie-Rachlin model and to the research described above.

We have already seen how a student can make a precommitment to attend an early morning class by arranging to have a classmate meet her and insist that she go. The strategy of precommitment can be used in may other self-control situations. People who wish to lose weight are advised to shop for food when they are not hungry, and to purchase only foods that are low in calories and require some preparation before they can be eaten (Stuart, 1967). The role of precommitment in this case should be obvious. A dieter cannot impulsively eat some high calorie snack if there are none in the house. If a food item requires, say, an hour of cooking, this delay between the time of choice and the time of eating may decrease the value of the food enough so that sticking to the diet seems preferable. People who habitually spend money impulsively are advised to make a list before they go shopping, to take only enough money to buy what they need, to destroy their credit cards, and to avoid going to a shopping center without some definite purpose in mind (Paulsen, Rimm, Woodburn, & Rimm, 1977). All of these strategies make it more difficult for the person to buy something on the spur of the moment because it seems appealing at the time.

As Figure 14-7 suggests, impulsive behaviors occur when the value of a delayed reinforcer is too small to compete with the currently high value of an immediate reinforcer. It follows that any strategy which either increases the value of the delayed alternative or decreases the value of the immediate alternative should make the choice of the delayed reinforcer more likely. One useful strategy is therefore to make an additional, more immediate reinforcer contingent upon the choice of the large delayed reinforcer. For instance, a dieter may make an agreement with himself that he will watch his favorite early evening television program only on those days when he foregoes dessert. A college student who wishes to improve her study habits may allow herself to go out with friends for a snack only after she has studied in the library for two solid hours. Psychologists have labeled this type of strategy *self-reinforcement* because it is the individual who delivers his or her own reinforcers for the appropriate behaviors. Although self-reinforcement can work, a frequent problem is that it is easy to "cheat"—to give yourself the reinforcer even when you have failed to perform the appropriate behavior. For this reason, it is advisable to enlist the help of a friend or family member. The dieter's wife might make sure he only watches his program if he did not have dessert. The college student may go to the library with a conscientious roommate who makes sure she has spent two hours studying (rather than reading magazines or talking with friends) before they go out for a snack.

The complementary strategy is to make the value of the impulsive option lower by attaching some form of punishment to it. Ross (1974) reports a case in which this technique was used to cure a woman of a nail-biting problem. The woman was unhappy with the way her nails looked after she chewed on them, but as with many nail biters she found the behavior inherently reinforcing in the short-run (for reasons that are unclear). As part of her treatment, the woman gave the therapist a deposit of 50 dollars, and she was told that the money would be donated to an organization she intensely disliked (The American Communist Party) if her nails did not grow a certain length each week.

Another strategy for improving self-control relates to the finding of Mischel and his colleagues that observing or even thinking about reinforcers can increase their attractiveness. Although Mischel found that thinking about *both* reinforcers increased impulsiveness, it has frequently been suggested that *selectively* thinking about the large, delayed reinforcer can forestall an impulsive action (Ainslie, 1975; Watson & Tharp, 1985). For instance, a person on a diet may be advised to visualize the attractive healthy body he or she is striving for before sitting down to eat. A similar tactic is to tape a picture of an attractive person in a swimsuit on the refrigerator door to remind you of your long-term goal each time you have the urge for a snack. A person who is trying to save money to buy a large item (such as a camera) might tape a picture of the item to the inside of his wallet, to be seen whenever he reaches for some money. The idea behind all of these tactics is that a picture or visual image somehow bridges the gap between the present and the long-term goal, thereby increasing the subjective value of that goal.

We have surveyed some of the major strategies recommended by behavior therapists for improving self-control. Readers interested in more details and additional strategies can refer to behavioral self-management books such as Watson and Tharp (1985). All of these strategies show that there is more to self-control than simple determination and willpower. People who blame their impulsive behaviors on a lack of willpower may actually be lacking only the knowledge of how to apply the appropriate strategies.

OTHER CHOICE SITUATIONS

Without the Ainslie-Rachlin model, people's behavior in self-control situations might appear paradoxical: Why should an individual's preference vacillate between a small, proximal reinforcer and a larger, more distant reinforcer? Which is the individual's true preference? With the help of the Ainslie-Rachlin model, however, self-control choices become less mysterious. An individual's vacillations in preference are seen as straightforward consequences of the changing delays to the two alternatives. To conclude this chapter on choice behavior, we will examine a few other situations where people's decisions seem paradoxical. In some cases, their decisions appear to be inconsistent; in others, they are self-defeating. We will examine how psychologists have tried to analyze these situations.

Choice with Substitutable Alternatives

Imagine a man who eats at his favorite restaurant about once a week. The food is excellent, but the menu is small: There are only two entrees, fillet mignon and lobster. Over the course of a year, we observe that the man chooses each entree about equally often, with no predictable pattern to his choices. Based on the matching law and similar theories of choice behavior (Luce, 1959), we would probably conclude that the two items have about equal value for this person. But now suppose that the restaurant decides to expand its menu, and it adds crab as a third entree. Observing the man's choices for another year, we find that he now chooses fillet mignon 50 percent of the time, lobster 25 percent of the time, and crab 25 percent of the time. Again using the matching law, we would have to conclude that for this man, the value of fillet mignon is about double the value of lobster, since he selects the fillet mignon about twice as often. The paradox is that we have reached two different conclusions about the relative values of fillet mignon and lobster, depending only on whether a third item is on the menu or not. How can we explain this man's behavior and his apparent inconsistencies in preference?

From an economist's standpoint, the apparent inconsistencies in the man's choices seem to stem from the fact that crab is more similar to lobster than to fillet mignon, so that it may act as a substitute for the former but not for the latter (see Chapter 8 for more on substitutability). In an effort to develop a better understanding of choices involving substitutable commodities, Tversky and Sattath (1979) developed their theory of *preference trees*. The first assumption of this theory is that in almost all choice situations, each alternative is composed of not one but several attributes or characteristics. For instance, the attributes of the fillet mignon on a menu would include the fact that it is a type of beef, the fact that it is tender, its unique flavor, the spices and seasonings with which it is prepared, and so on. The second major assumption of the theory is that in a choice situation a person actually chooses among attributes rather than among the alternatives themselves, and that this decision-making process is frequently hierarchical, involving several steps. Figure 14-10 depicts a simple preference tree for the restaurant example. According to this scenario the man's first level of

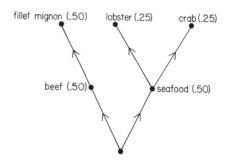

FIGURE 14-10. A preference tree for a choice among fillet mignon, lobster, and crab, for a person with the preferences described in the text.

decision is between the attributes of beef and seafood, which have equal value and are therefore each selected with a probability of .5. If seafood is selected, then a second decision must be made between the unique attributes of lobster and those of crab. Assuming that the unique features of these two alternatives have equal value, each type of seafood will be selected equally often (that is, each with an overall probability of .25). If beef is selected, the second level of decision is trivial, since fillet mignon is the only type of beef on the menu.

You should see how the preference tree in Figure 14-10 accounts for the man's behavior in our example. If crab is not on the menu, it cannot alter the probability of choosing beef versus seafood, so the two remaining items will be chosen with equal probability. Although we cannot predict in advance what a preference tree will look like (another person might have a strong preference for beef over seafood), once we have gathered enough data to construct a tree, we can use it to make new predictions. For instance, how will the man's choices change if another beef entree (such as prime ribs) is added to the menu? According to Figure 14-10, this should decrease the probability of selecting fillet mignon, but it should not alter the probabilities for either seafood item.

Tversky and Sattath did not apply their theory to any actual data on restaurant menu selections, but they did apply it with considerable success to research on people's choices of celebrities they would like to meet, of political parties (with European subjects who had many political parties among which to choose), and of academic disciplines. With regard to political decisions it is easy to see how the numbers and types of candidates can influence the outcome of an election. Suppose that 60 percent of the voters in one state favor the overall positions of the Democratic Party on the most important issues, and the other 40 percent favor the Republican positions. In an election for a Senate seat, the views of the majority would be served if a Democrat were elected. Suppose, however, that there are three candidates in the race—a Republican, a Democrat, and a former Democrat running on an independent ticket. If voters who favor the Democratic positions split their votes between the two latter candidates, they would each receive about 30 percent of the votes, and the Republican candidate would receive 40 percent and win the election. This sort of splintering of constituencies is not uncommon in elections, and it can have the unfortunate consequence of electing the candidate whom a majority of voters favor the least. In elections as well as in restaurants, the number of alternatives on the menu can have a major effect on the decision-making process.

Risky Decisions

The last section dealt with choice situations where the selected alternative would be delivered with certainty—if you order lobster, you can be fairly certain that the waiter will bring you lobster. However, in many everyday decisions the outcomes are not certain. If you invest in a company, you cannot be certain whether its stocks will increase or decrease in value. If you leave home without your umbrella, you cannot be certain whether or not it will rain. If you go to a party, you cannot be certain whether or not you will enjoy yourself. A popular theory which deals with choices among uncertain alternatives is *expected value theory*. Many economists and decision theorists have suggested that this theory offers guidance on what is the most "rational" choice to make in many situations (Edwards, 1955; von Neuman & Morganstern, 1953).

For simplicity, this discussion will be limited to choices where the alternatives are different

sums of money. A basic tenet of expected value theory is that the best estimate of the expected value of an alternative is the product of its dollar value times its probability of occurrence. For example, suppose that you have won a prize in a small contest, and you can select either (A) 4 dollars or (B) a .5 probability of receiving 10 dollars. According to the theory, the expected value of alternative (B) is .5 times 10 dollars, or 5 dollars. The logic behind this calculation is that if you had the opportunity to select alternative (B) again and again, you would earn 10 dollars on about half of the trials, so that the *average* amount earned per trial would be 5 dollars. Thus according to expected value theory, the rational decision would be to choose alternative (B), because the expected value of (A) is only 4 dollars.

The problem with expected value theory as a theory of behavior is that people often do not make the "rational" choice. Imagine that you have won a bigger contest and you can choose a prize of either (C) $3000 with a probability of 1.0, or (D) $4000 with a probability of .8. Stop and decide which you would choose. Kahneman and Tversky (1979) found that 80 percent of the people they surveyed preferred alternative (C), although the expected value of (D) is higher. This phenomenon, first discussed by Allais (1953), is called the *certainty effect* because people seem to prefer a certain reward over an uncertain one with a larger expected value. This preference suggests that whereas the expected value of alternative (D) is $3200, from a subjective viewpoint most people feel that it is worth less than a certain $3000 because of its riskiness.

To make matters more confusing, consider the fact that people are not always averse to choosing a risky alternative. Millions of people regularly play state lottery games, in which they are willing to trade small, certain amounts of money (the dollar bills in their wallets) for the exceedingly small chance of winning a large sum of money. Since the state keeps a certain percentage of the money gambled as its profit, it should be clear that the expected value of a one-dollar lottery ticket is less than one dollar. (That is, for every dollar that is gambled, less than one dollar is paid out as winnings.)

To summarize, it seems that people prefer a

guaranteed outcome to a risky outcome in some cases, but in other cases they prefer the risky outcome. In attempting to explain these and other peculiarities of human decision-making with risky options, Kahneman and Tversky suggested that people tend to use a distorted scale of probabilities when making such judgments. To be more specific, they claimed that very low probabilities are given more weight than they should be according to expected value theory, and intermediate probabilities are given less weight than they should be. The extra weight given to low probabilities accounts for the popularity of lotteries—people think they may get lucky and win even when their chances are miniscule. The lower weight assigned to intermediate probabilities is consistent with Allais's certainty effect. Of course, Kahneman and Tversky's theory provides just one of many possible explanations of people's risk-taking behavior. Regardless of which explanation is correct, it should be emphasized that while expected value theory may suggest choices that are rational in a statistical sense, they may not be the most sensible or adaptive ones. Given a choice between alternatives (C) and (D) above, a parent with bills to pay might be well advised to select the certain $3000 over the possibility of $4000. If she chose the latter and ended up with nothing, the knowledge that this strategy was the optimal one in a statistical sense would be little consolation.

The Tragedy of the Commons

When a person makes an impulsive choice in a self-control situation, the person is acting against his or her long-term interests. The following situations are similar, except here by acting in their short-term interests people make choices that are detrimental to society as a whole.

In an article entitled "The Tragedy of the Commons," Garrett Hardin (1968) described a situation that has far too many parallels in modern society. In many villages of colonial America, the commons was a grasslands owned by the village where any resident could allow his cows to graze freely. The commons was thus a public resource which benefited everyone as long as the number of grazing animals did not grow too

large. This might not happen for decades or for centuries, but according to Hardin it was inevitable that eventually there would be more animals than the commons could support. Then, because of overgrazing, the grass becomes scarce, erosion occurs, and the commons is destroyed, to the detriment of everyone.

Why did Hardin believe this unhappy scenario was inevitable? His reasoning was that it is to each herdsman's benefit to have as many cows as possible, for this will maximize his income. Now suppose an individual must decide whether to add one more cow to his herd. What are the benefits and costs to consider? The benefits are the profits to be earned from this cow, which go entirely to the owner of the cow. The cost is the extra strain imposed upon the commons, but one additional cow will not make much of a difference, and besides, this cost is shared by everyone who uses the commons. Hardin therefore concluded that the herdsman will experience a net gain by adding the additional cow to his herd, and by adding a second cow, and so on.

But this is the conclusion reached by each and every rational herdsman sharing a commons. Therein is the tragedy. Each man is locked into a system that compels him to increase his herd without limit—in a world that is limited. Ruin is the destination toward which all men rush, each pursuing his own best interest in a society that believes in the freedom of the commons. Freedom in a commons brings ruin to all. (Hardin, 1968, p. 1244)

The tragedy of the commons is a play that has been acted out many times in our civilization. The buffalo herds on the American plains were hunted nearly to the point of extinction. Excessive fishing has ruined many of the world's richest fishing areas. Whalers are killing off whales at a rate which may well lead to their extinction, which, besides being deplorable in its own right, will of course put the whalers out of business. With every acre of forest land that is turned into a highway or a shopping mall, there is less wilderness for everyone to enjoy.

Most problems of pollution have a similar structure. A company that must pollute the air in order to manufacture its product cheaply keeps the profits of its enterprise to itself; the air pollution is shared by everyone. Before we condemn big business, however, we should realize that individual people frequently make equally selfish decisions. Every person who drives to work in a large city (rather than walking or taking public transportation) contributes to the air pollution of that city. The reason that many people behave selfishly in this situation is obvious: The driver alone receives the benefits of convenience and comfort that come from driving one's own car. If the driver chose to walk, the reduction in air pollution would be so slight as to be undetectable.

Another instance of the commons tragedy involves a number of large American industries and their unionized workers. Because of the corporations' quests for ever-increasing profits and the unions' efforts to win higher and higher wages, the costs of manufacturing their goods have risen so high that imported goods have taken over a large portion of the domestic market. The result is often losses for corporations and unemployment for the workers. A related problem is the trade deficit of the United States, a consequence of the large amounts of foreign goods Americans buy. Most people know that the trade deficit hurts the economy, and that it would be eliminated if people bought fewer foreign goods. Nevertheless, when an individual consumer is deciding which product to purchase, alleviating the trade deficit usually seems far less important than getting the best buy, regardless of whether the product is domestic or foreign.

Rather than end on this pessimistic note, let us examine how it might be possible to rewrite the ending to the tragedy of the commons. Hardin (1968) and Platt (1973) have suggested several ways in which the tragedy can be averted. These suggestions will probably sound familiar, because in recent years our society has focused a good deal of attention on the problems of pollution, the extinction of wildlife, and the like, as well as on potential solutions. What is interesting, however, is the strong resemblance these solutions bear to the strategies individuals can use to avoid impulsiveness in a self-control situation.

We saw that one powerful technique for improving self-control is the precommitment strategy, in which an individual takes some action in advance that makes it difficult or impossible to make an impulsive choice later. Similarly, a society can decide to make it difficult or impossible for individuals to act in their selfish interests. Thus a society can pass legislation that simply makes it illegal to dump dangerous chemicals where they might seep into the water supply, to pollute the air, or to shoot a member of an endangered species. There will of course be people who complain that such laws are infringements of their freedom, but as Hardin points out, deciding what people are and are not free to do is one of the major tasks of society. Should an individual have any more right to kill another with a dangerous chemical than with a handgun?

Less coercive strategies for self-control situations are those that either attach a punisher to the small, immediate alternative or attach an additional (often immediate) reinforcer to the large, delayed alternative. These strategies do not make an impulsive choice impossible, only less likely. In a similar fashion, a city with traffic and pollution problems can punish the behavior of driving one's own car by prohibiting parking on city streets and by making it expensive to park in parking garages. Based on what we know about punishment, however, it would be advisable to couple such punishment with reinforcement for a desirable alternative behavior. For instance, the city should do all that it can to make public transportation convenient, reliable, safe, and inexpensive.

Finally, we should not underestimate the capacity of human beings to attend to and be influenced by the long-term consequences of their behaviors for society. Just as a picture on the refrigerator can remind a dieter of his long-term goal, educational programs and advertising campaigns can encourage individuals to alter their behaviors for the long-term benefits of the community. A good example is the personal sacrifices American civilians were willing to make for the war effort during World War II, not to mention the soldiers who gave their lives in the name of freedom. From a logical perspective, such behaviors may seem puzzling: Why should people behave in a way that is helpful to others but is harmful to them personally? One solution to this puzzle is simply to assert that, at least in certain circumstances, behaviors that benefit others can

References

Abbott, B. B. & Badia, P. (1986). Predictable versus unpredictable shock conditions and physiological measures of stress: A reply to Arthur. *Psychological Bulletin, 100,* 384–387.

Abbott, B. B., Schoen, L. S., & Badia, P. (1984). Predictable and unpredictable shock: Behavioral measures of aversion and physiological measures of stress. *Psychological Bulletin, 96,* 45–71.

Abelson, R. P. & Lesser, G. S. (1959). The measurement of persuasibility in children. In C. I. Hovland & I. L. Janis (Eds.), *Personality and Persuasibility.* New Haven: Yale University Press.

Abramovitch, R. & Grusec, J. E. (1978). Peer imitation in a natural setting. *Child Development, 49,* 60–65.

Abramowitz, A. J., O'Leary, S. G., & Rosen, L. A. (1987). Reducing off-task behavior in the classroom: A comparison of encouragement and reprimands. *Journal of Abnormal Child Psychology, 15,* 153–163.

Abramson, C. I. & Bitterman, M. E. (1986). The US-preexposure effect in honeybees. *Animal Learning & Behavior, 14,* 374–379.

Abramson, L. Y., Seligman, M. E. P., & Teasdale, J. D. (1978). Learned helplessness in humans: Critique and reformulation. *Journal of Abnormal Psychology, 87,* 49–74.

Adams, C. D. (1982). Variations in the sensitivity of instrumental responding to reinforcer devaluation. *Quarterly Journal of Experimental Psychology, 34B,* 77–98.

Adams, J. A. (1971). A closed-loop theory of motor learning. *Journal of Motor Behavior, 3,* 111–150.

Adams, J. A. (1976). *Learning and memory: An introduction.* Homewood, IL: Dorsey.

Adams, J. A. (1987). Historical review and appraisal of research on the learning, retention, and transfer of human motor skills. *Psychological Bulletin, 101,* 41–74.

Adams, J. A. & Reynolds, B. (1954). Effect of shift in distribution of practice conditions following interpolated rest. *Journal of Experimental Psychology, 47,* 32–36.

Ainslie, G. (1974). Impulse control in pigeons. *Journal of the Experimental Analysis of Behavior, 21,* 485–489.

Ainslie, G. (1975). Specious reward: A behavioral theory of impulsiveness and impulse control. *Psychological Bulletin, 82*, 463– 496.

Alberts, E. & Ehrenfreund, D. (1951). Transposition in children as a function of age. *Journal of Experimental Psychology, 41*, 30–38.

Alexander, A. B., Chai, H., Creer, T. L., Miklich, D. R., Renne, C. M., & Cardoso, R. (1973). The elimination of chronic coughing by response suppression shaping. *Journal of Behavior Therapy and Experimental Psychiatry, 4*, 75–80.

Allais, M. (1953). Le comportement de l'homme rationnel devant le risque, critique des postulats et axiomes de l'ecole Americaine. *Econometrica, 21*, 503–546.

Allaway, T. A. (1971). *Attention, information, and autoshaping.* Ph.D. dissertation, University of Pennsylvania.

Allison, J. (1976). Contrast, induction, facilitation, suppression, and conservation. *Journal of the Experimental Analysis of Behavior, 25*, 185–198.

Allison, J. (1983). *Behavioral Economics.* New York: Praeger.

Allison, J. & Boulter, P. (1982). Wage rate, nonlabor income, and labor supply in rats. *Learning and Motivation, 13*, 324–342.

Allport, D. A., Antonis, B., & Reynolds, P. (1972). On the division of attention: A disproof of the single-channel hypothesis. *Quarterly Journal of Experimental Psychology, 24*, 225–235.

Amiro, T. W. & Bitterman, M. E. (1980). Second-order appetitive conditioning in goldfish. *Journal of Experimental Psychology: Animal Behavior Processes, 6*, 41–48.

Ammons, R. B. (1947). Acquisition of motor skill: II. Rotary pursuit performance with continuous practice before and after a single rest. *Journal of Experimental Psychology, 37*, 393–411.

Ammons, R. B., Farr, R. G., Block, E., Neumann, E., Dey, M., Marion, R., & Ammons, C. H. (1958). Long-term retention of perceptual motor skills. *Journal of Experimental Psychology, 55*, 318–328.

Anderson, J. R. (1985). *Cognitive psychology and its implications* (2nd ed.) New York: Freeman.

Andrews, E. A. & Braveman, N. S. (1975). The combined effects of dosage level and interstimulus interval on the formation of one-trial poison-based aversions in rats. *Animal Learning and Behavior, 3*, 287–289.

Anger, D. (1956). The dependence of interresponse times upon the relative reinforcement of different interresponse times. *Journal of Experimental Psychology, 52*, 145–161.

Anisman, H., Hamilton, M., & Zacharko, R. M. (1984). Cue and response-choice acquisition and reversal after exposure to uncontrollable shock: Induction of response perseveration. *Journal of Experimental Psychology: Animal Behavior Processes, 10*, 229–243.

Annau, Z. & Kamin, L. J. (1961). The conditioned emotional response as a function of intensity of the US. *Journal of Comparative and Physiological Psychology, 54*, 428–432.

Annett, J. (1959). Learning a pressure under conditions of immediate and delayed knowledge of results. *Quarterly Journal of Experimental Psychology, 11*, 3–15.

Aristotle. *De memoria et reminiscentia.* Ca. 350 B.C. J. A. Smith (trans.) in W. D. Ross (Ed.) (1931). *The Works of Aristotle* (Vol. 3). Oxford: Clarendon Press.

Arthur, A. Z. (1986). Stress of predictable and unpredictable shock. *Psychological Bulletin, 100*, 379–383.

Averill, J. R. (1973). Personal control over aversive stimuli and its relationship to stress. *Psychological Bulletin, 80*, 286–303.

Ayres, J. J. B., Bombace, J. C., Shurtleff, D., & Vigorito, M. (1985). Conditioned suppression tests of context-blocking hypothesis: Testing in the absence of the preconditioned context. *Journal of Experimental Psychology: Animal Behavior Processes, 11*, 1–14.

Ayres, J. J. B., Haddad, C., & Albert, M. (1987). One-trial excitatory backward conditioning as assessed by conditioned suppression of licking in rats: Concurrent observations of lick suppression and defensive behaviors. *Animal Learning & Behavior, 15*, 212–217.

Azrin, N. H. (1956). Effects of two intermittent schedules of immediate and nonimmediate punishment. *Journal of Psychology, 42*, 3–21.

Azrin, N. H. (1960). Effects of punishment intensity during variable-interval reinforcement. *Journal of the Experimental Analysis of Behavior, 3*, 123–142.

Azrin, N. H. & Holz, W. C. (1966). Punishment. In W. K. Honig (Ed.), *Operant behavior: Areas of research and application.* Englewood Cliffs, N.J.: Prentice Hall.

Azrin, N.H., Holz, W.C., & Hake, D. F. (1963). Fixed-ratio punishment. *Journal of the Experimental Analysis of Behavior, 6*, 141–148.

Baer, D. M., Peterson, R. F., & Sherman, J.A. (1967). The development of imitation by reinforcing behavioral similarity to a model. *Journal of the Experimental Analysis of Behavior, 10,* 405–416.

Badia, P., Culbertson, S., & Harsch, J. (1973). Choice of longer or stronger signaled shock over shorter or weaker unsignaled shock. *Journal of the Experimental Analysis of Behavior, 19,* 25–32.

Bailey, C. H. & Chen, M. (1983). Morphological basis of long-term habituation and sensitization in *Aplysia. Science, 220,* 91–93.

Baird, I. S. & Hughes, G. H. (1972). Effects of frequency and specificity of information feedback on acquisition and extinction of a positioning task. *Perceptual and Motor Skills, 34,* 567–572.

Baker, A. G., Woods, W., Tait, R., & Gardiner, K. (1986). Punishment suppression: Some effects on alternative behaviour. *Quarterly Journal of Experimental Psychology, 38B,* 191–215.

Baker, K. E., Wylie, R. C., & Gagne, R. M. (1950). Transfer of training to a motor skill as a function of variation in rate of response. *Journal of Experimental Psychology, 40,* 721–732.

Baker, T. B. & Tiffany, S. T. (1985). Morphine tolerance as habituation. *Psychological Review, 92,* 78–108.

Balaz, M. A., Kasprow, W. J., & Miller, R. R. (1982). Blocking with a single compound trial. *Animal Learning & Behavior, 10,* 271–276.

Baldwin, J. M. (1906). *Mental development, methods, and processes.* New York: Macmillian.

Balsam, P. D. (1985). The functions of context in learning and performance. In P. D. Balsam & A. Tomie (Eds.), *Context and learning.* Hillsdale, N.J.: Erlbaum.

Balsam, P. D. & Tomie, A. (Eds.) (1985). *Context and learning.* Hillsdale, N.J.: Erlbaum.

Bandura, A. (1962). Social learning through imitation. In M. R. Jones (Ed.), *Nebraska symposium on motivation.* Lincoln: University of Nebraska Press.

Bandura, A. (1965). Influence of models' reinforcement contingencies on the acquisition of imitative responses. *Journal of Personality and Social Psychology, 1,* 589–595.

Bandura, A. (1969). *Principles of behavior modification.* New York: Holt, Rinehart, & Winston.

Bandura, A. (1986). *Social foundations of thought and action.* Englewood Cliffs, N. J.: Prentice-Hall.

Bandura, A., Blanchard, E. B., & Ritter, B. (1969). Relative efficacy of desensitization and modeling approaches for inducing behavioral, affective, and attitudinal changes. *Journal of Personality and Social Psychology, 13,* 173–199.

Bandura, A., Grusec, J. E., & Menlove, F. L. (1967). Vicarious extinction of avoidance behavior. *Journal of Personality and Social Psychology, 5,* 16–23.

Bandura, A. & Huston, A. C. (1961). Identification as a process of incidental learning. *Journal of Abnormal and Social Psychology, 63,* 311–318.

Bandura, A. & Kupers, C. J. (1964). The transmission of patterns of self-reinforcement through modeling. *Journal of Abnormal and Social Psychology, 69,* 1–9.

Bandura, A. & McDonald, F. J. (1963). Influence of social reinforcement and the behavior of models in shaping children's moral judgements. *Journal of Abnormal and Social Psychology, 67,* 274–281.

Bandura, A. & Menlove, F. L. (1968). Factors determining vicarious extinction of avoidance behavior through symbolic modeling. *Journal of Personality and Social Psychology, 8,* 99–108.

Bandura, A., Ross, D., & Ross, S. A. (1963). Imitation of film-mediated aggressive models. *Journal of Abnormal and Social Psychology, 66,* 3–11.

Bandura, A. & Walters, R. H. (1959). *Adolescent aggression.* New York: Ronald.

Bandura, A. & Walters, R. H. (1963). *Social learning and personality development.* New York: Holt, Rinehart, & Winston.

Barlow, H. B. (1972). Single units and sensation: A neural doctrine for perceptual psychology? *Perception, 1,* 371–394.

Barlow, D. H. (1984). Single case experimental designs: Strategies for studying behavior change. (2nd ed.). New York: Pergamon.

Baron, A., Kaufman, A., & Fazzini, D. (1969). Density and delay of punishment of free–operant avoidance. *Journal of the Experimental Analysis of Behavior, 12,* 1029–1037.

Bartlett, F. C. (1932). *Remembering: A study in experimental and social psychology.* Cambridge, England: Cambridge University Press.

Battalio, R. C. & Kagel, J. H. (1985). Consumption-leisure tradeoffs of animal workers: Effects of increasing and decreasing marginal wage rates in a closed economy experiment. In V. L. Smith (Ed.), *Research in experimental economics* (Vol. 2). Greenwich, Conn.: JAI Press.

Battig, W. F. & Montague, W. E. (1969). Category norms for verbal items in 56 categories: A replication and extension of the Connecticut category norms. *Journal of Experimental Psychology Monograph.* (No. 3 Part 2).

Baum, M. (1966). Rapid extinction of an avoidance response following a period of response prevention in the avoidance apparatus. *Psychological Reports, 18*, 59–64.

Baum, M. (1976). Instrumental learning: Comparative studies. In M. P. Feldman & A. Broadhurst (Eds.), *Theoretical and experimental bases of the behaviour therapies.* New York: Wiley.

Baum, M. (1987). Distraction during flooding (exposure): Concordance between results in animals and man. *Behavior Research & Therapy. 25*, 227–228.

Baum, M., Pereira, J., & Leclerc, R. (1985). Extinction of avoidance responding in rats: the noise-intensity parameter in noise-facilitation of flooding. *Canadian Journal of Psychology, 39*, 529–535.

Baum, W. M. (1973). The correlation–based law of effect. *Journal of the Experimental Analysis of Behavior, 20*, 137–153.

Baum, W. M. (1974). On two types of deviation from the matching law: Bias and undermatching. *Journal of the Experimental Analysis of Behavior, 22*, 231–242.

Baum, W. M. (1979). Matching, undermatching, and overmatching in studies of choice. *Journal of the Experimental Analysis of Behavior, 32*, 269–281.

Baum, W. M. (1982). Choice, changeover, and travel. *Journal of the Experimental Analysis of Behavior, 38*, 35–49.

Baum, W. M. & Rachlin, H. C. (1969). Choice as time allocation. *Journal of the Experimental Analysis of Behavior, 12*, 861-874.

Beatty, W. W. & Shavalia, D. A. (1980). Rat spatial memory: Resistance to retroactive interference at long retention intervals. *Animal Learning and Behavior, 8*, 550–552.

Beecher, M. D. (1988). Some comments on the adaptationist approach to learning. In R. C. Bolles & M. D. Beecher (Eds.), *Evolution and learning.* Hillsdale, N. J.: Erlbaum.

Beecher, M. D., Medvin, M. B., Stoddard, P. K., & Loesch, P. (1986). Acoustic adaptations for parent-offspring recognition in swallows. *Experimental Biology, 45*, 179–193.

Beidleman, W. B. (1981). Group assertive training in correctional settings: A review and methodological critique. *Journal of Offender Counselling, Services & Rehabilitation, 6*, 69–87.

Bekesy, G. von. (1964). Sweetness produced electrically on the tongue and its relation to taste theories. *Journal of Applied Physiology, 19*, 1105–1113.

Bekesy, G. von. (1966). Taste theories and the chemical stimulation of single papillae. *Journal of Applied Physiology, 21*, 1–9.

Bellack, A. S., Hersen, M., & Kazdin, A. E. (1982). *International handbook of behavior modification and therapy.* New York: Plenum.

Berger, D. E., Pezdek, K., & Banks, W. P. (Eds.) (1987). *Application of cognitive psychology: Problem solving, education, and computing.* Hillsdale, N.J.: Erlbaum.

Berger, T. W. & Weisz, D. J. (1987). Rabbit nictitating membrane responses. In I. Gormezano, W. F. Prokasy, & R. F. Thompson (Eds.), *Classical conditioning.* (3rd ed.). Hillsdale, N.J.: Erlbaum.

Bernstein, D. A. & Kleinknecht, R. A. (1982). Multiple approaches to the reduction of dental fear. *Journal of Behavior Therapy and Experimental Psychiatry, 13*, 287–292.

Bernstein, I. L., Webster, M. M., & Bernstein, I. D. (1982). Food aversions in children receiving chemotherapy for cancer. *Cancer, 50*, 2961–2963.

Bersh, P. J., Notterman, J. M., & Schoenfeld, W. N. (1956). Extinction of human cardiac-response during avoidance-conditioning. *American Journal of Psychology, 69*, 244–251.

Best, M. R. (1984). Associative and nonassociative sources of interference with the acquisition of a flavor aversion. In M. L. Commons, R. J. Herrnstein, & A. R. Wagner (Eds.) *Quantitative analyses of behavior: (Vol. 3). Acquisition.* Cambridge, Mass.: Ballinger.

Best, M. R. & Meachum, C. L. (1986). The effects of stimulus preexposure on taste-mediated environmental conditioning: Potentiation and overshadowing. *Animal Learning & Behavior, 14*, 1–5.

Bilodeau, E. A. (1954). Rate recovery in a repetitive motor task as a function of successive rest periods. *Journal of Experimental Psychology, 48*, 197–203.

Bilodeau, E. A. & Bilodeau, I. M. (1958). Variation of temporal intervals among critical events in five studies of knowledge of results. *Journal of Experimental Psychology, 55*, 603–612.

Bilodeau, I. M. (1956). Accuracy of a simple positioning response with variation in the number of trials by which knowledge of results is delayed. *American Journal of Psychology, 69*, 434–437.

Bilodeau, I. M. (1966). Information feedback. In E. A. Bilodeau (Ed.), *Acquisition of skill.* New York: Academic.

Bird, A. M. & Rikli, R. (1983). Observational learning and practice variability. *Research Quarterly for Exercise and Sport, 54*, 1–4.

Black, A. H. (1959). Heart rate changes during avoidance learning in dogs. *Canadian Journal of Psychology, 13*, 229–242.

Black, A. H. (1965). Cardiac conditioning in curarized dogs: The relationship between heart rate and skeletal behavior. In W. F. Prokasy (Ed.), *Classical conditioning: A symposium*. New York: Appleton-Century-Crofts.

Black-Cleworth, P., Woody, C. D., & Neimann, J. A. (1975). A conditioned eye-blink obtained by using electrical stimulation of the facial nerve as the unconditioned stimulus. *Brain Research, 90*, 45–46.

Blakemore, C. & Cooper, G. F. (1970). Development of the brain depends on the visual environment. *Nature, 228*, 477–478.

Blanchard, E. B. & Young, L. D. (1974). Clinical applications of biofeedback training: A review of evidence. *Archives of General Psychiatry, 30*, 573–589.

Blough, D. S. (1959). Delayed matching in the pigeon. *Journal of the Experimental Analysis of Behavior, 2*, 151–160.

Blough, D. S. (1982). Pigeon perception of letters of the alphabet. *Science, 218*, 397–398.

Boakes, R. A. & Halliday, M. S. (1975). Disinhibition and spontaneous recovery of response decrements produced by free reinforcement in rats. *Journal of Comparative and Physiological Psychology, 88*, 436–446.

Bolles, R. C. (1970). Species-specific defense reactions and avoidance learning. *Psychological Review, 77*, 32–48.

Bolles, R. C., Stokes, L. W., & Younger, M. S. (1966). Does CS termination reinforce avoidance behavior? *Journal of Comparative and Physiological Psychology, 62*, 201–207.

Bootzin, R. R. (1972). Stimulus control treatment for insomnia. *Proceedings of the 80th Annual Convention of the American Psychological Association, 7*, 395–396.

Bootzin, R. R. & Nicassio, P. M. (1978). Behavioral treatments for insomnia. In M. Hersen, R. M. Eisler, & P. M. Miller (Eds.), *Progress in Behavior Modification* (Vol. 6). New York: Academic.

Bossom, J. (1974). Movement without proprioception. *Brain Research, 71*, 285–296.

Bottjer, S. W. (1982). Conditioned approach and withdrawal behavior in the pigeon: Effects of a novel extraneous stimulus during acquisition and extinction. *Learning and Motivation, 13*, 44–67.

Bouton, M. E. & Bolles, R. C. (1985). Contexts, event–memories, and extinction. In P. D. Balsam & A. Tomie (Eds.), *Context and learning*. Hillsdale, N.J.: Erlbaum.

Bower, G. H. (1975). Cognitive psychology: An introduction. In W. K. Estes (Ed.), *Handbook of learning and cognitive processes* (Vol. 1). Hillsdale, N.J.: Erlbaum.

Bracewell, R. J. & Black, A. H. (1974). The effects of restraint and noncontingent preshock on subsequent escape learning in the rat. *Learning and Motivation, 5*, 53–69.

Braveman, N. S. (1977). Visually guided avoidance of poisonous foods in mammals. In L. M. Barker, M. R. Best, & M. Domjan (Eds.), *Learning mechanisms in food selection*. Waco, Tex.: Baylor University Press.

Breland, K. & Breland, M. (1961). The misbehavior of organisms. *American Psychologist, 16*, 681–684.

Brimer, C. J. (1970). Inhibition and disinhibition of an operant response as a function of the amount and type of prior training. *Psychonomic Science, 21*, 191–192.

Brogden, W. J. (1939). Sensory pre-conditioning. *Journal of Experimental Psychology, 25*, 323–332.

Brown, P. L. & Jenkins, H. M. (1968). Auto-shaping of the pigeon's key-peck. *Journal of the Experimental Analysis of Behavior, 11*, 1–8.

Brown, R. (1965). *Social psychology*. New York: The Free Press.

Brown, R. (1985). *Social psychology* (2nd ed.). New York: Free Press.

Brown, R. & Herrnstein, R. J. (1975). *Psychology*. Boston: Little-Brown.

Brown, T. (1820). *Lectures on the philosophy of the human mind*. (Vols. 1 and 2). Edinburgh: James Ballantyne.

Bucher, B. & Fabricatore, J. (1970). Use of patient-administered shock to suppress hallucinations. *Behavior Therapy, 1*, 382–385.

Budzynski, T. H., Stoyva, J. M., Adler, C. S., & Mullaney, M. A. (1973). EMG biofeedback and tension headache: A controlled outcome study. In L. Birk (Ed.), *Biofeedback: Behavioral medicine*. New York: Grune & Stratton.

Bullock, D. & Neuringer, A. (1977). Social learning by following: An analysis. *Journal of the Experimental Analysis of Behavior, 25*, 127–135.

Burish, T. G. (1981). EMG biofeedback in the treatment of stress-related disorders. In C. K. Prokop & L. A. Bradley (Eds.), *Medical psychology: Contributions to behavioral medicine.* New York: Academic.

Burnstein, E., Stotland, E., & Zander, A. (1961). Similarity to a model and self-evaluation. *Journal of Abnormal and Social Psychology, 62,* 257–264.

Bush, R. R. & Mosteller, F. (1955). *Stochastic models for learning.* New York: Wiley.

Butler, R. A. (1953). Discrimination learning by rhesus monkeys to visual-exploration motivation. *Journal of Comparative and Physiological Psychology, 46,* 95–98.

Bykov, K. M. (1957). *The cerebral cortex and the internal organs* (W. H. Gantt, Trans.). New York: Chemical Publishing Co.

Capaldi, E. J. (1966). Partial reinforcement: A hypothesis of sequential effects. *Psychological Review, 73,* 459–477.

Capaldi, E. J. (1967). A sequential hypothesis of instrumental learning. In K. W. Spence & J. T. Spence (Eds.), *The psychology of learning and motivation* (Vol. 1). New York: Academic.

Capaldi, E. J., Verry, D. R., & Davison, T. L. (1980). Memory, serial anticipation pattern learning and transfer in rats. *Animal Learning and Behavior, 8,* 575–585.

Carew, T. J., Hawkins, R. D., & Kandel, E. R. (1983). Differential classical conditioning of a defensive withdrawal reflex in *Aplysia californica. Science, 219,* 397–400.

Castellucci, V., Pinsker, H., Kupfermann, I., & Kandel, E. R. (1970). Neuronal mechanisms of habituation and dishabituation of the gill-withdrawal reflex in *Aplysia. Science, 167,* 1745–1748.

Catania, A. C. (1963). Concurrent performances: A baseline for the study of reinforcement magnitude. *Journal of the Experimental Analysis of Behavior, 6,* 299–300.

Catania, A. C. (1973). Self-inhibiting effects of reinforcement. *Journal of the Experimental Analysis of Behavior, 19,* 517–526.

Catania, A. C., Matthews, T. J., Silverman, P. J., & Yohalem, R. (1977). Yoked variable-ratio and variable-interval responding in pigeons. *Journal of the Experimental Analysis of Behavior, 28,* 155–161.

Catania, A. C. & Reynolds, G. S. (1968). A quantitative analysis of the responding maintained by interval schedules of reinforcement. *Journal of the Experimental Analysis of Behavior, 11,* 327–383.

Cerella, J. (1982). Mechanisms of concept formation in the pigeon. In D. J. Ingle, M. A. Goodale, & R. J. W. Mansfield (Eds.), *Analysis of visual behavior.* Cambridge, Mass.: MIT Press.

Champion, R. A. & Jones, J. E. (1961). Forward, backward, and pseudoconditioning of the GSR. *Journal of Experimental Psychology, 62,* 58–61.

Charbonneau, C., Robert, M., Bourassa, G., & Gladu-Bissonnette, S. (1976). Observational learning of quantity conservation and Piagetian generalization tasks. *Developmental Psychology, 12,* 211–217.

Charnov, E. L. (1976). Optimal foraging: Attack strategy of a mantid. *American Naturalist, 110,* 141–151.

Chomsky, N. (1959). Review of Skinner's *Verbal behavior. Language, 35,* 26–58.

Chomsky, N. (1972a). *Language and the mind.* New York: Harcourt, Brace, Jovanovich.

Chomsky, N. (1972b). Psychology and ideology. *Cognition, 1,* 11–46.

Church, R. M. (1978). The internal clock. In S. H. Hulse, H. Fowler, & W. K. Honig (Eds.), *Cognitive processes in animal behavior.* Hillsdale, N.J.: Erlbaum, 277–310.

Church, R. M. (1984). Properties of the internal clock. In J. Gibbon & L. Allen (Eds.), *Timing and time perception.* New York: Annals of the New York Academy of Sciences, Vol. 438.

Church, R. M., Getty, D. J., & Lerner, N. D. (1976). Duration discrimination by rats. *Journal of Experimental Psychology: Animal Behavior Processes, 4,* 303–312.

Church, R. M., Lolordo, V. M., Overmier, J. B., Solomon, R. L., & Turner, L. H. (1966). Cardiac responses to shock in curarized dogs. *Journal of Comparative and Physiological Psychology, 62,* 1–7.

Church, R. M. & Meck, W. H. (1984). The numerical attribute of stimuli. In H. L. Roitblat, T. G. Bever, & H.S. Terrace (Eds.), *Animal cognition.* Hillsdale, N.J.: Erlbaum.

Colwill, R. M. & Rescorla, R. A. (1985a). Postconditioning devaluation of a reinforcer affects instrumental responding. *Journal of Experimental Psychology: Animal Behavior Processes, 11,* 120–132.

Colwill, R. M. & Rescorla, R. A. (1985b). Instrumental responding remains sensitive to reinforcer devaluation after extensive training. *Journal of Experimental Psychology: Animal Behavior Processes, 11,* 520–536.

Colwill, R. M. & Rescorla, R. A. (1986). Associative structures in instrumental learning. In G. H. Bower (Ed.), *The psychology of learning and motivation* (Vol. 20). New York: Academic Press.

Colwill, R. M. & Rescorla, R. A. (1988). Associations between the discriminative stimulus and the reinforcer in instrumental learning. *Journal of Experimental Psychology: Animal Behavior Processes, 14*, 155–164.

Conger, R., & Killeen, P. (1974). Use of concurrent operants in small group research. *Pacific Sociological Review, 17*, 399–416.

Cook, M., Minecka, S., & Trumble, D. (1987). The role of response-produced and exteroceptive feedback in the attenuation of fear over the course of avoidance learning. *Journal of Experimental Psychology: Animal Behavior Processes, 13*, 239–249.

Cook, R. G. (1980). Retroactive interference in pigeon short-term memory by a reduction in ambient illumination. *Journal of Experimental Psychology: Animal Behavior Processes, 6*, 326–338.

Cook, R. G., Brown, M. F., & Riley, D. A. (1985). Flexible memory processing by rats: Use of prospective and retrospective information in the radial maze. *Journal of Experimental Psychology: Animal Behavior Processes, 11*, 453–469.

Creer, T. L., Chai, H., & Hoffman, A. (1977). A single application of an aversive stimulus to eliminate chronic cough. *Journal of Behavior Therapy and Experimental Psychiatry, 8*, 107–109.

Crossman, E. K. (1968). Pause relationships in multiple and chained fixed-ratio schedules. *Journal of the Experimental Analysis of Behavior, 11*, 117–126.

Crossman, E. K., Bonem, E. J., & Phelps, B. J. (1987). A comparison of response patterns on fixed-, variable-, and random-ratio schedules. *Journal of the Experimental Analysis of Behavior, 48*, 395–406.

Crowell, C. R., Hinson, R. E., & Siegel, S. (1981). The role of conditional drug responses in tolerance to the hypothermic effect of ethanol. *Psychopharmacology, 72*, 147–153.

Cunningham, C. E. & Linscheid, T. R. (1976). Elimination of chronic infant ruminating by electric shock. *Behavior Therapy, 1*, 231–234.

D'Amato, M. R. (1973). Delayed matching and short-term memory in monkeys. In G. H. Bower (Ed.), *The psychology of learning and motivation* (Vol. 7). New York: Academic.

D'Amato, M. R., Salmon, D. P., & Colombo, M. (1985). Extent and limits of the matching concept in monkeys (*Cebus apella*). *Journal of Experimental Psychology: Animal Behavior Processes, 11*, 35–51.

D'Amato, M. R. & Van Sant, P. (1988). The person concept in monkeys (*Cebus apella*). *Journal of Experimental Psychology: Animal Behavior Processes, 14*, 43–55.

Darwin, C. (1859). *On the origin of species by means of natural selection.* London: Murray.

Davenport, D. G. & Olson, R. D. (1968). A reinterpretation of extinction in discriminated avoidance. *Psychonomic Science, 13*, 5–6.

Davidson, E. S. & Smith, W. P. (1982). Imitation, social comparison, and self-reward. *Child Development, 53*, 928–932.

Davidson, T. L. & Rescorla, R. A. (1986). Transfer of facilitation in the rat. *Animal Learning & Behavior, 14*, 380–386.

Davis, H. & Albert, M. (1986). Numerical discrimination by rats using sequential auditory stimuli. *Animal Learning & Behavior, 14*, 57–59.

Davison, M. & Hogsden, I. (1984). Concurrent variable-interval schedule performance: Fixed versus mixed reinforcer durations. *Journal of the Experimental Analysis of Behavior, 41*, 169–182.

Davison, M. & Jenkins, P. E. (1985). Stimulus discriminability, contingency discriminability, and schedule performance. *Animal Learning & Behavior, 13*, 77–84.

Davison, M. & McCarthy, D. (1988). *The matching law.* Hillsdale, N. J.: Erlbaum.

DeCarlo, L. T. (1985). Matching and maximizing with variable-time schedules. *Journal of the Experimental Analysis of Behavior, 43*, 75–81.

Deluty, M. Z. (1976). Choice and the rate of punishment in concurrent schedules. *Journal of the Experimental Analysis of Behavior, 25*, 75–80.

Deluty, M. Z., Whitehouse, W. G., Mellitz, M., & Hineline, P. N. (1983). Self-control and commitment involving aversive events. *Behaviour Analysis Letters, 3*, 213–219.

den Brinker, B. P., Stabler, J. R., Whiting, H. T., & Van Wieringen, P. C. (1986). The effect of manipulating knowledge of results on the learning of slalom-type ski movements. *Ergonomics, 29*, 31–40.

Denny, M. R. (1971). Relaxation theory and experiments. In F. R. Brush (Ed.), *Aversive conditioning and learning.* New York: Academic.

Desimone, R., Albright, T. D., Gross, C. G., & Bruce, C. (1984). Stimulus-selective properties of inferior temporal neurons in the macaque. *Journal of Neuroscience, 4*, 2051–2062.

de Villiers, P. A. (1977). Choice in concurrent schedules and a quantitative formulation of the law of effect. In W. K. Honig & J. E. R. Staddon (Eds.), *Handbook of operant behavior*. Englewood Cliffs, N.J.: Prentice Hall.

de Villiers, P. A. (1980). Toward a quantitative theory of punishment. *Journal of the Experimental Analysis of Behavior, 33*, 15–25.

de Villiers, P. A. & Herrnstein, R. J. (1976). Toward a law of response strength. *Psychological Bulletin, 83*, 1131–1153.

Dews, P. B. (1962). The effect of multiple S^Δ periods on responding on a fixed-interval schedule. *Journal of the Experimental Analysis of Behavior, 5*, 369–374.

DiCara, L. V. (1970). Learning in the autonomic nervous system. *Scientific American, 222*, 30 –39.

Dinsmoor, J. A. (1954). Punishment: I. The avoidance hypothesis. *Psychological Review, 61*, 34– 46.

Dinsmoor, J. A. (1955). Punishment: II. An interpretation of empirical findings. *Psychological Review, 62*, 96–105.

Dinsmoor, J. A. (1977). Escape, avoidance, punishment: Where do we stand? *Journal of the Experimental Analysis of Behavior, 28*, 83–95.

Dodwell, P. C. & Bessant, D. E. (1960). Learning without swimming in a water maze. *Journal of Comparative and Physiological Psychology, 53*, 422– 425.

Domjan, M. (1983). Biological constraints on instrumental and classical conditioning: Implications for general process theory. In G. H. Bower (Ed.), *The psychology of learning and motivation* (Vol. 17). New York: Academic.

Domjan, M. & Best, M. R. (1980). Interference with ingestional aversion learning produced by preexposure to the unconditioned stimulus: Associative and nonassociative aspects. *Learning and Motivation, 11*, 522–537.

Domjan, M. & Burkhard, B. (1982). *The principles of learning and behavior*. Monterey, Cal.: Brooks/Cole.

Domjan, M. & Galef, B. G. (1983). Biological constraints on instrumental and classical conditioning: Retrospect and prospect. *Animal Learning and Behavior, 11*, 151–161.

Domjan, M. & Hollis, K. L. (1988). Reproductive behavior: A potential model system for adaptive specializations in learning. In R. C. Bolles & M. D.

Beecher (Eds.), *Evolution and learning*. Hillsdale, N. J.: Erlbaum.

Donegan, N. H. & Wagner, A. R. (1987). Conditioned diminution and facilitation of the UR: A sometimes opponent-process interpretation. In I. Gormezano, W. F. Prokasy, & R. F. Thompson (Eds.), *Classical conditioning*. Hillsdale, N. J.: Erlbaum.

Dore, L. R. & Hilgard, E. R. (1937). Spaced practice and the maturation hypothesis. *Journal of Psychology, 4*, 245–259.

Dorr, D. & Fey, S. (1974). Relative power of symbolic adult and peer models in the modification of children's moral choice behavior. *Journal of Personality and Social Psychology, 29*, 335–341.

Dougan, J. D., McSweeney, F. K., & Farmer-Dougan, V. A. (1986). Behavioral contrast in competitive and noncompetitive environments. *Journal of the Experimental Analysis of Behavior, 46*, 185–197.

Drabman, R. & Spitalnik, R. (1973). Social isolation as a punishment procedure: A controlled study. *Journal of Experimental Child Psychology, 16*, 236–249.

Drugan, R. C., Ader, D. N., & Maier, S. F. (1985). Shock controllability and the nature of stress-induced analgesia. *Behavioral Neuroscience, 99*, 791–801.

Dunham, P. J. (1972). Some effects of punishment on unpunished responding. *Journal of the Experimental Analysis of Behavior, 17*, 443– 450.

Dunham, P. J. & Grantmyre, J. (1982). Changes in a multiple-response repertoire during response-contingent punishment and response restriction: Sequential relationships. *Journal of the Experimental Analysis of Behavior, 37*, 123–133.

Dunn, R. M. (1982). Choice, relative reinforcer duration, and the changeover ratio. *Journal of the Experimental Analysis of Behavior, 38*, 313–319.

Durlach, P. J. (1986). Explicitly unpaired procedure as a response elimination technique in autoshaping. *Journal of Experimental Psychology: Animal Behavior Processes, 12*, 172–185.

Durlach, P. J. & Mackintosh, N. J. (1986). Transfer of serial reversal learning in the pigeon. *Quarterly Journal of Experimental Psychology, 38B*, 81–95.

Ebbinghaus, H. (1885). *Memory*. Leipzig: Duncker. H. A. Ruger and C.E. Bussenius (trans.) (1913). New York: Teachers College, Columbia University.

Edelstein, B. A. & Eisler, R. M. (1976). Effects of modeling and modeling with instructions and feedback on the behavioral components of social skills. *Behavior Therapy, 7*, 382–389.

Edwards, C. A., Jagielo, J. A., & Zentall, T. R. (1983). "Same/different" symbol use by pigeons. *Animal Learning & Behavior, 11,* 348–355.

Edwards, C. A., Jagielo, J. A., Zentall, T. R., & Hogan, D. E. (1982). Acquired equivalence and distinctiveness in matching-to-sample and related problems. *Journal of Experimental Psychology: Animal Behavior Processes, 8,* 244–259.

Edwards, W. (1955). The prediction of decisions among bets. *Journal of Experimental Psychology, 50,* 201–214.

Ehrenfreund, D. (1952). A study of the transposition gradient. *Journal of Experimental Psychology, 43,* 81–87.

Eibl-Eibesfeldt, I. (1975). *Ethology* (2nd ed.). New York: Holt, Rinehart & Winston.

Eikelboom, R. & Stewart, J. (1982). Conditioning of drug-induced physiological responses. *Psychological Review, 89,* 507–528.

Ellis, N. R., Detterman, D. K., Runcie, D., McCarver, R. B., & Craig, E. M. (1971). Amnesic effects in short-term memory. *Journal of Experimental Psychology, 89,* 357–361.

Ellison, G. D. (1964). Differential salivary conditioning to traces. *Journal of Comparative and Physiological Psychology, 57,* 373–380.

Elsmore, T. F., Fletcher, G. V., Conrad, D. G., & Sodetz, F. J. (1980). Reduction of heroin intake in baboons by an economic constraint. *Pharmacology, Biochemistry and Behavior, 13,* 729–731.

Epstein, R. (1983). Resurgence of previously reinforced behavior during extinction. *Behaviour Analysis Letters, 3,* 391–397.

Epstein, R. (1985a). Animal cognition as a praxist views it. *Neuroscience & Biobehavioral Reviews, 9,* 623–630.

Epstein, R. (1985b). Extinction-induced resurgence: Preliminary investigations and possible applications. *The Psychological Record, 35,* 143–153.

Epstein, R. (1985c). The spontaneous interconnection of three repertoires. *Psychological Record, 35,* 131–141.

Epstein, R. (1987). The spontaneous interconnection of four repertoires of behavior in a pigeon (*Columba livia*). *Journal of Comparative Psychology, 101,* 197–201.

Epstein, R., Kirshnit, C. E., Lanza, R. P., & Rubin, L. C. (1984). "Insight" in the pigeon: Antecedents and determinants of intelligent performance. *Nature, 308,* 61–62.

Epstein, S. M. (1971). Toward a unified theory of anxiety. In B. A. Maher (Ed.), *Progress in experimental personality research* (Vol. 4). New York: Academic.

Eron, L. D. (1987). The development of aggressive behavior from the perspective of developing behaviorism. *American Psychologist, 42,* 435–442.

Estes, W. K. (1944). An experimental study of punishment. *Psychological Monographs, 57,* (3, Whole No. 263).

Estes, W. K. (1950). Toward a statistical theory of learning. *Psychological Review, 57,* 94–107.

Estes, W. K. (1955). Statistical theory of spontaneous recovery and regression. *Psychological Review, 62,* 145–154.

Etscorn, F. & Stephens, R. (1973). Establishment of conditioned taste aversions with a 24-hour CS-US interval. *Physiological Psychology, 1,* 251–253.

Ettinger, R. H., Reid, A. K., & Staddon, J. E. R. (1987). Sensitivity to molar feedback functions: A test of molar optimality theory. *Journal of Experimental Psychology: Animal Behavior Processes, 13,* 366–375.

Ettinger, R. H. & Staddon, J. E. R. (1982). Behavioral competition, component duration and multiple-schedule contrast. *Behavioural Analysis Letters, 2,* 31–38.

Evarts, E. V. & Tanji, J. (1974). Gating of motor-cortex reflexes by prior instruction. *Brain Research, 71,* 479–494.

Evers, W. L. & Schwarz, J. C. (1973). Modifying social withdrawal in preschoolers: The effects of filmed modeling and teacher praise. *Journal of Abnormal Child Psychology, 1,* 248–256.

Fagan, A., Eichenbaum, H., & Cohen, N. J. (1987). Normal learning set and facilitation of reversal learning in rats with combined fornix-amygdala lesions: Implications for preserved learning abilities in amnesia. *Annals of the New York Academy of Sciences, 444,* 510–512.

Fanselow, M. E. (1980). Conditional and unconditional components of post-shock freezing. *Pavlovian Journal of Biological Science, 15,* 177–182.

Fanselow, M. S. & Lester, L. S. (1988). A functional behavioristic approach to aversively motivated behavior: Predatory imminence as a determinant of the topography of defensive behavior. In R. C. Bolles & M. D. Beecher (Eds.), *Evolution and learning.* Hillsdale, N. J.: Erlbaum.

Farley, J. (1980). Reinforcement and punishment effects in concurrent schedules: A test of two models. *Journal of the Experimental Analysis of Behavior, 33,* 311–326.

Ferchmin, P. A. & Eterovic, V. A. (1980). Four hours of enriched experience are sufficient to increase cortical weight of rats. *Society for Neuroscience Abstracts, 6,* 857.

Ferguson, J. M., Taylor, C. B., & Wermuth, B. (1978). A rapid behavioral treatment for needle phobics. *Journal of Nervous and Mental Disease, 166,* 294–298.

Ferster, C. B. (1958). Control of behavior in chimpanzees and pigeons by time out from positive reinforcement. *Psychological Monographs, 72*(461).

Ferster, C. B. & Skinner, B. F. (1957). *Schedules of reinforcement.* New York: Appleton- Century-Crofts.

Field, T., Goldstein, S., Vega-Lahr, N., & Porter, K. (1986). Changes in imitative behavior during early infancy. *Infant Behavior and Development, 9,* 415– 421.

Field, T. M., Woodson, R., Greenberg, R., & Cohen, D. (1982). Discrimination and imitation of facial expressions by neonates. *Science, 218,* 179–181.

Finch, G. (1938). Salivary conditioning in atropinized dogs. *American Journal of Physiology, 124,* 136–141.

Fisher, J. & Hinde, C. A. (1949). The opening of milk bottles by birds. *British Birds, 42,* 347–357.

Fitts, P. M. & Posner, M. I. (1967). *Human performance.* Belmont, Cal.: Brooks/Cole.

Ford, M. R. (1982). Biofeedback treatment for headaches, Raynaud's disease, essential hypertension, and irritable bowel syndrome: A review of the long-term follow-up literature. *Biofeedback and Self-Regulation, 7,* 521–536.

Fouts, R. S., Hirsch, A. D., & Fouts, D. H. (1982). Cultural transmission of a human language in a chimpanzee mother-infant relationship. In H. E. Fitzgerald, J. A. Mullins, & P. Gage (Eds.), *Child nurturance* (Vol. 3). New York: Plenum.

Fox, D. K., Hopkins, B. L., & Anger, W. K. (1987). The long-term effects of a token economy on safety performance in open-pit mining. *Journal of Applied Behavior Analysis. 20,* 215–224.

Fox, L. (1962). Effecting the use of efficient study habits. *Journal of Mathetics, 1,* 75–86.

Fraenkel, G. S. & Gunn, D. L. (1940). *The orientation of animals: Kineses, taxes, and compass reactions.* Oxford, England: Oxford University Press.

Frank, P. (1949). *Modern science and its philosophy.* Cambridge, Mass.: Harvard University Press.

Franks, J. J. & Bransford, J. D. (1971). Abstraction of visual patterns. *Journal of Experimental Psychology, 90,* 65–74.

Freedman, J. L. (1986). Television violence and aggression: A rejoinder. *Psychological Bulletin, 100,* 372–378.

Friedrich-Cofer, L. & Huston, A. C. (1986). Television violence and aggression: The debate continues. *Psychological Bulletin, 100,* 364–371.

Galbicka, G. & Branch, M. N. (1981). Selective punishment of interresponse times. *Journal of the Experimental Analysis of Behavior, 35,* 311–322.

Galbicka, G. & Platt, J. R. (1984). Interresponse-time punishment: A basis for shock-maintained behavior. *Journal of the Experimental Analysis of Behavior, 41,* 291–308.

Gamzu, E. R. & Schwartz, B. (1973). The maintenance of key pecking by stimulus-contingent and response-independent food presentation. *Journal of the Experimental Analysis of Behavior, 19,* 65–72.

Gamzu, E. R. & Williams, D. R. (1973). Associative factors underlying the pigeon's key pecking in auto-shaping procedures. *Journal of the Experimental Analysis of Behavior, 19,* 225–232.

Garcia, J., Ervin, F. R., & Koelling R. A. (1966). Learning with prolonged delay of reinforcement. *Psychonomic Science, 5,* 121–122.

Garcia, J., Hankins, W. G., Robinson, J. H., & Vogt, J. L. (1972). Bait shyness: Tests of CS-US mediation. *Physiology and Behavior, 8,* 807– 810.

Garcia, J. & Koelling, R. (1966). Relation of cue to consequence in avoidance learning. *Psychonomic Science, 4,* 123–124.

Garcia, J., McGowan, B. K., & Green, K. F. (1972). Biological constraints on conditioning. In A. H. Black and W. F. Prokasy (Eds.), *Classical conditioning II: Current theory and research.* New York: Appleton-Century-Crofts.

Gardner, R. A. & Gardner, B. T. (1969). Teaching sign language to a chimpanzee. *Science, 165,* 664 – 672.

Gardner, R. A. & Gardner, B. T. (1975). Early signs of language in child and chimpanzee. *Science, 187,* 752–753.

Gerbner, G., Gross, L., Eleey, M. F., Jackson-Beeck, M., Jeffries-Fox, S., & Signorielli, N. (1977). TV violence profile No. 8: The highlights. *Journal of Communication, 27,* 171–180.

Gibbon, J. & Balsam, P. (1981). Spreading association in time. In C. M. Locurto, H. S. Terrace, & J. Gibbons (Eds.), *Autoshaping and conditioning theory.* New York: Academic.

Gillan, D. J. (1981). Reasoning in the chimpanzee: II. Transitive inference. *Journal of Experimental Psychology: Animal Behavior Processes, 7,* 150 –164.

Gillan, D. J., Premack, D., & Woodruff, G. (1981). Reasoning in the chimpanzee: I. Analogical Reasoning. *Journal of Experimental Psychology: Animal Behavior Processes, 7,* 1–17.

Gittelson, B. (1977). *Biorhythm: A personal science.* New York: Warner Books.

Glasscock, S. G., Friman, P. C., O'Brien, S., & Christopherson, E. R. (1986). Varied citrus treatment of ruminant gagging in a teenager with Batten's disease. *Journal of Behavior Therapy and Experimental Psychiatry, 17,* 129–133.

Gleitman, H. (1971). Forgetting of long-term memories in animals. In W. K. Honig & P. H. R. James (Eds.), *Animal memory.* New York: Academic.

Glencross, D. J. (1977). Control of skilled movements. *Psychological Bulletin, 84,* 14–29.

Glueck, S. & Glueck, E. (1950). *Unravelling juvenile delinquency.* Cambridge, Mass.: Harvard University Press.

Goldiamond, I., Atkinson, C. J., & Bilger, R. C. (1962). Stabilization of behavior and prolonged exposure to delayed auditory feedback. *Science, 135,* 437–438.

Goldsmith, J. B. & McFall, R. M. (1975). Development and evaluation of an interpersonal skill-training program for psychiatric inpatients. *Journal of Abnormal Psychology, 84,* 51–58.

Gonzalez, R. C., Gentry, G.V., & Bitterman, M. E. (1954). Relational discrimination of intermediate size in the chimpanzee. *Journal of Comparative and Physiological Psychology, 47,* 385–388.

Goodall, G. (1984). Learning due to the response-shock contingency in signalled punishment. *Quarterly Journal of Experimental Psychology, 36B,* 259–279.

Gordon, W. C. (1983). The malleability of memory in animals. In R. L. Mellgren (Ed.), *Animal cognition and behavior.* Amsterdam: North-Holland Publishing.

Gordon, W. C., McGinnis, C. M., & Weaver, M. S. (1985). The effect of cuing after backward conditioning trials. *Learning and Motivation, 16,* 444–463.

Gordon, W. C., Smith, G. J., & Katz, D. S. (1979). Dual effects of response blocking following avoidance learning. *Behavior Research and Therapy, 17,* 479–487.

Gormezano, I. & Coleman, S. R. (1973). The law of effect and CR contingent modification of the UCS. *Conditional Reflex, 8,* 41–56.

Gould, M. S. & Shaffer, D. (1986). The impact of suicide in television movies: Evidence of imitation. *New England Journal of Medicine, 315,* 690–694.

Grant, D. S. (1975). Proactive interference in pigeon short-term memory. *Journal of Experimental Psychology: Animal Behavior Processes, 1,* 207–220.

Grant, D. S. (1976). Effect of sample presentation time on long-delay matching in the pigeon. *Learning and Motivation, 7,* 580–590.

Grant, D. S. (1981). Short-term memory in the pigeon. In N. E. Spear & R. R. Miller (Eds.), *Information processing in animals: Memory mechanisms.* Hillsdale, N.J.: Erlbaum.

Grant, D. S. (1982). Stimulus control of information processing in rat short-term memory. *Journal of Experimental Psychology: Animal Behavior Processes, 8,* 154–164.

Grant, D. S. (1984). Rehearsal in pigeon short-term memory. In H. L. Roitblat, T. L. Bever, & H. S. Terrace (Eds.), *Animal Behavior.* Hillsdale, N.J.: Erlbaum.

Grant, D. S., Brewster, R. G., & Stierhoff, K. A. (1983). "Surprisingness" and short-term retention in pigeons. *Journal of Experimental Psychology: Animal Behavior Processes, 9,* 63–79.

Grant, D. S. & Roberts, W. A. (1978). Sources of retroactive inhibition in pigeon short-term memory. *Journal of Experimental Psychology: Animal Behavior Processes, 2,* 1–16.

Green, L., Fischer, E. B., Perlow, S., & Sherman, L. (1981). Preference reversal and self control: Choice as a function of reward amount and delay. *Behavior Analysis Letters, 1,* 43–51.

Green, L. & Kagel, J. H. (Eds.) (1987). *Behavioral economics.* Norwood, N. J.: Ablex.

Green, L., Kagel, J. H., & Battalio, R. C. (1987). Consumption-leisure tradeoffs in pigeons: Effects of changing marginal rates by varying amount of reinforcement. *Journal of the Experimental Analysis of Behavior, 47,* 17–28.

Grinker, R. & Spiegel, J. (1945). *Men under stress.* London: Churchill.

Grosch, J. & Neuringer, A. (1981). Self-control in pigeons under the Mischel paradigm. *Journal of the Experimental Analysis of Behavior, 35,* 3–21.

Gross, C. G., Rocha-Miranda, C. E., & Bender, D. B. (1972). Visual properties of neurons in inferotemporal cortex of the macaque. *Journal of Neurophysiology, 35,* 96–111.

Gulliksen, H. (1932). Studies of transfer of response: I. Relative versus absolute factors in the discrimination of size by the white rat. *Journal of Genetic Psychology, 40,* 37–51.

Gunn, D. L. (1937). The humidity reactions of the wood-louse, *Porcellio Scaber* (Latreille). *Journal of Experimental Biology, 14,* 178–186.

Guthrie, E. R. (1935). *The psychology of learning.* New York: Harper.

Guthrie, E. R. & Horton, G. P. (1946). *Cats in a puzzle box.* New York: Holt, Rinehart and Winston.

Gutman, A. (1977). Positive contrast, negative induction, and inhibitory stimulus control in the rat. *Journal of the Experimental Analysis of Behavior, 27,* 219–233.

Guttman, N. & Kalish, H. I. (1956). Discriminability and stimulus generalization. *Journal of Experimental Psychology, 51,* 79–88.

Hake, D. F., Donaldson, T., & Hyten, C. (1983). Analysis of discriminative control by social behavioral stimuli. *Journal of the Experimental Analysis of Behavior, 39,* 7–23.

Hall, G. & Channell, S. (1985). A comparison of intradimensional and extradimensional shift learning in pigeons. *Behavioral Processes, 10,* 285–295.

Hall, G., Kaye, H., & Pearce, J. M. (1985). Attention and conditioned inhibition. In R. R. Miller & N. E. Spear (Eds.), *Information processing in animals: Conditioned inhibition.* Hillsdale, N. J.: Erlbaum.

Hall, G. & Pearce, J. M. (1983). Changes in stimulus associability during acquisition: Implications for theories of acquisition. In M. L. Commons, R. J. Herrnstein, & A. R. Wagner (Eds.), *Quantitative analyses of behavior: (Vol. 3). Acquisition.* Cambridge, Mass.: Ballinger.

Halliday, M. S. & Boakes, R. A. (1971). Behavioral contrast and response independent reinforcement. *Journal of the Experimental Analysis of Behavior, 16,* 429– 434.

Hamilton, A. L., Stellar, J. R., & Hart, E. B. (1985). Reward, performance, and the response strength method in self-stimulating rats: Validation and neuroleptics. *Physiology and Behavior, 35,* 897–904.

Hanson, H. M. (1959). Effects of discrimination training on stimulus generalization. *Journal of Experimental Psychology, 58,* 321–334.

Hanson, J. & Green, L. (1986). Time and response matching with topographically different responses. *Animal Learning & Behavior, 14,* 435– 442.

Hanson, S. J. & Timberlake, W. (1983). Regulation during challenge: A general model of learned performance under schedule constraint. *Psychological Review, 90,* 261–282.

Hardin, G. (1968). The tragedy of the commons. *Science, 162,* 1243–1248.

Harlow, H. F. (1949). The formation of learning sets. *Psychological Review, 56,* 51–65.

Harnick, F. S. (1978). The relationship between ability level and task difficulty in producing imitation in infants. *Child Development, 49,* 209–212.

Hatze, H. (1976). Biomechanical aspects of a successful motion optimization. In P. V. Komi (Ed.), *Biomechanics V-B.* Baltimore: University Park Press.

Hawkins, R. D., Carew, T. J., & Kandel, E. R. (1983). Effects of inter-stimulus interval and contingency on classical conditioning in *Aplysia. Society for Neuroscience Abstracts, 9,* 168.

Hawkins, R. D. & Kandel, E. R. (1984). Is there a cell-biological alphabet for simple forms of learning? *Psychological Review, 91,* 375–391.

Hayes, C. (1951). *The ape in our house.* New York: Harper.

Hayes, J. R. (1984). *Problem solving techniques.* Philadelphia: Franklin Institute Press.

Hayes, L. A. & Watson, J. S. (1981). Neonatal imitation: Fact or artifact? *Developmental Psychology, 17,* 655–660.

Hearst, E. & Jenkins, H. M. (1974). Sign tracking: The stimulus-reinforcer relation and directed action. *Monograph of the Psychonomic Society.* Austin, Tex.

Hebb, D. O. (1956). The distinction between "classical" and "instrumental." *Canadian Journal of Psychology, 10,* 165–166.

Hekimian, L. J. & Gershon, S. (1968). Characteristics of drug abusers admitted to a psychiatric hospital. *Journal of the American Medical Association, 205,* 125–130.

Heller, R. F. & Strang, H.R. (1973). Controlling bruxism through automated aversive conditioning. *Behavior Research and Therapy, 11,* 327–329.

Hendry, D. P. & Van-Toller, C. (1964). Fixed-ratio punishment with continuous reinforcement. *Journal of the Experimental Analysis of Behavior, 7,* 293–300.

Herman, L. M. (1975). Interference and auditory short-term memory in the bottlenosed dolphin. *Animal Learning and Behavior, 3,* 43– 48.

Herman, L. M. & Forestell, P. H. (1985). Reporting presence or absence of named objects by a language-trained dolphin. *Neuroscience & Biobehavioral Reviews, 9,* 667– 681.

Herman, L. M., Richards, D. G., & Wolz, J. P. (1984). Comprehension of sentences by bottlenosed dolphins. *Cognition, 16,* 1–90.

Herman, L. M. & Thompson, R. K. R. (1982). Symbolic, identity, and probe delayed matching of sounds by the bottlenosed dolphin. *Animal Learning & Behavior, 10,* 22–34.

Heron, W. T. & Skinner, B. F. (1940). The rate of extinction in maze-bright and maze-dull rats. *Psychological Record, 4,* 11–18.

Herrnstein, R. J. (1961). Relative and absolute strength of response as a function of frequency of reinforcement. *Journal of the Experimental Analysis of Behavior, 4,* 267–272.

Herrnstein, R. J. (1966). Superstition: A corollary of the principles of operant conditioning. In W. K. Honig (Ed.), *Operant behavior: Areas of research and application.* New York: Appleton-Century-Crofts.

Herrnstein, R. J. (1969). Method and theory in the study of avoidance. *Psychological Review, 76,* 49–69.

Herrnstein, R. J. (1970). On the law of effect. *Journal of the Experimental Analysis of Behavior, 13,* 243–266.

Herrnstein, R. J. (1974). Formal properties of the matching law. *Journal of the Experimental Analysis of Behavior, 21,* 159–164.

Herrnstein, R. J. (1977). The evolution of behaviorism. *American Psychologist, 32,* 593–603.

Herrnstein, R. J. (1979). Acquisition, generalization, and reversal of a natural concept. *Journal of Experimental Psychology: Animal Behavior Processes, 5,* 116–129.

Herrnstein, R. J. & de Villiers, P. A. (1980). Fish as a natural category for people and pigeons. In G. H. Bower (Ed.), *The psychology of learning and motivation* (Vol. 14). New York: Academic.

Herrnstein, R. J. & Heyman, G. M. (1979). Is matching compatible with reinforcement maximization on concurrent variable interval, variable ratio? *Journal of the Experimental Analysis of Behavior, 31,* 209–223.

Herrnstein, R. J. & Hineline, P. N. (1966). Negative reinforcement as shock-frequency reduction. *Journal of the Experimental Analysis of Behavior, 9,* 421–430.

Herrnstein, R. J. & Loveland, D. H. (1964). Complex visual concept in the pigeon. *Science, 146,* 549–551.

Herrnstein, R. J. & Loveland, D. H. (1974). Hunger and contrast in a multiple schedule. *Journal of the Experimental Analysis of Behavior, 21,* 511–517.

Herrnstein, R. J., Loveland, D. H., & Cable, C. (1976). Natural concepts in pigeons. *Journal of Experimental Psychology: Animal Behavior Processes, 2,* 285–302.

Herrnstein, R. J. & Mazur, J. E. (1987). Making up our minds: A new model of economic behavior. *The Sciences, 27,* 40–47.

Herrnstein, R. J. & Vaughan, W. (1980). Melioration and behavioral allocation. In J. E. R. Staddon (Ed.), *Limits to action: The allocation of individual behavior.* New York: Academic.

Hersen, M. & Van Hasselt, V. B. (Eds.) (1987). *Behavior therapy with children and adolescents: A clinical approach.* New York: Wiley.

Heth, C. D. (1985). Within-compound associations of taste and temperature. *Learning and Motivation, 16,* 413–422.

Heyman, G. M. (1979). A Markov model description of changeover probabilities on concurrent variable-interval schedules. *Journal of the Experimental Analysis of Behavior, 31,* 41–51.

Heyman, G. M. & Herrnstein, R. J. (1986). More on concurrent interval-ratio schedules: A replication and review. *Journal of the Experimental Analysis of Behavior, 46,* 331–351.

Heyman, G. M., Kinzie, D. L., & Seiden, L. (1986). Chlorpromazine and pimozide alter reinforcement efficacy and motor performance. *Psychopharmacology, 88,* 346–353.

Heyman, G. M. & Luce, R. D. (1979). Operant matching is not a logical consequence of maximizing reinforcement rate. *Animal Learning and Behavior, 7,* 133–140.

Heyman, G. M. & Monaghan, M. M. (1987). Effects of changes in response requirement and deprivation on the parameters of the matching law equation: New data and review. *Journal of Experimental Psychology: Animal Behavior Processes, 13,* 384–394.

Hilgard, E. R. (1936). The nature of the conditioned response: I. The case for and against stimulus-substitution. *Psychological Review, 43,* 366–385.

Hineline, P. N. (1970). Negative reinforcement without shock reduction. *Journal of the Experimental Analysis of Behavior, 14,* 259–268.

Hinson, J. M. & Staddon, J. E. R. (1983). Hill-climbing by pigeons. *Journal of the Experimental Analysis of Behavior, 39,* 25–47.

Hiroto, D. S. & Seligman, M. E. P. (1975). Generality of learned helplessness in man. *Journal of Personality and Social Psychology, 31,* 311–327.

Hobbes, T. (1651). *Leviathan, or the matter, forme and power of a commonwealth ecclesiasticall and civill.* London: Andrew Crooke.

Hobson, S. L. & Newman, F. (1981). Fixed-ratio-counting schedules: Response and time measures considered. In M. L. Commons & J. A. Nevin (Eds.), *Quantitative analyses of behavior, Vol. 1: Discriminative properties of reinforcement schedules.* Cambridge, Mass.: Ballinger.

Hoffman, M. L. (1960). Power assertion by the parent and its impact on the child. *Child Development, 31,* 129–143.

Hogan, D. E. (1986). Observational learning of a conditional hue discrimination in pigeons. *Learning and Motivation, 17,* 40–58.

Holder, M. D. & Garcia, J. (1987). Role of temporal order and odor intensity in taste-potentiated odor aversions. *Behavioral Neuroscience, 101,* 158–163.

Holland, P. C. (1980). Second-order conditioning with and without unconditioned stimulus presentation. *Journal of Experimental Psychology: Animal Behavior Processes, 6,* 238–250.

Holland, P. C. (1983). Representation-mediated overshadowing and potentiation of conditioned aversions. *Journal of Experimental Psychology: Animal Behavior Processes, 9,* 1–13.

Holland, P. C. (1985). Element pretraining influences the content of appetitive serial compound conditioning in rats. *Journal of Experimental Psychology: Animal Behavior Processes, 11,* 367–387.

Holland, P. C. (1986). Temporal determinants of occasion setting in feature-positive discriminations. *Animal Learning & Behavior, 14,* 111–120.

Holland, P. C. & Rescorla, R. A. (1975). The effect of two ways of devaluing the unconditioned stimulus after first- and second-order appetitive conditioning. *Journal of Experimental Psychology: Animal Behavior Processes, 1,* 355–363.

Holz, W. C. & Azrin, N. H. (1961). Discriminative properties of punishment. *Journal of the Experimental Analysis of Behavior, 4,* 225–232.

Homans, G. C. (1961). *Social behavior: Its elementary forms.* New York: Harcourt, Brace & World.

Homme, L. E., deBaca, P. C., Devine, J. V., Steinhorst, R., & Rickert, E. J. (1963). Use of the Premack principle in controlling the behavior of nursery school children. *Journal of the Experimental Analysis of Behavior, 6,* 544.

Honig, W. K. (1974). Effects of extradimensional discrimination training upon previously acquired stimulus control. *Learning and Motivation, 5,* 1–15.

Honig, W. K. (1978). Studies of working memory in the pigeon. In S. H. Hulse, H. Fowler, & W. K. Honig (Eds.), *Cognitive aspects of animal behavior.* Hillsdale, N.J.: Erlbaum.

Honig, W. K. (1984). Contributions of animal memory to the interpretation of animal learning. In H. L. Roitblat, T. G. Bever, & H. S. Terrace (Eds.), *Animal cognition.* Hillsdale, N.J.: Erlbaum.

Honig, W. K., Boneau, C. A., Burstein, K. R., & Pennypacker, H. S. (1963). Positive and negative generalization gradients obtained after equivalent training conditions. *Journal of Comparative and Physiological Psychology, 56,* 111–116.

Honig, W. K. & Dodd, P. W. D. (1983). Delayed discriminations in the pigeon: The role of within-trial location of conditional cues. *Animal Learning & Behavior, 11,* 1–9.

Honig, W. K. & Dodd, P. W. D. (1986). Anticipation and intention in working memory. In D. F. Kendrick, M. E. Rilling, & M. R. Denny (Eds.), *Theories of animal memory.* Hillsdale, N.J.: Erlbaum.

Houston, A. (1986). The matching law applies to wagtails' foraging in the wild. *Journal of the Experimental Analysis of Behavior, 45,* 15–18.

Hubel, D. H. & Wiesel, T. N. (1963). Receptive fields of cells in striate cortex of very young, visually inexperienced kittens. *Journal of Neurophysiology, 26,* 994–1002.

Hubel, D. H. & Wiesel, T. N. (1965). Binocular interaction in striate cortex of kittens reared with artificial squint. *Journal of Neurophysiology, 28,* 1041–1059.

Hubel, D. H. & Wiesel, T. N. (1970). The period of susceptibility to the physiological effects of unilateral eye closure in kittens. *Journal of Physiology, 206,* 419–436.

Hubel, D. H. & Wiesel, T. N. (1979). Brain mechanisms in vision. *Scientific American, 241,* 150–162.

Hull, C. L. (1934). Learning II: The factor of the conditioned reflex. In C. Murchison (Ed.), *A handbook of general experimental psychology.* Worcester: Clark University Press.

Hull, C. L. (1943). *Principles of behavior.* New York: Appleton-Century-Crofts.

Hulse, S. H. & Campbell, C. E. (1975). "Thinking ahead" in rat discrimination learning. *Animal Learning and Behavior, 3,* 305–311.

Hulse, S. H. & Dorsky, N. P. (1979). Serial pattern learning by rats: Transfer of a formally defined stimulus relationship and the significance of nonreinforcement. *Animal Learning and Behavior, 7,* 211–220.

Hundt, A. G. & Premack, D. (1963). Running as both a positive and negative reinforcer. *Science, 142,* 1087–1088.

Hunter, W. S. (1920). The temporal maze and kinaesthetic sensory processes in the white rat. *Psychobiology, 2,* 1–18.

Hursh, S. R. & Bauman, R. A. (1987). The behavioral analysis of demand. In L. Green & J. H. Kagel (Eds.), *Behavioral economics.* Norwood, N. J.: Ablex.

Isaacs, W., Thomas, J., & Goldiamond, I. (1960). Application of operant conditioning to reinstate verbal behavior in psychotics. *Journal of Speech and Hearing Disorders, 25,* 8–12.

Israely, Y. & Guttman, J. (1983). Children's sharing behavior as a function of exposure to puppet-show and story models. *Journal of Genetic Psychology, 142,* 311–312.

Iverson, I. H., Sidman, M., & Carrigan, P. (1986). Stimulus definition in conditional discriminations. *Journal of the Experimental Analysis of Behavior, 45,* 297–304.

Jackson, R. L., Alexander, J. H., & Maier, S. F. (1980). Learned helplessness, inactivity, and associative deficits: Effects of inescapable shock on response choice escape learning. *Journal of Experimental Psychology: Animal Behavior Processes, 6,* 1–20.

Jackson, R. L., Maier, S. F., & Coon, D. J. (1979). Long-term analgesic effects of inescapable shock and learned helplessness. *Science, 208,* 623–625.

Jacobson, N. S. & Dallas, M. (1981). Helping married couples improve their relationships. In W. E. Craighead, A. E. Kazdin, & M. J. Mahoney (Eds.), *Behavior modification: Principles, issues and applications.* Boston: Houghton Mifflin.

Jacobson, N. S., Follette, W. C., Revenstorf, D., Baucom, D. H., Hahlweg, K., & Margolin, G. (1984). Variability in outcome and clinical significance of behavioral marital therapy: A reanalysis of outcome data. *Journal of Consulting and Clinical Psychology, 52,* 497–504.

Jacobson, S. W. (1979). Matching behavior in the young infant. *Child Development, 50,* 425–430.

Jakubczak, L. F. & Walters, R. H. (1959). Suggestibility as dependency behavior. *Journal of Abnormal and Social Psychology, 59,* 102–107.

James, J. E. (1986). Review of the relative efficacy of imaginal and *in vivo* flooding in the treatment of clinical fear. *Behavioral Psychotherapy, 14,* 183–191.

James, W. (1890). *The principles of psychology.* New York: Holt, Rinehart & Winston.

Jarrard, L. E. & Moise, S. L. (1971). Short term memory in the monkey. In L. E. Jarrard (Ed.), *Cognitive processes of nonhuman primates.* New York: Academic.

Jarvik, M. E., Goldfarb, T. L., & Carley, J. L. (1969). Influence of interference on delayed matching in monkeys. *Journal of Experimental Psychology, 81,* 1–6.

Jenkins, H. M. (1962). Resistance to extinction when partial reinforcement is followed by regular reinforcement. *Journal of Experimental Psychology, 64,* 441–450.

Jenkins, H. M., Barrera, F. J., Ireland, C., & Woodside, B. (1978). Signal-centered action patterns of dogs in appetitive classical conditioning. *Learning and Motivation, 9,* 272–296.

Jenkins, H. M. & Harrison, R. H. (1960). Effects of discrimination training on auditory generalization. *Journal of Experimental Psychology, 59,* 246–253.

Jenkins, H. M. & Harrison, R. H. (1962). Generalization gradients of inhibition following auditory discrimination learning. *Journal of the Experimental Analysis of Behavior, 5,* 435–441.

Jenkins, H. M. & Moore, B. R. (1973). The form of the auto-shaped response with food or water reinforcers. *Journal of the Experimental Analysis of Behavior, 20,* 163–181.

Johnson, H. E. & Garton, W. H. (1973). Muscle re-education in hemiplegia by use of electromyographic device. *Archives of Physiological and Medical Rehabilitation, 54,* 320–325.

Johnson, R. & McCabe, J. (1982). Schema theory: A test of the hypothesis, variation in practice. *Perceptual and Motor Skills, 55,* 231–234.

Johnson, S. B. (1981). Enuresis. In D. Reid (Ed.), *Clinical behavior therapy and behavior modification* (Vol. 1). New York: Garland Publications.

Johnson, S. B., Hamm, R. J., & Leahey, T. H. (1986). Observational learning in *Gallus gallus domesticus* with and without a conspecific model. *Bulletin of the Psychonomic Society, 24,* 237–239.

Kagel, J. H., Dwyer, G. P., & Battalio, R. C. (1985). Bliss points vs. minimum-needs: Tests of competing motivational models. *Behavioral Processes, 11,* 61–77.

Kahneman, D. & Tversky, A. (1979). Prospect theory: An analysis of decision under risk. *Econometrica, 47,* 263–291.

Kamil, A. C. & Balda, R. P. (1985). Cache recovery and spatial memory in Clark's nutcrackers. *Journal of Experimental Psychology: Animal Behavior Processes, 11,* 95–111.

Kamin, L. J. (1956). The effects of termination of the CS and avoidance of the US on avoidance learning. *Journal of Comparative and Physiological Psychology, 49,* 420–424.

Kamin, L. J. (1968). Attention-like processes in classical conditioning. In M. R. Jones (Ed.), *Miami symposium on the prediction of behavior: Aversive stimulation.* Miami: University of Miami Press.

Kamin, L. J., Brimer, C. J., & Black, A. H. (1963). Conditioned suppression as a monitor of fear of the CS in the course of avoidance training. *Journal of Comparative and Physiological Psychology, 56,* 497–501.

Kanareff, V. T. & Lanzetta, J.T. (1960). Effects of success-failure experiences and probability of reinforcement upon the acquisition and extinction of an imitative response. *Psychological Reports, 7,* 151–166.

Kandel, E. R. (1979). Small systems of neurons. *Scientific American, 241,* 66–76.

Kandel, E. R. (1985). Cellular mechanisms of learning and the biological bases of individuality. In E. R. Kandel & J. H. Schwartz (Eds.), *Principles of neural science* (2nd ed.). New York: Elsevier.

Kandel, E. R., & Schwartz, J. H. (1982). Molecular biology of learning: Modulation of transmitter release. *Science, 218,* 433–443.

Kandel, E. R. & Tauc, L. (1964). Mechanism of prolonged heterosynaptic facilitation. *Nature, 202,* 145–147.

Kandel, E. R. & Tauc, L. (1965). Heterosynaptic facilitation in neurones of the abdominal ganglion of *Aplysia depilans. Journal of Physiology, 181,* 1–27.

Kanfer, F. H. & Goldstein, A. P. (1985). *Helping people change* (3rd ed.). Elmsford, N. Y.: Pergamon.

Kanner, L., Rodriguez, A., & Ashenden, B. (1972). How far can autistic children go in matters of social adaptation? *Journal of Autism and Childhood Schizophrenia, 2,* 9–33.

Kant, I. (1781). *Kritik der reinen Vernunft.* Riga. Max Muller (trans.) (1881). [*Critique of pure reason*]. London: Henry G. Bohn.

Kaplan, P. S. (1985). Explaining the effects of relative time in trace conditioning: A preliminary test of a comparitor hypothesis. *Animal Learning & Behavior, 13,* 233–238.

Kawai, M. (1965). Newly acquired pre-cultural behavior of the natural troop of Japanese monkeys on Koshima Islet. *Primates, 6,* 1–30.

Kazdin, A. E. (1977). *The token economy: A review and evaluation.* New York: Plenum.

Kazdin, A. E. (1980). *Behavior modification in applied settings* (Rev. ed.). Homewood, Ill.: Dorsey.

Kazdin, A. E. (1983). The token economy: A decade later. *Journal of Applied Behavior Analysis, 15,* 431–445.

Keele, S. W. (1973). *Attention and human performance.* Pacific Palisades, Cal.: Goodyear Publishing Company.

Keller, M. F. & Carlson, P. M. (1974). The use of symbolic modeling to promote social skills in preschool children with low levels of social responsiveness. *Child Development, 45,* 912–919.

Kellogg, W. N. & Kellogg, L. A. (1933). *The ape and the child: A study of environmental influence upon early behavior.* New York: McGraw-Hill.

Kemler, D. G. & Shepp, B. E. (1971). Learning and transfer of dimensional relevance and irrelevance in children. *Journal of Experimental Psychology, 90,* 120–127.

Kendler, H. H. & Underwood, B. J. (1948). The role of reward in conditioning theory. *Psychological Review, 55,* 209–215.

Kendler, T. S. (1950). An experimental investigation of transposition as a function of the difference between training and test stimuli. *Journal of Experimental Psychology, 40,* 552–562.

Kendrick, D. F. & Rilling, M. (1984). The role of interpolated stimuli in the retroactive interference of pigeon short-term memory. *Animal Learning and Behavior, 12,* 391–401.

Kendrick, D. F., Rilling, M., & Stonebraker, T. B. (1981). Stimulus control of delayed matching in pigeons: Directed forgetting. *Journal of the Experimental Analysis of Behavior, 36,* 241–251.

Kendrick, D. F., Tranberg, D. K., & Rilling, M. (1981). The effects of illumination on the acquisition of delayed matching-to-sample. *Animal Learning and Behavior, 9,* 202–208.

Keppel, G. (1968). Retroactive and proactive inhibition. In T. R. Dixon & O. L. Horton (Eds.), *Verbal behavior and general behavior theory.* Englewood Cliffs, N.J.: Prentice Hall.

Kerr, R. & Booth, B. (1978). Specific and varied practice of motor skill. *Perceptual and Motor Skills, 46,* 395–401.

Killeen, P. (1972). The matching law. *Journal of the Experimental Analysis of Behavior, 17,* 489–495.

Killeen, P. R. (1982). Incentive theory: II. Models for choice. *Journal of the Experimental Analysis of Behavior, 38,* 217–232.

Kimble, G. A. (1949). Performance and reminiscence in motor learning as a function of the degree of distribution of practice. *Journal of Experimental Psychology, 39,* 500–510.

Kimble, G. A. (1961). *Hilgard and Marquis' conditioning and learning* (2nd ed.) New York: Appleton-Century-Crofts.

Kintsch, W. (1965). Frequency distribution of inter-response times during VI and VR reinforcement. *Journal of the Experimental Analysis of Behavior, 8*, 347–352.

Kirk, R. E. (1982). *Experimental design* (2nd ed.). Monterey, Ca.: Brooks/Cole.

Kirkland, K. & Caughlin-Carvar, J. (1982). Maintenance and generalization of assertive skills. *Education & Training of the Mentally Retarded, 17*, 313–318.

Klass, E. T. (1979). Relative influence of sincere, insincere, and neutral symbolic models. *Journal of Experimental Child Psychology, 27*, 48–59.

Klein, M. & Kandel, E. R. (1978). Presynaptic modulation of voltage-dependent Ca^{2+} current: Mechanism for behavioral sensitization in *Aplysia californica. Proceedings of the National Academy of Sciences, U. S. A., 75*, 3512–3516.

Klein, M., Shapiro, E., & Kandel, E. R. (1980). Synaptic plasticity and the modulation of the calcium current. *Journal of Experimental Biology, 89*, 117–157.

Kohler, W. (1927). *The mentality of apes*, E. Winter (trans.). New York: Harcourt Brace.

Kohler, W. (1939). Simple structural function in the chimpanzee and the chicken. In W. D. Ellis (Ed.), *A source book of gestalt psychology*. New York: Harcourt Brace.

Konorski, J. (1967). *Integrative activity of the brain: An interdisciplinary approach*. Chicago: University of Chicago Press.

Konorski, J. & Miller, S. (1937). On two types of conditioned reflex. *Journal of Genetic Psychology, 16*, 264–272.

Kozlowski, L. T. (1979). Psychosocial influences on cigarette smoking. In N. A. Krasnegor (Ed.), *The behavioral influences on cigarette smoking*. NIDA Research Monograph 26. DHEW Publication No. (ADM)79–882.

Krebs, J. R. & Davies, N. B. (Eds.). (1978). *Behavioral ecology: An evolutionary approach*. Sunderland, Mass.: Sinauer.

Kremer, E. F. (1978). The Rescorla-Wagner model: Losses in associative strength in compound conditioned stimuli. *Journal of Experimental Psychology: Animal Behavior Processes, 4*, 22–36.

Kucharski, D. & Spear, N. E. (1985). Potentiation and overshadowing in preweanling and adult rats. *Journal of Experimental Psychology: Animal Behavior Processes, 11*, 15–34.

Kuhn, D. (1974). Inducing development experimentally: Comments on a research paradigm. *Developmental Psychology, 10*, 590–600.

Kuo, Z. Y. (1921). Giving up instincts in psychology. *Journal of Philosophy, 18*, 645–664.

Kushner, M. (1965). Desensitization of a post-traumatic phobia. In L. P. Ullman & L. Krasner (Eds.), *Case studies in behavior modification*. New York: Holt, Rinehart and Winston.

Kushner, M. (1968). The operant control of intractible sneezing. In C. D. Spielberger, R. Fox, & D. Masterson (Eds.), *Contributions to general psychology*. New York: Ronald.

Ladoucier, R. & Gros-Louis, Y. (1986). Paradoxical intention vs. stimulus control in the treatment of severe insomnia. *Journal of Behavior Therapy and Experimental Psychiatry, 17*, 267–269.

Larew, M. B. (1986). Inhibitory learning in Pavlovian backward conditioning procedures involving a small number of US-CS trials. Ph. D. dissertation. Yale University.

Lashley, K. S. (1917). The accuracy of movement in the absence of excitation from the moving organ. *American Journal of Physiology, 43*, 169–194.

Lashley, K. S. (1924). Studies of the cerebral function in learning: V. The retention of motor habits after destruction of the so-called motor areas in primates. *Archives of Neurology and Psychiatry, 12*, 249–276.

Lashley, K. S. (1929). *Brain mechanisms and intelligence: A quantitative study of injuries to the brain*. Chicago: University of Chicago Press.

Lashley, K. S. (1950). In search of the engram: Physiological mechanisms in animal behavior. In J. F. Danielli and R. Brown (Eds.), *Symposium of the Society for Experimental Biology*. Cambridge: Cambridge University Press.

Lashley, K. S. (1951). The problem of serial order in behavior. In L. A. Jeffress (Ed.), *Cerebral mechanisms in behavior*. New York: Wiley.

Lavond, D. G., Hembree, T. L., & Thompson, R. F. (1985). Effects of kainic acid lesions of the cerebellar interpositus nucleus on eyelid conditioning in the rabbit. *Brain Research, 326*, 179–182.

Lawicka, W. (1964). The role of stimuli modality in successive discrimination and differentiation learning. *Bulletin of the Polish Academy of Sciences, 12*, 35–38.

Lawrence, D. H. & DeRivera, J. (1954). Evidence for relational transposition. *Journal of Comparative and Physiological Psychology, 47*, 465–471.

Lea, S. E. G. (1978). The psychology and economics of demand. *Psychological Bulletin, 85*, 441–466.

Lea, S. E. G. (1983). The analysis of need. In R. L. Mellgren (Ed.), *Animal cognition and behavior*. Amsterdam: North-Holland.

Lea, S. E. G. & Roper, T. J. (1977). Demand for food on fixed-ratio schedules as a function of the quality of concurrently available reinforcement. *Journal of the Experimental Analysis of Behavior, 27,* 371–380.

Lee, B. S. (1950). Effects of delayed speech feedback. *Journal of the Acoustical Society of America, 22,* 824–826.

Lee, T. D., Magill, R. A., & Weeks, D. J. (1985). Influence of practice schedule on testing schema theory predictions in adults. *Journal of Motor Behavior, 17,* 238–299.

Lefkowitz, M., Blake, R. R., & Mouton, J. S. (1955). Status factors in pedestrian violation of traffic signals. *Journal of Abnormal and Social Psychology, 51,* 704–706.

Lefkowitz, M. M., Huesmann, L. R., & Eron, L. D. (1978). Parental punishment: A longitudinal analysis of effect. *Archives of General Psychiatry, 35,* 186–191.

Lemere, F. & Voegtlin, W. L. (1950). An evaluation of the aversion treatment of alcoholism. *Quarterly Journal of Studies on Alcohol, 11,* 199–204.

Lemere, F., Voegtlin, W. L., Broz, W. R., O'Hallaren, P., & Tupper, W. E. (1942). The conditioned reflex treatment of chronic alcoholism. VIII. A review of six years' experience with this treatment of 1526 patients. *Journal of the American Medical Association, 120,* 269–270.

Lett, B. T. (1973). Delayed reward learning: Disproof of the traditional theory. *Learning and Motivation, 4,* 237–246.

Lett, B. T. (1975). Long delay learning in the T-maze. *Learning and Motivation, 6,* 80–90.

Lett, B. T. (1979). Long-delay learning: Implications for learning and memory theory. In N. S. Sutherland (Ed.), *Tutorial essays in psychology* (Vol. 2). Hillsdale, N.J.: Erlbaum.

Lett, B. T. (1984). Extinction of taste aversion does not eliminate taste potentiation of odor aversion in rats or color aversion in pigeons. *Animal Learning & Behavior, 12,* 414–420.

Leventhal, H. & Cleary, P. D. (1980). The smoking problem: A review of the research and theory in behavioral risk modification. *Psychological Bulletin, 88,* 370–405.

Lewis, A. (1942). Incidence of neurosis in England under war conditions. *Lancet, 2,* 175–183.

Lewis, D., McAllister, D. E., & Adams, J. A. (1951). Facilitation and interference in performance on the modified Mashburn apparatus: I. The effects of varying the amount of original learning. *Journal of Experimental Psychology, 41,* 247–260.

Lockard, R. B. (1971). Reflections on the fall of comparative psychology: Is there a message for us all? *American Psychologist, 26,* 168–179.

Locke, J. (1690). *An essay concerning humane understanding: In four books.* London: Thomas Bassett.

Locurto, C. M., Terrace, H. S., & Gibbon, J. (Eds.) (1981). *Autoshaping and conditioning theory.* New York: Academic.

Loeb, J. (1900). *Comparative physiology of the brain and comparative psychology.* New York: Putnam.

Loftus, G. R. & Loftus, E. F. (1988). *Essentials of statistics* (2nd ed.). New York: Knopf.

Logue, A. W. (1979). Taste aversion and the generality of the laws of learning. *Psychological Bulletin, 86,* 276–296.

Logue, A. W. (1988). A comparison of taste-aversion learning in humans and other vertebrates: Evolutionary pressures in common. In R. C. Bolles & M. D. Beecher (Eds.), *Evolution and learning.* Hillsdale, N.J.: Erlbaum.

Logue, A. W. & Chavarro, A. (1987). Effect on choice of absolute and relative values of reinforcer delay, amount, and frequency. *Journal of Experimental Psychology: Animal Behavior Processes, 13,* 280–291.

Logue, A. W., Logue, K. R., & Strauss, K. E. (1983). The acquisition of taste aversions in humans with eating and drinking disorders. *Behavior Research and Therapy, 21,* 275–289.

Logue, A. W., Ophir, I., & Strauss, K. E. (1981). The acquisition of taste aversions in humans. *Behavior Research and Therapy, 19,* 319–333.

LoLordo, V. M. & Ross, R. T. (1987). Role of within-compound associations in occasion setting: A blocking analysis. *Journal of Experimental Psychology: Animal Behavior Processes, 13,* 156–167.

Lorge, I. & Thorndike, E. L. (1935). The influence of delay in the after-effect of a connection. *Journal of Experimental Psychology, 18,* 186–194.

Lovaas, O. I. (1967). A behavior therapy approach to the treatment of childhood schizophrenia. In J. P. Hill (Ed.), *Minnesota symposium on child psychology.* Minneapolis: University of Minnesota Press.

Lovaas, O. I. (1977). *The autistic child.* New York: John Wiley & Sons.

Lovaas, O. I. (1987). Behavioral treatment and normal educational and intellectual functioning in young autistic children. *Journal of Consulting and Clinical Psychology, 55,* 3–9.

Lovaas, O. I., Freitag, L., Nelson, K., & Whalen, C. (1967). The establishment of imitation and its use for the development of complex behavior in schizophrenic children. *Behavior Research and Therapy, 5,* 171–181.

Lubow, R. E. (1974). High-order concept formation in the pigeon. *Journal of the Experimental Analysis of Behavior, 21,* 475– 483.

Lubow, R. E., Markman, R. E., & Allen, J. (1968). Latent inhibition and classical conditioning of the rabbit pinna response. *Journal of Comparative and Physiological Psychology, 66,* 688– 694.

Lubow, R. E. & Moore, A. U. (1959). Latent inhibition: The effect of nonreinforced preexposure to the conditional stimulus. *Journal of Comparative and Physiological Psychology, 52,* 415– 419.

Lucas, G. A., Deich, J. D., & Wasserman, E. A. (1981). Trace autoshaping: Acquisition, maintenance, and path dependence at long trace intervals. *Journal of the Experimental Analysis of Behavior, 36,* 61–74.

Luce, R. D. (1959). *Individual choice behavior: A theoretical analysis.* New York: Wiley.

Luce, R. D. (1984). Behavior theory: A contradiction in terms? *Behavioral and Brain Sciences, 7,* 525–526.

MacCorquodale, K. & Meehl, P. E. (1954). Edward C. Tolman. In W. K. Estes, S. Koch, K. MacCorquodale, P. Meehl, C. G. Mueller, Jr., W. N. Schoenfeld, & W. S. Verplanck (Eds.), *Modern learning theory.* New York: Appleton-Century-Crofts.

Mackey, S. L., Glanzman, D. L., Small, S. A., Dyke, A. M., Kandel, E. R., & Hawkins, R. D. (1987). Tail shock produces inhibition as well as sensitization of the siphon-withdrawal reflex of *Aplysia*: Possible behavioral role for presynaptic inhibition mediated by peptide Phe-Met-Arg-Phe-NH_2. *Proceedings of the National Academy of Science, 84,* 8730–8734.

Mackintosh, N. J. (1975). A theory of attention: Variations in the associability of stimuli with reinforcement. *Psychological Review, 82,* 276–298.

Mackintosh, N. J. (1983). *Conditioning and associative learning.* Oxford: Oxford University Press.

Mackintosh, N. J. & Dickinson, A. (1979). Instrumental (Type II) conditioning. In A. Dickinson & R. A. Boakes (Eds.), *Mechanisms of learning and motivation.* Hillsdale, N.J.: Erlbaum.

Mackintosh, N. J. & Little, L. (1969). Intradimensional and extradimensional shift learning by pigeons. *Psychonomic Science, 14,* 5–6.

Maier, N. R. F. (1931). Reasoning in humans: II. The solution of a problem and its appearance in consciousness. *Journal of Comparative Psychology, 12,* 181–194.

Maier, S. F. & Jackson, R. L. (1979). Learned helplessness: All of us were right (and wrong): Inescapable shock has multiple effects. In G. H. Bower (Ed.), *The psychology of learning and motivation* (Vol. 13). New York: Academic.

Maier, S. F. & Keith, J. R. (1987). Shock signals and the development of stress-induced analgesia. *Journal of Experimental Psychology: Animal Behavior Processes, 13,* 226–238.

Maier, S. F. & Seligman, M. E. P. (1976). Learned helplessness: Theory and evidence. *Journal of Experimental Psychology: General, 105,* 3–46.

Maier, S. F. & Warren, D. A. (1988). Controllability and safety signals exert dissimilar proactive effects on nociception and escape performance. *Journal of Experimental Psychology: Animal Behavior Processes, 14,* 18–25.

Maki, W. S. (1979). Pigeons' short-term memories for surprising vs. expected reinforcement and nonreinforcement. *Animal Learning and Behavior, 7,* 31–37.

Maki, W. S. (1981). Directed forgetting in animals. In N. E. Spear & R. R. Miller (Eds.), *Information processing in animals: Memory mechanisms.* Hillsdale, N.J.: Erlbaum.

Maki, W. S. (1984). Some problems for a theory of working memory. In H. L. Roitblat, T. G. Bever, & H. S. Terrace (Eds.), *Animal cognition.* Hillsdale, N. J.: Erlbaum.

Maki, W. S. & Hegvik, D. K. (1980). Directed forgetting in pigeons. *Animal Learning & Behavior, 8,* 567–574.

Maki, W. S., Olson, D., & Rego, S. (1981). Directed forgetting in pigeons: Analysis of cue functions. *Animal Learning and Behavior, 9,* 189–195.

Marinacci, A. A. & Horande, M. (1960). Electromyogram in neuromuscular re-education. *Bulletin of the Los Angeles Neurological Society, 25,* 57–71.

Marks, I. M. & Gelder, M. (1967). Transvestism and fetishism: Clinical and psychological changes during faradic aversion. *British Journal of Psychiatry, 113,* 711–739.

Marsden, C. D., Merton, P. A., & Morton, H. B. (1972). Servo action in human voluntary movement. *Nature, 238,* 140–143.

Marsh, G. & Johnson, R. (1968). Discrimination reversal following learning without "errors." *Psychonomic Science, 10,* 261–262.

Martin, G. & Pear, J. (1983). *Behavior modification* (2nd ed.). Englewood Cliffs, N.J.: Prentice Hall.

Martin, J. A. (1971). The control of imitative and nonimitative behaviors in severely retarded children through "generalized-instruction following." *Journal of Experimental Child Psychology, 11,* 390 – 400.

Marx, M. H. & Hillix, W. A. (1979). *Systems and theories in psychology.* (3rd ed.). New York: McGraw-Hill.

Matsuzawa, T. (1985). Use of numbers by a chimpanzee. *Nature, 315,* 57–59.

Matthews, L. R. & Temple, W. (1979). Concurrent-schedule assessment of food preferences in cows. *Journal of the Experimental Analysis of Behavior, 32,* 245–254.

Matzel, L. D., Brown, A. M., & Miller, R. R. (1987). Associative effects of US preexposure: Modulation of conditioned responding by an excitatory training context. *Journal of Experimental Psychology: Animal Behavior Processes, 13,* 65–72.

Mawhinney, V. T., Bostow, D. E., Laws, D. R., Blumenfeld, G. J., & Hopkins, B. L. (1971). A comparison of students studying-behavior produced by daily, weekly, and three-week testing schedules. *Journal of Applied Behavior Analysis, 4,* 257–264.

May, R. (1950). *The meaning of anxiety.* New York: Ronald.

Mazmanian, D. S. & Roberts, W. A. (1983). Spatial memory in rats under restricted viewing conditions. *Learning and Motivation, 14,* 123–139.

Mazur, J. E. (1975). The matching law and quantifications related to Premack's principle. *Journal of Experimental Psychology: Animal Behavior Processes, 1,* 374–386.

Mazur, J. E. (1981). Optimization theory fails to predict performance of pigeons in a two-response situation. *Science, 214,* 823–825.

Mazur, J. E. (1983). Steady-state performance on fixed-, mixed-, and random-ratio schedules. *Journal of the Experimental Analysis of Behavior, 39,* 293–307.

Mazur, J. E. & Vaughan, W. (1987). Molar optimization versus delayed reinforcement as explanations of choice between fixed-ratio and progressive-ratio schedules. *Journal of the Experimental Analysis of Behavior, 48,* 251–261.

Mazur, J. E. & Wagner, A. R. (1982). An episodic model of associative learning. In M. L. Commons, R. J. Herrnstein, & A. R. Wagner (Eds.), *Quantitative analyses of behavior: Vol. 3. Acquisition.* Cambridge, Mass.: Ballinger.

McClelland, D. C. (1961). *The achieving society.* Princeton, NJ.: Van Nostrand.

McCormick, D. A. & Thompson, R. F. (1984). Neuronal responses of the rabbit cerebellum during acquisition and performance of a classically conditioned nictitating membrane-eyelid response. *Journal of Neuroscience, 4,* 2811–2822.

McCullagh, P. (1986). Model status as a determinant of observational learning and performance. *Journal of Sport Psychology, 8,* 319–331.

McDougall, W. (1908). *An introduction to social psychology.* London: Methuen.

McFarland, D. S. (1971). *Feedback mechanisms in animal behavior.* New York: Academic.

McGuire, R. J., Carlisle, J. M., & Young, B. G. (1965). Sexual deviations as conditioned behavior: A hypothesis. *Behavior Research and Therapy, 2,* 185–190.

McNamara, H. J., Long, J. B., & Wike, E. L. (1956). Learning without response under two conditions of external cues. *Journal of Comparative and Physiological Psychology, 49,* 477–480.

Mechner, F. (1958). Probability relations within response sequences under ratio reinforcement. *Journal of the Experimental Analysis of Behavior, 1,* 109–121.

Meck, W. H. & Church, R. M. (1983). A mode control model of counting and timing processes. *Journal of Experimental Psychology: Animal Behavior Processes, 9,* 320–334.

Meehl, P. E. (1950). On the circularity of the law of effect. *Psychological Bulletin, 47,* 52–75.

Meichenbaum, D. H. & Goodman, J. (1971). Training impulsive children to talk to themselves: A means of developing self-control. *Journal of Abnormal Psychology, 77,* 115–126.

Mellgren, R. L. (1983). *Animal cognition and behavior.* Amsterdam: North-Holland Publishing.

Meltzoff, A. N. & Moore, M. K. (1977). Imitation of facial and manual gestures by human neonates. *Science, 198,* 75–78.

Meltzoff, A. N. & Moore, M. K. (1983). Newborn infants imitate adult facial gestures. *Child Development, 54,* 702–709.

Miles, H. L. (1983). Apes and language: The search for communicative competence. In J. de Luce & H. T. Wilder (Eds.), *Language in primates: Perspectives and implications.* New York: Springer-Verlag.

Mill, J. (1829). *Analysis of the phenomena of the human mind.* London: Baldwin & Cradock.

Mill, J. S. (1843). *A system of logic, ratiocinative and inductive, being a connected view of the principles of evidence, and the methods of scientific investigation.* London: J. W. Parker.

Miller, G. A., Gallanter, E., & Pribram, K. H. (1960). *Plans and the structure of behavior.* New York: Holt, Rinehart, & Winston.

Miller, H. L. (1976). Matching-based hedonic scaling in the pigeon. *Journal of the Experimental Analysis of Behavior, 26*, 335–347.

Miller, J. T., Saunders, S. S., & Bourland, G. (1980). The role of stimulus disparity in concurrently available reinforcement schedules. *Animal Learning & Behavior, 8*, 635– 641.

Miller, N. E. (1948). Studies of fear as an acquirable drive: I. Fear as motivation and fear-reduction as reinforcement in the learning of new responses. *Journal of Experimental Psychology, 38*, 89–101.

Miller, N. E. (1951a). Comments on multiple-process conceptions of learning. *Psychological Review, 58*, 375–381.

Miller, N. E. (1951b). Learnable drives and rewards. In S. S. Stevens (Ed.), *Handbook of experimental psychology*. New York: Wiley.

Miller, N. E. (1959). Liberalization of basic S-R concepts: Extensions to conflict behavior, motivation, and social learning. In S. Koch (Ed.), *Psychology: A study of a science* (Vol. 2). New York: McGraw-Hill.

Miller, N. E. & DiCara, L. (1967). Instrumental learning of heart rate changes in curarized rats: Shaping, and specificity to discriminative stimulus. *Journal of Comparative and Physiological Psychology, 63*, 12–19.

Miller, N. E. & Dollard, J. (1941). *Social learning and imitation*. New Haven: Yale University Press.

Miller, N. E. & Dworkin, B. R. (1974). Visceral learning: Recent difficulties with curarized rats and significant problems for human research. In P. A. Obrist, A. H. Black, J. Brener, & L. V. DiCara (Eds.), *Cardiovascular psychophysiology*. Chicago: Aldine.

Miller, R. R. & Schachtman, T. R. (1985). The several roles of context at the time of retrieval. In P. D. Balsam & A. Tomie (Eds.), *Context and learning*. Hillsdale, N.J.: Erlbaum.

Miller, R. R. & Spear, N. E. (Eds.) (1985). *Information processing in animals: Conditioned inhibition*. Hillsdale, N.J: Erlbaum.

Miller, S. & Konorski, J. (1928). Sur une forme particuliere des reflexes conditionnels. *Compte Rendu Hebdomadaire des Seances et Memoires de la Societe de Biologie, 99*, 1151–1157.

Mineka, S. (1979). The role of fear in theories of avoidance learning, flooding, and extinction. *Psychological Bulletin, 86*, 985–1010.

Mineka, S. (1985). The frightful complexity of the origins of fears. In F. R. Brush & J. B. Overmier (Eds.), *Affect, conditioning, and cognition*. Hillsdale, N.J.: Erlbaum.

Minecka, S., Cook, M., & Miller, S. (1984). Fear conditioned with escapable and inescapable shock: Effects of a feedback stimulus. *Journal of Experimental Psychology: Animal Behavior Processes, 10*, 307–323.

Mineka, S., Davidson, M., Cook, M., & Kerr, R. (1984). Observational conditioning of snake fear in rhesus monkeys. *Journal of Abnormal Psychology, 93*, 355–372.

Mintz, D. E., Mourer, D. J., & Gofseyeff, M. (1967). Sequential effects in fixed-ratio postreinforcement pause duration. *Psychonomic Science, 9*, 387–388.

Mischel, W. (1961). Father-absence and delay of gratification: Cross-cultural comparisons. *Journal of Abnormal and Social Psychology, 63*, 116–124.

Mischel, W. (1966). Theory and research on the antecedents of self-imposed delay of reward. *Progress in Experimental Personality Research, 3*, 85–132.

Mischel, W. (1971). *Introduction to personality*. New York: Holt, Rinehart, & Winston.

Mischel, W. (1974). Processes in delay of gratification. In L. Berkowitz (Ed.), *Advances in experimental social psychology* (Vol. 7). New York: Academic.

Mischel, W. (1981). Objective and subjective rules for delay of gratification. In G. d'Ydewalle & W. Lens (Eds.), *Cognition in human motivation and learning*. Hillsdale, N.J.: Erlbaum.

Mischel, W. (1983). Delay of gratification as process and as person variable in development. In D. Magnusson & V. L. Allen (Eds.), *Human development*. New York: Academic.

Mischel, W. & Ebbeson, E. B. (1970). Attention in delay of gratification. *Journal of Personality and Social Psychology, 16*, 329–337.

Mischel, W., Ebbesen, E. B., & Zeiss, A. R. (1972). Cognitive and attentional mechanisms in delay of gratification. *Journal of Personality and Social Psychology, 21*, 204–218.

Mischel, W. & Grusec, J. (1966). Determinants of the rehearsal and transmission of neutral and aversive behaviors. *Journal of Personality and Social Psychology, 3*, 197–205.

Mitchell, W. S. & Stoffelmayr, B. E. (1973). Application of the Premack principle to the behavioral control of extremely inactive schizophrenics. *Journal of Applied Behavior Analysis, 6*, 419– 423.

Moore, B. R. (1973). The role of directed Pavlovian reactions in simple instrumental learning in the pigeon. In R. A. Hinde & J. Stevenson-Hinde (Eds.), *Constraints on learning*. New York: Academic.

Moore, B. R. & Stuttard, S. (1979). Dr. Guthrie and *Felis domesticus* or: Tripping over the cat. *Science, 205,* 1031–1033.

Moore, J. W. (1972). Stimulus control: Studies of auditory generalization in rabbits. In A. H. Black & W. F. Prokasy (Eds.), *Classical conditioning II: Current research and theory.* New York: Appleton-Century-Crofts.

Moore, J. W. (1979). Brain processes and conditioning. In A. Dickinson & R. A. Boakes (Eds.), *Mechanisms of learning and motivation: A memorial volume to Jerzy Konorski.* Hillsdale, N.J.: Erlbaum.

Morgan, C. L. (1894). *An introduction to comparative psychology.* London: W. Scott.

Morgan, C. L. (1896). *Habit and instinct.* London: E. Arnold.

Morganstern, K. P. (1973). Implosive therapy and flooding procedures: A critical review. *Psychological Bulletin, 79,* 318–334.

Morin, C. M. & Azrin, N. H. (1987). Stimulus control and imagery training in treating sleep-maintenance insomnia. *Journal of Consulting and Clinical Psychology, 55,* 260–262.

Morris, R. G. M. (1974). Pavlovian conditioned inhibition of fear during shuttlebox avoidance behavior. *Learning and Motivation, 5,* 424–447.

Morris, R. J. & Kratochwill, T. R. (1983). *Treating children's fears and phobias: A behavioral approach.* New York: Pergamon.

Mowrer, O. H. (1947). On the dual nature of learning—a reinterpretation of "conditioning" and "problem solving." *Harvard Educational Review, 17,* 102–148.

Mowrer, O. H. & Jones, H. (1945). Habit strength as a function of the pattern of reinforcement. *Journal of Experimental Psychology, 35,* 293–311.

Mowrer, O. H. & Mowrer, W. M. (1938). Enuresis: A method for its study and treatment. *American Journal of Orthopsychiatry, 8,* 436–459.

Moye, T. B, Hyson, R. L., Grau, J. W., & Maier, S. F. (1983). Immunization of opioid analgesia: Effects of prior escapable shock on subsequent shock-induced and morphine-induced antinociception. *Learning and Motivation, 14,* 238–251.

Mucha, R. F., Volkovskis, C., & Kalant, H. (1981). Conditioned increase in locomotor activity produced with morphine as an unconditioned stimulus, and the relation of conditioning to acute morphine effect and tolerance. *Journal of Comparative and Physiological Psychology, 96,* 351–362.

Muenzinger, K. F. (1928). Plasticity and mechanization of the problem box habit in Guinea pigs. *Journal of Comparative Psychology, 8,* 45–69.

Muir, D. W. & Mitchell, D. E. (1973). Visual resolution and experience: Acuity deficits in cats following early selective visual deprivation. *Science, 180,* 420–422.

Mulder, T. & Hulstijn, W. (1985a). Delayed sensory feedback in the learning of a novel motor task. *Psychological Research, 47,* 203–209.

Mulder, T. & Hulstijn, W. (1985b). Sensory feedback in the learning of a novel motor task. *Journal of Motor Behavior, 17,* 110–128.

Murray, F. B. (1983). Equilibration as cognitive conflict. *Developmental Review, 3,* 54–61.

Myers, A. K. & Miller, N. E. (1954). Failure to find a learned drive based on hunger; evidence for learning motivated by "exploration." *Journal of Comparative and Physiological Psychology, 47,* 428–436.

Myers, D. L. & Myers, L. E. (1977). Undermatching: A reappraisal of performance on concurrent variable-interval schedules of reinforcement. *Journal of the Experimental Analysis of Behavior, 27,* 203–214.

Nairne, J. S. & Rescorla, R. A. (1981). Second-order conditioning with diffuse auditory reinforcers in the pigeon. *Learning and Motivation, 12,* 65–91.

Neuenschwander, N., Fabrigoule, C., & Mackintosh, N. J. (1987). Fear of the warning signal during overtraining of avoidance. *Quarterly Journal of Experimental Psychology, 39B,* 23–33.

Nevin, J. A. (1969). Interval reinforcement of choice behavior in discrete trials. *Journal of the Experimental Analysis of Behavior, 12,* 875–885.

Nevin, J. A. (1979). Overall matching versus momentary maximizing: Nevin (1969) revisited. *Journal of Experimental Psychology: Animal Behavior Processes, 5,* 300–306.

Nevin, J. A. & Shettleworth, S. J. (1966). An analysis of contrast effects in multiple schedules. *Journal of the Experimental Analysis of Behavior, 9,* 305–315.

Newell, A. & Simon, H. (1972). *Human problem solving.* Englewood Cliffs, N.J.: Prentice Hall.

Newell, K. M. (1974). Knowledge of results and motor learning. *Journal of Motor Behavior, 6,* 235–244.

Newell, K. M. (1976). Motor learning without knowledge of results through the development of a response-recognition mechanism. *Journal of Motor Behavior, 8,* 209–217.

Newell, K. M. & Kennedy, J. A. (1978). Knowledge of results and children's motor learning. *Developmental Psychology, 14,* 531–536.

Nicholas, J. M. (1984). Lessons from the history of science? *The Behavioral and Brain Sciences, 7*, 530–531.

Nottebohm, F. (1970). The ontogeny of birdsong. *Science, 167*, 950–956.

O'Connor, R. D. (1969). Modification of social withdrawal through symbolic modeling. *Journal of Applied Behavior Analysis, 2*, 15–22.

O'Dell, S. L., O'Quin, J. A., Alford, B. A., O'Briant, A. L., Bradlyn, A. S., & Giebenhain, J. E. (1982). Predicting the acquisition of parenting skills via four training methods. *Behavior Therapy, 13*, 194–208.

Olds, J. & Milner, P. (1954). Positive reinforcement produced by electrical stimulation of septal area and other regions of rat brain. *Journal of Comparative and Physiological Psychology, 47*, 419 – 427.

O'Leary, D. E., O'Leary, M. R., & Donovan, D. M. (1976). Social skill acquisition and psychosocial development of alcoholics: A review. *Addictive Behaviors, 1*, 111–120.

O'Leary, K. D., Kaufman, K. F., Kass, R. E., & Drabman, R.S. (1970). The effects of loud and soft reprimands on the behavior of disruptive students. *Exceptional Children, 37*, 145–155.

O'Leary, K. D. & Wilson, G. T. (1987). *Behavior Therapy: Application and outcome.* Englewood Cliffs, N.J.: Prentice Hall.

Olton, D. S. (1978). Characteristics of spatial memory. In S. H. Hulse, H. Fowler, & W. K. Honig (Eds.), *Cognitive processes in animal behavior.* Hillsdale, N.J.: Erlbaum.

Olton, D. S., Collison, C., & Werz, W. A. (1977). Spatial memory and radial arm maze performance by rats. *Learning and Motivation, 8,* 289–314.

Olton, D. S. & Samuelson, R. J. (1976). Remembrance of places past: Spatial memory in rats. *Journal of Experimental Psychology: Animal Behavior Processes, 2,* 97–116.

Osgood, C. E. (1949). The similarity paradox in human learning: A resolution. *Psychological Review, 56*, 132–143.

Overmier, J. B. & Seligman, M. E. P. (1967). Effects of inescapable shock upon subsequent escape and avoidance responding. *Journal of Comparative and Physiological Psychology, 63*, 28–33.

Overmier, J. B. & Wielkiewicz, R. M. (1983). On unpredictability as a causal factor in "learned helplessness." *Learning and Motivation, 14*, 324–337.

Page, H. A. & Hall, J. F. (1953). Experimental extinction as a function of the prevention of a response. *Journal of Comparative and Physiological Psychology, 46*, 33–34.

Paletta, M. S. & Wagner, A. R. (1986). Development of context-specific tolerance to morphine: Support for a dual-process interpretation. *Behavioral Neuroscience, 100*, 611– 623.

Parker, G. A. (1978). Searching for mates. In J. R. Krebs & N. B. Davies (Eds.), *Behavioral ecology: An evolutionary approach.* Sunderland, Mass.: Sinauer.

Patten, R. L. & Rudy, J. W. (1966). The effect on choice behavior of cues paired with noncontingent reward. *Psychonomic Science, 6*, 121–122.

Patterson, F. G. (1978). The gestures of a gorilla: Language acquisition in another pongid. *Brain and Language, 5*, 72–97.

Patterson, F. G. & Linden, E. (1981). *The education of Koko.* New York: Holt, Rinehart, & Winston.

Patterson, G. R., Chamberlain, P., & Reid, J. B. (1982). A comparative evaluation of a parent-training program. *Behavior Therapy, 13*, 638– 650.

Patterson, G. R. & Reid, J. B. (1973). Intervention for families of aggressive boys: A replication study. *Behavior Research and Therapy, 11*, 383–394.

Paul, G. L. (1969). Outcome of systematic desensitization. II: Controlled investigations of individual treatment, technique variations, and current status. In C. M. Franks (Ed.), *Behavior therapy: Appraisal and status.* New York: McGraw-Hill.

Paulsen, K., Rimm, D. C., Woodburn, L. T., & Rimm, S. (1977). A self-control approach to inefficient spending. *Journal of Consulting and Clinical Psychology, 45*, 433– 435.

Pavlov, I. P. (1927). *Conditioned reflexes.* Oxford: Oxford University Press.

Pavlov, I. P. (1928). *Lectures on conditioned reflexes.* New York: International Publishers.

Pearce, J. M. & Hall, G. (1980). A model for Pavlovian learning: Variations in the effectiveness of conditioned but not unconditioned stimuli. *Psychological Review, 87*, 532–552.

Pedalino, E. & Gamboa, V. U. (1974). Behavior modification and absenteeism: Intervention in one industrial setting. *Journal of Applied Psychology, 59*, 694–698.

Peeke, H. V. S. & Veno, A. (1973). Stimulus specificity of habitual aggression in the stickleback (*Gasterosteus aculeatus*). *Behavioral Biology, 8*, 427–432.

Pepperberg, I. M. (1981). Functional vocalizations of an African gray parrot (*Psitticus erithacus*). *Zeitschirift fur Tierpsychologie, 55*, 139–151.

Pepperberg, I. M. (1983). Cognition in the African gray parrot: Preliminary evidence for auditory/vocal comprehension of a class concept. *Animal Learning & Behavior*, *11*, 179–185.

Pepperberg, I. M. (1987). Evidence for conceptual quantitative abilities in the African parrot: Labeling of cardinal sets. *Ethology*, *75*, 37–61.

Peterson, C. & Seligman, M. E. P. (1984). Causal explanations as a risk factor for depression: Theory and evidence. *Psychological Review*, *91*, 347–374.

Peterson, G. B., Ackil, J. E., Frommer, G. P., & Hearst, E. S. (1972). Conditioned approach and contact behavior towards signals for food or brain-stimulation reinforcement. *Science*, *177*, 1009–1011.

Peterson, L. R. & Peterson, M. J. (1959). Short-term retention of individual verbal items. *Journal of Experimental Psychology*, *58*, 193–198.

Peterson, N. (1962). Effect of monochromatic rearing on the control of responding by wavelength. *Science*, *136*, 774–775.

Peterson, S. K. & Tannenbaum, H. A. (1986). *Behavior management: Strategies and techniques*. Lanham, Mary.: University Press of America.

Pfautz, P. L., Donegan, N. H., & Wagner, A. R. (1978). Sensory preconditioning versus protection from habituation. *Journal of Experimental Psychology: Animal Behavior Processes*, *4*, 286–295.

Phillips, D. P. (1982). The impact of fictional television stories on U.S. adult fatalities: New evidence on the effect of the mass media on violence. *American Journal of Sociology*, *87*, 1340–1359.

Phillips, D. P. & Carstensen, L. L. (1986). Clustering of teenage suicides after television news stories about suicide. *New England Journal of Medicine*, *315*, 685–689.

Phillips, E. L. (1968). Achievement place: Token reinforcement procedures in a home-style rehabilitation setting for "pre-delinquent" boys. *Journal of Applied Behavior Analysis*, *1*, 213–223.

Piaget, J. (1926). *The language and thought of the child* (M. Gabain, Trans.). London: Routledge & Kegan Parel Ltd.

Piaget, J. (1929). *The child's conception of the world*. New York: Harcourt & Brace.

Piaget, J. (1932). *The moral judgment of the child*. London: Routledge & Kegan Paul.

Pitariu, H., Bostenaru, N., Lucaciu, L., & Oachis, A. (1984). The theory and practice of biorhythms are not confirmed. *Revista de Psihologie*, *30*, 166–171.

Platt, J. (1973). Social traps. *American Psychologist*, *28*, 641–651.

Platt, J. R. (1979). Interresponse-time shaping by variable-interval-like interresponse-time reinforcement

contingencies. *Journal of the Experimental Analysis of Behavior*, *31*, 3–14.

Polya, G. (1957). *How to solve it*. Garden City, N. Y.: Doubleday Anchor.

Popper, K. (1959). *The logic of scientific discovery*. New York: Harper.

Posner, M. I. & Keele, S. W. (1969). Attentional demands in movement. *Proceedings of the 16th Congress of Applied Psychology*. Amsterdam: Swets and Zeitlinger.

Postman, L. (1947). The history and present status of the law of effect. *Psychological Review*, *44*, 489–563.

Powell, R. W. (1969). The effect of reinforcement magnitude upon responding under fixed-ratio schedules. *Journal of the Experimental Analysis of Behavior*, *12*, 605–608.

Premack, D. (1959). Toward empirical behavioral laws: I. Positive reinforcement. *Psychological Review*, *66*, 219–233.

Premack, D. (1962). Reversibility of the reinforcement relation. *Science*, *136*, 235–237.

Premack, D. (1963). Rate differential reinforcement in monkey manipulation. *Journal of the Experimental Analysis of Behavior*, *6*, 81–89.

Premack, D. (1965). Reinforcement theory. In D. Levine (Ed.), *Nebraska symposium on motivation*. Lincoln: University of Nebraska Press.

Premack, D. (1971). Catching up with common sense or two sides of a generalization: Reinforcement and punishment. In R. Glaser (Ed.), *The nature of reinforcement*. New York: Academic.

Premack, D. (1971). Language in chimpanzee? *Science*, *172*, 808–822.

Premack, D. (1983). The codes of man and beasts. *The Behavioral and Brain Sciences*, *6*, 125–167.

Premack, D. (1986). *Gavagai!* Cambridge, Mass.: MIT Press.

Prewitt, E. P. (1967). Number of preconditioning trials in sensory preconditioning using CER training. *Journal of Comparative and Physiological Psychology*, *64*, 360–362.

Pribram, K. H. (1966). Some dimensions of remembering: Steps toward a neuropsychological model of memory. In J. Gaito (Ed.), *Macromolecules and behavior*. New York: Appleton-Century-Crofts.

Prochaska, J., Smith, N., Marzilli, R., Colby, J., & Donovan, W. (1974). Remote-control aversive stimulation in the treatment of head-banging in a retarded child. *Journal of Behavior Therapy and Experimental Psychiatry*, *5*, 285–289.

Qualls, P. J. & Sheehan, P. W. (1981). Electromyograph biofeedback as a relaxation technique: A critical appraisal and reassessment. *Psychological Bulletin, 90,* 21–42.

Rachlin, H. (1966). Recovery of responses during mild punishment. *Journal of the Experimental Analysis of Behavior, 9,* 251–263.

Rachlin, H. (1969). Autoshaping of key pecking in pigeons with negative reinforcement. *Journal of the Experimental Analysis of Behavior, 12,* 521–531.

Rachlin, H. (1970). *Introduction to modern behaviorism.* San Fransisco: Freeman.

Rachlin, H. (1974). Self-control. *Behaviorism, 2,* 94 –107.

Rachlin, H. & Green, L. (1972). Commitment, choice, and self-control. *Journal of the Experimental Analysis of Behavior, 17,* 15–22.

Rachlin, H., Green, L., Kagel, J. H., & Battalio, R. C. (1976). Economic demand theory and psychological studies of choice. In G. H. Bower (Ed.), *The psychology of learning and motivation, 10,* 129–154.

Rachlin, H. & Herrnstein, R. J. (1969). Hedonism revisited: On the negative law of effect. In B. A. Campbell & R. M. Church (Eds.), *Punishment and aversive behavior.* New York: Appleton-Century-Crofts.

Randich, A. & Ross, R. T. (1984). Mechanisms of blocking by contextual stimuli. *Learning and Motivation, 10,* 245–277.

Randich, A. & Ross, R. T. (1985). Contextual stimuli mediate the effects of pre-and postexposure to the unconditioned stimulus on conditioned suppression. In P. D. Balsam & A. Tomie (Eds.), *Context and learning.* Hillsdale, N.J.: Erlbaum.

Rashotte, M. E., Griffin, R. W., & Sisk, C. L. (1977). Second-order conditioning of the pigeon's keypeck. *Animal Learning & Behavior, 5,* 25–38.

Rashotte, M. E. & Surridge, C. T. (1969). Partial reinforcement and partial delay of reinforcement effects with 72-hour intertrial intervals and interpolated continuous reinforcement. *Quarterly Journal of Experimental Psychology, 21,* 156–161.

Razran, G. (1949). Semantic and phonetographic generalizations of salivary conditioning to verbal stimuli. *Journal of Experimental Psychology, 39,* 642–652.

Reese, E. S. (1963). The behavioral mechanisms underlying shell selection by hermit crabs. *Behaviour, 21,* 78–126.

Rescorla, R. A. (1966). Predictability and number of pairings in Pavlovian fear conditioning. *Psychonomic Science, 4,* 383–384.

Rescorla, R. A. (1967). Inhibition of delay in Pavlovian fear conditioning. *Journal of Comparative and Physiological Psychology, 64,* 114–120.

Rescorla, R. A. (1968). Probability of shock in the presence and absence of CS in fear conditioning. *Journal of Comparative and Physiological Psychology, 66,* 1–5.

Rescorla, R. A. (1969). Pavlovian conditioned inhibition. *Psychological Bulletin, 72,* 77–94.

Rescorla, R. A. (1973). Second order conditioning: Implications for theories of learning. In F. J. McGuigan and D. B. Lumsden (Eds.), *Contemporary approaches to conditioning and learning.* New York: Wiley.

Rescorla, R. A. (1982). Simultaneous second-order conditioning produces S-S learning in conditioned suppression. *Journal of Experimental Psychology: Animal Behavior Processes, 8,* 23–32.

Rescorla, R. A. (1984). Associations between Pavlovian CSs and context. *Journal of Experimental Psychology: Animal Behavior Processes, 10,* 195–204.

Rescorla, R. A. (1985). Inhibition and facilitation. In R. R. Miller & N. E. Spear (Eds.), *Information processing in animals: Conditioned inhibition.* Hillsdale, N. J.: Erlbaum.

Rescorla, R. A. (1986a). Facilitation and excitation. *Journal of Experimental Psychology: Animal Behavior Processes, 12,* 325–332.

Rescorla, R. A. (1986b). Two perceptual variables in within-event learning. *Animal Learning & Behavior, 14,* 387–392.

Rescorla, R. A. (1987). Facilitation and inhibition. *Journal of Experimental Psychology: Animal Behavior Processes, 13,* 250–259.

Rescorla, R. A. & Cunningham, C. L. (1978). Within-compound flavor associations. *Journal of Experimental Psychology: Animal Behavior Processes, 4,* 267–275.

Rescorla, R. A. & Durlach, P. J. (1981). Within event learning in Pavlovian conditioning. In M. E. Spear & R. R. Miller (Eds.), *Information processing in animals: Memory mechanisms.* Hillsdale, N.J.: Erlbaum.

Rescorla, R. A., Durlach, P. J., & Grau, J. W. (1985). Contextual learning in Pavlovian conditioning. In P. D. Balsam & A. Tomie (Eds.), *Context and learning.* Hillsdale, N.J.: Erlbaum.

Rescorla, R. A. & LoLordo, V. M. (1965). Inhibition of avoidance behavior. *Journal of Comparative and Physiological Psychology, 59,* 406– 412.

Rescorla, R. A. & Wagner, A. R. (1972). A theory of Pavlovian conditioning: Variations in the effectiveness of reinforcement and nonreinforcement. In A. H. Black and W. F. Prokasy (Eds.), *Classical conditioning II: Current research and theory*. New York: Appleton-Century-Crofts.

Restorff, H. V. (1933). Analyse von Vorgangen im Spurenfeld. I. Uber die Wirkung von Bereichsbildungen im Spurenfeld. *Psychologische Forschung, 18*, 299–342.

Revusky, S. H. (1977). Learning as a general process with an emphasis on data from feeding experiments. In N. W. Milgram, L. Krames, & T. M. Alloway, (Eds.), *Food aversion learning*. New York: Plenum.

Revusky, S. H. & Bedarf, E. W. (1967). Association of illness with prior ingestion of novel foods. *Science, 155*, 219–220.

Reynolds, G. S. (1961). An analysis of interactions in a multiple schedule. *Journal of the Experimental Analysis of Behavior, 4*, 107–117.

Reynolds, G. S. (1963). Some limitations on behavioral contrast and induction during successive discrimination. *Journal of the Experimental Analysis of Behavior, 6*, 131–139.

Richards, C. S. (1981). Improving college students' study behaviors through self-control techniques: A brief review. *Behavioral Counseling Quarterly. 1*, 159–175.

Richelle, M. M. (1984). Are Skinner's warnings still relevant to current psychology? *The Behavioral and Brain Sciences, 7*, 531–532.

Rilling, M. (1977). Stimulus control and inhibitory processes. In W. K. Honig & J. E. R. Staddon (Eds.), *Handbook of operant behavior*. Englewood Cliffs, N.J.: Prentice Hall.

Rilling, M. E. & Neiworth, J. J. (1986). Comparative cognition: a general process approach. In D. F. Kendrick, M. E. Rilling, & M. R. Denny (Eds.), *Theories of animal memory*. Hillsdale, N.J.: Erlbaum.

Rivera, D. M. & Smith, D. D. (1987). Influence of modeling on acquisition and generalization of computational skills: A summary of research findings from three sites. *Learning Disability Quarterly, 10*, 69–80.

Roberts, R. C., Boone, R. R., & Wurtele, S. K. (1982). Response uncertainty and imitation: Effects of pre-experience and vicarious consequences. *British Journal of Social Psychology, 21*, 223–230.

Roberts, S. (1980). Distribution of trials and intertrial retention in delayed matching to sample with pigeons. *Journal of Experimental Psychology: Animal Behavior Processes, 6*, 217–237.

Roberts, S. (1981). Isolation of an internal clock. *Journal of Experimental Psychology: Animal Behavior Processes, 7*, 242–268.

Roberts, S. (1982). Cross modal use of an internal clock. *Journal of Experimental Psychology: Animal Behavior Processes, 8*, 2–22.

Roberts, S. (1983). Properties and function of an internal clock. In R. L. Mellgren (Ed.), *Animal Cognition and Behavior*. Amsterdam: North-Holland Publishing.

Roberts, W. A. & Grant, D. S. (1974). Short-term memory in the pigeon with presentation time precisely controlled. *Learning and Motivation, 5*, 393–408.

Roberts, W. A. & Grant, D. S. (1978). An analysis of light-induced retroactive inhibition in pigeon short-term memory. *Journal of Experimental Psychology: Animal Behavior Processes, 4*, 219–236.

Roberts, W. A., Mazmanian, D. S., & Kraemer, P. J. (1984). Directed forgetting in monkeys. *Animal Learning & Behavior, 12*, 29–40.

Rodgers, W. & Rozin, P. (1966). Novel food preferences in thiamine-deficient rats. *Journal of Comparative and Physiological Psychology, 61*, 1–4.

Rogers, C. A. (1974). Feedback precision and postfeedback interval duration. *Journal of Experimental Psychology, 102*, 604–608.

Roitblat, H. L. (1980). Codes and coding processes in pigeon short-term memory. *Animal Learning and Behavior, 8*, 341–351.

Roitblat, H. L. (1987). *Introduction to comparative cognition*. New York: W. H. Freeman.

Roitblat, H. L., Bever, T. G., & Terrace, H. S. (1984). *Animal cognition*. Hillsdale, N.J.: Erlbaum.

Roitblat, H. L., Pologe, B., & Scopatz, R. A. (1983). The representation of items in serial position. *Animal Learning & Behavior, 11*, 489–498.

Roitblat, H. L., Scopatz, R. A., & Bever, T. G. (1987). The hierarchical representation of three-item sequences. *Animal Learning & Behavior, 15*, 179–192.

Rosch, E. (1973). On the internal structure of perceptual and semantic categories. In T. E. Moore (Ed.), *Cognitive development and the acquisition of language*. New York: Academic.

Rosch, E. (1975). Cognitive representations of semantic categories. *Journal of Experimental Psychology: General, 104*, 192–233.

Rosch, E. (1977). Human categorization. In N. Warren (Ed.), *Advances in cross-cultural psychology* (Vol. 1). London: Academic Press.

Rosellini, R. A., De Cola, J. P., & Warren, D. A. (1986). The effect of feedback stimuli on contextual fear depends upon the length of the minimum ITI. *Learning and Motivation, 17,* 229–242.

Rosellini, R. A., Warren, D. A., & De Cola, J. P. (1987). Predictability and controllability: Differential effects upon contextual fear. *Learning and Motivation, 18,* 392– 420.

Rosen, B. & D'Andrade, R. (1959). The psychosocial origins of achievement motivation. *Sociometry, 22,* 185–218.

Rosenthal, R. (1966). *Experimenter effects in behavioral research.* New York: Appleton-Century-Crofts.

Rosenthal, R. & Rosnow, R. L. (1984). *Essentials of behavioral research: Methods and data analysis.* New York: McGraw-Hill.

Rosenthal, T. L. & Zimmerman, B. J. (1972). Modeling by exemplification and instruction in training conservation. *Developmental Psychology, 6,* 392– 401.

Rosenthal, T. L. & Zimmerman, B. J. (1978). *Social learning and cognition.* New York: Academic.

Rosenzweig, M. R. (1966). Environmental complexity, cerebral change, and behavior. *American Psychologist, 21,* 321–332.

Rosenzweig, M. R. (1984). Experience and the brain. *American Psychologist, 39,* 365–376.

Rosenzweig, M. R.; Mollgaard, K.; Diamond, M. C.; & Bennet, T. E. L. (1972). Negative as well as positive synaptic changes may store memory. *Psychological Review, 79,* 93–96.

Ross, J. A. (1974). The use of contingency contracting in controlling adult nailbiting. *Journal of Behavior Therapy and Experimental Psychiatry, 5,* 105–106.

Ross, R. T. & Holland, P. C. (1981). Conditioning of simultaneous and serial feature-positive discriminations. *Animal Learning & Behavior, 9,* 293–303.

Rozin, P. & Kalat, J. W. (1971). Specific hungers and poison avoidance as adaptive specializations of learning. *Psychological Review, 78,* 459– 486.

Rozin, P., Reff, D., Mack, M., & Schull, J. (1984). Conditioned opponent responses in human tolerance to caffeine. *Bulletin of the Psychonomic Society, 22,* 117–120.

Rudolph, R. L., Honig, W. K., & Gerry, J. E. (1969). Effects of monochromatic rearing on the acquisition of stimulus control. *Journal of Comparative and Physiological Psychology, 67,* 50 –57.

Rudy, J. (1982). An appreciation of higher order conditioning and blocking. In M. L. Commons, R. J. Herrnstein, & A. R. Wagner (Eds.), *Quantitative analyses of behavior, Vol. 3: Acquisition.* Cambridge, Mass.: Ballinger.

Rudy, J. (1984). In M. L. Commons, R. J. Herrnstein, & A. R. Wagner (Eds.), *Quantitative analyses of behavior. Vol. 3. Acquisition.* Cambridge, Mass.: Ballinger.

Rumbaugh, D. M. (Ed.). (1977). *Language learning by a chimpanzee: The Lana project.* New York: Academic.

Rushford, N. B. (1965). Behavioral studies of the coelenterate *Hydra pirardi* Brien. *Animal Behaviour, 13,* 30 – 42.

Rushford, N. B., Burnett, A., & Maynard, R. (1963). Behavior in Hydra: Contraction responses of *Hydra pirardi* to mechanical and light stimuli. *Science, 139,* 760–761.

Rusiniak, K. W., Hankins, W. G., Garcia, J., & Brett, C. P. (1979). Flavor-illness aversions: Potentiation of odor by taste in rats. *Behavioral and Neural Biology, 25,* 1–17.

Russek, M. & Pina, S. (1962). Conditioning of adrenalin anorexia. *Natus, 193,* 1296–1297.

Sachs, D. A. & Mayhall, B. (1971). Behavioral control of spasms using aversive conditioning with a cerebral palsied adult. *Journal of Nervous and Mental Disorders, 152,* 362–363.

Salmon, D. P. & D'Amato, M. R. (1981). Note on delay-interval illumination effects on retention in monkeys (*Cebus apella*). *Journal of the Experimental Analysis of Behavior, 36,* 381–385.

Savage-Rumbaugh, E. S. (1984). Acquisition of functional symbol usage in apes and children. In H. L. Roitblat, T. G. Bever, & H. S. Terrace (Eds.), *Animal cognition.* Hillsdale, N.J.: Erlbaum.

Savage-Rumbaugh, E. S., McDonald, K., Sevcik, R. A., Hopkins, W. D., & Rubert, E. (1986). Spontaneous symbol acquisition and communicative use by pygmy chimpanzees (*Pan paniscus*). *Journal of Experimental Psychology: General, 115,* 211–235.

Schaefer, H. H. & Martin, P. L. (1966). Behavioral therapy for "apathy" of schizophrenics. *Psychological Reports, 19,* 1147–1158.

Schlosberg, H. (1928). A study of the conditioned patellar reflex. *Journal of Experimental Psychology, 11,* 468– 494.

Schlosberg, H. (1937). The relationship between success and the laws of conditioning. *Psychological Review, 44,* 379–394.

Schlosberg, H. & Katz, A. (1943). Double alternation lever-pressing in the white rat. *American Journal of Psychology, 56,* 274 –282.

Schmidt, R. A. (1975). A schema theory of discrete motor skill learning. *Psychological Review, 82,* 225–260.

Schmidt, R. A. (1982). *Motor control and learning.* Champagne, Ill.: Human Kinetics Publishers.

Schneider, J. W. (1973). Reinforcer effectiveness as a function of reinforcer rate and magnitude: A comparison of concurrent performances. *Journal of the Experimental Analysis of Behavior, 20,* 461– 471.

Schneiderman, N. (1966). Interstimulus interval function of the nictitating membrane response of the rabbit under delay versus trace conditioning. *Journal of Comparative and Physiological Psychology, 62,* 397– 402.

Schneiderman, N., McCabe, P. M., Haselton, J. R., Ellenberger, H. H., Jarrell, T. W., & Gentile, C. G. (1987). Neurobiological bases of conditioned bradycardia in rabbits. In I. Gormezano, W. F. Prokasy, & R. F. Thompson (Eds.) *Classical conditioning.* (3rd ed.) Hillsdale, N.J.: Erlbaum.

Schneirla, T. C. (1933). Some important features of ant learning. *Zeitschrift fur Vergleichenden Physiologie, 19,* 439–452.

Schoener, T. W. (1971). Theory of feeding strategies. *Annual Review of Ecology and Systematics, 2,* 27–39.

Schoenfeld, W. N. (1950). An experimental approach to anxiety, escape, and avoidance behavior. In P. H. Hoch & J. Zubin (Eds.), *Anxiety.* New York: Grune and Stratton.

Schrier, A. M. & Brady, P. M. (1987). Categorization of natural stimuli by monkeys (*Macaca mulatta*): Effects of stimulus set size and modification of exemplars. *Journal of Experimental Psychology: Animal Behavior Processes, 13,* 136–143.

Schroeder, S. R. & Holland, J. G. (1969). Reinforcement of eye movement with concurrent schedules. *Journal of the Experimental Analysis of Behavior, 12,* 897–903.

Schull, J. (1979). A conditioned opponent theory of Pavlovian conditioning and habituation. In G. H. Bower (Ed.), *The psychology of learning and motivation* (Vol. 13). New York: Academic.

Schuster, R., & Rachlin, H. (1968). Indifference between punishment and free shock: Evidence for the negative law of effect. *Journal of the Experimental Analysis of Behavior, 11,* 777–786.

Schusterman, R. J. & Krieger, K. (1984). California sea lions are capable of semantic comprehension. *The Psychological Record, 34,* 3–23.

Schwartz, B. & Gamzu, E. (1977). Pavlovian control of operant behavior: An analysis of autoshaping and its implication for operant conditioning. In W. K. Honig & J. E. R. Staddon (Eds.), *Handbook of operant behavior.* Englewood Cliffs, N.J.: Prentice Hall.

Sears, R. R., Maccoby, E. E., & Levin, H. (1957). *Patterns of child rearing.* New York: Harper.

Sechenov, I. M. [Reflexes of the Brain.] (1935). In I. M. Sechenov, *Selected Works* (A. A. Subkov, trans.). Moscow and Leningrad: State Publishing House for Biological and Medical Literature. (Originally published St. Petersburg: 1863).

Seligman, M. E. P. (1970). On the generality of the laws of learning. *Psychological Review, 77,* 406 – 418.

Seligman, M. E. P. (1975). *Helplessness: On depression, development, and death.* San Francisco: Freeman.

Seligman, M. E. P. & Campbell, B. A. (1965). Effects of intensity and duration of punishment on extinction of an avoidance response. *Journal of Comparative and Physiological Psychology, 59,* 295–297.

Seligman, M. E. P. & Hager, J. L. (1972). *Biological boundaries of learning.* New York: Appleton-Century-Crofts.

Seligman, M. E. P. & Johnston, J. C. (1973). A cognitive theory of avoidance learning. In F. J. McGuigan and D. B. Lumsden (Eds.), *Contemporary approaches to conditioning and learning.* Washington, D.C.: Winston-Wiley.

Shaffer, L. H. (1978). Timing in the motor programming of typing. *Quarterly Journal of Experimental Psychology, 30,* 333–345.

Shapiro, D. C. & Schmidt, R. A. (1982). The schema theory: Recent evidence and developmental implications. In J. A. S. Kelso and J. E. Clark (Eds.), *The development of movement control and coordination.* New York: Wiley.

Shaughnessy, J. J. & Zechmeister, E. B. (1985). *Research methods in psychology.* New York: Knopf.

Sheffield, F. D. (1948). Avoidance training and the contiguity principle. *Journal of Comparative and Physiological Psychology, 41,* 165–177.

Sheffield, F. D., Wulff, J. J., & Backer, R. (1951). Reward value of copulation without sex drive reduction. *Journal of Comparative and Physiological Psychology, 44,* 3–8.

Shepard, R. N. (1967). Recognition memory for words, sentences, and pictures. *Journal of Verbal Learning and Verbal Behavior, 6,* 156–163.

Shepp, B. E. & Eimas, P. D. (1964). Intradimensional and extradimensional shifts in the rat. *Journal of Comparative and Physiological Psychology, 57,* 357–361.

Sherrington, C. S. (1906). *The integrative action of the nervous system.* New Haven: Yale University Press.

Sherry, D. (1984). Food storage by black-capped chickadees: Memory for the location and contents of caches. *Animal Behaviour, 32,* 451– 464.

Sherry, D. F. (1987). Foraging for stored food. In M. L. Commons, A. Kacelnik, & S. J. Shettleworth (Eds.), *Quantitative analyses of behavior: Vol. 6. Foraging.* Hillsdale, N.J.: Erlbaum.

Sherry, D. F. (1988). Learning and adaptation in food-storing birds. In R. C. Bolles & M. D. Beecher (Eds.), *Evolution and learning.* Hillsdale, N.J.: Erlbaum.

Shettleworth, S. J. (1975). Reinforcement and the organization of behavior in golden hamsters: Hunger, environment, and food reinforcement. *Journal of Experimental Psychology: Animal Behavior Processes, 104,* 56–87.

Shettleworth, S. J. (1978). Reinforcement and the organization of behavior in golden hamsters: Punishment of three action patterns. *Learning and Motivation, 9,* 99–123.

Shettleworth, S. J. (1983). Function and mechanism in learning. In M. D. Zeiler & P. Harzem (Eds.), *Advances in analysis of behavior: Vol. 3, Biological factors in learning.* New York: Wiley.

Shettleworth, S. J. & Juergensen, M. R. (1980). Reinforcement and the organization of behavior in golden hamsters: Brain stimulation reinforcement for seven action patterns. *Journal of Experimental Psychology: Animal Behavior Processes, 6,* 352–375.

Shettleworth, S. J. & Krebs, J. R. (1982). How marsh tits find their hoards: The role of site preference and spatial memory. *Journal of Experimental Psychology: Animal Behavior Processes, 8,* 354–375.

Shettleworth, S. J. & Krebs, J. R. (1986). Stored and encountered seeds: A comparison of two spatial memory tasks in marsh tits and chickadees. *Journal of Experimental Psychology: Animal Behavior Processes, 12,* 248–257.

Shimp. C. P. (1966). Probabilistically reinforced choice behavior in pigeons. *Journal of the Experimental Analysis of Behavior, 9,* 443– 455.

Shimp, C. P. (1968). Magnitude and frequency of reinforcement and frequencies of interresponse times. *Journal of the Experimental Analysis of Behavior, 11,* 525–535.

Shimp, C. P. (1969). Optimal behavior in free-operant experiments. *Psychological Review, 76,* 97–112.

Shimp, C. P. (1973). Synthetic variable-interval schedules of reinforcement. *Journal of the Experimental Analysis of Behavior, 19,* 311–330.

Shurtleff, D., Warren-Boulton, F. R., & Silberberg, A. (1987). Income and choice between different goods. *Journal of the Experimental Analysis of Behavior, 48,* 263–275.

Sidman, M. (1953). Two temporal parameters of the maintenance of avoidance behavior by the white rat. *Journal of Comparative and Physiological Psychology, 46,* 253–261.

Sidman, M. & Stebbins, W. C. (1954). Satiation effects under fixed-ratio schedules of reinforcement. *Journal of Comparative and Physiological Psychology, 47,* 114–116.

Siegel, S. (1975). Evidence from rats that morphine tolerance is a learned response. *Journal of Comparative and Physiological Psychology, 89,* 498–506.

Siegel, S. (1982). Pharmacological habituation and learning. In M. L. Commons, R. J. Herrnstein, & A. R. Wagner (Eds.), *Quantitative analyses of behavior, Vol. 3: Acquisition.* Cambridge, Mass.: Ballinger.

Siegel, S. & Domjan, M. (1971). Backward conditioning as an inhibitory procedure. *Learning and Motivation, 2,* 1–11.

Siegel, S., Hinson, R. E., Krank, M. D., & McCully, J. (1982). Heroin "overdose" death: The contribution of drug-associated environmental cues. *Science, 216,* 436– 437.

Siegel S., Sherman, J. E., & Mitchell, D. (1980). Extinction of morphine analgesic tolerance. *Learning and Motivation, 11,* 289–301.

Silberberg, A., Hamilton, B., Ziriax, J. M., & Casey, J. (1978). The structure of choice. *Journal of Experimental Psychology: Animal Behavior Processes, 4,* 368–398.

Silberberg, A., Warren-Boulton, F. R., & Asano, T. (1987). Inferior-good and Giffen-good effects in monkey choice behavior. *Journal of Experimental Psychology: Animal Behavior Processes, 13,* 292–301.

Silberberg, A., Warren-Boulton, F. R., & Asano, T. (1988). Maximizing present value: A model to explain why moderate response rates obtain on variable-interval schedules. *Journal of the Experimental Analysis of Behavior, 49,* 331–338.

Silver, L. B., Dublin, C. C.,& Lourie, R. S. (1969). Does violence breed violence? Contributions from a study of the child abuse syndrome. *American Journal of Psychiatry, 126,* 404 – 407.

Skinner, B. F. (1935). The generic nature of the concepts of stimulus and response. *Journal of General Psychology, 12,* 40 –65.

Skinner, B. F. (1938). *The behavior of organisms.* New York: Appleton-Century-Crofts.

Skinner, B. F. (1948). "Superstition" in the pigeon. *Journal of Experimental Psychology, 38,* 168–172.

Skinner, B. F. (1950). Are theories of learning necessary? *Psychological Review, 57,* 193–216.

Skinner, B. F. (1953). *Science and human behavior.* New York: Macmillan.

Skinner, B. F. (1956a). What is psychotic behavior? In F. Gildea (Ed.), *Theory and treatment of the psychoses: Some newer aspects.* St. Louis: Washington University Press.

Skinner, B. F. (1956b). A case history in scientific method. *American Psychologist, 11,* 221–233.

Skinner, B. F. (1966). The phylogeny and ontogeny of behavior. *Science, 11,* 159–166.

Skinner, B. F. (1977). Herrnstein and the evolution of behaviorism. *American Psychologist, 32,* 1006–1012.

Skinner, B. F. (1985). Cognitive science and behaviourism. *British Journal of Psychology, 76,* 291–301.

Smith, K. (1954). Conditioning as an artifact. *Psychological Review, 61,* 217–225.

Smith, K. U. (1962). *Delayed sensory feedback and behavior.* Philadelphia: Saunders.

Smith, K. U. (1966). Cybernetic theory and analysis of learning. In E. A. Bilodeau (Ed.), *Acquisition of skill.* New York: Academic.

Smith, M. C. & Gormezano, I. (1965). *Conditioning of the nictitating membrane response of the rabbit as a function of backward, simultaneous and forward CS-UCS intervals.* Paper presented at the meeting of the Psychonomic Society, Chicago

Solomon, P. R. (1977). Role of the hippocampus in blocking and conditioned inhibition of the rabbit's nictitating membrane response. *Journal of Comparative and Physiological Psychology, 91,* 407–417.

Solomon, R. L. (1980). The opponent process theory of acquired motivation. *American Psychologist, 35,* 691–712.

Solomon, R. L. & Corbit, J. D. (1974). An opponent-process theory of motivation: I. Temporal dynamics of affect. *Psychological Review, 81,* 119–145.

Solomon, R. L., Kamin, L. J., & Wynne, L. C. (1953). Traumatic avoidance learning: The outcomes of several extinction procedures with dogs. *Journal of Abnormal and Social Psychology, 48,* 291–302.

Solomon, R. L. & Wynne, L. C. (1953). Traumatic avoidance learning: Acquisition in normal dogs. *Psychological Monographs, 67* (354).

Solomon, R. L. & Wynne, L. C. (1954). Traumatic avoidance learning: The principles of anxiety conservation and partial irreversibility. *Psychological Review, 61,* 353–385.

Soltysik, S. (1960). Studies on the avoidance conditioning: II. Differentiation and extinction of avoidance responses. *Acta Biologiae Experimentalis, 20,* 171–182.

Spear, N. E. (1971). Forgetting as retrieval failure. In W. K. Honig & P. H. R. James (Eds.), *Animal memory.* New York: Academic.

Spelke, E., Hirst, W., & Neisser, U. (1976). Skills of divided attention. *Cognition, 4,* 205–230.

Spence, K. W. (1937). The differential response in animals to stimuli varying within a single dimension. *Psychological Review, 44,* 430–444.

Spence, K. W. (1956). *Behavior theory and conditioning.* New Haven: Yale University Press.

Spinelli, D. H., Jensen, F. E., & DiPrisco, G. V. (1980). Early experience effect on dendritic branching in normally reared kittens. *Experimental Neurology, 1980, 62,* 1–11.

Sprinthall, R. C. (1987). *Basic statistical analysis.* (2nd ed.) Englewood, Cliffs, N.J.: Prentice Hall.

Squier, L. H. (1969). Autoshaping key responses with fish. *Psychonomic Science, 17,* 177–178.

Staddon, J. E. R. (1983). *Adaptive behavior and learning.* Cambridge: Cambridge University Press.

Staddon, J. E. R. (1988). Learning as inference. In R. C. Bolles & M. D. Beecher, (Eds.), *Evolution and learning.* Hillsdale, N.J.: Erlbaum.

Staddon, J. E. R. & Hinson, J. M. (1983). Optimization: A result or a mechanism? *Science, 221,* 976–977.

Staddon, J. E. R. & Simmelhag, V. L. (1971). The "superstition" experiment: A reexamination of its implications for the principles of adaptive behavior. *Psychological Review, 78,* 3–43.

Starr, M. D. & Mineka, S. (1977). Determinants of fear over the cause of avoidance learning. *Learning and Motivation, 8,* 332–350.

Staub, E. (1968). Duration of stimulus-exposure as determinant of the efficacy of flooding procedures in the elimination of fear. *Behavior Research and Therapy, 6,* 131–132.

Stelmach, G. E. (1969). Efficiency of motor learning as a function of intertrial rest. *Research Quarterly, 40,* 198–202.

Stewart, J., deWit, H., & Eikelboom, R. (1984). Role of unconditioned and conditioned drug effects in the self-administration of opiates and stimulants. *Psychological Review, 91,* 251–268.

Stuart, R. B. (1967). Behavioral control over eating. *Behavior Research and Therapy, 5,* 357–365.

Stuart, R. B. (1971). A three-dimensional program for the treatment of obesity. *Behaviour Research and Therapy, 9*, 177–186.

Stubbs, A. (1968). The discrimination of stimulus duration by pigeons. *Journal of the Experimental Analysis of Behavior, 11*, 223–238.

Summers, J. J. (1981). Motor programs. In D. Holding (Ed.), *Human skills.* New York: Wiley.

Swan, J. A. & Pearce, J. M. (1987). The influence of predictive accuracy on serial autoshaping: Evidence of orienting responses. *Journal of Experimental Psychology: Animal Behavior Processes, 13*, 407– 417.

Tait, R. W. & Saladin, M. E. (1986). Concurrent development of excitatory and inhibitory associations during backward conditioning. *Animal Learning & Behavior, 14*, 133–137.

Taub, E. & Berman, A. J. (1968). Movement and learning in the absence of sensory feedback. In S. J. Freedman (Ed.), *The neuropsychology of spatially oriented behavior.* Homewood, Ill.: Dorsey.

Taylor, A. & Noble, C. E. (1962). Acquisition and extinction phenomena in human trial-and-error learning under different schedules of reinforcing feedback. *Perceptual and Motor Skills, 15*, 31– 44.

Terhune, J. G. & Premack, D. (1970). On the proportionality between the probability of not-running and the punishment effect of being forced to run. *Learning and Motivation, 1*, 141–147.

Terrace, H. S. (1963). Errorless transfer of a discrimination across two continua. *Journal of the Experimental Analysis of Behavior, 6*, 223–232.

Terrace, H. S. (1966). Stimulus control. In W. K. Honig (Ed.), *Operant conditioning: Areas of research and application.* Englewood Cliffs, N.J.: Prentice Hall.

Terrace, H. S. (1972). By-products of discrimination learning. In G. H. Bower (Ed.), *The psychology of learning and motivation* (Vol. 5). New York: Academic.

Terrace, H. S. (1975). Evidence for the innate basis of the hue dimension in the duckling. *Journal of the Experimental Analysis of Behavior, 24*, 79–87.

Terrace, H. S. (1979). *Nim.* New York: Knopf.

Terrace, H. S. (1983). Simultaneous chaining. In M. L. Commons, R. J. Herrnstein, & A. R. Wagner (Eds.), *Quantitative analyses of behavior, Vol. 4: Discrimination processes.* Cambridge, Mass.: Ballinger.

Terrace, H. S. (1985). On the nature of animal thinking. *Neuroscience & Biobehavioral Reviews, 9*, 643–652.

Terrace, H. S., Petitto, L. A., Sanders, R. J., & Bever, T. G. (1979). Can an ape create a sentence? *Science, 206*, 891–902.

Terrace, H. S., Straub, R., Bever, T. G., & Seidenberg, M. (1977). Representation of a sequence by pigeons. *Bulletin of the Psychonomic Society, 10*, 269.

Terry, W. S. & Wagner, A. R. (1975). Short-term memory for "surprising" versus "expected" unconditioned stimuli in Pavlovian conditioning. *Journal of Experimental Psychology: Animal Behavior Processes, 1*, 122–133.

Thelen, M. H., Dollinger, S. J., & Kirkland, K. D. (1979). Imitation and response uncertainty. *Journal of Genetic Psychology, 135*, 139–152.

Thelen, M. H., Paul, S. C., & Dollinger, S. J. (1978). Response uncertainty and imitation: The interactive effects of age and task options. *Journal of Research in Personality, 12*, 370–380.

Thomas, D. R. (1981). Studies of long-term memory in the pigeon. In N. E. Spear & R. R. Miller (Eds.), *Information processing in animals: Memory mechanisms.* Hillsdale, N.J.: Erlbaum.

Thomas, D. R. & Lopez, L. J. (1962). The effect of delayed testing on generalization slope. *Journal of Comparative and Physiological Psychology, 44*, 541–544.

Thompson, R. F. (1986). The neurobiology of learning and memory. *Science, 233*, 941–947.

Thompson, R. F., McCormick, D. A., & Lavond, D. G. (1986). Localization of the essential memory-trace system for a basic form of associative learning in the mammalian brain. In S. H. Hulse & B. F. Green, Jr., (Eds.), *One hundred years of psychological research in America.* Baltimore, Mary.: Johns Hopkins University Press.

Thompson, R. F. & Spencer, W. A. (1966). Habituation: A model phenomenon for the study of neuronal substrates of behavior. *Psychological Review, 73*, 16 – 43.

Thorndike, E. L. (1898). Animal intelligence: An experimental study of the associative processes in animals. *Psychological Review Monograph Supplement, 2* (8).

Thorndike, E. L. (1911). *Animal intelligence.* New York: Macmillan.

Thorndike, E. L. (1927). The law of effect. *American Journal of Psychology, 39*, 212–222.

Thorndike, E. L. (1946). Expectation. *Psychological Review, 53*, 277–281.

Thorpe, W. H. (1963). *Learning and instinct in animals* (2nd ed.) London: Methuen.

Thurstone, L. L. (1919). The learning curve equation. *Psychological Monographs, 26* (114).

Tierney, K. J., Smith, H. V., & Gannon, K. N. (1987). Some tests of molar models of instrumental performance. *Journal of Experimental Psychology: Animal Behavior Processes, 13,* 341–353.

Timberlake, W. (1983). Rats' responses to a moving object related to food or water: A behavior-systems analysis. *Animal Learning and Behavior, 11,* 309–320.

Timberlake, W. (1984a). Behavior regulation and learned performance: Some misapprehensions and disagreements. *Journal of the Experimental Analysis of Behavior, 41,* 355–375.

Timberlake, W. (1984b). A temporal limit on the effect of future food on current performance in an analogue of foraging and welfare. *Journal of the Experimental Analysis of Behavior, 41,* 117–124.

Timberlake, W. & Allison, J. (1974). Response deprivation: An empirical approach to instrumental performance. *Psychological Review, 81,* 146–164.

Timberlake, W. & Grant, D. L. (1975). Auto-shaping in rats to the presentation of another rat predicting food. *Science, 190,* 690–692.

Tinbergen, N. (1951). *The study of instinct.* Oxford: Oxford University Press.

Tinbergen, N. & Perdeck, A. C. (1950). On the stimulus situation releasing the begging response in the newly hatched Herring Gull chick (*Larus argentatus argentatus* Pont). *Behaviour, 3,* 1–39.

Tinkelepaugh, O. L. (1928). An experimental study of representative factors in monkeys. *Journal of Comparative Psychology, 8,* 197–236.

Tolman, E. C. (1932). *Purposive behavior in animals and men.* New York: Appleton-Century-Crofts.

Tolman, E. C. (1951). *Collected papers in psychology.* Berkeley: University of California Press.

Tolman, E. C. (1959). Principles of purposive behavior. In S. Koch (Ed.), *Psychology: A study of a science* (Vol. 2). New York: McGraw-Hill.

Tolman, E. C. & Honzik, C. H. (1930). Introduction and removal of reward, and maze performance in rats. *University of California Publications in Psychology, 4,* 257–275.

Towe, A. L. (1954). A study of figural equivalence in the pigeon. *Journal of Comparative and Physiological Psychology, 47,* 283–287.

Tracy, W. K. (1970). Wavelength generalization and preference in monochromatically reared ducklings. *Journal of the Experimental Analysis of Behavior, 13,* 163–178.

Tranberg, D. K. & Rilling, M. (1980). Delay-interval illumination changes interfere with pigeon short-term memory. *Journal of the Experimental Analysis of Behavior, 33,* 39–49.

Trapold, M. A. & Spence, K. W. (1960). Performance changes in eyelid conditioning as related to the motivational and reinforcing properties of the UCS. *Journal of Experimental Psychology, 59,* 209–213.

Trinkaus, J. W. & Booke, A. L. (1982). Biorhythms: Another look. *Psychological Reports, 50,* 396–398.

Trowbridge, M. H. & Cason, H. (1932). An experimental test of Thorndike's theory of learning. *Journal of General Psychology, 7,* 245–260.

Tsuda, A. & Tanaka, M. (1985). Differential changes in noradrenaline turnover in specific regions of rat brain produced by controllable and uncontrollable shocks. *Behavioral Neuroscience, 99,* 802–817.

Turner, E. R. A. (1965). Social feeding in birds. *Behaviour, 24,* 1–46.

Turner, S. M. & Forehand, R. (1976). Imitative behavior as a function of success–failure and racial-socioeconomic factors. *Journal of Applied Social Psychology, 6,* 40–47.

Turney, T. H. (1982). The association of visual concepts and imitative vocalization in the mynah (*Gracula religiosa*). *Bulletin of the Psychonomic Society, 19,* 59–62.

Turnure, J. & Zigler, E. (1964). Outer-directedness in the problem solving of normal and retarded children. *Journal of Abnormal and Social Psychology, 69,* 427–436.

Tversky, A. & Sattath, S. (1979). Preference trees. *Psychological Review, 86,* 542–573.

Ulrich, R. E. & Azrin, N. H. (1962). Reflexive fighting in response to aversive stimulation. *Journal of the Experimental Analysis of Behavior, 5,* 511–520.

Urcuioli, P. J. & Zentall, T. R. (1986). Retrospective coding in pigeons' delayed matching-to-sample. *Journal of Experimental Psychology: Animal Behavior Processes, 12,* 69–77.

Vander Wall, S. B. (1982). An experimental analysis of cache recovery by Clark's nutcracker. *Animal Behaviour, 30,* 84–94.

Vaughan, W. (1976). *Optimization and reinforcement.* Ph. D. dissertation, Harvard University.

Vaughan, W. (1981). Melioration, matching, and maximization. *Journal of the Experimental Analysis of Behavior, 36,* 141–149.

Vaughan, W. (1982). Choice and the Rescorla-Wagner model. In M. L. Commons, R. J. Herrnstein, & H. Rachlin (Eds.), *Quantitative analyses of behavior, Vol. 2: Matching and maximizing accounts.* Cambridge, Mass.: Ballinger.

Vaughan, W. (1985). Choice: A local analysis. *Journal of the Experimental Analysis of Behavior, 43,* 383–405.

Vaughan, W. (1987). Dissociation of value and response strength. *Journal of the Experimental Analysis of Behavior, 48,* 367–381.

Vaughan, W. & Greene, S. L. (1983). Acquisition of absolute discriminations in pigeons. In M. L. Commons, A. R. Wagner, & R. J. Herrnstein (Eds.), *Quantitative analyses of behavior, Vol. 4: Discrimination processes.* Cambridge, Mass.: Ballinger.

Vaughan, W. & Greene, S. L. (1984). Pigeon visual memory capacity. *Journal of Experimental Psychology: Animal Behavior Processes, 10,* 256–271.

Vaughan, W. & Miller, H. L. (1984). Optimization versus response-strength accounts of behavior. *Journal of the Experimental Analysis of Behavior, 42,* 337–348.

Vienero, V. & Lagerspetz, K. (1984). The relation of parent background and TV-viewing habits to child aggression in six different countries. *Psykologia* (Finland), *19,* 414–419.

Voegtlin, W. L. (1940). The treatment of alcoholism by establishing a conditioned reflex. *American Journal of Medical Science, 199,* 802–810.

Volpicelli, J. R., Ulm, R. R., & Altenor, A. (1984). Feedback during exposure to inescapable shocks and subsequent shock-escape performance. *Learning and Motivation, 15,* 279–286.

von Holst, E. (1935). Uber den Lichtruckenreflex bei Fischen. *Publicazioni della Stazione zoologica di Napoli, 15,* 143–158.

von Neuman, J. & Morgenstern, O. (1953). *Theory of games and economic behavior,* (3rd ed.). Princeton: Princeton University Press.

Wagner, A. R. (1978). Expectancies and the priming of STM. In S. H. Hulse, H. Fowler, & W. K. Honig (Eds.), *Cognitive aspects of animal behavior.* Hillsdale, N.J.: Erlbaum.

Wagner, A. R. (1981). SOP: A model of automatic memory processing in animal behavior. In N. E. Spear & R. R. Miller (Eds.), *Information processing in animals: Memory mechanisms.* Hillsdale, N.J.: Erlbaum.

Wagner, A. R. & Brandon, S. E. (in press). Evolution of a structured connectionist model of Pavlovian conditioning (AESOP). In S. B. Klein and R. R. Mowrer (Eds.), *Contemporary learning theories.* Hillsdale, N. J.: Erlbaum.

Wagner, A. R. & Donegan, N. H. (in press). Some relationships between a computational model (SOP) and a neural circuit for Pavlovian (rabbit eyeblink) conditioning. In R. D. Hawkins & G. H. Bower (Eds.), *The psychology of learning and motivation: Vol. 22. Computational models of learning in simple neural systems.* Orlando: Academic.

Wagner, A. R. & Larew, M. B. (1985). Opponent processes and Pavlovian inhibition. In R. R. Miller & N. E. Spear (Eds.), *Information processing in animals: Conditioned inhibition.* Hillsdale, N.J.: Erlbaum.

Wagner, A. R., Rudy, J. W., & Whitlow, J. W. (1973). Rehearsal in animal conditioning. *Journal of Experimental Psychology, 97,* 407–426.

Wallin, J. A. & Johnson, R. D. (1976). The positive reinforcement approach to controlling employee absenteeism. *Personnel Journal, 55,* 390–392.

Walters, R. H., Leat, M., & Mezei, L. (1963). Inhibition and disinhibition of responses through empathetic learning. *Canadian Journal of Psychology, 17,* 235–243.

Warden, C. J., Fjeld, H. A., & Koch, A. M. (1940). Imitative behavior in cebus and rhesus monkeys. *Journal of Genetic Psychology, 56,* 311–322.

Warren, J. M. (1965). Primate learning in comparative perspective. In A. M. Schrier, H. F. Harlow, & F. Stollnitz (Eds.), *Behavior of nonhuman primates* (Vol. 1). New York: Academic.

Wasserman, E. A. (1973). Pavlovian conditioning with heat reinforcement produces stimulus-directed pecking in chicks. *Science, 81,* 875–877.

Watson, D. L. & Tharp, R. G. (1985). *Self-directed behavior: Self-modification for personal adjustment.* (4th ed.) Monterey, Cal.: Brooks/Cole.

Watson, J. B. (1916). The place of the conditioned-reflex in psychology. *Psychological Review, 23,* 89–117.

Watson, J. B. (1919). *Psychology from the standpoint of the behaviorist.* Philadelphia: J. B. Lippincott.

Watson, J. B. & Rayner, R. (1921). Studies in infant psychology. *Scientific Monthly, 13,* 493–515.

Webb, E. J., Campbell, D. T., Schwartz, R. D., Sechrest, L., & Grove, J. B. (1966). *Unobtrusive measures: Nonreactive research in the social sciences.* Chicago: Rand-McNally.

Webbe, F. M. & Malagodi, E. F. (1978). Second-order schedules of token reinforcement: Comparisons of performance under fixed-ratio and variable-ratio exchange schedules. *Journal of the Experimental Analysis of Behavior, 30*, 219–224.

Weisberg, P., Stout, R., & Hendler, M. (1986). Training and generalization of a "yes-no" discrimination with a developmentally delayed child. *Child & Family Behavior Therapy, 8*, 49–64.

Weisberg, P. & Waldrop, P. B. (1972). Fixed-interval work habits of Congress. *Journal of Applied Behavior Analysis, 5*, 93–97.

Weisman, R. G. & Litner, J. S. (1969). Positive conditioned reinforcement of Sidman avoidance in rats. *Journal of Comparative and Physiological Psychology, 68*, 597–603.

Weisman, R. G. & Litner, J. S. (1972). The role of Pavlovian events in avoidance training. In R. A. Boakes and M. S. Halliday (Eds.), *Inhibition and learning*. London: Academic Press.

Weisman, R. G., Wasserman, E. A., Dodd, P. W., & Larew, M. B. (1980). Representation and retention of two-event sequences in pigeons. *Journal of Experimental Psychology: Animal Behavior Processes, 6*, 312–325.

Weiss, J. M. (1971). Effects of coping behavior with and without a feedback signal on stress pathology in rats. *Journal of Comparative and Physiological Psychology, 77*, 22–30.

Weiss, J. M., Goodman, P. A., Losito, B. G., Corrigan, S., Charry, J., & Bailey, W. H. (1981). Behavioral depression produced by an uncontrollable stressor: Relationship to norepinephrine, dopamine, and serotonin levels in various regions of the rat brain. *Brain Research Reviews, 3*, 167–205.

Werner, G. E. & Hall, D. J. (1974). Optimal foraging and size selection of prey by the bluegill sunfish (*Lepomis macrochirus*). *Ecology, 55*, 1042–1052.

Wexler, D. B. (1973). Token and taboo: Behavior modification, token economies, and the law. *California Law Review, 61*, 81–109.

Whitaker, H. A. (1983). Towards a brain model of automatization: A short essay. In R. A. Magill (Ed.), *Memory and control of action*. Amsterdam: North-Holland Publishing.

White, C. T. & Schlosberg, H. (1952). Degree of conditioning of the GSR as a function of the period of delay. *Journal of Experimental Psychology, 43*, 357–362.

Wickelgren, W. A. (1979). Chunking and consolidation: A theoretical synthesis of semantic networks, configuring in conditioning, S-R versus cognitive learning, normal forgetting, the amnesiac syndrome, and the hippocampal arousal system. *Psychological Review, 86*, 44–60.

Wiens, A. N. & Menustik, C. E. (1983). Treatment outcome and patient characteristics in an aversive therapy program for alcoholism. *American Psychologist, 38*, 1089–1096.

Wilcoxon, H. C., Dragoin, W. B., & Kral, P. A. (1971). Illness-induced aversions in rat and quail: Relative salience of visual and gustatory cues. *Science, 171*, 826–828.

Wilkie, D. M. (1983). Pigeons' spatial memory: II. Acquisition of delayed matching of key location and transfer to new locations. *Journal of the Experimental Analysis of Behavior, 39*, 69–76.

Williams, B. A. (1981). The following schedule of reinforcement as a fundamental determinant of steady state contrast in multiple schedules. *Journal of the Experimental Analysis of Behavior, 35*, 293–310.

Williams, B. A. (1983). Another look at contrast in multiple schedules. *Journal of the Experimental Analysis of Behavior, 39*, 345–384.

Williams, D. R. & Williams, H. (1969). Auto-maintenance in the pigeon: Sustained pecking despite contingent non-reinforcement. *Journal of the Experimental Analysis of Behavior, 12*, 511–520.

Williams, J. L. & Lierle, D. M. (1986). Effects of stress controllability, immunization, and therapy on the subsequent defeat of colony intruders. *Animal Learning & Behavior, 14*, 305–314.

Wilson, D. M. (1961). The central nervous control of flight in a locust. *Journal of Experimental Biology, 38*, 471–490.

Wilson, P. N., Boakes, R. A., & Swan, J. (1987). Instrumental learning as a result of omission training on wheel running. *Quarterly Journal of Experimental Psychology, 39B*, 161–171.

Wing, L. (1972). *Autistic children: A guide for parents and professionals*. New York: Brunner/Mazel.

Winnick, W. A. & Hunt, J. McV. (1951). The effect of an extra stimulus upon strength of response during acquisition and extinction. *Journal of Experimental Psychology, 41*, 205–215.

Wolff, J. L. (1967). Concept-shift and discrimination-reversal in humans. *Psychological Bulletin, 68*, 369–408.

Wolpe, J. (1958). *Psychotherapy by reciprocal inhibition*. Stanford, Cal.: Stanford University Press.

Wolpe, J. & Lazarus, A. A. (1966). *Behavior therapy techniques: A guide to the treatment of neurosis*. Oxford: Pergamon.

Wood, D. C. (1973). Stimulus specific habituation in a protozoan. *Physiology and Behavior, 11*, 349–354.

Woodruff, G. & Williams, D. R. (1976). The associative relation underlying autoshaping in the pigeon. *Journal of the Experimental Analysis of Behavior, 26*, 1–13.

Wrisberg, C. A. & McLean, E. (1984). Training for the production of novel timing movements: Contextual considerations. *Psychological Research, 46*, 169–176.

Wyrwicka, W. (1978). Imitation of mother's inappropriate food preference in weanling kittens. *Pavlovian Journal of Biological Science, 13*, 55–72.

Yeo, C. H., Hardiman, M. J., & Glickstein, M. (1985). Classical conditioning of the nictitating membrane response in the rabbit. *Experimental Brain Research, 60*, 87–98.

Yerkes, R. M. & Morgulis, S. (1909). The method of Pavlov in animal psychology. *Psychological Bulletin, 6*, 257–273.

Yoshikubo, S. (1985). Species discrimination and concept formation by rhesus monkeys (*Macaca mulatta*). *Primates, 26*, 285–299.

Young, G. C. & Morgan, R. T. (1972). Overlearning in the conditioning treatment of enuresis: A long term follow-up study. *Behavior Research and Therapy, 10*, 419–420.

Yule, W., Sacks, B., & Hersov, L. (1974). Successful flooding treatment of a noise phobia in an eleven-year-old. *Journal of Behavior Therapy and Experimental Psychiatry, 5*, 209–211.

Zamble, E., Hadad, G. M., Mitchell, J. B., & Cutmore, T. R. H. (1985). Pavlovian conditioning of sexual arousal: First- and second-order effects. *Journal of Experimental Psychology: Animal Behavior Processes, 11*, 598–610.

Zener, K. (1937). The significance of behavior accompanying conditioned salivary secretion for theories of the conditioned response. *American Journal of Psychology, 50*, 384–403.

Zentall, T. R. (1983). Abstract codes are not just for chimpanzees. *The Behavioral and Brain Sciences, 6*, 157–158.

Zentall, T. R. & Hogan, D. E. (1978). Same/different concept learning in the pigeon: The effect of negative instances and prior adaptation to the transfer stimuli. *Journal of the Experimental Analysis of Behavior, 30*, 177–186.

Zentall, T. R., Hogan, D. E., & Edwards, C. A. (1984). Cognitive factors in conditional learning by pigeons. In H. L. Roitblat, T. G. Bever, & H. S. Terrace (Eds.), *Animal cognition.* Hillsdale, N.J.: Erlbaum.

Zimmerman, B. J. & Blom, D. E. (1983). Toward an empirical test of the role of cognitive conflict in learning. *Developmental Review, 3*, 18–38.

Zimmerman, B. J. & Koussa, R. (1979). Social influences on children's toy preferences: Effects of model rewardingness and affect. *Contemporary Educational Psychology, 4*, 55–66.

AUTHOR INDEX

SUBJECT INDEX